Critical Incidents in Counseling Children

Edited by

Suzanne M. (Hobson) Dugger

Laurie A. Carlson

AMERICAN COUNSELING ASSOCIATION
5999 Stevenson Avenue
Alexandria, VA 22304
www.counseling.org

Critical Incidents in Counseling Children

10   9   8   7   6   5   4   3   2   1

American Counseling Association
   5999 Stevenson Avenue
   Alexandria, VA 22304

Director of Publications
   Carolyn C. Baker

Production Manager
   Bonny E. Gaston

Copy Editor
   Rachel Fending

Editorial Assistant
Catherine A. Brumley

Cover and text design by Bonny E. Gaston

Library of Congress Cataloging-in-Publication Data
Critical incidents in counseling children / Suzanne M. (Hobson) Dugger and Laurie A. Carlson (editors).
   p. cm.
   ISBN-13: 978-1-55620-257-5 (alk. paper)
   ISBN-10: 1-55620-257-1 (alk. paper)
1. Child psychotherapy—Case studies. 2. Adolescent psychotherapy—Case studies. 3. Children—Counseling of—Case studies. 4. Youth—Counseling of—Case studies. I. Dugger, Suzanne M. II. Carlson, Laurie A.
   RJ504.C77 2006
   618.92'8914—dc22   2006009511

Contents

Acknowledgments   vii
Preface   ix
About the Editors   xiii
Contributor Listing   xv
In Memoriam   xxi

Part I

Anxiety, Mood, and Psychotic Disorders

1   "Get Off My Back": Childhood Depression   3
Laurie A. Carlson, Debbie Vernon, John M. Littrell

2   Differential Diagnosis: "Fantasies or Delusions?"   13
Angie D. Waliski, Deborah E. Renard, Suzanne M. (Hobson) Dugger

3   "Why Does She Behave This Way?":
Reactive Attachment Disorder   23
Chasity Amber Harris, Charles L. Thompson, Gary R. Mauldin

4   Separation Anxiety: "Helping Children
Feel Safe and Secure"   33
Elsa Soto Leggett, Karen E. Reed, Jon Carlson,
Matt Englar-Carlson, Karen Mackie, Maureen Finnigan Rundle

5   "There's a Monster Under My Bed!": Sleep Problems   45
Elysia V. Clemens, Adria E. Shipp, Laurie L. Williamson,
Imelda N. Lowe

Contents

■ Part II

Child Abuse and Other Trauma

6 Abuse Disclosure: "Walt Touched Me Down There" 57
Barbara J. Carlozzi, Krista M. Malott, Elizabeth U. Willingham

7 "He Blew Our House Down":
Natural Disaster and Trauma 71
Jennifer Baggerly, Courtney Green, Antoinette Rae Thorn,
William Steele

8 "Healing Visible and Invisible Wounds":
Physical Abuse 81
Serena M. Lambert, Erin Martin, Lonnie E. Duncan, Yolanda Duncan

9 "I Don't Know": Helping Reluctant Children
Tell Their Stories 93
Christina R. Marbach, Heather M. Helm, Laura R. Simpson

10 "Please Don't Make Me Go Home":
Sexual Abuse and Safety Issues 103
Vera B. Triplett, Heather C. Trepal, Emily Phillips

11 "My Pa-Pa Is an Alligator": Sexual Abuse Reporting 111
Laurie A. Carlson, Byron E. Norton, Carol C. Norton, Lisa Hinkelman

12 "Don't Talk!": Trauma and Dissociation in Play Therapy 121
Heather M. Helm, Marilyn S. Snow, Vera B. Triplett,
Michael M. Morgan, Serena M. Lambert

■ Part III

Diversity Issues

13 "My Name Is Samantha, Not Sammy!": Gender Identity 133
Linda L. Black, Hugh C. Crethar, Shannon B. Dermer, Melissa Luke

14 "In Big Mama's House": Intergenerational Issues 147
Angela D. Coker, Glenda Clare, Kevin O'Connor,
Vivian J. Carroll McCollum

15 "Gettin' Soft in the 'Burbs": Children Living in Poverty 159
Leann M. Wyrick-Morgan, Heidi S. Deschamps, Delila Owens

16 "Let's Dance": Race, Faith, and Sexual Orientation 169
Jolie Ziomek-Daigle, Linda L. Black, Michael M. Kocet

17 "People Say I'm Black": Racial Identity Development 181
Carmella Hill, Charles L. Thompson, Ramón Vega de Jesús

Part IV

Family Problems

18 "Please Don't Tell!": Custody Battles
and Confidentiality 197
Cynthia A. Reynolds, Kelly Duncan, Rita Sommers-Flanagan

19 "Outside the Castle": Divorce and Relocation 205
Nicole R. Hill, Heidi S. Deschamps, Tarrell Awe Agahe Portman

20 "When Home Is Not a Haven":
Addressing Domestic Violence 213
Darcie Davis-Gage, Scott W. Peters, Terry Kottman

21 "I Already Have a Real Mom":
Foster Care and Adoption 223
Glenda Clare, Nicole R. Hill, Kimberly Bundy-Fazioli

22 "Misguided Attempts to Love":
Intergenerational Substance Abuse 233
Glenda Clare, Katrina Cook, Christina Rosen Galvin

Part V

Grief and Loss

23 "I Never Got to Say Good-Bye": Death of a Sibling 247
Shawn Patrick, John Beckenbach, Nancy Boyd Webb, Jolie Ziomek-Daigle

24 "But All My Friends Are Here!":
Minimizing and Managing the Effects of Relocation 255
Jodi Ann Mullen, Diana H. Gruman, Michelle R. Holcomb

25 "We Can't Believe It Happened": Crisis Consultation 265
Susan A. Adams, Kathleen (Ky) T. Heinlen, S. Kent Butler

Part VI

Physical Ailments

26 "But He Needs Me": Responding to a Child's
Catastrophic Illness 277
LeAnne Steen, Heather M. Helm, Laurie Shepherd Johnson

27 "My Head Hurts—Come Pick Me Up
From School, Gramma!": Somatization 293
Suzanne E. Degges-White, JoLynn V. Carney, Constance J. Deuschle

Contents

■ Part VII

Protecting Children From Themselves

28 "Why Didn't You Tell Me?": School Responsibilities
in the Wake of Death by Autoerotic Asphyxiation   307
Susan A. Adams, Constance J. Deuschle, G. Kurt Moore

29 "I'm Too Fat": Body Images in Childhood   317
Jan R. Bartlett, Nicole R. Hill, Torey L. Portrie-Bethke

30 Self-Injury: "Cutting the Crazy Out of Me"   329
Heather C. Trepal, Elizabeth E. Shanahan, Emily Phillips, Ann Vernon

31 "Are You Saying Corey Is an Addict?":
Childhood Substance Abuse   337
Christina Rosen Galvin, John Sommers-Flanagan, Linwood G. Vereen

■ Part VIII

School-Based Counseling

32 Academic Difficulties: "The Boy's Just Lazy!"   351
Jody J. Fiorini, Rhonda M. Bryant, Carol A. Dahir

33 "Stan Is Driving Me Crazy!": Behavior Problems   363
Jill Bills, Larry Golden, Marie A. Wakefield

34 The Systemic Nature of Bullying:
"Handle Your Own Business, Punk!"   371
*Teah L. Moore, Shannon Casey-Cannon, Hardin L. K. Coleman,
Harvey Hoyo*

35 "And Who's Gonna Make Me?": Defiant Behavior   387
*Kenneth McCurdy, Nancy Bodenhorn, Stephen E. Craig,
Jennifer C. Mills, Lonnie E. Duncan*

36 "But I Was Just Kidding!": The School Counselor's Role
in Responding to Student Threats and the Potential
for Violence   399
*Linda M. Fortin, JoLynn V. Carney, Maureen Finnigan Rundle,
Karen Mackie, Walter B. Roberts Jr.*

Acknowledgments

With a total of 104 contributors to *Critical Incidents in Counseling Children,* our job as editors has been likened to the fine art of herding cats. Although this process certainly presented an organizational challenge, our task was made easier in large part by Kerry Ann Ryan. Ms. Ryan is an SpA candidate in Educational Leadership at Eastern Michigan University and serves as a graduate assistant to Dr. (Hobson) Dugger. Her enthusiasm for the project, her attention to detail, and her willingness to offer a noncounseling perspective have all served to strengthen the book. We offer our sincerest thanks and appreciation for the quality of her contributions as an editorial assistant.

Additionally, we would like to acknowledge Carolyn Baker, Director of Publications for the American Counseling Association, for her helpful guidance throughout the editing process and extend our appreciation to her and the rest of the ACA Publications Committee for supporting publication of this book.

Finally, we thank our friends and family—with a special thanks to Chandler, Kelly, Rochelle, and Corrie—for their support and understanding as we immersed ourselves in this project.

Preface

The practice of counseling children is decidedly complex, requiring that counselors use a theoretical orientation while adapting counseling techniques to match the developmental level of their young clients. In addition to the developmental differences in how children experience the world, how they learn, how they problem solve, and how they communicate, other complicating matters also challenge the counselor who works primarily with children. Children, as minors, have considerably less control over their lives and are deeply affected by the decisions made for them by the important adults in their lives. Unlike adult clients, children in counseling generally lack the maturity and legal rights to autonomously make major life decisions. In most cases, children cannot simply decide whether to change schools, to move to a new residence, to discontinue an unsatisfactory and possibly abusive relationship, or even to initiate or terminate counseling services.

As a result, it is necessary to approach the practice of counseling differently when the client is a child. One needs specialized training to effectively serve this population of clients. Unfortunately, though, it is my experience that the majority of master's degree programs in counseling focus primarily on the practice of counseling with adults. Programs in mental health and community agency counseling tend to focus on adolescent and adult clients, and even the specialization courses in school counseling programs tend to focus on middle and high school students. Almost universally, counseling techniques courses concentrate on communication and intervention skills better suited to adolescent and adult clients. Counselors who are schooled in such traditional training programs often find themselves lacking when it comes to counseling these "little boppers," children for whom words are not the primary mode of communication.

This book is intended for use in master's degree training programs as a textbook or supplemental textbook, for use by counselors who have graduated from traditional training programs and who want to enhance their skills when counseling children, and for use in specialization programs focused on counseling children. In addition to these intended uses, we recognize that this book has relevance in a number of other fields—including family studies, psychology, social work, and teacher education—and that it may be useful at the undergraduate, graduate, and postgraduate levels. Readers will benefit from this book's focus on actual cases that reflect the realities of counseling with children.

Indeed, *Critical Incidents in Counseling Children* is designed to address the many complexities involved in the practice of counseling children, with the goal of assisting counselors in more effectively working with their young clients. In particular, this book focuses on the practice of counseling children who have not yet reached the formal operational level of cognitive development and who therefore require counseling approaches not primarily rooted in conversation. Although all chapters focus on children 13 years of age and younger, they differ with regard to the setting in which the counseling occurs. The chapters explore counseling incidents with children in both school and nonschool settings, including governmental agencies (e.g., community mental health centers, protective services and child abuse agencies, and foster care agencies), children's homes, trauma centers, private practices, residential settings, and community agencies. The book also illustrates multiple treatment approaches, including various theoretical approaches to the practice of play therapy and other treatment modalities, such as sand tray therapy, art therapy, and family therapy. In addition to addressing these various settings and treatment approaches, *Critical Incidents in Counseling Children* also explores a wide range of issues faced by children. This book is arranged into eight sections, each of which focuses on an area of concern frequently encountered by mental health professionals who counsel children: (a) Anxiety, Mood, and Psychotic Disorders; (b) Child Abuse and Other Trauma; (c) Diversity Issues; (d) Family Problems; (e) Grief and Loss; (f) Physical Ailments; (g) Protecting Children From Themselves; and (h) School-Based Counseling.

Each of the chapters in these sections is designed to explore an actual issue encountered by a professional counselor, disguised only to protect the identity of the child client. The professional counselor begins by providing background information about the case, then focuses on a critical incident that occurred while he or she was counseling the child, and ends with questions about the incident. The chapter then turns to the opinions of other professional counselors, each of whom responds directly to the questions posed. This is known as a critical incident approach and is similar to a case study approach. The critical incident approach focuses the reader's attention on a specific aspect of a case and on questions that arose for the clinician. Instead of focusing only on success stories, the counselors in this book frequently reveal self-doubt and confusion about how to proceed. This approach is especially useful for training purposes because it allows students to witness the struggles of already seasoned clinicians, to grasp the complexities of counseling children, to discover divergent ways other counselors might proceed, and to begin conceptualizing how they might proceed as counselors working with the client described in the critical incident. In addition, the critical incident approach generally resonates with the experiences of more seasoned counselors, who have had enough clinical experience to discover that the counseling process rarely proceeds as smoothly as portrayed in a textbook.

Also appealing to graduate students and seasoned professionals alike are the high quality and depth of each of the responses to the cases presented in *Critical Incidents in Counseling Children*. Indeed, a quick review of the book's table of contents reveals a number of truly expert contributors whose previous work in the area of counseling with children is widely published and highly acclaimed. These nationally recognized counselors were invited to participate as expert respondents. In addition, many other highly qualified and accomplished individuals applied to contribute to the development of this book. These individuals responded to postings on the Counselor Education and Supervision NETwork and the International Counselors Network and were selected as contributors for chapters focused on areas in which they generally had significant experience and expertise.

In reading each chapter, take the role of an active participant rather than a passive observer. Before reading the responses, reflect on each of the questions posed by the counselor who worked with the child and formulate your own ideas about how you might respond. Consider how you might have handled the case. As you continue reading the chapter, compare your own responses with those offered by the contributors to this book. Also notice the similarities and differences of the two or three responses presented in each chapter. Reading the book in this manner will have the greatest impact on your skill development.

As editors, we hope that you will share in our enthusiasm for this book and will agree that the depth and breadth of this collection of critical incidents serve to enhance your understanding of counseling children. Although challenging, the practice of counseling children is also enormously rewarding and intensely meaningful. We wish you the best as you work to improve their lives!

Suzanne M. (Hobson) Dugger

About the Editors

Suzanne M. (Hobson) Dugger, EdD, NCC, LPC, LLP, is an associate professor in the Department of Leadership and Counseling at Eastern Michigan University in Ypsilanti, Michigan, and serves as the coordinator of the university's CACREP-accredited school counseling program. Outside the university, she serves as a member of the Michigan Board of Counseling (state licensure board) and as the chair of the Michigan Department of Education's School Counselor Educators Committee.

Prior to accepting the lead editor responsibilities for this book, Dr. Dugger served for 4 years as the editor of the journal *Dimensions in Counseling: Research, Theory and Practice* and has served on the editorial boards for the *Professional School Counseling* and *Elementary School Guidance & Counseling* journals. In addition, she has been a contributor to *The School Counselor Handbook,* to *Critical Incidents in Group Counseling,* and to *Case Studies in Child and Adolescent Counseling* and has published articles in *The Journal of Humanistic Counseling, Education and Development,* in the *American Journal of Health Studies,* in *College Teaching,* in *Elementary School Guidance & Counseling,* and in *Professional School Counseling.*

In addition, Dr. Dugger is currently the chair of the American Counseling Association's (ACA's) Midwest Region and has served as the ACA Human Rights Committee Chair. She has also served as the president of the Michigan Counseling Association, as president of the Michigan Association for Counselor Education and Supervision, and as a Governing Board Member of the Michigan School Counselor Association. Dr. Dugger is the founding member of the Association of Michigan School Counselors.

Dr. Dugger received her bachelor's degree in psychology from Harvard University, where she also earned a teaching certificate. She earned her master's degree in counseling from Central Michigan University and her doctorate in counseling psychology from Western Michigan University. Before pursuing her doctoral studies, Dr. Dugger served as an elementary school counselor for 5 years.

She also has 3 years of experience in university counseling centers and 8 years of experience in private practice.

Dr. Dugger may be reached at emudugger@yahoo.com.

■ *Laurie A. Carlson*, PhD, NCC, NCSC, is an associate professor in the School of Education's Counseling and Career Development Program at Colorado State University in Fort Collins, Colorado. In addition to her faculty responsibilities, Dr. Carlson serves on the executive board of the Colorado School Counselors' Association as state conference coordinator.

Dr. Carlson has made varied contributions to literature in the field, including chapters in *Spirituality as a Fifth Force in Counseling and Psychology: Implications for Practice, Training and Research*; in *Unfocused Kids: Helping Students to Focus on Their Education and Career Plans*; in *Professional School Counseling: A Handbook of Theories, Programs & Practices*; and in *Measuring Up: Resources on Testing for Teachers, Counselors, and Administrators*. Dr. Carlson's work has also appeared in various journals, including *The International Journal of Testing*; the *Journal of Counseling & Development*; *Professional School Counseling*; the *Rural Educator*; and *The Journal of Humanistic Education, Counseling, and Development*. Editorial duties have included serving as Web editor for the National Career Development Association Web site and serving on the guest editorial board for special issues of the *Journal of Counseling and Development* and the *E-Journal of Teaching and Learning in Diverse Settings*. In addition to these contributions, Dr. Carlson serves as an external reviewer for school counseling and assessment titles published by Houghton Mifflin: Lahaska Press and Prentice Hall.

National service is also a large part of Dr. Carlson's professional life. In 2000–2002, Dr. Carlson helped to establish the ACA task force on women in counseling. Since 2003, Dr. Carlson has served as a national trainer for the American Psychological Association/Centers for Disease Control–Division of Adolescent and School Health's Healthy Gay, Lesbian, and Bisexual Student Project, and in 2004 Dr. Carlson was appointed cochair of ACA's Sexual Minority Youth Taskforce.

Dr. Carlson earned her bachelor's degree in English education from Moorhead State University (now Minnesota State University—Moorhead), and taught 7th through 12th grade language arts in northern Minnesota for 5 years. She then received her master's degree in school counseling from Western Washington University in Bellingham. Following this degree, Dr. Carlson served as a kindergarten through 12th grade school counselor for 4 years in Minnesota before attaining her PhD in counselor education from the University of Arkansas, Fayetteville, in 2000.

Dr. Carlson can be reached at laurie.carlson@colostate.edu.

Contributor Listing

We would like to extend our deepest appreciation to the following contributors for sharing their experience and expertise about the world of counseling children. Each of these contributors was selected on the basis of his or her expertise with regard to a clinical issue, theoretical orientation, or treatment modality. Although space constraints do not allow for the inclusion of a biography about each contributor, we applaud the impressiveness of the contributors' individual and collective experience and expertise. As you read each chapter, we hope you will share in our appreciation for the insights contributed by the following individuals.

It should be noted that each contributor should be considered an equal coauthor of the chapter to which he or she contributed. The order in which the contributors are listed is simply a reflection of the order in which their contributions appear rather than an indication of the importance of their contribution.

Susan A. Adams, PhD, LPC, NCC, ACS
    Texas Woman's University (Denton, TX)

Jennifer Baggerly, PhD, LMHC-S, RPT-S
    University of South Florida

Jan R. Bartlett, PhD
    Oklahoma State University

John Beckenbach, EdD, NCC, LPC
    Texas State University—San Marcos

Jill Bills
    Almont Community Schools (Almont, Michigan)

Linda L. Black, EdD, LPC
    University of Northern Colorado

Nancy Bodenhorn, PhD
    Virginia Tech

Rhonda M. Bryant, PhD, LPC, NCC, NCSC
Albany State University (Albany, GA)

Kimberly Bundy-Fazioli, LCSW, PhD
Colorado State University

S. Kent Butler, PhD, NCC, NCSC
University of Missouri—St. Louis

Barbara J. Carlozzi, PhD
Oklahoma State University

Jon Carlson, PsyD, EdD
Governors State University

Laurie A. Carlson, PhD, NCC, NCSC
Colorado State University

JoLynn V. Carney, PhD, LPCC-S
Pennsylvania State University

Shannon Casey-Cannon, PhD
California School of Professional Psychology at Alliant International University

Glenda Clare, MA
Doctoral Candidate, College of William and Mary

Elysia V. Clemens, MAEd, NCC
University of North Carolina at Greensboro

Angela D. Coker, PhD, LPC, NCC
University of Missouri—St. Louis

Hardin L. K. Coleman, PhD, LPC
University of Wisconsin—Madison

Katrina Cook, LPC, LMFT
University of Texas at San Antonio

Stephen E. Craig, PhD, LPC, LLP
Western Michigan University

Hugh C. Crethar, PhD
University of Arizona

Carol A. Dahir, EdD
New York Institute of Technology

Darcie Davis-Gage, PhD, LPC
University of Northern Iowa

Suzanne E. Degges-White, PhD, LMHC, LPC-NC, NCC
Purdue University Calumet

Shannon B. Dermer, PhD, LMFT
Governors State University

Heidi S. Deschamps, LPC, NCC
University of New Mexico

Constance J. Deuschle, EdD, NCC, CADAC II, RN
Indiana University South Bend

Suzanne M. (Hobson) Dugger, EdD, NCC, LPC, LLP
Eastern Michigan University

Kelly Duncan, PhD, LPC, NCC
Northern State University (Aberdeen, South Dakota)

Lonnie E. Duncan, PhD, LP
Western Michigan University

Yolanda Duncan, MA, LPC
Grand Rapids Community College (Grand Rapids, Michigan)

Matt Englar-Carlson, PhD
California State University, Fullerton

Jody J. Fiorini, PhD, LMHC, NCC, ACS
State University of New York at Oswego

Linda M. Fortin, BS, MS Ed, CAS in School Counseling
Merton Williams Middle School, Hilton Central School District
(Hilton, New York)

Christina Rosen Galvin, EdD, LPCP, ICRC
Idaho State University

Larry Golden, PhD, Licensed Psychologist (Texas)
University of Texas at San Antonio

Courtney Green
Zolfo Springs Elementary School, Hardee District Schools (Wauchula, Florida)

Diana H. Gruman, PhD, NCC
Western Washington University

Chasity Amber Harris, MS, NCC
Graduate, University of Tennessee

Kathleen (Ky) T. Heinlen, MEd, PCC-S, Psychology Fellow
Parmadale Family Services (Bay Village, Ohio)
Cleveland State University

Heather M. Helm, PhD, LPC, NCC, RPT
University of Northern Colorado

Carmella Hill, MEd
Kent State University

Nicole R. Hill, PhD, LPC
Idaho State University

Lisa Hinkelman, PhD, LPC
Ohio State University

Michelle R. Holcomb, LPC
University of Texas at San Antonio

Harvey Hoyo, EdD, PPSC
National University

Laurie Shepherd Johnson, PhD, LMHC, NCC
Hofstra University (Hempstead, New York)

Michael M. Kocet, PhD, LMHC, NCC
Bridgewater State College (Bridgewater, Massachusetts)

Terry Kottman, PhD, NCC, RPT-S, LMHC
The Encouragement Zone (Cedar Falls, Iowa)

Serena M. Lambert, PhD, LPC, NCC
University of Wyoming

Elsa Soto Leggett, PhD, LPC, CSC
Texas Southern University

John M. Littrell, EdD
Colorado State University

Imelda N. Lowe, MEd, Licensed School Counselor
Doctoral Student, Idaho State University

Melissa Luke, MA, MS, LMHC
Doctoral Student, Syracuse University

Karen Mackie, PhD, NCC
University of Rochester

Krista M. Malott, PhD, NCC
Villanova University

Christina R. Marbach, MS, LPC
Private Practice and Doctoral Student at the University of Texas at San Antonio

Erin Martin, PhD, NCC, LPC, RPT
Louisiana State University Health Science Center

Gary R. Mauldin, PhD, LPC, LMFT
Holston Conference Pastoral Counseling Center (Knoxville, Tennessee)

Vivian J. Carroll McCollum, PhD, LPC-S, LPC-P, NCC
Albany State University

Kenneth McCurdy, PhD, LPC(C), NCC, ACS
Gannon University

Jennifer C. Mills, MS, LLPC
Doctoral Student, Counselor Education, Western Michigan University

G. Kurt Moore, PhD, NCC, LPC
Walter R. McDonald & Associates, Inc. (Greenwood Village, Colorado)

Teah L. Moore, PhD, LPC, NCC
East Tennessee State University

Michael M. Morgan, PhD, LMFT
University of Wyoming

Jodi Ann Mullen, PhD, NCC, LMHC, RPT-S
State University of New York at Oswego

Byron E. Norton, EdD, Licensed Psychologist, RPT/S
Family Psychological Services, PC (Greeley, Colorado)

Carol C. Norton, EdD, Licensed Psychologist, RPT/S
Family Psychological Services, PC (Greeley, Colorado)

Kevin O'Connor, PhD, RPT-S
California School of Professional Psychology at Alliant International University

Delila Owens, PhD, LPC
Wayne State University

Shawn Patrick, EdD, NCC, LPC
Texas State University—San Marcos

Scott W. Peters, MA, LPC-S
University of Texas at San Antonio

Emily Phillips, PhD, NCC
State University of New York at Oneonta

Tarrell Awe Agahe Portman, PhD, LMHC, NCC
University of Iowa

Torey L. Portrie-Bethke, MCoun, LPC, NCC
Idaho State University

Karen E. Reed, MS
Corpus Christi Independent School District (Corpus Christi, Texas)

Deborah E. Renard, PhD, CRC, LPC
University of Wisconsin—Milwaukee

Cynthia A. Reynolds, PhD, NCC, RPT-S, Licensed Psychologist, LPCC Supervisor,
Certified School Counselor
University of Akron

Walter B. Roberts Jr., EdD, LPC, LSC, NCC, NCSC
Minnesota State University, Mankato

Maureen Finnigan Rundle, MSEd, CAS
Merton Williams Middle School, Hilton Central School District (Hilton, New York)

Elizabeth E. Shanahan, MSEd
State University of New York College at Oneonta

Adria E. Shipp, MAEd, NCC, NCLSC
Western Carolina University and Buncombe County School System
(North Carolina)

Laura R. Simpson, PhD, LPC, NCC, ACS
Delta State University

Marilyn S. Snow, PhD, NCC, LPC, RPT/S
University of Mississippi and Oxford Play Therapy Training Institute
(Oxford, Mississippi)

John Sommers-Flanagan, PhD
University of Montana

Rita Sommers-Flanagan, PhD
University of Montana

William Steele, MSW, PsyD
National Institute for Trauma and Loss in Children
(Grosse Pointe Woods, Michigan)

LeAnne Steen, PhD, LPC, RPT
Loyola University

Charles L. Thompson, PhD (Deceased; see in memoriam on page xxi)
University of Tennessee

Antoinette Rae Thorn, PhD, LPC, NCC
Rogers Public Schools (Rogers, Arkansas) and the University of Arkansas

Heather C. Trepal, PhD, LPC
University of Texas at San Antonio

Vera B. Triplett, PhD, LPC, RPT
Our Lady of Holy Cross College (New Orleans, Louisiana)

Ramón Vega de Jesús, PhD
California State University, Stanislaus

Linwood G. Vereen, PhD, NCC, LPC
Idaho State University

Ann Vernon, PhD, LMHC, NCC
University of Northern Iowa

Debbie Vernon, PhD, PCC-S, ACS
Hudson Middle School (Hudson, Ohio)

Marie A. Wakefield, MS
University of Nevada, Las Vegas

Angie D. Waliski, PhD, LPC, NCC
Ozark Guidance (Springdale, Arkansas) and University of Arkansas

Nancy Boyd Webb, DSW, BCD, RPT-S
Child Welfare Studies, Fordham University

Laurie L. Williamson, EdD, LPC, ACS
Appalachian State University

Elizabeth U. Willingham, EdS, LAPC, NCC
Georgia State University

Leann M. Wyrick-Morgan, PhD, LPC, NCC
Northern Illinois University

Jolie Ziomek-Daigle, PhD, LPC, RPT-S
University of Georgia

In Memoriam

Charles L. Thompson, PhD

1937–2005

When Dr. Charles "Chuck" Thompson agreed to serve as an expert respondent for this book, I was nothing less than thrilled. By coincidence, my very first publication was a piece that he had accepted while serving as the editor of the IDEA Exchange in the *Elementary School Guidance & Counseling* journal. To now have him contribute to a book I edited was quite the honor. We are saddened that Dr. Thompson died suddenly, soon after submitting his contributions to Chapter 3 and Chapter 17. By offering this memoriam, we hope to honor his many professional contributions and express our appreciation of his participation in this particular project.

Dr. Thompson had been a professor of counselor education and educational psychology at the University of Tennessee for 39 years. Licensed as a psychologist and school counselor and board certified by the National Board of Certified Counselors, Dr. Thompson held memberships in the American Counseling Association, the Association for Counselor Education and Supervision, the American Mental Health Counselors Association, the American School Counselor Association, and the American Psychological Association.

Dr. Thompson was the senior author of *Counseling Children*, a textbook that has been used around the world and that is currently in its eighth edition. In addition, Dr. Thompson has coauthored four other books, published numerous professional articles, was editor of the IDEA Exchange in the *Elementary School Guidance & Counseling* journal from 1979 to 1997, and was widely considered the source for expert opinion and information relative to his field. Dr. Thompson received the 1996 Counselor Educator of the Year award from the American Mental Health Counselors Association and the 2001 Writer of the Year award from the American School Counselor Association.

Indeed, Dr. Thompson's friendly, spirited nature, his many professional contributions, and his ability to stay at the forefront of developing knowledge in the area of counseling children will long be remembered by those of us who have had the good fortune of working with him. Godspeed!

Part

Anxiety, Mood, and Psychotic Disorders

"Get Off My Back": Childhood Depression

This incident demonstrates that childhood depression can be masked in misbehavior and that the way this misbehavior is addressed by schools may result in a failure to recognize serious underlying mental health issues. The chapter explores the use of solution-focused brief counseling, the identification of serious mental health issues, and the impact of special education placement on children's self-esteem.

◼ Critical Incident

Laurie A. Carlson

"Gage Thompson" was a 10-year-old fifth grader in our small, kindergarten through 12th grade midwestern school. Although school had never come easy for him, Gage had been a model student until halfway through the 4th grade. Gage was well liked by his peers and his teachers, and he appeared to be a generally happy, although academically frustrated, child. During his 4th-grade year, Gage was tested for special education and classified as learning disabled. Although he expressed relief for the extra academic support, Gage's classroom behavior began to deteriorate almost immediately after his placement in the special education program.

One day early in November Gage walked into my school counseling office visibly upset. It was lunch period for his class, and he had asked his teacher for permission to come down to see me. Gage had come to my office because he was upset that some of his classmates had gotten him "in trouble with the teacher." He said that two classmates near him were throwing wads of paper while the teacher was facing away from the class. Because Gage was giggling when the teacher became aware of the behavior, he was told that he would have to stay in from recess along with his two classmates.

This was not the first time that Gage had come to see me for disruptive behavior that he perceived as the fault of his classmates. I had previously tried reality therapy and problem-solving approaches, exploring with Gage the motivations for his behavior, the logical consequences, and strategies for avoiding future incidents. Although he was visibly upset on this particular visit to my office, his distress was unusual. More typically, Gage would be "sent down" by his frustrated teacher, and, rather than seeming upset, he would appear apathetic and resigned to the fact that he was "just a bad kid." My prior counseling strategies sometimes resulted in short-term improvement, but they were more often frustrating and fruitless. I concluded that focusing on "the problem" in the past had not really worked. Shortly before this particular incident, I had been to a workshop to learn more about solution-focused brief counseling, so I decided to try this approach with Gage.

Using concepts from one of the interventions in the book I had acquired on solution-focused counseling (Metcalf, 1995), I identified a metaphor that might appeal to Gage. Knowing that Gage—like most young men in this rural, northern plains community—enjoyed deer hunting with his father and brothers, I began by asking him, "If you were out deer hunting and saw two bucks, one much larger than the other, which would you aim at?" Gage responded incredulously, "The big one, of course." When I asked him why he would make that choice, he responded, "Because bigger is better—it would have more meat and probably a larger rack." "Any other reason?" I asked. "Not that I can think of," Gage responded in a rather puzzled voice.

I then offered, "I would shoot at the bigger one because I would have a better chance of success. It would be a bigger target." Gage laughed out loud, smiled broadly, and agreed. I then went on to explain, "I think that might be what's happening with your friends. It's like you have a large target on your back that says, 'Pick me! Get me in trouble!' I don't know whether we can completely eliminate the target from your back, but perhaps we can make it smaller."

I had him hooked. Gage completely related to the metaphor I had chosen and seemed open to the idea of solving this problem. Unlike our previous sessions, I was not focusing on his accountability or addressing his problematic behavior. I had observed Gage in his classroom and on the playground, so I knew that when he was interacting with his peers, Gage was sullen, unexpressive, and periodically childish. I firmly believed that this seeming lack of social skills contributed to his frequent discipline struggles. Nevertheless, in this moment, I was accepting his explanation and moving from there with a metaphor that worked for him.

I continued, "Why do you think that there is such a large target on your back?" "Dunno," he mumbled. "I have a theory," I started. "I think that sometimes when you are in school you act like you don't care about what happens to you. You usually don't tell your classmates to stop if they are doing something that might get you all in trouble. You don't look them in the eyes when you talk to them to let them know that you mean business." "Uh-huh," came the weak affirmation. I continued, "I think that we can take at least two circles off of the outside of your target if you would be able to just speak up for yourself and look your friends in the eyes." Gage shrugged. "I dunno," he said and then continued, "In some ways I think it is OK. It doesn't always bother me to get into trouble. I know that helping my friends have fun at school instead of just being bored all day is at least one thing I am good at. Lots of times, I can get kids to laugh, and most times I don't get into real trouble."

I reflected for a moment and then, in my inexperience, responded, "I am sure you are good at many things." "Name one thing," Gage challenged. Gage had caught me in what I later came to realize was a therapeutic error: trying to convince a client of something he or she did not believe without having proof or "ammunition." I had to think fast. I knew that Gage lived on a farm and that his younger brother helped Gage's father in the field. I was unsure of Gage's situation, but it seemed reasonable that he did the same. "You are good at farming, at helping your dad in the field," I quickly responded. "Nope," Gage said. "He doesn't trust a retard running our machinery." I was astonished by his curt reply, realized my mistake, and knew I needed to steer our conversation back to where it had been just minutes ago.

To my relief, Gage let me off the hook and allowed me to redirect the conversation. "Back to the target," I said, "How do *you* think you can make it smaller?" He responded, "I think that the best thing would be to just try to stay away from all of them. They have been getting on my nerves lately anyway." "OK," I responded. This seemed like a reasonable strategy, one that adults often suggest to students. "Do you have a plan, then?" I asked. "Yep," replied Gage. "Good," I said, "I will check in with you once in a while to see how it is working." Gage left my office apprehensively, and, as I watched him retreat, I hoped that his days of getting in trouble were over.

I checked in with Gage and his teacher over the following weeks. Gage had not been sent down to my office, he said he was doing "fine," and his teacher reported that the intervention was obviously working because she seldom even remembered he was in class anymore. I was encouraged by the seeming success.

Four weeks after my solution-focused session with Gage, however, his teacher entered my office with concern written all over her face. With her hand trembling, she handed me a crumpled piece of notebook paper. "I found this in Gage's desk when doing a desk check during recess." I looked at the picture and felt my heart sink to the pit of my stomach. On the paper was a very detailed pencil drawing of a young boy standing on a 55-gallon fertilizer drum, noose around his neck and rope tied to a tree branch above.

I immediately contacted Gage's parents and helped support the family through the subsequent evaluation and intervention at the regional mental health agency. Gage was diagnosed with major depressive disorder and hospitalized for suicidal tendencies. Although the solution-focused session had succeeded in solving the teacher's problem and had helped Gage stay out of trouble, it did nothing to address his internal emotional state. In my haste to address Gage's behavioral issues, I had missed his deep pain and sadness.

Questions

1. How might one be able to use brief counseling and still identify serious underlying mental health issues?
2. Are the kinds of behavioral problems that Gage presented common for depressed children?
3. It has occurred to me that Gage's placement in special education might have contributed to a decreasing sense of self-esteem and possibly directly to his depression. How likely is this? What suggestions do you have for school counselors who want to address this possibility in a preventive manner?

■Response

Debbie Vernon

My first thought on reading this incident is that Gage seems to be having difficulty managing the social and emotional transition into special education programming. As a school counselor, I have found that this response is not unusual. Students and parents are often relieved when academic supports are provided to address learning disabilities. Nevertheless, in the midst of attending to these academic needs, educational personnel can easily overlook other social and emotional responses to this change.

When a placement change is made, I believe it is important to talk with the students to explore (a) what they think the reasons are for making the change, (b) what the change means to them, (c) how the change affects the way they see themselves, and (d) how they think it will affect how others see them. Exploring these issues can allow the counselor to identify student concerns and address any myths or questions that the student may have about what it means to receive special education services. This is also important from a preventive standpoint, as I can troubleshoot any concerns ahead of time and alert teachers and parents to any potential issues. It also helps me begin to establish a relationship with the student and act as a resource to him or her when future issues arise. In addition to telling students that I will check in with them periodically to see how they are doing, I also like to work with students individually or in short-term small groups to help them anticipate change. In most cases, students are able to navigate the changes and manage them quite well with a bit of assistance and support.

I was impressed with how Gage took the initiative and sought such assistance and support by visiting his school counselor to talk about his recent difficulties. The school counselor had built a relationship with Gage that allowed him to feel comfortable approaching her and to jointly explore possible solutions to his complaints. Because of this relationship and the school counselor's previous interactions with Gage, she had developed an understanding of his typical behaviors and the responses she was likely to elicit. Using this as a baseline, the school counselor was quick to note that Gage's level of emotional distress was unusual and observed some indications of hopelessness. At this point, I likely would have erred on the side of caution and told Gage about my concerns. In particular, I would have commented that his responses seemed different from what I had noticed before.

The school counselor's use of metaphor with Gage was a good way to connect with him. By using Gage's interest in hunting, she was able to communicate with him at a level he understood. This is important, developmentally speaking, as children this age vary widely in their ability to cope with abstraction. The counselor's use of metaphor also enlisted Gage's cooperation in working toward resolving the concern. He was now more involved and more likely to take responsibility for what he wanted to be different. Nevertheless, I became increasingly concerned about Gage's responses as the school counselor discussed the target with him. Gage's "I dunno" responses suggested that he had begun to shut down. I also sensed to some extent that Gage did not feel good about himself, as compared with his peers. I began to wonder whether Gage's decrease in self-confidence was an unanticipated response to his change in placement at school.

I often find that solution-focused brief therapy techniques, such as scaling questions, exploring exceptions to the problem, and asking the miracle question, can help school counselors identify the students' perceptions of their emotional state and current level of functioning. It can also help them begin to look toward possible solutions (Davis & Osborn, 2000). In Gage's case, I would have invited him to measure his current mood and adjustment level through the use of a scaling question such as the following: "Gage, you say that getting in trouble with the teacher is a challenge for you and that your feelings about getting into trouble have affected your feelings about school as a whole. On a scale of 1 to 10, where 10 means you feel really great about school and 1 means you feel really bad about school, where would you rank your feelings today?" By using such a scaling question, I could get a sense of what Gage thought about his own feelings and goals as well as what things he would like to do differently.

The second solution-focused brief therapy approach I would use involves looking for exceptions. I would help Gage look for exceptions to his problem by identifying those times when he was not getting in trouble or disliking school, and identifying what he was doing at those times. This approach would provide me with valuable information about attempted solutions and student strengths.

Finally, the miracle question is another tool I would use to help Gage begin to identify his goals for change. In the miracle question, I would ask Gage the following: "Gage, suppose you went to sleep tonight, and while you were sleeping a miracle took place and your problems at school disappeared. You didn't know a miracle happened, though, because you were asleep when it happened. When you awoke in the morning, what would you notice that would be different for you that would tell you that a miracle had happened?"

Depending on how Gage responded to these three solution-focused techniques, I would likely also do a mini risk assessment to get a sense of his level of functioning and any potential risk of harm to himself or others. If it was warranted, I would also make contact with his parents to let them know about my encounter with Gage that day. This parental contact would allow me to explore their perceptions of Gage's adjustment to special education and to find out about any other concerns they might have about him. Information from the mini risk assessment and parental contact would also provide me with useful feedback for Gage's teachers to help them better support his needs in school.

Although I tend to use solution-focused brief counseling when working with students, I cannot rely on any one approach alone. I still need to use my clinical judgment to assess the seriousness of a concern and determine whether there is a significant risk involved. Furthermore, depending on the outcome of my assessment, I may need to consult with key others, such as parents, teachers, administrators, school nurses, fellow counselors, or mental health providers. Thank goodness for teachers, who act as extra sets of eyes and ears, alerting counselors to student concerns. By finding his picture, Gage's teacher allowed the school counselor to respond immediately and to provide support to the parents in getting Gage the help that he needed.

In addition to working with his teacher, I would also emphasize the importance of collaborating with Gage's parents. Despite their best efforts, educators do not always get the complete picture of what is going on with the whole student; rather, they get only a glimpse of what is going on at school. There may be, for example, previous history and family factors unknown to the counselor that could alert him or her to potential concerns.

Finally, because of their age and developmental level, children may lack a certain level of emotional awareness and have difficulty putting words to feelings. It is often through their behavior, rather than their words, that students may communicate a concern. An example of this in Gage's case is the school counselor's observation of his sullen and unexpressive behavior. Irritability is also a common sign of depression in children. Students in distress may complain that others get on their nerves, or they may seem moody or irritable to teachers. Gage's increasing level of irritability, as evidenced by his comments that others were "getting on his nerves," could have been recognized by a counselor as a potential symptom of depression. Both Gage's sullen, unexpressive behavior and his comments reflecting irritability could be considered red flags pointing to the need for a more thorough assessment.

In summary, although Gage seems to have had significant difficulties with the transition, and although his placement in special education might have been a stressor that contributed to his declining self-esteem and, perhaps, depression, direct causality is unlikely. As I mentioned earlier, there might have been a history of prior mental health issues or family problems that were not brought to light until a crisis situation such as this occurred. Furthermore, there may be other chronic or acute stressors affecting Gage that were unknown to the school counselor. A thorough assessment was warranted and might have helped prevent Gage from reaching a level of distress that involved him drawing pictures depicting suicide.

Nevertheless, for all of the reasons detailed in this response, it can be difficult to assess depression and risk of harm to self or others in children Gage's age. Not all school counselors have been trained to clinically assess for mental health concerns; even if they have training, they may not feel confident handling these situations. School counselors need to consult with counseling colleagues and continue to update and hone their clinical skills through reading and professional development. Case studies and role playing involving other key school staff members can be great ways to problem solve appropriate responses to various student crises from a multidisciplinary team approach.

 Response

John M. Littrell

I applaud the counselor for presenting a case that she dealt with as a beginning school counselor. The process of learning to be a school counselor is laden with situations that challenge the awareness, knowledge, and skills of experienced counselors, let alone novices. In her case presentation, the counselor acknowledged that she was surprised when the teacher discovered Gage's cry for help, a detailed pencil drawing of a suicidal boy, and was distraught that she missed Gage's "deep pain and sadness."

The counselor's first question was "How might one be able to use brief counseling and still identify serious underlying mental health issues?" This question assumes a dichotomy between practicing brief counseling and identifying serious underlying mental health issues. I do not believe that such a dichotomy exists. Perhaps the dichotomy arose in this particular case because the counselor conceptualized brief counseling as a set of techniques (e.g., using a metaphor) and as a time-limited intervention (e.g., using a single session). I find it more useful to think of brief counseling as a theory designed to help people more quickly experience greater choice (Littrell, 1998). As a major theory, brief counseling lends itself to two complementary approaches. The first approach is more *problem focused* (Watzlawick, Weakland, & Fisch, 1974). The counselor helps the student through four stages: (a) identifying problems, (b) eliciting the student's attempted solutions, (c) setting a goal, and (d) using various strategies to help the student achieve the goal. The second brief counseling approach is more *solution focused* (Berg & Steiner, 2003). The counselor spotlights the student's strengths and resources. The counselor might ask the miracle question to identify the student's goal and then use techniques such as scaling questions and exploring exceptions to help the student move in the direction of the goal.

I believe that if one conceptualizes brief counseling as a way of thinking about problems and solutions, rather than as a set of techniques, the seeming dichotomy between a behavioral problem and a serious underlying mental health issue is resolvable. Effective counselors of all theoretical persuasions take time when counseling begins to figure out what students want to change in their life. In this case, the counselor explains that she had worked with Gage in the past and that his disruptive behavior continued. I suspect that when the reality therapy and the problem-solving approaches she had tried so far were not working, the counselor quickly moved to the technique of metaphor, which she had recently learned in a solution-focused brief counseling workshop. With respect to alternatives to becoming technique focused, the practice of brief counseling does not exclude the use of the following alternatives to assist students who present challenging problems:

- using diagnostic and assessment work to clarify and understand the student's world,
- consulting with or making referrals to other professionals when one is stumped or overwhelmed,
- cycling back and renegotiating the counseling contract with the student if the initial approach is not working,
- rethinking the student's situation more deeply and generating new ideas by returning to theory, and
- being aware of the signs and symptoms of serious problems so that one can be more alert to situations in which one should not use time-limited approaches.

I propose four ways to use brief counseling in this case while remaining alert to serious mental health issues:

1. Rather than the counselor selecting the metaphor (i.e., a target) and proceeding to an action for Gage to take, I believe the counselor needed to assess where Gage was in the change process. Prochaska, Norcross, and DiClemente (1994) offered a six-stage framework for understanding the process of change: precontemplation, contemplation, preparation, action, maintenance, and termination. Gage seems to be at the precontemplation stage in dealing with his problem of getting into trouble in the classroom. Instead of encouraging contemplation and preparation, the counselor jumped ahead to having Gage make efforts to change his behavior (action). For his part, Gage's statement "I know that helping my friends have fun at school instead of just being bored all day is at least one thing I am good at" seems to suggest that he had more reasons not to change than to change. The counselor could have helped Gage generate more reasons to change, and this would have assisted Gage in moving to the contemplation stage of the change process. Small steps toward an immediate goal help ensure success.

2. Gage does not seem to be a motivated student. In brief counseling, one often asks oneself, "Who is the client?" The answer is that the client is the person who has a problem. In this case, the person with the problem was not Gage; it was the teacher. Consulting with the teacher is one alternative to working with someone who has little motivation to change.

3. One way to have Gage become more involved with counseling is to tell him the following: "Gage, you're in my office because the teacher thinks you have a problem with getting into trouble. Your teacher wants us to deal with that. However, there could be other problems or concerns that you think are more important. What could we talk about in this office that would really help you?" Talking in this way places more responsibility on Gage, not the teacher or counselor, to identify relevant issues for him.

4. One aspect of a counselor's job in elementary schools involves the socialization of students. If Gage has poor social skills, it would be very appropriate to have him work on these skills with a small group. The small group may be an opportunity for Gage to begin to make friends whom he does not have to amuse.

In response to the counselor's second question, "Are the types of behavioral problems that Gage presented common for depressed children?" childhood depression may manifest itself in numerous ways. Gage persistently exhibited several signs of depression that the American Academy of Child and Adolescent Psychiatry (1994) has listed. The signs of childhood depression include

- frequent sadness, tearfulness, crying
- hopelessness
- decreased interest in activities; or inability to enjoy previously favorite activities
- persistent boredom; low energy
- social isolation, poor communication
- low self-esteem and guilt
- extreme sensitivity to rejection or failure
- increased irritability, anger, or hostility
- difficulty with relationships
- frequent complaints of physical illnesses such as headaches and stomachaches
- frequent absences from school or poor performance in school
- poor concentration
- a major change in eating and/or sleeping patterns
- talk of or efforts to run away from home
- thoughts or expressions of suicide or self-destructive behavior. (American Academy of Child and Adolescent Psychiatry, 1994)

Although any single sign may not indicate depression, school counselors must be attuned to the possibility and recognize persistent signs. Counselors not trained in recognizing childhood and adolescent depression have a professional responsibility to obtain such training through workshops or in-service training led by experts. To her credit, on learning of the suicide drawing, the counselor took the required steps to ensure the student's safety.

The counselor's third question addresses the impact of special education placement on children's self-esteem and on the development of mood disorders as well as ways counselors might work to prevent such problems from occurring in the transition from regular to special education services. In particular, she offered, "It has occurred to me that Gage's placement in special education might have contributed to a decreasing sense of self-esteem and possibly directly to his depression. How likely is this? What suggestions do you have for school counselors who want to address this possibility in a preventive manner?"

To be successful, placement in special education requires skill, sensitivity, and follow-up on the part of teachers, administrators, counselors, and parents. Gage's placement in special education might have had the unintended effects of cutting him off from peer support and familiar surroundings, sparking verbal harassment by other children, and undermining Gage's self-esteem. His self-labeling of "retard" may be an assessment of his new standing or an internalization of messages being delivered by others. Both could be understood as warning signs of depression.

In this case, there were several ways the school counselor could have used a prevention modality. These include the following:

- enlisting the cooperation of Gage's parents so that they can act in concert with the counselor.
- including Gage in a small social-skills group led by the counselor. This would be particularly appropriate as Gage seems to have poor social skills. School counselors can find a curriculum detailing how to organize a social-skills group in our book (Littrell & Peterson, 2005) about Claudia Vangstad, an exemplary elementary school counselor.
- identifying and then increasing the focus on Gage's internal and external strengths and resources.
- eliciting Gage's solutions rather than relying on those of the counselor. I have occasionally thought myself clever in thinking of ways for clients to change. Inevitably, though, the client's world is much richer than my limited understanding of it. As a result, I have found it much more effective to brainstorm with the student and to let the student have the last say as to what will really work in his or her world.
- helping Gage be explicit rather than vague in setting goals and planning actions to reach them. The more vague the goals and actions are, the less likely the student is to carry them out. Piaget's (2000) concrete operations stage would be useful in understanding and helping Gage. Children at this stage are capable of concrete, sequential problem solving. First, what is Gage's specific goal? Second, what small, specific steps can Gage take to move himself in the direction of his goal?

In summary, adherence to a particular theoretical framework (e.g., brief counseling) should not blind counselors to other valuable ways of understanding the change process. Although a counselor uses the strengths of a given theoretical approach, he or she must be aware of its limits. My suggestion to school counselors is to acquire a strong counseling foundation by first mastering the strategies and techniques in their favorite theoretical approach. Building on this foundation, they can then fill in any gaps by acquiring further knowledge and skills from supplementary approaches.

References

American Academy of Child and Adolescent Psychiatry. (1994). *The depressed child.* Retrieved May 16, 2006, from http://www.aacap.org/publications/factsfam/depressd.htm

Berg, I. K., & Steiner, T. (2003). *Children's solution work.* New York: Norton.

Davis, T. E., & Osborn, C. J. (2000). *The solution-focused school counselor.* Philadelphia: Accelerated Development.

Littrell, J. M. (1998). *Brief counseling in action.* New York: Norton.

Littrell, J. M., & Peterson, J. S. (2005). *Portrait and model of a school counselor.* Boston: Lahaska Press/Houghton Mifflin.

Metcalf, L. (1995). *Counseling toward solutions: A practical solution-focused program for working with students, teacher, and parents.* Englewood Cliffs, NJ: Center for Applied Research in Education.

Piaget, J. (2000). Piaget's theory. In K. Lee (Ed.), *Childhood cognitive development: The essential readings* (pp. 33–47). Malden, MA: Blackwell.

Prochaska, J. O., Norcross, J. C., & DiClemente, C. C. (1994). *Changing for good.* New York: William Morrow.

Watzlawick, P., Weakland, J., & Fisch, R. (1974). *Change: Principles of problem formation and problem resolution.* New York: Norton.

Differential Diagnosis: "Fantasies or Delusions?"

This incident explores the complexities of distinguishing between normal developmental reliance on fantasy play and delusions indicative of childhood psychosis.

■ Critical Incident

Angie D. Waliski

"Joey Jacobs," a 4.5-year-old Caucasian boy, first came to our county's community mental health agency when his parents were having severe marital issues, including domestic violence. I was a brand new employee at the agency, and Joey was my very first client. As such, I sat in and observed while a more experienced counselor conducted the initial intake session. Joey's father and paternal grandmother attended the intake session and explained their reasons for seeking our assistance. During this session, we learned that Joey was displaying a vast array of symptoms. In particular, Joey was exhibiting hyperactivity, impulsivity, somatic complaints, separation anxiety from his grandmother, encopresis, enuresis, nightmares, temper tantrums, aggression toward his siblings, regressive behaviors (e.g., sucking his thumb and chewing on clothing), attachment to inanimate objects, and frequent immersion in fantasy play.

Next, the intake counselor inquired about Joey's health and family history. In terms of prenatal health, no complications with pregnancy or the birth were reported, but Joey did experience some mild jaundice and colic as an infant. Exploration of Joey's family history revealed a number of mental health concerns for both parents. Both of Joey's parents had received inpatient treatment for psychological disorders as adolescents. Joey's father had been diagnosed with borderline personality disorder, bipolar disorder, and schizoaffective disorder; Joey's mother had a history of depression and past suicide attempts and an early diagnosis of schizophrenia. In addition, both Mr. and Mrs. Jacobs had a history of drug abuse. Indeed, in conducting the interview with Mr. Jacobs, we detected that he seemed to be under the influence of alcohol.

During this intake session, we also had the opportunity to experience firsthand the conflict within Joey's family. Joey's father and grandmother had brought Joey to this intake session and reported that Joey needed counseling because of the severe conflict in the home. In fact, Mr. Jacobs claimed that Joey's mother had held them all against their will for a week in their home. Toward the end of the intake session, Joey's mother also arrived at the clinic. Mrs. Jacobs was irate and aggressive toward the office staff. She demanded that Joey be released into her care and threatened to prevent him from receiving counseling.

Because Joey's symptoms seemed a likely response to the marital conflict and violence in the family unit, the intake counselor diagnosed Joey with adjustment disorder with mixed disturbance of emotion and conduct (Code 309.4 in the *Diagnostic and Statistical Manual of Mental Disorders*; 4th ed., text rev.; *DSM–IV–TR*; American Psychiatric Association, 2000) and child–parent relationship problems (Code V61.20) and referred him to me. Although I was unsure whether he would actually receive his mother's consent for treatment, I found myself both enthusiastic and rather daunted as I anticipated working with Joey.

I was both relieved and nervous when Joey's father contacted our clinic and scheduled Joey's first appointment with me. Mr. Jacobs explained that he had moved out of the family home and that he and his children were now living with his mother. Joey's grandmother brought him to our appointment, and, just as described in the initial intake session, Joey was reticent to leave his grandmother. As his grandmother encouraged him to "go to the playroom with the nice lady," Joey was visibly anxious and refused to enter the playroom with me. Unable to persuade him to enter alone, I finally invited his grandmother into the playroom as well. Joey's grandmother and I sat down to talk, and Joey immediately curled up into a fetal position on the floor. He then urinated on himself. Thus began our work.

As a new counselor, I found myself using a combination of behavior modification techniques, designed to reduce Joey's separation anxiety, and child-centered play therapy techniques, designed to engage him in the counseling process. Over the course of the next couple of months, Joey gradually became comfortable entering the playroom with me and engaging in play behaviors. As he did so, I became increasingly aware of Joey's reliance on fantasy.

Soon, Joey's sessions with me consisted primarily of fantasy play involving action figures and superheroes. Although this is not necessarily unusual for a child of Joey's age, his almost exclusive involvement in these fantasies was notable. On entering the playroom, he would immediately launch into detailed fantasy play, and this play would continue for the duration of our session.

As Joey's parents decided to divorce and began a custody battle, Joey's fantasy play was no longer limited to our counseling sessions. In fact, his fantasy play increased to the point that he was functioning as fictional movie characters throughout the entire day. At this point, I referred Joey to a therapeutic preschool. At this preschool, Joey received group counseling every day in addition to the individual or family counseling I was providing once or twice a week.

Feedback from Joey's preschool teachers was consistent. They indicated that he seemed to be immersed in fantasy almost constantly. These fantasies generally featured Joey as the superhero, on the lookout for villains and other bad guys, conquering evil and dodging danger. One day he might be Frodo from *Lord of the Rings* and exhibit the magical ability to become invisible. Another day, Joey might be frightened by a *Jurassic Park* tyrannosaurus rex dinosaur that causes "earth-shakes" when it walks. At school, at home, and in sessions, he engaged in conversations with these fictional characters and was often so immersed in this fantasy play that he was unaware of the activities happening around him. His preschool case manager contacted me to share her perception that Joey was exhibiting signs of a psychotic disorder and to suggest that he needed hospitalization.

In our sessions, I was able to help Joey identify ways his real life resembled fantasies. For example, he explained, "Grandma is like the T-rex because whenever she comes over, I want to run and hide because of all the yelling." This conversation allowed me to understand that, although he clung to her and resisted separation at times, Joey also feared his grandmother a great deal. Although I was finding the fantasy play useful in our sessions and was gaining some insight into the fantasies, I found myself still struggling with my confidence about the correct diagnosis. Was Joey's fantasy play merely a developmentally age-appropriate strategy for coping with his life, or was it indicative of delusional thinking and a possible psychotic disorder? Although the case came to a successful conclusion through the use of child-centered play therapy, I find myself still wondering about these issues.

Questions

1. How can a counselor best determine whether immersion in fantasy play is adaptive or instead indicative of a psychotic disorder?
2. What are other approaches that have been demonstrated to be effective with clients presenting such behaviors and issues?

■ Response

Deborah E. Renard

The issue of fantasy play seems to be one of the most salient aspects of this case, and it is a serious concern for Joey's preschool personnel and for the novice counselor. I discuss this issue first in terms of diagnosis and case conceptualization and second in the context of how it can be most effectively managed by those who have face-to-face contact with Joey.

As the counselor noted, interest and involvement in fantasy play are not unusual given Joey's age and developmental status. Concerns about the frequency and intensity of his immersion in fantasy play led to the need to determine whether these behaviors were indicative of a psychotic disorder, as suggested by the preschool case manager, or whether they were essentially an elaborate yet somehow adaptive coping mechanism, as the counselor believed. On the basis of the data presented in this critical incident, I view Joey's fantasy-related behavior not as psychotic but rather as a means of coping with the multiple stressors and threats he has experienced in his chaotic home life.

A few comments about diagnosis and clinical assessment are in order. Although the scope of practice for professional counselors varies from state to state with regard to the diagnosis and treatment of mental disorders, it is my opinion that all counselors benefit from knowledge of psychopathology, psychodiagnostics, and the associated terminologies and criteria. Even when the professional counselor is not in a position to conduct formal diagnosis, his or her awareness of behaviors that warrant further assessment via referrals is important for appropriate client care; moreover, the counselor's observations and input are often sought by the psychologist or psychiatrist who is conducting the formal diagnostic assessment. In a professional context in which counselors are not always accorded the prestige, status, and respect extended to other helping professionals, familiarity with psychodiagnostics and the ability to communicate with other mental health care providers in terms they understand can be essential elements of the counselor's credibility and capacity to be an effective advocate for the client. Finally, when counselors are trained and capable of conducting mental health diagnosis and treatment, they are in a strong position to influence the disposition of the case. Having credibility and the ability to articulate clinical judgments in the language of the medical model (i.e., the current *DSM–IV–TR*) enhances the impact and acceptance of the counselor's opinions. Having the knowledge necessary for accurate diagnosis also equips the counselor with the power to avert misdiagnosis and the inappropriate pathologizing of clients and their behaviors.

In this case, the stakes associated with misdiagnosis are quite high for Joey. At least one member of his treatment team is advocating psychiatric hospitalization. An unwarranted hospitalization would put Joey at risk for unnecessary medication, increased separation anxiety issues, and long-lasting stigma associated with being labeled with a mental illness and having a history of psychiatric hospitalization. There is a strong likelihood that this pathologized perspective of Joey would influence important decisions (especially around schooling and special educational placement) that would follow him for years to come. The counselor, who views Joey's diagnosis as an adjustment disorder, needs to present a credible assessment of Joey's mental status and behaviors as nonpsychotic to the preschool personnel and perhaps as part of the custody hearings as well.

Children of Joey's age frequently engage in fantasy play. They often talk aloud with their imaginary friends, invent and play out elaborate scenarios in which they may play important fantasy roles, and express affect that is congruent with the fantasy play. Indeed, immersion in such play and a blurring of "the line between fantasy and reality" (Benham, 2000, p. 255) are not uncommon. To be considered psychotic, Joey's thought processes, affect, and behavior should show significant deviance both from developmentally typical behaviors and from the objective reality of his experiences. There is no evidence that Joey was experiencing hallucinations or paranoid ideation. However strange his imaginary conversations and fantasy identifications may seem on the surface, the underlying thematic issues of power, safety, and danger do match closely with Joey's actual experiences with caretakers who had been exhibiting unpredictable, irrational, and sometimes violent behaviors. One can understand this child's reality-based desire for peace and safety and the preoperational cognitive processes that could give rise to both his vigilance and his desire to have magical powers and strengths that would render the unpleasantries of his life harmless.

It is therefore my opinion that the content and expression of Joey's fantasy play are not indicative of childhood psychosis. The data better fit with a conceptualization of Joey's symptoms as indicative of his difficulties with adjustment, overlaid on insecure attachment to parental figures. Insecure attachment (Bowlby, 1988) is indicated not only by direct behavior observation but also by his separation anxiety, regressive behaviors, somatic complaints, nightmares, fantasy play, and externalizing problematic behaviors (e.g., hyperactivity, impulsivity, temper tantrums, aggression toward siblings). Such expressions of distress and insecurity are not uncommon modes for boys of Joey's age. In their discussion of adjustment to parental separation and divorce,

O'Halloran and Carr (2000) noted that children are especially vulnerable in cases in which there is insecure attachment and "exposure to chronic family problems, including parental adjustment problems, marital discord, domestic violence, [and] family disorganization" (p. 282). I consider Joey's lack of appropriate bladder and bowel control as secondary symptoms—that is, regressive behavior. Noting that enuresis and encopresis are not typically diagnosed until after ages 4–5, Murphy and Carr (2000) stated that these behaviors can present as "part of a wider set of adjustment problems primarily related to a chaotic, stressful, or abusive psychosocial environment" (p. 49). Conceptualizing Joey's various symptoms as issues of adjustment rather than frank psychopathology provides the best fit with the data and the best guide to appropriate counseling interventions.

Turning now to the matter of intervention, I note that Joey's fantasy immersion—however effective it may be as a psychological coping mechanism—interferes with his ability to fulfill expected social roles, especially in the preschool and home environments. Of all the reported symptoms, Joey's fantasy play and his separation anxiety seem to be creating the greatest amount of concern, and thus it is on these areas that the counselor should focus first.

In my opinion, three distinct components are important to include in treatment. First, the counselor must deal with the issue of getting Joey into the treatment room without undue distress related to separation from the caregiver who accompanied him to the appointment. A graduated approach to familiarizing Joey with the new environment and creating rapport with the counselor, without the immediate presence of his caregiver, could be accomplished through the use of behavioral shaping and contingency management. Over the course of several sessions, it would be expected that Joey would be willing and able to comfortably engage in treatment in the counseling office without the presence of his caregiver.

The second treatment component involves the actual counseling interventions that are used with Joey. The ability to engage in treatment without the presence of the caregiver is important not only because it is a significant step toward healing the separation anxiety but also because it allows the counselor to begin the intervention process in an environment in which Joey can safely express the full range of feelings in a nonjudgmental, unconditionally accepting environment. I would most likely use child-centered play therapy (Landreth, 2002) as the primary modality, just as the novice counselor chose to do in the critical incident. I would expect to observe a transformation of his fantasy immersion into more discrete play sessions, with themes evolving over time to reflect his changing feelings, his perceptions of others, and an increased realistic sense of self-efficacy. I have found this modality to be effective with a wide range of children, and I especially prefer it in cases in which the child has experienced trauma or chaotic environments, which tend to engender complex feelings and atypical or dysfunctional thoughts and beliefs about self, others, and the way the world works. Child-centered play therapy allows but does not coerce children to find their own unique ways of expressing and understanding their experiences and potential, with the counselor as an affirming witness to this process of growth and psychological development. In addition to nondirective, individual child-centered play therapy, I would also consider the incorporation of some cognitive-behavioral elements (Friedberg & McClure, 2002) in middle therapy—for example, modeling, role play, and behavioral rehearsal of alternative scenarios, expressed as variations of the play scenarios that the child has created. In later therapy, I would weigh the risks and benefits of bringing the caregiver into part of the session to observe and learn to play and interact more constructively with the child.

The third treatment component requires attention to the child's environment outside the therapy room. As I noted earlier, the preschool staff members need to shift their conceptualization and approach to working with Joey. In an ideal world, the behaviors of concern to them would simply resolve via the counselor's skillful work; in the real world, it is more likely that the counselor needs to educate the preschool staff about Joey's status and collaborate with them in establishing achievable goals and expectations for his behavior.

More important, the counselor should address Joey's relationships with his parents and his grandmother. In my opinion, Joey is not at risk as much from the potential genetic transmission of his parents' own mental health problems as he is from his chaotic home environment, especially his exposure to marital discord, parental intoxication, and domestic violence. It is essential to Joey's mental health that the counselor, in collaboration with others who may be involved with the child, form a plan for maintaining a more stable and less conflictual home life. His caregivers' engagement in individual, group, or family counseling might be in order. For example, if the grandmother has assumed parental responsibilities for Joey, she might benefit from a group for grandparents raising grandchildren (Renard, 1995). Joey's father might benefit from substance abuse treatment, and his mother might benefit from mental health assessment and treatment. Psychoeducational interventions about the experience of divorce might benefit all parties; parenting and behavior management skill training should be strongly recommended for the custodial caregivers. Given the parents' decision to divorce and the pending custody issues, Joey would certainly benefit from ongoing individual supportive treatment until his home life is more settled.

Response

Suzanne M. (Hobson) Dugger

I can only imagine the counselor's internal reactions to receiving such a difficult first client. I am assuming that, in addition to being brand new, this counselor was also trained in a program that de-emphasized the medical model approach to diagnosis and treatment and that instead emphasized the wellness-based, developmental model of assessment and intervention that has long been the hallmark of the counseling profession. As such, developing a diagnostic impression of such disordered behavior and determining an appropriate course of treatment would undoubtedly prove daunting. In my response, I hope to (a) normalize and validate the counselor's sense of being overwhelmed, (b) address the counselor's question of differential diagnosis using a developmental perspective, and (c) briefly discuss treatment options in the context of wraparound services.

Indeed, Joey presented with quite the list of symptoms: "hyperactivity, impulsivity, somatic complaints, separation anxiety from his grandmother, encopresis, enuresis, nightmares, temper tantrums, aggression toward his siblings, regressive behaviors (e.g., as sucking his thumb and chewing on clothing), attachment to inanimate objects, and frequent immersion in fantasy play"(p.13). Joey's symptoms, whether or not they are indicative of a psychotic disorder, are certainly severe enough in nature to challenge even the most seasoned counselor. Referral of such difficult clients to novice counselors is, unfortunately, all too commonplace in the mental health system. In my more cynical moments, I might even speculate that the more seasoned counselors use their seniority to pass along the most challenging of cases to maintain their own comfort level.

That being said, the counselor is nevertheless still faced with the challenge ahead of her: understanding and helping Joey. To do so, it is essential that the counselor not suffer a crisis of confidence but instead recognize the normative nature of her initial reaction. Although the counselor might have initially worried that her sense of feeling overwhelmed was simply a product of being so new to the profession, the fact is that Joey was an extremely challenging client. He presented with a wide array of symptoms that were clearly interfering with his functioning to a significant degree. He was unable to participate in the social and cognitive aspects of school in a developmentally appropriate way. Whenever one is faced with difficult clients, it is important to avoid functioning in isolation. I would encourage the counselor to reach out—both to a supervisor and to the literature. In doing so, she should explore diagnostic and treatment issues that would assist her in counseling Joey.

In approaching the diagnostic process, it is important to note that the *DSM–IV–TR* diagnostic classification system is based on the principles of hierarchy and parsimony (Maxmen & Ward, 1995). The principle of hierarchy requires that the counselor rule out more severe disorders before arriving at a less severe diagnosis. In this case, it seems that the novice counselor did not consider the possibility of a psychotic disorder (i.e., schizophrenia) until prompted by the case manager at Joey's preschool. To diagnose properly, however, it is essential that the counselor address and, if appropriate, rule out a diagnosis of a psychotic disorder before arriving at a less severe diagnosis. The principle of parsimony urges counselors to "seek the single most elegant, economical, and efficient diagnosis that accounts for all the available data . . . [and] when a single diagnosis is insufficient, [seek] the fewest number of diagnoses" (Maxmen & Ward, 1995, p. 45).

Especially given the severity of Joey's immersion in fantasy play and the fact that both of his parents had a history of psychotic symptoms (as evidenced by his mother's one-time diagnosis of schizophrenia and his father's diagnosis of schizoaffective disorder), it is essential to explore the possibility that Joey could indeed be displaying signs of a childhood psychotic disorder. By consulting the *DSM–IV–TR* (American Psychiatric Association, 2000), the counselor would discover that, to be diagnosed with schizophrenia, an individual must display at least two characteristic symptoms and experience significant impairment for at least 6 months in at least two areas of functioning. In addition, for the client to qualify for a diagnosis of schizophrenia, the symptoms cannot be better explained by other mental disorders, substance use, or medical conditions. This process of ruling out other potential explanations is known as *differential diagnosis*.

The determination of whether Joey has schizophrenia (or another psychotic disorder) therefore needs to be based both on an assessment of the nature of Joey's symptoms and on a differential diagnosis. With regard to symptoms, a diagnosis of schizophrenia requires that an individual display two or more characteristic symptoms for a minimum of 1 month. Some of the characteristic symptoms are known as *positive symptoms* because their presence is notable during psychotic episodes (McClellan, McCurry, Speltz, & Jones, 2002; Wicks-Nelson & Israel, 2003). Positive symptoms include delusions, hallucinations, disorganized speech, and disorganized or catatonic behavior (American Psychiatric Association, 2000). Other characteristic symptoms are known as *negative symptoms,* or "a lack of normally occurring behaviors" (Wicks-Nelson & Israel, 2003, p. 353). Negative symptoms are grouped together in the *DSM–IV–TR* as a single criterion and include "diminished affect, speech content, and goal-directed activities" (Wicks-Nelson & Israel, 2003, p. 353).

Key to Joey's case is whether his immersion in fantasy play represents two or more of the characteristic symptoms of schizophrenia. The information about Joey offers no indication that his speech had become disorganized or otherwise incoherent; that his behavior was disorganized or catatonic; or that he was exhibiting negative symptoms, such as flattened affect or diminished speech. The question, therefore, is whether Joey's interactions with fictional movie characters represent delusions or hallucinations. Ideally, the assessment process would involve determining whether Joey believed the fantasy play to be real or whether he knew it was make believe. Given the fact that Joey is only 4.5 years old and that it is developmentally appropriate for children his age to experience confusion about what is real and what is pretend, such a determination is made much more difficult (Volkmar & Tsatsanis, 2002). Making such a determination is indeed challenging for mental health professionals, because it is possible that the fantasies represent delusions or hallucinations or, alternatively, that they simply represent an altered, problematic adaptation to challenging developmental circumstances (Erk, 2004; Findling, Schulz, Kashani, & Harlan, 2001).

My sense in reading about Joey's case, however, is that his fantasy play does not represent hallucinations and delusions. The counselor indicated that Joey was able to connect his fantasy play with real-life events, as when he likened his grandmother to the tyrannosaurus rex and talked about how he sometimes wanted to run and hide when she visited. This suggests to me that there was a connection in Joey's mind between reality and his fantasy life. I was struck by the absence of any other symptoms characteristic of schizophrenia and would want to see signs of disorganization (in his speech and behavior, not in his bedroom) or some negative symptoms before I would be inclined to offer a diagnosis of schizophrenia for someone so young. In not diagnosing Joey with a psychotic disorder, I would also take into consideration the findings of McClellan et al. (2002) that the negative symptoms are "the best predictor of diagnosis" (p. 797), because positive symptoms, although they are hallmark features of schizophrenia, are also found in a number of other disorders.

Even if I were unable to rule out the presence of hallucinations or delusions, a diagnosis of schizophrenia would still require that the symptoms not be better explained by other mental disorders, substance use, or medical conditions. It is my belief that Joey is more likely suffering from an adjustment disorder with mixed disturbance of emotions and conduct, chronic type. Adjustment disorders "involve maladaptive reactions to psychosocial stressors" (Maxmen & Ward, 1995, p. 458) that occur within 3 months of the onset of the stressor and that persist no longer than 6 months after cessation of the stressor. The stressors present in Joey's life include his parents' marital conflict, violence in the home, and conflict related to his grandmother. I find it especially telling that Joey's increased immersion in fantasy play occurred when his parents began the divorce process, and I attribute the increased severity in his symptoms as indicative of adjustment difficulties.

From a developmental and psychological perspective, the timing of the parents' divorce is especially challenging to a child of Joey's age and developmental history. With regard to developmental history, Joey seems to have had a rather insecure attachment with his caretakers (parents and grandmother), as evidenced by his separation anxiety and regressive behaviors. Further disruption of the family unit would therefore predictably increase Joey's anxieties and insecurities. With regard to age, parental separations and divorces are especially difficult for children in the age range of 4 to 6 years. This difficulty arises because children's developmental processes at this stage generally involve expanding their relational circles to include peers and school personnel. This expansion process, although desirable, also challenges children to become less vigilant about whether their parents are present (Trembley, 1996). Again, this expansion requires a certain level of security. Major changes at home during this transitional time predictably result in less security and more anxiety about school. This is also consistent with Joey's case.

Moving on to a discussion of treatments, I note that it is especially fortunate that Joey and his family sought treatment at a community mental health agency. Although there are certainly disadvantages to such agencies (e.g., high turnover of overworked and underpaid mental health professionals), a prime advantage in this case is the feasibility of wraparound services. Wraparound services represent an ideal treatment approach for Joey and his family. In addition to receiving individual counseling, Joey will benefit from the collaborative involvement of other professionals. Case management services to ensure appropriate assessment of his home environment and adequate support of his parents are important. Regular communications with the therapeutic preschool personnel are essential. Educational and cognitive assessments might be deemed appropriate. Custody evaluations may be necessary. Parent education seems essential.

With regard to individual counseling approaches to working with Joey, the counselor has made an appropriate choice to use play therapy. I specifically recommend the use of experiential play therapy, as described by Norton and Norton (1997). In this approach, the counselor enters the child's world of play to develop an understanding of and ability to intervene in the child's struggles. With Joey, for example, the counselor could become part of the fantasy play. Initially, she would allow Joey to be directive of her and to teach her what to do. As she developed an understanding of the dynamics of this play, however, she could begin to act more independently to assist Joey in making changes. When Joey's play involved the arrival of the terrifying tyrannosaurus rex (grandma), for example, the counselor could help Joey shift from his current run-and-hide response to a more adaptive response. She could get out her (pretend) camcorder, point it at the tyrannosaurus rex, and shout out that she is recording everything and will show it to the safari hunters if the tyrannosaurus rex tries to hurt anyone. In this way, the counselor could use this play experience to help Joey recognize that another source of protection involves telling others about his grandma's scary visits. This, of course, would metaphorically parallel Joey's current "run and hide into fantasy" approach to coping and would encourage him to instead turn to others for assistance.

References

American Psychiatric Association. (2000). *Diagnostic and statistical manual of mental disorders* (4th ed., text rev.). Washington, DC: Author.

Benham, A. L. (2000). The observation and assessment of young children including use of the Infant-Toddler Mental Status Exam. In C. H. Zeenah Jr. (Ed.), *Handbook of infant mental health* (2nd ed., pp. 249–265). New York: Guilford Press.

Bowlby, J. (1988). *A secure base: Parent–child attachment and healthy human development.* New York: Basic Books.

Erk, R. R. (2004). *Counseling treatment for children and adolescents with* DSM–IV–TR *diagnoses.* Upper Saddle River, NJ: Pearson Education, Inc.

Findling, R. L., Schulz, S .C., Kashani, J. H., & Harlan, E. (2001). *Psychotic disorders in children and adolescents.* Thousand Oaks, CA: Sage.

Friedberg, R. D., & McClure, J. M. (2002). *Clinical practice of cognitive therapy with children and adolescents: The nuts and bolts.* New York: Guilford Press.

Landreth, G. L. (2002). *Play therapy: The art of the relationship* (2nd ed.). New York: Brunner-Routledge.

Maxmen, J. S., & Ward, N. G. (1995). *Essential psychopathology and its treatment* (2nd ed.). New York: Norton.

McClellan, J., McCurry, C., Speltz, M. L., & Jones, K. (2002). Symptom factors in early-onset psychotic disorders. *Journal of the American Academy of Child & Adolescent Psychiatry, 43,* 1026–1029.

Murphy, M., & Carr, A. (2000). Eneuresis and encopresis. In A. Carr (Ed.), *What works with children and adolescents: A critical review of psychological interventions with children, adolescents, and their families* (pp. 49–64). New York: Brunner-Routledge.

Norton, C. C., & Norton, B. E. (1997). *Reaching children through play therapy: An experiential approach.* Denver, CO: Publishing Cooperative.

O'Halloran, M., & Carr, C. (2000). Adjustment to parental separation and divorce. In A. Carr (Ed.), *What works with children and adolescents: A critical review of psychological interventions with children, adolescents, and their families* (pp. 280–299). New York: Brunner-Routledge.

Renard, D. E. (1995). *Group work with grandparents raising grandchildren.* Unpublished manuscript.

Trembley, E. L. (1996). *Relational therapy concepts.* Kalamazoo, MI: Author.

Volkmar, F. R., & Tsatsanis, K. (2002). Psychosis and psychotic conditions in childhood and adolescence. In D. T. Marsh & M. A. Fristad (Eds.), *Handbook of serious emotional disturbance in children and adolescents* (pp. 266–283). New York: Wiley.

Wicks-Nelson, R., & Israel, A. C. (2003). *Behavior disorders of childhood* (5th ed.). Upper Saddle River, NJ: Pearson Education, Inc.

"Why Does She Behave This Way?":
Reactive Attachment Disorder

The following critical incident involves an 11-year-old girl diagnosed with reactive attachment disorder (RAD). Her treatment and prognosis are complicated by the lack of information currently available on RAD and by the myriad cultural, environmental, and developmental factors that typically accompany such a diagnosis.

■ Critical Incident

Chasity Amber Harris

"Lauren," an 11-year-old female African American, presented for treatment at a child and adolescent residential care facility after her aunt and custodial guardian, "Grace," became increasingly concerned about Lauren's behavior. As an intern, I met Lauren and Grace for the first time during Lauren's initial assessment. Grace's frustration was evident in her opening statement: "I have finally had enough of trying to parent her." Grace complained that Lauren had been harming herself, including several suicide attempts, and had been angry and aggressive toward teachers and peers. Through subsequent interactions with Lauren during her treatment, I came to learn that these behaviors were common for her.

I obtained a thorough history of the client and her family during the initial intake, with both Grace and Lauren present. I discovered that Lauren was born 4 weeks prematurely and experienced all of the physical challenges accompanying premature birth. Grace attributed the complications during pregnancy and during labor and delivery to the fact that Lauren's mother was an alcoholic and drug addict who had failed many attempts at treatment. Lauren's mother had also been diagnosed with bipolar disorder, but there were no other indications of familial mental health problems. I had no information concerning Lauren's father at the time of her treatment.

Grace shared with me a number of facts about family history, past medical care, and therapeutic treatment history. Grace stated that she and her husband, who are now separated, adopted Lauren at the age of 2 after Lauren, extremely underweight and neglected, was left on their doorstep by her mother. From that moment, Grace was responsible for everything in Lauren's life, including her primary medical and psychological care. Grace took Lauren to a pediatrician for an examination and immunization series. It was discovered that Lauren had a history of childhood ear infections that had not been treated, and the physician placed tubes in her ears to cure the infection. Over the next few months, Lauren's health improved, and she started to gain weight. Grace told me that Lauren had always exhibited difficult behaviors, which Grace attributed to the volatile changes in Lauren's early childhood environment, and that she had believed that with time, love, and affection Lauren would make progress.

When Lauren was about 6, Grace became increasingly concerned with Lauren's lack of progress and sought help to address some of her behavioral problems. Although she was doing well academically, Lauren spent much of her time in an in-school suspension program and eventually was sent to a more restrictive alternative school. After 4 years of individual, family, and in-home therapy with three different counselors, there was little improvement in Lauren's behavior. Lauren was hospitalized in an acute care facility twice during this time period because of suicide attempts and was also placed in foster care for a very short time after she ran away from home. Increasingly, Grace became discouraged about the possibilities for Lauren's future and the chance for her to live a meaningful and fulfilling life. According to Grace, nothing seemed to work, and when I met them for the first time, it seemed that Grace had lost her sense of hopefulness for Lauren.

As our initial assessment began, Lauren stared at the floor and refused to speak or look at me. Occasionally, she scowled and looked annoyed when I asked her a question. As a Caucasian counselor, I contemplated the role that race played in Lauren's reaction to the session. As the session continued, I learned more from Grace about Lauren's history involving problems with anger, impulse control, cruelty to animals, false allegations of abuse, and destruction of others' property. It became increasingly clear to me that she had difficulty understanding the relationship between negative or positive behavior and the respective consequences. As Grace left my office, I noted that Lauren refused her aunt's gesture of affection as they parted and, furthermore, did not seem to display any emotion at being left at the facility. On the basis of Lauren's current behaviors, previous treatment history, and early childhood neglect, my diagnostic assessment was reactive attachment disorder (RAD; Code 313.89 in the *Diagnostic and Statistical Manual of Mental Disorders*; 4th ed., text rev.; *DSM–IV–TR*; American Psychiatric Association, 2000).

I escorted Lauren from the intake room to my office, where I explained the rules of the facility. I also explained to her what my job was and that she would be able to come to see me for anything she needed. Lauren did not respond but continued to sit in the corner chair with her head down. Our initial few weekly sessions mirrored the first, as I summarized our work in prior sessions and continued to probe to obtain more information while Lauren sat sullenly with her head down.

As the sessions progressed, Lauren gradually began to express her hatred toward others and contended that her previous behaviors were, in reality, attempts to shock. I remained calm, consistent, and emotionally nonreactive, showing little change in facial expression or tone in hope of allowing Lauren the therapeutic space to build rapport. Occasionally, I prompted her to determine the focus of our session, and Lauren began to respond more positively with this strategy. Her behavior with others, however, did not improve; she was combative, sometimes several times a day, and was not able to manage change. Lauren spit and cursed at the staff in addition to kicking, screaming, and pinching anyone who approached her. Lauren was able to work at her ability level in the educational component of our program but not up to her grade level. The first few weeks were exceptionally challenging for Lauren, and she was easily frustrated by schoolwork.

Over the next few months, Lauren began to make progress, and I was impressed that the number of acting-out episodes decreased, shortening in duration and diminishing in intensity. Lauren eventually began to trust herself and others as more responsibility was given to her. I worked with her to understand the consequences of her negative behavior. The weekly family therapy sessions were also more productive, as evidenced by how receptive Lauren became to affection from her aunt. I shared information about RAD with Grace so that she could learn about the syndrome and develop effective parenting skills, such as setting limits and ignoring negative behaviors.

I noticed that Lauren seemed to give up her acting-out behaviors if they were ignored. I noted further improvement when she addressed issues related to her abandonment by her mother and as she developed strategies for controlling her behavior and angry outbursts. Lauren progressed from almost daily outbursts to choosing more appropriate behavior.

Lauren met several of the developmental criteria indicative of developing RAD. Not only was her mother a drug and alcohol addict during and after pregnancy, but Lauren was also born prematurely, had a difficult delivery, and failed to thrive. In addition, Lauren experienced severe physical and emotional neglect and possible physical abuse during the first 2 years of her life. Given that her mother was abusing drugs and alcohol and was not being treated for bipolar disorder, I suspected that Lauren's early family situation was probably chaotic and that her mother had few parenting skills.

In addition to this history, Lauren's behavior was typical of someone struggling with RAD. Initially, she avoided making eye contact, needed to control others, and overreacted with anger when her routine was even slightly altered. Lauren was argumentative over the smallest things, even when they did not concern her. She was very demanding of me during her treatment, insisting that she see me whether or not I was available, typically when she did not get her way with other residents or staff. Furthermore, Lauren had a difficult time learning to connect her negative behavior to our program consequences. For example, she did not understand how her physical aggression led to her being physically restrained for her safety and the safety of others. Lauren would destroy anything in her path when she became angry, and if nothing were available, she would scratch at her skin until she bled or stab her arms with pencils, staples, and anything else that she could find. Many times, Lauren found these items and stored them up for a temper outburst later in the day. Lauren had difficulty making friends and often attempted to triangulate one staff member against another.

RAD may be more common than researchers once believed, so it is important for all counselors to be aware of this syndrome (Reber, 1996). Wilson (2001) suggested that behavior associated with RAD may be misdiagnosed as a conduct disorder, oppositional–defiant disorder, or attention-deficit/hyperactivity disorder, and misdiagnosis might have been why Lauren's early experiences in therapy were not productive. Children with RAD, such as Lauren, often do not learn how to bond with others; therefore, Lauren's failure to bond in the past and the building of rapport with me were both major foci during our sessions. I believe this was key to the progress we made.

Lauren was in treatment for a total of 9 months. Appointments were set up to continue therapy following her discharge, and Lauren was told that she could call me to maintain the relationship we had established. It is likely that Lauren may need therapy for the remainder of her youth and young adulthood; nevertheless, I am hopeful that her chances of being a successful adult have increased dramatically because of the patience and creativity of the staff involved in her care and treatment. According to Kierkegaard, one must truly understand another's worldview to be the most helpful. This statement is particularly salient for counselors who are challenged when helping children with RAD.

Questions

1. How can counselors conceptualize a case such as Lauren's and determine the diagnosis that is most reflective of her issues?
2. What are some ways to determine when presenting concerns that are not necessarily a result of mental disorders may disguise underlying issues with children?
3. What other treatment modalities could have been used in Lauren's case?

■ Response

Charles L. Thompson

The counselor is to be commended for her persistence, patience, and skill in working through several potential barriers to establish a trusting relationship with Lauren. These barriers included a background of severe neglect from her birth mother, uninformed parenting practices from a well-meaning aunt drafted into motherhood, three failed attempts with therapy, and failure in two schools. In addition, with no prior experience of developing trust with adults other than her aunt, Lauren found herself in a residential treatment center facing a fourth counselor, who was White. The task of building a trusting relationship with Lauren would challenge many counselors.

The basic trust between a child and his or her parents, which should develop before age 2, never happened for Lauren. Toddlers need to be able to trust their parents to be there to take care of them and to be consistent and predictable caregivers. Lauren had neither of these needs met. Although there is no irreversible critical period for developing trust, the job is more easily done in those first 2 years of life. It is also apparent that there were no consistent limits placed on Lauren's behavior at home. For example, in Lauren's case, limits should have been set and enforced on any behavior that infringed on the rights of others. Limits help establish trust between parents and children. Trust also develops when children can depend on their parents to set firm limits to protect them from common dangers in the home and community. Lacking consistent limits on her behavior, Lauren might have felt that she had to test her aunt on a daily basis to define the limits of the moment. Lauren's behaviors of testing limits and angry outbursts might have worked at home, but they did not work well for her in making friends and doing well in school. Consequently, at age 11, Lauren found herself in a treatment center as the last resort for remediation of her situation.

Lauren, however, was not without assets. In accord with the Nietzschean philosophy "That which does not defeat you will make you stronger," Lauren was a survivor and fighter, determined not to be defeated. The problem was that she was fighting those who were trying to help her. Lauren had one other asset: that her aunt declared child-rearing bankruptcy. Parents who acknowledge that they are bankrupt in knowing what to do with their children generally are highly motivated to learn better parenting practices.

Case Conceptualization

Counselors practicing choice theory reality therapy, choosing not to base their case conceptualization on the *DSM–IV–TR*, would opt instead for an assessment of (a) how well Lauren is meeting her needs for survival, love and belonging, power, freedom, and fun; (b) how Lauren handles the pain of not getting what she wants; and (c) how her symptoms relate to her attempts to meet her needs or compensate for not meeting her needs (Glasser, 2000a). Lauren's case conceptualization should not be based on treating symptoms without supporting pathology. With no supporting pathology for RAD in the *DSM–IV–TR*, I would begin with an assessment of how well Lauren is meeting her needs.

Without the early intervention of her aunt, it is doubtful that Lauren would have lived. Grace provided the medical care, food, shelter, and protection that Lauren needed to survive. Presently, Lauren seems to be doing well in meeting her survival needs. Meeting her need for love and belonging is, perhaps, the area requiring the most attention by Lauren's counselor. Lauren has a long history of being unable to initiate and maintain relationships. Her lack of friendships and support from friends may be the reason Lauren seems to work hard to reject others before they can reject her. Much of the treatment plan should be focused on those behaviors that move her away from her peers and what she could do to move closer to them.

Power is the need for one to have things one's way. Currently, Lauren tries to get what she wants with aggressive acts and temper outbursts. She needs to learn that there is more power in getting along with people than in trying to force them to do what she wants. There is also power in doing better work in school—another main focal point for Lauren's treatment plan.

Freedom is the need to have choices in how one lives one's life. Lauren's behavior has resulted in severe reductions in her opportunities to engage in choice. Infringing on the rights of others has cost her friendships as well as the trust she needs to earn to be given the freedom to make choices.

Fun results from learning and laughing, which provide the foundation for all successful long-term relationships (Glasser, 1998). Clearly, Lauren is close to bankruptcy with regard to having fun in her life, and, as such, fun should become another focal point in her treatment plan. Much of Lauren's plan should be focused on helping her have a better day tomorrow at the treatment center, which includes her work at the center's school. Longer term goals should center on the generalization of her improvement to her home and school settings.

Presenting Concerns and Underlying Mental Health Needs

Presenting concerns are generally symptoms children adopt to compensate for not being able to meet their basic needs. Two primary needs children have are the needs to feel loved and capable. Difficulty meeting these two needs may result in attention-getting and revenge behaviors that land children in further difficulty. Discouraged children fight back until their discouragement overwhelms them to the point of giving up. Adlerian counselors have a useful read on what children are trying to achieve through their misbehavior (presenting symptoms) and how the goals of their misbehavior can be determined (Dreikurs & Soltz, 1964; Thompson, Rudolph, & Henderson, 2004).

Children who have been discouraged in meeting their needs may seek one or more of the following four goals of misbehavior: attention, power, revenge, and withdrawal. Each goal is based on faulty reasoning and can be recognized by how the child's behavior makes the parents or other adults feel. Attention-getting behavior, based on the faulty logic that life is good only when one is the center of attention, annoys adults. Power struggles, based on the faulty logic that life is good only when one gets one's way, angers or threatens adults. Revenge-seeking behaviors, based on the faulty logic that the only way to handle hurt feelings is to hurt back, hurts adults' feelings. Withdrawal, based on the faulty logic that the best way to avoid failure is to fail everything until adults stop asking the child to perform, discourages adults. Treatment plans based on personal needs assessments and analysis of what children are trying to achieve through their presenting symptoms are my preference for counseling children.

Intervention Options

With regard to possible alternative treatment modalities, my preference would be choice theory reality therapy, augmented with parent education for Grace. In addition, a quality schools approach (Glasser, 2000b) for Lauren's remedial academic work would be my preference for her treatment plan. I would focus on building my relationship with Lauren by having her teach me what it is like being her. We would talk about what people and things she would like to have in her quality world. Eventually, we would begin to work on evaluating how well her behavior is helping her get what she wants and what behaviors might serve her better.

Choice theory reality therapy is not so structured that it cannot accommodate effective interventions from other counseling approaches. Adlerian methods of parent education would be excellent for Lauren's aunt. She would learn how to set and enforce limits that would strengthen her relationship with Lauren. She would learn to enforce limits through logical consequences rather than illogical punishments, and Lauren would be given a range of choices that her aunt could manage. Grace would also learn the importance of using encouragement rather than criticism to motivate Lauren to make better choices. Catching Lauren in appropriate rather than inappropriate behavior would be a first step in helping the aunt move away from what Glasser (2005) called the seven relationship breakers: criticizing, blaming, nagging, complaining, threatening, punishing, and rewarding to control. He suggested replacing these behaviors with the caring behaviors of supporting, encouraging, listening, accepting, trusting, respecting, and negotiating differences.

Child-centered play therapy, adapted to Lauren's level of development, could be another excellent plan for establishing a working relationship with her. Making choices within the limits of the play therapy setting, including selecting activities and games she enjoyed playing with the counselor, would address her needs for power, fun, love, and belonging. Play therapy could be expanded into some adventure-based counseling interventions, including team games, rope courses, and favorite sports. Regardless of the treatment modality chosen, the eventual effectiveness of any counseling approach is the degree to which the counselor is able to establish a strong working and trusting relationship with Lauren.

Response

Gary R. Mauldin

In responding to the question of how to conceptualize Lauren's case, I first express my curiosity about the meaning of the terms that are used to frame this question. The question assumes a reality (story) whereby the counselor has expertise and knowledge separate from that of the client. I assume that what we take to be a person is socially constructed and constituted through the language and stories we use to construct and give meaning to our world (Gergen, 1994; Hoffman, 1995; White & Epston, 1990).

I noted that the counselor described the client as African American and female. She described herself as Caucasian. I was curious about the stories that were imbedded in each of these scripts. The terms *African, American, female,* and *Caucasian* are value-laden stories that connote a cultural context. These systems of interlocking relationship (stories) are reflective of the difficulty in describing a person separately from context. We are all born into a story. People's sense of what they are and how they behave is imbedded in and defined by socially, culturally, politically, and economically constructed stories (Gergen, 1994). Indeed, the patterns of acceptable and unacceptable behavior are products of social and cultural systems (Berger & Luckmann, 1966).

I argue that case conceptualizations should always begin by valuing and understanding the impact of culture, ethnicity, and context. The counseling relationship begins at the intersection and interchange of conflicting social and cultural systems. When our clients present for therapy, we invite them into our story with the hope of opening the space for compassion and becoming a part of their story. Counselors who ignore the impact of culture demean the counseling process, devalue its importance, and threaten meaningful case conceptualization. There is nothing more powerful than family and the broader culture from which both client and counselor emerge. The counselor can ignore it, to the harm and detriment of the client, but the impact of culture is always present.

Second, the question assumes a hierarchy in the client–counselor–agency context whereby the counselor attempts to diagnose from a position that is separate from that of the client. I am also curious about the meaning of the terms *counselor* and *client.* These terms assume a context in which the counselor is the helper and evaluator, but the relationship context among the client, counselor, and agency seems to be ignored. I noted that Lauren had difficulty in maintaining the agency's program standards. The assumption was made that Lauren's failure was due to RAD. The imbedded assumption is that children with RAD always fail to maintain program standards.

How does one know whether the program standards are good or bad? Is it possible that the standards were good for some persons but not good for Lauren? Is it possible that the standards assumed a set of dominant cultural values that were different from Lauren's ethnic background and cultural values? I also reject the notion of counselor as expert evaluator and diagnostician and would assume, as Anderson (1997) suggested, that Lauren is the expert on her life and what she needs. I assume that power is always an issue in counseling. It is the counselor's failure to understand the impact of culture and the power of the dominant culture that may lead to failure in therapy.

I was curious about Lauren's years of ineffective and unhelpful counseling, hospitalization, and educational programs. If one assumes that counselors are experts, then the failures were due to deficits within Lauren. The assumption is that her other counselors could not help her because she was a child with RAD. She was misdiagnosed, but had she been properly diagnosed, the counselors would have known from the beginning why she did not get better. What if the problem was not in Lauren but in her relationship with the prior counselors?

I assume that clients have all they need to construct a life that is meaningful for them and that one cannot know what is best for someone else. As Watzlawick (1984) argued, meaning is not discovered but invented and socially constructed in relationship. Therefore, RAD is not a real thing but constitutes a socially constructed relationship that involves the counselor, client, and therapeutic community. Counselors have expertise in conducting therapeutic conversations with persons, and these conversations just may be helpful and meaningful (Anderson, 1997). However, as Hoffman (1995) suggested, the client decides what is helpful and meaningful. RAD and similar descriptions of unhappiness are meaningful only to the degree that they are helpful to the client, not to the counselor or therapeutic community.

Finally, the question assumes the client has issues. I am curious: Are these issues in the mind of the counselor, the mind of the client, or the context? The counselor used the term *RAD* in her description of her client. No doubt this *DSM–IV–TR* category accurately describes much of the unhappiness and many of the struggles that Lauren had endured. *RAD* may accurately describe Lauren's behavior, but it does not describe her. As Keeney (1983) and Gergen (1994) both observed, it is a small step from using such pejorative definitions to understand and describe behavior to beginning to think the definitions are describing a person. *RAD* is the description of a relationship (story) and not a syndrome. It describes a story involving Lauren, her aunt, the counselor, and the therapeutic community in which she is being treated. It may be useful to help one understand Lauren, but it will never fully describe her, because humans are more complex and wonderful than anything found in the *DSM–IV–TR*.

In addressing the question related to presenting concerns that are not resultant of mental disorders, I am curious about what the counselor means by the term *mental disorder*. The concept assumes that there is an order to human behavior that is preferred and normal. It also assumes that there is a reality of disordered behavior. The *DSM–IV–TR* is an example of this culturally derived story. Although I agree that the behaviors described in the *DSM–IV–TR* do exist, one needs to take care because it is impossible to separate one's own bias and prejudice from what one observes (Von Foerster, 1982). In some sense, counseling is always political. Counselors need to acknowledge their premises, points of view, and biases. Through this self-acknowledgment of bias, counselors can begin to observe their own way of constructing and influencing phenomena (Gergen, 1994).

Counselors will always be responsible for the decisions they make and the distinctions they draw as they attempt to describe persons under their care. Keeney (1983) referred to this as an ethic of responsibility. Gergen (1994) described it as an ethic of relationship. They argued that counselors should not come to know too quickly what is best or normal because their descriptions may in fact become the thing that binds their clients to their difficulties.

I was impressed to learn that when those in authority over Lauren ignored her negative behavior, her behavior improved. Bateson (1972) suggested that all behavior is communication. Is it possible that Lauren's change in behavior was an attempt to invite those who cared for her into a conversation about her struggle for hope and change? The best way to differentiate context from behavior is to explore the meaning of the behavior with the client. I would want to hear from Lauren what the term *RAD* meant to her. I would be interested in having her tell me about the times when she had control over her RAD and also about the times the RAD controlled her. The effect of these conversations would be to separate Lauren from the RAD so that she could see ways that she could choose to control her own behavior.

I was troubled to read how hopeless it is for children who have been labeled as having RAD. I would want to work with Lauren to identify stories in which she does have hope and in which she believes she can change. These conversations would lead Lauren away from a deficit and mental disorder conversation (story) and toward a conversation (story) in which she experiences possibility and hope.

In choosing a treatment modality, I would assume the importance of using a positive and hopeful dialogue with Lauren to elicit her perspective, resources, and unique experiences that are not problem saturated (White & Epston, 1990). I would encourage the use of reflective questions that would help empower Lauren and her family members to speak and to express their diverse positions. I would also want to find ways to enhance awareness of the impact of various aspects of the dominant culture on her family, the counselor, and the therapeutic community that had been attending to Lauren's concerns.

Therapeutic conversations (restory) are both deconstructive and generative. Initially, the goal is to deconstruct the power the difficulty has over the person. As the counselor was describing Lauren, there were times when I had trouble differentiating Lauren from the RAD. A major focus in these initial conversations would be to deconstruct and minimize power differences within the counselor–client relationship and the problem–person relationship (story). I would also encourage Lauren to see how the RAD label contributes to her lack of hopefulness and possibility for change. The key would be to identify those choice points where Lauren has been or could be free of RAD (White & Epston, 1990).

A second goal would be to invite Lauren and her family into a generative conversation (restory) around gaining new meaning and purpose. I would attempt to codevelop, with Lauren, solutions that were unique to the situation and meaningful to her. The goal would be to empower Lauren to reauthor a liberating or alternative story to the dominant, problem-saturated story within which she is currently living (White & Epston, 1990). I would hope for her that she could begin to view her life free of RAD rather than being controlled by it. Therefore, my conversations with Lauren would be designed to highlight new and rediscovered understandings and previously unnoticed choice points that are valued by her and that she could use to weave a new story for her life (White & Epston, 1990).

As I read Lauren's story, I was struck by how resilient she was despite all that she had been through in the past. I was impressed that there had been so many failed attempts at therapy. I would want to hear from Lauren and her aunt about what they believed was helpful and not helpful within the context of these past experiences. I also noticed Lauren's response when she developed a sense of rapport with her present counselor. The relationship she had with her counselor had a positive effect that began to affect her life at the center and her learning at school. I was impressed that the counselor discovered that what seemed to work best was the facilitation of a positive relationship between her and Lauren. This confirms the research of Hubble, Duncan, and Miller (1999), who found that a positive counselor–client relationship accounted for 40% of the variance in positive therapeutic outcomes.

Finally, I encourage counselors to focus on exceptions and not pathology with persons who carry a RAD label. The list of sufferings related to this disorder is lengthy. The challenge is to listen carefully, seek to understand, and see how the client has remained resilient even under difficult circumstances.

References

American Psychiatric Association. (2000). *Diagnostic and statistical manual of mental disorders* (4th ed., text rev.). Washington, DC: Author.

Anderson, H. (1997). *Conversation, language, and possibilities: A postmodern approach to therapy.* New York: Basic Books.

Bateson, G. (1972). *Steps to an ecology of the mind.* New York: Ballantine.

Berger, P. L., & Luckmann, T. (1966). *The social construction of reality: A treatise in the sociology of knowledge.* New York: Doubleday.

Dreikurs, R., & Soltz, V. (1964). *Children: The challenge.* New York: Hawthorn/Dutton.

Gergen, K. J. (1994). *Realities and relationships: Soundings in social construction.* Cambridge, MA: Harvard University Press.

Glasser, W. (1998). *Choice theory: A new psychology of personal freedom.* New York: HarperCollins.

Glasser, W. (2000a). *Counseling with choice theory.* New York: HarperCollins.

Glasser, W. (2000b). *Every student can succeed.* Chatsworth, CA: William Glasser, Inc.

Glasser, W. (2005). *Treating mental health as a public health problem.* Chatsworth, CA: William Glasser, Inc.

Hoffman, L., (1995). A reflexive stance for family therapy. In S. McNamee & K. J. Gergen (Eds.), *Therapy as social construction* (pp. 7–24). London: Sage.

Hubble, M. A., Duncan, B. L., & Miller, S. D. (Eds.). (1999). *The heart and soul of change: What works in therapy.* Washington, DC: American Psychological Association.

Keeney, B. P. (1983). *Aesthetics of change.* New York: Guilford Press.

Reber, K. (1996). Children at risk for reactive attachment disorder: Assessment, diagnosis, and treatment. *Progress: Family Systems Research and Therapy, 5,* 83–98.

Rygaard, N. P. (2005). *A practical handbook in therapy for children with severe attachment disorder.* Brussels, Belgium: Deboeck University.

Thompson, C., Rudolph, L., & Henderson D. (2004). *Counseling children.* Belmont, CA: Thomson Learning

Von Foerster, H. (1982). *Observing systems* (2nd ed.). Seaside, CA: Intersystems Publications.

Watzlawick, P. (1984). *The invented reality: How do we know what we believe we know?* New York: Norton.

White, M., & Epston, D. (1990). *Narrative means to therapeutic ends.* New York: Norton.

Wilson, S. L. (2001). Attachment disorders: Review and current status. *Journal of Psychology, 135,* 37–51.

Separation Anxiety: "Helping Children Feel Safe and Secure"

This incident addresses a school counselor's work with a child exhibiting symptoms of separation anxiety that are complicated by special education placement and frequent moves by his family. The respondents discuss the diagnosis and treatment of separation anxiety disorder and explore alternative ways to conceptualize the case. In particular, Adlerian counseling, gender socialization, family systems, and narrative therapy approaches are explored.

■ Critical Incident

Elsa Soto Leggett and Karen E. Reed

As a new school counselor being assigned midyear, I first met "Jack Williams" when he was halfway through the first grade. This tall African American boy was the oldest child in an active military family. On my arrival at this small, rural elementary school, I was instructed that my duties included meeting the counseling needs of special education students, including Jack, as described in their Individualized Education Programs. Jack's primary identification for special education services was emotionally disturbed (ED) with a secondary diagnosis of learning disabled (LD), and he was to receive weekly counseling sessions to help him cope with stressors in his life. Jack had developed a strong relationship with the school counseling interns who preceded me; they met with him each morning before school to help him begin the day with encouragement and direction. This had been a positive routine for Jack, and because he did not adjust well to change, it was going to be difficult not to continue this custom.

In preparation for working with Jack, it was important to learn more about his background, his diagnosis, and the reasons for his placement in special education. I first consulted with Jack's teacher, "Ms. Trotman." She had been with Jack through kindergarten and first grade in a unique academic program that allowed teachers to stay with each class for 2 years. Ms. Trotman shared that her greatest concern about Jack involved those instances in which he withdrew from interacting with the other students and pulled away from small group and instructional activities. She indicated that he would begin by becoming disengaged from those around him and would sometimes intensify his withdrawal by crawling under the tables or desks and refusing to respond to any requests. Ms. Trotman indicated that Jack would only respond to his mother during those times and that, when hiding under a desk or table, he would often voice a request for his mother's presence or a concern for her well-being. On the basis of these behaviors, first observed during Jack's kindergarten year, a school counselor referred him for a special education evaluation.

To best serve Jack, I also contacted Jack's mother to get a better picture of his home life. She shared that Jack was the oldest of four children in a blended family, two children from her previous marriage and two from her marriage to Jack's stepfather. Mrs. Williams indicated that Jack responded well to her remarriage, seemed to accept the role of his stepfather in the family, and had been very excited about the birth of his younger siblings.

Jack's stepfather, however, was often gone because of his active military work with the Navy. Mrs. Williams reported that Jack was clearly affected by the absence of his stepfather when Mr. Williams's assignments drew him away from the family. During these absences, Jack required more of his mother's attention, and he expressed distress by whining, clinging to his mother, and complaining about not feeling well. Although the family was accustomed to frequently moving because of changes in Mr. Williams's military assignments, Jack's mother hoped to stay at this location as long as possible to provide more stability for her children, especially Jack.

The school counselor and the school psychologist under whom Jack received his diagnosis were no longer a part of the school district, so I was unable to consult with them to obtain additional background information about his diagnosis and treatment. In reading Jack's special education record and psychological report, however, I learned that there had been a suspicion of sexual abuse at an earlier time in Jack's life and that the primary diagnosis that qualified Jack to receive special education services was emotional disturbance.

Nevertheless, as I read through the report, I noted a number of characteristics associated with separation anxiety. Jack's frequent requests for his mother and his clingy behaviors toward her were the first things that alerted me. Jack also needed daily contact with his younger sister at school to ensure that she was present and safe. In addition, he continued to be reluctant to interact with other students or teachers and often reported physical symptoms, such as headaches or stomachaches. As a school counselor, I did not make a formal diagnosis, but these diagnostic impressions guided my counseling sessions with Jack.

For the remainder of first grade, I saw Jack for counseling sessions on a consistent schedule. Because I was someone new to Jack, he did not respond to me quickly. He was quiet and withdrawn and did not respond to talk therapy with any depth. Knowing that he was a good artist, I encouraged Jack to draw pictures and explain the details of the pictures. He enjoyed this kind of session, and this allowed us to build a caring, productive relationship that proved to be useful in the moments when Jack became anxious in response to challenges in the classroom or changes in his home life. During these times of stress, Jack would again become withdrawn and cry for his mother. Afterward, Jack would sit in my office for a period of time, sometimes curled up on the floor and other times simply sitting silently. When he was ready to respond to me, he would draw pictures of himself and his mother or his family. He would share the details of the pictures and eventually would feel comfortable enough to return to class. Jack sometimes left his picture with me and other times took the picture with him to help him remember the positive feelings he experienced in his work with me.

When Jack entered the second grade, I placed him in a small group for counseling. I alternated each session between directive play therapy and relaxation. Both of these approaches resulted in positive outcomes for Jack. The directive group play therapy helped him understand how to interact and cope with other students. The relaxation provided him with a method or process for controlling his responses to stressful situations. In addition to receiving group counseling, Jack also began participating in individual play therapy with a private practitioner after I provided his mother with a referral. This was a good year developmentally for Jack. He made progress both personally and academically.

The third grade began well for Jack. His transition was smooth, due in part to the school program that allowed him to maintain his same teacher and many classmates from the previous year. During the school year, his mother had her fifth child, and his stepfather was home more often. Jack still participated in directive group play therapy and relaxation, but his required minutes of counseling had been reduced, given that his progress was reflected on his updated Individualized Education Plan. Indeed, it appeared that Jack was more in control of his behaviors and felt secure about the well-being of his mother and his family.

Then, in February, the unwelcome but always anticipated occurred. Mr. Williams learned that he would once again be transferred. The family began to prepare for the move to another state, and Jack slowly began to show signs of regression. He started withdrawing from interactions with his classmates in both educational activities and play, refused to respond to the requests of his teachers, and often sat in my office silently. Jack was no longer comforted by the activities he and I had used in the past, and his mother was also called to school more frequently to calm or reassure him. On the worst days, Jack would shrink down under his desk and wait there until his mother arrived at school to comfort him.

When it reached this point, Jack's mother took the initiative to offer a plan to help Jack manage the rest of the school year. In particular, Mrs. Williams told the school and Jack that she had decided she would stay behind with the children so they could complete the school year and that she would then follow her husband when summer vacation began. Mr. and Mrs. Williams felt this proposal would work best for Jack and help him return to a stable mind-set, and the school concurred. Fortunately, Jack was also satisfied with this plan, and his behavior began to show improvements.

Nevertheless, it later became apparent that Mrs. Williams made these statements only to appease Jack and that she had not actually planned to stay for the remainder of the school year but had instead been secretly continuing with the moving arrangements. Without any forewarning, she appeared at school one day in early May to withdraw the children from school and join her husband within the next few days. Before I knew what was happening, Jack was leaving. I was able only to say good-bye and wish him well.

I did not know whether Jack's new school would meet his emotional needs or whether he would remember the coping skills he began to demonstrate with me. I believe I addressed Jack's need to feel that he and his family were safe and to help him develop skills to cope with his anxiety. The directive group play therapy coupled with the relaxation treatments offered Jack the opportunity to cope with his anxiety and feelings of insecurity, which then allowed him to focus his attention on his studies. Nevertheless, I still have concerns about some of the issues Jack was facing and how we dealt with them together on a daily basis. I continue to wonder how he fared in the move and how he is today.

Questions

1. Is there a time or age when a child will naturally grow out of separation anxiety? Is this equally true for children with a diagnosis of ED? Is this equally true for children who face frequent moves throughout their childhood?
2. What are some other appropriate treatments for separation anxiety that may work well in school settings? Which ones may be particularly helpful to a child with an emotional disturbance?
3. What suggestions do you have for dealing with my own feelings related to Jack's sudden move and my worries about his welfare?

■ Response

Jon Carlson and Matt Englar-Carlson

We want to start by recognizing the conscientious effort and dedication of the school counselor in this case. Clearly, she felt close to Jack and wanted to make a difference in his life. Over the 2 years detailed in the critical incident, it seems that intervention efforts helped Jack adjust to school and begin to feel more safe and secure when he was away from his family. Even with the return of symptoms triggered by another move, it seems that the school counselor was serving as a strong advocate for Jack's emotional and psychological well-being.

Even so, it is apparent that the school counselor remains somewhat troubled by a number of questions related to her work with Jack. Her questions reflect a desire for additional information about the course of the separation anxiety disorder, about how this disorder may be affected by special education diagnoses and by environmental stressors such as frequent moves, and about how children with separation anxiety might best be treated. In addition, her question about how to deal with her own feelings about Jack's welfare suggests some discomfort with unnatural endings with clients. In our response to this incident, we address each of these concerns and also offer additional thoughts related to ways the case of Jack might be reconceptualized.

Diagnostic Issues

The case of Jack provides a good example of how children can be negatively affected by their environment. Jack has dealt with the separation from his birth father and his mother's subsequent remarriage, geographical moves, changes in the family constellation, and alleged sexual abuse. Furthermore, he has been given several diagnoses and placed in special education because of his inability to manage these and other variables. Yet, as we read through the vignette, we wondered whether the counselor's diagnosis and treatment plan were accurate. Furthermore, we doubt the appropriateness of Jack's placement in an ED/LD classroom. On reading the facts of the case, we questioned the validity of the ED/LD diagnosis, which must have been made during Jack's kindergarten year or before.

The counselor seems to accept the fact that Jack is the problem, not his environment. From an Adlerian perspective, however, Jack seems to us to be underfunctioning and acting out to adhere to family and school expectations. We were impressed with Jack's resilience, his ability to make positive gains, and his development of a strong relationship with a counseling intern. This would not be likely if the diagnosis were truly emotional disturbance and separation anxiety. Placing him in a special class further alienates him from his peers and does not directly resolve the real issues in his family and environment.

We also had many questions that were not answered in the vignette. We wanted to know more about Jack's attachment to and suggested enmeshment with his mother; his role as oldest child in the family; his relationship with his birth father and his birth father's family; the level of acceptance, rejection, and oppression he might have experienced as an African American in a rural area; his status as a military child in the classroom; and the possible pattern of family dishonesty. Additional details are necessary to develop a deeper understanding of Jack and to create an effective treatment plan.

Treatment Issues

In the event that Jack does indeed exhibit separation anxiety disorder, it is important to comment on accepted standards of practice with regard to treating the disorder. Anxiety disorders (including separation anxiety) have been labeled as the most common type of childhood psychopathology (Christophersen & Mortweet, 2001). Many children progress through childhood with fears and worries about developmentally appropriate issues, but only some develop more significant symptoms that impair their emotional functioning.

Before beginning any treatment, it is always prudent to begin with a complete medical examination to rule out any organic problems. Whereas many children are receiving antianxiety and other psychotropic medications to help them deal with many of the presenting symptoms of separation anxiety, there is limited empirical support and documentation on the efficacy and safety of pharmaceutical interventions with children. Therefore, at this time, nonpharmacological treatments are considered the primary forms of intervention (Christophersen & Mortweet, 2001).

According to Christophersen and Mortweet (2001), children with diagnoses of separation anxiety and emotional disturbance often get worse as they mature. Whereas mentally healthy children get along with the significant adults in their life, children with these diagnoses become alienated from family and friends. Furthermore, children who move frequently often develop a belief that relationships are temporary and learn not to invest or risk much of themselves. If frequent moves occur at critical points in a child's development of social skills (e.g., preschool, kindergarten, or first grade), he or she may miss out on some of the developmentally appropriate lessons and skills of middle childhood.

Jongsma, Peterson, and McInnis (1996) outlined a variety of counseling protocols for separation anxiety that set the following long-term goals. Many of these can be tailored for work in a school setting:

1. Together, the counselor and child eliminate the anxiety and expression of fears when a separation is anticipated or occurs.
2. The child tolerates separation from attachment figures without exhibiting heightened emotional distress, regressive behaviors, temper outbursts, or pleading.

3. The counselor and child work together to eliminate the somatic complains associated with separation.
4. The child manages the nighttime fears effectively, as he or she evidences by remaining calm, sleeping in his or her own bed, and not attempting to go into the attachment figure's room at night.
5. The counselor and child resolve the core conflicts or traumas contributing to the emergence of the separation anxiety.
6. The child participates in extracurricular peer group activities and spends time in independent play on a regular, consistent basis.
7. The parents establish and maintain appropriate parent–child boundaries and set firm, consistent limits when the client exhibits temper outbursts or manipulative behaviors around separation points.

It is our belief that schools often need to teach children appropriate social and coping skills. Cognitive-behavioral interventions have been the most well-established treatments for children experiencing anxiety symptoms (Christophersen & Mortweet, 2001). These interventions include behavioral control, calming and relaxation techniques, visualization techniques, thought-stopping exercises, anxiety management, and self-concept-building exercises that teach children coping skills in response to stress and anxiety. Instead of teaching these skills, however, most schools put such children into small special education classes, where they are taught basic academic subjects. We contend that most children need social and coping skills before they can benefit from academic instruction. In the case of Jack, meeting his emotional needs seems to be a necessary first step to meeting his academic ones.

Reconceptualizing Jack's Case

The preceding comments were related to the treatment of properly diagnosed separation anxiety disorder. As we noted earlier, however, we question whether Jack was indeed properly diagnosed. We are concerned with the possibility that Jack's behavior might have been unnecessarily pathologized as an individual's disorder rather than conceptualized in a wider context as a misguided response to difficult environmental challenges.

In many ways, we are not surprised by the attachment and connection Jack expressed for his mother. She seems to be the one constant adult in his life, and Jack's attempts to emotionally connect with his father and stepfather seem to be hampered by physical and emotional inaccessibility. This seems to be highlighted by the frequent disruption of the bond between Jack and his stepfather because of military service. It also seems that the parenting in this family has been left to Jack's mother. With the absence of his father (we are assuming his absence because of the lack of information in the case), the military schedule of his stepfather, the frequent family moves, and even the rotation of significant adults at school (e.g., classroom teachers, counseling interns), Jack's mother seems to be his only consistent emotional resource. In light of the alleged sexual abuse, it seems that Jack has been disappointed and even harmed by many adults in his life, which has led to distrust. Thus, in an environment in which there are few constants and questionable safety, it is understandable and normal that Jack is anxious about his mother's well-being and wants to stay near her for his own sense of security.

It does seem that the role and relationship of Jack's father and stepfather require further attention. We wondered about the lack of involvement of either man in the counseling interventions. Although it is often the case that fathers are excluded from counseling services, engaging both fathers and mothers in counseling and other services can enhance the therapeutic effectiveness of any intervention (Duhig, Phares, & Birkeland, 2002). Furthermore, the role of fatherly love and acceptance with children has been indicated as a buffer against psychological adjustment problems. Conversely, the withdrawal of fatherly love has been indicated in a myriad of adjustment problems, including anxiety, social and emotional withdrawal, and negative self-concept and self-esteem (Rohner & Veneziano, 2001). Therefore, we would look for ways to get Jack's father and stepfather more engaged with the counseling process.

This case also seems to represent the difficulties many young boys have in expressing their emotions and fears in a society that actively socializes boys to internalize and repress their emotions. In particular, Pollack (1998) suggested that many boys are pressured to separate from their parents and forced into pseudoindependence before they are emotionally ready. When boys rebel against the push to separate by showing fear, worry, or tears, they are often made to feel ashamed by adults who encourage boys to grow up and toughen up. This shame can undermine a boy's self-esteem and confidence, leading to feelings of loneliness and disconnection. Furthermore, repressed emotions can lead to disruptive behaviors, such as the ones displayed by Jack. It seems that Jack was expressing his understandable fears and worries about being separated from his parents, but the response to these concerns was ED/LD placement and a subsequent diagnosis of separation anxiety. We wondered whether Jack would have been treated and viewed the same way if he were a young girl.

Adlerian counselors understand that all behavior has a purpose. Behaviors such as hiding or curling into a ball and even physical symptoms such as stomachaches develop because they in some way work or pay off for the individual. It seems that Jack received a lot of adult attention and involvement because of his negative behaviors. We wondered whether, alternatively, Jack's positive behaviors could have been reinforced through more adult involvement and attention. Of course, for this to be effective, coordination and consistency between family and school would be required.

We believe that Jack's problems could have been managed more effectively through teacher and parent consultation and possibly family therapy. Given the role of the family in childhood behavioral problems, treatments that include the family or look to alter the family dynamics are often among the most effective interventions (Nichols & Schwartz, 2006; Northey, Wells, Silverman, & Bailey, 2003). Direct individual service (although logical) seems to be more of a Band-Aid approach if the existing environmental dynamics are left unaddressed. Although most school counselors are not able to provide long-term individual counseling for complex problems because of other demands on their time, we advocate regular individual consultation sessions (Dinkmeyer & Carlson, 2006) with the teacher and parents. These sessions would focus on helping these significant adults deal effectively with the problems that they are having with Jack. The focus of the consultation would be on the significant adults, not on Jack. Family therapy could also be provided intermittently by the school counselor or more consistently by a referral to a community family counselor. Treatment topics might include examining the possibility that Jack is being triangulated, encouraging Jack's father and stepfather to become more involved in Jack's life, and exploring how the family would respond to the arrival of a new child. Other issues to be discussed might include the need for appropriate boundaries, personal space, and privacy; the improvement of communication skills; and the establishment of clear disciplinary consequences.

Unnatural Endings and Lingering Feelings

We finish this response by addressing the school counselor's question regarding her own feelings about the ending of the case. At this time, it is hard for us to say whether the school counselor got too close to Jack. It is our hope that the school counselor would have recognized any feelings of countertransference during the treatment and sought appropriate professional consultation with a past or current supervisor. Whereas it is truly sad and unfortunate that Jack was in this situation, the ending of this case is by no means uncommon. More often than not, counselors do not know what happens to clients beyond the course of the current treatment. In situations of unnatural endings (e.g., with Jack), both counselor and client are often faced with a feeling of unfinished work without a proper chance to say good-bye. Yet it is our hope that counselors can believe in the power of counseling relationships and honor the notion that clients gain from the counselor's attention and commitment to them. At the end of treatment, counselors need to detach and believe in children and their resiliency. Unfortunately, too many counselors provide direct services to children without believing in the potential of a child to grow emotionally. This unintentionally perpetuates rather than reduces the presenting problem.

Response

Karen Mackie and Maureen Finnigan Rundle

We appreciate the efforts of the school counselor to draw on treatment methods that would help Jack both at school and in the community, and we commend her referral of Jack's family for other sources of help. The effective counseling of children with separation anxiety disorder commonly requires a combination of treatment modalities to address children's deep fears and the uncertainty about trust and security that seems to underlie the symptoms they manifest. Ideally, play therapy, relaxation techniques, cognitive therapy, and behavioral therapy are used together to modify the child's thoughts, feelings, and direct experiences of relationship. There are a number of clues and cues in Jack's case that signal the need for a more systemic and communication-based interpretation of Jack's difficulties to supplement the individually focused treatment modalities we have listed. Two more systemic and communication-based approaches that also have merit in the treatment of young children with persistent distress are family systems therapy and narrative counseling. We focus our response to this critical incident by addressing the counselor's second question about other appropriate treatments for separation anxiety that may work well in school settings. In particular, we offer recommendations for family systems therapy and narrative counseling approaches to Jack's case.

Before describing these approaches further, we would like to add two caveats. First, we want to briefly address the counselor's question about the impact of an ED diagnosis on children exhibiting separation anxiety. We believe there is a tendency in schools to create categories for instructional programming purposes (e.g., ED and LD) that are suspect from both diagnostic and systemic perspectives. The counselor struggles with whether her understandings of Jack's anxious behavior and its resolution have to be modified or uniquely considered because he bears these two additional identifiers (ED and LD) in the school setting. We believe this constitutes a red herring from the point of view of therapeutic approach and responsiveness and that the counselor should consider these designators of limited utility to her helping purposes.

The second caveat is that there is a difference between separation anxiety and separation anxiety disorder. It seems to us that Jack shares features of separation anxiety that are normal for children of his age and circumstances as well as features of the diagnosed disorder. For example, it is common for children in the 5–7-year-old age bracket as well as those in the 11–14-year-old age bracket to engage in school refusal after a time of particular closeness to a parent, such as during a vacation or school break. Therapeutically speaking, it may be good to consider both elements as real factors in devising a treatment plan.

That being said, we now turn to our recommendations for the use of family systems therapy and narrative counseling approaches. A family systems or interpersonal approach to problems differs from the individualist perspective of most counseling approaches in that it assumes that problems reside not in individual family members (e.g., Jack) but instead in the wider family system (e.g., the Williams family). From this perspective, an individual's maladaptive behaviors are conceptualized as representing imperfect solutions to difficulties in interpersonal dynamics among family members or to difficulties between the family and the larger social systems that surround and embed the family. From this perspective, problems in children serve a metaphoric or signaling function in that the child may give evidence of distress that exists in other components of the family's relationship system.

When one looks at the case from a family systems perspective, it is interesting to note that when his stepfather was home, Jack did well with the positive routines he had experienced with the school counseling interns and again with the counselor during the art and play therapy and the group counseling in second grade. However, the family pattern of inconsistency related to his stepfather's military transfers and deployments was unintentionally replicated by the instability of counseling personnel. In this context, it makes sense that Jack reacted and had difficulties adjusting to changes at school. Rather than identifying this as an individually based problem of separation anxiety, the counselor would do well to consider Jack's difficulties as reflective of a more systemic problem both at home and at school. It seems to us that Jack's misbehavior signals a systemic problem related to multiple comings and goings of people with whom he was in close relationship. In particular, his problematic behavior calls attention to the problem of instability both at home and at school. Rather than conceptualizing Jack as having trouble adjusting to change, one might instead conceptualize Jack's family and school environments as having difficulty maintaining consistency and stability.

Another interesting illustration of the relational and metaphoric nature of children's distress may be found in the school counselor's mention of suspected sexual abuse in Jack's history. Again, rather than interpreting Jack's behaviors from an individual perspective, the counselor could consider them as signaling wider, systemic failures to offer him protection and safety. From this perspective, Jack might have been responding to his own experiences with sexual abuse in relational ways. Especially if the abuse occurred outside of the home, Jack's concern for the safety of his sister at school might be reflective of his reactions to the abuse he experienced. We wonder about how Jack, as an African American youngster in a rural school, interprets his sibling role as brother to his younger sister and about how contact and safety in the school environment factor in for him generally. In relation to the abuse incident, we wonder whether Jack fears he will not be adequately protected if his stepfather is not around. Does he perhaps ask for his mother specifically because she is the other adult in his life who knows about this incident and could protect him? From a family systems therapy approach, a counselor would ask whether Jack's behaviors actually make sense from a relational systems understanding of his history and its meaning to the family.

We move now to a discussion of the narrative counseling perspective, noting that this approach starts with the premise that problems have real effects on an individual's life. Like the family systems therapy approach, narrative counseling sees the problem as localized not inside the person but rather outside of the person. In narrative counseling, however, the problem is viewed as a force to be reckoned with through the relationship the person develops with the problem. This view frees clients, families, and counselors from wrestling with the stigmatizing effect of identifying the problem as residing in the client. Perceiving the client as a damaged person with an internal problem and an associated, labeled identity (e.g., ED or LD) risks having the label become an all encompassing identity story and thereby limiting the client's coping options. In contrast, perceiving the client as struggling with an external problem allows the counselor to tap into the inner resources of the client, family, or counselor and deploy these resources against the externalized problem that is distorting what the client would otherwise be experiencing.

Because narrative counseling assumes that problems are not "totalizing" in their impact—that is, they are not ever present, completely powerful, and the only activity going on in a person's life—it is important to help clients notice the times when their life is not taken up by dealing with the problem and to amplify these times of exception. These other moments can be developed into stories (narratives) about resources and capacities that can be invoked to improve the client's capacity to deal with the influence of the problem in his or her life. A narrative approach invites clients and families to discern their meanings and explanations for events and to construct an alternative understanding of their experience and identity that includes their resistance to the dominating effects of the problem, their preferred life values, and their commitments and self-definitions.

In Jack's case, a narrative approach could be used fruitfully. For example, clues about exceptions to the problem and Jack's internal resources include the fact that Jack had adjusted well to his mother's remarriage and the birth of new siblings. Both of these represent transitions that frequently pose challenges for children, and, in both cases, Jack adjusted in adaptive ways. How was Jack able to manage these changes, and how was his family able to help him be successful with these transitions? These are examples of counterstories that contradict the dominating story offered by the school counselor: that Jack is unsuccessful at adapting to change in his life.

Another clue to the utility of combining a family systems and narrative approach in helping Jack is found in the counselor's comment that, during episodes of withdrawal at school, Jack responded only to his mother's arrival to assist. What did the mother do at these times? How did she understand how her presence helped Jack? In addition, how did she understand his concern for her well-being? What strengths does this interactional sequence reveal about the relationship between Mrs. Williams and Jack?

Some counselors might conceptualize this interactional sequence as an example of Jack wielding power over his mother and the school system. They might speculate that the school should stop calling Jack's mother to avoid reinforcing his misbehavior (withdrawal and requests for his mother). They might label this as an inversion of the power hierarchy and suggest that Jack's parents were not sufficiently empowered to put limits around his unproductive behavior. However, we rather doubt that such an interpretation captures the full meaning of these interactions, and we prefer to view all parties (Jack, his mother, and the school system) as acting competently. From this perspective, the challenge becomes understanding how each party's actions can be conceptualized as a competent response and understanding what each party is responding to. Rather than only relying on the counselor's and school's interpretation of the interactional sequence, in which Jack withdraws, requests his mother, and is comforted only by her presence, it would be wise to involve both Jack and his mother in developing a "thicker" description of the meaning of their actions. This might really help design an intervention.

We suggest that a thicker description is also needed to better understand the bigger picture. Mrs. Williams believes Jack is affected by the absence of his stepfather during his active duty. This is her *theory of change,* her account of what is going on. If one accepted this premise as equally authoritative as one's own, what use could one make of it? Similarly, Mrs. Williams seems anxious to help Jack feel more stability, and, to accomplish this, she selects a strategy related to concealing the moving time frame. What might she, as a parent, know about Jack that nobody else does? What does she want for him, and how does she think about this episode of moving in relation to her military family life and its realities? Before opposing Mrs. Williams's strategy and setting up a school versus parent dynamic, we would want to align with Mrs. Williams to better understand her strategy. We were not shocked by her strategy but rather curious about her own rationale for this choice. We wondered about the possible impact of her family's cultural minority status relative to the culture of the school. We wondered about how lifestyle circumstances relative to military family patterns affected her choice of action. We would say that elevating the local knowledge of the parent is more productive as an intervention strategy for helping Jack than the strategy of questioning her choice or seeing her as fearful or unable (i.e., incompetent) to help Jack cope with the move.

In summary, to assess a client's problems from a narrative and family systems perspective, we suggest first listening carefully to the client story, staying alert for details that relate to the client's competence as well as to oppressive problems, and asking questions such as these (Madsen, 1999; Winslade & Monk, 1999):

- In what situations is the problem most or least likely to occur?
- What is the effect of the problem on you and your relationships?
- How does this problem interfere with your preferred life?
- How do you explain the problem?
- How have you attempted to cope with the problem?
- What feelings of delight or pride in small achievements or victories over the problem have you experienced? What about feelings of anger, grief, or discouragement about the strength the problem appears to hold?
- What broader cultural support does the problem receive? How do cultural discourses operate in this problem story?
- Where would you like your life to be headed? What future would you like to have?
- What constraints stand in the way of you getting to that future?
- What strengths, resources, and knowledge do you have to deal with those constraints?

References

Christophersen, E., & Mortweet, S. (2001). *Treatments that work with children: Empirically supported strategies for managing childhood problems.* Washington, DC: American Psychological Association.

Dinkmeyer, D., & Carlson, J. (2006). *Consultation* (3rd ed.). New York: Routledge.

Duhig, A., Phares, V., & Birkeland, R. (2002). Involvement of fathers in therapy: A survey of clinicians. *Professional Psychology: Research and Practice, 33,* 389–395.

Jongsma, A. E., Peterson, L. M., & McInnis, W. P. (1996). *The child and adolescent treatment planner.* New York: Wiley.

Madsen, W. (1999). *Collaborative therapy with multi-stressed families: From old problems to new futures.* New York: Guilford Press.

Nichols, M. P., & Schwartz, R. C. (2006). *Family therapy: Concepts and methods.* Boston: Allyn & Bacon.

Northey, W. E., Wells, K. C., Silverman, W. K., & Bailey, C. E. (2003). Childhood behavioral and emotional disorders. *Journal of Marital and Family Therapy, 29,* 523–545.

Pollack, W. (1998). *Real boys.* New York: Random House.

Rohner, R., & Veneziano, R. (2001). The importance of fatherly love: History and contemporary evidence. *Review of General Psychology, 5,* 382–405.

Winslade, J., & Monk, G. (1999). *Narrative counseling in schools: Powerful and brief.* Thousand Oaks, CA: Corwin Press/Sage.

"There's a Monster Under My Bed!": Sleep Problems

This incident explores how one counselor helped a child conquer nighttime fears using a sensorimotor developmental approach. Issues of collaborative intervention and effective play therapy as well as bibliotherapeutic strategies are discussed.

■ Critical Incident

Elysia V. Clemens and Adria E. Shipp

"Sara Lawson," a first grade student at a rural elementary school, was referred to the school counseling office by her mother, a teacher at the elementary school. Sara's mother expressed concern about nightmares her daughter had been experiencing since Sara's classroom teacher had read a Halloween story to the class. I scheduled an appointment with Sara for later that day and looked through her cumulative folder, hoping to learn more about Sara's history at the school.

Sara was of typical age for her grade, 6 years old with a March birthday. She first enrolled at our school as a kindergartner the year before. All of Sara's grade reports indicated that she had made above average progress while in kindergarten, and she had achieved perfect attendance during both years of school. Teachers' comments such as "a pleasure to teach" and "works well with others" decorated each progress report. Nothing in her cumulative file indicated significant family changes or an atypical medical history.

Sara greeted me excitedly at her classroom door and eagerly asked whether her mom had told me about the ghost. I barely got through my standard introduction before Sara began talking about the book her teacher had read and the images of ghosts that continuously ran through her mind, especially at night. She explained, "The words weren't bad. It was just the pictures that scared me." As Sara described vivid images of the ghost, I identified her use of the sensorimotor developmental orientation (Ivey, 1991) to tell her story.

Sara continued to explain that she was afraid that the ghost from the story would come into her bedroom while she was sleeping in the dark. She reported having trouble falling asleep and said she had awoken—scared by bad dreams—for the past 3 nights. Sara was now sleeping with her light on to help ward off the ghost. Her difficulty sleeping had occurred consistently since her teacher had read the Halloween book to Sara's class.

Rather than focusing on the nightmares or the strategy of sleeping with the light on, I tried to address the antecedent of the sleep problems (the story) and, in doing so, to match Sara's sensorimotor orientation. I decided to take a constructivist approach that allowed Sara to recreate and reexperience the book in a way that allowed her to control the pictures and, in turn, the images that repeatedly ran through her mind.

The following is transcription of parts of the counseling session.

> *Me:* Would you be willing to draw another book? I have some paper and some markers and some crayons.
> *Sara:* Yeah, that would be fun.
> *Me:* OK.
> *Sara:* We could make a book.

We worked together to recreate the story that had initially frightened Sara. As she told me a revised version of the story as she wished it to be, I wrote her words on a handmade book made of white drawing paper and staples.

> *Sara:* First let's see . . . I don't know how to write that. Can you write it for me? How about I'll pick the colors and you write the story.
> *Me:* OK.
> *Sara:* I'll make the pictures. You'll write the story.
> *Me:* OK. That sounds good to me.
> *Sara:* How about we use this color for the title?

Once the story was rewritten, Sara and I proceeded to illustrate the new book with pictures that were, in Sara's words, "not so spooky." Once the book was complete, Sara and I read the new version of the book together. Through this process of recreating a not-so-scary ghost story, Sara was able to craft a developmentally appropriate book for herself.

Sara went on to verbalize her thoughts about the new images replacing the old images in her head. She indicated that she would remember the friendly ghost from the new story rather than the "spooky" ghost from the original story. Sara decided, before leaving the session, that she would read the new book every night before going to bed, and she felt this would help her to feel less frightened at night.

> *Me:* And maybe that way you could remember the new book . . .
> *Sara:* The new book, I could keep it beside my bed and I could read it every night.
> *Me:* OK, and then you wouldn't have to remember the other book.
> *Sara:* The old book . . . Yikes! The new book is going to be great!

I checked in with Sara and her mother every day for 1 week, then once a week for 4 additional weeks. Sara and her mom reported reading the new version of the ghost story each night before Sara went to sleep. Sara's nightmares about the ghost story decreased in frequency, and after 2 weeks Sara was able to go to sleep with her bedroom light off.

Questions

1. If there is not a clear antecedent to sleep problems, such as a scary story, where might counselors begin when addressing the "monster under the bed"?
2. How can school counselors help teachers and parents to determine which books (or other forms of media) are developmentally appropriate for children?
3. How can counselors differentiate between the typical monsters under children's beds and fears that are grounded in reality?
4. In this case, the child was allowed to choose the colors she wanted to use for the pictures she was drawing. In what other ways might a counselor give young clients control over small decisions to help them feel empowered?
5. If the child had continued to have nightmares after recreating the book, what are some other techniques that could be tried?

■ Response

Laurie L. Williamson

I would approach this situation from a client-centered perspective. In working with children, I primarily use play therapy techniques and expressive modalities, including music, drawing, writing, role play, and movement. I frequently incorporate cognitive-behavioral components (e.g., relaxation techniques, cognitive restructuring, and rehearsal activities) into an intervention as necessary. My belief is that play therapy techniques and expressive modalities can help children identify the problem and explore its solution. The cognitive-behavioral components reinforce the new learning. I firmly believe children can and should be actively involved and empowered throughout the entire intervention process. Increasing a child's sense of self-efficacy and confidence needs to be the cornerstone of any intervention.

The first step in this case is to accept Sara's concerns as real and valid and empathetically respond to her experience. I would develop a trusting relationship with her, encouraging open communication and allowing for mutual problem solving. Play therapy approaches support developmental levels by offering children creative and nonthreatening ways to express themselves (Landreth, 2002; Norton & Norton, 1997). Furthermore, the use of imagination and fantasy can offer powerful metaphors to assist children in coping constructively with the many challenges they face (Lankton & Lankton, 1989).

If there was not a clear antecedent to Sara's sleep problems, such as the frightening story, I would ask Sara to tell me more about her nightmares. First and foremost, I would ask Sara to describe her fear. What about the monster is scary? What happens? What does the monster do? In addition, what does Sara do? I would have her fully describe the experience to me. It is often educational as well as rapport building to ask all the sensory questions. What does the monster look like? What does the monster sound like? I would include touch, smell, and even taste. This method challenges the child to consider nontraditional perspectives and also may provide useful information to me regarding how the child is processing a situation. Follow-up questions can assist me in making a differential diagnosis about whether the child's monster is fantasy or reality based.

The more information I gathered, the better I would understand Sara's experience. I would allow myself to be creative. I would provide Sara with the opportunity to draw, act, or sculpt her fear. The more we defined the fear, the more she could externalize it. Once it had a form and shape, it could have a name. We could begin to contain it, control it, and revise it. Why, we could even capture it in a box.

Chances are that Sara is experiencing normal, developmental anxiety in regard to first grade. Her mother works at the school, Sara appears to come from a stable home environment, and she is not reported to exhibit any other concerning behaviors. It is still important, especially if there is no clear antecedent, to explore whether Sara's fear is grounded in reality. Important questions I would ask myself include the following: How well developed is this fear? For how long and at what intensity level has Sara exhibited the fear? Was Sara exposed to an overt event, such as an emergency or accident? Does Sara have any other fears? Does the same bad dream reoccur, or does the theme change? Have I learned anything that makes me suspicious of a covert traumatic event, such as abuse or a threat (Mindell & Barrett, 2002)?

Distressing dreams and sleep disturbances can be symptomatic of posttraumatic stress disorder (PTSD). Pediatric PTSD may result from exposure to sexual abuse, physical abuse, natural disaster, urban violence, school violence, or terrorism. Studies show that children with PTSD may exhibit such symptoms as numbing or avoidance (marked diminished level of interest in regular activities), hypervigilance (increased arousal levels to environmental stimuli), and flashbacks of the trauma or intrusive thoughts (reexperiencing or a sense of reliving the experience). Reexperiencing trauma may manifest in generalized nightmares of monsters, rescuing others, or threats to self and others. Severe to moderate levels of PTSD are associated with depression, and girls are twice as likely as boys to report symptoms (Chemtob, Nakashima, & Carlson, 2002; Cook-Cottone, 2004; Guilleminault, Palombini, Pelayo, & Chervin, 2003; Russoniello et al., 2002). Practitioners need to be aware of the research on pediatric PTSD. Research shows that many professionals, from pediatricians to school counselors, underestimate posttraumatic stress in children (Ziegler, Greenwald, DeGuzman, & Simon, 2005).

If the situation was severe, a child this age would be expected to exhibit comorbid symptoms, possibly including regressive behaviors, such as bed wetting or frantic clinging. Children can also exhibit aggressive behaviors, such as defiance, bullying, or self-harm. Cook-Cottone (2004) provided counselors with diagnostic and treatment criteria designed to assist students with PTSD reintegrate into the school setting. In addition, the author identified assessment tools that can be used to evaluate children for PTSD.

Whether the nightmares are ever fully understood or given a rational explanation, the counselor still needs to intervene to relieve Sara's stress. There are several books that deal specifically with bad dreams. One that I have used and recommend is *Jessica and the Wolf* (Lobby, 1993). In this story, a young girl, with her parents' support, finds self-reliance in conquering a reoccurring bad dream. Narrative techniques, such as journaling, bibliotherapy, and memory scrapbooks, may also be helpful.

I have also used a technique called *cartoon magic*, a constructivist approach similar to the one used by the counselor in this incident. The process involves working with the child to recreate the dream and revise it to become less scary. The first step in cartoon magic would be to have Sara identify her favorite cartoon or comic book character. She would then identify the character's special talents (e.g., Spider Man could tie the bad guys up in a web, or Clifford the Big Red Dog could bark and scare them away). We would next fully explore the cartoon character's profile using art or drama. In doing so, Sara already would be focusing on more positive and empowering images. I would then ask Sara to consider what would happen if this cartoon character showed up in the dream. How would this ally intervene, support her, or even rescue her? We would develop a complete story line, through to a constructive ending. I would suggest that Sara review the drawing or reenact the scene regularly before bedtime, an example of a cognitive-behavioral component (rehearsal) in this intervention plan. Many children have returned in a week or 2 and reported that their dreams have improved. Often, a cartoon character arrives just in time to save the day. In more severe situations, such as abuse, regular and collaborative monitoring and more involved interventions may be required.

Dreams are one's conversations with oneself, and I have found children to be ready listeners. I knew a 9-year-old girl who, one morning, came into my office intent on sharing her dream. I thought it unusual for a 9-year-old to remember a dream from hours before and knew it must have been a powerful one. Unless they take diligent notes, most people will only briefly remember their dreams. The young girl shared a nightmare in which she was to walk between two buildings where there was an open, grassy area. As she walked toward the other building, she was attacked by squirrels. They climbed on her and bit her. She could knock some off, but more took their place. She was horrified and felt afraid and helpless; the squirrels were relentless. I listened to her story with a heavy heart and tried to soothe her. She had recently been diagnosed with lupus and died a short time later. Lupus is an autoimmune disorder in which the body attacks itself. In Jungian psychology, dreams represent an "ongoing dialectic which occurs between conscious and unconscious dynamics" (Whitmont & Perera, 1989, p. 73), or, in this case, a conversation between body and mind. I share this experience to encourage the reader to view children and their dreams as a means of legitimate communication and deserving of attention.

In respect to selecting developmentally appropriate materials, parents and teachers need to take a proactive role. Children should be involved in helping parents and teachers select books and films. Adults should teach children how to best choose books or films by accessing review lists and recommendations from respected authorities. There are numerous lists available to ensure that quality children's literature or film is selected. After taking the children's developmental level and areas of interest into consideration, one should provide an appropriate list and allow the children to choose. Parents and teachers can model good skills and promote communication with children by discussing the story. They could throw in some outrageous questions, such as, "How would the story be different if we read it backward?" This helps keep children's attention and encourages critical and creative thinking. Try telling *Goldilocks and the Three Bears* backward. It comes out completely different and, by the way, not so frightening.

In regard to other techniques to help with bedtime, routines are helpful. Assist the child in taking an inventory of the day and processing his or her activities. Ask thoughtful questions, such as, "What was the highlight of your day?" "Who helped you today, and how?" "Who did you help today, and how?" and "On a scale of 1 to 10, how well did you take care of your body today?" Repeat this scaling question asking about social, emotional, intellectual, and even spiritual well-being. "If you could live today over, what would you do differently?" or "What are your plans for tomorrow?"

These kinds of practices make one more mindful and are helpful for adults as well as children. Soft, soothing music (especially baroque) and aromatherapy candles can calm a restless body. A warm bath and relaxation with imagery can go a long way in facilitating a good night's sleep. Some children respond to a transitional object, such as a favorite stuffed animal or reassuring nightlight. One child I know loves to sleep with a flashlight—safety and control at the push of a button. When parents consistently implement bedtime routines, children can learn to make a smooth transition and settle in for a restful night's sleep.

■ Response

Imelda N. Lowe

Typically, children are not able to identify the cause of nightmares at the beginning of counseling; nevertheless, I describe Sara as a unique client who was able to identify the presenting problem and its cause. Initially, I would begin with an intake interview with the parent or guardian addressing issues of physical or sexual abuse or trauma. If the parent were unaware of any such event or did not disclose this information, I would look for themes to emerge during play therapy sessions to help me address the "monster under the bed." Identifying metaphors of fear and struggles in the child's play can help the counselor formulate a hypothesis of inner conflict. Commenting on and reflecting these thoughts to the child provides an opportunity to explore the counselor's hypothesis. The use of bibliotherapy has been effective in my experience. I would consider using a book such as *Go Away Big Green Monster!* (Emberly, 1993) or *Let's Talk About Feeling Afraid* (Berry, 1995) to introduce the topic of monsters or feeling scared. Art techniques have also been effective with children who experience nightmares. Having the child draw kinetic family drawings, school drawings, serial drawings, or drawings of how he or she would like things to be (Allan, 1988; Kottman, 1995), may be helpful in identifying and resolving fears.

Piaget (Lefrancois, 1996) would describe Sara as being in the period of intuitive thinking (4–7 years of age). During this stage, logical thinking is not fully developed, and the child's thinking is egocentric (unable to be objective) and perception dominated (the child's perception is reality). Sara's nightmares are an example of the inability to distinguish what is real from what is make believe. Because children develop at different rates, I hypothesize that Sara is unable to differentiate the pictures as fantasy or make believe.

School counselors have a unique opportunity to interact on a regular basis with the child's school environment. Staff development training can be offered to provide a review of the developmental stages that children progress through. Examples of developmentally appropriate and inappropriate books or videos can be presented for school-age children at different grade levels. Discussing the rationale for what makes the books appropriate can be useful in clarifying information. In working with elementary-age children over the past years, I have heard children describe graphic scenes from R-rated movies that I would not consider watching. Providing parents with information similar to that provided to teachers and other staff may facilitate an awareness of the impact that developmentally inappropriate material can have on children.

The American Academy of Family Physicians (2005) stated that one in four children has nightmares at least once a week and that these nightmares can be viewed as metaphoric communication indicating internal, physical, or emotional distress. Given the information that it is developmentally appropriate for children to experience nightmares, I would attempt to discover whether the nightmares were somatic symptoms of trauma, anxiety, abuse, or normal childhood fears.

In considering the criteria for nightmare disorder, as described by the *Diagnostic and Statistical Manual of Mental Disorders* (4th ed., text rev.; American Psychiatric Association, 2000), my primary goal at intake with the parent or guardian is to assess the frequency, recall, and time of occurrence for the dream as well as to obtain a description of the child's behavior after awakening. I further conduct a thorough assessment of possible mental and medical conditions.

If the child does not meet the formal diagnostic criteria, I use various techniques, including a consideration of themes in play therapy, to assess possible abuse. Bibliotherapy provides a nonthreatening opportunity for the child to discuss any issues of concern, including abuse, and using the Touch Survey (Hewitt, 1999) can provide a formal assessment of sexual or physical abuse. I carefully observe the child's reactions when using these techniques because, many times, nonverbal responses can indicate more than words can. If I do not see any indication that the child has experienced abuse or any other traumatic event, I may consider the nightmares to be developmental. However, I do not easily dismiss abuse or trauma as a possibility.

Sara was invited to design a new story to replace the previous, scary version. In recreating the story, she was invited to use her own pictures and themes in a version that was less scary to her. Sara dictated her story to the counselor and chose the colors to use, which provided her the opportunity to control the story, facilitating empowerment.

As described in *Play Therapy: The Art of the Relationship* (Landreth, 1991), to promote strength development, I allow my clients the freedom to set the pace and direction for the counseling process as well as to choose which toys or tools are used during the session. When a child looks to me for direction, I respond, "In here you decide what to use." To further promote empowerment, I always assure my young clients that they have the choice of whether to answer questions or participate in role play during the counseling session. During role playing, I use the whisper technique, which allows the child to direct my actions. I believe this technique offers the child an opportunity to make decisions he or she may not be permitted to make outside of the counseling session, thereby promoting empowerment and self-responsibility.

If recreating the book does not alleviate the nightmares for Sara, there are additional techniques that may be used. One such technique is the use of therapeutic stories that use metaphors to indirectly provide insight and suggestions (Mills & Crowley, 1986). Therapeutic metaphors provide the child with an opportunity to identify with the character, removing the belief that he or she is the only one who feels this way. A conflict is presented in the story that parallels the child's real-world struggle. Heroes and villains are integrated into the story to metaphorically represent the child's inner resources and beliefs, and situations or conflicts occur in the story to present alternative solutions to the problem. Metaphors provide a child with the opportunity to reframe his or her experience and allow him or her access to inner resources to alleviate distress. Conversely, to promote Sara's personal power more directly, I might develop my own metaphor story using information gathered from her during our sessions.

Another technique I could use with Sara is to have her draw a representation of the monster on paper. I would encourage Sara to draw the scariest monster she could imagine, and if this became too difficult for her, I would draw the monster for her as she described it. Next, I would place the picture on the floor for Sara to jump on, kick, or hit. Again, if Sara were unable to begin, I would model jumping on the picture as I made statements such as, "You will not scare me anymore." After this process, I would encourage Sara to tear the picture into as many little pieces as she could. We would then burn the pieces or flush them down the toilet. This process might need to be repeated at home or during the following counseling sessions as many times as Sara deemed necessary (Davis, 1990).

References

Allan, J. (1988). *Inscapes of the child's world: Jungian counseling in schools and clinics.* Dallas, TX: Spring Publications.

American Academy of Family Physicians. (2005). *Nightmares and night terrors in children.* Retrieved December 14, 2005, from http://www.aafp.org/afp/20051001/1322ph.html

American Psychiatric Association. (2000). *Diagnostic and statistical manual of mental disorders* (4th ed., text rev.). Washington, DC: Author.

Berry, J. (1995). *Let's talk about feeling afraid.* New York: Scholastic.

Chemtob, C. M., Nakashima, J., & Carlson, J. G. (2002). Brief treatment for elementary school children with disaster-related posttraumatic stress. *Journal of Clinical Psychology, 58,* 99–112.

Cook-Cottone, C. (2004). Childhood posttraumatic stress disorder: Diagnosis, treatment and school reintegration. *School Psychology Reviews, 33,* 127–139.

Davis, N. (1990). *Once upon a time . . . therapeutic stories to heal abused children* (rev. ed.). Burke, VA: Author.

Emberly, E. (1993). *Go away big green monster!* New York: Little, Brown.

Guilleminault, C., Palombini, L., Pelayo, R., & Chervin, R. (2003). Sleepwalking and sleep terrors in prepubertal children: What triggers them? *Pediatrics, 111,* 17–25.

Hewitt, S. (1999). *Assessing allegations of sexual abuse in preschool children.* Thousand Oaks, CA: Sage.

Ivey, A. E. (1991). *Developmental strategies for helpers.* Belmont, CA: Brooks/Cole.

Kottman, T. (1995). *Partners in play: An Adlerian approach to play therapy.* Alexandria, VA: American Counseling Association.

Landreth, G. (1991). *Play therapy: The art of the relationship.* Bristol, PA: Accelerated Development.

Landreth, G. L. (2002). *Play therapy: The art of the relationship* (2nd ed.). New York: Brunner-Routledge.

Lankton, C. H., & Lankton, S. R. (1989). *Tales of enchantment: Goal-oriented metaphors for adults and children in therapy.* Bristol, PA: Brunner/Mazel.

Lefrancois, G. (1996). *The lifespan* (5th ed.). Belmont, CA: Wadsworth Publishing.

Lobby, T. (1993). *Jessica and the wolf: A story for children who have bad dreams.* Milwaukee, WI: Stevens.

Mills, J., & Crowley, R. (1986). *Therapeutic metaphors for children.* New York: Brunner/Mazel.

Mindell, J. A., & Barrett, K. M. (2002). Nightmares and anxiety in elementary-aged children: Is there a relationship? *Child: Care, Health, & Development, 28,* 317–322.

Norton, C. C., & Norton, B. E. (1997). *Reaching children through play therapy: An experiential approach.* Denver, CO: Publishing Cooperative.

Russoniello, C. V., Skalko, T. K., O'Brien, K., McGhee, S. A., Bingham-Alexander, D., & Beatley, J. (2002). Childhood posttraumatic stress disorder and efforts to cope after Hurricane Floyd. *Behavioral Medicine, 29,* 61–71.

Whitmont, E. C., & Perera, S. B. (1989). *Dreams: A portal to the source.* London: Routledge.

Ziegler, M. R., Greenwald, M. H., DeGuzman, M. A., & Simon, H. K. (2005). Posttraumatic stress responses in children: Awareness and practice among a sample of pediatric emergency care providers. *Pediatrics, 115,* 1261–1267.

Part

II

Child Abuse and Other Trauma

Abuse Disclosure: "Walt Touched Me Down There"

This incident describes the disclosure of child sexual abuse by a 10-year-old Native American boy. The respondents explore treatment issues as well as the difficulties of assessing auditory hallucinations in a culturally sensitive way.

Critical Incident

Barbara J. Carlozzi

"Matthew Lightfoot" and his sister "Jennifer" appeared at my office door unannounced. I was working as a school counselor in a small, suburban school in the Midwest, having been hired 2 years previously when the community experienced a sexual abuse case with multiple victims. My rather vague job description was to "meet the needs of the students," and I was given a great deal of flexibility in the amount of time allotted to treatment and prevention activities. The nearest counseling services were 30 minutes away, and many families had difficulty traveling this distance, either because of unreliable transportation or because of work schedules that did not allow enough leave time.

"We need to talk to you," said Jennifer. The principal had just called to see whether I could talk to a parent who was in tears in his office, so I was hurrying to leave and deal with that possible crisis. "What is it about?" I asked Jennifer. "Something private," she responded. Today was the annual Thanksgiving dinner at our school, and my office was located off the cafeteria. Just outside the door, I could hear the voices of parents and grandparents coming to meet their children for lunch. My office would be anything but private, so, despite my concern that Jennifer and Matthew should be my highest priority at the moment, I checked to see whether we could postpone our conversation until later in the day. "Is this something that could wait until lunch is over and we have a little more privacy?" I asked. Neither of them seemed visibly upset, and they said they could wait, so I arranged to meet them shortly after 1:00 that afternoon.

As they entered later that day, Jennifer said, "Go on, tell her." Matthew and Jennifer whispered together briefly, and Jennifer gave her brother a gentle nudge in my direction. I had seen both students in guidance classes over the last 2 years. Matthew was 10 and Jennifer 12. Like many of the children in this school, Matthew and Jennifer's parents had registered them as Caucasian–European American, even though, when asked, the children would readily acknowledge that a grandparent was a full-blood American Indian. In Matthew and Jennifer's case, both of their paternal grandparents were Cherokee.

"Matthew has something he wants to tell you," said Jennifer. I looked to Matthew and tried to assess how willingly he had come. "Matthew," I asked, "do you want to talk to me about something?" He nodded his head yes. "Would you like to talk alone, or do you want Jennifer here, too?" "I want her to stay," he said. We all looked to Matthew as he looked down and remained silent. "It looks like this is something that's hard to talk about," I said. Matthew nodded. "Is this something that happened to you, Matthew?" Again, he nodded yes. "Maybe you could start by telling me where you were when this happened." With this suggestion, Matthew began the story of how he had been molested by a male friend of the family.

Matthew told me about "Walt and Linda Talyard." They were friends of Jennifer and Matthew's parents and had invited Jennifer and Matthew to spend the night with them and go with them to a local bakery the next day. After the two children had gone to bed and Matthew was apparently almost asleep, Walt had moved Matthew into bed with him and his wife. At this point in the story, Matthew had difficulty continuing. He said it was embarrassing. He continued by saying that Walt had started "rubbing" on him. When asked where Walt had rubbed, Matthew remained silent. "Was it above or below the waist?" I asked. "Down there," said Matthew, pointing to his genital area. "How long did he rub?" I asked. Matthew stammered, "Uuh, not long." "What did you do?" I asked.

"I pretended I was asleep," said Matthew.

Me: And Walt's wife, where was she?
Matthew: Asleep.
Me: In the same bed?
Matthew: Uh-huh.

At this point I began to think about how our conversation might affect a future investigation by child protective investigators, but I felt it was therapeutically important to allow Matthew to tell me his story. I therefore chose to continue with our session rather than immediately calling Child Protective Services. Nevertheless, I told Matthew that what he was telling me was very important and asked him whether I could take some notes. He consented, and I continued by asking whether anything had happened before Walt stopped. Matthew said, "He put his thing in me." Matthew went on to describe anal intercourse that had taken place in Walt and Linda's bed. According to Matthew, Linda had remained asleep while Walt fondled Matthew, penetrated him anally, and attempted to French kiss him.

I replied that it must have been difficult to tell me this story. Matthew looked me straight in the eye when I said, "Adults are not supposed to do this to children . . . *no matter what*. That means you're not to blame. Walt is." When I asked how he was doing, Matthew said he was OK. Because he had not previously made eye contact with me, I wondered about the impact of my previous comment about Walt's culpability. Was he checking my facial expression to see whether he could believe me? Was he in doubt about Walt's responsibility for the abuse? By his behavior, I could not assess how Matthew felt about the sexual abuse, and he was not in a talkative mood. Some students who had been sexually molested had clearly been terrorized, others appeared to feel guilty about their involvement, some refused to talk about it and displayed marked behavioral changes, and one or two refused to talk about it and showed no evidence of any problems.

I asked Matthew whether he would like to draw what happened to him, and he said, "Yes." He drew three pictures in boxes, like a cartoon drawing in sequence. The first picture showed Matthew and Walt in bed side by side, with Walt smiling and Matthew looking scared. The next picture showed Walt with his hand on Matthew's pelvic area, and the third picture showed the two figures on top of one another and read, "He kissed me." At the bottom of the picture, it read, "I do not remember all of it." When I commented that Matthew looked scared and unhappy in the pictures, Matthew did not respond.

I had lots of questions, but I decided to stop at this point and begin the process that I hated—preparing the client for reporting his story to Child Protective Services. "Matthew," I said, "it seems like Jennifer encouraged you to come talk to me about this. What did you think would happen?" "Don't know. Guess you'll call DHS." Apparently, Matthew already understood that this was something I had to report to the Department of Human Services (i.e., DHS). I believed that this was because students were aware of the aforementioned case with multiple victims and because I had talked to students in guidance classes about issues of sexual abuse and about the limits of confidentiality.

I asked Matthew whether he had told anyone else about the incident with Walt, and he indicated that he had already told his mother, an aunt, and his sister. He said that his mother had simply told him to yell if it ever happened again but that his sister, Jennifer, suggested that they come tell me. I explained that I would call their home to let his parents know that I would be calling Child Protective Services and that someone would be coming to their house to talk with them about it. Matthew told me that his mom would not answer the phone. When asked why, Jennifer said her mom did not want to talk to people. I had talked to Mrs. Lightfoot in person, so I assumed Jennifer meant that her mom screened phone calls by not answering them.

"Is there anything else you want to say or ask me?" I asked. "No," Matthew replied. I was surprised that he did not seem to object to my calling Child Protective Services. I said that I would check in with him on the next school day to see how things were going. He and Jennifer then went back to their respective classrooms.

Feeling the anxiety mounting in my chest, I took a few minutes alone to collect my thoughts and then called Child Protective Services and asked to speak with one of the investigators I knew. Fortunately, I was able to reach him and explain the situation. He reminded me that this was not one of their cases. This was a criminal case because the perpetrator was unrelated to Matthew. I had never dealt with a disclosure that was criminal in nature, so I asked about the process. The investigator told me that the police often asked for child protective workers to accompany them on an investigation of this nature but that I would have to call the police with the report. I then called the police. It was 4 days before I saw Matthew again, and it was in the principal's office with a local police officer.

Matthew relayed the same story to the police officer, much of it through drawing. Although I considered this to be a credible sexual abuse story, no legal action took place after the report. Weeks went by, and I heard nothing about any follow-up. I called the police officer and was told they were checking whether there were other victims. Matthew left a note for me that said, "You are my favorite teacher. Thank you for your help." He came to see me once and asked me when the police were going to arrest Walt. I told him I did not know and hoped it would be soon. He said that his mom and dad had gotten into a fight and that Child Protective Services had been to their house (apparently for domestic violence). He said he was going to see a counselor at a community agency.

Several weeks after the winter holiday break, Matthew asked to speak with me. He said he was grumpy, he was losing friends, and his mom was mad at him. I told him that it was normal to feel angry after having been abused and talked about how counseling could help. At this point, Matthew revealed that his parents had not followed through and taken him to see the counselor at the community agency. I suggested that Matthew again ask his parents about seeing a counselor, but I learned later that they never did take him for counseling. Matthew reported that his father had said that no one was going to tell him how to raise his kids.

Over the next 2 months, I saw Matthew seven times. I was impressed with Matthew's ability to talk about the abuse, to discuss the impact it had on his family and his awareness of his changing emotions. It seemed that after the initial disclosure, a barrier had been overcome, and he was now quite able to process the event and its consequences.

One day, a month after my last session with Matthew, I was asked by the school principal to speak with Matthew. A teacher had brought Matthew to the office after discovering him shaking and visibly upset on the playground during recess. When the teacher went to check on him, Matthew told her he had heard an evil voice that was threatening to kill him. During my subsequent conversation with Matthew, he explained that the voice sounded like a local man whom Matthew had recently seen at a ball game. Matthew told his mother that he felt afraid of this man and did not like him, but his mom had reportedly laughed at him and indicated that the man was harmless. Matthew also talked with me about the unrest at home and said that his parents were either at work or arguing. He said he really did not have a mom, that Jennifer took care of his younger siblings and that he was on his own. He wanted to know why he had heard that voice. Did it mean that this man was really going to kill him? He expressed concern that I would think he was weird.

I told Matthew that there are differing beliefs about why people hear voices. I suggested that some people hear voices after something scary happens to them. I speculated that maybe, after all he had been through, the voice was his own mind trying to protect him from the possibility of something scary happening to him again. Frankly, at this point, I felt I was getting in over my head. I knew the family had some American Indian heritage and wondered how that might influence this situation, especially the issue of voices. I did not know, however, how to distinguish between culturally sanctioned responses to stress and actual hallucinations. Child Protective Services had told me they had recommended that the parents get counseling for Matthew, but this had not happened.

Questions

1. How should I respond to Matthew's report about hearing voices? Are Matthew's voices a functional response to his abuse, or are they indicative of increasing dysfunction?
2. Should I request a psychiatric evaluation? I have no confidence that Matthew's parents will get outside help for him, and I risk further alienation between the parents and the school if I make another request that they seek psychological help for Matthew. What is more, might a referral for a psychiatric evaluation communicate to Matthew that I think he is "weird"?
3. What part might the cultural component play in this case, and how might that have been incorporated into Matthew's treatment?

Response

Krista M. Malott

Matthew showed great courage in seeking support after an extremely difficult experience. In turn, the counselor showed sensitivity and respect in gaining the client's permission to address and explore this event. She was also able to normalize subsequent reactions by openly acknowledging diverse beliefs regarding symptomatology—in this case, the hearing of voices. The counselor also provided a key element of support by facilitating Matthew's exploration of the impact of the abuse.

Nevertheless, Matthew remains isolated and vulnerable to additional problems because of increasing conflict in his family, the loss of friends, and a lack of parental support with regard to the sexual abuse. The counselor could brainstorm with Matthew to assess his perception of personal strengths and external supports. Building on his suggestions, she could broaden his support network, urging his involvement in school and community activities or matching him with an adult or student mentor.

Connecting Matthew with American Indian individuals or community programs would strengthen his sense of heritage and American Indian identity—an essential factor in building his resiliency and self-esteem. Additionally, the counselor could create a support group for Matthew and the other American Indian youths who experienced sexual abuse. Ashby, Gilchrist, and Miramontez (1987) suggested guidelines for establishing such a group using Native traditions, such as the Indian talking circle, meal sharing, and traditional Indian art and free expression.

Matthew's reports of grumpiness and difficulty with relationships are not in themselves sufficient evidence of depression. Nonetheless, a further exploration of symptomatology, including assessment of potential suicidal ideation, is warranted. This is culturally relevant when one considers that the suicide rate among American Indian youths is more than double the national rate for non-Indian youths (Grossman, Milligan, & Deyo, 1991). Other culturally relevant factors in this case may include Matthew's compliance, silence, lack of eye contact, and lack of expressiveness in the sessions. These factors could all be interpreted as American Indian communication traits. Should Matthew adhere to his Native heritage, the counselor must also be aware of the following American Indian beliefs (J. T. Garrett & Garrett, 1994; Irwin & Roll, 1995):

- the belief that an individual chooses to make himself or herself well or unwell;
- the belief that no one may tell another individual what to do;
- the perception of emotional restraint and silence as signs of maturity;

- the importance of harmony and balance and the belief that same-sex and intergenerational sexual activity destroy that harmony and balance;
- the essential role of spirituality, ritual or ceremony, and family and community in a client's healing process;
- the belief in immanent justice and the importance of refraining from negative comments or actions toward another;
- the belief that direct confrontation disrupts harmony and balance;
- an emphasis on living or being in the moment;
- a belief that family and tribal group take precedence over the individual.

J. T. Garrett and Garrett (1994) suggested that counselors working with American Indian clients offer advice and interpretation only when invited by the client. They further indicated that advice should be presented as possibilities and solutions. Additional recommendations included the following:

- Ask permission whenever possible and always give thanks.
- Never interrupt—allow sufficient time for completion of thoughts.
- Be patient.
- Use silence whenever it seems appropriate (or even when it does not).
- Use descriptive statements rather than questioning.
- Model self-disclosure through anecdotes or short stories.
- Make use of metaphors and imagery when appropriate. (p. 143)

Nonetheless, before drawing conclusions regarding the cultural components of this case, the counselor must determine to what extent Matthew and his family identify with their American Indian heritage. This should include exploration of their use of the Cherokee American Indian language, their practice of Native American cultural traditions, and their adherence to American Indian beliefs and values. To build trust and establish a connection with the family, the counselor could organize a meeting in a setting chosen by the family. Additionally, because many American Indians believe that extended family, friends, and community members play an essential role in an individual's healing, the counselor could ask the family to invite all persons they consider important.

During the meeting, the counselor could clarify her role as a helper and provide written and verbal education regarding sexual abuse. In preparation for the meeting, she could enrich her understanding of American Indian clientele and culturally appropriate interventions by

- consulting with a professional experienced in tribe-specific mental health issues and culturally appropriate interventions (many reservations employ mental health professionals).
- reviewing historical discriminatory practices against American Indians and the cumulative effects of these past and ongoing practices on American Indians' current mental health status.
- reviewing tribe-specific traditions, values, and worldviews.
- identifying interventions suggested as appropriate for American Indians. These include group therapy (Manson, Walker, & Kivlahan, 1987), family systems therapy (Ivey, Ivey, & Simek-Morgan, 1997), social–cognitive interventions, traditional healing (LaFromboise & Dizon, 2003), and cognitive therapy (Burke, Chauvin, & Miranti, 2005).

In response to the question of hearing voices and the need for psychiatric evaluation, there are a couple of factors to consider. Matthew's symptoms could be in response to an increasingly dysfunctional setting, and such symptoms could be influenced by his American Indian heritage. If the counselor decides to proceed with a referral for a psychiatric evaluation, only a referral to a professional familiar with culture-bound syndromes (Dana, 1998) is recommended. This referral, if addressed sensitively, would not necessarily result in Matthew feeling that the counselor perceived him as "weird." For example, in making the referral, the counselor could explain to Matthew that an evaluation by an "expert in voices" could be helpful.

Nevertheless, before seeking an outside evaluation, the counselor should first consult with the individuals closest to Matthew. These include (a) Matthew's family and extended family members; (b) relevant community members, including tribal leaders, if appropriate; and (c) healing or mental health professionals specifically versed in the illness beliefs and healing practices of the Cherokee Nation. In addition to providing cultural insight, consultation with these individuals could help the counselor establish a relationship of trust with Matthew's family, thereby lowering the risk of alienating them should the counselor decide to pursue a psychiatric evaluation for Matthew.

Once a relationship was established with the family, the counselor could then explore any perceived barriers to obtaining additional help. Cultural barriers to seeking help may include distrust of dominant-culture practices and establishments, American Indian beliefs about illness and healing that differ from Western beliefs, and a fear of dishonoring the perpetrator (Walt Talyard, who may be perceived as a family member). Independent of culture, Matthew's family may not understand the impact of sexual abuse or may feel immobilized by shame concerning the topic. They also simply may not have the energy, money, transportation, or available time to obtain outside services. Once barriers are identified, the counselor could work with the family to remove them or to create alternative, culturally appropriate solutions.

In summary, the counselor could have provided additional resources and supports for Matthew; assessed for suicidal ideation; and involved him in Native-specific group, school, and community activities. Additionally, the counselor could have (a) assessed Matthew's and his family's level of identification with their Cherokee heritage, (b) educated herself about the culture through written material and consultation with Cherokee tribal experts, and (c) met with the family off site to collaborate with them in designing culturally appropriate interventions.

The voices reported by Matthew could be addressed through consultation with family and community members or tribal-specific individuals. Should the auditory hallucinations prove to be nonculture specific or should the family identify mainly with dominant cultural beliefs, the counselor could seek a psychiatric evaluation. She could also assess the family's perceptions of barriers in obtaining further assistance and work with them to overcome those barriers.

Response

Elizabeth U. Willingham

For counselors, one of the most difficult stories to hear is a child's disclosure of sexual abuse. For children, one of the most difficult stories to tell is about sexual abuse. For families, one of the most difficult situations to face is sexual abuse. For communities, one of the most widespread concerns is sexual abuse. Although it is painful for everyone involved on every level, with the appropriate response to child abuse, a new story about courage, empowerment, protection, and healing can be created.

When a child discloses sexual abuse, the counselor must be present with and attend to the child. While listening, observing, empathizing, and conveying acceptance, the counselor must also be aware of the many ethical, legal, and multicultural issues that warrant critical attention in cases of child sexual abuse. At times, this can be extremely stressful and frightening for counselors, especially if they have not had much specialized training or experience dealing with child sexual abuse. Personally, I always try my best to focus on the most important piece—the child. If I am feeling stressed and frightened as an adult, I can only imagine how terrified the child must feel. I think about the courage it takes for a child to face the fear, break the silence, give up the secret, and tell the story. Through the child's strength and courage I find my own strength and resolve, knowing that I can help a child to have a voice when children's voices so often go unheard.

As a 10-year-old boy of Native American heritage who was severely victimized by a trusted male adult, Matthew Lightfoot possessed tremendous courage to disclose sexual abuse. It is evident that Matthew felt a close connection with his school counselor, given that he not only disclosed this abuse to her but also continued to see her for therapeutic guidance and support. Her calm and reassuring response communicated genuine caring, acceptance, and respect for Matthew's privacy as well as her concern for his safety. She reassured him that he was not responsible for what happened and offered him another way to communicate his story, by drawing. The counselor also took concrete steps by making a report first to Child Protective Services and then to the police. Unfortunately, although Matthew clearly benefited from his ongoing interactions with the counselor, the responses of other adults involved do not seem to have been as helpful to him. Perhaps as a result of this, Matthew continued to exhibit symptoms of distress.

Symptoms and Diagnostic Implications

Matthew's symptoms of distress, although marked, are common in children whose abuse experience has been traumatic, especially those children whose safety is still uncertain. Intrusive reexperiencing of the trauma, avoidance, and physiological arousal are the hallmark characteristics of traumatic stress and were observed with Matthew. For example, when he wrote "I do not remember" on his drawing, this was indicative of avoidance of the painful memories associated with the abuse. Similarly, the incident at recess when Matthew was upset and shaking and reported hearing a voice reflects intrusive thoughts and heightened physiological arousal. Increased arousal was also evident in Matthew's heightened sensitivity to the local man at the ball game.

Matthew's emotional response shows how fear and anxiety that is abuse specific can generalize and overwhelm a child's coping skills. I believe that many children are misdiagnosed when their symptoms of traumatic stress mimic symptoms of other diagnoses. In this vein, I believe that it is unlikely that Matthew was experiencing true psychosis when he heard the voice on the playground. In my experience, when traumatized children do not feel safe and their extreme fear and anxiety are not adequately addressed, these emotions can intensify and, at times, present like psychosis. Although Matthew admitted to having the hallucination, he also seemed reality oriented in his conversation with the counselor. Additionally, such hallucinations are generally less indicative of psychosis in children (Kronenberger & Meyer, 2001). More specific to Matthew's cultural heritage, the fact that some Native American children may report hearing "bad spirits" and might not eat when they experience distress (Amanda Wolfe, personal communication, September 7, 2005) may be culturally relevant in understanding Matthew's response and in determining the best approach for his evaluation and treatment.

Therapeutic Issues

Matthew was physically, psychologically, and emotionally violated. Several factors are noteworthy as they relate to Matthew's abuse and functioning after disclosure. First, there are the nature and severity of the abuse. Matthew was fondled, kissed, and anally penetrated. Multiple kinds and levels of abuse can be more traumatic to a child. Second, the alleged perpetrator was a man. This is significant because it may confuse Matthew's ideas and feelings about sexuality. Matthew may also struggle with power and control issues related to his inability to protect himself. Third, Walt was a trusted family friend. This may cause Matthew to feel confused about, unsafe with, betrayed by, or ambivalent toward Walt. Walt's wife, Linda, who was in the bed during the abuse, did not protect Matthew. He may conclude that adults close to him cannot or will not protect him in the future.

Matthew's perceptions about the abuse also influence his level of distress. The school counselor noted embarrassment and guilt. Matthew probably feels helpless, powerless, and unsafe because a trusted adult abused him and he could not protect himself. He may question the trustworthiness of the system, given that the police did not respond in the manner he hoped by arresting Walt. Matthew may also blame himself for not stopping the abuse or not telling someone sooner. He may be worried about how "telling on" Walt will affect his family and community. In some Native American cultures, family friends are responsible for helping to raise children (J. T. Garrett & Garrett, 1994). Matthew may also feel like the domestic violence and arguing between his parents are his fault. Matthew disclosed to his mother, aunt, and sister. Although his mother told him to yell if it happened again, it is unclear whether the abuse was further addressed or reported by the family. Only his 12-year-old sister, Jennifer, encouraged him to tell the counselor. The one adult who responded to Matthew by reporting the abuse to authorities in an effort to keep him safe was the counselor. Matthew likely perceives that the other adults in his life cannot keep him safe. In addition, these adults may be unaware that this is the way he perceives their responses to his disclosure.

Additional Cultural Issues

Native Americans have a long history of social, economic, and political oppression and victimization. European Americans' brutal attempts to assimilate or "civilize" Native Americans have had devastating and traumatic effects on their social and family structures. This trauma and loss of identity, culture, language, and land directly contribute to the challenges Native American families and communities face, such as limited resources; high levels of stress; unemployment; increased rates of drug and alcohol abuse; and increased incidences of domestic violence, suicide, and homicide. In addition, Native peoples experience increased rates of hate crimes, gang violence, incarceration, and child abuse (BigFoot, 2000). It is not surprising that the overwhelming feelings of powerlessness, helplessness, and distrust experienced by many Native Americans factor into their underuse of mental health services.

The traditional Native American value system conflicts considerably with American mainstream culture, which values power over nature, competition and success, individual gain, scientific explanations, and orientation to the future. There is much diversity among Native Americans, yet they share many of the same traditional values, beliefs, and practices. Among these are harmony with nature, cooperation, group focus, humility, reliance on extended family, supernatural explanations, and orientation to the present. When working with Native Americans, it is also essential to consider the client's specific cultural heritage and explore the client's level of acculturation (M. T. Garrett, 2006). In Matthew's case, it is important to explore his perceptions of his Cherokee heritage and assess his level of acculturation. I wonder, for example, about the acculturation implications of his parents' decision to register their children in school as Caucasian. On the basis of the Native American value of reliance on the extended family and my belief that caregiver and family involvement is critical to Matthew's healing process, I would want to connect with his family. Understanding the family perspectives about their culture, their acculturation process, and Matthew's abuse would be important to ensuring that my counseling practices were culturally sensitive, appropriate, and helpful.

Treatment Recommendations

Providing counseling that is culturally sensitive and developmentally appropriate is essential in all cases. Demonstrating cultural sensitivity within our counseling relationship, I would validate Matthew's feelings, reassure him that he was having a normal response to abuse, emphasize that he was not alone, and reaffirm my willingness to be a witness to his story and to help him feel better. In treating Matthew, I would also draw on play therapy, filial therapy, family consultation, and collaboration with a multidisciplinary team.

Play therapy and filial therapy (Landreth, 2002), which teaches parents play therapy skills to enhance the parent–child relationship, have been implemented effectively with some Native American populations. These approaches are respectful of the traditional Native American culture because they involve nonverbal and symbolic expression and are nondirective, holistic, family oriented, and collaborative (Glover, 2001). I believe play therapy is a powerful and effective approach for expression, growth, and healing for almost all ages and populations. There is nothing more incredible and sacred than witnessing a child's story and watching the child's self-directed healing process unfold in just the way the child needs. Play therapy would give Matthew a safe and protected space to express, explore, and resolve issues related to his distress. The playroom provides a safe haven from the negative images, messages, and interactions children experience and internalize in the outside world. The comfortable and peaceful atmosphere of the playroom would give Matthew the opportunity to temporarily leave the scary, discordant outside world. Through relationship and play, he could create and experience positive healing images and interactions so that he could reenter the outside world with a greater sense of inner strength, understanding, and coping.

The freedom to direct the healing process at their own pace is vital for children who have experienced abuse or trauma. Using toys and expressive materials provides children with a mode of symbolic expression that does not force them to talk about their experience. It also gives them a way to distance themselves from their pain when it becomes too much (Ater, 2001; Webb, 2001). This is crucial because it returns the control to the child. In play therapy, Matthew could use toys, dolls, puppets, art, sand trays, and storytelling to explore his being, find his strength, and make sense of and integrate his traumatic experiences (Gil, 1991). Art, for example, is a very helpful mode of expression for children who may not have words to verbally describe their experience. My toys and materials in the playroom would reflect cultural diversity and be relevant to Native American culture—for instance, natural objects, leather, beads, feathers, dolls, utensils, clay, and various types of cloth. Matthew could choose to use these materials to symbolically communicate his experiences and needs.

When I am counseling a child who has been sexually abused, my immediate goals are to address the child's safety and reduce the child's distress, keeping in mind the ultimate goals of resolution, healing, and prevention. I believe that healing is facilitated in the context of a therapeutic relationship and that caregiver involvement in the healing process is critical to the child's recovery. I also believe in treating the whole child. This means not only focusing on abuse-related concerns but also viewing the child holistically and addressing all of the child's emotional, social, mental, and spiritual needs in the sociocultural context of his or her life. With this in mind, there are many factors pertinent to Matthew's experience of, reaction to, and treatment for the abuse. These factors include his Native American heritage, the kind and extent of the sexual abuse he endured, his perceptions about the abuse, his relationship with the perpetrator, his disclosure process, the response to his disclosure, and his symptoms of distress.

In deciding whether to refer Matthew for a psychiatric evaluation, I would consider how an evaluation might benefit him and how it could be potentially harmful. Many tests do not include Native American norming samples; thus, the tests may not be culturally appropriate or valid (Wasserman, 2000). Would the person conducting the evaluation have knowledge about Native Americans, in particular those of Cherokee descent? Would an evaluation increase Matthew's anxiety or reduce it? Would his family view my request as helpful or imposing? If they again did not follow through, how might this affect Matthew? Before referring Matthew for an evaluation, I would attempt to connect with Matthew's family to better understand their perspective on the situation as it related to their beliefs, values, and practices. I would also contact a nearby child advocacy center (CAC) for consultation or referral sources specific to Native Americans.

CACs use a multidisciplinary team approach to minimize the trauma for children, families, and communities dealing with child abuse. Collaborative efforts among community members help to heal children and to restore balance and harmony. Many tribal communities have CACs with trained interviewers, investigators, child protective services, health services, and victim advocates and can conduct forensic medical exams. There are also experts in the community and tribal elders who can provide traditional healing practices. Tribal CACs can be a helpful link between the federal government and tribal governments in investigating, prosecuting, and treating cases of child abuse (Wasserman, Cain, & Bubar, 2000).

Summary

In closing, I would view the opportunity to work with Matthew and his family as an honor. I believe in Matthew's power to heal. I believe in Matthew's parents' and family's strength, ability, and power to help him heal. I believe that understanding the cultural implications is critical to grasping the complexity of the responses to Matthew's case. I would research and use consultation to explore the cultural dynamics that might influence my response as a counselor and affect the response of Matthew, his family, and the community. I would use the freedom and flexibility offered at the school for treatment and prevention to extend services to Matthew, Jennifer, and their family. I would embrace the opportunity to learn from the family and hope that I could build their trust. I would use my knowledge of the prior multivictim case and my connections with the child protection investigator to advocate on behalf of Matthew, his family, and his culture. I would try to heighten awareness and improve the response of my school and community by promoting increased involvement and education. No doubt this endeavor would be a great challenge, but it would be one worth taking for Matthew's sake and for the sake of other children who might not have found their voice.

References

Ashby, M. R., Gilchrist, L. D., & Miramontez, A. (1987). Group treatment for sexually abused American Indian adolescents. *Social Work With Groups, 10,* 21–32.

Ater, M. K. (2001). Play therapy behaviors of sexually abused children. In G. L. Landreth (Ed.), *Innovations in play therapy: Issues, process, and special populations* (pp. 119–129). Philadelphia: Brunner-Routledge.

BigFoot, D. S. (2000). History of victimization in Native communities. *Native American Topic-Specific Monograph Series.* Retrieved February 14, 2006, from http://ccan.ouhsc.edu/History%20of%20Victimization%20Issues.pdf

Burke, M. T., Chauvin, J. C., & Miranti, J. G. (2005). *Religious and spiritual issues in counseling: Applications across diverse populations.* New York: Brunner-Routledge.

Dana, R. H. (1998). *Understanding cultural identity in intervention and assessment.* Thousand Oaks, CA: Sage.

Garrett, J. T., & Garrett, M. W. (1994). The path of good medicine: Understanding and counseling Native American Indians. *Journal of Multicultural Counseling and Development, 22,* 134–144.

Garrett, M. T. (2006). When eagle speaks: Counseling Native Americans. In C. C. Lee (Ed.), *Multicultural issues in counseling: New approaches to diversity* (3rd ed., pp. 25–53). Alexandria, VA: American Counseling Association.

Gil, E. (1991). *The healing power of play: Working with abused children.* New York: Guilford Press.

Glover, G. J. (2001). Cultural considerations in play therapy. In G. L. Landreth (Ed.), *Innovations in play therapy: Issues, process, and special populations* (pp. 31–41). Philadelphia: Brunner-Routledge.

Grossman, D. C., Milligan, B. C., & Deyo, R. A. (1991). Risk factors for suicide attempts among Navajo adolescents. *American Journal of Public Health, 81,* 870–874.

Irwin, M. H., & Roll, S. (1995). The psychological impact of sexual abuse of Native Americans. *Journal of the American Academy of Psychoanalysis, 23,* 461–473.

Ivey, A. E., Ivey, M. B., & Simek-Morgan, L. (1997). *Counseling and psychotherapy: A multicultural perspective* (4th ed.). Boston: Allyn & Bacon.

Kronenberger, W. G., & Meyer, R. G. (2001). *The child clinician's handbook* (2nd ed.). Needham Heights, MA: Allyn & Bacon.

LaFromboise, T., & Dizon, M. R. (2003). American Indian children and adolescents. In J. Y. Gibbs & N. L. Huang (Eds.), *Children of color: Psychological interventions with culturally diverse youth* (3rd ed., pp. 45–90). San Francisco: Jossey-Bass.

Landreth, G. L. (2002). *Play therapy: The art of the relationship* (2nd ed.). New York: Brunner-Routledge.

Manson, S. M., Walker, R. D., & Kivlahan, D. R. (1987). Psychiatric assessment and treatment of American Indians and Alaska Natives. *Hospital and Community Psychiatry, 38,* 165–173.

Wasserman, E. B. (2000). *Evaluations: Child and family's best interest and use in court proceedings.* Retrieved August 8, 2005, from University of Oklahoma Health Sciences Center, Center on Child Abuse and Neglect, Web site: http://ccan.ouhsc.edu/PsychEVAL.pdf

Wasserman, E. B., Cain, T., & Bubar, R. (2000). *Children's advocacy centers in Indian country.* Retrieved August 8, 2005, from University of Oklahoma Health Sciences Center, Center on Child Abuse and Neglect, Web site: http://ccan.ouhsc.edu/CAC.pdf

Webb, P. (2001). Play therapy with traumatized children: A crisis response. In G. L. Landreth (Ed.), *Innovations in play therapy: Issues, process, and special populations* (pp. 289–302). New York: Brunner-Routledge.

"He Blew Our House Down":
Natural Disaster and Trauma

This incident illustrates the treatment of a child who experienced a natural disaster and witnessed terrorist events on television. Interventions were provided in the context of a comprehensive guidance and counseling approach and included traumatic play reenactment. The chapter responses focus on therapeutic issues and interventions related to childhood trauma.

Critical Incident

Jennifer Baggerly and Courtney Green

"Miguel Rodriquez" was an 8-year-old Hispanic boy in the third grade at an elementary school in a rural area of Florida that sustained extensive damage during Hurricane Charley. The hurricane destroyed his family's mobile home, shattering windows and blowing the entire roof off, while Miguel and the rest of his family took shelter in the bathroom. Miguel's parents were undocumented migrant farmers from Mexico and refused to take the family to a hurricane shelter because they feared deportation. As a result, Miguel's family was now residing in an overcrowded Federal Emergency Management Agency trailer with relatives who had documented status.

Miguel's third grade teacher, "Ms. Garcia," referred him to me because she was concerned about his poor hygiene, inability to concentrate, hyperactivity, and constant requests to phone his mother. Ms. Garcia reported that Miguel had begun displaying these symptoms when school reconvened after Hurricane Charley. Initially, I reassured Ms. Garcia that these were normal responses by a normal child after an abnormal event. Nonetheless, Miguel's symptoms became worse after the subsequent Hurricanes Francis, Ivan, and Jeanne. Because of the reoccurring hurricane threats,

I was unsure whether these symptoms were still considered typical or whether they were more severe. Most of the other children in the school were also experiencing symptoms. Even teachers, including Ms. Garcia, showed signs of fatigue, irritability, and impatience as a result of significant damage to their own homes. Because it seemed that the whole community was traumatized, it was difficult for me to ascertain what was "normal."

I tried calling Miguel's mother on several occasions but did not receive a response. Ms. Rodriquez spoke limited English and was hesitant to speak with school personnel because she feared deportation. After several weeks, however, I was able to catch up with Ms. Rodriquez when she dropped Miguel off at school. I informed her that community members had donated a number of $100 Wal-Mart gift certificates for hurricane survivors and asked whether she would like one. Ms. Rodriquez began to cry in gratitude and told me that her children needed new clothes, shoes, and toiletries, because they had lost everything in the hurricane.

When I informed her about the teacher's concerns with Miguel's hygiene, inattentiveness, and other symptoms, Ms. Rodriquez said that Miguel has refused to take a bath ever since Hurricane Charley. When family members tried to make him bathe, she explained, Miguel would kick, hit, cry, and scream, "He blew our house down and I'm not going in there." Ms. Rodriquez explained that during Hurricane Charley, Miguel and his 12-year-old brother, Carlos, were hunkered down in the bathtub.

Unsure how to best serve Miguel and address such serious issues in the school counseling setting, I consulted with a former professor. Together, we developed a comprehensive counseling intervention plan for Miguel. In keeping with the American School Counselor Association (ASCA) national model (ASCA, 2003), we agreed that I should organize my interventions into the areas of guidance curriculum, individual student planning, responsive services, and systems support. First, I initiated classroom guidance lessons and started with Miguel's class. In these lessons, I used puppets and art activities to teach students about typical responses after a hurricane and about common coping strategies. We talked about responses such as nightmares and inattentiveness and coping strategies such as drawing and physical affection with family. I also read the book *A Terrible Thing Happened,* by Margaret Holmes (2000), to classes to reassure the students that they would recover.

Second, for individual student planning, I administered the Children's Depression Inventory (CDI; Kovacs, 1985) and the Revised Children's Manifest Anxiety Scale (RCMAS; Reynolds & Richmond,1985) to Miguel. His scores indicated significant departure from the norm in the CDI subscales of Negative Mood and Anhedonia as well as the RCMAS Total Anxiety score and subscales of Physiological Anxiety, Worry/Oversensitivity, and Social Concerns/Concentration.

Third, for responsive services, I initiated weekly individual child-centered play therapy sessions with Miguel. In the first two sessions, he explored most of the toys and focused on kicking and punching the bop bag. In the third session, Miguel carefully placed toy furniture and dolls in the dollhouse. Then he grabbed a wolf puppet and said, "I'm going to huff and puff and blow your house down." He knocked everything down in the house and threw the people and furniture out. Afterward, he used blocks to build two large towers and made the wolf blow the towers down as well. Finally, he used the wolf to knock over the toy school bus. During these sessions, I reflected his play content and feelings of fear and anger. I also interpreted the meaning of his play by offering, "It just seems like everything will get blown down. Perhaps you feel out of control and helpless and need some protection." Miguel nodded his head as if to agree. In the next few sessions, he repeated the theme of destruction, but for shorter periods of time, and ended the sessions by playing with Legos.

I informed Miguel's mother that he was playing out his worries in the play sessions and asked her about the family situation during September 11, 2001. Ms. Rodriquez said that, because Miguel was only 4 years old at the time, he stayed home with a relative who constantly watched television reports of the September 11, 2001, terrorist attacks. Consequently, Miguel became frightfully preoccupied with the Twin Towers collapsing and would repeatedly say, "The bad guys blew the buildings down." Hence, the hurricane's destruction of their family mobile home seemed to have reactivated his previous fears related to the September 11, 2001, terrorist attacks.

Finally, for systems support, I provided a training workshop for school personnel to assist them in identifying their worries and developing individual compassion fatigue resiliency plans. Not only were the teachers exhausted from their own hurricane-related home repairs, they were also feeling pressure to catch up on their students' preparation for the state standardized testing, the Florida Comprehension Assessment Test. Last year, the students' test scores had resulted in a low grade for the school. With all the lost school days and disruption, teachers feared this might happen again. After facilitating the teachers' expression of these concerns, I encouraged them to identify two methods to pamper themselves; two friends who are supportive; and two coping strategies in the realms of cognitive, emotional, behavioral, physical, and spiritual coping.

Nevertheless, despite my implementation of this comprehensive plan, Miguel continues to refuse to take baths, is inattentive in class, fights with peers, and repeatedly asks to call his mother. I attempted to refer Miguel for community services, but his family does not have insurance, and the local counseling agencies have a very long waiting list. In addition, the entire community continues to be emotionally and financially overwhelmed with recovery efforts. Unfortunately, this year's hurricane season threatens to be worse than last year's.

Questions

1. Given the ongoing trauma of hurricane threats in a community that has not yet recovered, how can a counselor know whether a child's symptoms are "normal" and will subside after the traumatic events end?
2. What are other approaches that have been demonstrated to be effective with children presenting such behaviors and issues?
3. How should a counselor respond when an entire community, including teachers and community agencies, seems to be overtaxed?

■ Response

Antoinette Rae Thorn

The elementary counselor who responded with such a comprehensive set of interventions to this situation should be commended for her actions. The counselor not only addressed the initial and ongoing needs of the teacher but also collaborated with a professional in the field to create responses that addressed a variety of areas outlined in the ASCA (2003) national model. The counselor provided counseling and consultation that addressed issues concerning the client, his mother, and the school faculty. As school counselors struggle to meet the needs of an ever-increasing student–counselor ratio, it is nothing short of amazing to observe the incredible amount of time and energy the counselor invested in solving the problems that Miguel's mother and teacher were having with Miguel. In addition, the counselor was part of the community experiencing ongoing disruption from hurricanes in the region. While dealing with the issues at school, she undoubtedly needed the same support she offered her fellow staff members.

The variety of ways the counselor attempted to help Miguel indicates that she does not see Miguel in the same light as the other children or as having "normal" symptoms. Having provided classroom guidance lessons concerning human reactions and responses to the hurricane to all students in the school, the counselor provided specific therapeutic activities to address Miguel's distress. Information provided by the teacher, in conjunction with the mother's comments regarding Miguel's reaction to watching television during the events associated with the collapse of the Twin Towers in New York on September 11, 2001, points toward potential posttraumatic stress disorder, a condition best addressed through appropriate diagnosis and therapy.

What remains uncertain is whether the events associated with the hurricanes produced all of Miguel's inappropriate behaviors or whether some of these behaviors existed previously. The teacher brought Miguel's behaviors to the attention of the counselor sometime after school reconvened following the August 13th hurricane. However, the teacher had only 4 days' experience with the child prior to the hurricane. Apart from repeated requests to phone his mother, the teacher might not have known whether the behaviors were new or old. It is possible that the hyperactivity and inability to concentrate were normal for him in a school setting. The only change in Miguel, according to his mother, is that he "refused to take a bath ever since Hurricane Charley." Isolating the behaviors that began after the hurricane would help the counselor focus on the behaviors that likely are the direct result of the hurricane. I would suggest Miguel's requests to phone home and his reluctance to bathe be remediated through more direct, behavioral techniques. Ongoing behaviors, such as hyperactivity and inability to concentrate, should be dealt with through multiple, long-term techniques. Consultation with previous teachers and counselors and further consultation with the mother regarding previous behavior would help the counselor to isolate recent changes in behavior. Additionally, it is important to ascertain the language in which counseling be provided. Miguel may be able to communicate most successfully in his native language, which would thereby make counseling in Spanish much more effective.

As part of the counselor's plan for individual student planning, she administered a depression and an anxiety scale to Miguel. Both scales are appropriate for use with young children and do not require advanced training to administer. The counselor reported that both scales indicated "significant departure from the norm." Although both inventories provide helpful information, I suggest research on the scales be taken into advisement. Fristad, Emery, and Beck (1997) advised that clinicians use caution when interpreting the results of the CDI, noting both the need to have a variety of instruments to diagnose depression and the need to be cautious about the self-report nature of the inventory. Additionally, the test administrator needs to ensure that young children have the capacity to complete this self-report inventory. Because Miguel is a child of immigrants, I recommend that the counselor take into consideration his age, language, and cultural background when assessing his ability to understand the statements in the inventory. The same cautions should be applied to the results of the RCMAS, because test instructions indicate the inventory should be used in conjunction with data from a complete clinical evaluation and should be read to young children.

Techniques associated with behavior therapy, such as role playing and diversion techniques, have successfully ameliorated a variety of abnormal behaviors (Corsini & Wedding, 1995). Additionally, techniques such as sand tray therapy, using puppets to act out situations, and drawing have been effectively used with children (Gilliand & James, 1997). I suggest the school counselor first focus on the issue most easily corrected—the requests to call home. Inappropriate behavior may be ameliorated through a behavioral contract. Working in conjunction with the mother, the counselor could first explain to Miguel why he cannot call his mother from school. Miguel could attempt to explain why he wants to call his mother and what benefits he obtains by talking to her. Thompson and Rudolph (1996) described *token economics* to address behavioral issues in children. Token economics allows children to earn tokens for targeted behaviors. In Miguel's case, the teacher and counselor could create a behavioral contract with Miguel, giving him several phone call tokens to use during the day. He could choose when to call by presenting a token to the school secretary for a 1-minute call. Miguel would receive verbal praise when he no longer requested to use the phone after using up his tokens for the day. Should Miguel display inappropriate behavior (asking to call when the tokens are exhausted), an additional token would be taken from the following day's tokens. Should Miguel end the day with leftover tokens, he would receive a reward for each one. Each week, the number of tokens would be reduced, with Miguel receiving praise from both the school and home for reducing phone calls, until no more tokens were needed.

I recommend systematic desensitization as a method of dealing with Miguel's reluctance to bathe (Wolpe, 1969). The issue could be addressed via a team approach (parent, school nurse, teacher, and counselor), and Miguel could be cleaned with a damp washcloth. As he became comfortable with this method, he could begin dampening the cloth and cleaning himself. Eventually, increasing the exposure to water in small steps, Miguel could again be comfortable around water and develop appropriate hygiene skills.

As previously mentioned, the counselor in this situation has implemented a variety of strategies and interventions addressing Miguel's issues. Although I recognize and commend the extraordinary measures the counselor has taken to address the problem, it is important that school counselors make referrals when necessary. According to ASCA's (2004) *Ethical Standards for School Counselors*, school counselors must make "referrals when necessary or appropriate to outside resources." The situation reflects two difficulties the school counselor must address: (a) having the time to work with Miguel while supporting all students in the school, and (b) providing counseling "within the boundaries of individual professional competence" (ASCA, 2004). Multiple hurricanes, lack of resources in the community, and the family's lack of resources because of their immigration status all combine to limit the school counselor's ability to assist Miguel, his teacher, and his family. The school counselor must balance the demands of the position with professional and personal demands.

The counselor's entire community and adjacent communities experienced multiple traumas because of four successive hurricanes. In addition, succeeding years promise to bring additional hurricanes to the community because of its location on the coast of Florida. The counselor herself has undoubtedly suffered her own hurricane-related losses and should be certain to address her own needs. She needs to be as mentally and physically healthy as possible to help others. Suggestions include participating in daily and weekly physical or mental activities, such as exercising at a club, playing card games, receiving massages, or learning yoga. By attending to her own needs, she gives herself the best opportunity to help others.

Response

William Steele

My recommendations for Miguel, his mother, and the community are based on my understanding of the experience of trauma, the importance of implicit versus explicit approaches, and the need to become a witness to the unique ways each individual might have experienced the same situation. I believe it is critical to avoid making the assumption that we know what is best for trauma survivors. It is not our experience. It is difficult, if not impossible, to know what it has been like for the child unless we can give that child or parent the opportunity to bring us into their experience. We must let them walk us through their experience in a way that allows us to truly see what they see as they look at themselves and the world around them. This intervention approach is detailed in *Structured Sensory Intervention for Traumatized Children, Adolescents, and Parents (SITCAP)* (Steele & Raider, 2001).

I believe both mother and son fit the primary experience of trauma. The one word that best describes the experience of grief is *sadness*. The one word most associated with the experience of trauma is *terror*. The two predominant sensory components of terror are (a) feeling totally unsafe and (b) feeling powerless to do anything about the situation (Steele, 2003).

My first impression of Miguel and his mother is that a consistent sense of safety has eluded them for many years, even prior to the September 11, 2001, terrorist attacks cited as Miguel's first exposure to terror. We know that a critical factor in recovery from trauma is the ability of the parent to communicate resilience and the behavioral and emotional expression of confidence that the family will get through this adversity (Perez Foster, 2001). The mother's fears of being deported, her sense of being unsafe in the community, and her readiness to run and hide certainly have been transmitted to her son, leaving him far more vulnerable to trauma and to the arousal reactions he is now exhibiting. I believe his fear of deportation is a far stronger contributor to his prolonged reactions than the ongoing threat of hurricanes. If the fear of being deported cannot be eliminated, the counselor unfortunately may continue to see inappropriate arousal reactions in Miguel because of his mother's constant hypervigilance.

Given that this condition may not change, it still remains important that intervention be structured (for safety) and directed at restoring a sense of safety and power to Miguel and his mother. This needs to be done at a sensory, implicit level, which is actually where trauma is experienced. The majority of children as well as some adults experience trauma in implicit memory. In implicit memory there is no language. There are simply no words to describe or communicate what is being experienced. Position emission tomography scans have found that trauma also creates changes in the Broca area of the brain that lead to difficulties in identifying and verbalizing experiences (VanDalen, 2001). It is difficult to process trauma in explicit memory, the type of memory that supports primary cognitive functions, because trauma is often contained in implicit memory. In implicit memory, one's senses contain the experience—what one sees, hears, smells, touches, and tastes become the implicit containers of that experience (Rothchild, 2000).

If there is no language in implicit memory to help verbalize what that experience is like, how, then, is it defined and explained? It is defined through an implicit process referred to as *iconic symbolization* (Michaesu & Baettig, 1996). Iconic symbolization is the process of giving one's experience a visual identity. Images are created to contain all the elements of that experience. The trauma experience, therefore, is more easily communicated through imagery (Kaplan, 2000; Malchiodi, 2003; Silver, 2000; Steele & Raider, 2001). Van der Kolk (1988) explained, "When a terrifying incident such as trauma is experienced and does not fit into a contextual memory, a new memory or dissociation is established" (p. 289). When a memory cannot be linked linguistically into a contextual framework, it remains at a symbolic level, with no words to describe it. The memory must first be retrieved and externalized in its symbolic, iconic form before it can be encoded, given a language, and then integrated into consciousness, also known as explicit memory (Steele, 2003).

To access children's implicit memories, counselors must use sensory interventions that allow children the opportunity to present the counselor with their iconic representations and, thereby, make the counselor a witness to their experiences. Such interventions give the counselor the opportunity to see how the children see themselves and their world after experiencing trauma. In this sense, a picture is worth a thousand words. Drawings provide a representation of those iconic symbols that implicitly define what an experience was like for a child.

When one understands trauma as an implicit experience versus an explicit (cognitive) experience, it follows that drawing is an effective and essential technique for helping children to release the horrid, terror-filled, iconic memories of their traumatic experiences. Byers (1996) cited numerous studies that illustrated the use of drawing to help children access those traumatic memories and channel them into a trauma narrative that could then be reworked explicitly (cognitively) in ways that became manageable for them. In response to September 11, 2001, the World Trade Center Children's Mural Project was unveiled in March 19, 2002, and depicted over 3,100 portraits drawn by children. This drawing project "served to lessen feelings of isolation and helplessness felt among those children who had difficulty understanding (cognitively) the complexity of this tragedy" (Berberian, Bryant, & Landsberg, 2003, p. 111). These children could not explicitly communicate the many ways September 11, 2001, affected them, but they could implicitly define these ways through their self-portraits. This, by the way, is one technique that could be used to help the community collectively grieve and also regain some sense of power and ability to survive (i.e., be prepared for) the next crisis. I would involve school personnel in this process as well. At some point, talking is no longer helpful. People need to do something. Community campaigns promoting the theme "We are survivors" are helpful in the grieving and empowerment process.

For this intervention to be effective, it must be structured, and activities must focus on the major sensations of trauma—fear, terror, worry, hurt, anger, insecurity, powerlessness, desire for revenge or accountability, and survivor versus victim thought processes. Child-centered play therapy can be a very valuable intervention, as Miguel demonstrated by trying to master his experience through repetitious reenactment. However, in Miguel's case, the counselor was left to interpret his behaviors herself. In such situations, one must be extremely careful not to lead the child to conclusions that are not necessarily his or her own.

I personally would want Miguel to communicate to me what his experience was like in detail by making me a witness to the many elements of his experience through drawing pictures of what happened that day and the days that followed. I would have him tell me what each element of his drawing (lines, dots, scribbles, figures, faces, etc.) represented. I would not interpret nor lead him in his story with statements such as, "Your face looks really scared," but instead would simply say, "Tell me about your face." I would use questions related to the trauma experience, keeping the intervention focused on the sensory experiences. A few of the questions I would ask in this approach are, "When this first happened, where did you feel the hurt or fear most on your body?" "What was the worst part of what happened?" and, "Since this happened, what has been your biggest worry?" This approach of drawing accompanied by such questioning allows the child to walk the counselor through his or her experience and to experience relief from trauma's many elements as a result of the sensory activities that allow him or her to externalize that iconic representation of the trauma by placing it into a container (drawing paper). This container of the traumatic experience now becomes something outside the child, because it is concrete and tangible. The child can begin to manage it and to experience a renewed sense of safety from and power over his or her trauma in the past and present.

I would help this child move from the past to the present by asking questions such as, "What was the worst part for you then? What is the worst part for you now?" I would also want to give the mother the opportunity to process her traumas in the same way, while being carefully sensitive to the cultural elements this family brings to the situation. Since 1990, the National Institute for Trauma and Loss in Children has been field testing, researching, and teaching the sensory approach to healing from trauma, primarily in children exposed to multiple traumas (www.tlcinsitute.org). Its short-term, structured intervention programs allow children the opportunity to address the many sensory experiences of trauma that explicitly driven interventions do not. So often in trauma, the healing begins when the survivor can bring someone into his or her experience and no longer be alone in it. One can only do that at the sensory level. Working in the sensory level on implicit memory allows the counselor and the child this opportunity. I therefore recommend more of a structured, sensory, implicit approach with Miguel. I further recommend, if possible, that the counselor work with him in a sensory-directed intervention group with other survivors. This would provide Miguel the opportunity to connect as a survivor to other survivors, something that is difficult for him to experience with his mother. Finally, there is no discussion about how Miguel's mother understands her son's experience. She also needs to hear his story as he uses his many drawings to tell her what this experience was like for him—what his hurt looks like. Only then can she better understand and accept what she needs to do to help her son feel safer and more empowered.

References

American School Counselor Association. (2003). *The ASCA national model: A framework for school counseling programs*. Herndon, VA: Author.

American School Counselor Association. (2004, June 25). *Ethical standards for school counselors*. Retrieved September 10, 2005, from http://www.schoolcounselor.org/content.asp?contentid=173

Berberian, M., Bryant L. L., & Landsberg, M. (2003). Interventions with communities affected by mass violence. In S. Straussner & N. Phillips (Eds.), *Understanding mass violence: A social work perspective* (pp. 105–115). New York: Pearson.

Byers, J. (1996). Children of the stones: Art therapy interventions in the West Bank. *Art Therapy: Journal of the American Art Therapy Association, 13*, 238–243.

Corsini, R. J., & Wedding, D. (1995). *Current psychotherapies* (5th ed.). Itasca, IL: F. E. Peacock.

Fristad, M. A., Emery, B. L., & Beck, S. J. (1997). Use and abuse of the Children's Depression Inventory. *Journal of Consulting and Clinical Psychology, 65*, 699–702.

Gilliand, B. E., & James, R. K. (1997). *Crisis intervention strategies* (3rd ed.). Pacific Grove, CA: Brooks/Cole.

Holmes, M. (2000). *A terrible thing happened*. Washington, DC: Magination Press.

Kaplan, F. (2000). *Art, science and art therapy: Repainting the picture*. London: Jessica Kingsley.

Kovacs, M. (1985). The Children's Depression Inventory (CDI). *Psychopharmacology Bulletin, 21*, 995–998.

Malchiodi, C. (Ed.). (2003). *Handbook of art therapy*. New York: Guilford Press.

Michaesu, G., & Baettig, D. (1996). An integrated model of posttraumatic stress disorder. *European Journal of Psychiatry, 10*, 243–245.

Perez Foster, R. M. (2001). When immigration is trauma: Guidelines for the individual and family clinician. *American Journal of Orthopsychiatry, 71*, 2.

Reynolds, C. R., & Richmond, Bert, O. (1985). The Revised Children's Manifest Anxiety Scale (RCMAS). *Mental Measurements Yearbook, 10*.

Rothchild, B. (2000). *The body remembers*. New York: Norton.

Silver, R. (2000). *Art as language*. New York: Brunner-Rutledge.

Steele, W. (2003). Helping traumatized children. In S. Straussner & N. Phillips (Eds.), *Understanding mass violence: A social work perspective* (pp. 42–56). New York: Pearson.

Steele, W., & Raider, M. (2001). *Structured sensory intervention for children, adolescents, and parents (SITCAP)*. New York: Mellen Press.

Thompson, C. L., & Rudolph, L. B. (1996). *Counseling children* (4th ed.). Pacific Grove, CA: Brooks/Cole.

VanDalen, A. (2001). Juvenile violence and addiction: Tangled roots in childhood trauma. *Journal of Social Work Practice in the Additions, I*, 25–40.

Van der Kolk, B. (1988).The trauma spectrum: The interaction of biological and social events in the genesis of the trauma response. *Journal of Traumatic Stress, 1*, 273–290.

Wolpe, J. (1969). *The practice of behavior therapy*. New York: Pergamon Press.

"Healing Visible and Invisible Wounds": Physical Abuse

■ Critical Incident

Serena M. Lambert

This incident brings to light the reality that childhood physical abuse has multifaceted and long-term effects on the cognitive, emotional, and social well-being of children. The child in this case suffered from traumatic brain injury resultant of physical abuse and, as a consequence of violent behavior, was placed in a residential treatment facility.

"Jay," a 12-year-old Caucasian and Native American boy, was placed in our community-based, intensive-level, therapeutic group home by his youth court probation officer. Jay came from a rural community in our state, over 100 miles away from our facility. He had broken into a home in his neighborhood 3 days before Christmas and did thousands of dollars' worth of damage to property and the home itself. The police report stated that it looked like Jay had "flown into a rage" in the home. He destroyed the family's Christmas presents and decorations, emptied the contents of the refrigerator onto the floor, and did structural damage to the home. Until this point, Jay did not have a prior record with juvenile probation and had not been reported to be in any trouble at school. He was in some remedial courses in school and had a recorded full-scale IQ in the low 90s.

Child Protective Services (CPS) reports indicated that the family had been investigated for concerns regarding neglect and physical abuse. One report indicated that Jay had been locked in the bathroom as a punishment for poor behavior. Another stated that he had been found by a neighbor wandering in the cold because he had did not want to be at home. CPS had previously removed Jay from the home because of substantiated reports of physical abuse by his father. The records stated that Jay was allowed to return home after his parents successfully participated in a parent education program offered by the department. These reports indicated that although Jay's parents were mildly impaired in their cognitive functioning, they were capable of caring for their children and of benefiting from the parent training provided.

When I became the clinician for the group home, my first position as a professional counselor, Jay had already been residing there for several months. The staff and prior clinician stated that he "refused to discuss" his destruction of his neighbor's property and became "agitated and aggressive" when pressed to do so. He was reported to have frequent outbursts of anger when he was redirected by staff or when he felt that he was not "being heard," which seemed to mean that he was simply not getting his way. These outbursts included threatening to hit staff members, actually hitting other residents, and destroying property by throwing objects and kicking or hitting the walls. As a result of the initial incident of property destruction and his outbursts in the group home, he had been diagnosed with intermittent explosive disorder (Code 312.34 in the *Diagnostic and Statistical Manual of Mental Disorders*; 4th ed., text rev.; American Psychiatric Association, 2000). Jay also seemed to have some physical tics; he frequently cleared his throat, had involuntary facial contractions, seemed awkward in gait, and was markedly uncoordinated for his age.

The group home staff and clinical notes also indicated that Jay had been masturbating excessively and was exposing himself to others in the process. When the staff addressed this with Jay, he was very reluctant to engage in these conversations and became quickly agitated. In these discussions, the staff and previous counselor informed Jay about his body and masturbation as a normal part of his development. They also directed him to use the bathroom while masturbating and instructed him to lock the door so that he could have some privacy for this behavior.

When I began working with Jay, it was obvious that he had some difficulty interacting with his peers. He reported being "picked on" by kids at school, and this was supported by another resident who attended the same school and by Jay's teacher. Jay's teacher observed that he "just doesn't seem to pick up on social cues." She said that his occasional attempts to connect with peers seemed "stilted and inappropriate." In the group home, Jay often kept to himself; he enjoyed playing video games on the computer. His attempts to connect with his peers in the group home frequently missed the mark. He would try to join in the teasing and humor of the other boys and would instead be bluntly insulting or overly literal. When these attempts failed, he would quickly become angry and would be directed to remove himself from the situation to take a time-out and calm down. Given enough time alone, he seemed to be able to deescalate. However, if Jay was asked to process the incident too soon, his anger and agitation could increase dramatically and result in a violent outburst. Such outbursts were generally followed by a police intervention, in which he was often cited for property damage and ungovernable conduct.

In contrast, Jay was eager to engage with staff and made attempts to do so appropriately, especially when he was not allowed to play computer games. He seemed to prefer to spend time interacting with staff members, likely because they were more patient and less threatening for him than fellow residents. He developed a strong relationship with a particular female staff member, showed genuine appreciation for their time together, and seemed especially grateful for any shopping trips to meet his needs for personal items or clothing.

Jay was consistently open to individual and group counseling, and he seemed to enjoy the attention. In spite of these social successes, his inability to communicate a range of emotions seemed to contribute to a sense of isolation. When we discussed feeling lonely, Jay became tearful at times, and this could escalate into agitation. I suspected that Jay was often lonely and had limited experience with feeling safe enough to express this level of vulnerability. I feared that much of this resulted from having few experiences with caregivers who were available and responsive to his needs.

In individual and group counseling, I observed what seemed to be a deficit in Jay's ability to cognitively process social cues as well as cause and effect relationships. I wondered about the appropriateness of the diagnosis that he had been given. Although the diagnosis of intermittent explosive disorder did seem to explain the incident that had brought him to this setting, it did not take into account the developmental issues and concerns we were observing. I wondered about possible fetal alcohol effect issues, but these did not seem to be indicated anywhere in his history. My early individual sessions with Jay focused on the exploration of his cognitive and verbal abilities and on learning more about his relationships with family members.

After a couple of months of working together, Jay began to tell me more about what it had been like to live in his home. He stated that he had observed his parents having sex on a regular basis and that it was common for him to see both of his parents naked around the house. He said that he felt "uncomfortable" at these times and that he was now "confused" by this. Jay typically used the word *confused* to describe himself in the moment. Jay also reported that his father frequently yelled at and hit him. He was reluctant to discuss the physical abuse but eventually disclosed that his father had "slammed" his head into the wall when he was about 5 years old. This was part of the incident that resulted in his removal from his home by CPS. After hearing this, I began to wonder about possible brain injury. The CPS worker stated that Jay had received medical attention at the time of the injury and had been diagnosed as having a concussion as well as visible bruising.

My supervisor and I requested that Jay undergo a neuropsychological evaluation to rule out possible neurological explanations for his cognitive, social, and behavioral challenges, but obtaining this was a lengthy process. In the meantime, the frequency of Jay's masturbation increased to multiple times per day. In individual sessions, Jay stated that he had not been sexually abused and became silent or agitated when asked to discuss the masturbation. On an outing to another group home, Jay stole a female resident's underwear from the laundry room. When asked about this incident, he again became quiet and sullen. When asked whether he could communicate his feelings in any other way, such as art or writing, he stated that he could not. The typical behavioral interventions used in the group home were not effective for Jay. When he received restrictions, he frequently became agitated, angry, and violent. At these times, it seemed as though he did not care whether he lost all of his privileges. Any therapeutic progress was very slow and seemed to involve two steps forward followed by one or two steps back.

The results of the neuropsychological evaluation were not surprising; they indicated that Jay had suffered a traumatic brain injury (TBI) as a younger child and that the injury affected his frontal lobe region. The neuropsychologist attributed Jay's emotional liability, social challenges, cognitive deficits, and physical symptoms to this injury and its resulting impact on his development. Recommendations in the evaluation included behavioral interventions that would emphasize experiential learning. I tried to educate myself on TBIs and found that most of the healing and recovery occurs within the first few months immediately after the injury. I also found that the lists of behavioral symptoms of children who had suffered a TBI seemed to account for all of the cognitive, social, and physical symptoms that Jay exhibited.

Regarding Jay's frequent masturbation, my supervisor and I decided to consult with a local clinician with a master's degree in social work who specialized in sexual development and sexual behavior disorders. Frankly, we were not sure whether this was a compulsion associated with the brain injury, a symptom of sexual abuse that needed to be addressed, or in the bounds of what could be normal male sexual development. I also considered the seeming correlation between the frequency with which Jay became angry and the frequency of his masturbation and was concerned that sexual behavior and anger were being combined in Jay's experience. As a new counselor, I felt the need to refer Jay to a clinician with a specialization in this area.

The consulting clinician was also concerned about the frequency of the masturbation and the fact that Jay reported some physical discomfort of his genitals. She agreed to see him weekly to address the masturbation issue through continued education about sexual development in boys, fantasy exploration, and boundary issues regarding sexuality. She felt that his frequent masturbation was possibly an emotionally self-soothing behavior. Simultaneously, I began working with Jay behaviorally to identify and communicate a range of emotions.

For example, we started this process by renting the movie *Stand By Me* and stopping the film frequently to have Jay identify the emotion that a particular character was feeling and how he saw the character express these emotions (behaviors). I asked Jay to identify the last time that he had felt the same emotion and how he had expressed it. Jay then role-played ways he might express that emotion more effectively. It took us several weeks to view the entire film, and, for the first time, Jay seemed genuinely engaged in our sessions. With the staff, he also completed homework assignments that involved more emotion identification and practice regarding how he might express those emotions. Initially, his emotional vocabulary increased, but his in-the-moment expression of emotion continued to look like anger. Eventually, Jay began to develop the skill of asking for a time-out when he felt himself become frustrated; he would then try to identify other feelings and triggers that contributed to his emotional response.

Jay's stay in the group home was approximately 1 year long. During that time, he did progress in his ability to identify his emotions, and his angry outbursts decreased in frequency and intensity. He seemed to benefit from the work with the consulting clinician, and his masturbating behaviors were limited to the bathroom and decreased in frequency. I attributed Jay's progress to the stable and consistent living environment that he experienced in the home, which included available and responsive caregiving by both counseling professionals and the child care staff. I believe his progress was also the result of individual and group counseling that focused on emotional expression, social skill development, sexual development education, and effective modeling by both peers and adults.

Before he left the group home, Jay discussed the night that he had destroyed his neighbor's home, but he did so with little insight. He identified feeling angry but was unaware of how he had become angry. He said that he did not know the family or have any prior negative experiences with them. When he talked about breaking the Christmas presents, he identified feeling jealous of the children in that home and angry with his own parents. Jay moved to a less restrictive group home closer to his family, which facilitated access to family counseling sessions, with a goal of reunification. Although Jay did seem to progress during his stay in our treatment home, I was left with several questions regarding his treatment.

Questions

1. What is the prevalence of brain injuries related to physical abuse in children? How can counselors best assess for and address behaviors associated with these injuries?
2. What approaches have been found to be effective in addressing the emotional and attachment needs of children with a history of abuse and neglect similar to Jay?
3. As a new counselor, I did not feel adequately prepared to address the sexual development issues in this case and had more concerns than answers. How can counselors prepare themselves to effectively assess and address the sexual development needs of clients who have a history of abuse, neglect, and inappropriate exposure to sexual situations?

◼ Response

Erin Martin

Assessing the behavioral, emotional, cognitive, and developmental needs of children with multifaceted issues can be very challenging for counselors. Nevertheless, I applaud this counselor's determination and willingness to pursue Jay's case. It is not often that novice counselors, just entering into the profession, agree to pursue cases that require so much research, consultation, and supervision. I can closely relate to the counselor's lack of experience and her wish to seek assistance from external resources, such as supervisors, professional colleagues, and the professional literature.

Jay's case presented an extensive list of symptoms that the counselor needed to take into consideration. His case presented not only visible wounds but also invisible wounds, including cognitive, behavioral, emotional, and developmental wounds and symptoms. Jay's cognitive symptoms included his limited ability to process incidents as they occur, difficulty cognitively processing social cues as well as cause and effect relationships, his confusion when asked to recount feelings he experienced, and a reluctance to discuss the physical abuse he experienced. With respect to emotions, Jay's symptoms included rage, agitation, impulsivity, loneliness, jealousy, and a lack of insight into his own intense feelings—especially those related to the destruction of his neighbor's house. He also displayed some positive emotional attributes, including an eagerness to appropriately engage with staff and the development of strong relationships with female staff members. In terms of behavior, Jay's symptoms included aggressive acts, sudden outbursts, threats, object throwing, kicking and hitting, physical tics, and the making of bluntly insulting or overly literal comments. Jay also exhibited developmentally inappropriate behavior related to masturbation and the exposure of his genitals to others. As the counselor in this case discovered, this entire list of symptoms can be directly related to Jay's childhood experiences of abuse, neglect, and exposure to inappropriate sexual situations.

In addressing the counselor's questions, I hope to encourage other novice professional counselors to view such multifaceted cases not as hindrances but as opportunities to gain experience. My discussion focuses on (a) the prevalence of brain injuries related to physical abuse in children and the best ways to assess and address behaviors associated with these injuries, (b) the approaches that have been found to be most effective in addressing the emotional and attachment needs of children with a history of abuse and neglect similar to Jay, and (c) ways counselors can prepare themselves to effectively assess and address the sexual developmental needs of clients who have a history of abuse, neglect, and inappropriate exposure to sexual situations.

Child Abuse and TBIs

Physical abuse and neglect have become a widespread problem both nationally and internationally. Understanding and conceptualizing the impact of physical abuse and neglect on children is complex and challenging. Physical abuse and neglect affect children's physical, cognitive, social, and emotional development. Often, children experiencing abuse or neglect are deprived not only of basic needs but also of a "normal" childhood. These children are said to have a "lost childhood," a childhood filled with fear and anger instead of play and enjoyment. When assessing the treatment needs of children who have been physically abused or neglected, counselors need to consider a number of issues. Gil (1991) suggested that counselors should consider the "impact of the abuse, the family's level of dysfunction, the environmental stability, the age of the child, and the child's relationship to the offender" (p. 37) before beginning therapy with the child. In particular, depending on the level of abuse, neglect, and exposure to inappropriate sexual behaviors, children may suffer from brain injuries, attachment disorders, and inappropriate sexual development.

Neglected children experience low self-concept, disorganization, and a lack of self-discipline, structure, and consistency (Roscoe, Peterson, & Shaner, 1983). Physically abused children exhibit symptoms of withdrawal, apathy, aggression, and estrangement from peers. Additionally, children who experience intense physical abuse and recurrent attacks may suffer TBI. According to Martin and Rodeheffer (1980), "it is estimated that between 25 and 30% of abused children who survive the attack have brain damage or neurological dysfunction resulting directly from physical trauma about the head" (p. 207). As the counselor discovered on researching TBI, many of the cognitive, behavioral, and physical symptoms exhibited by Jay could be directly linked to this physical trauma in childhood.

Children suffering from TBI are negatively affected both emotionally and socially; sometimes, they are scarred for life. Many researchers have suggested that social and emotional support is the best treatment for children who have experienced TBI. Community-based support in a residential treatment center also enables a team of professionals, including counselors, social workers, and case managers, to assess and address the presenting issues regarding social and medical problems.

In addressing the emotional, social, and attachment needs of physically abused and neglected children, it is important to consider not only their presenting issues but also the intensity of the abuse experienced (Gil, 1991). With or without sustaining a TBI, children who experience intense physical abuse often experience cognitive and developmental symptoms. Likewise, children suffering from emotional deprivation may exhibit symptoms including oppositional defiance, self-mutilation, property destruction, aggression, impulsivity, dishonesty, stealing, poor peer relationships and socialization, and a lack of self-control, empathy, remorse, or compassion (Twaite & Rodriguez-Srednicki, 2004). When children present with these various emotional needs and challenges, they typically have what is termed an attachment disorder.

Attachment and Treatment Issues

The attachment period (typically the child's first 2 years of life) plays a significant role in the child's development whereby he or she is able to relate to the rest of the world, on the basis of his or her attachment with the primary caregivers. This first attachment relationship serves as the foundation for the development of future relationships (Bowlby, 1988). Ideally, the attachment is developed securely and allows the child to experience the world as safe, loving, and caring. Conversely, when an infant develops an insecure attachment to his or her primary caregiver, the child constructs a view of the world as unsafe. Often, the child concludes that he or she is incapable of being loved. These children, who have been deprived of a strong, central figure in their life, seem desperate to connect with someone. In this case, Jay seems to present with an insecure attachment not only to his parents but also to the rest of the world.

Because the "elusive sensation" (Gil, 1991, p. 57) of intimacy is something neglected children desire, counselors must be cautious in facilitating the development of a therapeutically intimate relationship with these children. It is important for the counselor to assess the child's attachment needs early in the treatment process so that the child does not develop an unhealthy attachment to the counselor. To avoid this, Gil (1991) suggested setting appropriate limits for these children so that they begin to understand the therapeutic relationship. It is therefore wise for the counselor to become educated about how to respond to neglected and needy children so that appropriate limits and boundaries can be established.

Although no single treatment has been proven to be effective for children with attachment disorders (O'Connor & Zeanah, 2003), several treatments have been found helpful in addressing the needs of these children. Child-centered play therapy (Landreth, 2002) is one approach that offers a safe, nonthreatening environment in which children can gain a sense of control over their traumatic experiences. Depending on external factors, play therapy may lead to greater self-regulation and empowerment, decreasing visible presenting issues. Other treatments that have been found helpful for working with attachment-disordered children include holding therapies, parent training and family support, and social–cognitive approaches (O'Connor & Zeanah, 2003). According to Gil (1991), counseling should continue far beyond the elimination of presenting issues to ensure that the child learns how to construct a healthy sense of the world and his or her relationships.

Sexual Development

Although it is common for children of Jay's age to engage in some form of sexual curiosity, children who are exhibiting inappropriate sexual behaviors require behavior modification, feelings identification, and education to help them properly understand their need to display such behaviors. Jay's inappropriate public masturbation and history of exposure to his parents' sexual behaviors suggest the need for therapeutic intervention. Engaging in role playing, puppetry, or art allows children the freedom to displace these feelings onto another object.

Nevertheless, working with any child who has suffered abuse, neglect, or inappropriate exposure to sexual behaviors is difficult and complex. To effectively address the sexual developmental needs of clients who have a history of being exposed to inappropriate sexual behaviors, counselors should either have specific training or seek much supervision and consultation. Counselors should consider their resources when approaching such cases. Far too often, important details are overlooked or concerns go unanswered.

In summary, it is the counselor's responsibility to provide a nurturing, therapeutic environment for the child suffering from abuse and neglect. Additionally, it is the counselor's responsibility to provide as much therapy as the child requires. Because of the complexity of issues facing children like Jay—including the possibility of TBI, attachment issues, and sexual development issues—a collaborative effort involving several mental health professionals is advisable. Counselors must work together as a team to provide the stability, consistency, and therapy that abused and neglected children need.

 Response

Lonnie E. Duncan and Yolanda Duncan

We can only imagine being a beginning therapist and having to deal with the treatment and diagnostic issues related to this case. It does seem that this counselor had some formal diagnostic training, given that she was able to recognize that the previous diagnosis of intermittent explosive disorder did not capture the range of problems that Jay was experiencing at the treatment center. The counselor appropriately brought these concerns to her supervisor and then requested further diagnostics to rule in or out TBI. The most salient issues in this case seem to be the distinction between TBI and mental illness, effective treatment strategies, and the counselor training experiences required to address the unique challenges associated with TBI, childhood abuse, and sexual development issues. In responding to this incident and the counselor's questions, we first provide a framework for diagnosing TBI. We then provide effective treatment strategies for dealing with the issues experienced by Jay and conclude with ways counselors can prepare themselves for working with this population.

TBI and Mental Illness

TBI and physical abuse are major problems affecting the quality of life for many children and adolescents. According to the U.S. Department of Health and Human Services Administration on Children, Youth, and Families (2003), physical abuse was identified in nearly 19% of cases of child maltreatment that were substantiated by CPS. As noted by the American Academy of Pediatrics Committee on Child Abuse and Neglect (2001), "head injuries are the leading cause of traumatic death and the leading cause of child abuse fatalities" (p. 206).

In this case, the incident that prompted Jay's removal from his home included a head injury that resulted in a concussion as well as other bruising. Because problems of TBI may not manifest themselves initially, it is not uncommon for children of abuse to be sent to temporary housing without an immediate assessment for TBI (Hibbard, Gordon, Martin, Raskin, & Brown, 2001). In cases like Jay's, in which children sustain relatively less severe TBIs, it is not uncommon for these children to slip through the cracks without an accurate diagnosis. Often, the onset of behavioral problems resulting from TBI is delayed, and these problems are then attributed to other causes. This is particularly true for those, like Jay, who experience TBI early in life. Like Jay, these children often score in the normal range on most cognitive tests, and problems arise only later, in the middle to high school years, as the environment demands more from the child living with TBI (Hibbard et al., 2001).

TBI generally cannot be recognized through standard cognitive testing. Traditional cognitive assessments (e.g., the Wechsler Intelligence Scale for Children—Fourth Edition; Wechsler, 2003) are generally based on assumptions that are inappropriate for the purpose of diagnosing TBI. For example, standard cognitive tests assume that a child's ability to learn new information progresses over time. According to Hibbard et al. (2001), information learned prior to brain injury most often remains intact. As such, the immediate administration of a traditional cognitive test would reveal no decline in intelligence. Nonetheless, TBI children learn new information at a slower rate than non-TBI children, and this results in declines in IQ scores over time. Unfortunately, these declines are normally attributed to psychosocial problems other than TBI. Therefore, traditional assessment fails to determine the extent of the cognitive problems underlying IQ declines. To determine the extent of the damage in TBI, a neuropsychologist should conduct tests to evaluate attention deficits, information processing speed, memory and learning, and problem solving and organization.

Assessment approaches should also include a systematic examination of the level of functional impairment and the degree to which the child is struggling in his or her functioning at home or school and in his or her interactions with others. Increasing environmental demands often contribute to the development of difficulties dealing with cognitive changes (e.g., remembering and comprehending), emotional challenges (e.g., depression, anxiety, poor impulse control, aggressive tendencies, explosive verbal or physical outbursts toward others), physical challenges (e.g., fatigue), and developmental challenges (e.g., understanding complex social rules) in children who have sustained a TBI. If one examines the critical incident, it is clear that Jay is struggling with some of these transitions and challenges. These issues are further exacerbated by the fact that Jay was approximately 5 years old when he acquired his brain injury. At this age, Jay had not yet mastered the foundations of learning (i.e., learning to listen, question, and engage socially), and he had to acquire these skills after he sustained his brain injury.

Distinguishing between TBI and mental illness typically involves looking at the psychosocial history of the abused child. Because physical abuse involves some form of violence, it is important to find out as much as one can about the nature of the physical abuse and the area of the body that was injured. Additionally, any information that can establish the onset of difficulties, functional changes, emotional difficulties, behavioral difficulties, peer interactions, and so forth can go far in determining whether behavioral problems are caused by TBI or mental illness. For example, in persons with TBI, the onset of difficulties is sudden. Cognitive functioning involves marked and sudden changes between pre- and postonset. Emotional difficulties include labile mood, depression, and anxiety. Relational interactions are affected not only by behavioral difficulties but by a reduction in social skill acquisition; behavioral difficulties consist of unpredictability, impulsiveness, and aggression. In contrast, for persons with mental illness, the onset of difficulties is typically gradual and reactive to the environment, the functional changes emerge slowly, emotional reactions result from distortions in reality, and relational interactions are affected only by behavioral difficulties (Hibbard et al., 2001).

Treatment Issues

Effectively treating abused children is complicated when a brain injury is part of the larger trauma. It can be difficult to distinguish whether the TBI or the abuse has the most impact on the child, but more than likely there is an interaction effect between TBI and the residual effects of the abuse. In Jay's case, he experienced ongoing physical abuse, a TBI, and inappropriate exposure to his parents' sexual behavior. Treatment needs to address each of these areas. In addition, attention to resultant attachment issues and Jay's racial identity should be considered.

As the critical incident indicates, the residential treatment center used various behavioral interventions, but these interventions seemed to create more problems with Jay rather than decrease his problematic behavior. The group home did a good job of offering Jay alternatives to his negative behavior. One suggestion we might offer for improving the treatment is to examine more closely what Jay was trying to communicate when he engaged in counterproductive behavior. Although his behavior might have been inappropriate, it is possible that he was attempting to communicate something that was a legitimate emotional response to some environmental stimuli.

Also, asking Jay to demonstrate insight into his behavior is probably stressful because he may be unable to make connections because of his acquired brain injury. Using insight as an indicator of therapeutic progress may not be appropriate. Rather, observable behavioral changes are better indicators of therapeutic progress. In Jay's case, his behavioral changes suggest that he responded well to some interventions, such as individual and group counseling. Overall, the staff involved did a good job under the circumstances. Generally, in working with a child like Jay, counselors try to identify the patterns that produce the counterproductive behavior. They normally do this through observation and talking with other staff. This seemed to have been a part of the treatment plan for Jay.

The counselor noted that Jay had many emotional and attachment needs, which is not unusual under the circumstances. These issues can be challenging to any counselor, especially for a beginning counselor. In general, adolescents like Jay have had—at best—inconsistent relationships with their caregivers. In normal psychosocial development, these emotional needs are worked out between the child and primary caregivers. As we noted earlier, abused children have emotional developmental delays that have to be resolved. It is not surprising that Jay had problems relating to his peers, because he was emotionally in a different stage of development. Transference to a surrogate caregiver (e.g., counselor) is a normal response. Ways of responding to transference vary by theoretical orientation, but the counselor can use this transference to help Jay work through this developmental stage. Saunders, Berliner, and Hanson (2004) detailed a variety of therapy approaches for working with child physical and sexual abuse.

We would also like to comment on Jay's frequent masturbation. The counselor noted in the critical incident that there was a question about whether Jay's behavior was sexually appropriate. It was determined that his frequent masturbation was possibly an emotionally self-soothing behavior. When determining the appropriateness of a child's sexual behavior, it is important to note that one third of children who have been sexually abused have sexual behavior problems (U.S. Department of Health and Human Services National Center on Childhood Abuse and Neglect, 1996). It is important, as noted in the critical incident, that determinations of normal sexual behavior should be developmentally informed. According to Saunders et al. (2004), a consequence of abuse or the reaction to abuse by the sexually abused child delays his or her projected psychosocial and sexual development. This delay can cause aggression or early sexualized behavior.

Last, we believe that interventions should be culturally appropriate. The counselor mentioned that Jay was biracial. It was unclear how this affected the case. We suspect it might have had to do with the original conceptualization of Jay's problem. Saunders et al. (2004) specifically stated that cultural competence is critical to the treatment paradigms of clients from diverse religious, racial–ethnic, and cultural backgrounds.

Preparing to Work With Abused Children

In closing, we note that this is a very difficult case that has many complex layers. Most counseling programs would have a difficult time in preparing a beginning counselor for this kind of client. Indeed, we think that this would be a difficult case to manage and treat for a seasoned counselor, let alone a beginning counselor. If counselors want to engage in this kind of work, it is important that they be well grounded in human development and the various models that address physical, mental, and sexual development. Also, as with anything, experience is critical. We therefore suggest that prospective counselors interested in working with this population use their internship to gain supervised experiences in treating abused children. An internship site that specializes in child and adolescent treatment or even in child abuse and neglect would be a good place to have a field placement.

References

American Academy of Pediatrics Committee on Child Abuse and Neglect. (2001). Shaken baby syndrome: Rotational cranial injuries—technical report. *Pediatrics, 108*, 206–210. Retrieved April 13, 2006, from http://aappolicy.aappublications.org/cgi/content/full/pediatrics;108/1/206

American Psychiatric Association. (2000). *Diagnostic and statistical manual of mental disorders* (4th ed., text rev.). Washington, DC: Author.

Bowlby, J. (1988). *A secure base: Parent–child attachment and healthy human development.* New York: Basic Books.

Gil, E. (1991). *The healing power of play: Working with abused children.* New York: Guilford Press.

Hibbard, M., Gordon, W. A., Martin, T., Raskin, B., & Brown, M. (2001). *Students with traumatic brain injury: Identification, assessment and classroom accommodations* [Brochure]. New York: Research and Training Center on Community Integration of Individuals With Traumatic Brain Injury.

Landreth, G. (2002). *Play therapy: The art of the relationship* (2nd ed.). New York: Brunner-Routledge.

Martin, H. P., & Rodeheffer, M. A. (1980). The psychological impact of abuse on children. In G. J. Williams & J. Money (Eds.), *Traumatic abuse and neglect of children at home* (pp. 205–212). Baltimore: Johns Hopkins University Press.

O'Connor, T. G., & Zeanah, C. H. (2003). Attachment disorders: Assessment strategies and treatment approaches. *Attachment and Human Development, 5*, 223–245.

Roscoe, B., Peterson, K. L., & Shaner, J. M. (1983). Guidelines to assist educators in identifying children of neglect. *Education, 103*, 395–399.

Saunders, B. E., Berliner, L., & Hanson, R. F. (Eds.). (2004, April). *Child physical and sexual abuse: Guidelines for treatment (revised report).* Charleston, SC: National Crime Victims Research and Treatment Center.

Twaite, J. A., & Rodriguez-Srednicki, O. (2004). Understanding and reporting child abuse: Legal and psychological perspectives: Part 2. Emotional abuse and secondary abuse. *Journal of Psychiatry & Law, 32*, 443–481.

U.S. Department of Health and Human Services Administration on Children, Youth, and Families. (2003). *Child maltreatment 2003.* Retrieved March 22, 2006, from http://www.acf.hhs.gov/programs/cb/pubs/cm03/index.htm

U.S. Department of Health and Human Services National Center on Childhood Abuse and Neglect. (1996). *Third national incidence study of child abuse and neglect: Final report (NIS-3).* Washington, DC: U.S. Government Printing Office.

Wechsler, D. (2003). *The Wechsler Intelligence Scale for Children—Fourth Edition.* San Antonio, TX: Psychological Corporation.

"I Don't Know": Helping Reluctant Children Tell Their Stories

This incident illustrates how one counselor used musical lyrics and storytelling to reach a resistant child client and help her heal from the pain of multiple stressors. The expert respondents support the use of such bibliographic techniques and outline the efficacy of such an approach with a broad variety of client issues.

■ Critical Incident

Christina R. Marbach

"Samantha Daniels," a 12-year-old Caucasian girl, was referred to my office by Child Protective Services to receive counseling after an incident of sexual abuse by her female cousin. Documentation received from Child Protective Services stated that Samantha had alleged "touching" by her female cousin and that the alleged incidents occurred several times during the summer when Samantha was 10 years of age. When Samantha arrived for her scheduled appointment, her biological mother and stepfather accompanied her. The family revealed that Samantha's biological father had died 3 years prior after a long battle with cancer. Samantha's mother had remarried 1 year ago. During the session, I also learned that Samantha was experiencing conflicts in her new family structure, peer difficulties at school, and academic problems. When discussing Samantha's developmental history, her mother reported a normal pregnancy without complications, developmental milestones attained within normal limits, and no history of previous counseling. However, an inquiry into Samantha's family history revealed anxiety and depression-like symptoms for her mother, maternal grandmother, and paternal grandfather.

After obtaining informed consent and background information from Samantha's mother, I met individually with Samantha. Samantha denied experiencing any difficulties, blamed "Mom and her husband" for being "too strict" regarding her grades, and complained that kids at school were "always messing" with her. Samantha further stated that she did not need a counselor because she had "friends to talk to." In response, I praised Samantha for having such a good support network of friends and focused the remainder of our session time on more innocuous topics, such as favorite activities, favorite movies, favorite places, and happiest memories. Samantha answered each of my questions but did so with a look of, "Are you really this stupid, lady?"

When I asked how she would like to use the time in our future sessions, she commented, "I don't know." When I offered possible goals of counseling, such as improving friendships at school, getting better grades, or "getting your mom off your back," Samantha again shrugged and said, "I don't know." As the session ended, I again encouraged Samantha to consider how she would like to use our time together and asked her to return next week with one or two goals. When Samantha arrived for her appointment the following week, I began the session by meeting with her individually. After Samantha spent a significant portion of this session alternating between silence and responses of "I don't know," I met with her mother to obtain any additional information, and I then scheduled another appointment for the following week.

After this rather frustrating session, I reflected on what I had learned about Samantha. Despite her claims of not needing a counselor and not having any problems, she had clearly undergone a series of difficult events in her life. Given these multiple stressors, her family history of depression, and the fact that she was exhibiting problems both at home and at school, counseling services were likely needed. However, counseling could only be effective if I could actually reach this young client. The question–nonresponsive answer pattern we had begun to establish would not be effective. I knew I needed to use a different approach to effectively engage Samantha in the counseling process.

At the third session, as Samantha moved to sit on the couch in my office, I sat on a large floor pillow at one corner of my office, facing Samantha. I purposely avoided any discussion of goals or objectives for counseling and instead asked Samantha what station she would like to listen to on the radio. She laughed and said, "Yeah . . . right." When I assured her that I was serious, she said, "96.1." As I tuned the radio, we began discussing music. She told me that she liked hip hop and laughed when I told her I liked heavy metal, saying it was old music. Our discussion about music turned into a discussion about lyrics. Samantha discussed lyrics she saw as similar to her life. For example, we talked about the following lyrics from "One Day" by Simple Plan: "Sometimes this house feels like a prison/ That I just can't leave behind/There's so many rules I gotta follow/ Cuz you can't let go."

She explained that this song captured her feelings of resentment toward her parents and her anger about their strict rules. Now we were getting somewhere.

During our discussion of lyrics, Samantha also revealed that she liked to write stories. Although Samantha was certainly not fond of the idea of talking to a counselor, she did like the idea of writing "fictional" stories, such as "Tiffany's Best Accomplishment" or "Denise's Family," and discussing them in our sessions. Because they were about other people and not about herself, Samantha's stories were a way for her to express herself without risking embarrassment, reprimand, or—even worse to Samantha—sympathy.

As I continued to use this approach with Samantha for several more sessions, her stories expressed improved family communication, increased self-esteem, and more kinds of emotion. Through her stories, Samantha was able to cope with the multiple changes, losses, and stressors in her life. In the end, goals and objectives were not verbally stated, but the goals were attained, as evidenced by Samantha's endings to her stories.

Questions

1. How else might a counselor effectively use stories in individual and family counseling?
2. What other approaches might be effective with clients who are silent, reluctant, or resistant?
3. What are your diagnostic impressions of Samantha?

■ Response

Heather M. Helm

To begin, I applaud the creativity of the counselor in her efforts to reach this young woman, because reluctant clients, particularly adolescents, can be difficult. Often, the reluctant adolescent client has little historical evidence to uphold with any confidence a belief that adults can be supportive and understanding. Society's responses and attitudes toward adolescents tend to be directive instead of empowering and untrusting rather than trusting. With no prior counseling experience, Samantha had no reason to believe that this experience, with this adult, would be any different. Often, adolescents ascribe to the belief that something is wrong with them or that they are at fault for their struggles or the struggles of their family. Samantha experienced a series of significant events in a short period of time, and trust would naturally come, if at all, reluctantly. Additionally, because the events in Samantha's life were out of her control, the need to control each new situation is also a natural response. The focus of my response is on (a) approaches for working with silent, reluctant, or resistant clients; (b) diagnostic impressions of Samantha; and (c) the use of storytelling and creative narratives in individual and family counseling.

Many clients, regardless of their degree of motivation, enter counseling maintaining a self-protective stance. Therefore, as I mentioned earlier, perhaps Samantha's silence and reluctance can be viewed as a normal response to a stressful situation—that is, counseling. In particular, Samantha has faced situations that have accompanied a great loss of control over the outcome. The death of her father after what sounds like a long struggle and during such a critical time in her physical, social, and psychological development likely left Samantha with a sense of the world not being right and of situations as something she was unable to exert any control over. The perpetration against her is another way she was clearly out of control, along with the development of her new family and her eventually expressed feelings of being suffocated and controlled at home. Given the context, it is easy to understand why Samantha appears resistant; nevertheless, this does not provide any clear clinical direction in working with her.

I believe one of the first steps in considering the direction of a clinician's effort with silent or reluctant clients is to first try to determine the intent of the silence. On the basis of the information presented in the case study, for Samantha the intent seems to be control, yet it may also be transference of rejection, the child's perception of permissiveness to talk about problems, debilitating guilt and anxiety, or fear of being found out as the one who is in fact the cause of the family's problems or to blame for the events that have occurred in her life. Samantha was clearly perceived as having problems (perhaps even as the identified patient) and might have accepted that perception; therefore, she might have assumed that the therapist, having spoken with her family, also believed this to be true.

To determine the intent of a client's silent, resistant, or reluctant behavior, it is important for the therapist to recognize his or her personal reactions to the child's behavior. In particular, if the therapist feels rejected, then it is important to consider whether the child is experiencing a sense of rejection in his or her own life and therefore representing that rejection in the therapy room. Conversely, if the therapist feels silenced and limited in his or her capacity to express himself or herself in the room, it may be that the child comes to therapy with powerful messages not to talk about problems, inside or outside of the family environment. Regardless of the intent of the silence, the most important thing the therapist can do is to use joining techniques that clearly validate for the child who he or she is, how he or she feels, and how he or she acts. Joining techniques allow the therapist to send a clear message of acceptance and understanding while normalizing the client's response. Like opposing magnets, a therapist can "chase" the reluctant client with any level of energy and receive the same response: futile efforts at approach and continued resistance.

I clearly believe the therapist in this incident did the right thing by not trying to draw the client into interaction through direct questioning. The therapist's initial instinct to engage the client in any dialogue whatsoever (a natural instinct, given that adolescents typically do want to talk about themselves) is a trap all of us have fallen into at one time or another and is counterproductive, as clients can clearly see through a counselor's surface-level inquires. Given that many of the efforts to draw out a young, silent, and reluctant client often result in frustration on the part of the therapist and the client, traditional talk therapy may not be the modality of choice. I have found that children of Samantha's age respond quite well to a nondirective play environment. Giving adolescents the opportunity to engage in nonthreatening activities that allow for a creative outlet for the emotions they are experiencing as well as giving them control over one environment, even if they feel control nowhere else, does wonders for establishing a sense of empowerment and for strengthening the therapeutic relationship.

Clients of Samantha's age are sometimes reluctant to engage in spontaneous play, depending on their developmental level; nonetheless, people of all ages, when presented with the opportunity to play and explore, eventually use the materials to express themselves in some way, even if it is only to provide themselves another place to gaze. Despite occasional reluctance, given Samantha's age, it is likely that she will still find it easier to express herself through play, a child's natural expressive language (Erikson, 1963; Ginott, 1959; Landreth, 2002). My experience has also been that when the environment is age appropriate and not the typical office, fear and resistance diminish. Silence sometimes does not go away, but words are not necessary when the client has an opportunity to express himself or herself in another way. Additionally, in a nondirective environment, the client is not asked to develop and subsequently articulate goals for therapy because nondirective play therapy maintains an unwavering belief in the child's capacity to naturally move toward growth and healing (Landreth, 2002).

Although it is not a diagnostic impression in the traditional sense as based on the current *Diagnostic and Statistical Manual of Mental Disorders* (4th ed., text rev.; American Psychiatric Association, 2000), it seems that Samantha is experiencing prolonged grief from the loss of her father and the events following his death. Additionally, regardless of what diagnostic category she would fall into (if any), Samantha seems to be reacting to several traumatic events that occurred in a short period of time, exacerbated by the developmental crises considered normal for her age. Obviously there are several foci to which one could choose to attend: the death of her father, movement to a step-family, perpetration by her cousin, and a familial history of depression and anxiety. All of these could, independently of one another, create significant difficulties, but in conjunction they may lead to substantial difficulties. Although, as I have stated, there is a familial history of depression and anxiety, I would be reluctant to jump to such diagnoses given Samantha's age and the recent events in her life.

To rule out any biologically based explanations and to better assess the impact of the events on her life, it is important to know whether Samantha's difficulties at home and with her peers began over the course of the 3 years in which she experienced trauma and significant life changes or whether there was any indication of these struggles prior to these events. Naturally, a different course of action would be indicated depending on the answer to this inquiry, particularly further assessment. Again, I encourage a thoughtful and discriminating approach to diagnosis, because misdiagnosis in this case could potentially lead to inappropriate pathologizing and additional feelings of isolation and alienation on Samantha's part. I cannot emphasize enough how important it is to acknowledge the impact of life events and not rush toward a formal diagnosis that would be with Samantha for many years.

The spontaneous and creative use of storytelling in this incident was a powerful and useful medium of great therapeutic value. In general, children and adults organize life experiences as narratives that assist in creating meaning of events and in guiding actions in relationships. As Samantha was able to find the necessary distance from her struggles through creative narratives, she was able to rewrite the current state of her life narrative. It may be that Samantha had created a self-narrative that she applied as a true representation of self. If Samantha felt any sense of responsibility for her father's death or the perpetration against her, her self-narrative might have been one that maintained her grief and loss in the interest of maintaining her view of reality. Perhaps by telling stories of children whom she created and likely identified with, Samantha was able to change the language of her self-narrative and open herself up to a different assessment of self and perhaps to more satisfying relationships with her parents and her peers. In her article on the therapeutic use of stories in counseling children, Carlson (2001) wrote, "In the story, children can see the main character struggle with a problem, explore various solutions, and arrive at a resolution. They react and experience feelings while thinking about what they would do in the same situation. This experience validates the child's feelings, illustrating that other children share the same feelings" (p. 92).

In my opinion, because all people create personal narratives based on their experiences, there is no limit to the use of storytelling in therapy, regardless of whether the work is with children, adolescents, adults, individuals, or families. Any technique that allows for joining and a greater interpersonal connection is a useful one, particularly for silent and reluctant clients. There are many techniques in the child therapy and family therapy literature that make use of storytelling and personal narratives. One limitation of these techniques is, of course, that some verbal skills and abstract reasoning must be present. Therefore, they are not appropriate for clients with limited abstract reasoning skills.

Samantha found a way to express the complexity of her emotions over the events in her life through the use of stories. Additionally, the therapist found a way to connect with Samantha beyond verbal expression of emotions, which, for a child Samantha's age (or for anyone, for that matter), can be challenging. The therapist in this case was willing to think outside of the box and create a comfortable environment by demonstrating her commitment not to be like all other adults. Through the use of music, the therapist connected with Samantha (they did not even have to like or know each other's music) and symbolically demonstrated her commitment to Samantha. Music also tells a story; this is a large part of the visceral experience of listening to a given piece of music. By allowing Samantha to express herself through the lyrics of her favorite song, the therapist opened the door to further storytelling. To me, Samantha's initial presentation in therapy was no more than an adaptive coping mechanism. Given the amount of frustration and, at times, anger that a silent, resistant, or reluctant client can draw from a therapist, the use of creative techniques is paramount.

Response

Laura R. Simpson

Few occasions are more likely to remind a counseling professional of the tenuous nature of building a therapeutic relationship than coming face to face with a brooding, silent adolescent. The initial contact with this type of client is ominous and may cause a variety of reactions in the counseling professional. My response explores the counselor's question of diagnostic impressions of Samantha as well as the use of writing as a counseling technique. Additionally, I examine pertinent issues that can arise when counselors attempt to work with resistant clients and explore a potentially effective approach for working with clients who are reluctant to participate in the therapeutic process.

Samantha has certainly experienced more than her share of challenges. The death of her father, her molestation by a family member, and the interpersonal discord in her relationships with peers and family are each enough to challenge the coping resources of even the most resilient individual. The combination of these issues certainly seems to have stunted Samantha's ability to engage in relationships, which has put her in a position of being vulnerable and has resulted in a suspicious and wary young woman who has closed herself off from her family and all but a few friends. The family history of depression, in conjunction with Samantha's current dysfunctional coping mechanisms, suggests that Samantha is experiencing depression herself. Samantha's depression is multidimensional and likely complicated by unresolved grief, anger, and guilt. She presents as having limited affective skills and has a tendency to be negative toward authority figures at home and at school. Furthermore, she is prone to blaming others and accusing them of being hostile toward her. Her treatment needs are complex, and her resistance makes addressing these issues daunting at best. As the counselor noted, counseling could only be effective if she could reach the client.

Before one considers how to actually do the work, it is important to be reminded that a counselor's state of mind is critical to the potential for successful therapy with a resistant client. Developing the ability to work with children who are resistant requires learning to balance meeting the youths on their own terms and maintaining a mature response to the challenges they send one's way (Chambers, 2005). Counselors must remember that everyone tends to put up resistance in the presence of a threat or the suggestion of change (Otani, 1989). If youths perceive an adult as threatening, resistant behavior is set in motion. Resistance is a healthy sign and is usually protective in intent. Youths attempt to protect themselves physically, and it should come as no surprise that they are protective psychologically as well. Thus, the manner in which a counselor conceptualizes resistance plays a critical role in his or her approach to working with the client.

If resistant behavior is viewed as indicative of feeling scared or cautious, the counselor is likely to approach working with the client more positively than if resistance is defined as difficult or uncooperative behavior (Corey & Corey, 2006). Resistance can cause counselors to express doubts in their ability to work with the client or to have empathy for the client (Chen & Giblin, 2002). After all, it is not always easy to respond empathically to the client whose verbalizations seem primarily resistant or defensive. Viewing the resistant behavior as information the client is sharing and as an opportunity as opposed to a problem can be the foundation of building a successful working relationship. Additionally, when resistance is present, the widespread urge is to "speed up the session and break through resistance" (Mitchell, 2003, p. 11). Maintaining patience, being creative, and setting a pace that allows the client to move through the change process are critical to a successful counseling outcome. Counselors need the ability to communicate caring and trust while allowing the client an opportunity to design a personal solution to life's difficulties.

With this client, the counselor had great insight into the need to step outside of traditional client–counselor interaction and elected to build on Samantha's interest in writing as a technique for developing the relationship and creating a safe, neutral space for addressing issues. Although Samantha was not comfortable writing about her own experiences, examining her fictional stories gave the counselor an opportunity to normalize the narrative (Ivey & Ivey, 2003). The use of these stories normalized such concerns and the reality of difficult situations. Samantha certainly benefited from the opportunity to see that issues are a natural and logical result of life situations. Through her characters, Samantha increased her understanding of herself. In addition, the counselor gained an opportunity to analyze the thoughts, feelings, and psychological meanings of the story, thus gaining a new way of understanding Samantha's lifestyle and goals. This technique ultimately resulted in an opportunity to point out that although everyone has challenges, the concerns are solvable.

Writing is a very common technique used in therapeutic process (Scorzelli & Gold, 1999). For example, survivors of abuse are frequently encouraged to use writing as part of healing. Some examples of writing include journal writing, story writing, and letter writing. Keeping a journal can serve several purposes. Writing allows an individual an opportunity to express repressed feelings, confront the offender, and keep track of thoughts and feelings between sessions (Pearson, 1994). The experience of writing the story of what transpired, although painful, has the power to be a non-threatening way for survivors to begin to express and vent abuse-related feelings. Survivor narratives have personal meaning and may allow survivors of abuse to begin to reconnect with feelings from childhood (Bhuvaneswar & Shafer, 2004). Finally, writing letters, with or without intent to send, can be a safe way for the client to confront the perpetrator or the nonprotective parent (Davis, 1990). In general, writing can enhance communication between client and counselor, particularly with clients who have difficulty expressing themselves verbally.

In addition to being reluctant to enter the therapeutic relationship, clients are often resistant to participating in the process. When counselors suggest incorporating change to clients who are ambivalent, they are likely to ignite the clients' arguments for the opposite side of their ambivalence. In other words, the more evidence we offer our clients about the benefits of change, "the more likely they are to argue with us" (Roes, 2003, p. 46). A manner of addressing this reality is through the use of paradoxical interventions, which are often the opposite of what the client is expecting. They may surprise clients and sometimes seem to defy common sense. Indeed, sometimes this approach does not go as planned, yet at times such strategies are appropriate when one meets a therapeutic impasse. This kind of reverse psychology is designed to promote "statements of problem recognition, intention to change, and optimism" (Roes, 2003, p. 46). It stands to reason that when counselors are making an argument for change, it leaves them wide open for counterarguments from clients of all the reasons change cannot or will not work (Cade & O'Hanlon, 1993). Ultimately, advising a client to intentionally increase the symptom he or she wants to get rid of can allow the client an opportunity to take control of a situation. For example, if one were working with an adolescent to overcome dishonesty, one might give the assignment of telling one extra lie per day. This is certainly not the type of homework one would expect, yet it creates an opportunity for the client to increase self-awareness of his or her behavior. Potentially, although this may seem risky, it heightens the client's perception of actions he or she wants to change and helps promote the self-confidence that the change is within his or her power to achieve.

Finally, as Samantha's counselor experienced, resistant clients often fear embarrassment, reprimand, or sympathy. Regardless of how irrational, inappropriate, or illogical the counselor feels the client's resistance is, the client has a perceived need to cling to it. To not respect the client's resistance is to reject the client. "One of the best predictors of counseling outcomes is the client's experience of the counselor's acceptance" (Mitchell, 2003, p. 11). Showing a genuine respect for the client's resistance is typically the counselor's first opportunity to do the unexpected.

References

American Psychiatric Association. (2000). *Diagnostic and statistical manual of mental disorders* (4th ed., text rev.). Washington, DC: Author.

Bhuvaneswar, C., & Shafer, A. (2004). Survivor of that time, that place: Clinical uses of violence survivors' narratives. *Journal of Medical Humanities, 25,* 109–127.

Cade, B., & O'Hanlon, W. H. (1993). *A brief guide to brief therapy.* New York: Norton.

Carlson, R. (2001). Therapeutic use of story in therapy with children. *Guidance and Counseling, 16*(3), 92–99.

Chambers, J. C. (2005). The art of kid whispering: Connecting with adult-wary youth [Electronic version]. *Reclaiming Children and Youth, 13,* 241–248.

Chen, M., & Giblin, N. (2002). *Individual counseling: Skills and techniques.* Denver, CO: Love Publishing Company.

Corey, M. S., & Corey, G. (2006). *Process and practice: Groups.* Belmont, CA: Thompson Brooks/Cole.

Davis, L. (1990). *The courage to heal workbook.* New York: Harper & Row.

Erikson, E. (1963). *Childhood and society.* New York: Norton.

Ginott, H. (1959). The theory and practice of "therapeutic intervention" in child treatment. *Journal of Consulting Psychology, 23,* 160–166.

Ivey A. E., & Ivey, M. B. (2003). *Intentional interviewing and counseling: Facilitating client development in a multicultural society.* Pacific Grove, CA: Brooks/Cole-Thompson Learning.

Landreth, G. (2002). *Play therapy: The art of the relationship* (2nd ed.). New York: Brunner-Routledge.

Mitchell, S. W. (2003). Tips for treating highly resistant clients. *Advocate, 26*(11), 1, 10–11.

Otani, A. (1989). Client resistance in counseling: Its theoretical rationale and taxonomic classification. *Journal of Counseling & Development, 67,* 458–461.

Pearson, Q. (1994). Treatment techniques for adult female survivors of childhood sexual abuse. *Journal of Counseling & Development, 73,* 32–37.

Roes, N. A. (2003). Breaking your own rules. *Counselor: The Magazine for Addiction Professionals, 4*(4), 46–51.

Scorzelli, J., & Gold, J. (1999). The mutual storytelling writing game. *Journal of Mental Health Counseling, 21,* 113–124.

10

"Please Don't Make Me Go Home": Sexual Abuse and Safety Issues

This incident explores a situation in which a novice counselor was faced with deciding whether to release a child into her mother's care following the child's expression of fear. It also addresses dynamics related to sexual abuse by a relative.

■ Critical Incident

Vera B. Triplett

"Lakeesha Williams" was an 8-year-old African American girl who had been molested by an 18-year-old female relative named Safiya. I began counseling her as a doctoral student while employed under a grant obtained by an inner city child advocacy center. The grant had been written to expand the center's services beyond the investigation and forensic interviewing process to also provide counseling services for sexually abused children and their nonoffending immediate family members. The treatment modality of choice at the center was play therapy.

My working pattern is to have three sessions with the child alone and then meet with the parents and child every fourth session. My rationale for having these family sessions is to open up a safe and secure line of communication between the child and the parents about issues that may arise in session to which they should be privy. Because I primarily work with children, I know that parents will inquire about session particulars. I often encourage them to let their children reveal whatever information they feel comfortable revealing. I also give my assurances that if anything comes up in session that may be harmful to their child or that would put anyone else in danger, I will inform them immediately. This allows me to create an atmosphere of trust both between the child and me and between me and the parent.

As such, I met with Lakeesha for three sessions and then met with Lakeesha and her mother, a single parent, every fourth session. Although her mother occasionally requested that I also address issues surrounding school behavior, our work focused on Lakeesha's reactions to the molestation she had experienced. Lakeesha presented with issues of anxiety, shame, and dangerously diminished boundaries.

After approximately 10 sessions, Lakeesha shared with me that she was very upset about some things that had occurred at a sleepover party that she had attended. She revealed to me in session that she felt like "doing to the other little girls at the party what Safiya did to me." Lakeesha said that she knew that it was wrong to do but that she could not help feeling that way. In this session, we discussed her feelings of shame surrounding her desire to touch other children in sexual ways, and I normalized some of the urges she had to practice these behaviors on others. We discussed how she could use self-talk and other coping mechanisms to keep herself from acting on these urges. I also encouraged her to decline future sleepover invitations until we felt that this issue was under control. Because I had some concern about safety issues for Lakeesha and her friends, I also informed her that we needed to talk with her mother about this at our next family meeting.

The session with Lakeesha's mother started off fairly routinely, with me facilitating dialogue between them. Approximately 20 minutes into the session, I noticed that Lakeesha's body language had become very tense and her eyes were downcast. When I encouraged her to express what she was feeling at that moment, she burst into tears. She then began to yell at her mother in a very loud voice, saying that her mother had been mean to her and had yelled at her. She went on to say that her mother had too many boyfriends coming over to the house. She then collapsed into hysterical crying and curled up into a ball in the corner of the room.

Her mother explained that she had yelled at Lakeesha the day before for being irresponsible with her schoolwork. She apologized to Lakeesha and attempted to comfort her. Lakeesha, however, rebuffed all of her mother's attempts and told me that she did not want to go home with her. Ms. Williams then began to cry as well and assured me that she would never do anything to hurt her daughter. She admitted that she did date often but indicated that she never brought a date home unless he was a serious boyfriend. She then asked her daughter whether any of her boyfriends had ever done anything sexual to her.

Lakeesha responded with an emphatic and convincing "no," but she still refused to go home with her mother. She continued to cry and remained curled into a ball in the corner. At that time, Ms. Williams attempted to physically pick her up. I told Ms. Williams that I did not think that this course of action would help matters and asked her to let me talk with Lakeesha alone.

Once Ms. Williams had left the room, I began to talk with Lakeesha and asked her to take some deep breaths in an effort to calm her. Once she had calmed enough to begin to speak, I asked her why she did not want to go home with her mother. She said that she just did not and that she was not going to. I then went out to talk with Ms. Williams alone. I explained to her that children who have been sexually victimized often develop pent up emotions such as this kind of anger and suddenly express them. I further explained that, on some level, all children feel that their parents should have been there to protect them from the abuse, regardless of whether the parents were aware of the danger.

In addition, I explained that I felt that I was in a precarious situation because, although I suspected that this was what was happening, I could not be certain and had a responsibility to err on the side of caution to ensure Lakeesha's safety. I then brought

Ms. Williams back into the room with Lakeesha so that I could again talk with both of them at the same time about their options. I explained to them that I would have to call in the Office of Child and Family Services (OCS). I explained that I would like to defer to another person's judgment about the matter of Lakeesha refusing to leave voluntarily with her mother.

At this point, Ms. Williams became very upset and began to assure me that Lakeesha was in no danger from her. I then turned my attention to my young client and asked Lakeesha whether she felt that her mother would harm her when they left the facility. She softly answered, "No." I then asked whether her mother had ever hurt her in the past, and she again softly answered, "No."

I then explained to Lakeesha that, if I called OCS, it was likely that she would be taken to a foster home until this issue was sorted out. I told Lakeesha that her safety was my first priority and that, if she did not feel safe going home with her mother, I would call the necessary authorities. After about 2 to 3 minutes of silence, she raised herself from the floor. I offered and she accepted a drink of water, and I asked her again whether she was willing to return home with her mother. This time, she said, "Yes." Lakeesha and her mother then departed. Our session had begun at approximately 6:00 p.m. When all was said and done, it was approximately 8:30 p.m.

The day after the incident, I called to follow up with Ms. Williams. She told me that Lakeesha was exhausted from the events of the night before and that she therefore had allowed Lakeesha to stay home from school. She also wanted to make it quite clear that she did not have a lot of men "coming in and out of the house" and that she was willing to do anything to help Lakeesha through this difficult time.

I also called my clinical supervisor and gave her a brief synopsis of the incident. We agreed that we would discuss it at length in our next supervision session. My feelings about the incident ranged from feeling like I had handled it appropriately to feeling as if I should have done some things differently. I ultimately made the decision to allow my client to leave with her mother because my experience has been that children who have been sexually abused often reach a stage in their healing process when they become extremely angry with their parents or parent. Young children do not know how to express anger that their parents did not protect them, so they often take a relatively small incident and use it to express their overwhelming sense of anger and grief.

Nevertheless, I did have a few concerns. Most important, I wondered whether I should have made the decision (to allow Ms. Williams to take Lakeesha home that night) on my own without consulting with anyone. I realized that I had asked Lakeesha about her feelings of safety while her mother was present and wondered whether this might have inhibited her. I was also concerned that I did not address the issue of Lakeesha's fears of becoming a perpetrator until the following session.

Questions

1. As a doctoral student intern, should I have consulted with my supervisor or called OCS before making a decision to release Lakeesha to her mother's care?
2. Would it have been appropriate and helpful to have Lakeesha write a statement saying that she did not feel that she was in any danger from her mother?
3. Would I have been liable if Ms. Williams had ultimately harmed Lakeesha?
4. Would I have been culpable if Lakeesha had perpetrated against another child if I did not inform her mother that this was a concern?
5. How would you have handled this incident?

Response

Heather C. Trepal

As with almost any case involving sexual abuse by a relative, the issues in this case are complex. Because of complicated family dynamics, there are often multiple crises that can and do arise during the healing process. Lakeesha is a young child who has already been through a lot in her short life. She is coping, albeit struggling in some areas. The doctoral student counselor was facing uncharted territory on two levels when she encountered Lakeesha that night. First, there was Lakeesha's disclosure of urges that she was experiencing at the slumber party, and, second, there was the issue of Lakeesha's unwillingness to go home with her mother.

I think it is a sign of strength and trust that Lakeesha was able to tell her counselor about her urges to do to other girls at the slumber party what had been done to her. The counselor did a nice job normalizing Lakeesha's feelings. Regarding culpability, I am not sure the counselor would be held responsible if Lakeesha were to act on her urges before the counselor had discussed them with Lakeesha's mother. Lakeesha's anger toward her mother might have been a reflection of her fears related to the counselor's intention to disclose Lakeesha's slumber party urges to Ms. Williams. Given that so many boundaries have been violated and that trust has been broken in their life, abused clients often test their counselors. Lakeesha's actions that night might have been a test to see what her counselor would do. Would the counselor protect her secrets or tell her mother about the issues that she had disclosed in session? The counselor had told Lakeesha that they needed to address the issue in the next session with her mother. Lakeesha might have been attempting to avoid this discussion by turning the focus onto anger toward her mother and onto issues of her mother's social life.

Even so, I think that the counselor, as a student intern, should have consulted with her supervisor before making the decision to release Lakeesha into her mother's care. Such decisions are complicated, and, although the counselor thought through the issues involved, consulting first with a supervisor is almost always the recommended course of action. The supervisor could have provided some guidance on the basis of prior experience with children who have been sexually abused by a relative and on the basis of knowledge of the family dynamics involved in healing. In addition, the intern could have discussed with the supervisor the idea of calling the child protective agency.

It should be noted that Lakeesha did not directly say that she was afraid of her mother. She did display nonverbal behavior (e.g., looking down, curling up, soft voice) that suggested that she was afraid. She also displayed angry behavior toward her mother (e.g., shouting, tears) and made accusations that her mother was mean and had too many boyfriends over. Sometimes sexual abuse is part of a pattern of abuse and dysfunction in a family. Given the contradictory messages, consulting with her supervisor would have been a reasonable thing for the counselor to do.

I am not sure that having Lakeesha write a statement about not being afraid of her mother would have been helpful in this case. I have to wonder about the goal of such an intervention. If the counselor wanted to get information privately from the client, she could have asked her without her mother being present. If the counselor's goal was for legal protection, the counselor should have conferred with her supervisor or called the child protective agency. Such consultation would provide much better legal protection than a written statement from a minor client.

If I were in the student counselor's shoes that night, I think I would have first consulted with the client regarding disclosing her urges toward other children to her mother. If the confidentiality policy had been clearly discussed with all parties involved (the mother, Lakeesha, and the counselor) and perhaps even put in writing, then I would have first consulted with Lakeesha about how and when to go about discussing the issue with her mother. The American Counseling Association's (2005) *Code of Ethics* clearly indicates that "counselors should seek the assent of clients (who are unable to give consent themselves) to services and include them in decision making as appropriate" (Section A.2.d.). Ideally, I would have liked to have Lakeesha be the one to initiate the discussion; I would also have liked to discuss with Lakeesha her feelings about the urges and about disclosing them to her mother. Maybe she was ashamed. Maybe she did not want the counselor to tell her mother just yet. This information might have been important for the counselor to know.

After having this discussion and making the ensuing decision to either (a) have Lakeesha initiate the discussion with her mother or (b) formulate with Lakeesha a plan for telling her mother and continuing with the session, I would have brought in Ms. Williams. If Lakeesha had acted the way she did in the incident, then I would have immediately consulted with my supervisor regarding my course of action. Depending on his or her recommendations, I would have either assisted Lakeesha to calm down and released her to her mother or called the child protective agency to make an assessment.

Response

Emily Phillips

The story of 8-year-old Lakeesha Williams, who was molested by a female relative, would challenge the most experienced counselor, let alone a doctoral student. The field of sexual abuse is quite complex and also involves the laws of the particular state in which a counselor works. Therefore, I couch my comments in the knowledge that my response to this incident could be affected by variations in state law and by differing university policies regarding doctoral students in field placements.

In the incident provided, there is no discussion of the actual play techniques that were used or the thematic material that arose. As an elementary school counselor, mental health clinician, and counselor educator, I have found that play therapy is an effective medium for children to work through issues of trust, protection, and power. Nondirective play allows children to work through these issues in a safe, supportive, and nonthreatening atmosphere. Including the mother every few sessions is an excellent idea because there needs to be healing in this primary relationship. However, caution must be exercised, as the child needs to know that this is his or her time and that the counselor will not reveal the child's confidences in these joint sessions.

Issues of "anxiety, shame, and dangerously diminished boundaries" are typical challenges to be addressed in cases of sexual abuse. That the abuse occurred with a family member adds additional stress and shame, as it is nearly impossible to isolate the child from this family member without other relatives also finding out what happened. This can be very divisive in a family system. In addition, anger toward the custodial parent is common and often hard for a child to identify or acknowledge.

First, let me state that it makes no sense to have Lakeesha write a statement that she feels safe. A written statement by an 8-year-old is not considered a legal document and could be viewed as coercion on the counselor's part. It would only give the doctoral student some false sense of security against possible legal challenge. In addition, there is no evidence that Lakeesha's mother ever harmed her, barring her failure to realize the threat posed to her daughter by the female relative. As long as Ms. Williams is now keeping the perpetrator away from Lakeesha and not exposing Lakeesha to any additional risk (and this seems to be the case), there is no reason to involve Social Services. Indeed, unless someone is currently molesting Lakeesha, I doubt that Social Services would investigate a call made to report that a child does not want to go home with her mother.

If, as presented in this vignette, there are no concrete grounds for removing the child from the home, I highly doubt that a supervisor would suggest calling Social Services. In fact, in my opinion, there was no urgent reason for the supervisor to be contacted during the client visit. However, the counselor should contact each supervisor (faculty and clinical supervisor) soon afterward. The parent has a right to take his or her own child, especially if no imminent danger is evident. Moreover, the counselor cannot insist on keeping the child at the clinic because, in most states, this could be considered kidnapping.

Additionally, Social Services surely would not place a child in foster care without evidence of imminent danger. Indeed, it is generally not a good idea for counselors to tell children they will go into foster care. First, this is not a common occurrence anymore. Also, this could be viewed as a threat, not as information, and could serve to shut the child down and encourage him or her to lie to remain at home. Children's primary loyalty is to their parents, even under horrible circumstances.

I see three additional issues with this case: (a) the counselor's status as a doctoral student, (b) Lakeesha's urge to perpetrate against other children, and (c) Lakeesha's anger toward her mother. With regard to the counselor's status as a doctoral student, her clinical supervisor at the child advocacy center is ultimately responsible for her caseload. In addition, the counselor's mentor and her university department are also liable for her actions. This is why counselors are required to keep case notes on each client and have supervisory meetings and why they should carry liability insurance. Given the counselor's status as a student, she needed to discuss this case with both of her supervisors.

With respect to the second issue, the urge to perpetrate against other children is often a signal that an abused child needs to act out his or her sense of power–powerlessness. This theme repeats itself throughout the critical incident. Attention paid in play therapy to Lakeesha's feelings of powerlessness and her need to gain power would be beneficial. Indeed, I strongly suspect that Lakeesha's refusal to go home with her mother was a way to gain a sense of power over her life and her mother. She needs to feel that she is in control of herself and her world. It could be that a 2.5-hour session in which she was the center of attention might have innocently reinforced Lakeesha for seeking power in an unhealthy way.

It is not uncommon for children who have been molested to reenact this with other children. The counselor needs to address this issue to break the cycle. At 8 years old, Lakeesha's sense of empathy and moral development are relatively primitive, and the counselor needs to be explicit in stating what is okay and not okay for her to do. Providing Lakeesha with information about her body rights would be helpful. If the abuse had been ongoing, Lakeesha might also have been unsure about what constitutes appropriate social interaction. Teaching Lakeesha to use "self-talk and other coping mechanisms" is certainly in order. The counselor in this incident does not specify which coping mechanisms she taught Lakeesha, but one such strategy should involve an identification of who is in her support system and who she can talk to when she experiences these urges. In addition, Lakeesha needs to know about the consequences for herself and others if she were to act on these urges, and therapy must be continued until she has them under control.

The counselor was right to inform the mother about these urges, but both the counselor and the mother must remember that urges are not actions. Once the mother has been informed of the potential, it would in all likelihood be considered neglect if Lakeesha's mother's allowed her to continue attending sleepovers or to participate in other social activities in which Lakeesha might be tempted to act on these urges. The counselor relieved her responsibility by disclosing this information to the mother (and documenting it). Disclosure to Lakeesha's mother is necessary because the child expressed urges that could potentially harm someone else. There is absolutely no evidence from this case that the mother put Lakeesha at risk for abuse, and there is no reason to suspect that the mother would not be sympathetic and supportive and continue with treatment in the future.

I have saved the third issue for last, but it is probably the primary issue in this case. Lakeesha, like many children who have been sexually abused by someone they know, has lost a sense of security, love, and trust. Even if she is not fully aware of it, she likely feels a great deal of anger toward her mother for failing to protect her. This is evidenced by her complaint that her mother has lots of boyfriends. She is sensitive to this because she has been sexualized at an early age. Although the abuse incident was with a female relative, she may be concerned that her mother's boyfriends could also abuse her and that her mother does not have the ability or power to keep her safe from sexual abuse in the future. Lakeesha needs to express through play her anger at her mom for not protecting her.

The counselor needs to work with Lakeesha's mother to help her understand this anger and to allow Ms. Williams to apologize and reassure Lakeesha that she would never allow this to happen again. Lakeesha needs to know she does not have to scream to be heard by her mother. The counselor does not mention in the incident how the abuse was disclosed. If Lakeesha disclosed to a school counselor and not to her own mother, this would be further evidence that the child believes her mother is powerless to protect her. Anything the counselor can do to help Lakeesha identify ways to feel powerful in her life without abusing others would be helpful.

Therefore, if this were my case, I would allow Lakeesha to explore this anger toward her mother. I would work on helping her find ways of feeling powerful without harming others. I would also work with Ms. Williams to assure Lakeesha that, as her daughter, she is first in her mother's life and that her mother is willing to do all she can to protect Lakeesha. I would also advise Ms. Williams to keep her own sex life more private for a while and to continue with therapy to deal with her own guilt and to support her daughter. Lakeesha may have a long road ahead of her while trying to heal from this.

Reference

American Counseling Association. (2005). *ACA Code of ethics.* Alexandria, VA: Author.

"My Pa-Pa Is an Alligator": Sexual Abuse Reporting

This critical incident presents the case of a young boy who was repeatedly sexually molested by a family member. The incident also presents the complicated and sometimes frustrating nature of the reporting process. The respondents to this case stress the importance of consistent and multifaceted approaches to issues regarding a familial history of abuse.

Critical Incident

Laurie A. Carlson

"Bobby Harris," a slight and pale Caucasian kindergartner from a very poor family in rural Mississippi, was the only child of his single mother. At the age of 6, he had been expelled from school because of disruptive classroom behavior. As a result of his expulsion, Bobby was enrolled in the district's behavior modification classroom for students in kindergarten through fifth grade. I was a licensed school counselor employed half time by the school district to provide counseling services exclusively to the students in this classroom. On review of Bobby's file, I learned that Bobby had a long history of self-harming behaviors, including cutting his hair and skin, ripping his clothing, drawing on himself, and pouring glue on himself and peeling it off until lesions appeared. Further review of the school's records revealed that previous interventions included suspensions, time-outs, elaborate reward systems, and regular paddling by the principal. I also learned that Bobby had enrolled in kindergarten the previous year but had been expelled for these problematic behaviors. That expulsion was followed with no further intervention because, at that time, the current behavior modification program was not in place. The school's records indicated that

Bobby's teacher, principal, and mother felt that he "just wasn't ready for school yet" and that he would be more successful if given another year to mature before attending kindergarten.

In beginning my counseling work with Bobby, I used nondirective play to establish rapport and to better understand Bobby's troublesome behaviors. During our early sessions, Bobby's activities included dollhouse play with human figures, drawing, clay, sand play, and painting. By the third session, he had begun to play almost exclusively with the human figures in the sand box. Bobby identified the smallest of the figures as himself, and he repeatedly buried and then excavated the figure. When I asked him about this, Bobby explained that he sometimes wished he could disappear but that he was afraid of the darkness when buried. The sand play sessions seemed to be very therapeutic for Bobby, and the frequency of his angry outbursts and self-harming behaviors significantly decreased after these sessions.

During our sixth session, Bobby began to attack the representation of himself with an aggressively postured alligator figure. These enactments were unique in that the alligator always burrowed into the sand to bite the Bobby figure when he was buried "in the dark." It was at this point that Bobby began calling the alligator "Pa-Pa." My suspicions of sexual abuse grew as the Pa-Pa figure's aggression increased over the next several sessions and transformed from biting to impaling with the long, sharp tail. Shortly after the impaling actions began, Bobby announced, "Pa-Pa hurts Bobby with his tail in the dark." At this point, I asked Bobby to "tell me more about that." Bobby reported that Pa-Pa was his maternal grandfather and that Bobby spent most days after school and every weekend at Pa-Pa's. Bobby further clarified that the alligator's tail represented his grandfather's "thing" while pointing toward his genital area and said, "Pa-Pa puts his thing in my butt and it hurts." I reminded Bobby of the limits of confidentiality that we reviewed during the first session, explained to him that I would have to talk to some other people to help him, and then immediately called the statewide child abuse hotline.

Because Bobby was scheduled to go to his grandfather's after school that day, the Department of Human Services (DHS) intake worker informed me that an interviewer would be sent to the school immediately. A novice interviewer was dispatched, and when she arrived at about 11:00 a.m., she requested that I sit in on the interview because of her inexperience and anxiety. This request was uncomfortable for me, yet I believed that, considering the circumstances, my presence was in Bobby's best interest. During the interview, I became painfully aware that several of the interviewer's questions might be construed as leading, and I worried that the credibility of Bobby's report might subsequently be questioned.

At that point, I requested a personal conversation with the interviewer, secured an aide to sit with Bobby, and, in a private location, engaged in a dialogue with the interviewer concerning whether a more experienced interviewer should be summoned. The interviewer informed me that my presence actually increased her anxiety, and she requested to continue the interview alone. I was confused and unsure about what to do. I called the hotline again to express my concern regarding the interview, and the intake worker assured me that all interviewers were well trained and qualified to carry out their duties. Almost immediately after I hung up the phone, Bobby returned to the classroom, appearing at ease and hope filled.

Shortly before dismissal, Bobby's very angry mother appeared in the classroom. She immediately began yelling cuss words at classroom staff and threatened her son with "a paddling he would never forget." The DHS interviewer had contacted her at work to inform her that a report had been filed against the grandfather. In an attempt to defuse the situation, I suggested that Bobby, his mother, and I go into an adjoining room to process what had happened during the day. Bobby sat straddling his mother's lap, facing her, with tears running down his cheeks as she kept yelling at him to "quit telling lies about Pa-Pa." Ms. Harris repeatedly reminded Bobby that his grandparents were the only family they had and that without the child care and financial support they provided she and Bobby likely would not be able to stay together.

The more Bobby tried to share with his mother what he was experiencing, the more distant she seemed to become. I had a gut feeling that Ms. Harris's response to her son was as much about her as about protection of her father. It occurred to me that there was a very real possibility that, as a child, she had experienced incest at the hands of her father and that she was terrified of the memories. Eventually, out of frustration and fervor, Bobby cradled his mother's face in his hands and cried in her face, "Please listen to me!" This behavior invoked an open-handed slap across Bobby's face from his mother.

I immediately summoned the school resource officer, who removed the mother and secured a safe place for Bobby. I then completed a third call to the child abuse hotline to report subsequent happenings, including the slap by Bobby's mother. I was not privy to where Bobby was taken that afternoon, and he was absent for 5 days after the incident. When Bobby returned, his previous disruptive behaviors also returned. In addition, Bobby seemed more sullen and easily outraged. I eventually learned that DHS had conducted a follow-up interview with Bobby's mother after school that day. Because of her interview, allegations in the case had been dismissed, and Bobby had been returned to his previous environment the very night of the report.

Questions

1. Discuss the options available to a professional counselor who finds himself or herself faced with an interview situation as I have described.
2. Were my gut feelings regarding childhood sexual abuse of the mother something I should have followed up on, and, if so, what is the proper way to do that?
3. What other therapeutic techniques likely would be effective in a case with such presenting conditions?

■ Response

Byron E. Norton and Carol C. Norton

Counselors are faced with an array of issues in conveying concerns around child abuse. As in this case, a counselor's observations are mandated to be conveyed to another authority or agency. The first thing that the counselor should do is make a list of concerns that have been surfacing over the course of her observations, including concerns of the teacher, principal, or other school personnel. This would lend credibility to the report and give the intake worker impetus to inquire on the dynamics of this case rather than the immediacy of the situation and the emotional state of the mother. This case could be investigated from a multivariable perspective. Data could be collected from the school personnel we have mentioned. A home environment and neighborhood assessment should also be considered, and a medical–pediatric consult would be valuable. These aspects would also state a historical concern that would give this case an overall perspective rather than an incident focus, as the intake worker may perceive the situation. The school social worker would be a valuable asset in obtaining information about the home and neighborhood. An assessment of post-traumatic stress disorder by a professional outside the school setting would support the chronicity of this case.

The interview with the child should have been conducted at a safe house or Kids Place. This would remove the issue of the school as the referral point, and the interview could be viewed by other professionals or videotaped for review by supervisory staff. DHS as well as the police have basic standards of interviewing in sexual abuse cases and could then review the quality of the interview.

When the mother slapped Bobby in the interview with the counselor, the counselor could have called the police directly because she had observed violence being perpetrated on a student. With the police involved, this incident would have another formal complaint source, which would support a pattern of abuse that is part of the parent–child relationship and the transfilial dynamics of at least two generations. In addition, this case needs to be refiled in the future because abuse is a pattern and not an incident. These records will build credibility for the counselor's concerns and may be used in an appeal to DHS at this time or in the future.

Academic interventions, such as an Individualized Education Program (IEP), are also important. The plan may state concerns about the child's behavior and include a statement of the family history that has been collected by the school social worker. The importance of the parent's involvement can be emphasized. This would also provide an official document that would address many of the dynamics previously introduced. The IEP would state requirements of the mother relative to her son's academic progress, which would be monitored and reassessed at a future date. A representative of DHS should be asked to attend the IEP meetings so that a spirit of cooperation could develop between the two agencies. This DHS caseworker could observe the concerns around Bobby's behaviors and develop the historical perspective that was lacking in the crisis interview model. Also, concerns are more likely to be acknowledged by a case worker who has an ongoing relationship with school personnel.

Bobby's at-risk behavior indicates an underlying concern of suicidal risk. Bobby should remain in some form of counseling, which would allow for ongoing assessment of his current risk factors. The classroom teacher must also be informed of possible behaviors that may indicate a change in his risk level. Coordination could be administered through the IEP or a 504 plan if no formal IEP is in place. Bobby should remain in play therapy with the counselor, who could evaluate his status.

This counselor needs the support of her administrative staff, including the immediate staff (i.e., principal and teachers). In addition, the support of the district-level administrators would be valuable. In this case, the principal should have been more involved as part of the reporting process. The safety of students is the jurisdiction of the principal, and a greater team effort would have conveyed the importance of the issue to all involved. Furthermore, this counselor also needs a supportive colleague with whom she can vent her frustrations regarding the ineptness of a system that does not always hear her concerns or respond to the cries of a child in need. The tendency is to resent the system rather than to develop a process that responds to children. The counselor cannot afford to become defeated or jaded by this incident because several children will need this process in the future.

The counselor's gut reactions that the mother also experienced childhood abuse are most likely accurate. Nonetheless, the immediate protection of Bobby is a higher priority than focusing on mother's prior sexual abuse. The family would better be served by a focus on how the mother's prior abuse (not identified to her as victimization) is affecting her parenting style. The dynamics and defense system of the mother's history are too deeply ingrained for the focus of the school counselor. What the counselor can do is support the fears and frustrations of the mother and move these fears toward better care of Bobby. At this time, Ms. Harris would benefit more from support of the counselor on the appropriate parenting she is doing. If confronted with her failings as a parent, the mother would not integrate what she needs to understand to change her adversarial position with the school.

One can observe that Ms. Harris operates on a stress and survival model of living. At this time, she has absolutely no capacity to transcend the immediate situation nor to have empathy for the experiences Bobby is enduring. One can see that she has little ability to respond to Bobby's world. Ms. Harris needs support for her efforts to give Bobby a better life. Bobby's mother would benefit from guidance on how she can focus her concerns toward Bobby, which would also help her reach her personal goals. Referral to DHS would be helpful in facilitating the mother in locating other resources so she does not have to rely so heavily on her parents.

Ms. Harris is a "frozen," or emotionally immobilized, parent because of her history of abuse. She may need someone to care about her immediate situation so she can be more available to respond to Bobby's concerns. Assessment of the mother's parenting style indicates that she is unable to nurture Bobby in any beneficial manner that gives him a sense of identity or self-worth. In essence, Ms. Harris is self-fulfilling the prophecy of her own shattered life. Bobby's mother needs to see a personal benefit to change for Bobby. Obviously, Bobby is a burden to her struggling existence, and she experiences very little pride in having a son. The mother's capacity to nurture and respond to Bobby in a reciprocal manner is crucial in their relationship. Bobby is in a parentalized mode with his mother, which means that his needs are secondary to his mother's needs. Ms. Harris needs assistance with meeting the primary needs of her family so that she has energy available to attend to Bobby's basic emotional needs. In the school counselor role, I would "feed" his mother aspects of Bobby that she could respond to and feel any sense of pride in as a mother. In keeping with this, Bobby's mother needs to see models of ways to comfort and soothe him. Perhaps asking Ms. Harris what she needed or wanted as a child would open the way to providing that for Bobby. Cooperation on the mother's part will probably be slow and resistive in the early stages, but persistence in providing encouragement for her is necessary and is more likely than other approaches to shift her perspective of the meaning of living.

Once Bobby's mother has some degree of trust in the counselor, we might recommend that she join a support group for single mothers or mothers who are survivors of abuse early in life. Ms. Harris needs a support system outside her dysfunctional family system. Intense counseling is necessary, but she has to realize the benefits to achieve successful results. Indeed, it is likely that any effective intervention needs to be on a human relations level because the mother would probably not read books on parenting at this point. Conversely, encouraging her to read to or with Bobby could enhance their relationship and create an engagement that would fill a currently existing void.

The principal would benefit from being informed of the dynamics behind Bobby's acting out in order that he understand that spanking Bobby will be ineffective. Bobby's inappropriate behavior is a result of his stress environment and trauma conditions. Expressions of his trauma should not be punished. If corporal punishment were the solution, Bobby would have changed from his mother's harsh punishment and control. Bobby would benefit more from encouragement and validation of his importance from school staff than from attempts at behavior management through control and demand. School may be Bobby's only positive source of relationships and encouragement. If the school environment is viewed as a second family setting for Bobby, then school may represent the only safe haven for Bobby from the dilemma he experiences at home.

Bobby is in need of continuous counseling, which could be provided outside the school setting. This would give assistance to the abuse issues from another agency; nevertheless, Bobby's mother would need to cooperate with this process, and it seems she views community resources as a threat to her patterns of functioning.

It is also important for the school counselor to maintain a close relationship with Bobby. The counselor may want to provide Bobby with a security object as a reminder to him that someone cares about him. The object could be anything that represents something positive in his life. It could be a symbolic key chain containing a teddy bear, an animal of his choosing, or a race car if that were his interest. Attached to the object would be a message for him to call if he needed to contact someone for help. If the school counselor runs a children's group, Bobby could make immeasurable gains by learning of the impact that his behaviors have on other children. In addition, Bobby could learn that other children can care about him when they are able to see beyond his aggressive behaviors.

Because abuse is a pattern of behavior, the issues will emerge again, and the counselor will be required to make another report. Some states have requirements that repeatedly reported abuse has to be reinvestigated after three separate reports. The process of resolving Bobby's predicament will likely take time and good documentation.

Response

Lisa Hinkelman

The counselor in this situation has a tremendous responsibility. Not only must she correctly handle the allegations of abuse that Bobby shared with her, she must also ensure his safety and protection while attempting to maintain an effective therapeutic relationship with Bobby. Of additional importance is securing the trust and cooperation of Bobby's mother. In delicate situations concerning sexual abuse allegations, extraordinary care is required on the part of the counselor. One minor misstep can result in additional harm to the child or in the parent's refusal to let the child continue counseling. In this incident, an already difficult situation became more intense because of a visceral reaction from the counselor, the inexperience of the DHS interviewer, and the ensuing reaction from Bobby's mother.

Many counselors feel ill prepared to handle allegations of child abuse (England & Thompson, 1988). It is emphasized to students during counselor preparation programs that reporting allegations of child abuse is a mandate of the profession. However, it is less clear how to actually make this report and how to do so efficiently and effectively while supporting and protecting the abused child. Oftentimes, when child abuse is disclosed in a counseling session, the initial reaction of the counselor is, "I need to report this immediately!" Although it is imperative that the abuse allegation is reported to the proper authorities in a timely manner, the counselor who makes the report must ensure that he or she takes the time to gather the necessary information from the client, document this information, make contact with client's guardian (if appropriate), and then provide support to the client throughout this process.

The counselor working with Bobby should first be commended for listening to him, believing him, and taking swift action. Most children who are experiencing sexual abuse do not report their abuse for fear of not being believed (Finkelhor, 1994). Additionally, sexual abuse survivors may experience anger, guilt, or feelings of responsibility for the abuse (Winton & Mara, 2001). Thus, the most important thing the counselor can do in this situation is communicate to the child that he is believed and that the abuse was not his fault. At such a young age, it is very difficult for Bobby to understand that he did not do anything wrong in this situation. This is particularly true because, as is the case with most incidents of child sexual abuse, it is quite likely that his grandfather told him not to tell anyone or told him something bad would happen to him or his mother if he ever told. Thus, I would reassure Bobby that he did not do anything wrong and that he was brave and strong for telling me about the abuse.

Next, I would want to talk to Bobby a bit more about the interactions with his grandfather and to let him know that it was safe for him to discuss this with me. Some questions I might ask him are, "How long has Pa-Pa been touching you like this?" "When is the last time you can remember this happening?" and, "Have you ever told anyone else what you just told me?" Taking the time to gain this valuable information would assist the counselor in discussions with Child Protective Services and would serve as further documentation in the abuse investigation. If my initial reaction to the abuse allegations is to interrupt the session to call Child Protective Services, it is likely that I have just given Bobby the message that there is big trouble on the horizon and that perhaps he should have kept his secret. It had taken several counseling sessions for Bobby and the counselor to build the appropriate rapport necessary for him to feel that he could share this information; thus, the preservation of the counseling relationship is paramount in this situation.

An explanation to Bobby about what happens next is also vital to the integrity of the counseling relationship. Because of his age, Bobby is unlikely to understand the impact of these disclosures on his young life, and a whirlwind of questions from caseworkers and investigators may serve to further traumatize him. As such, the counselor not only should remind Bobby of the limits of confidentiality but also may want to explain to Bobby the logistics of the investigation. This explanation may include the kinds of questions he may be asked by the investigators, whether he will be required to have a physical exam or go to the hospital, and whether his mother will be present during all of these activities. This should be done in age-appropriate language and in a manner that will serve to reassure him rather than frighten him. Bobby may have questions about what will happen to him or his grandfather. These are difficult questions to answer because the counselor is likely unsure of what, in particular, might happen. It is important once again to preserve the counseling relationship by ensuring that no false promises are made, such as "Everything is going to be okay," "You are going to be safe," or "No one is going to hurt you now."

The uncertainty and apprehension that accompany the act of reporting child abuse exist because the child welfare system is imperfect. Caseworkers and investigators in child protection agencies and human services departments are generally social service workers who lack rigorous training and are underpaid and overworked (Winton & Mara, 2001). There are high rates of burnout and turnover in the child protective agencies, and, despite the best of intentions, many ill-qualified individuals are called onto very serious cases. In this instance, the investigator from DHS was apprehensive to meet with Bobby alone and lacked the requisite skills to conduct an effective interview. Careful questioning and information gathering are vital to the appropriate handling of abuse accusations. Perhaps a more seasoned investigator would have handled this case with greater ease, and the resulting actions taken would have been different.

Personally contacting Bobby's mother is imperative in this situation. His mother is his legal guardian, and, at the outset, there is no indication that she knows about the abuse. Getting Ms. Harris involved with the situation as an ally from the beginning might have served to defuse the blow-up that ensued after the counselor contacted Child Protective Services. Although the counselor is still required to report the abuse to the proper authorities, a personal contact with Bobby's mother may be helpful both in ensuring Bobby's safety and in learning more about Ms. Harris's knowledge of the abuse or about her own history of abuse.

Sexual molestation by a family member accounts for 80% of the child sexual abuse cases in the United States (U.S. Department of Health and Human Services Administration of Children, Youth, and Families, 2005). In interfamilial sexual abuse cases, there are often multiple victims in the same family (Finkelhor, 1994). Because sexual abuse is often a hidden, shameful secret, there can be multiple family members who have been abused by the same perpetrator. On the basis of the reaction of Bobby's mother, this may be the case in the Harris family. The gut reaction of the counselor in assessing the situation after the arrival of Bobby's mother indicated that she believed that Ms. Harris also might have been sexually abused by her father. Although this information may be illuminating to the counselor, a confirmation of the abuse is not required to appropriately address the needs of Bobby, the identified client. Confronting Ms. Harris regarding her own abuse and encouraging her disclosure could be viewed as questionable practices on the part of the counselor. Although knowledge of previous sexual abuse history in the family would assist in the explanation of the present dynamics, the ethical responsibility of the counselor is to her primary client, Bobby— not his mother. Ms. Harris may be wrought with memories from her past and may be blaming herself for her abuse (if this is the case) and for the abuse of her child. As I stated earlier, I would want to involve Ms. Harris immediately in the situation, and perhaps at this point I could talk to her about the fact that perpetrators in the family tend to abuse multiple family members. Other children in the home are also at risk for abuse and should be protected. I would refer Ms. Harris to her own counselor in the event that she was ready to discuss her personal issues.

What is particularly troubling about this case is that Bobby was returned to his home and to the abusive environment. If there is no acknowledgment of the abuse, the message that Bobby received is, "We don't believe you, and we aren't going to protect you." As long as the abuse remains a secret, there is little the counselor can do to help Bobby. There is no therapeutic advancement that can be made if Bobby is still being abused. I expect that the troubling behaviors that Bobby evidenced in counseling will continue and perhaps increase after this incident.

I would continue to be an advocate for Bobby. Clearly, he does not have anyone else in his life who is willing to protect him at this time. I would meticulously document each of our sessions, including Bobby's behavior throughout the session and any disclosures that he made during our work together. Because he is in a therapeutic school environment, I would also speak with the teachers at the school and request that they do the same. In addition to the disruptive behaviors Bobby has evidenced, I would be keenly aware of further behaviors indicative of sexual abuse. These behaviors may include an increased awareness of sexuality compared with other children his age, masturbation while at school, inappropriate sex play with peers, guilt, shame, increased anxiety, and self-destructive behaviors (Tower, 1999; Winton & Mara, 2001).

If I continued to believe that the sexual abuse was present, I would once again call Child Protective Services and make a formal report. As Bobby's counselor, my ability to have a therapeutic impact or provide helpful interventions for Bobby would be limited if he were not free from the abusive environment.

References

England, L. W., & Thompson, C. L. (1988). Counseling child sexual assault victims: Myths and realities. *Journal of Counseling & Development, 66,* 370–373.

Finkelhor, D. (1994). The international epidemiology of child sexual abuse. *Child Abuse and Neglect, 18,* 409–417.

Tower, C. C. (1999). *Understanding child abuse and neglect* (4th ed.). Boston: Allyn & Bacon.

U.S. Department of Health and Human Services Administration on Children, Youth, and Families. (2005). *Child maltreatment 2003.* Washington, DC: U.S. Government Printing Office.

Winton, M. A., & Mara, B. A. (2001). *Child abuse and neglect: Multidisciplinary approaches.* Boston: Allyn & Bacon.

12

"Don't Talk!": Trauma and Dissociation in Play Therapy

This incident explores the manifestation of dissociation in play therapy and examines the complexities and potential dangers of reporting suspected child abuse when a custodial parent is the suspected perpetrator.

▪ Critical Incident

Heather M. Helm and Marilyn S. Snow

Benjamin Briggs, a 4-year-old Caucasian boy, began play therapy sessions with me while his parents were in the process of getting a contentious divorce. His father and paternal grandmother initiated contact and reported that Benjamin was acting "bizarre" and having frequent outbreaks of rage. During an intake session with the director of the play therapy center, Benjamin's father and grandmother explained that he was hitting his cousins and had, at one point, beaten the family dog with a coat hanger. Additionally, Mr. Briggs reported that he found Benjamin in the bedroom "playing with himself." When he asked Benjamin where he learned that, Benjamin reportedly said his mother did "it" to him in the bathtub.

Concerned about possible child abuse, Mr. Briggs indicated that he had immediately contacted his lawyer about Benjamin's disclosure. The attorney advised Mr. Briggs to have Benjamin examined by a local physician who specialized in forensic examinations of abuse. On the basis of his examination of Benjamin, the doctor made a report to the Department of Human Services (DHS), and a DHS caseworker then interviewed Benjamin. During the DHS interview, Benjamin reported to them that his mother touched him when he was in the bathtub. On questioning Ms. Briggs about Benjamin's allegations, however, DHS closed the case and indicated that Ms. Briggs explained that she "had to touch him when giving him a bath" and that she was not abusing her son.

Although DHS was satisfied with the explanation offered by Benjamin's mother, Mr. Briggs remained concerned and decided to pursue sole custody of his son. During his initial intake at our play therapy center, he explained that, given DHS's response, he believed that the only way he could protect Benjamin was to bring up the sexual abuse allegation in court. He further explained that the court date to finalize the divorce would be occurring approximately 1 month from the date of our intake.

After a brief time on our waiting list, Benjamin began play therapy sessions with me. I was a master's level counselor and worked under the supervision of the center's director. At the beginning, I was able to see Benjamin only every 2 weeks because these were the weeks his father had physical custody of him. During our child-centered play therapy sessions, Benjamin showed a great deal of aggression toward the stuffed animals in the playroom. He pretended to cut them up and described in detail how he was cutting them: "I'm cutting him down the middle." During his initial sessions, Benjamin also routinely played out a scene with the bathtub in the dollhouse. He would make no comments about this play even though I would verbally track the activity.

Shortly after we began, Benjamin's father and mother went to court to finalize their divorce. Although the judge apparently refused to admit the medical report from the doctor who performed the initial examination and made the report to DHS, the judge did stipulate that Benjamin's parents must continue his counseling and required his mother to also bring him every other week. From that point forward, I was able to meet with Benjamin on a weekly basis and to compare his play during weeks with his dad and during weeks with his mom.

After the divorce settlement, Benjamin's mother contacted the center and arranged to meet with the director while Benjamin was in a play therapy session with me. During this meeting, Ms. Briggs maintained that she did not see anything wrong with Benjamin. When confronted about situations such as Benjamin's violent behavior toward the dog, she responded that she thought that was "simply what little boys do." Regarding the sexual abuse allegations, Ms. Briggs simply stated that they were not true and alleged that her ex-husband was making them up in an attempt to "take Benjamin away."

On this same day, when I told Benjamin that our time together was over for the day and that his mother was waiting for him in the consultation room, he became visibly upset, handcuffed himself to me, and picked up a sword before allowing us to proceed to the consultation room where his mother was meeting with the director. As Benjamin entered the room, he went directly to his mother, pointed the sword at her face, and told her he did not want to leave. He remained upset and refused to leave the center. When the director asked Ms. Briggs about Benjamin's current aggressive behavior, she again stated that she thought that was "just how little boys act." I walked Benjamin to the car, watched while his mother had to physically put him in the car, and listened helplessly while Benjamin cried and pleadingly screamed, "I don't want to go home." He had not demonstrated any such reluctance to leave our previous sessions, all of which he attended while accompanied by his father. I was curious to see whether he would display similar distress in future sessions when accompanied by either parent.

As we continued with our sessions, I began to notice a substantial difference in Benjamin's behavior and his themes in the playroom depending on which parent brought him to the center. When his mother brought him, Benjamin's play was aggressive, and he consistently demonstrated more dissociative behaviors. When his father brought him, Benjamin demonstrated a greater capacity to self-regulate emotion and to remain present in his play.

Although Benjamin was frequently dissociative in his sessions, one session in particular stands out in my mind. To begin his session, Benjamin pulled the table close to the paint board, put the paint on the table, and began to chaotically paint the board. Benjamin explained that he was painting different animals. At one point, he painted a "fence" around the animal so it "couldn't get out." Throughout this process, Benjamin told me repeatedly that his mother would like the painting. After saying this, he would step back from his painting and flail his arms and hands in quick, jerking movements while jumping up and down. At one point in the session, Benjamin spilled the paint. When he eventually noticed the paint on the floor, he looked confused and asked me, "Who spilled that paint?" Similar behavior continued throughout this session.

When I informed Benjamin that only 5 minutes were remaining in this session, he became extremely distressed and again told me that he did not want to go home. When I said it was time to end the session, Benjamin started painting the door, stating, "They can't get in and we can't get out." As I continued to call time, he painted the doorknob and then a line in front of the door. At one point Benjamin looked directly at the camera and, with a distressed look on his face, said, "I don't want to go home."

After reviewing the video with me, the center director decided that it was imperative that another forensic interview be conducted. Many of Benjamin's behaviors seemed to point to ongoing abuse. Because DHS in the county where Benjamin lived had closed the case, the director of the center contacted the police department of the county where the center was located and asked whether the report could be given in that county. The police officer stated that he would take the report, and, after reviewing the tape, the officer agreed to investigate the case. Benjamin's father was notified that a report was being made, but his mother was not notified at that time because of concerns for Benjamin's safety. Unfortunately, despite the police officer's desire to pursue the investigation, he notified the center director that ultimately he could not do so because the judge who was initially involved in the case refused to order the forensic interview as requested.

In desperation, Benjamin's father contacted his lawyer, and they decided to make contact with Ms. Briggs's lawyer in an attempt to persuade Benjamin's mother to consent to another forensic interview. In response, Ms. Briggs's attorney contacted the director of our play therapy center. When the director expressed our concerns about Benjamin's welfare, the attorney responded by reminding the director that the role of a counselor is not to engage in investigative work and suggested that we focus on maintaining the therapeutic relationship with Benjamin rather than investigating his client. Just a few days after this conversation, Benjamin's mother brought him to his session. She did not mention any conversation with her lawyer, yet Benjamin played out the following scenario.

At the beginning of the session, Benjamin was aggressive toward me. As he angrily gathered all the knives and swords in the room and moved them to the table and I attempted to verbally track his play, he said to me, "Don't talk!" Each time I spoke, he put a knife up to my throat and said, "Don't talk!" He continued gathering the swords and moving them around the room while intermittently pointing them at my throat. When I set limits and reminded him that I am not for cutting, he pointed a knife at me and yelled, "I said . . . *don't talk*!" Throughout this play, Benjamin threatened to cut me up and put me in the oven or freezer. At one point, he turned to me and said that someone was going to come and let me out. Benjamin proceeded to get the handcuffs and a handful of beaded necklaces to tie my hands. He continued to tell me not to talk.

About 25 minutes into the session, after he tied my hands together, he briefly turned his back toward me. When he turned back around, he asked, "Who tied you up?" and immediately untied me. He appeared confused and asked many questions about his surroundings. He then sat down in the chair at the table and offered me Kool-Aid. I asked Benjamin whether he knew who tied me up, and the following conversation ensued.

Benjamin: I don't know. I was in my mama's car.
Me: You were in your car when I was tied up.
Benjamin: Yeah, I was coming here.
Me: So you don't know who tied me up.
Benjamin: Yeah, Benjamin.
Me: Oh, Benjamin tied me up?
Benjamin: (clearly frustrated) No, I'm Benjamin (and he pointed at himself).
Benjamin: The bad man tied you up.

Benjamin then gathered up the weapons and stated that he would "make the bad man go away." I asked, "You know how to protect yourself?" "No, I know how to protect you," he replied. Benjamin spent the remainder of the session creating ways to keep the bad man away. During the last 5 minutes of the session, Benjamin began "cutting up the bad man" and cooking him, and he offered me body parts to eat.

In this session, it seemed that Benjamin might have been threatened to keep quiet. His repeated admonition to not talk seemed to indicate that not only had he been threatened, he was also concerned about what I might be telling. I, along with my director, continued to be greatly concerned about Benjamin's safety and vulnerability. The center director and I continued to believe that Benjamin had been abused by his mother and that the posttraumatic stress disorder symptomatology and dissociative features of his play indicated significant traumatic material. After this session, we also became increasingly concerned that our efforts to protect Benjamin had ultimately resulted in his exposure to additional trauma. If only the detective had been able to convince the judge to order the forensic evaluation, his mother would not have been alerted to our concerns and might not have retaliated.

Benjamin's mother did not agree to the forensic evaluation as requested by Mr. Briggs. Instead, she took Benjamin to a neighboring city for a psychological evaluation. The psychologist assessed Benjamin's symptoms as representative of a significant degree of psychological distress and recommended that she continue to bring him to play therapy at the center.

After this evaluation, Benjamin's mother became increasingly compliant with therapy. As therapy progressed, Benjamin's behavior at home became much less disturbed. He was less dissociative in the playroom, and his affect was significantly less frightened and anxious. It was reported that he stopped torturing animals and became more socially appropriate with other children. When trying to make sense of the reasons for Benjamin's significant improvement, we speculated that either his mother became increasingly aware of appropriate versus inappropriate behavior with Benjamin or, despite ongoing abuse, Benjamin was able to use therapy to find new ways to cope.

Questions

1. How can we protect vulnerable children from becoming even more victimized when we have to involve the law and the legal system?
2. Because the role of the nondirective play therapist is not one of investigator and the abuse was not substantiated in any way, would it have been better not to push for the forensic evaluation or try to uncover what was happening to Benjamin?
3. From a nondirective perspective, which de-emphasizes diagnosis and maintains a firm belief in a child's capacity to heal given the right conditions, how are dissociative symptoms best managed in the playroom?

■ Response

Vera B. Triplett

The case of young Benjamin, although startling to some, is a relatively common one faced by professional counselors. Unfortunately, because child abuse laws vary from state to state, there is no universal format to follow in situations such as the one described in the incident. Nonetheless, professional counselors are mandatory reporters, and the mandate is clear: If we have a reasonably good faith suspicion that a child is being abused, it is our statutory responsibility to report it. Experience has taught me that we cannot always protect children like Benjamin from the wrath of their abusers, at least not in the way suggested by the counselor in this case. The best way that we can protect them is by continuing to do our jobs as counselors and advocates. On the basis of the description of events, the counselor's course of action was warranted and appropriate. Conversely, the description of the actions of others involved in this case reinforces my view that there needs to be a more multidisciplinary approach to all child abuse investigations. When a child's case is discussed, all professionals involved in the case—including the forensic interviewer, the district attorney's office, and the detective—should be present to hear the facts of the case. Perhaps then the district attorney or a representative of his or her office would be able to make a more convincing argument to a judge.

Given this information, the short answer to this question is that the best way to protect children like Benjamin is to do one's job the best one can. Do not be discouraged by bureaucracy. Remember that counselors are trained to see what others cannot. If a counselor stays the course, he or she will see results and ultimately provide both physical and emotional safety to the client.

In regard to the question about the role of the play therapist and whether it would have been better not to push for the forensic evaluation, the answer is clear. The counselor absolutely should not attempt to help a child by not pursuing an investigation. To ignore the implications of what was happening to this child would have been criminally negligent. As the counselor stated in the critical incident, play therapists are not investigators. Nevertheless, counselors who work with children should always have a direct line to someone who is. In most states, there are police units assigned specifically to investigate child abuse suspicions and allegations. Those units are responsible for investigating or uncovering what is happening to children like Benjamin. The counselor's request for another forensic evaluation was a responsible and reasonable response to Benjamin's behavior in sessions.

The thing to always keep in mind is that a counselor's actions as advocate should not undermine the therapeutic process. Once a judicial ruling has been handed down related to a request for child abuse investigation, one can only operate within the confines of that ruling. If new information comes to light, of course, a new judicial ruling may be rendered. Counselors should never lose sight of the big picture; any action taken on behalf of a client should focus on the best interest of the client and the therapeutic relationship.

With respect to the counselor's question about how dissociative symptoms might be best managed in a nondirective play therapy approach, it is important to recognize that dissociative behavior can provide valuable information about the inner world of a client. As a nondirective play therapist, the counselor's charge is to operate in the reality the child is displaying at that time. In Benjamin's case, his dissociative tendencies were so severe that he did not immediately remember them. Some children never remember the behaviors they exhibit when they are in that zone. For the counselor, the education is priceless. Witnessing the dissociative behaviors provides the counselor with an educational opportunity to learn about the client from these behaviors. For the child, the opportunity to express the anomalies of his or her subconscious in a safe environment may be critical to therapeutic healing. I feel that the best approach is not to interfere unless the child is a true danger to the counselor, himself or herself, or others. These dissociative episodes can provide important information about the child and his or her capacity for healing.

Response

Michael M. Morgan and Serena M. Lambert

In his classic tale of environmental destruction, *The Lorax*, Geisel (1971) introduced the reader to the Lorax, a typical Dr. Seuss character, who declared, "I am the Lorax, I speak for the trees. I speak for the trees, for the trees have no tongues" (p. 23). As play therapists who work with abused or neglected children, we often find ourselves in the position of the Lorax—speaking for those who cannot speak for themselves. The story of Benjamin Briggs clearly illustrates not only how heart wrenching and difficult this can be but also how essential. As respondents, we appreciate the quality of care and services Benjamin received, from both a therapeutic and an advocacy standpoint.

The counselor posed three thoughtful questions about her work. Most of us who have worked with children have probably asked these very questions, either to a colleague or to ourselves. In addressing these questions, we begin with the second. In essence, this question asks, "How far should we go to uncover abuse?" The question does not seem to be about the propriety of reporting. With mandatory reporting laws, counselors have no choice but to report any abuse that they suspect, just as this counselor did. Instead, the question seems to ask whether counselors should continue to pursue an investigation of suspected abuse after an initial report is not substantiated. We believe that, within reasonable limits, such efforts serve the vulnerable child. The issue of substantiation has more to do with legal standards and prosecutorial decisions than with whether the abuse occurred. As such, when additional clinical evidence suggests a continuing problem, as in Benjamin's case, we argue that the counselor has an ongoing duty to alert those who can protect the child.

One of the interesting things about this case is that Benjamin, in what seems to have been a dissociative state, explicitly demanded that the therapist keep quiet. Such a passionate demand by a 4-year-old child, particularly in the context of the case, might suggest an increased sense of urgency for help. We were pleased to see that the counselor felt likewise and made an additional effort to legally substantiate what seemed so clear clinically. Although legally nothing happened, we believe that this additional effort likely encouraged Benjamin's mother to alter her behavior. Few counselors want to adopt an investigative role, but we are duty bound—both ethically and morally—to do whatever we can to protect our child clients because they cannot protect themselves.

Nonetheless, we are also aware of the need to be very careful when reporting abuse. Working with children in abusive situations often triggers powerful emotional reactions in counselors (Gil, 1991), and it can be easy to let one's emotional countertransference control one's decision making. In our mind, there are two important ways to protect against this. First, we strongly believe that all counselors need to constantly work on their own self-awareness and emotional and mental health (Lum, 2002). Counselors who do so are less likely to be controlled by their emotional reactions to clients. Second, as the counselor did in this case, consultation with trusted colleagues and supervisors is essential to inform one's appropriate response to legal, ethical, and moral dilemmas.

Given mandatory reporting requirements and our belief that additional reports may be warranted in some cases, how should counselors protect children from additional trauma caused by the reporting process? This concern is likely responsible for some counselors deciding not to report suspected abuse. Although we advocate fulfilling the mandatory reporting responsibility, we understand the concern and the desire to protect children from further harm. It seems that the counselor's continued efforts to protect Benjamin through legal means, although never legally successful, indeed might have provided the safety he needed. In essence, the counselor demonstrated that as long as Benjamin's behavior clearly suggested ongoing harm, she was going to advocate for his safety.

Our own approach to working with children relies heavily on attachment theory. One of the features shared by attachment theory and child-centered play therapy is the importance of the relationship with the therapist. Both theories assert that the relationship plays a major role in therapeutic change (Landreth, 2002; Munns, 2003). For us, the fact that Benjamin has in the counselor an adult who is readily and consistently available and who responds appropriately to his needs is perhaps the most important thing, next to ending the abuse, that can be done to protect him. Stern's (2002) concept of attunement—an accurate recognition of and response to the child's needs—suggests that Benjamin's therapist was building the kind of healthy attachment relationship he needed. Evidence is growing that such a relationship can serve as a protective factor against long-term negative impacts of abuse (Rak & Patterson, 1996). Counselors who work with abused children may feel powerless when they are unable to stop the abuse, but they should know that in their sensitive, responsive work with these children, they are perhaps doing everything possible to facilitate resiliency.

The final question posed by the counselor was about how dissociative symptoms are best managed in the playroom. Leading play therapists consider dissociation a common reaction to sexual and other forms of abuse (Homeyer & Landreth, 1998). Nonetheless, there is very little in the literature to suggest how best to work with children who present dissociative symptoms. Perhaps the best source is Gil's (1991) classic on working with abused children, in which she outlined several techniques for addressing dissociation. We highlight a few of these techniques on the basis of the specifics of Benjamin's case and our own beliefs about working with children.

In our view, the first thing for counselors to remember is that the dissociation is an adaptive coping mechanism, providing often powerless children with a means for containing unmanageable experiences and emotions. For Benjamin, this might have meant two things. First, the abuse itself was likely so overwhelming psychologically that it led to a pressure valve sort of dissociation. Thoughts or feelings too closely linked to the abuse, or even just spending time with his mother, might have triggered Benjamin's dissociative coping states. Second, Benjamin might have felt powerless to directly communicate with the counselor his experiences related to her attempts to legally substantiate the abuse. His behavior suggests the possibility that his mother was forcefully demanding his silence. To complicate matters, Benjamin might have felt anxious and ambivalent about the counselor's advocacy efforts and their possible impact on his mother's behavior and his own relationship with her.

In both cases, Benjamin was faced with a double bind—a desire to avoid and escape the abuse and a need to maintain the important relationships with his mother and with the play therapist. To directly name and address this situation and the emotional conflict it created seems to have been too threatening for Benjamin and is likely beyond any 4-year-old's developmental abilities. As a consequence, a dissociative state provided a safe way for Benjamin to communicate his experience and conflicted feelings about both his mother and his counselor while not having to directly deal with them. It was Benjamin saying and doing those things, but, at the same time, it was not Benjamin.

How should a counselor respond? Although the state is dissociative, the needs and emotions being expressed are very much a part of Benjamin's (or any other dissociative child's) experience and should be given the same sort of care and attention as nondissociative material. Returning to the attachment idea of attunement, we note that what the child needs is a caring adult who will consistently recognize and then appropriately attend to her or his needs. When the child is in a dissociative state, the limits and rules for the playroom should still apply, although they might need to be reintroduced and reinforced. Barring safety needs, we do not believe that any attempt should be made to "bring the child back" while he or she is dissociating. The child is dissociating for a reason, and counselors do better to respond at the level of that need rather than to react to the dissociation itself. This belief appears to echo Benjamin's counselor's stated belief that, with a healthy therapeutic relationship, children have an inherent capacity to heal.

Dissociation may be frightening to children, who may "come to" not knowing where they are or what is going on. Gil (1991) encouraged therapists to normalize and find a language to speak about the dissociation with the child. We might say to Benjamin, "Sometimes when we feel scared, we might 'space out' or 'go away' for a while, and this can be nice," or, "Sometimes part of us needs to say something, but another part of us is afraid to, so part of us might space out." Then, when Benjamin dissociates in session, we could afterward say, "It seems like you spaced out for a little while, but you're back now," and then address the child's underlying needs. Gil also suggested that counselors help children recognize that dissociation can be a choice and then help them develop other coping skills for dealing with the difficult emotions that trigger their dissociations.

With Benjamin, we would work to name the emotions he is likely having. Because of his age, we might need to work more at a nonverbal level—perhaps with colors, puppets, facial expressions, or other symbolic means that could help identify and normalize his emotions. This perhaps falls somewhat outside the normal routine of a strictly nondirective play therapist, who may instead wish to identify and name those emotions as they emerge in the child's play. We would also work to identify Benjamin's repertoire for self-soothing. If he has a comfort object (blanket, stuffed animal, etc.), we would invite him to bring it to therapy and suggest that he always take it to his mom's house. If he brought such an object to therapy, we would watch to see whether he spontaneously used it in the course of the play and, if not, might suggest its use with a question when we noticed emotional struggles: "I wonder whether holding teddy would help?"

We might invite Benjamin to create a safe place in the play room, which would communicate our confidence in his ability to create some safety for himself while also helping us to understand how he uniquely perceives safety. We would also likely work closely with Benjamin's father to develop some special rituals that communicate safety, nondemanding love, and caring. Appropriate touch through cuddling or hand games might be particularly important, given that touch might have been powerfully corrupted in the abuse yet is such an important part of healthy human attachment. If ever possible, we would love to make Benjamin's mom a part of the process and help her develop some healthy ways of connecting with her son, perhaps with a filial approach.

Our goal with these more active interventions would be to acknowledge the function of the dissociation and then to strengthen other coping resources so that the child had some choice for how to manage the situation. We were touched by Benjamin's story; as we read it, we saw the faces of many children with whom we have worked and whose voices were also silenced by their abuse. We applaud Helm and Snow for their tender approach with Benjamin, their faith in his ability to heal, and mostly for their willingness to be his surrogate voice.

References

Geisel, T. (1971). *The Lorax.* New York: Random House.

Gil, E. (1991). *The healing power of play: Working with abused children.* New York: Guilford Press.

Homeyer, L. E., & Landreth, G. L. (1998). Play therapy behaviors of sexually abused children. *International Journal of Play Therapy, 7,* 49–71.

Landreth, G. L. (2002). *Play therapy: The art of the relationship* (2nd ed.). New York: Brunner-Routledge.

Lum, W. (2002). The use of self of the therapist. *Contemporary Family Therapy, 24,* 181–197.

Munns, E. (2003). Theraplay: Attachment-enhancing play therapy. In C. E. Schaefer (Ed.), *Foundations of play therapy* (pp. 156–174). Hoboken, NJ: Wiley.

Rak, C. F., & Patterson, L. E. (1996). Promoting resilience in at-risk children. *Journal of Counseling & Development, 74,* 368–373.

Stern, D. N. (2002). *The first relationship: Infant and mother.* Cambridge, MA: Harvard University Press.

Part

III

Diversity Issues

13

"My Name Is Samantha, Not Sammy!": Gender Identity

This incident explores the dynamics of childhood gender identity development and its impact on a child and the foster parents. Complexities regarding language, case conceptualization, and differential diagnoses are discussed, and multiple intervention strategies are considered.

■ Critical Incident

Linda L. Black

"Sammy Ramos," a bright-eyed 10-year-old boy, sat in the corner of the waiting room tightly clutching a much-loved teddy bear. His foster parents, "Sue and Jason Sadler," sat next to him, quietly paging through magazines. I had met the Sadlers 2 months earlier at a foster parent education and training seminar and was now assigned to Sammy's case as a residential support therapist (RST). The position of RST was created through the collective efforts of the local Department of Social Services (DSS) and the county mental health center to serve and maintain the placements of children in foster care. My role with this family was to provide counseling services for Sammy, his family of origin, and his foster parents, with the goal of supporting his eventual return to his family of origin.

Because the treatment approach focused on the family as a system, it was important that all family members have the opportunity to provide information. I therefore invited Mr. and Mrs. Sadler to accompany Sammy into my office for the intake evaluation. As I called them by name, Sammy mumbled something that was inaudible to me. When I bent over and quietly asked him to repeat what he had said, he rolled his eyes and clucked his tongue with what seemed to be mild disdain. At the same time, Mr. and Mrs. Sadler exchanged a glance that clearly communicated, "Oh, here we go again." I began the intake session by describing my role in serving them as a family and in serving Sammy individually. I explained that we would meet sometimes in my office and at other times in their home. I emphasized that I wanted to see Sammy in multiple settings (foster home, school, agency) for treatment. Mr. and Mrs. Sadler looked simultaneously relieved and anxious. Sammy seemed mildly interested in this information yet detached. I asked what was going on in their family and how I could be helpful.

I then asked Mr. and Mrs. Sadler to begin by sharing basic information about themselves and Sammy. They indicated that they had been married 20 years and had two children—"Elyse," age 14, and "Tom," age 16. They reported that their marriage was stable and strong. Mr. Sadler worked for a local high-tech company as a midlevel manager, and Mrs. Sadler had taught elementary school for 12 years before deciding to resign and become a foster parent. They reported having had a total of five foster children in their home over the past 2 years and expressed that they generally enjoyed the experiences. In addition to Sammy and their two children, Mr. and Mrs. Sadler were also providing foster care for a 6-year-old boy named "Gus."

Mr. and Mrs. Sadler indicated that Sammy had been in foster care with them for 8 months after he was removed from his mother's home for the third time in 5 years. Mr. Sadler reported that Sammy was occasionally anxious and sometimes had difficulty sleeping. When he first arrived in their home, Sammy had some occasional bed wetting and nightmares, but he had not had any difficulty with either behavior for the past 2 months. The Sadlers described Sammy's daytime behavior as clingy toward Mrs. Sadler and cautious toward Mr. Sadler. Often, Sammy was in the kitchen or followed Mrs. Sadler around as she did her household tasks. Mr. Sadler recounted that, each time he invited Sammy to play a board game or participate in an activity with him, Sammy simply said, "No thanks, I don't like sports."

Mr. and Mrs. Sadler also reported that his teachers described Sammy as "shy to the point of painfulness." He seemed to have few friends and was reluctant to engage in play with same-gendered peers. Mrs. Sadler added that his teacher believed that Sammy's social behavior was more like that of a second or third grader instead of a fourth grader. Academically, Sammy was just at or slightly below grade level in all subject areas.

As I listened to Mr. and Mrs. Sadler, I noticed that Sammy sat quietly and engaged appropriately when asked to confirm or add detail. When I had heard from the Sadlers, I then focused the intake evaluation on Sammy. Sammy said he had no problems to talk about and stated that he liked the Sadlers' house. He specifically offered that he really liked having an older sister around.

By this point, I was uncertain why this family had been referred for counseling. The issues described by Mr. and Mrs. Sadler seemed normal for children in foster placements, and the Sadlers already seemed to be effectively addressing the concerns with a fair degree of skill. When I wondered out loud how my services could help them, a stillness set over the room. Mrs. Sadler cleared her throat and was about to say something when Sammy burst out, "My name is Samantha, not Sammy, and I am a girl!"

"Sammy!" Mrs. Sadler said in an elevated tone, "We have been over this a hundred times. You are a boy, not a girl! Girls have different bodies than yours. You are a boy!" Mr. Sadler slumped back in his chair, seemingly embarrassed and frustrated, while Mrs. Sadler recounted how Sammy's behavior had grown increasingly odd in the last

6 months. She said it began 6 months ago, when Sammy announced that he wanted to be called Samantha because he was a girl. He refused to answer to any other name. (Ah! This explained his disdain with me in the waiting room. To him, I had called him by an inappropriate name.) Next, Mrs. Sadler found Sammy trying on Elyse's clothing, makeup, and perfume. Then, on the school bus 6 weeks ago, Sammy announced to his seatmate that he was really a girl and that his name was Samantha. This led to a great deal of teasing and harassment from his classmates and the older kids on the bus and at school. Finally, 10 days ago, while shopping with the family, Sammy was stopped by store security and was found to have shoplifted girls' clothing and a purse.

Mr. and Mrs. Sadler stated that they were at their wits' end. "That's why we're here," said Mr. Sadler in a resigned tone. "Sammy thinks he's a girl, and we wonder if he may be . . .," and continued in a hushed tone, "homosexual. We don't know what to do for him. There's no cure for that, right? Is he just, you know, that way?"

I responded by saying, "All we know for sure is that Sammy has been through a lot in his life and, up to 6 months ago, thought he was a boy. Now he feels that he is a girl and wants to be called Samantha." I let the Sadlers and Sammy know that I would need to be in contact with Sammy's DSS caseworker and his biological parents to gather more information. At this point, Sammy got out of his chair, came over to me, and softly said, "Tell my mom I said hi."

I shared with Sammy and the Sadlers that gender identity and sexual orientation are related but separate processes of human development. I explained that gender identity is typically considered a general, internal sense that people have regarding their maleness or femaleness and the degree of congruence between their biological sex and societally based gender roles. I further explained that sexual orientation describes the affectional orientation of a person toward the same or different gender. Mr. and Mrs. Sadler looked at me blankly. Thus ended our first session.

Following the intake evaluation, I contacted Sammy's caseworker and learned that Sammy's mother had been a victim of repeated domestic violence and that she had a history of drug abuse, theft, and prostitution. She was currently serving a 2-year sentence in the state women's correctional facility and had 16 months remaining. The caseworker indicated that Sammy's mother did not know who Sammy's father was. Therefore, if Sammy were to be returned to his family of origin prior to his mother's release from prison, it would be into the kinship care of his maternal grandmother.

As I synthesized what I had so far learned about Sammy, the nature and etiology of his symptoms seemed to indicate a history of mild to moderate anxiety, dysthymia, and occasional disturbance in his conduct. His symptoms seemed to worsen when he was removed from his mother's home. I diagnosed Sammy with an unspecific adjustment disorder, chronic type (Code 309.9 in the *Diagnostic and Statistical Manual of Mental Disorders*; 4th ed., text rev.; *DSM–IV–TR*; American Psychiatric Association, 2000), given the diffuse yet chronic nature and intensity of his symptoms. I decided to consider gender identity disorder in children (Code 302.6) as a rule-out or provisional diagnosis because (a) some of Sammy's behaviors might be reflective of separation anxiety as a result of his removal from his home rather than as a result of gender confusion, (b) the extent and pervasiveness of Sammy's gender dysphoric symptoms did not yet seem to have reached a profound level, and (c) Sammy had not specifically articulated a desire to have his penis or testicles removed.

I also decided to use a nondirective play therapy approach, partly because Sammy seemed to be developmentally younger than his chronological age. I described my treatment approach to Sammy and the Sadlers, and I explained that Sammy would be allowed to move at his own pace. When Sammy arrived for our first individual session, he entered the play therapy room with some hesitation and caution. He asked me to call him Samantha, and I agreed to do so. After investigating all the toys in the room, Samantha then focused on the dollhouse, girls' dress-up clothes, and tea sets. Samantha appeared to play comfortably with toys, rarely looking at me for confirmation, and, by the third session, began to talk freely about "being a girl." Samantha said s/he liked that girls were soft and how good they smelled. S/he asked me frequently whether I liked being a girl.

Prior to every play therapy session, I met with Mr. and Mrs. Sadler to discuss Sammy's behavior at home and school. In our second meeting, I had intended to discuss the printed information I had given them about social learning theory, gender identity formation, and the development of sexual orientation in children. When we met, Mrs. Sadler said that she and her husband really wanted me to just tell Sammy to "stop this behavior" because allowing him to engage in it only made it worse. They said that Sammy had become even more isolated at school and that they were very worried that Sammy's behavior would "encourage Gus to be a girl as well." Mrs. Sadler said that they believed that Sammy was only behaving this way to "get attention" or because maybe he "was gay."

Mr. Sadler reported that he had told Sammy that God had made him a boy and that by wanting to be a girl or by being gay, he would anger God. Mr. and Mrs. Sadler remarked sadly that they were not sure they could keep Sammy in their home unless he changed his behavior. I discussed with them that their support of him was crucial to his progress in treatment, even though his contention that he was female seemed difficult to understand and perhaps even odd and troubling. I indicated that I was not certain of the origins or reasons for Sammy's behavior at this time and that to simply quash his behavior could be counterproductive. We discussed that his behavior could be related to a disordered adjustment to his previous environment and recent placement in foster care or a sign that he felt safe enough in their home to express who he really was. When my comments seemed to provide little relief, I asked what part of Sammy's behavior was most troublesome for them. They responded that, because Sammy knew he was a boy, supporting this behavior was akin to allowing him to lie. At this point, Mr. and Mrs. Sadler also refused my request to conduct a home visit.

In Play Therapy Sessions 4 through 8, Sammy dressed up in girls' clothing and used a falsetto voice to play out scenes in which male characters violently attacked female characters, who were, in turn, rescued by a strong female champion. Sammy's play was graphic in its violence, but by the end of each session, the female victims had been dramatically rescued from harm. From time to time during his play, Sammy remarked, "Girls are better than boys because they are not so mean." The manifest content of Sammy's play paralleled the real life events reported by his caseworker. He seemed to be working through much of what he had witnessed earlier in life.

After the fourth session, Mr. and Mrs. Sadler declined to meet with me for presession case management. They mentioned in passing, however, that Sammy had not had any nightmares and that, although still odd, he seemed calmer. Despite my repeated attempts to reengage them in the process by having them attend presession case management sessions, Mr. and Mrs. Sadler refused and expressed a preference for remaining in the waiting room. Contacts with Sammy's school counselor and teacher indicated that he was making friends with a couple of girls in his class but that he was still demonstrating gender-incongruent behavior (speaking in a falsetto voice and asking to be called Samantha). Sammy seemed to be making progress despite his foster parents' discomfort and reluctance to join treatment.

In the 8th week of treatment, Mrs. Sadler called to cancel Sammy's standing appointment. The next week, his DSS caseworker called to tell me that Sammy had been hospitalized after threatening suicide and would not be returning to foster care. Apparently, Sammy had worn a dress to church under his pants and shirt. After Sunday school, he removed his pants and shirt and joined Mr. and Mrs. Sadler in the sanctuary wearing a dress. He was immediately taken home, and a family fight ensued. When Sammy then threatened to kill himself, Mr. and Mrs. Sadler asked that he be permanently removed from their home. Because Sammy's treatment did not come to a successful completion with me, I am left wondering whether he truly was experiencing gender identity disorder or whether he was simply coping with a previously violent environment in the best way he knew.

Questions

1. What are additional approaches I could have used to determine whether Sammy was experiencing a gender identity disorder?
2. How can counselors best determine whether gender dysphoria represents a gender identity disorder, is reflective of the developmental process, or is symptomatic of another underlying problem?
3. How can counselors help parents and/or caregivers understand the nature of gender identity development in the context of childhood development, homophobia, and the narrow societal images of gender?
4. How can one distinguish, early on, between gender identity and sexual orientation?

■ Response

Hugh C. Crethar and Shannon B. Dermer

The case of Samantha is an interesting one because it challenges one's notions of sex, gender, and affectional (sexual) orientation and how they are related. If one defines these concepts in dichotomous terms (e.g., a person is either a boy or a girl, masculine or feminine, heterosexual or homosexual), then it is easy to define whether someone fits or does not fit into one category. Although it is easier to categorize people using dichotomous terms, it negates diversity and is not an accurate reflection of human variance. What should we do with the Samanthas of the world, and how should we define health when a child does not fit the socially prescribed concepts of normal? Is intervention most appropriate at the individual or the societal level?

The case description of Samantha and her foster parents presents examples of insightful work with gender-variant children as well as areas for increased sensitivity and improvement. The RST approached both the foster parents and Samantha with kindness, understanding, and a psychoeducational perspective. Nonetheless, we have suggestions for additional information that should have been gathered and suggestions for how to present the case in a manner more embracing of gender-variant people.

Sex, Gender, and Affectional Orientation

This counselor, to her credit, explained the difference between gender identity and affectional orientation and tried to give more developmental information to the foster parents. She did not, however, demonstrate the same clarity regarding the constructs of sex and gender. For many, the terms *sex*, *gender*, and *affectional (sexual) orientation* are confusing. Although they are related in some ways, they are not the same.

Although *sex* and *gender* tend to be used interchangeably, they have quite different meanings. Sex is the system of classification based on biological and physical differences, such as primary and secondary sexual characteristics, which create the categories male and female. Between these categories exist a wide variety of people with more ambiguous sexual characteristics. An intersex person is one whose genitalia, reproductive organs, or secondary sex characteristics are not exclusively male or female. A more archaic and less preferred term for intersex people is *hermaphrodite*.

Gender, conversely, is a system of sexual classification based on the social construction of the polar categories masculine = men and boys and feminine = women and girls. Between these categories exist combinations of gender, with androgyny located at the center. The term *androgyny* refers to two concepts: (a) the blending of masculine and feminine characteristics, or (b) a person who is perceived as neither masculine nor feminine. Thus, androgynous traits are commonly seen as those that either have no gender value or have some aspects generally attributed to the opposite gender. A person's gender does not inherently correspond with a person's sex. This is because sexual identity is more objective in nature, whereas gender identity is more subjective. Gender is defined on the basis of sociocultural norms and expectations.

This counselor also used the terms *sexual orientation* and *affectional orientation* in an interchangeable fashion. Of the two, the term *affectional orientation* is more accurate because human relationships go beyond to whom one is attracted sexually. A person's orientation is defined by the sex of the person with whom he or she is predisposed to share personal affection and emotional bonds. Using the term *sexual orientation* connotes that the relationship is only about sex rather than also about affection; thus, the preference is for *affectional orientation*. Similar to the constructs of sex and gender, affectional orientation also resides on a continuum from homosexual to bisexual to heterosexual.

Gender Identity

When gender is defined on a continuum rather than dichotomously, it raises the question of the validity of gender identity disorder. Is gender identity disorder more about the individual or more about his or her family's and society's discomfort with nonconformity? Where is the line between nonconformity and pathology? These are important questions to consider when deciding whether gender-variant persons have an identity disorder or are merely outside of socially prescribed notions of gender.

For argument's sake, let us imagine that Samantha has a cleft palate instead of possible gender variance. The cleft palate is considered a medical abnormality when compared with typical development but does not cause emotional distress for Samantha, and she does not want to have an operation to make her look more like others. Although the cleft palate does not bother Samantha, the variation in her physical looks bothers her parents, makes other adults uncomfortable, and opens her up to teasing from other children.

Should one intervene with Samantha and convince her that she needs to change and have an operation, or should one perhaps look at the parental distress, societal expectations of physical appearance, and the definition of beauty? Should one collude with society to make an individual feel ashamed of being different from the majority, or should one help the individual to embrace variation? Finally, is the psychological and physical pain of making Samantha conform to societal expectations worth making others more comfortable? Our perspective is to embrace diversity rather than advocate conformity.

The basic question, with respect to mental health, is whether clinicians should diagnose people on the basis of individual distress or nonconformity (societal distress). This question was debated when homosexuality was included and then removed from the *Diagnostic and Statistical Manual of Mental Disorders*. With homosexuality, it was decided that an affectional orientation different from that of the dominant society should not constitute a mental disorder. Instead, the amount of personal distress to Samantha caused by the incongruence between gender identity and societal expectations should be the determining factor in diagnosing a disorder.

Case Feedback

The case of Samantha is challenging because of societal confusion and judgmental attitudes toward gender-variant people as well as the misunderstanding of the relationship among sex, gender, and affectional orientation. Aside from previously stated issues, we also have concerns regarding language consistency, case conceptualization, and assessment.

Although the RST respected Samantha's wish to be referred to as a girl when they met in session, the case write-up continued to refer to Samantha as Sammy and to use masculine pronouns. In addition, Samantha was sometimes referred to as *s/he*. We believe people should be identified in accordance with their own self-identification.

Nevertheless, we do realize that there is a need to counterbalance the wishes of parents and children. This issue is particularly complicated for people under the age of legal consent because children can sometimes wish for things that are not in their best interest. A question that comes to mind is, "At what age do people have the right to proclaim their own identity?" One could argue that Samantha, at age 10, has reached an age of basic consent to decide her own identity.

In addition to language, we had several concerns regarding case conceptualization and assessment. For instance, the foster parents were consulted, and information was gathered from them, but we were surprised that ongoing family sessions were not conducted, particularly because the counselor stated that she focused on the family as a system. Furthermore, the counselor seemed to presumed that Samantha "thought he was a boy" until 6 months ago, when, in actuality, there was no evidence presented that the counselor or the foster parents actually knew whether Samantha had been identifying as a girl prior to her placement in the foster home.

Conclusion

The case of Samantha offers readers an excellent opportunity to reflect on issues of gender, sex, and affectional orientation. Overall, the RST appropriately handled the case within the confines of the *DSM–IV–TR*. We were particularly pleased with her decision not to label Samantha with gender identity disorder because there was no clear evidence of clinically significant distress or impairment. This case seems to be more about societal distress than about individual distress; thus, more of a family systems approach rather than an individual approach would be appropriate.

■ Response

Melissa Luke

What a difficult case this would be under any circumstance. Nonetheless, I can imagine that this RST was left feeling particularly unsettled, given her client's suicide threat, foster care placement breakdown, and premature termination of treatment. Although most training programs educate students to expect these kinds of complex issues at some point in their career, the didactic instruction is often insufficient when it comes to preparing counselors for dealing with the range of personal and professional concerns that can result. In this instance, it seems as if 10-year-old Samantha was positively responding to the initial seven sessions of nondirected play therapy, yet, after the unanticipated turn of events, the RST had residual questions surrounding processes related to diagnosis and case conceptualization as well as treatment selection and implementation. Circumstances like these underscore the importance of accessible clinical supervision and consultation for counselors at all levels of experience. The ensuing response aims to provide a synthesis of the current literature related to gender identity in children, clarify common misconceptions, and elucidate the recommended procedures related to assessment, treatment, and prognosis.

Although clinical supervision is an integral part of all counseling training, its importance does not end when a counselor obtains employment (Bernard & Goodyear, 2004). Regular and ongoing supervision can enhance the quality of services provided to clients and, as in this instance, provide an opportunity for the counselor to process reactions as well as address questions and concerns regarding complicated cases. Given the rarity and complexity of gender identity disorders in children (Di Ceglie, Freedman, McPherson, & Richardson, 2002; Rekers & Kilgus, 1998; Zucker, 2005; Zucker, Owen, Bradley, & Ameeriar, 2002), it is quite likely that this counselor had little, if any, exposure to the myriad developmental, psychological, biological, social, and familial issues related to the presentation of atypical gender identity prior to working with this case.

If one presumes that the RST was currently participating in either individual or group supervision, she would have already gained support and assistance in conceptualizing the salient issues related to the case, including distinguishing Samantha's symptomatic behavior from normative development. In supervision, the RST likely would have examined the recommended procedures for the evaluation and treatment of a range of possible diagnoses applicable in this case (i.e., adjustment disorder, separation anxiety disorder, gender identity disorder, and posttraumatic stress disorder), explored a variety of potential referral resources, and ascertained ideas for how to further implement and evaluate her therapeutic interventions with Samantha. In addition, the supervisor might have offered experienced insight regarding the depth or source of Mr. and Mrs. Sadler's disapproval and apprehension as well as provided potential strategies for reengaging them in Samantha's treatment. Moreover, at this point in the case, supervision could provide this RST with a beneficial place and space to deal with any of her unresolved thoughts, feelings, or professional behaviors, minimizing the likelihood that they could interfere with her future counseling work (Bernard, 1997).

As indicated through the case presentation, the RST was appropriately in the process of using differential diagnosis to rule out Samantha's presenting behaviors as indicative of the more severe diagnosis of gender identity disorder in children (Code 302.6). Nonetheless, the complexity of this case might have complicated these matters. Although the RST noted that her role in this case included the provision of counseling for Samantha, her family of origin, and her foster family, the extent of contact that she made with Samantha's family of origin is unclear. It is particularly relevant for Samantha's diagnosis and treatment that the RST obtain the most comprehensive familial and developmental history possible. This assessment should include appraisal of pertinent information regarding Samantha's mother's medical history, including her pregnancy and Samantha's birth and early developmental history, and any previous evidence of gender dysphoria as well as any other indicators of familial physical and mental health, including the manifestations and expressions of gender identity. Although it is reported that the identity of Samantha's biological father is unknown, it is possible that, with recognition of its salience, Samantha's mother may be able to provide some information pertinent to the case. Moreover, given Samantha's documented history of abuse and neglect, a more complete understanding of the exact nature of this exposure is needed when one considers the context of her current symptoms.

If I were working with Samantha, I would be particularly interested in understanding the extent of the domestic violence that Samantha had witnessed and potentially experienced herself. Given the possibility that Samantha's symptoms are a manifestation of separation anxiety disorder, more information about her earlier attachment to her mother, the gender of the perpetrators of the related domestic violence, and the people with whom Samantha identifies in relation to these instances would be useful to conceptualize the case. Previous medical and school records could be helpful in this regard as well as used in corroborating reports of her earlier development, in particular with respect to her current symptoms. Additionally, as Samantha's eventual reunification with her family of origin is a long-term treatment goal regardless of the diagnosis, the inclusion of Samantha's mother and potentially her grandmother in some aspect of Samantha's treatment seems warranted. By engaging them in the process of assessment, the RST may begin to establish a respectful and trusting therapeutic relationship that could positively influence Samantha's treatment outcomes (Bernard & Goodyear, 2004; Di Ceglie, 2000; Landreth, 2002).

It is also reported that, after two meetings, Samantha's foster parents, Mr. and Mrs. Sadler, refused participation in the established consultative presession meetings and later denied requests for a home visit, such that the residential support services seem to have gone underused. This is obviously problematic for several reasons. Regardless of the etiology or diagnosis of Samantha's symptoms, the literature supports that Samantha and both her family of origin and her foster family should receive services to cope with and reduce distress associated with her presenting dysphoric gender identity development as well as to address the comorbid difficulties (Cohen-Kettenis, Owen, Kaijser, Bradley, & Zucker, 2003; Di Ceglie, 2000; Zucker et al., 2002). Thus, the multidisciplinary services proposed to the family at their initial visit, including treatment at home, school, and the clinic, are quite fitting. Moreover, because the Sadlers reported an increase in the frequency and intensity of the cluster of gender-atypical behaviors over the past 6 months, an argument could be made that Samantha's gender-dysphoric symptoms are interfering with her familial, social, and intrapersonal experiences. At this point, Samantha's symptoms can be viewed as approaching a profound level, indicating that, in addition to counseling services, Samantha needs further evaluation. In keeping with best practice as recommended in the literature, a referral for more thorough medical and psychological testing is warranted (Di Ceglie, 2000; Meyer et al., 2001; Vitale, 2001).

Although they are relatively rare, there are numerous intersex conditions that can first manifest themselves with emotional and behavioral presentations similar to those evidenced in Samantha's case (Meyer et al., 2001). Through physical examination, radiographic assessment, and endocrine and chromosomal testing, such conditions can be assessed. Because children with atypical gender identity development often display numerous associated emotional and behavioral features (Cohen-Kettenis et al., 2003; Di Ceglie, 2000; Di Ceglie et al., 2002; Zucker et al., 2002) and have by the age of 8 most typically developed an awareness of how these conflict with familial and societal norms, direct questioning regarding gender-dysphoric symptoms can be confounded by social desirability. Consequently, Samantha's lack of expressed desire for removal of her penis or testicles can be understood as possibly resulting from her experienced pressure to conform. Although adults with gender identity disorder often internally wish for removal of their genitalia, consistent with children's developmental capabilities and awareness, children frequently do not voice such a preference.

Current data on gender identity disorder in children suggests that boys are more than six times as likely as girls to be diagnosed (Cohen-Kettenis et al., 2003; Zucker, Bradley, & Sanikhani, 1997; Zucker et al., 2002). Researchers do not yet understand whether this reflects a physiologic, socially constructed, or psychologically influenced predisposition or results from limitations in contemporary methodological design. There is some evidence to suggest that there is a complex interaction among these factors (Di Ceglie et al., 2002; Zucker, 2005). Nonetheless, qualified professionals are advised to consider a number of issues in making a differential diagnosis, according to either the *DSM–IV–TR* (American Psychiatric Association, 2000) or the *International Statistical Classification of Diseases and Related Health Problems* (10th ed.; World Health Organization, 1992) nomenclature, to accurately assess children with a possible gender identity disorder (Meyer et al., 2001).

Although the *DSM–IV–TR* includes the most comprehensive description of associated problems and diagnostic criteria, the material was not designed for use as a checklist. The kind and age of onset of the gender-dysphoric symptoms, their temporal relation to other development events, and their longitudinal duration are important considerations. It is also imperative that professionals examine the ratio of gender-dysphoric behaviors to gender-congruent ones because the number of expressions is not solely relevant for diagnosis (Rekers & Kilgus, 1998; Zucker, 2005). In this case, it is possible that the eye rolling and tongue clucking observed by the RST in the first encounter were in fact a cross-gendered display of disdain, as described. Nonetheless, there is less confusion regarding Sammy's request to be called Samantha; her declaration that she is in fact a girl; her trying on her older foster sister's clothing, makeup and perfume; or her having recently attempted to steal similar items from a store. The Sadlers clearly indicated that although this cluster of behaviors first appeared 2 months after Samantha moved in, it had become increasingly problematic to all involved over the past 6 months.

It seems that the RST aptly began engaging the foster family in Samantha's treatment using presession psychoeducational consultation (Di Ceglie, 2000; Zucker, 2005). In their first meeting, the Sadlers expressed their discomfort with and disapproval of Samantha's behavior as well as their concern regarding its meaning. In particular, Mr. Sadler asked whether Sammy's belief he was a girl had implications for homosexuality. The RST adeptly explained the orthogonal relationship between gender identity and sexual–affectional orientation; nonetheless, the Sadlers gave her no indication that they understood or accepted this information. This is when, in retrospect, the Sadlers might have benefited from a referral to a parent support group or some other forum for group psychoeducation. A filial therapy parenting group might have been one possible way for the RST to facilitate multiple aims (Rennie & Landreth, 2000). Such a group could be creatively formatted, possibly combining a structured portion that was more didactic and psychoeducationally focused with a more open portion that, although counselor facilitated, allowed for parents to express and explore specific issues and concerns with one another. Through such a group, the Sadlers might have been able to continue to receive both information and support as well as obtain the parenting and behavioral training necessary to remain engaged in Samantha's treatment.

Because children exhibiting gender identity disturbances also manifest other behavioral difficulties (Cohen-Kettenis et al., 2003; Di Ceglie et al., 2002; Zucker et al., 2002), one treatment recommendation is to establish a behavior-shaping system by which all caregivers are active in the positive reinforcement of gender-consistent behaviors (Rekers & Kilgus, 1998, 2001). This is not incompatible with the RST's selection of nondirective play as the primary treatment intervention for Samantha. Used in combination with other treatment components, nondirective play therapy could communicate acceptance and facilitate Samantha's identity exploration (Di Ceglie, 2000; Landreth, 2002; Rennie & Landreth, 2000). Such an environment could create the permissiveness for Samantha to experiment with a variety of social roles and explore concepts and behaviors related to her gender identity.

Examining a case retrospectively can allow a more comprehensive perspective, thus making clearer possible points of intervention. Accordingly, when, after one session, the Sadlers expressed misgivings about how play therapy seemed to be encouraging Samantha's inappropriate behavior, I might have inquired more about what was underlying this. On more than one occasion, Mr. Sadler expressed concern regarding the likelihood of Samantha being gay, further expressing to Samantha that her cross-gendered behavior might anger God. Mrs. Sadler also suggested that Samantha knew better and might simply be trying to get attention. I would be inclined to join with the Sadlers by complimenting their ability to see multiple ways to possibly understand Samantha's behavior and then use this as a place to expand their conceptualization, reframing some of the more troubling behaviors. The RST seemed to astutely recognize that the Sadlers were at risk for disengaging from the treatment when she asked them about what part of Samantha's behaviors were most troubling. Recognizing the meaning that the Sadlers attribute to Samantha's behavior is necessary in supporting their treatment involvement and assisting them in responding to Samantha in a manner that facilitates her open communication and healthy development (Di Ceglie, 2000; Rekers & Kilgus, 1998; Vitale, 2001; Zucker, 2005).

Gender identity disturbances have an outcome that is not easily predicted (Meyer et al., 2001; Vitale, 2001), nor is there consistent agreement as to the aims or modalities of recommended treatment (Di Ceglie et al., 2002; Meyer et al., 2001; Rekers & Kilgus, 1998). There is recognized fluidity in the gender identity of prepubescent children, and although gender identity confusion has frequently been believed to be intractable, it does not necessarily lead to homosexuality or gender identity disorders in adolescence or adulthood (Cohen-Kettenis et al., 2003; Di Ceglie, 2000; Zucker, 2005). It is, however, the case that, in adults with gender identity disorder, there is overwhelming support that these symptoms began in early childhood (Vitale, 2001). Although longitudinal research on gender identity disorder in children is scant, there is some evidence to suggest that more positive adjustment occurs with earlier treatment (Rekers & Kilgus, 2001; Vitale, 2001; Zucker, 2005). Although altering the gender identity of any child is not a therapeutic aim in itself, assisting the child experiencing atypical gender identity, as well as his or her family, in tolerating and openly communicating about the associated ambiguity, possible social disapproval and isolation, and the likelihood of concomitant clinical features needs to be an integral focus of treatment.

References

American Psychiatric Association. (2000). *Diagnostic and statistical manual of mental disorders* (4th ed., text rev.). Washington, DC: Author.

Bernard, J. M. (1997). The discrimination model. In C. E. Watkins Jr. (Ed.), *Handbook of psychotherapy supervision* (pp. 310–327). New York: Wiley.

Bernard, J. M., & Goodyear, R. K. (2004). *Fundamentals of clinical supervision* (3rd ed.). Boston: Allyn & Bacon.

Cohen-Kettenis, P. T., Owen, A., Kaijser, V. G., Bradley, S. J., & Zucker, K. J. (2003). Demographic characteristics, social competence, and behavior problems in children with gender identity disorder: A cross-national, cross-clinic comparative analysis—1. *Journal of Abnormal Child Psychology, 31,* 41–53.

Di Ceglie, D. (2000). Gender identity disorder in young people. *Advances in Psychiatric Treatment, 6,* 458–466.

Di Ceglie, D., Freedman, D., McPherson, S., & Richardson, P. (2002). Children and adolescents referred to a specialist gender identity development service: Clinical features and demographic characteristics. *International Journal of Transgenderism, 6*(1). Retrieved June 20, 2006, from http://www.symposion.com/ijt/ijtvo06no01_01.htm

Landreth, G. L. (2002). *Play therapy: The art of the relationship.* New York: Brunner-Routledge.

Meyer, W., III, Bockting, W., Cohen-Kettenis, P., Coleman, E., Di Ceglie, D., Devor, H., et al. (2001, February). The standards of care for gender identity disorders: Sixth version. *International Journal of Transgenderism, 5*(1). Retrieved June 20, 2006, from http://www.symposion.com/ijt/soc_2001/index.htm

Rekers, G. A., & Kilgus, M. D. (1998). Diagnosis and treatment of gender identity disorders in children and adolescents. In L. VandeCreek, S. Knapp, & T. L. Jackson (Eds.), *Innovations in clinical practice: A sourcebook* (Vol. 16, pp. 127–141). Sarasota, FL: Professional Resource Press.

Rekers, G. A., & Kilgus, M. D. (2001, December). Early identification and treatment of gender identity disorder. *Psychiatric Times, 18*(12). Retrieved June 20, 2006, from http://www.psychiatrictimes.com/p011244.html

Rennie, R., & Landreth, G. (2000). Effects of filial therapy on parent and child behaviors. *International Journal of Play Therapy, 9*(2), 19–37.

Vitale, A. (2001, Spring). Being gender dysphoric: A developmental review. *Gender and Psychoanalysis: An Interdisciplinary Journal, 6*(2), 121–141.

World Health Organization. (1992). *The international statistical classification of diseases and related health problems* (10th ed.). Geneva, Switzerland: Author.

Zucker, K. J. (2005). Gender identity disorder in children and adolescents. *Annual Review of Clinical Psychology, 1,* 467–492.

Zucker, K. J., Bradley, S. J., & Sanikhani, M. (1997). Sex differences in referral rates of children with gender identity disorder: Some hypotheses. *Journal of Abnormal Child Psychology, 25,* 217–227.

Zucker, K. J., Owen, A., Bradley, S. J., & Ameeriar, L. (2002). Gender-dysphoric children and adolescents: A comparative analysis of demographic characteristics and behavioral problems. *Clinical Child Psychology and Psychiatry, 7,* 398–411.

14

"In Big Mama's House": Intergenerational Issues

This incident examines issues related to intergenerational family conflict, grief and loss issues, and anger management as related to counseling one African American multi-generational family. Respondents discuss family dynamics in which a parent is drug addicted as well as the advantages and difficulties facing grandparents raising grand-children. The use of an ecosystemic theoretical framework is also explained as a way to effectively address the mix of individual, developmental, dyadic, familial, social, and cultural issues involved in this incident.

Critical Incident

Angela D. Coker

"Twanna" was a beautiful 12-year-old African American girl. She was referred to me for counseling to deal with issues of grief and loss related to being removed from the custody of her mother by a local social service agency. At the time of my initial contact with Twanna, she had lived in the home of her maternal grandmother for close to 5 months. Her emotional state was upbeat, and she exhibited all of the characteristics of a young girl curious about herself and the world. She loved music, especially old TLC songs. Her favorite television show was *American Idol*.

As I met with Twanna, I also had discussions with her grandmother, whom Twanna referred to as "Big Mama." (*Big Mama* is a term of affection used in many African American families to describe and pay homage to the respected and elevated status of elderly mothers.) As a sign of cultural respect, I spoke to Twanna's grandmother at length during our first few sessions. After all, child counseling is in many ways family counseling, especially when one is dealing with African American families. I wanted to use that time to explain the counseling process, allow an opportunity for Twanna and Big Mama to get to know me, and answer any questions they might have about confidentiality. Equally as important, I wanted to get a sense of how Big Mama thought Twanna was coping with her present living situation. Big Mama was a 70-year-old woman whose heart and mind were vibrant but whose physical abilities and use of her legs were diminishing. Big Mama reminded me of my own grandmother. She was wise, loving, and protective. Also living in the home was Twanna's Aunt Betty, who was there temporarily until she was able to get on her feet financially. Twanna was very close to her aunt and often shared how much she loved her aunt and valued her help and advice. I liked this family instantly. There was an obvious love and warmth among all family members. Nonetheless, Twanna's issues and this family's love for each other were complicated by a variety of situational challenges.

First, there were issues related to the reasons for Twanna's removal from her mother's care. Twanna was placed in the care of Big Mama because her mother had been a habitual crack cocaine user for several years and could no longer care for her. Twanna blamed Big Mama for reporting her mother to the social service agency. Twanna was angry at being separated from her mother and blamed Big Mama for intervening. Big Mama also expressed some feelings of guilt. Her decision to report her daughter's behavior put her in a difficult position. She wanted the safety of her granddaughter but feared the emotional and legal consequences such a decision would bring.

A second concern was associated with challenges inherent in grandparents raising grandchildren. Big Mama never thought she would have to care for a teenager at the golden age of 70. Big Mama's new family situation put additional strains on her financially, emotionally, and physically. She was on a fixed income and had to be resourceful with every penny that entered the house. In addition, Big Mama had issues regarding her own parenting. She felt a sense of guilt, regret, and sadness about how her daughter's life had turned out. Big Mama's health was fair but declining as a result of meeting the logistical demands of having a teenager in the home (e.g., driving Twanna to school functions, hairdressers, church events).

A third family issue was related to child discipline and house rules established by Big Mama. Twanna's mother had been permissive and underinvolved because she was frequently under the influence of drugs. In contrast, Big Mama was much stricter. In fact, Twanna's chief complaint was that Big Mama did not allow her any social freedom. Twanna felt smothered and "locked up." The only social outlets Twanna had were church functions, choir rehearsals, extended family gatherings, and other supervised social affairs. Big Mama would say, "Ain't nothing out there in the streets but some trouble. I don't want Twanna courtin' and messing around with those boys. That's what happened to her mama . . . and then she started on that stuff [drugs]." Big Mama was very protective, fearing that what had happened to her daughter might happen to her grandchild. Twanna was not allowed to socialize with other teenagers unless Big Mama personally knew their family. This was causing Twanna the greatest developmental discomfort and the most family conflict in the household. Twanna felt that she did not have the freedom she would like to have. In fact, Twanna had become quite disrespectful to Big Mama, saying inappropriate things and refusing to listen to advice or complete chores. In turn, Big Mama's health was deteriorating—her blood pressure was rising, and she complained of frequent headaches. She also had mobility issues and often used a cane to walk around her home. Big Mama warned Twanna that if Twanna's negative behaviors and attitude did not change, she would eventually have to leave her home. As Big Mama stated, "I want to help my granddaughter, but I don't want to be disrespected . . . my heart can't take it."

A fourth challenge involved issues related to the disappearance of Twanna's mother. She had not been heard from in several weeks after a suspected marathon bout with drug use. In response, Twanna was experiencing anxiety and fear regarding the safety of her mother as well as a sense of abandonment. Twanna longed for the embrace of her mother, who Twanna said was very affectionate when she was sober. Nevertheless, Twanna began to question her mother's commitment to her. Twanna felt that if her mother really loved her, she would stop using drugs, come back home, and reclaim her. Finally, Twanna was only doing marginally well at school. Her teachers and school counselor all agreed that Twanna could do better if she buckled down.

I worked with Twanna and her grandmother for over a year. Although there were some difficult times, there were also some incredibly rewarding moments. As a 12-year-old, Twanna had been exposed to many of the pitfalls of urban life. She had experienced the pain of seeing her beloved mother's life be diminished by drug use. She was also going through the normal developmental stages of constructing her own sense of identity during the turbulent period of adolescence. As the reader ponders Twanna's situation, it is important not to stereotype. Twanna's story is not the narrative of all African American girls. Many African American families never experience the pain of seeing their loved ones fall victim to drug use. Nonetheless, Twanna's conflict and intergenerational family structure represent a growing reality in American households. These challenges occur in many families, irrespective of race and ethnicity, transcending socioeconomic boundaries.

Questions

1. How would you have assisted Twanna during this difficult time? What strategies might you have used? In particular, how would you assist Twanna in the grieving and separation from her mother? How would you assist Twanna in dealing with her feelings of anger and abandonment? How would you have dealt with the intergenerational issues regarding Twanna's social freedom and supervision? How would you encourage Twanna to show more engagement in school?
2. What cultural issues are present in this incident, particularly as they relate to respect for elders in the African American community and the wisdom provided by families? How would you instill in Twanna a greater sense of respect for her grandmother, who is her primary source of support and guidance?
3. What are some other issues I have not addressed?

◼Response

Glenda Clare

Substance abuse is a family disease. Although neither Twanna nor her grandmother was abusing substances, they were both significantly affected by Twanna's mother's substance abuse. Twanna's mother took center stage, and the grandmother's and daughter's life revolved around her actions. Twanna and her grandmother need to learn more about the family disease of drug addiction to improve their life. A number of specific issues related to substance abuse, the family disease, come to mind.

The use and abuse of substances by Twanna's mother affect not only Twanna but also her grandmother. Although Twanna feels alone and mourns her mother's absence, she is not alone in her situation. Twanna's grandmother, Big Mama, shares many of Twanna's feelings. I think it took a lot for her to report her own daughter to Child Protective Services. Big Mama's actions were motivated by love of her granddaughter and fear of her daughter's behavior. Twanna needs to hear this perspective. Big Mama has the additional guilt of knowing that she raised a child who neglects the needs of her daughter in deference to the use of drugs. Twanna needs to be asked what she would have done if she were in her grandmother's place.

Big Mama, likewise, needs to learn more about what is going on with Twanna. Children of substance abusers often assume the role of parent. In the absence of adequate care from a substance-abusing parent, children of substance abusers learn to take care of themselves as well as their biological parent. Twanna has learned, out of necessity, to care for herself. She has learned to set her own standards and make her own rules. Depending on the length of her mother's substance use, she may also have attachment issues and feel that she really cannot trust the decision-making skills of adults. This being the case, Twanna's grandmother needs to learn to make adjustments in her parenting style; otherwise, she and her grandchild will always be engaged in battle. Twanna needs to learn, with time and reassurance, that she can trust the nonsubstance-abusing adults in her life.

Twanna's conflicting feelings of abandonment, love, hate, anger, concern, fear, relief, grief, and loss are all natural and normal. Learning about substance abuse and hearing the stories of other children who have substance-abusing parents would help Twanna to see that she is not alone in having these feelings. Having feelings is one thing, but inappropriately expressing these feelings is something else. Twanna needs to be confronted with the consequences of her current choice of expression of feelings. She needs to be asked what she wants in life and whether her current course of action will result in what she wants. She needs to be confronted with her current school performance and asked whether she is meeting her potential. Twanna needs assistance to weigh and balance her current choices. This is her life, and only she can determine her path. Nonetheless, she needs to have someone ask her pointed questions to inspire deeper thought so that she can determine whether she can live with the consequences of her current actions or whether she needs to make adjustments to her behavior. If Twanna determines that she needs to make adjustments, she needs to be taught new, more positive ways to channel her feelings and express her emotions.

The granddaughter and grandmother have a lot of issues on their plate. At 70, the grandmother has assumed the role of parent. At 12, Twanna is unfamiliar with having a responsible parental role model and has to make adjustments to live in her grandmother's household. These are not easy tasks. Twanna needs to be aware of the sacrifice her grandmother is making to protect Twanna's well-being. With family counseling, family rules can be established. Twanna will have to learn that she is not in charge and that every individual has to make adjustments to live with others. If she is not willing to live with her grandmother's rules, she can leave and enter foster care. All possibilities must be examined. Both parties must learn to understand the perspective of the other. If Twanna earns her grandmother's trust, her grandmother may decide to be more lenient in her rules.

As I stated earlier, Twanna is not alone her situation. Her grandmother is experiencing considerable turmoil. In the African American family, the grandmother is often considered the matriarch. She is to be honored and respected. All abide by her word and follow her rules. Twanna's actions are considered disrespectful. She talks back, she is rude, and she does not follow her grandmother's rules. Twanna needs assistance in seeing what is actually happening in her family. She needs help to understand that she is not alone in her pain and that her grandmother is experiencing many similar feelings. She needs to be reminded of her grandmother's age and how Big Mama is affected by taking on child-rearing responsibilities at her age. I think understanding her grandmother's perspective will help Twanna to settle down and make the adjustments needed to get her through a challenging period in her life.

Nonetheless, both grandmother and granddaughter also need to be realistic; Big Mama is more than 70 years old. Can Twanna really feel assured that her grandmother will be there to meet her needs as she grows and matures? Because it is unlikely that Twanna's mother will stop getting high, it might be a good idea to develop a permanency plan for Twanna. I would be surprised if Big Mama were able to care for Twanna up to the age of 21.

■ Response

Kevin O'Connor

I operate from an ecosystemic theoretical framework, which conceptualizes cases such as Twanna's from a multisystemic perspective. Rather than attempting to summarize all the dimensions of the theory, I refer the reader to O'Connor (2000; O'Connor & Ammen, 1998) and focus on just three dimensions that seem particularly relevant to Twanna's treatment. These dimensions are (a) the significant developmental issues involved, (b) the need to take a phenomenological perspective to develop a strong working alliance with Twanna and her grandmother, and (c) the balancing of each individual's needs across the generations in a cultural context.

No information is given about the early relationship between Twanna and her mother or when her mother's substance abuse began. It would be helpful to know this to assess the degree to which early developmental difficulties—particularly those related to the development of attachment, affect, behavior, and relationship skills—may be underlying Twanna's current relationship difficulties with her grandmother. The fact that Twanna is close to her aunt suggests that she has good attachment capacity, and this bodes well for both her treatment and her future. Nevertheless, it is clear that separation from her mother has triggered a number of early developmental issues. Twanna is experiencing the fundamental sort of sadness any child experiences when abandoned by a parent. This is complicated by her perception that her mother is choosing drugs over her. Having her parent make such a choice is a terrible blow to Twanna's self-esteem. Although Twanna's grandmother has provided her with a place to live, there remains a two-pronged threat of further abandonment that keeps Twanna's separation anxiety at the forefront. Her grandmother has directly told her that if she continues to act out Twanna may have to live elsewhere and has also indicated that her "heart can't take" Twanna's behavior. Although it is important for Twanna to know there are absolute limits to what her grandmother can tolerate, the sense of impermanence and Twanna's acting out tend to feed one another in a slowly escalating cycle.

As Twanna struggles with some very early developmental issues connected to abandonment and separation anxiety, she is also struggling with two very age-appropriate developmental tasks. One of these involves working on establishing a new balance between dependence on adults and independence from them. On the one hand, Twanna has been forced to be completely independent from her mother. She has no way of getting any kind of input from the person who should be central in her life at this point. On the other hand, her grandmother has asserted a level of control Twanna has never before experienced, making Twanna uncomfortably dependent. Twanna has not yet figured out how to take responsibility for her own behavior, to exert much personal control, or to engage in active problem solving with her grandmother. All three of these are critical developmental tasks for young adolescents (Wood, Davis, Swindle, & Quirk, 1996). The other important developmental task Twanna has not yet achieved is the development of a significant relationship with a group of peers with whom she can experience success. Her very restricted social life does not give her room to address some of her emotional issues with age-mates who might be able to give her a very different and useful perspective.

The critical incident identifies the treatment as being focused on helping Twanna deal with issues of grief and loss. In applying ecosystemic theory, it is important to develop a very specific, phenomenologically framed treatment goal. Phenomenology is a philosophy of science that takes the position that there are no absolute facts; instead, there are only a person's individual perceptions (Georgi, 1985). What are the negative emotions experienced most by Twanna? Is she sad, angry, lonely, or frustrated? Which of these negative emotions could she commit to work toward reducing in therapy? Which ones bother her so much that she would be willing to work hard to make them go away to make room for more fun and happiness in her life?

Last, from an ecosystemic perspective, it is clear that neither Twanna nor her grandmother is getting her needs met adequately. In Twanna's case, her emotional, social, and developmental needs are not being satisfied. In Big Mama's case, her basic living, emotional, and social community needs are not being satisfied. Making these the focus of active problem solving in at least some of the treatment sessions may help both Twanna and her grandmother feel better connected, more empowered, and less anxious and deprived.

The first therapeutic goal I would address is the need to establish an attachment relationship between Twanna and her grandmother; simultaneously, I would address the rupture in the attachment between Twanna and her mother. This is not an easy task. Twanna blames her grandmother for the loss of her mother, yet she is old enough to understand that her grandmother did what she thought was best. Twanna may also perceive attaching to her grandmother as betraying her mother. Attachment-building activities between Twanna and her grandmother that focus on the present should help reduce this fear of betrayal. They could identify things they enjoy doing together and ways to spend positive time interacting. Additionally, the counselor might address some of Twanna's separation anxiety and her grandmother's basic living needs at some point in therapy by having Big Mama apply to become Twanna's official foster parent. This would demonstrate to Twanna her grandmother's commitment to keeping her and provide extra income so that Big Mama experienced less stress. Last, I would spend at least one session having Big Mama and Twanna develop a written contract delineating those behaviors that would make it impossible for Big Mama to continue to raise Twanna. The purpose of this activity would be threefold: (a) to make Twanna aware of just how extreme her behavior would really have to become before her grandmother would actually move her out of the home, (b) to identify other resources Big Mama could activate for support to help her keep Twanna in the home, and (c) to shift the control of the decision to stay or go from Big Mama to Twanna.

At some point, Twanna may resist attaching too closely to her grandmother because it exacerbates the sadness she feels over the neglect she has experienced in the past or the abandonment she is experiencing in the present. That is, she might not have been really aware of just how little she was getting from her mother until she began to get those needs met by her grandmother. It will be important then to actively look for opportunities in therapy to address the underlying sadness. This sadness is often more difficult to address than the anger the child uses to cover it. The intensity of the sadness is often a product of an unrealistic view of what has been lost. The child idealizes the parent to some degree, which makes the loss all that much more painful. Additionally, children may blame themselves for being unlovable, turning the loss into an attack on the self.

In treatment, I would help Twanna build a reality-based view of her mother that included both the positives and the negatives. Creating a scrapbook in which she recalls both aspects of her mother might be a good project for Twanna and her grandmother to work on together. As Twanna's reality-based assessment of her mother stabilizes, her anger may become more focused and may need to be vented in an age-appropriate way. The simplest way might be to have her write letters to her mother expressing her thoughts and save them until they can be delivered. The letters might also be buried or burned in a ceremony in which Twanna grieves the loss of her idealized, perfect mother and accepts the mother she actually has.

It is also important to ensure that Twanna's grief and anger do not interfere with her addressing the age-appropriate goal of developing and attaching to a group of peers. If she can find ways to make functional contributions to a positive peer group, such an attachment will decrease her separation anxiety and provide a source of self-esteem. Treatment could facilitate her developing three types of peer attachments. One possibility is to include Twanna in a therapy group for other teens coping with either parental loss or substance abuse. The second is to encourage her to develop a peer social group near her home, potentially with her grandmother's assistance. As a starting point, maybe Twanna and her grandmother could work on identifying a group of girls Twanna likes from church. Last, Twanna needs to develop a peer group at school to help motivate her to go to school and to perform well. Joining either a club or a sports team at school might provide an excellent connection. The advantage of these options is that they meet Twanna's developmental needs without challenging her grandmother's need to feel in control of Twanna's safety at this point in time.

I perceive two African American cultural issues at play in this case. One is the cultural value placed on elders and their wisdom. The other is the usual value placed on extended family and community as sources of support in time of need. In this incident, the first seems to be overemphasized and the second underemphasized.

In African American culture, children are expected to respect their elders. In Twanna's case, adherence to that value is complicated by two factors. It was Big Mama's wisdom that resulted in Twanna being separated from her mother in the first place. Fair or not, Twanna sees that wisdom as a source of pain; therefore, asking Twanna to unilaterally respect Big Mama's wisdom violates the reality of her emotional experience. The other factor is that Big Mama is using the cultural value to make idiosyncratic and overprotective decisions that are interfering with Twanna's healthy movement through age-appropriate developmental challenges. By promoting greater attachment between the two family members, I would hope to promote Twanna's desire to respect her grandmother as she relinquishes her sadness and anger and comes to value her grandmother's desire to care for her. Attachment is a much more powerful motivator than a cultural value promoting respect. It is also important to help Big Mama see that she cannot mask her anxiety and guilt over her daughter's problems by relying on a cultural value to restrict Twanna's social contacts and independence. Every culture allows for some sort of problem solving. I would help Twanna and her grandmother discover a method that works for them, allowing them both to get their needs met without violating cultural norms.

In African American culture, there is also great value placed on the support one can garner from one's extended family and community. In this case, it is unclear how much either Twanna or her grandmother is taking advantage of this cultural value. Some mention is made of church, but is Big Mama pulling those people in to help her? Is she meeting with other women or other grandparents who are raising teens? Is she asking for support in providing supervision? There is also mention of Aunt Betty and of extended family gatherings. Again, to what extent are these family members being asked to provide real support to ease both Twanna's and her grandmother's burdens? I would strongly encourage them to have at least periodic sessions in which some extended family members are included to assist them all in brainstorming ways they can create a mutual support network.

In conclusion, this case lends itself very well to an ecosystemic conceptualization because there is such a mix of individual, developmental, dyadic, familial, social, and cultural issues involved. Stepping back and looking at these variables and their unique interaction allowed me to generate a range of potential direct and collateral interventions that Twanna and her grandmother might find helpful. My goal would be to ensure that both are getting their needs met in ways that do not violate either the other's needs or their basic cultural values.

■ Response

Vivian J. Carroll McCollum

Twanna is a 12-year-old African American who lives with her grandmother and her Aunt Betty. Intergenerational living arrangements are common among African American families. "African American children are often taken into the household of their grandparents" (Baruth & Manning, 2003, p. 109). These living arrangements are a sign of the value placed on family responsibility in the African American family and happen for a number of reasons, including economics, parental disability, need for child care or elder care, and family tradition. This living arrangement became the best solution for Twanna's care when she was removed from her mother, who was unable to care for her.

Twanna was referred to counseling to help her deal with grief and loss related to the custody issue. As Twanna's counselor, I would first determine whether some of the behaviors exhibited (disrespect, saying inappropriate things) were linked to the normal psychosocial developmental stage of early adolescence. According to psychosocial development theory, at 12 years old, Twanna should be working through issues of group identity versus alienation, which means that she is struggling to find her place in society as well as dealing with peer pressure (eSSORTMENT, n.d.). This developmental stage may account for Twanna's difficulty in reconciling her grandmother's strictness with the autonomy to which she had become accustomed while in her mother's custody.

In addition to these developmental challenges, Twanna has to resolve the anger issues related to her removal from her mother's custody. Twanna's anger is tridirectional; she is angry with her grandmother for initiating the process of removal, with her mother for abandoning her, and with herself for being helpless and powerless to change her living arrangements. I would use several anger management techniques, including "tear it up," an exercise in which the counselor gives the client a telephone book or magazine to tear up as the client verbalizes what he or she is angry about (Vernon, 2004). I would encourage Twanna to identify why she is angry and at whom her anger is directed. I would then ask her how she might replace the words of anger with words of love.

Twanna may also be feeling unwanted, despite the fact that her grandmother took her in when her mother could not care for her. Her grandmother indicated that if Twanna's behavior and attitude did not change, she would have to eventually leave the house. Unfortunately, Twanna's acting-out behaviors made the grandmother respond in a way that became a self-fulfilling prophecy for Twanna. I would help Twanna to explore her familial relationships, identifying individuals in her family who she feels care about her welfare. I would do this by having Twanna make a list of her family members and, next to each name, write their relationship to her and one thing they have done to show they care. We would then discuss how she felt about the list she made. The purpose of this exercise is to show Twanna that she has family support even if her mother is not there.

I would assist Twanna in the grieving process by helping her to picture her mother and putting this picture into a tangible form. I could accomplish this by having Twanna journal her feelings, write poetry, make a scrapbook, develop a photo journal, or make a memory box. A memory box is decorated inside and out with pictures and other memorabilia that assist the client in coming to grips with the loss of a loved one. The box memorializes the loved one through artifacts that can serve as fond reminders of a better time in the life of the client and provide a way to honor or remember the loved one. Twanna could make the box during individual counseling sessions—she could talk while affixing the pictures or artifacts—or as a homework project between sessions.

In family counseling sessions with Twanna, Big Mama, and Aunt Betty, I would mediate family problem-solving discussions. These sessions could help Big Mama and Twanna come to a reasonable compromise concerning social time issues, such as curfew and developing like-valued friends (maybe from church) with whom the grandmother could be comfortable. Because Twanna is fond of Aunt Betty, Aunt Betty could possibly relieve Big Mama of some of the day-to-day responsibilities related to Twanna's care, such as taking her shopping, picking her up from school, chaperoning social outings, and being an advocate for Twanna at school.

I would encourage Twanna to be more engaged in school by exploring her future goals. I would have Twanna indicate what she would like to accomplish each year for the next 2 or 3 years to help her realize the importance of doing well in school. Given that Twanna is interested in music, one way to hook her on school may be through the music department. In a future family counseling session with Big Mama and Aunt Betty, I would suggest that Aunt Betty make an appointment for her and Twanna to visit the music teacher to see whether Twanna would be a candidate for one of the vocal or instrumental music programs at school. Participation in the school music program would help Twanna connect with other students who share her interest in music and would provide the opportunity for Twanna to develop healthy peer relationships.

African American cultural values, such as strong family kinship networks, respect for elders, and emphasis on education, are embedded in this case. Nevertheless, other issues are not addressed. These include the importance of the church in decision making and the problem of the negative stereotyping of African American culture. Often, social critiques focus only on the negative aspect of the absence of parents in the home and fail to see the positive historical benefit of multigenerational child rearing. In these family arrangements, African American children receive multigenerational life lessons that contribute to the development of self-esteem and a strong sense of self. As Twanna's counselor, I would encourage her to have conversations with her grandmother about her relatives and ancestors to learn about her family's history. This would allow Twanna and Big Mama to enter into casual, nonadversarial conversations that could enhance their relationship, reflect a sense of family and group pride, and make each of them feel valued by the other.

The church has historically played an integral role in African American life. The church has served as a source of leadership in the community and as a major social outlet, particularly for African American seniors and children, providing positive peer group interaction (Baruth & Manning, 2003). I would suggest to the family that the church might be a place where Twanna and Big Mama could participate in shared or parallel activities. At church, Twanna could interact with her peers under the watchful eye of Big Mama without peer group ridicule.

In summary, while counseling Twanna, I would remember where she is in her psychosocial development and provide interventions that complemented her need to find her place in society and to have positive peer interaction. It would also be important for me to respect the cultural values of the African American family by allowing both individual and family sessions with Twanna, Big Mama, and Aunt Betty during which individuals could speak freely without fear of embarrassing or belittling each other. Family sessions are especially important because group-oriented solutions and family member support are valued among African Americans. Twanna's recognition that her mother is not in the picture for her at the moment is of utmost importance to her socioemotional growth. I would allow Twanna and Big Mama to express and work through their feelings about Twanna's mother. Working through these feelings would help Big Mama to avoid making decisions concerning Twanna on the basis of transference of feelings toward Twanna's mother. Likewise, Twanna could begin to recognize and work through some of the misplaced anger she has directed toward Big Mama.

I would also give particular attention to Twanna's feelings toward school. Many African Americans view a good education as a key strategy for fighting racism. A culturally sensitive education would help Twanna to better appreciate her African American culture, to develop positive self-identity, and to improve her self-esteem and self-efficacy while teaching her appropriate developmental skills. In addition, bibliotherapy could be used with Twanna to show African Americans in positive roles.

Finally, I must be aware of any biases I may have relating to the cultural values of this family and be open to accepting methods that may be different from those used with mainstream populations. For instance, I must be open and accepting of the family's religious values and receptive of any need they may express to involve their minister or religious leader as a resource for helping Twanna. The key to helping Twanna is facilitating her increased awareness of and use of her extended family support network. This network not only includes Big Mama, Aunt Betty, and other family members but also includes friends, the church, and the community at large and is important in helping Twanna better understand herself and cope with her feelings.

References

Baruth, L., & Manning, M. L. (2003). *Multicultural counseling and psychotherapy: A life-span perspective* (3rd ed.). Upper Saddle River, NJ: Merrill Prentice Hall.

eSSORTMENT. (n.d.). *Erik Erikson and psychosocial development.* Retrieved September 29, 2005, from http://aza.essortment.com/psychosocialdev_rijk.htm

Georgi, A. (1985). *Phenomenology and psychological research.* Pittsburgh, PA: Duquesne University Press.

O'Connor, K. (2000) *The play therapy primer* (2nd ed.). New York: Wiley.

O'Connor, K., & Ammen, S. (1998) *The play therapy treatment planning workbook: An ecosystemic model.* San Diego, CA: Academic Press.

Vernon, A. (2004). *Counseling children & adolescents* (3rd ed.). Denver, CO: Love Publishing Co.

Wood, M., Davis, K., Swindle, F., & Quirk, C. (1996). *Developmental therapy–developmental teaching* (3rd ed.). Austin, TX: ProEd.

15

"Gettin' Soft in the 'Burbs": Children Living in Poverty

The counselor in this case helps a young client acclimate to middle-class living during his stay in a residential treatment center and then questions the humanity and efficacy of facilitating such acclimation. This chapter explores the challenges of counseling children living in poverty from a systemic and social justice perspective.

■ Critical Incident

Leann M. Wyrick-Morgan

On accepting a position as a counselor in a private agency, I was assigned a caseload of six boys in one group home and two in another. The home where "Jimmy Sanchez" lived was a residential treatment facility for boys ages 6–12 who were, for various reasons, wards of the state. I am not in the habit of thoroughly reading a child's file prior to meeting him or her for the first time because I like to form my own opinion of where I think the child is before reading what others have identified as the challenges for the child. This case was no exception, so I had only been provided a brief oral history of what had happened to Jimmy's parents and siblings and how he ended up in the state's care.

According to this brief oral history, Jimmy was 9 years old and had been in and out of foster care homes and residential treatment facilities since the age of 6. Jimmy had never known his father, and his mother had lost her parental rights over a year before I met him. He had been raised in an area of the city known for gang violence, drugs, and extreme poverty. Jimmy had endured a history of repeated physical abuse, resulting in several broken bones, and there was speculation among caregivers that Jimmy had also been sexually abused, but there was no documentation to substantiate this suspicion. A series of lengthy hospital stays after hostile outbursts toward teachers and caregivers led to Jimmy's eventual placement in the group home setting.

In terms of diagnostic impressions, I was told Jimmy had attachment issues and would initially test the boundaries of our relationship. The final remarks from my supervisor regarding my work with Jimmy included cautions about his behavior, the kinds of medication he had been prescribed, and the ways he had manipulated his other counselors. In short, Jimmy was what my colleagues and I referred to as a child who had been "therapized." This meant that Jimmy knew what words counselors wanted to hear to perceive him as cooperative and worthy of praise. In spite of the apparent barriers inherent in establishing a truly therapeutic relationship with Jimmy, I welcomed the challenge. I was determined to avoid taking his words only at face value and instead hoped to listen more deeply in order to melt away his self-protective facade and really understand what he was experiencing.

I decided to leave at the door the baggage of prior therapeutic experiences involving Jimmy and just spend some time with him. I discovered that he was a bright boy with a wonderful sense of humor who was understandably guarded and unwilling to offer unearned trust. As our sessions progressed and his trust in me developed, Jimmy revealed that he struggled with his place not only in the residential treatment facility but also in his world back home. As Jimmy explained how he grew up with his brothers and sisters in his Nana's care, it became apparent to me that there was a stark discrepancy between the surroundings of the suburban group home in which he was currently living and the oppressive poverty of the place he still called home.

Jimmy and I explored the way he navigated the struggles with peers and adults in his life and how the way he dealt with fear was important if he were to make progress toward his goal of being reunited with his brothers and sisters in an urban foster care home in the neighborhood where he was born. This issue became a major focus in our therapy sessions, as Jimmy began to equate the fears of past abuse with the reality that returning to the neighborhood represented potential for the abuse cycle to be repeated.

Through our counseling conversations, we also came to realize that Jimmy was not struggling with his ability to follow the rules under which he currently lived. Instead, Jimmy was struggling with the fact that the group home rules were made for living in the group home, in suburbia, rather than for living in the impoverished housing projects of the inner city to which he yearned—and simultaneously feared—to return. In the group home, Jimmy was being asked to abandon the defenses that he had learned from his mother, his Nana, his peers, and those who came and went in his life. Abandonment of these coping strategies contributed to Jimmy's fear and insecurity.

While respecting Jimmy's need to regain control of his emotions in the context of his current placement, I began to understand that for him to reconcile this transition in himself he needed someone to understand the effects of poverty on his belief system. I spent the next 14 months working with Jimmy addressing his concerns about "getting soft in the 'burbs" while his peers back in the city were getting tougher and stronger. What I learned was that a child living in poverty can tell you what food stamps can (and cannot) buy, what it is like to make a box of cereal feed three children for 3 days, and how to make sure that no one steals all the clothes you own while they wash in the community laundry room in your building. This was the life that Jimmy had left and to which, as a reward for making enough progress toward his goals, he would return. It was a life that in no way resembled the suburban group home life to which he had become accustomed over the past 3 years.

Jimmy had become accustomed to getting new clothes each season thanks to do-
nations from wealthy humanitarians. He was used to three nutritious meals each day,
to basic assurances of safety, and to consistency resulting from house rules. This
would not be the case when Jimmy returned back home. The home and neighborhood
in which he lived during treatment were a lifestyle so foreign to him that it was beyond a hope or dream. Now that he was living the dream and enjoying the comforts
of suburban life, Jimmy was not sure whether he wanted to give it up by proving to
everyone that he was well enough to go home. Going back to the housing project
where his brother and sister still lived would be extremely difficult given that he had
become accustomed to the security of middle class living and the status that it afforded him.

It is not surprising that Jimmy seemed to have regressive episodes each time attempts were made to begin the transition process of returning him home. As a result,
I began to question whether his team of counselors and case workers was doing him
a disservice by treating his issues in the context of a middle class safety net, only to return him to an environment that represented compound issues that were not likely
present in the group home environment. Transition from one socioeconomic environment to another and back again is likely confusing and scary for an adult, let alone for
a child, whose social development may be far less sophisticated. When we encounter
children in our office or our suburban residential treatment center, we see them
through the lens of what we hope for them. Nevertheless, children who have lived
most of their life without basic necessities present different needs than children who
have not experienced the effects of poverty.

Jimmy tried to help me understand his concerns about going back home, but, with
my growing yet still limited understanding of the residual effects of poverty on the
life cycle of a child, I felt incompetent in my approach to dealing with his transitional
concerns. I sought supervision from both the residential treatment team in the group
home and the team of counselors with whom I engaged in regular supervision on a
weekly basis. To both groups, I posed the same question: "What message are we sending to kids when we take them away from their home, tell them they need to change
the behaviors that they developed as a result of surviving in their environment, and
then return them to the original environment once they master the skills to navigate
middle class living?"

These supervision discussions focused on the effects of this practice on children as
well as on the wider social justice system. On the basis of our discussions, I was able
to identify a possible strategy for assisting Jimmy with the transition from his suburban treatment setting back to his impoverished home environment. I recognized that
it was essential to help Jimmy resolve the confusion about which protective characteristics he needed to maintain and which he could abandon. Toward this end, we made
frequent visits to his home neighborhood, even if just to drive around and see what
there was to see.

Jimmy began to realize that being with his siblings, even if the environment was
not as comfortable as the group home, was what he truly wanted. He also began to
verbalize that our trips to his neighborhood, especially the ones in which there was no
actual visit to his prospective foster home, were comforting and helped relieve his
fears of return. Jimmy was once again familiar with what the neighborhood looked
like, smelled like, sounded like, and felt like. Returning in this way represented power
to Jimmy, power over the behaviors that led to his removal from his siblings so long

ago. Jimmy gradually gained confidence in his ability to contain himself back in his neighborhood, even without the luxuries he had become accustomed to in the group home. He continued to express desires that he understood would not be fulfilled back home. For instance, Jimmy knew that luxuries such as getting a new team jersey for making good grades at school or for accomplishing predetermined behavioral goals would not be afforded him once he returned home. Jimmy was able to verbalize this loss without regret, and his enthusiasm for returning to what he perceived as normal began to outweigh his desire for the luxuries of the treatment environment.

After 3 years and 8 months of treatment, Jimmy began overnight visits with his siblings in the foster care home. The reunification with his siblings was not without setbacks, but, overall, Jimmy presented as ready for his permanent transfer into their home. I was unsure about the transition, but it was determined after hours of dialogue with other supervisors and counselors that this course of action was appropriate.

Jimmy's return home was deemed a success when he reached the 6-month marker without any major regressive episodes that required hospitalization or return to residential treatment. It is uncertain whether my strategy of reintroduction contributed to Jimmy's initial success. Either way, the effect that Jimmy had on my life continues to shape the way I approach children in general, especially those children who have been affected by poverty.

I left the agency to pursue a doctoral degree not long after Jimmy's transition was complete, but I continue to revisit my role in his life and his in mine. As I teach new counselors in training the art of developing a relationship with a client, I am reminded how poverty uniquely affects each individual and that the counselor must address it to fully understand the client's worldview. It is impossible to truly understand the full experience of a child without admitting that one may not understand how poverty has touched him or her. I do not claim to completely understand poverty, but, by recognizing that the long-term effects of poverty are as real as the children I treat, I am one step closer to helping them on their journey. The questions that continue to linger in my mind, even after all these years, are more about the treatment modalities than about the impact that poverty has on the mind-set and behaviors of children. They include the following.

Questions

1. Do counselors do children a disservice by removing them from an impoverished environment for the sake of treatment, just to return them to poverty with skills they have only practiced in the context of the treatment environment?
2. What are the long-term effects of showing children a different way of life? Does it help them overcome poverty in adulthood?
3. How can counselors truly understand the world of a child living in poverty to provide the most appropriate level of care?
4. Did the visits to the neighborhood with Jimmy have a lasting effect on his life there, or did they merely calm his immediate fears about the changes that had taken place in the 3 years he was away?
5. Can counselors ensure that children will not become more confused by learning a new way of living by including the children's home environment in every phase of treatment?

Response

Heidi S. Deschamps

The questions presented by this counselor are questions that must be addressed by the counseling profession on several levels. First, we must examine the common, every-day practices of counselors as they relate to counseling children living in poverty. Second, we must explore the personal reactions of counselors as they encounter the culture of poverty. Finally, it is crucial that we address the broader issues of social justice and client advocacy.

It has been my experience that much of counseling is conducted in a way that is far closer to the traditional, stereotypical image of psychotherapy than one might want to admit: A client lies on a couch as the counselor listens intently, with occasional inter-jections of, "I see," and, "Mmm hmm." Of course, this is an exaggeration; I have also seen inventive, dynamic, and innovative approaches in my profession, especially in work with children. Nevertheless, it is time that counselors more directly challenge the notion of the 50-minute hour at a cozy suburban office. The reality is that the life of many clients is simply not representative of the quiet and controlled environment called the counseling room. Conducting counseling outside of the counseling room may expose the counselor to the reality of his or her child client's life in a more direct way. Sometimes, not involving oneself in the everyday reality faced by children is a greater disservice than removing them from their home environment. There are times when the safety of a child necessitates removal from his or her home. This seems to have been the case with Jimmy. When a child is removed from his or her environment, there might be more creative ways to maintain connections with the home environ-ment during the course of treatment. This requires counselors to engage with that en-vironment in a more direct way.

Jimmy seemed to benefit from the visits to his neighborhood. In addition, these visits enhanced the counselor's ability to understand Jimmy's worldview and to con-ceptualize a better avenue of treatment. When counselors remain removed from the contexts in which clients are situated, they lose crucial information about the clients' experience. It was necessary to remove Jimmy from his home environment because it was unsafe for him to stay there. Providing him a safe and secure home, basic neces-sities, and exposure to compassionate people is not a disservice to him. Nonetheless, not attending to the reality of the life he was living or the life to which he will return could be detrimental to his growth and development. Attending to this aspect of his experience or the experiences of children in similar circumstances may require more than listening and empathic responding. It may require counselors to more fully en-gage with the environment of clients, just as this counselor did. When the counselor began to shift the counseling process into the context of Jimmy's home environment, his fears decreased, and he began to experience power over his behaviors.

Counselors need to find more innovative ways to do counseling in the context of their clients' everyday experiences. If one truly hopes to understand the world of poverty, there is no better way than experiencing the world of a child living in poverty. This requires a dramatic shift from the traditional construct of counseling. Models of in-home counseling have been created (Vass, Jacobs, & Slavek, 1984). It might be useful to use these underdeveloped methods and explore other approaches to counseling children that incorporate the family and the environment throughout the counseling process. Although it is impossible to know whether the neighborhood visits had a long-term effect on Jimmy, it is clear that doing counseling in the context of his environment eased his transition. Conducting counseling in the environments of the clients requires counselors to face several personal and professional challenges.

When counseling takes place in a cozy suburban office, the reality of children living in poverty is somewhat removed from our vision. Yes, we hear the heartbreaking stories. We see children wearing clothes that do not always fit and realize that it is because the family does not have money to keep up with growth spurts. We wonder whether they are getting enough to eat. We know that they might not get the attention they need because their mom works two low-wage jobs. Yet, at the end of the day, we go home to our middle class way of life. As counselors, we are genuinely attempting to understand, but we may not fully get it. If a counselor walks into a home of poverty, drives through the neighborhood, or goes to the school and sits in the yard at recess, it is much more difficult to avoid the reality of poverty. Facing this reality can feel overwhelming and frightening. Some counselors might also experience a sense of guilt or shame for living a life without such hardship. Even more difficult to overcome is the often intense sympathy (rather than empathy) that rises up when one witnesses poverty. Helping children overcome poverty requires that counselors face these fears and discomforts. If they are to help children apply the learning that is possible through counseling, they must understand and engage with the environment in which the children will have to apply it.

The counselor in this incident came to realize that asking Jimmy to abandon all of his defenses was not a reasonable request. In reality, these defenses kept him safe in many ways. It is important that counselors examine what behaviors they expect from the children they see in counseling. Jimmy knew what one could buy with food stamps and how to keep his clothes safe when doing laundry in communal areas. The counselor might not possess or understand these abilities, but she realized that these are valuable skills that can be shaped and built on in counseling. In addition, there are other skills that can be experienced in counseling that might enhance Jimmy's life in fundamental ways. To help the transfer of learning from counseling to home, the counselor must have an understanding of the challenges children might encounter in their everyday world. Showing Jimmy another way of life could be detrimental, if it is assumed that this way of life will easily fit into the distinctive cultural context from which he came or if it is assumed that every aspect of the new way of life is better or healthier for Jimmy. There are many aspects of the culture of poverty that are healthy and growth promoting. Counseling is not about asking Jimmy to choose one way of life over another. It is about giving him an opportunity to explore new ways of being that might better serve him as he continues to develop. As he makes these choices, he becomes better equipped to face life's challenges.

Although it is important to consider the nature of treatment and the everyday practices of counseling, it is crucial that one also examine Jimmy's experience from a broader perspective. There are larger social and systemic issues that directly contribute to Jimmy's experience. If counselors want to make an impact on the life of children like Jimmy, they must examine and challenge the larger social and political structures that sustain poverty in their country and in the world around them. This struggle can create feelings of hopelessness and confusion. It is difficult to know where to begin in the attempt to make systemic change for marginalized and underprivileged groups. Yet if counselors do not begin working for change at a larger, systemic level, they will continue to see children like Jimmy come into their offices, schools, churches, agencies, and group homes. I find it maddening to live in such a wealthy nation yet see children every day without resources to meet their basic needs or access to opportunities for continued growth. I have struggled to find means and methods to challenge the social and political structures that maintain such conditions. Yet it is possible to make change in small movements. It is exciting to be part of a profession with organizations such as Counselors for Social Justice, which provides avenues for addressing issues related to poverty. This counselor furthered the social justice movement the moment she left the comfort and predictability of the group home in an attempt to understand how Jimmy's life of poverty was affecting his transition. Overcoming poverty is not just a struggle for those who experience poverty directly; it is a struggle for all who are affected by poverty. It is difficult not to feel affected by the struggle of children like Jimmy. Through engagement and a willingness to face the discomforts of really trying to understand, the counselor's perspective was forever changed, and her willingness to engage in this way will have a lasting impact on Jimmy.

# Response

Delila Owens

Determining the most effective way to assist children of low socioeconomic status seems to be one of the most important issues in this case. I first discuss my initial reactions on reading this case. I then address three core issues: the long-term effects of exposing children from impoverished homes to new environments, the effects of returning these children to their impoverished home environments, and the counselor's role in understanding and assisting children such as Jimmy.

Working with children from impoverished environments can be both challenging and stimulating. Sometimes, working with children from what a counselor perceives to be chaotic environments can leave the counselor feeling drained, frustrated, and uncertain. It is understandable that the counselor in this case questioned whether her interventions were effective.

This case was challenging in that it presented an array of counseling issues, including attachment and anxiety problems, disconnection from birth parents, physical and possibly sexual abuse, and poverty. Given Jimmy's background, it is not surprising that he reacted the way he did. I believe that Jimmy's humor was a gift that he used as an effective coping mechanism to deal with the reoccurrences of trauma in his life.

The counselor in this critical incident did a terrific job pointing out some of the key issues with which Jimmy struggled. In fact, she was quite brave to take on such a challenging case. The counselor's advocacy skills were especially impressive given Jimmy's vulnerabilities. Children dealing with such circumstances need an advocate to give them a voice and to protect their interests. In addition, Jimmy's symptoms seem to go beyond adjustment problems.

Jimmy has dealt with abuse and abandonment on so many levels that I would have considered a diagnosis of posttraumatic stress disorder (PTSD) in addition to adjustment issues. His behavioral manifestations, such as irritability, detachment from others, and angry outbursts, are common responses to posttraumatic stress in children (Yule, 2001). Unfortunately, the diagnostic criteria for PTSD are largely geared toward adults, not children. Children understandably are less sophisticated in their ability to communicate and express the effects of trauma on their psychological well-being. It has been recommended that the criteria for PTSD be altered to accommodate work with young children (Scheeringa & Zeanah, 1995).

Childhood is a critical time for learning and development. Children are constantly absorbing information and creating meaning from their experiences. In my opinion, with proper support and encouragement, Jimmy can surmount his difficulties despite his circumstances and background. This is certainly the perspective that I use in my work with children of low socioeconomic status. I also draw from aspects of Adlerian theory, because this modality has proven effective for me with a range of children. This approach allows children both to assist the counselor in setting goals and to understand that they are ultimately responsible for their own behavior. In essence, this approach gives children who might otherwise feel powerless the power to control their own actions.

There are various other aspects of Adlerian theory that I would use in assisting Jimmy. For example, Adlerian theory stresses the effects of birth order on children's personality. By understanding these effects, one can perceive children's unique beliefs, correct mistakes in their logic, and help them to overcome feelings of inferiority. In this modality, the counselor is seen as the teacher, informer, and encourager (Corey, 2001). Therefore, using some aspects of Adlerian theory might assist the counselor in getting a well-rounded picture of Jimmy. In addition, it is important to understand Jimmy's current environment and family background. I believe that counselors must always view a client in his or her own environment to gain a more holistic understanding of the client's needs.

I want to elaborate on three key points in this case. First, I want to consider the long-term effects of showing children who live in poverty a different way of life. Second, I address the counselor's concern about whether she did Jimmy a disservice by placing him back in his home environment. Finally, I discuss the need for counselors to broaden their understanding of the frame of reference shared by children from impoverished communities.

In my opinion, it is not damaging to remove a child from his or her environment for treatment purposes. Children from impoverished environments benefit from exposure to lifestyles outside of their existing circumstance and need the opportunity to develop life skills beyond those used in their current home environment. I believe counselors would be doing children from impoverished homes a disservice by not exposing them to new environments. The effects of nonexposure would be more damaging than removing the child from his or her environment. In Jimmy's case, he needs to be shown how to find harmony between the two environments. It is not surprising that Jimmy had mixed feelings about returning to his distressed home environment. Unfortunately, there will be some social losses, such as friends, but there will also be some positive gains, such as the application of new skills. Helping Jimmy to understand the dynamics of both environments and how his new skills can be transferable to his original home environment is crucial.

Counselors should actively seek ways to allow all children to develop higher order thinking skills. These higher order thinking and problem-solving skills can only come from exposure to new environments. The skills that children learn through a counselor's work with them are transferable (Ray, Alson, Lantieri, & Roderick, 1996). Jimmy needs new skills to make more effective choices. I was most impressed by the way the counselor allowed Jimmy to tell his story. She did not automatically begin viewing Jimmy from a deficit model because of his background. All children are capable of flourishing. It takes a skilled counselor to bring out the uniqueness and capabilities in each child.

Permanently moving to the suburbs would not protect Jimmy from some of the same societal issues that plague inner city children. One added challenge for Jimmy is that he may not be readily embraced by the suburban community. There is an assumption that children who move from impoverished areas to the suburbs will be welcomed. This is not always the case, and Jimmy needs coaching on how to transfer the skills he has learned in treatment to his posttreatment environment. It would certainly be beneficial for Jimmy to have ongoing counseling services once the services at the treatment facility are terminated. Continued counseling services would allow Jimmy to have a trained professional assist him in further processing his feelings and navigating his successful transition. There is a notable lack of recent research investigating the long-term effects (including affluence in adulthood) of temporary placement of poor children in more affluent environments. However, the Gautreaux program and the U.S. Department of Housing and Urban Development's Moving to Opportunity (MTO) program, which relocated families of low socioeconomic status to low-poverty communities, produced some positive results.

The Gautreaux program was created in the 1970s as a result of a court-mandated desegregation of public housing. The research of Dr. James Rosenbaum of Northwestern University on this program contributed to the creation of the MTO program in 1994. One aspect of these studies was an investigation of the educational outcomes of the children who participated. The results from the Gautreaux study indicated that there were several positive long-term effects for children who moved from impoverished, urban areas to suburban areas. These children were more likely to take college prep courses, less likely to drop out of high school, more likely to attend college or university, and more likely to gain full-time employment after high school graduation (Ludwig, Ladd, & Duncan, 2001; Rosenbaum, 1991). Although the MTO program had more ambiguous results, participating children showed improvements in math and reading test scores (Ludwig et al., 2001). Education is one mechanism for getting out of poverty because it provides increased access and opportunity. Although more current research is warranted, I believe that exposure to new environments broadens a child's frame of reference and increases opportunity through educational advancement.

Finally, I want to elaborate on the importance of counselors being knowledgeable and empathetic toward children from impoverished backgrounds. I am reluctant to use the term *at risk* when describing children who grow up in poverty. I believe that even the child with the most privilege can be at risk for something. It is challenging to fully understand the worldview of a child living in poverty, and this is particularly true if a counselor has never resided in an impoverished community. The counselor in this case was wise to consult with a treatment team because consulting is always beneficial. In addition to consulting, attending workshops and conferences about poverty can prove to be valuable.

As a novice counselor, I attended the Framework for Understanding Poverty Workshop by Dr. Ruby Payne. Dr. Payne's workshop and book (Payne, 2001) do a phenomenal job of discussing the hidden rules of class in the United States. Poverty and its effects on children and families are explained with great detail, and the book presents many practical applications for counselors. Although most of the claims made in Dr. Payne's book were based on observations and have not been validated by hard research, she described many of the characteristics of children and families living in poverty that I have observed in my own work. Reading related literature, attending workshops, and consulting with other professionals can prove to be beneficial in enhancing one's knowledge and understanding of children such as Jimmy. In addition to educating themselves on the individual effects of poverty, it is a must that counselors become more aware of the institutional barriers and multiple oppressions faced by children and families living in poverty.

References

Corey, G. (2001). *Theory and practice of counseling and psychotherapy* (6th ed.). Pacific Grove, CA: Brooks/Cole.

Ludwig, J., Ladd, H. F., & Duncan, G. J. (2001). *The effects of urban poverty on educational outcomes: Evidence from a randomized experiment.* Washington, DC: Georgetown Public Policy Institute.

Payne, R. K. (2001). *A framework for understanding poverty.* Highlands, TX: Aha! Process Inc.

Ray, P., Alson, S., Lantieri, L., & Roderick, T. (1996). *Resolving conflict creatively: A teaching guide for grades kindergarten through six.* New York: Educators for Social Responsibility Metropolitan Area.

Rosenbaum, J. E. (2001). Black pioneers: Do their moves to the suburbs increase economic opportunity for mothers and children? *Housing Policy Debate, 2,* 1179–1214.

Scheeringa, M. S., & Zeanah, C. H. (1995). Symptom differences in traumatized infants and young children. *Infant Mental Health Journal, 16,* 259–270.

Vass, M., Jacobs, E., & Slavek, N. (1984). Live in family counseling: An integrated approach. *Personnel & Guidance Journal, 62,* 429–431.

Yule, W. (2001) Posttraumatic stress disorder in the general population and in children. *Journal of Clinical Psychiatry, 62,* 23–28.

16

"Let's Dance":
Race, Faith, and Sexual Orientation

This incident explores ways one school counselor attempted to help a young student begin to address conflicts among his race, faith, and sexual orientation. Counseling interventions, systemic interventions, and advocacy issues are addressed by the respondents.

■ Critical Incident

Jolie Ziomek-Daigle

I was in my 5th year as a middle school counselor in an urban public school system when I first met "Ricky Randolph," an 11-year-old, African American sixth grader. The school was located in a predominately poor area of the city, and the school, along with the local Baptist church, served as the center of many community activities. Reflective of the community, 95% of the students and 50% of the faculty members were African American, with the remainder of the faculty primarily Caucasian. Approximately 850 students attended the middle school and were enrolled in Grades 6–8.

There were two school counselors for the building: Ms. Smith and me. Ms. Smith was a 62-year-old African American with strong religious beliefs. She had been a teacher for 20 years and a school counselor for 12 years. Ms. Smith had a master's degree in counseling and did not hold any other certifications or licenses in the field. In contrast, I was a 30-year-old Caucasian and had been a school counselor for only 5 years. I had a specialist degree in counseling and was a licensed professional counselor–school and held certifications as a nationally certified counselor, nationally certified school counselor, and registered play therapist–school. We divided our caseload across the alphabet; I was responsible for students whose last names began with *A* through *L,* and Ms. Smith was responsible for students whose last names began with *M* though *Z.*

Ricky Randolph, of course, was on Ms. Smith's caseload. I became involved in working with Ricky, however, after a rather disturbing incident occurred. It was October, and the sixth graders were abuzz with excitement about their first after-school dance. Crushes were being revealed, hopes were high, and rejected invitations were accompanied by emotional stinging. Ms. Smith and I had been "putting out fires" and finding the need to assist many students with the developmental transition. Ricky was popular and well liked by his peers and teachers alike. The school dance, however, proved to be challenging even for a student like Ricky. In many ways, Ricky was just another kid dealing with the excitement of the first school dance. In other ways, though, Ricky presented an unusual case.

Ms. Smith was called to the principal's office for an emergency conference with Ricky and his mother, Mrs. Randolph. It had been reported that Ricky had asked another boy to accompany him to the school dance. There were four witnesses to the account, and Ricky admitted to the incident. During the conference, the principal and Ricky's mother were sternly talking with Ricky and making statements such as, "What's wrong with liking a woman?" "God did not make you to be with men," "It's a sin to like men and not women," and, "You're just scared of girls." After listening to the conversation, Ms. Smith facilitated discussion about how this was to be handled. The principal agreed not to treat the incident in a disciplinary fashion, and the adults all agreed that it was in Ricky's best interest to receive counseling from an elder at the Baptist church. Over lunch, while we were discussing the various dance-related crises that had arisen that day, Ms. Smith recounted the story to me.

My initial shock was unimaginable as I listened to my coworker tell the story of what happened. "Can you believe it?" she gasped. "What that boy needs is some good religious education!" Although I was admittedly a bit surprised on hearing that Ricky had asked another boy to the dance, my shock was prompted by how the situation was handled by the school staff. Ricky had been told in no uncertain terms that the only acceptable option was to be heterosexual, and he was now being sent for counseling at the local church. Where were the counseling, education, and referrals for Ricky and his mother? I realized that this was a sensitive situation, given that many of the reactions and solutions were culturally, religiously, and educationally based, but I was nonetheless motivated to do something to help Ricky. He needed an advocate, a counselor who would not impose her values on him.

Sensitive to the fact that Ricky was on Ms. Smith's caseload, I asked whether she was going to provide individual counseling to Ricky or refer him to an agency. When she expressed her belief that there was no need for counseling in this situation because the matter was being handled by Mrs. Randolph, I told Ms. Smith that I would be happy to screen Ricky and have him join a self-esteem group I was facilitating. My hope was that this would provide a means through which I could legitimately interact with Ricky and that I could provide follow-up sessions as needed.

With Ms. Smith's agreement, I screened Ricky for the group and met with his mother to discuss the consent form. He joined the group, seemed to enjoy listening to the other group members, and eventually opened up about his own struggles. In response to Ricky's disclosure that he was questioning his sexual orientation, I invited a representative of Parents, Families and Friends of Lesbians and Gays (PFLAG) to talk with the group about differences, sensitivity, and tolerance. The students were inspired and, with the principal's permission, presented this information to other students during their homeroom sessions. After the PFLAG presentation, Ricky asked me about support groups outside of school. I suggested that we meet with his mother together to discuss the community resources. During the meeting, Mrs. Randolph cautiously agreed to allow Ricky to attend PFLAG support groups as long as he continued with his church obligations. To normalize the situation and help Mrs. Randolph better understand her son, I also suggested that she attend the parent support group meetings.

Finally, recognizing that there were also some systemic issues to be addressed, I met with the coordinator of school counselors for the district. I told her about the incident, and we discussed the possibility of arranging sensitivity trainings for principals, school counselors, and social workers. Teachers were not targeted for the initial trainings simply because of how difficult it is for teachers to attend such trainings during the school day. We agreed that the staff members who did participate in the trainings could, in turn, relay the information to the teachers during a faculty meeting. As a result of this meeting, the trainings were scheduled for the beginning of the next school year.

As I reflect on the incident, I think of the many issues related to my involvement with Ricky Randolph. First, there were cultural issues related both to Ricky being raised in a southern Baptist, African American family and to Ricky and I differing across nearly all demographic categories. He and I were different in terms of ethnicity, religion, gender, sexual orientation, and socioeconomic status. Second, there were issues related to the fact that Ricky was not on my caseload. Because I thought it was so imperative that he and his family receive information regarding counseling services, I sought involvement with Ricky and his family. Finally, there were systemic issues. Students who identified as lesbian, gay, or bisexual or who were questioning and unsure of their sexual orientation were obviously being neglected and even harmed by the school system's approach to them. Because I advocated for this group to my supervisor, trainings were conducted, and awareness was raised.

Questions

1. How does the intersection of race, faith, and sexual orientation affect students who do not identify as heterosexual? How can a counselor help students reconcile these multiple identities?
2. How should I have handled my disagreement with Ms. Smith's approach to Ricky? What are your thoughts about the way I gained access to Ricky?
3. How can counselors best advocate for students and achieve systemic changes?
4. What would you have done differently?

■ Response

Linda L. Black

As I read the case of Ricky Randolph, I experienced multiple and conflicting emotions: profound sadness, disbelief, anger, irritation, regret, and hope. Of these, the two emotions that were most salient were profound sadness and deep regret. I felt profound sadness that gay, lesbian, bisexual, and transgendered (GLBT) children and adults continue to be subjected to overt oppression and discrimination and deep regret that, despite years of education and training, some counselors continue to do harm to GLBT youths because of their homophobia and heterosexist beliefs.

The intersection of one's identities—in this case, race, faith, and sexual orientation—is dynamic and presents opportunities as well as obstacles for individuals and their counselors. Coming to grips with these intersecting identities becomes even more challenging when child developmental processes must also be considered. When adults discuss these intersecting identities with a child, they should take into account the child's developmental level. For example, prepubescent children like Ricky are often considered to be concrete thinkers who are unable to think abstractly. Therefore, they often require adult intervention to sort out the complexities of what they think and feel. In addition to taking into account developmental levels, counselors must consider the culture of the child's family (e.g., parental attitudes, communication style) when deciding on a course of action.

One's race is often more readily identified than one's sexual orientation or religious beliefs. In this culture, children of color grow up in conditions of racism and oppression. They learn from their family and their experiences that others who are not like them may distrust or harm them. They learn to be cautious around others and to seek support from family and close friends. Within this support network, they can openly discuss the racial oppression and rejection they may feel. There are support and mutuality in the shared difference.

Children who begin to question their sexual orientation or to identify as something other than heterosexual, however, do not generally experience this same level of support and understanding in their support network. With respect to sexual orientation, adults are likely to dismiss or reject children's questions or behavior related to sexual orientation because they view such behavior as immature, confused, imitative, foolish, wrong, or deviant. Furthermore, many adults have difficulty accepting that prepubescent children, in general, are sexual beings with feelings, attractions, and questions. When issues of sexual orientation emerge, many adults become confused or reactionary in their response to children. In my experience, the reactionary response usually takes the form of a blame game, with the media, culture, heredity, or the child's upbringing taking the blame.

Religious or faith-based beliefs provide many people with a guide to living and rules by which to live. Many people find comfort and solace in these rules, but these rules often come into direct conflict when applied literally to the life of humans. For example, Ricky's religion likely taught him to always tell the truth. When he followed the rule to live truthfully and asked a boy to the dance, however, he was sternly admonished, told of his personal and moral failings before God, and "sentenced" to counseling with a church elder to correct his ways. I can only imagine Ricky's compounded confusion.

The impact of reactionary and punitive adult behavior on GLBT youths can be devastating and long lasting, and, when race and faith are added to the mix, it can create conditions for the "perfect storm" of rejection, depression, and confusion. GLBT youths learn very quickly and often dramatically that who they are and what they feel are considered wrong. They also learn that they must conceal these feelings for fear of condemnation and even assault. Thus, confusion and conflict emerge as the twin pillars of GLBT adolescent sexual development. GLBT youths, just like heterosexual youths, are drawn to fulfill their emotional and sexual developmental needs and desires. What is different for GLBT youths is that they fear (often rightly) that they will be ridiculed or worse but may not fully understand why. How could what they feel be considered so wrong and threatening to others? Concealment of their desires and behavior becomes a survival strategy, forcing GLBT youths to go outside of the mainstream for acceptance, connection, and information about their sexuality.

Homophobia and heterosexism are pervasive in Western culture. The power of these cultural views can be particularly oppressive for GLBT youths from families or backgrounds with strong religious beliefs. Granted, there are some religious and faith-based communities that are sensitive and inclusive of GLBT persons, but the sad truth is that those are the exception, not the rule. Condemnation that is religious or faith based in nature compounds the negative impact of prevailing cultural attitudes on GLBT youths. These youths begin to perceive that not only are they considered culturally deviant, even God thinks they are bad.

For youths coming out of families and communities with these beliefs, the weight of rejection and abandonment can be soul crushing. The impact of such societal rejection is profound. Gibson's (1989) benchmark study found that "gay youth are 2 to 3 times more likely to attempt suicide than other young people" and "comprise up to 30 percent of completed youth suicides annually" (p. 110). It is sad that "suicide is the leading cause of death among gay male, lesbian, bisexual and transsexual youth" (p. 110). Several recent research studies have also found that GLBT adolescents are significantly more likely to attempt suicide than their heterosexual peers (Bagley & Tremblay, 1997; Garofalo & Wolf, 1998; Lebson, 2002; Remafedi, French, Story, Resnick, & Blum, 1998).

To address the issues faced by GLBT youths, counselors must first evaluate and address their own heterosexist beliefs and attitudes. Counselors can look to the multicultural competencies (Sue, Arredondo, & McDavis, 1992) for a framework for addressing their own attitudes, knowledge, and skills in this area. Next, counselors must focus on the needs and welfare of GLBT youths, who may be isolated and potentially at risk. Counselors can assist GLBT youths by being overt in their recognition and acceptance of the youths' experiences as individuals. GLBT youths need to know it is safe to be visible and to let someone know them. They need to be able to voice who they are and discuss their confusion, fears, and conflicts without judgment, embarrassment, or punishment. Counselors may also provide reading materials as well as referrals to outside agencies and support groups where GLBT youths can feel validated for all aspects of themselves. In general, dealing with one's own complexity as an individual takes time, education, clarification, feedback, and support. GLBT youths deserve nothing less.

Because of counselors' roles as advocates and educators, they should approach system-level intervention next. It would be great if all counselors worked in settings that welcomed all persons regardless of their demographic characteristics, but the truth is they do not. Like the counselor in this case, one's ability to proceed is influenced by the attitudes and beliefs of the school administrator, faculty, and school community. Some examples of system-level intervention are displaying "safe space" placards in offices and around the school building; providing for the education of students, faculty, and staff through speakers from PFLAG; and forming gay–straight alliance groups in school communities. These activities can demonstrate to GLBT youths that they matter and that their needs and security are taken seriously.

In the case of Ricky, I was uncertain whether the counselor ever directly discussed her feelings and concerns with Ms. Smith. Clearly, the counselor was concerned and caring enough to get directly involved, yet I wondered whether issues of race, religion, history with the school system, or possibly respect for one's elders inhibited her from addressing Ms. Smith directly. I recognize that issues of race, faith, and sexual orientation can be difficult to discuss even in the abstract, let alone face to face with one's colleagues. Nonetheless, if counselors truly wish to ameliorate the negative consequences of heterosexism and homophobia, they must at least be willing to discuss such issues with those around them. I would have had a dialogue with Ms. Smith regarding my concerns about how she reconciles her personal beliefs with the ethical code counselors are bound to follow. It seems obvious that Ms. Smith cares for Ricky, but she needs to examine the potential consequences of her form of caring.

These conversations need to happen on a personal level, with understanding and accountability as a foundation. No doubt this would be a tough conversation to have, yet I believe counselors are ethically required to discuss perceived ethical violations with their peers (American Counseling Association, 2005). At a minimum, Ms. Smith violated the moral principles of autonomy, justice, and nonmaleficence in this case, and she infringed on the spirit of the free speech and establishment (separation of church and state) clauses of the U.S. Constitution. By failing to address Ms. Smith directly, the counselor in this case allowed herself to become complicit in these ethical violations. Although the counselor was able to address Ricky's own short-term needs by gaining access to him through a self-esteem group, she might have left other students at risk. Finally, I wondered how Ms. Smith responded when she heard about the PFLAG classroom presentations. Might Ms. Smith view the counselor's efforts to improve the system without having directly consulted her as undercutting and disrespectful?

On a more personal level, I am mystified how counselors who hold conservative religious beliefs stating that homosexuality is a sin or an abomination before the Lord can view their clients nonjudgmentally or work to promote and accept diversity, as required by the profession's *Code of Ethics* (American Counseling Association, 2005). Clearly, Ms. Smith did not meet these ethical requirements in her response to Ricky. How can she reconcile these requirements with her personally held belief that Ricky is doomed to hell if he does not change his ways? How can she avoid imposing her values on Ricky and his mother? Although I understand that she was concerned about Ricky on the basis of her personal religious beliefs, I believe her response was misplaced and psychologically harmful to Ricky. Furthermore, I submit that Ms. Smith, in her current state and without direct intervention, does not belong in the field of counseling. My strong reactions to Ms. Smith highlight the dilemma facing counselors whose faith-based beliefs differ from the teachings, beliefs, and ethics code of the profession. Just as Ricky must struggle with the intersection of his race, faith, and sexual orientation, so must our profession.

In conclusion, I believe that counselors can best advocate for their students by understanding and attempting to diminish the devastating impact of homophobia and heterosexism. Systemic change on behalf of GLBT youths starts with one individual who is self-aware, educated, compassionate, passionate, accountable, and resourceful. School counselors face many challenges as they balance the competing needs of parents and students, the public education system, and prevailing community norms. For me, it is most important that counselors take an educative rather than militant stance by inviting parents, administrators, peers, and students into discussion and dialogue about the needs of GLBT youths. We must; the kids are counting on us.

Response

Michael M. Kocet

In this critical incident, it is evident that the issues of race, faith, and sexual orientation do in fact intersect and sometimes conflict with one another. From a multicultural perspective, it is important to keep in mind that all people hold memberships in a variety of cultural identities, and one should not attempt to segment each of these characteristics into separate and distinct categories. Ricky is not African American on Mondays and Fridays, gay or questioning on Wednesdays, a boy on Thursdays and Saturdays, and Baptist on Sundays. All aspects of Ricky's identity—his race, gender, sexual orientation, socioeconomic status, religion, and spirituality—are interwoven in shaping his identity and self-concept. Counselors have the responsibility of helping students like Ricky learn to understand, manage, and reconcile multiple identities. This is especially challenging when some aspects of identity are in conflict with one another.

In presenting Ricky's case, the counselor asked how his multiple identities may affect him and how she could help him reconcile the conflict that exists among his race, faith, and sexual orientation. When it comes to helping children who identify as gay, lesbian, bisexual, or questioning (GLBQ), it is vital that counselors become familiar with the identity development literature (Cass, 1979; McCarn & Fassinger, 1996; Reynolds & Hanjorgiris, 2000; Troiden, 1989) related to sexual orientation and understand that the process of coming out is not a fixed event but takes place over a lifetime, in each new encounter or social interaction (Reynolds & Hanjorgiris, 2000). This literature suggests that a common struggle for people in coming out is reconciling their sexual orientation with the societal messages and mores that suggest that being anything other than heterosexual is wrong. These messages tend to exist regardless of a person's racial or religious background, but they are particularly profound in communities of color and in communities that practice conservative religions (Boykin, 1996, 2005; Crouteau & Constantine, 2005).

Establishing a Safe Environment for All Students

In these situations, it is essential that counselors help foster a supportive environment in which students can explore their identity without fear of judgment. This is important not only in counseling sessions but also in the school environment at large. One of the cruelest words that students can use to taunt or insult another student is *faggot*. Unfortunately, this word is heard all too often in classrooms, hallways, cafeterias, locker rooms, and playgrounds. Although it is most often used to insult another student without actually referring to the student's real or perceived sexual orientation, the word becomes synonymous with *bad*. By the time students reach an age at which they begin questioning sexual orientation, the message that being a faggot is bad is already deeply ingrained. School counselors, teachers, parents, and school administrators should all unite to promote dialogue about and awareness of the deeply harmful impact of hateful words and violence on sexual minority youths and to establish a sense of safety and security for all students in schools, regardless of sexual orientation.

Systemic Interventions

In the absence of such an environment, incidents with students like Ricky often prompt an awareness that diversity training is needed. I was pleased that the counselor chose to work with the other counselors and administrators in the district to create sensitivity training addressing gay and lesbian issues. Conversely, I disagree with the school's decision to exclude teachers from the training. Teachers are on the front line in terms of witnessing the teasing, taunting, and bullying of sexual minority youths by peers. If teachers do not go through sensitivity training themselves, they may overlook instances of bigotry and prejudice, thereby perpetuating GLBQ students' feelings of invisibility and shame. The school administrators need to value the sensitivity training and provide teachers with an opportunity to participate in such activities during school hours.

Most school districts require teachers to have some kind of continuing education, usually provided through in-service trainings, and sensitivity training on GLBQ issues is greatly needed. The book *How Homophobia Hurts Children: Nurturing Diversity at Home, at School, and in the Community* (Baker, 2002) and the video *It's Elementary: Talking About Gay Issues in Schools* (Chasnoff, 1999) are useful resources for teachers, counselors, administrators, and parents regarding sexual minority youth issues and may be helpful in developing the in-service trainings.

Counselors can also advocate for GLBQ students and help create change by challenging administrative policies on a number of levels. For example, counselors can advocate for a school district–wide policy of no tolerance for bullying, including the harassment of GLBQ students. Alternatively, like the counselor in the incident, counselors can help develop staff trainings that foster greater understanding and respect for all kinds of differences. There is often the narrow view that sexual orientation should not be discussed in school settings, particularly in elementary and middle schools. Trainings provide parents, teachers, counselors, school staff, and administrators with a formal opportunity to have their assumptions challenged and to share accurate information about GLBQ youths and their development (Fairchild & Hayward, 1998; Perrotti & Westheimer, 2001). Also, as Baker's (2002) book and Chasnoff's (1999) video have demonstrated, children of all ages have the superb capacity to teach adults how to be inclusive, respectful, and wise beyond their years. Children's literature is an important way to introduce young students to the subject of sexual identity in a normative and safe manner with which children can positively identity (De Paola, 1979; Skutch, 1995). Gay and lesbian students often feel marginalized and invisible. By advocating for GLBQ students, counselors can help to foster a more welcoming and nurturing environment for all students (Human Rights Watch, 2001).

Counseling Interventions

Ricky was apparently not fortunate enough to attend a school in which such sensitivity training had already been conducted and in which safety for all students, regardless of sexual orientation, had already been established. In asking another boy to the dance, he suddenly found himself confronted by strong messages of disapproval. Counseling interventions are especially important at this time.

It can be very difficult for students like Ricky to manage the mixed messages that they may be receiving from their family, church, school officials, and peers and their own internal messages. One way a counselor can be supportive and not leading is to use the language of the student. For example, if a young girl in a session identifies herself as a free spirit rather than saying, "I am a lesbian," then the counselor should explore what being a free spirit means to that student.

It is also important, as I stated earlier, not to attend exclusively to sexual orientation but instead to also address multiple identities. In Ricky's case, affirming his cultural identity and religious upbringing was also important. Although the school counselor may have different personal beliefs about sexual orientation, she must be culturally sensitive and recognize the different ways that sexual orientation issues are understood, particularly in the African American community. Some African Americans, for example, do not engage in traditional counseling or psychotherapy and often seek counsel from a pastor or church elder. According to the *ACA Code of*

Ethics (American Counseling Association, 2005) Section A.1.d., Support Network Involvement, "Counselors recognize that support networks hold various meanings in the lives of clients and consider enlisting the support, understanding, and involvement of others (e.g. religious/spiritual/community leaders, family members, friends) as positive resources, when appropriate, with client consent" (p. 4).

One recommendation for the school counselor in the incident is (with student and parental consent) to contact the religious elder with whom Ricky has been speaking to partner with him or her in addressing Ricky's struggles. It may be important for the counselor to do more research and locate local, state, or national organizations and resources that are offered specifically for GLBQ people of color. Ricky needs to meet other GLBQ youths and adults who are also persons of color and who are able to make religion, race, and sexual orientation compatible and interconnected.

I support the counselor's decision to invite a speaker from PFLAG to talk with the support group. It is vital that students be exposed to healthy role models from a variety of backgrounds. The PFLAG speaker, for example, provided all the students—gay, straight, and questioning—the opportunity to discuss the importance of celebrating differences and the uniqueness of human beings. This experience also served to increase the students' sensitivity toward those who may be questioning their sexual orientation.

Resources

It is critical for counselors to have available local, state, and national resources on GLBT issues. Building a library of affirming and inclusive books, movies, Web sites, documentaries, and resource people is very important. Organizations such as the Gay, Lesbian & Straight Education Network (www.glsen.org), PFLAG (www.pflag.org), and The Point Foundation (www.thepointfoundation.org) sponsor outstanding Web sites that feature education and resource sections. Web sites designed for GLBQ youths are also important for peer support, such as *Oasis Magazine,* an online queer magazine (http://www.oasismag.com/). A visit to such a Web site might have helped Ricky's counselor, for example, to discover an organization specifically geared toward helping Baptist individuals reconcile their faith with their nonheterosexual identity (the Association of Welcoming & Affirming Baptists; www.wabaptists.org) or an organization focused on the intersection of race and sexual orientation (Lesbian, Gay, Bisexual and Transgender People of African Descent; www.blackstripe.com).

Dealing With Issues Openly and Honestly

I believe that the school counselor missed an opportunity to help educate her colleague, Ms. Smith, about the importance of respecting cultural differences and to have an authentic dialogue about issues surrounding sexual orientation. It would have been helpful for the counselor to talk with Ms. Smith about healthy exploration of sexual identity issues for children. Ms. Smith displayed her own cultural and religious biases by stating, "What that boy needs is some good religious education!" and failing to address the principal's and Ricky's mother's comments, "What's wrong with liking a woman?" and, "It's a sin to like men and not women." Ms. Smith needs to understand the implications of such attitudes for Ricky and his ability to form a healthy sexual identity and to synthesize it into his overall identity. It might have been helpful for the counselor to share with Ms. Smith current books, articles, and other resources that address sexual minority issues in schools. Destigmatizing sexuality is an important component in understanding the emotional, social, and psychological needs of gay youths. Another way the counselor could have improved the situation with Ms. Smith is to do her own research with regard to sexual orientation issues in the Black community (Boykin, 1996, 2005; Crouteau & Constantine, 2005). Talking with colleagues and experts in this area as well as consulting the literature in the field would have provided the counselor with the knowledge and background necessary to better resolve the issue. Although it seems that Ricky is on the road to receiving the help he needs, the counselor did not fully involve all members of Ricky's support system in a way that would be most effective.

It also seems that the counselor was not very forthright with Ms. Smith, Ricky, or his mother about the reasons for her desire to have Ricky join her support group. Of course, the counselor needed to be sensitive to the nature of the problem, but she also needed to help her colleague understand why Ricky should participate in this support group. In other words, the support group was not only to improve his self-esteem but also to provide him with counseling and a supportive environment to explore his struggles and to help him normalize his own questioning. Additionally, what was Mrs. Randolph told about the support group? It seems that the counselor used the guise of a self-esteem group to help Ricky explore his sexual orientation but did not discuss this intention with the other school counselor, Ricky, or his mother. There needed to be more direct and honest communication about the counselor's reasons for having Ricky join the support group. Ricky clearly needs affirmation and support as he works to build (with the counselor's help) a positive self-esteem, but this is not the whole story. Creating a positive self-esteem can enable Ricky to develop the internal ego strength needed to face discrimination and prejudice about his sexual orientation.

If I were the counselor working directly with Ricky, his mother, and the other school counselor, I would have been more forthright in discussing the importance of Ricky getting the formal support services he needed to help him explore his identity. I would have fostered more direct and honest communication with Ms. Smith by voicing my concerns about how the situation with Ricky was handled. With Ricky's and his mother's permission, I also would have consulted with the church elder to create a team approach that would hopefully empower Ricky and help him feel safe and supported through this process. Finally, I would have done my own homework as a counselor to gather more appropriate resources to help Ricky and his mother normalize and better understand Ricky's emerging sexual identity, particularly focused on how GLBQ issues intersect with Ricky's racial, gender, religious, and socioeconomic identities.

References

American Counseling Association. (2005). *ACA code of ethics*. Alexandria, VA: Author.

Bagley, C., & Tremblay, P. (1997). Suicidal behaviors in homosexual and bisexual males. *Crisis, 18*(1), 24–34.

Baker, J. M. (2002). *How homophobia hurts children: Nurturing diversity at home, at school, and in the community.* Binghamton, NY: Harrington Park Press.

Boykin, K. (1996). *One more river to cross: Black & gay in America.* New York: Anchor Books.

Boykin, K. (2005). *Beyond the down low: Sex, lies, and denial in Black America.* New York: Carroll & Graf.

Cass, V. (1979). Homosexual identity formation: A theoretical model. *Journal of Homosexuality, 4*, 219–235.

Chasnoff, D. (Director). (1999). *It's elementary: Talking about gay issues in schools* [Documentary]. United States: New Day Films.

Crouteau, J., & Constantine, M. (2005). Race and sexual orientation in multicultural counseling: Navigating rough waters. In J. Croteau, J. Lark, M. Lidderdale, & Y. B. Chung (Eds.), *Deconstructing heterosexism in the counseling professions: A narrative approach* (pp. 159–185). Thousand Oaks, CA: Sage.

DePaola, T. (1979). *Oliver Button is a sissy.* San Diego, CA: Voyager Books.

Fairchild, B., & Hayward, N. (1998). *Now that you know: A parents' guide to understanding their gay and lesbian children* (3rd ed.). New York: Harcourt Brace.

Garofalo, R., & Wolf, C. (1998). The association between health risk behaviors and sexual orientation among a school-based sample of adolescents. *Pediatrics, 101,* 895–902.

Gibson, P. (1989). Gay male and lesbian youth suicide. In M. R. Feinleib (Ed.), *Report of the secretary's task force on youth suicide* (Vol. 3, pp. 110–142). Washington, DC: U.S. Department of Health and Human Services.

Human Rights Watch. (2001). *Hatred in the hallways: Violence and discrimination against lesbian, gay, bisexual, and transgender students in U.S. schools.* New York: Author.

Lebson, M. (2002). Suicide among homosexual youth. *Journal of Homosexuality, 42,* 107–117.

McCarn, S., & Fassinger, R. (1996). Revisioning sexual minority identity formation: A new model of lesbian identity and its implications for counseling and research. *Counseling Psychologist, 24,* 508–534.

Perrotti, J., & Westheimer, K. (2001). *When the drama club is not enough: Lessons from the safe schools program for gay and lesbian students.* Boston: Beacon Press.

Remafedi, G., French, S., Story, M., Resnick, M. D., & Blum, R. (1998). The relationship between suicide risk and sexual orientation: Results of a population-based study. *American Journal of Public Health, 88,* 57–60.

Reynolds, A., & Hanjorgiris, W. (2000). Coming out: Lesbian, gay, and bisexual identity development. In R. Perez, K. DeBord, & K. Bieschke (Eds.), *Handbook of counseling and psychotherapy with lesbian, gay, and bisexual clients* (pp. 35–55). Washington, DC: American Psychological Association.

Skutch, R. (1995). *Who's in a family?* Berkeley, CA: Tricycle Press.

Sue, D. W., Arredondo, P., & McDavis, R. J. (1992). Multicultural counseling competencies and standards: A call to the profession. *Journal of Counseling and Development, 70,* 477–486.

Troiden, R. (1989). The formation of homosexual identities. *Journal of Homosexuality, 17,* 43–73.

17

"People Say I'm Black":
Racial Identity Development

Many concerns exist for multiracial children with regard to their racial identity development. These factors are even more complex in a culturally insensitive environment, such as a school. This incident relates the case of a young boy whose identity development journey led him to be inappropriately diagnosed. The expert respondents offer insight into appropriate intervention using reality theory and systemic consultation.

■ Critical Incident

Carmella Hill

"Gerald Collins," a 10-year-old biracial child whose mother was Caucasian and whose father was African American, lived in a predominantly African American community. Gerald was an only child. His mother was a homemaker, and his father was in the Army Reserves. The family had lived in the community for 2 years. In the neighborhood, there were two other bicultural families. Each of the families had one biracial child who had at least two other single-race siblings. Gerald's school was racially mixed, with African American students accounting for approximately 50% of the student population.

Mr. and Mrs. Collins sought counseling for Gerald at the insistence of his school. Apparently, Gerald had been getting into frequent fights with classmates and had been suspended several times. As a condition for his return to school, he was referred for counseling in the community. I was an intern at the community mental health (CMH) agency, and the case was referred to me. Gerald was diagnosed by the CMH intake worker as having oppositional defiant disorder (ODD; Code 313.81 in the *Diagnostic and Statistical Manual of Mental Disorders;* 4th ed., text rev.; *DSM–IV–TR;*

American Psychiatric Association, 2000), and I was directed to work on anger management skills with him because he was aggressive toward his peers and teachers.

In preparation for my work with Gerald, I met with his parents. Gerald's parents described him as "a good kid." They indicated that they rarely had trouble with him and were firm in stating that they had never witnessed any aggressive behavior on his part. Mrs. Collins acknowledged that Gerald sometimes showed "attitude" when he did not get what he wanted, but she expressed her opinion that "it is normal behavior for children."

Although they had no problems at home with Gerald, Mr. and Mrs. Collins acknowledged that this school year had been different. In particular, Gerald seemed to be having difficulties at school, frequently getting in fights with classmates and displaying a disrespectful attitude toward his teacher. They indicated that he had been suspended several times during the year for fighting with his peers and once for attempting to assault his female Caucasian teacher.

On receiving Mr. and Mrs. Collins's written consent, I contacted Gerald's teacher and school counselor to inquire about his difficulties at school. Both described Gerald as being "temperamental but very intelligent." He was doing fine academically and faithfully completed his work in class and turned in homework assignments. Nevertheless, they indicated that Gerald began having behavioral difficulties in school after a racial incident between two African American boys and one Caucasian boy. They shared that the incident caused tension in the school because of rumors that the Caucasian boy was not punished in the same manner as the two African American boys. Eventually, the atmosphere in the school settled and returned to normal, but Gerald's behavior did not.

As instructed by my supervisor, I began holding weekly sessions with Gerald and focused our sessions on anger management and self-control. Toward this end, I used cognitive-behavioral therapy to help Gerald decrease his aggressive behavior and angry feelings. I also maintained contact with Gerald's school to monitor his progress. To my dismay, Gerald's school continued to report that Gerald's behavior was not changing.

After about 2 months, however, when Gerald and I had formed a solid therapeutic relationship, we had a breakthrough. Gerald told me that he hated himself. When I explored this with him, he began to reveal his inner feelings, and I helped him connect these inner feelings with his external behaviors. In the process, I asked what was really going on with him in school.

Gerald shared that he was being teased about being Black. When I asked how he identified himself, he stated, "Well, people say I am Black." When I asked again and emphasized my interest in how he saw himself, he stated, "Mixed." Gerald then began to cry. He said that he was not only African American but Caucasian too.

Remembering that his misbehavior began just after the racial incident at his school, I asked Gerald to tell me about what had happened. He told me about the fight between the three boys, two of whom were African American and one of whom was Caucasian. He explained that he was friends with all three boys but thought "it was unfair" that his Caucasian friend "got off free" and his Black friends got punished. Gerald also told me that, shortly after the incident, he started to have problems with some Caucasian students calling him a "nigger" and "slave boy." To keep the boys from talking about him, Gerald told them he was not Black and to stop calling him a nigger. He said that he was Caucasian as well as African American and that he did not like the fact that some Caucasian students were being mean to him given that he was "one of them," at least partially.

Gerald also talked about how the African American students started to hate him because he said he was not Black. He explained that this was not what he meant, that he did not mean to offend them. He explained that he simply meant that being mixed is different than being Black. Nonetheless, Gerald said his African American friends would no longer play with him at recess. In addition, he complained that some of the Caucasian students had threatened to "kick my butt." Gerald said he told his teacher, but he felt she was ignoring him. Gerald stated, "I know she was looking out for them [the Caucasian students]." Gerald reported that he had also tried talking to his mother about the incidents, but she told him "people are ignorant" and to ignore them. Feeling that his teacher was protecting the Caucasian students and that his mother was ignoring the situation, Gerald became quite frustrated, and his anger increased. As a result, he resorted to defending himself by fighting with the Caucasian students as well as with the African American students.

In response to his fights and suspensions, Gerald's teacher referred him to the school counselor. Unfortunately, the school counselor was Caucasian, and Gerald refused to see her. Despite several conferences with Gerald's parents, his behavior continued to escalate, to the point that the school insisted he attend counseling for anger management at a CMH center. Having met with Gerald for nearly 2 months and coming to understand how the racial incident had affected him, I started to rethink Gerald's ODD diagnosis.

In light of Gerald's new information, I wanted to work with him on his self-esteem and identity issues. I really felt Gerald was misdiagnosed. He was labeled aggressive, angry, and defiant. Instead, in my opinion, Gerald was having identity problems. In supervision, I expressed my belief that Gerald's diagnosis should be identity problem (Code 313.82) and that I should work on his self-esteem and identity issues. Nevertheless, because I was a novice counselor who was perceived as overly zealous, I was directed to continue to work on the anger and aggression issues that had landed Gerald in counseling. My supervisor reminded me that the purpose of counseling in Gerald's instance was to keep him from being suspended or even expelled from school.

Although I continued to help Gerald work on decreasing his anger and aggressive behaviors, as directed by my supervisor, I also worked on his self-esteem and identity issues. We talked about what it means to be biracial, about his feelings of not fitting anywhere, and about his desire to express his whole racial identity rather than only part of it. We also role-played situations in which someone might make a racist comment to him. In these role plays, I focused not only on how Gerald could control his external reaction (behavior) but also on how he could process his feelings and respond internally.

After about 10 more sessions, Gerald's school reported that he was behaving differently; he was not as angry or aggressive toward his peers or teachers. I believe Gerald's changes were a direct result of self-esteem and identity work. Again, in my opinion, his anger and aggressive issues were Gerald's external way of dealing with his internal identity struggles.

Questions

1. How can counselors, particularly new counselors, effectively conceptualize a case and determine the diagnosis that is most reflective of a client's issues?
2. What are some ways to determine when presenting concerns that are not necessarily a result of mental disorders may disguise underlying issues with children?

3. What other diagnosis and treatment modalities could I have used with this particular case?
4. What are other techniques that counselors can use to help children struggling with their racial identity development?
5. With the increasing number of bi- and multiracial children, how can training programs better prepare counselors to address racial identity and multicultural issues in counseling?

■ Response

Charles L. Thompson

I congratulate Gerald's counselor for exercising the wisdom to try something different despite being directed to stay the course with what seems to have been an extreme case of misdiagnosis, followed, of course, by the corresponding wrong treatment plan. It is unfortunate that 2 months passed before the two errors were corrected and the counseling process was finally put on track. It is, however, a credit to the counselor that she made the midcourse corrections that led to the success Gerald was able to realize from his counseling experience. Just how was the counselor able to turn the situation around? First, she maintained contact with the school to get feedback on the progress, or lack thereof, that Gerald was making. Second, she worked on connecting with Gerald and building a trusting relationship with him. This connection was especially significant for a child who basically was friendless in his school. He was not fitting in with his peers, and he did not feel cared for by any of the adults in the school. Gerald needed a buddy other than his parents, and I think the counselor was a good start toward filling that need. Third, once the trusting relationship was established, Gerald was able to open up and talk about what was really going on with him. In a sense, one could say that Gerald and the counselor established the important therapeutic alliance that is needed to meet counseling goals. Somehow, when one is working with children, *having a buddy* sounds better than *therapeutic alliance,* especially when one is not working to heal a sickness. Gerald felt free to talk about his feelings of frustration as a result of being ignored by his teacher, misunderstood by his mother, and unable to stop the teasing and harassment by his former friends. We all know from Psychology 101 and personal experience that the very normal reaction to frustration is aggression, especially when the frustration reaches the level it did with Gerald. Fourth, the counselor was very skillful in pleasing her supervisor without compromising her job or Gerald's progress in counseling.

Diagnostic Considerations

First, I think all counselors can learn from the lesson presented in Gerald's case. Reliance on an intake interview, which obviously lacked input from Gerald, resulted in a misdiagnosis and, therefore, a mistreatment plan. At the risk of having my health provider status removed from my license, I need to be forthright regarding my thoughts about the *DSM–IV–TR*. I agree with Glasser's (2004, 2005) view that the *DSM–IV–TR* is basically a book of unhappiness (presenting symptoms), which should not be treated with the medical model because there is no underlying pathology. Exceptions are Parkinson's disease, Alzheimer's disease, and Huntington's disease as well as brain injury when there is pathology. When mental illness or disorders are diagnosed from symptoms alone (as in Gerald's case) with no supporting pathology, a basic tenet of medical science is ignored. Clients are better served if counselors view symptoms, such as aggressive behavior, as manifestations of unhappiness caused by failure to meet one or more of the client's basic human needs. Removing the symptom does not necessarily solve the problem. Both Maslow's (1970) and Glasser's (1998) lists of human needs included love and belonging. Gerald was having difficulty meeting his need for love and belonging in his school situation. He was not finding his place in his peer group or feeling cared for by his teacher. Wubbolding (2005), writing about the power of love and belonging, stated that he believed human relationships that are liberating, gratifying, empowering, and fun provide the royal road to mental health. The need for love and belonging motivates people to be relentless in their pursuit of human closeness. Gerald, frustrated in meeting his need to belong, tried to change the behavior of his friends through his aggressive behavior, which worsened the situation. More frustration resulted from the teacher's apparently differential treatment of Black and White students for the same misbehavior.

Treatment Approach

As Gerald's counselor, with a reality therapy orientation to counseling, my immediate task would be to work on our relationship to the point that he would feel free to "tell me what it is like being Gerald in your school." Toward that end, I would spend some time talking about the assets Gerald has going for him. He does well at home with his parents, has a history of good school behavior, and is an excellent, responsible student. We also might talk about interests and hobbies that Gerald would be willing to share with me. When we did get to the point at which Gerald would share with me his relationship problems with his former friends, I would try to avoid minimizing the seriousness of his situation or fixing his problem with advice. Gerald's mother attempted to downplay the relationship problems, and the anger management program aimed to fix the behavior problem. Minimizing the problem carries the possible side effect of making Gerald think there is something wrong with him for feeling the way he does. Only when Gerald confirmed that I understood the problem the way he did, his feelings about the situation, and what he would like to have happen would I initiate the following problem-solving plan (Thompson, Rudolph, & Henderson, 2004).

First, I would have him evaluate what he was doing that was helping the situation and what he was doing that did not help. If things Gerald was doing were not working very well, I might have him consider stopping them. Next, we could discuss some new things he could do to fill the free time created by stopping his ineffective behaviors. For example, we might examine how Glasser's (1998, 2000) choice theory provides two options. One can change what one wants, or one can change what one is doing to get what one wants. Because the only behavior people can change is their own, we could shift our focus from changing the former friends' behavior to changing what Gerald could do that would help. Of course, changing one's behavior often effects change in others' behavior. We could examine what Gerald's tormentors were trying to get him to do with their harassment—possibly to get him in trouble for fighting. We might consider finding a new set of friends and a support group in the school by focusing on making one friend at a time or joining a club or a team. Each counseling session would end with a commitment to try something different. For example,

Gerald might help a classmate who needed tutoring. A basic tenet of reality therapy is that bad feelings are not likely to change unless one changes one's behavior.

If I were required to use a *DSM–IV–TR* diagnostic label for a child, I would probably use adjustment disorder with depressed mood, which, in my opinion, has the least potential to harm the child. Three things about diagnostic labels seem to be true. First, they are difficult to remove from a person's record. The client has them for life. Second, people often live down to their diagnostic labels and never improve beyond that point. Third, if a psychiatrist is involved, there is likely to be a prescription for medication. As I have noted, I think choice theory reality therapy could work well with Gerald, provided that I could connect with him and that we had the same quality of relationship he had with his counselor. The counselor became an important part of Gerald's quality world. Without that relationship, I doubt any treatment modality would be very effective.

Solution-focused brief counseling is a second possible treatment modality. Often, clients like Gerald respond well to solution-focused brief counseling when the counseling agenda is based on the miracle question: "What if during the night, while you were sleeping, a miracle happened and your problem went away and you did not know the miracle had happened; what would be your first clue that there was no longer a problem?" Cognitive-behavioral therapy, which was used by the counselor, and rational emotive behavior therapy could be useful in helping Gerald examine his thinking or self-talk that was leading to his frustration, anger, and aggressive behavior.

Establish a Network

For all children, a strong sense of identity regarding who they are and where they fit in is important. Erickson (1968) listed identity formation as a major developmental task for the adolescent period of development. Glasser (1965) based his treatment program at the Ventura School for Girls, a reform school, on moving the girls from a failure identity to a success identity. His program focused on giving his students two important qualities of a success identity: being lovable and being capable. He hired staff who would care about the girls and instructed the teachers to make sure each student had some success in each class each day. Going into counseling, Gerald had mastered the academic side of the success identity equation, but he still had to work on filling his need to belong to his peer group.

Several things have been done to help students struggling with racial identity. Many of these interventions could be used in Gerald's situation, including consultation with Gerald's parents and teacher as well as group interventions with his classmates. Interventions with Gerald's parents could include having them listen at length to how things are going for him at school. His mother's attempts to downplay his feelings of frustration and anger by dismissing the harassment of his former friends as ignorance are not working for Gerald. His parents have a significant role in helping Gerald clarify and resolve his racial identity confusion. Many communities have active support groups for biracial children and their parents. Mothers of biracial children have a support group online. There also are a wealth of resources online for biracial children and their parents. One such Web site is http://www.diversitydtg. com/artides/interracial_families.htm#top. *Interracial Voice* is a periodical that publishes articles on biracial children and families. The January–February 2002 issue contained an article titled "Educating Those Who Educate Biracial Children," which parents and teachers of biracial children should read (Williamson, 2002). I would encourage Gerald and his family to make a scrapbook of all the famous biracial people who have made it through situations similar to Gerald's. Such people include Senator Edward W. Brooke, Booker T. Washington, Tiger Woods, Halle Berry, Vin Diesel, Derek Jeter, Jason Kidd, Andre Watts, Mariah Carey, and Mya. Some of this information can be found at http://www.mixedfolks.com/.

One family I contacted emphasized how lucky their children were to have the best of both Black and White worlds. The children had bulletin boards in their room that had the biracial flag, biracial identity statement, and pictures of both sides of their family. The family tried to integrate both races (via books, toys, TV shows, and friends). The mother went to her children's classes, read books to the students about being different, and had the children do a craft on what they learned. The family also involved their children in cultural events for all races, and they attended an integrated church. I recommend three sources on racial identity models: Cross (1971), Helms (1993), and Poston (1990).

In addition to having the parents work with the classroom teacher, I would consult with the school counselor about what could be done individually with Gerald and with his classmates. First, if there is one no-tolerance rule I can tolerate, it is the one about no tolerance for bullying. If bullying is happening, it needs to be stopped, and the perpetrators should receive group counseling about ways to meet their needs that neither violate school policy nor interfere with other students' rights. Second, I would like the school counselor and Gerald's teacher to work on becoming part of Gerald's quality world of people he can trust when he needs help and support.

Third, I would like the school counselor to hold some problem-solving classroom meetings with Gerald's class, focusing on the identity of each child in the classroom. One such meeting could focus on all the subgroups to which each student belongs. Example groups are Irish on mother's side, English on father's side, gender, eye color, hair color, age group, favorite foods, activities, and skills. The purpose of the activity is to teach the children how each of them is unique and that race is only one of several ways people differ from each other. Some elementary school teachers conduct classroom meetings on the basis of which of two groups each student belongs to: workers or disturbers. Of course, each student's identity as a worker or disturber cannot be determined until the students define the difference between the groups and what one would do to claim an identity in either group. Fourth, I would work with the teacher and school counselor in finding school or community groups, clubs, or teams Gerald could join. Being part of such groups working together for a common purpose provides an instant feeling of belonging and self-esteem in contributing to the team effort.

Preparing to Work With Multiracial Children

Seven million (2.4%) Americans described themselves as multiracial in the 2000 census (U.S. Census Bureau, 2001). Among Americans under 18 years old, 4.2% were multiracial, compared with 1.9% of adults. Clearly, counselor preparation programs should address the kind of problems experienced by Gerald in his school and community. Programs accredited by the Council for the Accreditation of Counseling and Related Educational Programs are required to provide training in multicultural counseling but could err in neglecting children and adults who struggle with trying to find their racial identity in one group or another. It is becoming evident that the best solution for many is to seek a biracial identity instead of trying to adapt to a bad fit in a single-identity group. Of course, the focus of the first American system of psychotherapy, Carl Rogers's (see Moss, 1999) person-centered counseling, always has been to treat people as unique individuals with their own culture and family history. Our job as counselors is to let our clients teach us about their uniqueness. Counselors are not supposed to enter a counseling relationship blinded by assumptions, hypotheses, and preconceptions about clients based on their racial or cultural identities. Personally, I think this works best for me; nonetheless, I do find cultural information helpful in modifying my counseling style to fit my clients' preferences.

In summary, Gerald's case is a good one to include in this book. It is clear that the increase in the number of biracial children will likely result in more incidents similar to Gerald's. Nevertheless, the upside of increased numbers is that, in the future, biracial children will have an easier time than Gerald did in finding his biracial identity. In fact, biracial children are now in the majority in some American communities.

Response

Ramón Vega de Jesús

Recent U.S. Census Bureau (2001) statistics depicted a pronounced increase of bi- and multiracial children directly affecting school population and society in general. Gerald Collins is one of them. This signals a change in counseling strategies for students who are part of this growing trend. This trend not only poses additional classification challenges for the U.S. Census Bureau regarding the proper identification of new demographic groups; more important, for counselors it means the need for fresh approaches to the unique problems faced by multiracial and multiethnic children.

This topic is of personal interest to me because I am a father of Latino–Caucasian children and a veteran counselor and counselor educator with extensive supervisory experience. I specialize in working with racial and ethnic minority youths in the urban setting and its school systems. My research centers on issues of cultural and ethnic identity, migration, transborder identity, and transnationality issues. I have been involved for many years in binational research on Puerto Rican circular migrant students, who have experiences similar to those of Gerald (Vega de Jesús, 2004, 2005; Vega de Jesús & Sayers, 2005; Vega de Jesús, Sayers, & Brown, 2005). The following sections deal with the questions posed at the conclusion of this critical incident.

The question regarding case conceptualization is an excellent one, with a complex answer that merits some pondering of other questions, such as the following: (a) What is diagnosable, and what is not? (b) Why diagnose and label Gerald? (c) Does the *DSM–IV–TR* have an accurate diagnosis for the racism in Gerald's environment? (d) Why think of Gerald as a case and not as a person?

Part of the problem this counselor encountered, besides being an intern with low status on the counseling pole, is that agencies have a business side that requires justification for third-party liability payment. Agencies submit to diagnosis guidelines established by the insurance companies and health maintenance organizations. Another possibility, which the supervisor in charge did not see or did not care about, is the incorrect labeling and the potential negative consequences of this in Gerald's life. The counselor inherited someone else's wrong intake assessment, and her supervisor made her stick with it. She is not an overzealous counselor but rather a brave intern who stood up for what she believed was the better diagnosis given the circumstances that she uncovered with Gerald. She found the context of Gerald's behavior and found him with no one to advocate for him but her. I give kudos to Gerald's counselor.

The real question is, is this a diagnosable issue? To me, it is clear that it is not, and, therefore, the *DSM–IV–TR* cannot do justice to Gerald because the problem is not Gerald. The real problem is the racist, toxic environment to which he was exposed and the emotional trauma it inflicted on him. Judging from the information given, it seems that Gerald is the only one in his bi/rational frame of mind in his school and home. (The term *bi/rational* was coined in a personal conversation I had with social worker Jenny Duncan Rojano on October 18, 2005, when, by mistake, Mrs. Rojano used the term *bi/rational* instead of *biracial*. *Bi/rational* refers to the psyche of biracial individuals.) The problem is that others are not bi/rational, as Gerald is, and would like him to assimilate to conform to one of the two compartments that African American and Caucasian children in his school have constructed. Gerald's biracial identity construct does not fit with the offered compartments, and he is not capitulating his position. To this, I say bravo for Gerald. I would hate to think of Gerald as a case that needs to be diagnosed. I like to think of Gerald, and of any client, as a person and his circumstance. Gerald is an individual with an inalienable right to express his voice and to express his biracial identity to its fullest.

This case study illustrates the need for proper supervision of interns (and, I might add, for counselors in general) because many supervisors do not posses any supervisory training and depend on their own experience as their supervisory north. *Supervision* is loosely defined, or not defined at all in many cases, which opens the door for situations such as the one presented to take place. This counselor had her heart in the right place, but, like Gerald, she found herself parallel processing with no advocates for her revised diagnosis because of the contextualization of Gerald's behavior. She was forced to accept an imposed diagnosis that she disagreed with.

My advice to Gerald's counselor is to find additional supervision beyond her agency, maybe at a local higher education institution, which could have given her some insight concerning how to present her case more convincingly to her supervisor. The focus is Gerald's well-being. Although this counselor's rationale might have fallen on deaf ears, one should not prejudge the outcome of the intervention. Confronting is not easy to do for many and is especially difficult when so much is at stake—when one's field supervisor has a say in one's internship grade. This might call for political muscle flexing that the intern has no recognized power to execute.

The answer to distinguishing between a mental disorder and other underlying issues might seem somewhat simplistic a priori, but it lies in the *DSM–IV–TR* itself. Knowing the descriptions of the disorders covered in the *DSM–IV–TR* is paramount to this answer. If one looks carefully at the descriptors offered for ODD (Code 313.81), one will find that there are time and setting definitions for manifestation of the disorder that are simply not met in Gerald's situation (American Psychiatric Association, 2000). There should be at least 6 months of manifestation, and oppositional manifestation must take place in different settings across the board, not just in school. Knowledge of the ODD descriptors was the first sign for me that ODD was the wrong diagnosis. Gerald did not exhibit behavior consistent with an ODD diagnosis because he was having behavior problems only with other schoolchildren and with his teacher and only on one occasion. The fights with other children were in response to racial bullying and were not oppositional in nature because they were with his peers, who were not in a position of authority to be challenged by Gerald. Knowing the *DSM–IV–TR* well is a must if one is to be able to discern cases and ascertain whether they really fit a mental disorder. Gerald's situation is social in nature and does not necessarily require a diagnosis per se, at least not ODD.

I believe the ODD diagnosis to be a mistake for the reasons mentioned in the previous section. ODD has a labeling effect that will stay with Gerald forever. I believe identity problem (Code 313.82) to be a more benign label, but I do not concur with that assessment because it might not tell the whole story (American Psychiatric Association, 2000). Gerald was reacting to the racial bullying directed at him by African American and Caucasian children in his school. Anyone who has had experience with racism knows that these kinds of dynamics do not easily go away without structured and systematic intervention, as the school administration seems to suggest. The administration blamed Gerald as the one with the problem, but the school has a racism problem that it has not addressed; inexperience or denial could be the culprit. The perception of the school administration was that racial problems in the school had subsided, but closer to the truth could be that the administrators had turned their attention away from racism, which would mean that they were in denial of the problems. Gerald was still struggling with racism, and he is part of the school; therefore, it was not resolved.

In my experience as a school administrator and as founder and past director of the Student and Family Assistance Center of an urban middle school with problems similar to those in Gerald's school, it is not reasonably plausible that the dynamics of racism would simply vanish without a systemic intervention. It is racist to ignore racism. Many students I encountered as a counselor and an administrator were hard to classify because they were African American–Puerto Rican, living their biracial, bi-ethnic life in a highly racially compartmentalized world. Some opted for one culture or the other, whereas many embraced both cultures and experienced problems similar to the one Gerald confronted.

Gerald has been the victim of racial bullying or harassment and is experiencing the emotional trauma associated with it. From this case study, I gathered that Gerald accepts his biracial reality and describes himself as mixed, as opposed to just being African American or Caucasian. The conflict originates not from Gerald but rather from situational stress and the fact that no one in school or at home advocated for him. Mrs. Collins dismissed Gerald's problem by telling him not to pay attention to ignorance, ending her intervention there and not responding to Gerald's emotional status. Gerald reported the problems to a teacher, who did nothing to intervene; in fact, he saw her as defending the Caucasian children. Gerald then took matters into his own hands, as many would, to survive and save face in the school community, and he did so after being turned down by the very people who could do something about the problem.

Gerald seemed clear about his biracial identity, but the African American and Caucasian peers in his school had a problem with this. This problem is social in nature and not a mental disorder per se, but if I were forced to use a diagnosis, I would use adjustment disorder not otherwise specified (Code 309.9) with situational stressors specifically located in the racial bullying and harassment he experienced (American Psychiatric Association, 2000). This is a transient diagnosis with high resolution possibilities that would not remain in Gerald's record. I would stay away from impulse control issues (Code 312.34) and intermittent explosive disorder (Code 312.30) because he is not showing impulse problems in different settings, only as a reaction specific to the racism he is experiencing at school. In this way, I would avoid giving Gerald an inaccurate and unnecessary label and would work with him in finding more appropriate manifestations of his anger. As it turns out, anger is an appropriate response in this case; it is what Gerald does with this anger that needs to be addressed. Systematic desensitization is contraindicated. Gerald should not be programmed not to feel anger as a recipient of racism. Instead, his sense of alarm regarding this should remain intact.

Additionally, I would work with the reasons for Gerald's anger from a person-centered existential approach rather than a cognitive-behavioral approach. Racism is an emotionally laden issue; these emotions need to be addressed and the feelings examined. Anger is a secondary emotion, and, as such, Gerald needs to get in touch with his primary emotions first. Some of these primary feelings could be embarrassment, sadness, and rejection. The behavioral approach of anger management, prescribed by the school in its referral, needs to be reconsidered. Anger management should be considered the secondary intervention, so that Gerald, after dealing with his emotions and feelings, could learn to effectively deal with the externalization of his emotions. Anger management is meant not to teach Gerald to deny and repress feelings so that the school administrators are satisfied but rather to help Gerald deal with his feelings in a healthier, more functional fashion.

Racial identity issues do not occur in a vacuum in a school setting. There is a high probability that others are also struggling with these issues. One way to approach this is to use group counseling. Children can benefit greatly from sharing their feelings with others who are experiencing similar challenges and those who have dealt successfully with racial issues.

Another way to approach these issues is to address the school racism problem from a systems perspective. This is an excellent opportunity to provide consultation. One could create a task group to address racism issues, with the expected outcome of raising consciousness as well as increasing racial and ethnic sensitivity in students, parents, teachers, staff, counselors, administrators, school officials, and, possibly, the larger community. This could start with a peace project, such as Help Increase the Peace (HIP) (http://www.afsc.org/hipp.htm) or the Peace Pole. The beauty of these programs is that they have trained personnel who can provide training of trainers for the counselor and the school. HIP became the anticipatory set in my school before we delved into issues of racism and discrimination. Programs such as HIP could help alleviate and possibly resolve some of these emotionally charged issues around race, ethnicity, diversity, and sensitivity present at Gerald's school.

It is sad that counselor education programs across the nation need to do more to address racial and multicultural issues in counseling. Although accrediting institutions such as the Council for the Accreditation of Counseling and Related Educational Programs have addressed this in their elaborations, many universities and colleges fail to meet this expectation or meet it marginally. Often, this results from the overuse of transient faculty or adjunct faculty, not tenure track faculty, who could provide consistent delivery of multicultural curricula and who might have a higher commitment to the department's mission supporting diversity.

Counselor education programs across the nation should commit to diversity issues and reflect this in their curricula. I have learned that it is a very different experience for the client when he or she has a counseling relationship with someone from the same racial, ethnic, or cultural background—someone who not only can understand what the client is going through but has had experience, survived, and known resiliency. I also believe that any perceptive counselor with experience and sensitivity toward racial issues can be just as effective in reaching someone like Gerald.

The practice of having one or two courses that deal with diversity is outdated and naive at best. Multicultural issues should be taught in a context, not as a compartmentalized course or one focusing only on *DSM–IV–TR* material. I pose a challenge to counselor education programs in the United States and internationally as well: Be innovative and make multicultural diversity the thread that holds all courses together. A course in assessment should also be multiculturally contextual. All counseling relationships are cross-cultural, and the undeniable fact is that children like Gerald will be the norm in the near future. Counselor education programs must adjust and realize that new counseling approaches are needed for the sake of Gerald and others.

References

American Psychiatric Association. (2000). *Diagnostic and statistical manual of mental disorders* (4th ed., text rev.). Washington, DC: Author.

Cross, W. (1971). The Negro to Black conversion experience: Toward the psychology of Black liberation. *Black World, 20,* 13–27.

Erickson, E. (1968). *Identity, youth, and crisis.* New York: Norton.

Glasser, W. (1965). *Reality therapy.* New York: Harper & Row.

Glasser, W. (1998). *Choice theory: A new psychology of personal freedom.* New York: HarperCollins.

Glasser, W. (2000). *Reality therapy in action.* New York: HarperCollins.

Glasser, W. (2004). *Warning: Psychiatry can be dangerous to your health.* New York: HarperCollins.

Glasser, W. (2005). *Treating mental health as a public health problem: A new leadership role for the helping professions.* Chatsworth, CA: William Glasser Inc.

Helms, J. (1993). *Black and White racial identity: Theory, research, and practice.* Westport, CN: Praeger.

Maslow, A. (1970). *Motivation and personality* (2nd ed.). New York: Harper & Row.

Moss, D. (1999). Carl Rogers, the person-centered approach, and experiential therapy. In D. Moss (Ed.), *Humanistic and transpersonal psychology: A historical and biographical sourcebook* (pp. 41–48). Westport, CT: Greenwood Press.

Poston, W. (1990, November–December). The biracial identity development model: A needed addition. *Journal of Counseling & Development, 69,* 152–155.

Thompson, C., Rudolph, L., & Henderson, D. (2004). *Counseling children.* Belmont, CA: Thomson Learning.

U.S. Census Bureau. (2001). *Profiles of general demographic characteristics: 2000 census of population and housing, United States.* Retrieved August 25, 2005, from http://www.census.gov/prod/cen2000/ index.html

Vega de Jesús, R. (2004). *Voices: A crosscultural bi-national study of Puerto Rican circular migrant students.* Unpublished doctoral dissertation, University of Connecticut.

Vega de Jesús, R. (2005, July). *¿La frontera? ¡Sí, se puede!* [The border? Yes we can!] Paper presented at the National California Association for Bilingual Education Conference on Two-Way Bilingual Immersion Programs, Monterey, CA.

Vega de Jesús, R., & Sayers, D. (2005, October). *Voices: Bilingual youth constructing and defending their identities across borders, a bi-national study of Puerto Rican circular migrant students.* Paper presented at the Border Pedagogy Conference, San Diego, CA.

Vega de Jesús, R., Sayers, D., & Brown, K. R. (2005, November). *Voices of Puerto Rican circular migrant students: A crosscultural bi-national study.* Paper presented at the La Cosecha Annual National Conference, Albuquerque, NM.

Williamson, A. (2002, January–February). Educating those who educate biracial children. *Interracial Voice.* Retrieved August 22, 2005, from http://www.webcom.com/!invoice/Williamson.html

Wubbolding, R. (2005). The power of belonging. *International Journal of Reality Therapy, 24*(2), 43–44.

Part

IV

Family Problems

18

"Please Don't Tell!": Custody Battles and Confidentiality

This incident explores the use of an ethical decision-making model by a school counselor struggling with whether to honor a child client's confidentiality or to testify in a custody hearing. Respondents address the use of ethical decision-making models, the importance of allowing clients to offer their informed consent, and issues related to the confidentiality rights of minors.

■ Critical Incident

Cynthia A. Reynolds

"Evelyn Hunter," an 11-year-old Caucasian girl, first came to see me, the elementary school counselor, when she was in first grade. After a series of classroom guidance lessons on friendship, she and another classmate wanted help resolving issues in their relationship. Evelyn returned to see me once in the second grade with her concerns about another child in her classroom who was being bullied and whom she wanted to help. In third grade, she asked to see me about a comment a substitute teacher had made to her. In fourth grade, she talked about the long hours that her father worked and how much the family needed him at home. In the 5 years of my contact with Evelyn, I also spoke to her mother several times. Evelyn's father was a businessman who worked a great deal. Mrs. Hunter was a well-educated woman who had chosen to stay home with her four children. Evelyn was the oldest of the four and was very intelligent, attractive, popular, mature, and eager to please adults. Mrs. Hunter dedicated many hours to assisting in the school and was parent–teacher association president one year. School faculty regarded the family as ideal.

Mrs. Hunter called me one Monday morning in October about an incident that had happened over the weekend. Evelyn was home, but the other children were spending the night at their grandparents' house. Mrs. Hunter explained that she and her husband had quarreled about his affair with a coworker. The quarrel ended with domestic violence against Mrs. Hunter. Police and Child Protective Services (CPS) were called. Mr. Hunter was removed from the home, and Mrs. Hunter was filing for a divorce. Mrs. Hunter wanted me to speak to Evelyn as soon as she arrived to help her to ease into her day at school and to assess the impact of this event on her daughter.

Evelyn was relieved to speak with me and shared her anger, disgust, and fear of her father. She was heartbroken about his violent behavior and his affair with another woman. Evelyn felt sad about the family breaking up. She had already spoken to both the police and CPS, who scheduled an appointment for her with a clinical counselor.

Over the next few months, Evelyn met with me on several occasions to talk about visitations with her father and her sadness, anger, grief, and uncertainty about the future. She had spoken with the clinical counselor several times, and it had been suggested that Evelyn attend a divorce group at school. She was released from the clinical counselor's care after four sessions and was scheduled to begin attending a divorce group at school 2 weeks after the holiday break.

During the month of December, Mr. Hunter filed a report with CPS and alleged that Mrs. Hunter failed to keep the children clean. He also contested Mrs. Hunter's custody of the children and asked for full custody. When investigating this claim, CPS discovered that Mr. Hunter was assisting Evelyn with her showers, often scrubbing her back for her. He told Evelyn that there was "nothing wrong with it" and that "the human body is beautiful to behold." Upset with CPS's investigation of him, he had a high-powered attorney threaten to bring charges against CPS. It was common knowledge in the community that Mr. Hunter had friends who were judges in the district court.

When I spoke to Evelyn after the school break, she was ecstatic about her father's new "friend," chattering on about the details of the new bedroom for her that was being planned in the house her father was building. She said that she would like to live with her father so that he would not be sad about living alone. When I mentioned how much she had changed over the break and introduced concerns about Mr. Hunter helping her shower, Evelyn became sullen and said, "I don't have to talk to you about that. I am not going to be in your divorce group either." She intimated that her dad needed her, that she was very happy to be spending so much time with him, and that he had told her to stop talking to "that nosy school counselor."

The next day I got a call from a frantic Mrs. Hunter. She felt that her children had been turned against her. She had taken Evelyn back to the clinical counselor, but Evelyn refused to talk. Two days later, I got a subpoena from Mrs. Hunter's attorney to testify at the custody hearing.

Evelyn asked to see me the following week. Her father had found out about the subpoena and asked Evelyn whether she had told me anything bad about him. She emphatically stated that she did not want me to testify or reveal anything she had said about her father or the divorce because I had told her that was confidential material. She stated she would never trust another counselor again if I talked without her permission. She was angry and distant and would not even make eye contact with me. I was distraught that a child whom I had known for 5 years was so upset with me. I worried about the influence that her father was wielding over her. I felt sympathy for her mother and what she was going through. I had a tough decision to make. Evelyn was demanding that I give her an answer. I told her I needed a day to think about it.

I used Kitchener's (1999) ethical decision-making model. This model is designed to assist counselors in recognizing and reconciling ethical dilemmas and focuses on the moral principles of beneficence, nonmaleficence, fidelity, justice, and autonomy. On the intuitive level, I wanted to assist Evelyn's mother with her struggle because I felt that the children had been alienated from her. If my decision were to testify, I would have the law on my side, given that, in our state, the parent is the holder of the confidentiality privilege and one parent was granting a release for me to testify. One of the exceptions to confidentiality is a court order, so by testifying in court, I would be on solid legal grounds. Conversely, because I was not trained as a custody evaluator, my testimony might be challenged anyway. Although the law would permit me to testify, ethics demanded that I maintain the confidentiality of my client (American Counseling Association, 2005). I also needed to look at the issue from Evelyn's point of view. Evelyn and I had a long relationship, and she had come to trust and rely on me. She was asking me to do only what I had promised her that I would do: keep our talks confidential except in instances involving harm to self, harm to others, or abuse.

I began to reflect on my decision by considering the five ethical principles of the counseling profession (Kitchener, 1999). If I were to be faithful and true to Evelyn and to my promise, I would refuse to testify and thereby uphold my fidelity to her and my word. In terms of autonomy, should I grant Evelyn her wish because she was certain that was what she wanted? Is an 11-year-old who is under pressure from her father capable of making an autonomous decision regarding custody? If I had confidence in her ability to make an autonomous decision, I would refuse to testify.

Counselors are asked to practice beneficence. Whom would I be helping if I testified? By not testifying, I would help both Evelyn and her father. Evelyn was worried that my testimony would harm both her and her father. She felt an intense need to take care of him and guarantee that he would get custody of her. By testifying, I could help Evelyn's mother in the case but would harm my relationship with Evelyn.

In terms of nonmaleficence, would I do less harm by testifying or by refusing to testify? By testifying, I could destroy my relationship with Evelyn and her trust in counselors. By not testifying, I could be putting Evelyn in harm's way with her father. I could put myself in harm's way by refusing to testify; I could be jailed for contempt of court. By not testifying, I could harm my relationship with Mrs. Hunter as well.

I could not find resolution, so I continued to the next level of Kitchener's (1999) model. In terms of justice, it would only be fair to honor Evelyn's desire that her counseling sessions be held confidential. With regard to universality, if Evelyn were my daughter, I would want the counselor to testify. I would want the judge to have confirmatory evidence about how the children had been unduly influenced and turned against me. From the father's point of view, I would want that nosy school counselor to stay out of my family business. If I were Evelyn, I would not want my counselor to testify because I had never been told that what I was sharing could be subpoenaed.

After a sleepless night, consultation with another counselor, and a review of the state laws, I came up with the following by balancing these principles. I informed Mrs. Hunter that I would not honor the subpoena and that I would refuse to testify unless the judge ordered me to. If ordered, I would request an in-chambers hearing so that the parents and child would not be present to hear my testimony. I also strongly suggested that, in the meantime, Mrs. Hunter schedule an appointment with an area psychologist who specialized in parental alienation syndrome (Darnall, 1998; Gardner,

Sauber, & Lorandos, 2005) and indicated that I would be more than willing to consult with him.

I met with Evelyn and shared my decision. I told her how much I liked her and how connected I felt to her after working with her for so many years. I told her that I wanted to honor my promise to her and would only testify if it meant keeping myself out of jail. Evelyn seemed to appreciate this. I also told her that if I did testify, it would not be in front of her or her father. She became visibly relieved. I did challenge her, however, to start making decisions on the basis of what was best for her rather than what might be best for either parent. I assured her that it was not her job to take care of either parent. I stressed the importance of privacy when showering. Finally, I encouraged Evelyn to attend the divorce group, but she declined. The subpoena was withdrawn.

Questions

1. Did I make the right decision? Did my actions do the least possible harm to the parties involved?
2. What is the proper role of the school counselor in custody cases?
3. What is the school counselor's obligation to children during litigious divorces?

■Response

Kelly Duncan

It has been my experience that school counselors find themselves in ethical dilemmas more often than their colleagues employed in other counseling settings. The issues that face school counselors are complex and often fraught with complications. One of the confounding factors facing school counselors has at its core a common thread—the age of the clients school counselors serve. Their clients are predominantly minors, and although ethically they deserve the right to confidentiality, their parents legally hold this right. Neither the American Counseling Association's (2005) *Code of Ethics* nor the American School Counselor Association's (2004) ethical guidelines define the term *minor.* State laws vary as well on what is considered the age of majority or age of consent.

This counselor finds herself in an ethical dilemma that is somewhat common for counselors employed in school settings. She and her client, Evelyn, began a counselor–client relationship focusing on school-related issues. The relationship was further fostered as Evelyn's family situation changed and she sought counseling from her school counselor related to her feelings regarding those issues. Throughout the 5 years of their acquaintance, Evelyn was this counselor's client, and a school counselor's first responsibility is to the students. Although the school counselor had consulted with the mother on more than one occasion, the focus of her work was appropriately focused on Evelyn.

It is good counseling practice to explain the limits of confidentiality to one's clients at the onset of the relationship. Counselors must always explain to clients—in language that is developmentally appropriate—the limits of their ability to keep information confidential. They must keep in mind that, although they might have shared this information with their clients in the initial phases of the work, it is imperative that they continually revisit this issue so that clients are cognizant of the counselors' duties and the limits of their ability to keep information confidential.

Sections A.2.a. and A.2.b. of the American School Counselor Association's (2004) *Ethical Standards for School Counselors* pertain to confidentiality. According to these sections, the professional school counselor

a. Informs students of the purposes, goals, techniques and rules of procedure under which they may receive counseling at or before the time when the counseling relationship is entered. Disclosure notice includes the limits of confidentiality such as the possible necessity for consulting with other professionals, privileged communication, and legal or authoritative restraints. The meaning and limits of confidentiality are defined in developmentally appropriate terms to students.

b. Keeps information confidential unless disclosure is required to prevent clear and imminent danger to the student or others or when legal requirements demand that confidential information be revealed. Counselors will consult with appropriate professionals when in doubt as to the validity of an exception.

In reviewing this section as it relates to this critical incident, one must keep in mind that Evelyn assumed that what she was sharing was to be held in confidence. It is unclear whether the school counselor did indeed explain the limits of confidentiality to Evelyn, as required by counselors' ethics codes. A lesson we can all learn from this case is the importance of explaining to clients the limits of confidentiality and the reasons we may need to revisit this issue periodically throughout the counseling relationship.

Whenever one is faced with an ethical dilemma, it is useful to follow an ethical decision-making model. In this case, the school counselor followed Kitchener's (1999) model. It is fair to assume that this school counselor followed acceptable standards of practice. To determine this, one can ask oneself, "What would another school counselor with my level of training do in a similar situation?" This school counselor followed the steps of an ethical decision-making model and consulted with another counselor. As an added measure to show that she followed an appropriate ethics code, the school counselor should also document this consultation in her case notes.

Additionally, the school counselor needs to clarify who her client is in this case. Although she shows some empathy for the situation in which the parents find themselves, her duty is to her client—Evelyn. It is not the school counselor's responsibility to assist one parent or the other in a lawsuit. It is always in the school counselor's best interest to remain neutral and avoid siding with one parent over the other. Not knowing the potential outcome of any custody battle, it is important for a school counselor to maintain a neutral stance. Regardless of the outcome, the school counselor must preserve a working relationship with both parents so that she or he can continue to be helpful to the entire family.

The school counselor initially began seeing Evelyn about issues related to relationships with classmates. Her association with Evelyn later shifted to Evelyn's concerns with her situation at home. Nonetheless, at no time was the counselor engaged in this relationship as a professional appointed to do a custody evaluation. This was outside of the scope and practice of her position and outside of the intent of this relationship. Because it was not the intent, the counselor would not have been able to make any recommendations or comments with respect to the custody of Evelyn. If she is asked to share her opinion about custody, she may want to reply that she was serving in her capacity as a school counselor and not as someone employed to assess custody. As such, she can explain that she is unprepared to offer a qualified opinion or judgment about custody.

Whenever they are subpoenaed by the court, school counselors should consult with the attorney under retainer by their school district, school board, or professional liability insurance company. Depending on the law related to privilege in one's state, the relevant state statutes can be cited. If the school counselor finds himself or herself having to testify, the school attorney should be able to assist him or her in preparing for the process. The school board's attorney, however, ultimately represents the school district. If school counselors feel the school board's attorney is not acting in their best interest, they may wish to consult an attorney of their own. Professional liability insurance generally provides counselors with access to an attorney for these purposes.

In conclusion, school counselors hold a unique role in the school community. They assist children in a variety of situations and as they cope with a variety of conflicting emotions. The developmental level of each client varies and, as such, makes each situation and child unique. During times of trauma in a child's life, such as the litigious divorce referred to in this example, a school counselor can help the student learn coping skills. School counselors can also provide students with emotional support and encouragement. In this case, the school counselor has modeled the process that other professional counselors should follow when faced with an ethical dilemma. Following the steps of an ethical decision-making model, coupled with consulting with other professionals, would be considered best practice.

Response

Rita Sommers-Flanagan

As a former custody evaluator, I found this incident difficult to consider because of the many layers of emotion that surface whenever I think about the challenges facing parents and children as marriages dissolve and families reconfigure. Did the school counselor make the right decision? In my opinion, she did; choosing not to testify unless court ordered was the right decision. The reasoning offered for the decision is sound, although more current decision-making models exist. These more current models might have enriched the counselor's analysis, especially because they were developed by and for counselors and counselor educators. I especially like the combination of linear and constructivist options offered by Cottone and Tarvydas (2003) in their ethics text.

If the school counselor in this case had decided to testify or been court ordered to testify, the testimony would have been quite limited, and the counselor would have needed to be very careful not to insinuate any opinion whatsoever about the best custodial arrangement for Evelyn. The school counselor did not have an evaluative role in the life of this family and could therefore only testify as to the content of the counseling interactions with Evelyn and the phone contact with her parents. To offer any professional opinions about the best parental contact or arrangements would have been unethical and could be considered malpractice.

The second part of the counselor's question, "Did my actions do the least possible harm to the parties involved?" is a harder question to answer unequivocally. It takes one to a much deeper realm of ethics, where one wrestles with the life-altering consequences of such decisions. On the surface, the counselor has taken the ethical and legal course, but there will always be lingering doubts and troubling "what ifs" with which professionals have to live. What if the father was a sexual predator? What if the mother became so distraught that she committed suicide? What if Evelyn, years later, told the counselor, "I was only 11 years old. I needed you to see through my father's manipulation and say something to someone. You were the only person who could have made a difference. I tried to hint as much as I dared"? Counselors live with these haunting possibilities. They also live with the fact that, in custody fights, there are no easy answers, and the best outcome usually leaves everyone somewhat unhappy. Children are not commodities that can be divided into equal shares, and their best interests often get mangled in the legal process.

The second and third questions the counselor asks are related. In my opinion, the proper role of the school counselor in custody cases should include clearly defining the counselor's obligation to children during litigious custody battles. The school counselor is a professional with mental health expertise who works to help all students have the best educational opportunities possible. School counselors are generally not trained to do custody evaluations, and the school counselor's job description typically does not include the provision of family or individual therapy for students or their family. Therefore, the proper role of the school counselor is to provide nonjudgmental support to children experiencing divorce. The following is a nonexhaustive list of possible ways school counselors can help children in divorcing families.

1. School counselors should keep plenty of child-oriented divorce literature available to loan to children.
2. Divorce and life-transition counseling groups can offer children a safe place to universalize and begin to overcome their losses, grief, anger, and shame.
3. Counselors can assist students in explaining their situation and special needs to teachers.
4. Counselors can help students focus on how to make it through tough times without losing too much ground academically.

The school counselor showed compassion and wisdom in handling this incident. One area in which she could have improved, however, is related to informed consent. It may be a product of brevity rather than omission, but as the incident reads, there does not seem to have been an informed consent process that would have alerted Evelyn to the limits of confidentiality. Although informed consent practices are relatively new in the school setting, I am a great believer in having informed consent forms developed and available for all students and parents. Informed consent is a process that offers respect and empowerment to clients and clarity to administrators, colleagues, and other interested parties.

If Evelyn were not informed, in an age-appropriate manner, that her conversations with her counselor might not be confidential under certain circumstances, this would be a legal and clinical mistake. States vary in their laws regarding reportable child sexual and physical abuse, but if Evelyn's father had gone just a bit further with his shower assistance, it might have been reportable. If the police had not been called and Evelyn told the counselor of being very afraid when her father hurt her mother, the domestic violence might have been reportable. In the event of a court order, the counselor usually breaks confidentiality and testifies, given that the consequences of refusing to comply with a subpoena include being charged with contempt of court and being fined or jailed. Thus, a court order is another limit to confidentiality. Finally, states vary in their laws regarding parental access to children's counseling records and materials, so the school counselor is obliged to find out what can and cannot be kept confidential according to state law and school policy. It is good ethical practice to let students know what the counselor will and will not disclose to parents or school administrators.

In the ethics course I teach, every student must develop a client-friendly informed consent form. The schools in our region are gradually coming to expect that counselors will have a sound and understandable informed consent form that accurately reflects school policy and current state law. Exceptions to confidentiality almost universally include unreported instances of child abuse and a stated intent to harm oneself or others. State laws and school policies may dictate other exceptions. Students should be neither led nor allowed to believe that everything they say to a counselor will be kept private. These exceptions should be listed and explained in the informed consent process. Because of the high likelihood that school counselors will work with many children in divorcing families, a statement about what the school counselor will and will not do can also be a helpful part of the informed consent process. The following is a sample statement that might be appropriate for middle school students.

"Students often talk to me about troubles their families are going through. As your school counselor, I want to be helpful to anyone going through hard times. However, I will not take sides if your parents are divorcing. I will not judge either of your parents, and I do not provide any kind of evaluations about where you should live. I am here to help you make it through the best way you can. I hope you will ask me any questions you have about this." This statement could be embedded in a comprehensive informed consent form that would also include a careful explanation of the limits of confidentiality, or it could be developed further in pamphlet form as an adjunct to a more general informed consent form.

In summary, custody battles are a common, emotionally trying counseling situation. The counselor offers a well-reasoned ethical decision and raises important concerns regarding the school counselor's role in the life of students facing difficult family changes.

References

American Counseling Association. (2005). *ACA code of ethics.* Alexandria, VA: Author.

American School Counselor Association. (2004). *Ethical standards for school counselors.* Alexandria, VA: Author. Retrieved July 5, 2006, from http://www.schoolcounselor.org/content.asp?contentid=173

Corey, G., Corey, M. S., & Callanan, P. (2003). *Issues and ethics in the helping professions* (6th ed.). Pacific Grove, CA: Brooks/Cole.

Cottone, R. R., & Tarvydas, V. M. (2003). *Ethical and professional issues in counseling* (2nd ed.). Upper Saddle River, NJ: Merrill/Prentice Hall.

Darnall, D. (1998). *Divorce casualties: Protecting your children from parental alienation syndrome.* Dallas, TX: Taylor Trade.

Gardner, R. A., Sauber, S. R., & Lorandos, P. (Eds.). (2005). *International handbook of parental alienation syndrome: Conceptual, clinical, and legal considerations.* Binghamton, NY: Haworth Press.

Kitchener, K. (1999). *Foundations of ethical practice, research, and teaching in psychology.* Mahwah, NJ: Erlbaum.

Remley, T., & Herlihy, B. (2005). *Ethical, legal, and professional issues in counseling.* Upper Saddle River, NJ: Pearson.

Sommers-Flanagan, R., Elander, C., & Sommers-Flanagan, J. (2000). *Don't divorce us!: Kids' advice to divorcing parents.* Alexandria, VA: American Counseling Association.

Welfel, E. R. (2006). *Ethics in counseling and psychotherapy* (3rd ed.). Pacific Grove, CA: Brooks/Cole.

19

"Outside the Castle": Divorce and Relocation

This incident addresses the losses inherent in a divorce, especially when it necessitates a move to a new home. The authors consider the impact of divorce from a grief and loss perspective as well as from a cultural perspective.

◼ Critical Incident

Nicole R. Hill

"Ahmed Akhtar," a 4-year-old Pakistani American boy, was brought in for counseling at our mental health agency after his parents divorced. His mother, Mrs. Akhtar, explained that Ahmed had become "more and more needy, demanding, and dishonest" since the divorce and that complaints from his day care facility prompted her to seek counseling for him. Although the family had recently moved out of the house in which they had lived for the past 4 years, Ahmed was still attending the same day care that he began last fall, and his mother expressed confidence in the perceptions of his day care workers that he needed some additional assistance to adjust to the divorce.

During the initial intake session, I spent approximately 2 hours with Ahmed and his mother. Throughout this time, Ahmed presented with flat affect, and he rarely spoke. Although he did not interact with me or with his mother much during the intake, he did play with the toys that were available and created images of family scenes. Ahmed's mother explained that he "used to be such a sweet, nice kid. He was helpful at home, and I never heard one bad thing about him from his day care." Ahmed's mom explained that she had been contacted four times now by the day care teacher because Ahmed had been hitting other kids and breaking toys. Mrs. Akhtar also reported, "Ahmed has become really clingy. As soon as I go to leave in the morn-

205

ing, or any time for that matter, he runs up to me and grabs my leg. He starts to cry and cry, and I can't seem to calm him down. The other day, his uncle practically had to hold him down so I could leave the house."

When questioned about the divorce, Mrs. Akhtar said that she and her husband had been separated for the last 7 months, that she had just been granted primary custody of Ahmed, and that Ahmed's father picked him up every other weekend. She explained that she was not currently speaking with Ahmed's father, so she was uncertain whether Ahmed's behaviors were occurring when he was with his father as well.

As I was finishing the intake, Mrs. Akhtar remembered that she was also concerned about Ahmed's lying. She indicated that Ahmed had been telling other kids at the mosque that his parents still lived together. She expressed frustration and said that she had explained the divorce and the change in living and child care arrangements to Ahmed on several occasions. Mrs. Akhtar said she was confident that Ahmed understood and that his statements to others were lies rather than reflections of confusion.

On the basis of the initial intake information and Ahmed's interaction with the toys, I recommended weekly play therapy sessions. When they arrived for our first play therapy session, Ahmed showed marked distress in response to leaving his mother in the waiting room, but I assured him that she would be waiting out in the lobby and that he could check on her if needed. Once in the playroom, Ahmed seemed genuinely interested in the toys and began to play with them. He would temporarily become engrossed in his creations and would then sporadically want to check on his mother. I reflected to him, "You're worried about your mom leaving," and Ahmed responded by nodding and then refocusing on the toys in front of him. At the conclusion of the first session, I commended Ahmed on the courage he showed by staying in the counseling session for the entire 45 minutes.

As I reflected on the play session, I realized that Ahmed's play changed from toy to toy with no consistent play theme. He did not directly interact with me but would nod and look at me at times during the session. Ahmed seemed to be getting to know me and the play materials.

In my most recent session with Ahmed, he chose to play with the dinosaurs. He created a castle out of blocks and had three dinosaurs stay within the parameters of the castle, whereas the other two were not allowed inside. As Ahmed played, the "outside" dinosaurs kept asking and asking to be let in, but the answer of "no" remained the same. When I reflected that "this [outside] dinosaur seems really sad," Ahmed paused and then demolished the castle with the dinosaur I had described as sad. He then picked up the six foam balls in the play therapy room and started throwing them one after the next at the wall. His affect seemed sad, but his behaviors seemed to be expressing anger.

When I then reflected anger to Ahmed, he sighed and started to pick up the dinosaurs again. He started to build the castle again. Ahmed immediately set up the dinosaurs that were on the inside and the outside even before the castle construction was completed. For the remainder of the session, Ahmed enacted the scene of the outside dinosaurs asking to come in and then trying to find ways to sneak in.

For the last three counseling sessions, Ahmed had arrived with his Uncle Jamal. At one point during play therapy, Ahmed indicated that he and his mother were living with Uncle Jamal's family. Puzzled and wondering about possible connections with the dinosaur play, I met briefly with Uncle Jamal after the most recent session. Uncle Jamal did not seem as open to counseling as was Ahmed's mother, however, and was reluctant to disclose information about the family. He did acknowledge that Ahmed and Ahmed's mother were living with him and his family. He also asserted that there was nothing "crazy" about Ahmed or his behavior at day care.

Questions

1. How might one conceptualize this case from a grief and loss perspective? How developmentally appropriate were Ahmed's expressions of grief and reactions to the divorce? What would constitute behaviors that are developmentally inappropriate expressions of grief and loss?
2. What are some potential cultural issues emerging in this case? How might they be affecting Ahmed? How might one ethically, legally, and competently attend to these issues?
3. How might one approach this counseling relationship from a systems perspective? What other systems might be included to best support therapeutic work with Ahmed? How could a counselor best advocate for Ahmed and his ongoing development?

Response

Heidi S. Deschamps

When considering the typical responses to loss, one often generates visions of a man silently crying over a picture of his dead wife, a woman wailing in anguish as she buries her child, or a family honoring the life of their beloved grandmother through the retelling of her stories. The grief expressed by children is often overlooked or forgotten. This is especially true when the grief is not attached to the physical loss of a person through death.

Ahmed has recently experienced a dramatic change in his everyday living, including the loss of everyday interactions with his father, given that these are now limited to every other weekend, and the loss of the only home he has ever known. Any adult placed in this position might express a range of emotions, including fear, anger, sadness, and confusion. Because Ahmed is only 4 years old, he does not possess the verbal or intellectual capacity to express his thoughts and feelings associated with this loss. Instead, he expresses these emotions in ways that are developmentally appropriate for a 4-year-old child.

Ahmed may feel afraid of future loss, so he clings to his mother when she attempts to leave in the morning. He may feel angry that his life is so dramatically changed, so he occasionally breaks toys and hits other children. He may feel confused and wish that life could go back to what was familiar and comfortable, so he tells other children that his parents are still together. He may feel sad that he does not feel part of Uncle Jamal's family system, so he expresses this sadness in a dinosaur world. Young children often express their emotions through behavior rather than words. Ahmed's changes in behavior are representative of normal responses to loss for young children. When Ahmed's feelings are empathically acknowledged, the behavior may decrease in frequency and intensity or stop completely. When Ahmed's feelings of anger were acknowledged in counseling, he at first threw balls at the wall, expressing his anger, but then returned to his expression of sadness (playing with the castle and dinosaurs). Through empathic response and acknowledgment, over time, his expressions of sadness may decrease as well. Nonetheless, there is the possibility that his behavior could worsen.

Ahmed may begin to demonstrate developmentally inappropriate expressions of loss. Regressive behaviors, such as bed wetting, soiling, or acting far younger than his age, would be symptoms of greater concern. Ahmed might also begin to have nightmares, be unable to sleep, or lose his appetite for extended periods of time. He may stop playing with toys, isolate himself from other children, or demonstrate intensely violent and hostile behavior. Should these behaviors persist, other avenues of intervention might need exploration. An essential part of the therapeutic process would be to help Mrs. Akhtar and other family members understand how Ahmed might express his grief, how to appropriately acknowledge these reactions, and how to monitor for developmentally inappropriate responses to grief and loss. Normalizing Ahmed's behavior might go a long way toward enhancing Mrs. Aktar's relationship with Ahmed during this transitional time.

I would also explore Ahmed's behavior in the context of the family culture. The Pakistani culture may be influencing Ahmed's current experience as well as the responses from the adults in his life. I would attempt to gain a better understanding of the values, expectations, and perceptions of the family, including how Pakistani culture is experienced in the family context. Different cultural responses to divorce range along a broad continuum, from finding it extremely shameful to finding it fully acceptable. Young children can be sensitive to the subtle, and not so subtle, communication between adults regarding social norms. Depending on the particular expectations of the family regarding divorce, Ahmed's responses may be associated with the climate he is experiencing in the new family context. It would be vital to ascertain how Uncle Jamal's family and other social networks (including mosque, friends, and school) have responded to the divorce of Ahmed's parents. The expectations of these social groups may have a decisive impact on the ways Mrs. Akhtar and Ahmed navigate this important transitional time.

In addition, all cultures have various expectations regarding the role of children in society. I would work to understand how Mrs. Akhtar and the family view children and their various behaviors. Some cultures extend great lenience to children's actions, whereas other cultures find particular behaviors to be disrespectful and shameful to the entire family system. Ahmed's behaviors or unknown circumstances may be creating increased challenges toward Ahmed becoming fully integrated into Uncle Jamal's family system. This could result in feelings of instability and confusion for Ahmed. He may be crying, "Let me in," through his play in an effort to reconcile his feeling that he is not part of the new family system in which he finds himself.

Another area of consideration is the degree to which the family considers itself acculturated to the American culture. Being Pakistani American could mean a variety of things to different generations of Pakistani Americans. The ways the family gives meaning to their existence in the American culture may have important implications for Ahmed. The family may carry values and expectations that coincide or conflict with those of other important social groups. Ahmed's behaviors could be understood in the context of these various expectations. For example, Ahmed has told children at the mosque that his parents are still together, but he has not done so with children at day care. Perhaps he perceives different expectations in each setting. These potential differences and the possible impact on Ahmed and his family require further examination.

There are also important cultural considerations regarding counseling in particular. There are assorted cultural perspectives concerning the meaning and purpose of counseling. The observation that Uncle Jamal seemed less open to the counseling process might be an important piece of information. Should the family believe that counseling is an indication that Ahmed is crazy, counseling could serve as a barrier to Ahmed's development and integration into the family system. It is important to examine the family perspectives regarding counseling and how these perspectives are affecting Ahmed. At times, advocating for the counseling profession is a way of advocating for one's clients. Working with Uncle Jamal may represent an opportunity to increase understanding about counseling while simultaneously strengthening the relationships in Ahmed's social network.

Although Mrs. Akhtar does not maintain contact with Ahmed's father, he is still an important part of Ahmed's social system. Furthermore, if he has shared custody of Ahmed, he may have legal rights to be involved in the counseling process. Attempting to build relationships with both parents following a divorce can be very challenging for a counselor. Nonetheless, it may be in Ahmed's best interest to gain further understanding about the role his father is playing in his life. Ahmed may be experiencing grief as a result of diminished daily contact with his father. Depending on the circumstances of the divorce, Ahmed may feel torn between his parents. Mr. or Mrs. Akhtar might unknowingly convey that Ahmed should not love the other parent, creating a sense of confusion and betrayal for Ahmed. These possibilities require further investigation. I would begin by speaking with Mrs. Akhtar about her perceptions regarding Ahmed's relationship with his father. I would advocate for Ahmed by discussing the ways his father could become involved in the counseling process. It would be necessary to navigate this aspect of the counseling process with respect, compassion, and honesty, because there is the risk of becoming triangulated between parents.

Providing individual play therapy would be a necessary aspect of the counseling process because this would offer Ahmed an opportunity to express his thoughts and feelings. Nevertheless, taking additional steps to involve important adults in Ahmed's life might promote increased development and growth. I would conduct several filial play therapy sessions with Ahmed's parents (separately if necessary) and other adults in the family. Filial play therapy is a great way to involve caregivers in the counseling process and creates an opportunity to enhance parenting strategies. It requires that the counselor teach caregivers basic listening skills and types of empathic responses. Each caregiver then has the opportunity to practice these skills with the child, under the supervision of the counselor. These skills can be used for many years to come and might have long-term positive effects on the relationships in Ahmed's life.

Currently, Ahmed is encountering grief and loss that could challenge his growth and development, yet he is dealing with this situation in developmentally appropriate ways. Education, encouragement, and compassionate responses on the part of the counselor may further promote Ahmed's development and growth. Addressing these issues from a cultural and systemic perspective indicates the need to involve several social networks in Ahmed's life. I would anticipate and trust that Ahmed, with the support of his mother and family, could face this situation with resiliency and the capacity to strengthen his sense of self.

Response

Tarrell Awe Agahe Portman

My first inclination with this case is to carefully consider Ahmed's grief and loss issues as embedded in a Pakistani cultural context. As an existentialist grounded in social constructionism, I need more information to determine possible meanings behind

Ahmed's behaviors. For instance, there is no mention of the mother's ethnicity in the critical incident. There is no indication of the generational acculturation of the family. Is this a second or sixth generation Pakistani American family? Does Ahmed have any siblings? To conceptualize this case requires many assumptions based on the case. For a counseling professional, these questions would need to be answered to provide a more holistic view to Ahmed's background and socially constructed worldviews.

Ahmed Akhtar's case can be conceptualized as a 4-year-old, male Pakistani American child who currently resides with his biological mother in the home of an uncle and aunt. His estranged parents are divorced. Ahmed has visitation with his biological father every other weekend. Ahmed entered counseling because of behavior changes, reported by his mother as neediness, demandingness, and dishonesty, as a result of adjustment issues related to the divorce. Ahmed is demonstrating fears of abandonment by his mother. Ahmed's uncle reported there was nothing wrong with Ahmed. Ahmed's day care workers, according to the mother, reported that Ahmed needs help with adjusting to the divorce.

My professional judgment requires me to consider the level of anxiety being placed on Ahmed by his presenting issues and the reports of different adults in his life. I would assess the order of importance of Ahmed's counseling issues to be primarily related to grief and loss issues and normal developmental issues in a cultural context.

Child Development

Normal developmental behaviors should be assessed, and the counselor should determine whether they are related to grief and loss issues or just typical developmental milestones. Typical 4-year-old developmental issues can be divided into three relevant categories: emotional, social, and cognitive development. Ahmed seems to be on developmental target related to emotional development, given that he seems to exhibit behaviors similar to those of other 4-year-olds. For instance, Ahmed's periodic regression to "baby behavior" is demonstrated by his increased neediness, as described by his mother. Ahmed's display of new fears, as demonstrated by his worrying about maternal abandonment, may be developmentally appropriate. The counselor would need to watch to determine whether these fears are on target or beyond target for a 4-year-old. If they are off target, then one could consider the possibility of a relationship between the parental divorce and the child's behavior. Social development issues typical of 4-year-olds and displayed by Ahmed seem to be presented by the mother as concerns. Ahmed seems to test parental limits, and, with his mother in the primary caregiver role, he may test his mother more frequently. Ahmed also seems to be imitating adult activity by using a demanding tone, as reported by his mother. Ahmed may be a witness to demands placed on his parents by each other.

Ahmed's mother reported issues related to dishonesty. The case conceptualization suggests that Ahmed's cognitive development is on target with that of other 4-year-olds. Examples of this are Ahmed's fantasy play and exaggerated stories, as illustrated by the castle and dinosaurs session description. Indeed, even incessant "why" questions, which are a cognitive developmental task typical of 4-year-olds, could be interpreted as demanding by Ahmed's mother. Another cognitively developmental task of 4-year-olds is the beginning acknowledgment of differences between right and wrong. Ahmed's reported telling of stories at the mosque that his divorced parents are still living together may or may not be indicative of cultural stigmatism related to divorce. It may be a developmentally appropriate instance of a 4-year-old telling tall tales, or it may be demonstrative of the inability to distinguish between honesty and dishonesty.

Grief and Loss Issues

Grief and loss issues for Ahmed must be considered in a cultural context. These issues include (a) loss of the family unit and (b) cultural stigmatism related to divorce or alienation from cultural group value systems. Environmental factors in Ahmed's case include sources of stress as a result of loss. First, Ahmed seems to grieve his father's absence and alienation, as depicted by the dinosaur play during therapy sessions and the reported lack of communication between his estranged parents. Ahmed, however, does have sources of family support, as indicated in the case conceptualization. His aunt and uncle are apparently a strong support for Ahmed and his mother. His day care providers and members of the mosque also seem to be concerned about Ahmed's well-being.

Additional grief and loss issues may be directly related to Pakistani culture, and this is an important factor for Ahmed's counselor to consider. Islam does not consider divorce to be *Haram*, or forbidden, although there are rules surrounding divorce between couples and how many times the same two people can divorce. Nonetheless, even though Islam does not consider divorce forbidden, Pakistani culture frowns on divorce. Depending on the cultural and religious involvement of Ahmed's parents, the counselor may need to consider these conflicts. One of the basic commitments of Muslims is to take good care of children. This commitment includes a statement of protecting the child's life, spirit, mind, morals, and manners. Therefore, the counselor should consider this systems perspective when working with Ahmed's parents.

Response to the Child

As a counselor, I would implement the following plan in regard to Ahmed's treatment:

1. cultural awareness and understanding: (a) Research Pakistani American Web sites to educate myself on basic principles of the culture, and (b) meet with the leader of the mosque to gain understanding of the differences between Islam and Pakistani values related to divorce.
2. systems interventions: (a) Request a family meeting with both parents present to discuss open communication regarding Ahmed's parenting and develop a plan using the words presented in the basic principles of Muslims (protecting the child's life, spirit, mind, morals, and manners), (b) request a meeting with the aunt and uncle to gather further information regarding Ahmed's development, and (c) educate Ahmed's mother and father on normal 4-year-old developmental behaviors.
3. individual sessions: (a) Help Ahmed recognize the people who are supportive of him by using strategies and interventions to strengthen these relationships, (b) encourage Ahmed to talk or use play to express his feelings, and (c) continue play therapy but observe Ahmed's interactions with peers, in particular with Pakistani American children.

The school counselor will be able to make a significant difference in Ahmed's life if she approaches this case in a reflective manner. Alleviating or decreasing Ahmed's familial and cultural anxiety may help him to journey through this life change in a healthier manner. Success with this critical incident is dependent on the school counselor's ability to focus and reflect on the necessary treatment. Reflection and knowledge of cultural issues are essential to this child's progress in adjusting to familial changes.

"When Home Is Not a Haven": Addressing Domestic Violence

This critical incident involves a counselor who was working with a child from a home where domestic violence was occurring. An abrupt end to the counseling sessions left the counselor wondering whether she was able to help the child in such a short time and how she could have involved the school counselor in the treatment plan. Respondents address therapeutic issues specific to counseling children about domestic violence and provide a myriad of strategies for assisting these children.

■ Critical Incident

Darcie Davis-Gage

"Rachel Garrison," an 11-year-old Caucasian girl, was admitted to a domestic violence shelter with her mother, Eva, and her three younger siblings. The Garrison family was brought to the shelter after the police were called to their house to respond to a physical confrontation between Rachel's mother and father. The shelter was part of a community mental health center that provided counseling services to families affected by domestic violence, substance abuse, and child abuse. I was working as a professional counselor at the center and had worked there for about 2 years. This was my first job as a counselor, and I had recently started counseling children at the center.

This was the Garrison family's third admission to the shelter. Although Rachel's mother had previously received counseling at the center, her children had not received any counseling interventions while staying at the shelter. This time, however, Eva requested counseling services for Rachel, and I therefore met with Mrs. Garrison for a brief intake interview to gather background information regarding her daughter.

During the intake, I explained the limits of confidentiality and how they applied to minors. I also shared that I would explain confidentiality and its limits to Rachel.

During the intake, Eva indicated that she had had a normal pregnancy with Rachel. Physically, Rachel had developed normally over the years and remained healthy, with the exception of occasional, normal childhood illnesses. Mrs. Garrison reported that Rachel did quite well socially; she easily made friends and was quite popular. Although Eva said that Rachel usually did very well academically, she had recently received a call from the school counselor, who expressed concerns about Rachel. The school counselor told Eva that, according to her teachers, Rachel was now having difficulty concentrating and staying on task. I asked Eva whether she would be willing to sign a release of information so I could speak with the school counselor, and she agreed.

As we discussed Rachel's family background, Eva reported that her husband had been verbally abusive toward her for many years and that the physical abuse had started only about 3 years ago. Eva reported that her husband was never abusive toward the children but acknowledged that Rachel had recently witnessed him being physical violent toward her mother. To Eva's knowledge, this was the first time Rachel had witnessed an incident of violence between the two of them. Mrs. Garrison said that she had tried to talk with her daughter about the incident, but Rachel had been unwilling to discuss it with her. Given this, she was hoping it might be helpful for Rachel to talk with me. I agreed to do so, and, because the family's previous visits to the shelter had been very short in duration, I arranged to see Rachel twice a week.

At our first session, I told Rachel that her mom wanted me to meet with her and asked her whether she would be willing to talk with me. She readily agreed, and I then explained confidentiality and indicated that her mother had signed a release of information so that I could also speak with her school counselor. Rachel expressed that she liked her school counselor and that it would be fine for me to talk with her. I then explained the process of counseling and shared that we would spend this session getting to know one another and setting some goals for counseling.

I asked Rachel what had brought her family to the shelter, and she explained that her father had gotten very angry with her mother and started hitting her. One of the neighbors apparently overheard the fight and called the police. When the police arrived, they took her father to jail and brought Rachel, her mother, and her siblings to the shelter. Rachel shared that she had been in the shelter two times before, but only for a couple of days. The first time, they returned to their home, and the second time, they left and stayed with her grandmother for a couple of weeks before returning home. Rachel said that her dad was always "very sorry" for hitting her mom and that her mom always forgave him, but Rachel seemed convinced he was not going to change. Rachel told me that she had recently seen her father punching her mother in the face and expressed a fear that her mother was going to be seriously injured. Rachel confirmed that her father had never hit her but complained that he yelled at her quite a bit. She said she wished her parents would divorce.

Rachel then abruptly changed the subject, as if to tell me she was finished talking about the violence. I did not push her to continue talking about the violence or about her feelings toward her father because I felt she had already shared a significant amount of information about her family situation and did not want to overwhelm her. In my experience, most children do not initially share much about the violence in their home or the feelings related to that violence.

Next, Rachel began asking me questions about the artwork on my desk. Because she expressed an interest in art, I suggested that we might be able to incorporate some art projects into the counseling. Rachel seemed excited. I then asked her about school, and she seemed relieved to start discussing this safer topic. She said she had lots of friends but did not like to have them over to the house because she was worried her parents would start fighting. She also indicated that she liked school and said that she usually did well but lately had had trouble concentrating because she had been worried about her mother. Rachel also mentioned recent trouble sleeping and frequent nightmares. As our session ended, I asked Rachel what goals she had for counseling. She said she wanted to feel safer, sleep better, and stop worrying about her parents fighting. We decided those would be our goals, and she agreed to meet with me again in a couple of days.

After my session with Rachel, I phoned her school counselor to discuss Rachel's case. Ms. Jacobson shared that teachers had contacted her to report that Rachel seemed distracted and needed to be reminded many times to work on her assignments. These problems had started recently and were beginning to affect her grades. When Ms. Jacobson met briefly with Rachel to discuss these concerns, Rachel shared that she was having trouble sleeping but denied any family problems. Although Ms. Jacobson had suspected some family problems, she was not aware that the difficulties had escalated into physical violence. We decided that I would continue to meet with Rachel regularly to work on issues surrounding the family violence and that Ms. Jacobson would continue to monitor Rachel's progress at school.

On the basis of the information from the intake and the discussion with the school counselor, I diagnosed Rachel with adjustment disorder with anxiety (Code 309.24 in the *Diagnostic and Statistical Manual of Mental Disorders*; 4th ed., text rev.; American Psychiatric Association, 2000). It is typical for children in violent homes to report some of the same feelings, but Rachel's anxiety was causing her some significant problems. On the basis of my interaction with Rachel and my conversations with her mother and Mrs. Jacobson, I believed that Rachel needed a safe place in which to discuss the violence. Given her unwillingness to speak with her mother about the violence and her ability to do so in the context of counseling, I hypothesized that using counseling as an outlet would alleviate some of her anxiety, in that she would no longer need to keep it bottled up.

I decided to use a person-centered approach in counseling. I believed Rachel needed a warm, caring environment, so she would be able to explore some of her anxiety and fears related to the family violence. I hoped counseling would help her develop ways to express her feelings and learn some coping skills to deal with her feelings. I also decided to incorporate some expressive techniques. Rachel had expressed an interest in art, and I had found some expressive techniques to be very helpful with other children from violent homes. Many times, children were able to express feelings they had difficulty verbalizing through the various art projects they created.

During our next session, Rachel made a collage. She cut out magazine pictures of things that made her feel safe. The collage included a picture of an older woman, one of a large door, and many photos of stuffed animals. I asked her to tell me how each of these pictures made her feel safe. She explained that she had lots of stuffed toys in her room at home and often held them and slept with them, especially when her parents fought. She would also give them to her siblings to help them feel better. I commended her for being thoughtful regarding her siblings' feelings. The large door symbolized her attempts to shut out her parents' fighting. She told me she always kept the doors in the house shut so she did not have to see her parents fight. I encouraged her to continue this practice because it was a good way to remain safe, but I encouraged her not to shut out her emotions. Rachel concluded the session by discussing the picture of the older woman. Rachel said the woman reminded her of her grandmother and that she felt most safe when she was at her grandmother's house. We ended the session by making a safety plan. We listed the various things she could do to make herself feel safe in her own home and discussed other people she could share her feelings with, such as the school counselor and her grandmother.

During the next session, Rachel informed me she was not having trouble going to sleep anymore but was still having difficulty with nightmares. She said the nightmares were usually about her parents fighting. In the past, I had made dream catchers with children when they were having bad dreams or nightmares, so I decided this might be a good activity for this session. I usually gave children a hoop and then allowed them to choose from a variety of materials, such as netting, feathers, and beads. Rachel chose a variety of materials to use for her dream catcher. While constructing her catcher, Rachel shared that she had started to feel a little better. She had been more relaxed at school and was able to concentrate on her work. Rachel said she was glad to be in the shelter and had found it helpful to meet other children who had experienced family violence. We ended the session with a complete dream catcher. Rachel seemed very proud of herself and could not wait to try it out.

Unfortunately, when I arrived at work on Monday, I was informed that Rachel and her family had returned home on Saturday. Exiting the shelter over the weekend was a common occurrence, as women often decided to return home to try to reconcile their relationship. At the center, we try to empower women by allowing them to make their own choices while providing them with as much information as possible so they are able to make informed, safe, and healthy decisions. Although it was unknown whether Rachel was able to be a part of the decision to return home, I hoped that she had become empowered by finding some ways to keep herself safe and developing some ways to cope with her emotions.

As I closed out Rachel's chart, I also noticed that the release for me to speak with the school counselor had been revoked. I was disappointed and wished I had set up a more formal treatment plan with the school counselor. I wondered whether I had prepared Rachel for her possible return home and whether she would use some of the recourses we had discussed. As I reflected on this case, the following questions came to my mind.

Questions

1. How do you help children prepare to return to a home where family violence is occurring?
2. As a counselor, how do you handle an abrupt exit from counseling?
3. How can agency counselors work collaboratively with school counselors to help children deal with family violence in their home?

Response

Scott W. Peters

Providing counseling services to children victimized directly or indirectly by domestic violence presents many challenges to a counselor. Safety is always paramount with children in these situations. In addition to safety issues, the counselor needs to address the impact that domestic violence is having on the child emotionally, psychologically, behaviorally, academically, and socially. Furthermore, the counselor must prepare the child for the possibility that he or she may return to a home where family conflict is ongoing. Fortunately, in my experience working with women and children in domestic violence situations, I have been able to address many of these areas simultaneously.

Domestic violence places many demands on children, their mother, and counselors. The unpredictability that is inherent in these families often creates anxiety and fear in children. The possibility that there may be an explosive incident at any time may exacerbate that fear and anxiety. Many children simply lack the tools to cope with such stress and often rely on their mother to provide support, consistency, stability, and safety. Often the target of the abuse, the mother is thereby faced with the stress of attending to her own safety issues as well as the needs of her children. In these cases, the mother has to balance the safety of the children, her own safety, attempts to keep the father or significant other calm in an effort to avoid further altercations, and the need to maintain some semblance of order in the chaos.

As this case illustrates, one of the biggest challenges for a counselor is that mothers and their children often return to the abuser (D. J. Anderson, 2003; Giles-Sims, 1983; Hilbert & Hilbert, 1984; Snyder & Scheer, 1981). This has also been true in my experience as a counselor working both at a battered women's shelter and at an agency dealing with children and domestic violence for the past 6 years. As D. J. Anderson (2003) found in her study, women with children may be even more inclined than those with no children to return to their abuser. Consequently, the focus of intervention needs to revolve around safety planning and coping skills to ready a child for potential return to an abusive situation.

Preparing a child to return to a family in which domestic violence is an ongoing issue can be very difficult. No counselor in this situation feels completely comfortable knowing that a client may be in harm's way. Nonetheless, there are several strategies that a counselor may use to help mitigate these concerns while addressing a client's needs. My philosophy when working with children affected by domestic violence is to assume that the first session may also be the last. This means that safety planning should be an integral part of the first session—and all future counseling sessions— with children facing domestic violence (Wilson, 1997). In each session, counselors should talk with children about escape routes, safe places to go, people to contact whom they trust, and emergency phone numbers. In addition to discussing these issues, it is helpful to role-play and practice these safety and survival strategies. Children usually enjoy the role plays, and, by practicing, they become quite adept at keeping themselves safe. They tend to become less anxious and feel more in control. Making a safety kit composed of a card with phone numbers for police, shelters, and relatives whom the children can contact, with a phone card or quarters taped to it, helps to empower children by giving them a sense of control.

The second strategy is aimed at teaching coping skills. Home is not a safe haven for children confronted with domestic violence. It is well documented that exposure to domestic violence can lead to internalizing and externalizing problems, cognitive delays, poor socialization, and posttraumatic stress disorder symptoms in children (S. A. Anderson & Cramer-Benjamin, 1999; Margolin & Gordis, 2000; Wilson, 1997). To help these children better cope, the counselor may find it useful to explore ways to help them feel safe while in their home. In this case, helping Rachel create a collage and a dream catcher were both good ways to accomplish this. Oftentimes, I use a narrative approach with the children at the counseling center. Helping them to create new narratives that do not involve violence gives them a sense of control and hope. Additionally, the idea of externalizing the problem can help to separate the problem from the abuser. My experience is that sometimes these children are quite conflicted; they love their abusive parent but hate (or fear) what the parent does. By learning to consider the problem (abuse and anger) and the (abusive) parent separately, children may be better able to cope with what the parent does when behaving in angry and abusive ways. These strategies are wonderful opportunities to develop trust with children who may not be able to easily trust adults.

Despite the utility of these approaches, there are times when clients in abusive families discontinue counseling before a significant amount of change has occurred. Especially when faced with premature terminations, even seasoned counselors frequently wonder about the status of their clients after the clients stop attending counseling. Because safety issues are of such vital importance for children from abusive families, it can be particularly troubling when counseling abruptly ends in these cases. As with Rachel and her family, exits from shelters sometimes happen over the weekend, when counselors or shelter staff cannot do exit interviews. This may also happen in agencies and other counseling settings that treat survivors of domestic violence. When subsequent appointments are often not kept, one may struggle over whether one's interventions have been enough to meaningfully affect one's clients.

There are some strategies that I use to help ensure that the children I see are prepared should they not return to counseling. First, I always end every session by highlighting safety planning, exit strategies, and coping skills, such as those provided by Rachel's counselor. Second, I visit with the mother both individually and with her child during the crucial initial session. I do this to help identify support systems both in and outside the family (Wilson, 1997). The focus is to raise the mother's awareness of the effects of domestic violence on her child, its effects on the child's present and future relationships, the importance of her role in her child's healing, and the implications of returning to an unsafe environment. When a child stops coming to see me, I think of other adults with whom the child may likely come into contact. Because most children attend school, I often consult the school counselor as one of the child's primary contacts.

School counselors provide an important and sometimes critical role in children's lives. As an agency-based children's counselor, I depend on good relationships with school counselors. They are often wonderful resources and can give valuable information on a child's social, behavioral, and academic performance, which may provide insight into how the child may or may not be coping in an abusive household. Furthermore, school counselors may be the first adults to whom a student turns in times of crisis. In turn, both our agency and the shelter receive many referrals from school counselors when a student presents with actual or suspected domestic violence in the home. The school counselor, like all other counselors, is a mandated reporter and must report all suspected cases of abuse (Remley & Fry, 1993; Wilder, 1991), and making such referrals is one of his or her primary responsibilities. School counselors also can play a pivotal role in providing direct service to children affected by domestic violence. The interface between counseling professionals may be invaluable in the prevention and treatment of domestic violence.

There are several strategies that can help to facilitate even more collaboration between professionals in the area of families and domestic violence. One strategy is for schools to invite domestic violence counselors to provide in-service workshops for school faculty and staff members to increase awareness of the problem. Another strategy is for school counselors from area districts to visit battered women's shelters and counseling centers that service domestic violence survivors to build professional relationships across settings. Finally, another powerful way to collaborate and raise awareness of the issue of domestic violence is to have domestic violence counselors and school counselors cofacilitate student groups discussing topics related to family violence.

Unfortunately, in this case, Rachel's mother chose to revoke the release, precluding the shelter counselor from speaking any further with the school counselor. Although such occurrences are disappointing, it can be heartening to know that the counselor at the domestic violence shelter did a commendable job of helping Rachel learn to stay safe and feel more empowered while living in a family facing the ongoing issue of domestic violence.

■Response

Terry Kottman

I am an Adlerian counselor who uses the modalities of Adlerian play therapy (Kottman, 2003), art therapy, sand tray therapy (Homeyer & Sweeney, 1998), and coactive life coaching strategies (Whitworth, Kimsey-House, & Sandahl, 1998) with children and adolescents. Most of my ideas about how I would work with Rachel and other children who live in families in which domestic violence is a factor are informed by these approaches. At 11 years old, Rachel is at an age for which some combination of playful activities, art, sand tray therapy, and a few directive coaching strategies would compose my most likely intervention.

As an Adlerian, I believe that counseling should proceed through a four-phase process: (a) building an egalitarian relationship; (b) exploring the client's lifestyle; (c) helping the client gain insight into his or her lifestyle; and (d) reorienting and re-educating the client, teaching new attitudes and behaviors that might better serve the client's life. In some cases, such as when a child may not be allowed to stay in the counseling relationship over an extended period of time, this process may be a bit truncated, but even in a one-session relationship, I would want to progress through all four phases.

Part of my intervention with a child almost always involves regular and consistent consultation with parents (and sometimes school personnel). This consultation is designed to help the adults in the child's life to gain a better understanding of the child and his or her lifestyle and to learn more appropriate strategies for interacting with and encouraging the child. I would work with Mrs. Garrison to (a) build a relationship, (b) explore her ideas about Rachel's lifestyle, (c) examine her own lifestyle and how it affects Rachel, and (d) teach her parenting skills designed to help Rachel deal with her anxiety and life situation. In working with a child in a shelter or another setting in which there is a good chance of an abrupt departure from counseling, I believe that this consultation is extremely important. If I establish a strong enough relationship with the parent, providing encouragement, support, and skills, the parent might continue to bring the child to counseling even after the family is no longer living in the shelter.

In response to the author's initial question about preparing children to return to a home in which family violence occurs (or to other situations in which the children do not feel emotionally or physically safe), I use art, visualization, sand tray therapy, role playing, and cognitive restructuring to work with children to develop and operationalize a safety plan, explore feelings, and teach anxiety management skills. I also do regular consultation with school personnel and shelter staff as a vehicle for reinforcing what I am doing in my sessions with the children.

I would start with some of the same interventions that the counselor in this case used, especially the collage, the safety plan, and the dream catcher. To increase the probability that Rachel would use the safety plan we developed, it might be helpful to use the coactive coaching strategy of creating a structure to remind her of the ideas we had generated. At her age, it would be fun to make a bracelet together, with beads on it to represent what she could do to help her feel more safe, even when her parents were fighting.

I might even have Rachel practice with the dream catcher by having her act out a bad dream coming into her bedroom and demonstrating how the dream catcher would pursue and capture the dream, complete with sound effects. I might also use some drawing or sand tray techniques in which she could show me what happens in her dreams. I could then help her to consider what she could change in the drawing or sand tray to help her keep safe in the dream. Sometimes it is helpful to teach children that they can influence their own dreams and include a superhero or other character (e.g., a grandmother or school counselor) who could help them in the dream. Another strategy I use with traumatized children experiencing dreams and memories of traumatic events is a drawing technique developed by the National Institute for Trauma and Loss in Children (Steele & Raider, 2001). In this structured sensory intervention, I ask children to draw the dream or memory and ask a series of questions designed to help them gain mastery of the feelings connected with the traumatic event.

Especially when they must return to a situation in which the violence is ongoing, many children who live in families with domestic violence struggle with their feelings. In these cases, it is essential to help children explore their feelings and to provide them with coping strategies. One such strategy is the color-your-life technique (O'Connor, 1983), in which children are invited to fill a piece of paper with colors that represent their feelings. This gives them a way to examine their feelings and to explore the relative amounts of time each feeling occupies. It is also helpful to use body outline drawings as a way to help children explore where they feel their emotions in their body and where they store anxiety and stress. I have them lie down on a large piece of paper and draw an outline of their body. Then they can use crayons, markers, stamps, stickers, or pictures cut out of magazines to illustrate where they experience specific feelings in their body and the kinds of experiences that evoke those feelings. This activity enhances children's ability to recognize feelings as they manifest themselves in the children's body.

I also like to help children realize that they often experience simultaneously different (and sometimes contradictory) feelings. For example, Rachel might really love her father, and at times she might also hate him. She might be excited to see him again and afraid of how he is going to act. She might feel protective of her mother and also be angry with her for putting herself in harm's way. I often use a sand tray to help children see that all of these feelings can happen at the same time, asking them to pick a figure for each feeling that they experience in a situation. Sometimes I may ask them to make a layered collage of different colors of construction paper, having them assign a feeling to each color and then construct a multilayered sculpture of the paper to show the layers of feelings they experience all at the same time.

As they become more adept at recognizing their feelings, I also teach these children self-soothing strategies. Some children like to carry small stones, pieces of soft material, or beads in their pockets as worry objects, to be held or rubbed in stressful situations. Some children like to visualize themselves surrounded by an energetic shield that can repel worry and protect them from negative vibrations. Some children like to make a box into which they can put pictures of anxiety-provoking situations and re-lationships as a way of symbolizing letting go of their worries.

I might also use cognitive restructuring activities as a way to help provide children in this population with a vehicle for coping with their feelings. Many of these children take on responsibility for situations and relationships that are not legitimately their responsibility. It might be helpful for Rachel to explore whether it is really her job to keep her mother safe and whether her parents' relationship is really her responsibility.

As I talk about feelings with children, I am always careful to avoid using the phrase "makes you feel," because this implies that outside factors are responsible for their feelings. I believe that it is essential in working with children to communicate that nothing makes them feel a certain way, so I prefer to use the phrase "you feel." I think this is especially important in families in which domestic violence occurs be-cause so often the violent parent blames other people in the family for outbursts, and I do not want to reinforce this pattern of thinking.

The counselor in this incident also asked about handling abrupt exits from coun-seling. With children whose situation seems to presage an early departure from counseling, I tend to treat each session as potentially the last session I will have with them. I end every session by reviewing ways for them to use the skills we have been cultivating and telling them that I believe in their ability to apply those skills. Depending on my relationship with the parent or parents, I might also call and ask for a termination session with the child. I usually argue for time to consolidate all of the insights that the child has had and the skills he or she has learned in our sessions. If I have built a solid relationship with the parents in my parent consultation, they are often willing to allow one final session with the child.

When I have a child client abruptly exit from counseling, the biggest task for me can often be related to managing my own feelings. I frequently experience a sense of loss when I have not had a chance to wind down my relationship with the child. I may worry about whether the child will be able to cope without the supportive structure of counseling. I may feel guilty or anxious about whether I did everything I could have done for the child during the relationship or whether I did everything I could with the parents to keep the child in therapy. As a way of helping myself explore my own feel-ings about the abrupt termination and to release any personal emotions evoked by the termination, I often do a drawing or sand tray myself. If my reaction went on for an extended period of time, I would also seek supervision to explore potential counter-transference issues.

Finally, in response to the counselor's inquiry about collaborative efforts to help children deal with family violence in their home, the primary roles of agency coun-selors in working collaboratively with school counselors seem to be educative, infor-mative, and supportive (Andrea Christopher, personal communication, September 2005). School counselors need information and educational materials that explain the effects of family violence on children. They can use this information to inform teach-ers so that they can be more aware of the classroom implications of such situations. It can also be helpful for the agency counselor to keep the school counselor informed about insights and strategies that the child is planning on applying to his or her life so that school personnel can provide support to the child in using the strategies and reinforcement for progress made with the agency counselor. If there are numerous children in a school who are experiencing domestic violence at home, the agency counselor can also encourage the school counselor to develop a group counseling program for them. By attending school team meetings in which school personnel develop intervention plans for school situations, the agency counselor can serve as an advocate for the child and provide a different (sometimes more positive) perspective on the child. Because the agency counselor is outside the educational system, he or she may be able to contribute ideas that would not normally be generated by school personnel.

References

American Psychiatric Association. (2000). *Diagnostic and statistical manual of mental disorders* (4th ed., text rev.). Washington, DC: Author.

Anderson, D. J. (2003). The impact of subsequent violence of returning to an abusive partner. *Journal of Comparative Studies, 34*(1), 93–112.

Anderson, S. A., & Cramer-Benjamin, D. B. (1999). The impact of couple violence on parenting and children: An overview and clinical implications. *American Journal of Family Therapy, 27*(1), 1–20.

Giles- Sims, J. (1983). *Wife battering.* New York: Guilford Press.

Hilbert, J. C., & Hilbert, H. C. (1984). Battered women leaving shelter: Which way did they go? *Journal of Applied Social Sciences, 8,* 291–297.

Homeyer, L., & Sweeney, D. (1998). *Sandtray: A practical manual.* Canyon Lake, TX: Lindan Press.

Kottman, T. (2003). *Partners in play: An Adlerian approach to play therapy* (2nd ed.). Alexandria, VA: American Counseling Association.

Margolin, G., & Gordis, E. B. (2000). The effects of family and community violence on children. *Annual Review of Psychology, 51,* 445–480.

O'Connor, K. (1983). The color-your-life technique. In C. Schaefer & K. O'Connor (Eds.), *Handbook of play therapy* (pp. 251–258). New York: Wiley.

Remley, T. P., & Fry, L. J. (1993). Reporting suspected child abuse: Conflicting roles for the counselor. *The School Counselor, 40,* 253–259.

Snyder, K. S., & Scheer, N. S. (1981). Predicting disposition following a brief residence at a shelter for battered women. *American Journal of Community Psychology, 9,* 559–566.

Steele, W., & Raider, M. (2001). *Structured sensory interventions for children, adolescents, and adults (SITCAP).* New York: Edwin Mellen Press.

Whitworth, L., Kimsey-House, H., & Sandahl, P. (1998). *Co-active coaching: New skills for coaching people toward success in work and life.* Palo Alto, CA: Davies-Black.

Wilder, P. (1991). A counselor's contribution to the child abuse referral network. *The School Counselor, 38,* 203–215.

Wilson, K. J. (1997). *When violence begins at home.* Alameda, CA: Hunter House Inc.

21

"I Already Have a Real Mom": Foster Care and Adoption

The incident explores issues related to assisting children with the transition from bio-logical families to foster care or adoptive families. A complicating factor for this partic-ular case is multiple transitions resulting from the drug addiction of the young client's mother and the death of her maternal grandmother. The respondents offer diverse ap-proaches, including developmentally appropriate individual sessions focusing on self-esteem and grief as well as attachment.

■ Critical Incident

Glenda Clare

Adoption Services requested home-based services for 9-year-old "Ralphaela Hernandez" and her preadoptive mother, Ms. Telafero. The owner of the intensive home-based counseling service completed the initial intake assessment (to obtain de-mographic information, review policies and procedures, and sign required paper-work) and assigned me to work with Ralphaela and Ms. Telafero. As I completed a more thorough clinical assessment with them, I learned that Ralphaela had become available for adoption as a result of her maternal grandmother's death 1 year ago. With the exception of two short-term foster care placements ranging from 2 to 6 months, Ralphaela's 66-year-old grandmother (Abuelita) had been Ralphaela's pri-mary caretaker since birth. Ralphaela had been born at 8 months gestation, addicted to crack cocaine. Miraculously, Ralphaela seemed to suffer no unusual physical or mental health problems as a result of this perinatal addiction.

Ralphaela was reported to be a bright child who did well in school when she at-tended. Nevertheless, she often missed school while in Abuelita's care for one of three reasons: (a) her grandmother did not feel well, (b) her mother came to get her for a mother–daughter excursion, or (c) she and her grandmother were hiding out to avoid Ralphaela's mother. Ralphaela's biological mother, Sophia, had an extensive history of mental illness and crack cocaine use. She sometimes visited Abuelita's house at unexpected hours of the day or night and was known to harass and threaten Abuelita and Ralphaela. They therefore sometimes felt a need to hide from Sophia, avoiding being seen in the neighborhood and staying inside the house—even refusing to turn the lights on in the house after dark—with the hope that she would stay away.

Because Ralphaela's father was unknown and Sophia's parental rights had been terminated, Ralphaela was put in foster care when no biological relatives made themselves available to assume custody after Abuelita's death. At this point, Ralphaela became available for adoption. Ms. Telafero, a single parent and supervisor at a local homeless shelter, expressed a desire to adopt Ralphaela and requested home-based services to transition her into the Telafero family.

I met Ralphaela on my first visit to the Telafero home. She was a beautiful girl with a smooth olive complexion and sparkling brown eyes. As I entered the home, I commented on her good looks. She told me, "I look just like my real mother." As we sat down to conduct the assessment, she told me that she was not interested in being adopted. She explained that she had been kidnapped from her real mother and that she needed my assistance to return to her real mother's care. Ralphaela sulked as I reminded her that my purpose was to help her to transition into the Telafero family. Ms. Telafero shared that she wanted to make a home for Ralphaela. I attempted to validate the feelings of each individual as I outlined my strategy for treatment sessions. I shared that we would address these issues in family therapy. I shared that there would be times when I would meet them separately but that I mostly intended to meet with them together. I asked to meet with them separately for my next scheduled session and scheduled Ralphaela to spend the first hour with me.

When I arrived for our session, Ralphaela seemed irritated. She rolled her eyes as she reminded me that she had no interest in being adopted. She thought this was a waste of her time. She said that she had a real mother who loved and wanted her. She said that her real mother did not know where she was and that I needed to help them reunite. I let Ralphaela know that I did not believe that Sophia was a bad person. I expressed a belief that she probably did love and want to care for her daughter, just as Ralphaela had shared. Her disease, however, did not allow her to take proper care of a 9-year-old child.

I then started to share information (in a nonjudgmental tone) about substance abuse—a disease that affects the entire family. At first, Ralphaela listened quietly as I shared information from Bradshaw's (1990) work on substance abuse and the family. Eventually, Ralphaela began to ask questions and share memories of encounters she had had with her mother while living with her grandmother. I told her that there was a lot to learn about this disease, which affected her entire family. I told Ralphaela that we needed to share information about this session with her new mom, Ms. Telafero. I asked whether she wanted to share what had happened or whether she would prefer that I take the lead. Ralphaela decided to take the lead.

As we talked with Ms. Telafero, I shared that I thought it might help our work for mother and daughter to learn together about substance abuse, the family disease. I recommended that we attend a couple of Narcotics Anonymous meetings and discuss what we saw and heard. In a separate session with Ms. Telafero, I explained that I thought that we needed to get beyond Ralphaela's system of denial as it related to her mother before we could really work on integrating her into the Telafero family. I shared that I thought that Ms. Telafero's support in helping Ralphaela to learn about her birth family's disease of substance abuse might help to build a foundation on which the new Telafero family could grow.

Although it was unplanned, I thought the decision to have mother and daughter learn together about substance abuse was a good one. It provided an opportunity for Ms. Telafero to listen and learn as Ralphaela reflected on her past experiences dealing with her biological mother's substance abuse. When I came to conduct the initial assessment and begin family work, Ralphaela was not ready to accept Ms. Telafero as her mother. As time passed and Ralphaela saw that Ms. Telafero supported her need to learn more about why her biological mother was incapable of parenting, Ralphaela's appreciation for Ms. Telafero grew. At the Narcotics Anonymous meetings, Ralphaela was able to hear about others' experiences and to express her need for a mother in her life. Gradually, she allowed herself to become closer to Ms. Telafero and build the foundation for integrating into the Telafero family.

Questions

1. I chose to focus on Ralphaela's concerns related to Sophia rather than her new relationship with Ms. Telafero. What other approaches should I have considered given this particular situation?
2. What are the developmental needs of children as they transition from biological families to foster care or adoptive families? What counseling interventions can be particularly helpful in addressing these needs?
3. What are the implications and issues related to having multiple transitions of caretakers and to adoption later in childhood? How might these factors affect a child's capacity for attachment and intimacy in future relationships?

 Response

Nicole R. Hill

Some of the hallmarks of resilient youths include high self-esteem, insight into the feelings of self and others, and capacity to express feelings (Flach, 1988). Ralphaela's childhood has been characterized by chaos and uncertainty. Her experiences engender a series of unresolved feelings and questions about who she is and where she belongs. Although the counselor in the case study chose to focus on the relationship between Ralphaela and Ms. Telafero, another approach would be to work individually with Ralphaela and to focus on enhancing her sense of self, generating insight into her experiences and the resulting feelings, and encouraging her healthy expression of feelings.

I believe that it is important that counselors working with children encourage self-awareness, self-acceptance, and expression of feelings. Grief and loss constitute one important aspect of Ralphaela's experience that has not been addressed given the focus on substance abuse and the building of the relationship with the adoptive mother. In her 9 years, Ralphaela has experienced a series of losses, beginning with the cyclic absence of her biological mother, continuing with the transition to and from interim foster homes, and culminating with the death of her grandmother. My clinical sense is that Ralphaela has not had an opportunity to express or to resolve her feelings of grief. Such unresolved grief can complicate attempts to build new relationships, including the attachment with Ms. Telafero. In the context of individual counseling, the counselor and

Ralphaela could work collaboratively to express the grief and loss and to create meaningful experiences to say good-bye to past relationships. Such good-bye experiences could include a therapeutic letter written to her grandmother or to her biological mother as well as a loss time line in which Ralphaela explores her past experiences with grief. An important aspect of the grief and loss process is that people tend to respond to all future losses as they experienced their first loss. Given Ralphaela's experience with her biological mother, which included inconsistency and fear, her subsequent grief experiences could be clouded by feelings of fear and insecurity, which would compound the already challenging experience of loss.

Individual counseling focused on empowering Ralphaela could also explore Ralphaela's developmental confusion. Some critical questions with which Ralphaela seems to be struggling include the following: Who am I? Who loves me? Is it my fault that no one wants me? Where do I belong? Having the focus of counseling be on exploring these issues and coconstructing with Ralphaela her responses to these questions prepares her to reach out and develop a relationship with Ms. Telafero. A counselor might appropriately choose to address these issues before working on building a relationship with other significant figures in Ralphaela's life.

The primary developmental needs that stand out to me center around attachment. Ralphaela needs assistance in developing secure attachments with adult figures and peers, developing a sense of self and belonging, defining a new role in a family, and satisfying basic needs. In terms of transitioning to an adoptive family, the developmental shift for each family member is critical in that both Ralphaela and Ms. Telafero must define the family responsibilities, roles, traditions, and rules. Typically, the creation of a new family unit is characterized by expectations, past experiences, and unfinished business. When one combines all of these forces for each person involved, the process can be tedious and unexpectedly complicated.

Counseling interventions that specifically address family roles and boundaries would help Ralphaela and Ms. Telafero both understand their perspectives and how they converge. Rules and traditions could be coconstructed. Interventions that focus on communication and parenting skills could also be very helpful. Educating and role playing new skills with both Ralphaela and Ms. Telafero simultaneously could provide a shared experience and could begin to define how they interact as a family. Careful attention needs to be applied to making certain that this process is shared. For example, it might be unrealistic to demand initially that Ralphaela address Ms. Telafero as *mother*. The profound shift in having Ms. Telafero as a parental figure might be undermined if Ralphaela is forced to interact in a manner for which she is not ready. The counselor can function as an advocate to encourage a smooth transition that involves gradual establishment of a relationship.

Any counseling interventions must be implemented in the context of Ralphaela's past experiences with family. For example, her sense of self and belonging has been compromised by the repeated exposure to her biological mother's erratic and dangerous behavior. She may struggle to conceptualize and articulate what healthy relationships are and to understand what belonging in a family is like. Also, Ralphaela might be especially sensitive to any situation that suggests that her basic survival needs are not being met. Because of the chaotic home environment, Ralphaela and her grandmother seem to have coped by avoiding crises. For example, Ralphaela and Abuelita would hide from Sophia. Such repeated behaviors modeled to Ralphaela that a method for managing stressful situations and maintaining safety is to avoid at all costs the source of stress. Another factor that needs to be addressed for counseling interventions to be effective is the magical thinking in which Ralphaela engages.

Magical thinking tends to be developmentally appropriate for younger children, but it can manifest in older children as a result of grief and loss experiences or as a result of trauma. The counselor needs to consider how magical thinking (e.g., "I have been kidnapped") could jeopardize any attempts to support the developmental process of creating a new family unit.

Experiencing multiple transitions is equated with experiencing multiple losses because all change includes a component of loss. The long-term placement with Abuelita has enhanced Ralphaela's experience of consistency, yet the erratic and threatening emergence of Sophia throughout this time period has engendered a sense of insecurity. Additionally, one might expect that Ralphaela has a very confused perspective on family roles and processes. Many life experiences have disrupted the continuity of care that she has received. She has been expected at a young age to exercise rapid adjustment to unsettling experiences. Her senses of safety and self have been compromised by these experiences.

A child's working model for attachment is developed at an early age and sets the interaction pattern for future relationships. Given Ralphaela's tendency to avoid direct stressors, as modeled by Abuelita, it may be that she perceives others as not really being responsive and attentive to her needs. If this is the case, then her future relationships will be filtered through this philosophy of not being able to count on others. The counseling relationship provides a powerful vehicle for broadening Ralphaela's sense of belonging and attachment in significant relationships. Experiencing a counselor who is consistent, predictable, and responsive could substantially shift Ralphaela's working model of attachment. Again, embracing an empowering and strength-based perspective when counseling Ralphaela would have a multifaceted impact. First, it would provide a proactive and healthy model for attachment. Second, it would encourage her development of resiliency and self-acceptance.

Response

Kimberly Bundy-Fazioli

The counselor's focus on the biological mother, Sophia, seems to be a sound approach on the basis of Ralphaela's reaction to adoption. Clearly, Ralphaela is conflicted about her birth mother's role in her life, especially after the death of her grandmother. In reviewing this case, I am struck by the number of traumatic incidents Ralphaela is struggling with: (a) the death of her primary caretaker, (b) confusion about her birth mother's role, (c) abrupt foster care placement after the death of her grandmother, and now (d) the pressure to adjust to an adoptive home.

I believe that Ms. Telafero's request for home-based services was a positive and proactive move. Her intent was to help Ralphaela transition to her new home. As the counselor in this case, before I would pursue the issue of attachment and bonding with the preadoptive mother, I would first assess how Ralphaela is handling her grief around her grandmother's death. I suspect that her grief might have been compounded by an abrupt foster care placement; therefore, I would attempt to understand what happened before her grandmother's death. Did she know that her grandmother was going to die? What does she remember? What did she experience? Did she know that she would be going to a new home? Did her grandmother talk to her about this? What has been her understanding of her birth mother's role in her life? Using an ecological systems perspective, I would want to assess how the pieces of Ralphaela's life fit together. One of the challenges for the counselor working with

Ralphaela is to develop rapport and trust with a 9-year-old girl who has already experienced significant trauma.

Although time is of the essence for children waiting for a permanent home, the reality is that adoption disruption occurs all too frequently and is heartbreaking for the adoptive family and the child. In their seminal research on adoption disruption, Barth and Berry (1988) found that if the focus in counseling is on finalizing the adoption without considering the child's emotional needs, it affects the ability of the child and parent to bond effectively. Smith and Howard (1991) studied successful and disrupted adoptions and found that one of the contributing factors to disruption was the child's strong attachment to the birth mother. It is safe to speculate that Ralphaela does not have a close relationship with her birth mother; nonetheless, she was probably very attached to her grandmother, the only mother figure she knew. Therefore, if she has not grieved the loss of her grandmother, it is questionable whether she can successfully bond with a new mother figure. If the grief is not addressed, it could potentially contribute toward a fantasy that Ralphaela's birth mom will get better and come to rescue her.

A key to ensuring a successful adoption is attending to the matching of the child and the preadoptive parents, in this case a single mother. Matching involves identifying the compatibility between an adoptive parent's strengths and resources and the child's vulnerabilities and needs (Barth & Berry, 1988). Therefore, it is also important for the counselor to understand Ms. Telafero's expectations for this adoption. Ms. Telafero will have completed an adoption home study. I would want to read this and learn what motivated Ms. Telafero to adopt at this point in her life. I would want to know how she envisions her future with Ralphaela. Finally, I would want to know Ms. Telafero's experience with grief and loss issues. Is she comfortable honoring Ralphaela's memory of her grandmother? Alternatively, is she hoping that Ralphaela will forget and move on?

The National Adoption Information Clearinghouse (1994) estimated that 5% of all adoptions were by single parents. Although single-parent adoptions are more prevalent today, the adoptive parent still needs to be prepared. Thus, it is important to meet individually with Ms. Telafero to identify her strengths and resources as well as challenges and obstacles. I would assess Ms. Telafero's ability to take care of herself during stressful periods. Who does she identify as her support system? It is important that she is able to strike a new balance in juggling her new parenting role with her other responsibilities (National Adoption Information Clearinghouse, 1994).

In the critical incident narrative, I noted a change in the language the counselor used, moving from *Ms. Telafero* and to *preadoptive mom* and *mother*. I would want to know whether the use of *mother* was introduced by the foster–adoptive agency, the counselor, the preadoptive mom, or Ralphaela. When a child begins to use this name, it provides information that needs to be explored. Is the child expected to use this name, or did she initiate use of the word on her own? Is she seeking to please her preadoptive mom in fear of being moved again and rejected, or is she ready for this familial closeness? I believe it is important for the child to have permission to use the language of *mother* only when he or she is ready.

In my work with foster–adoptive families and children who have experienced multiple placements, I find it is important to understand the world of the parent and child, individually and as a unit. Using the ecological systems approach, I gather as much information as I can to begin to determine the most effective interventions. It is important to remain curious; new information is always forthcoming as the child and adoptive parent feel more comfortable and safe in the therapeutic setting.

Developmental Needs

When a child's world is abruptly changed and he or she is placed in foster care, the event can have devastating and lasting effects. This is not to say that there are not incredibly wonderful and effective foster parents. What it speaks to is the disruption and turmoil of living in one place one night and another place the next night. Imagine what this experience would be like for you at this point in your life. Now imagine that you are 8 years old. To put this in perspective, note that a recent study found that adults with a foster care history face rates of posttraumatic stress disorder twice that of U.S. war veterans (Casey Family Programs, 2005). Although not every child in foster care will experience posttraumatic stress disorder, this finding highlights how traumatic this upheaval can be in a child's life. Therefore, it is crucial that counselors working with children who have experienced multiple placements address issues of grief and loss, separation and healing, and lasting recovery.

Considering the trauma children endure from an abrupt upheaval in their life, it follows that their developmental needs will be delayed or interrupted. In the world of a typical 9-year-old child, it is normal to begin focusing less on the family and more on peer friendships and relationships. A girl at this age is also becoming prepubescent, with changing hormones and bodily symptoms. Clearly, these significant developmental milestones are complicated when a child's world has been turned upside down, as Ralphaela's has. The death of her grandmother, her entrance into the foster care system, and her adjustment to a new home all contribute to unresolved grief and loss. A child's response to grief, similar to adults' response, is individualistic, as each person responds differently to grief and loss; nonetheless, there are some characteristics that are common for this age group. Black (2005) found in her grief research that 9- to 11-year-old children may attempt to hide their sadness but exhibit more anger. She also found that grief can become complicated and prolonged when the child begins to avoid friends and shows increased irritability 3 to 6 months after the death of a loved one.

I anticipate that Ralphaela is experiencing numerous emotions, such as sadness, fear, and despair as well as hope and anticipation. The challenge for the counselor is helping Ralphaela to identify and express these emotions and work with her preadoptive mother to anticipate and accept these emotions. It is also normal for Ms. Telafero to express some grief and loss issues of her own because she is also making drastic changes in her lifestyle and perhaps hoping for an easy transition and instant family.

Individual sessions with Ms. Telafero would focus on helping her develop a trusting relationship with Ralphaela. The goal is for Ralphaela to eventually feel safe and secure in her new home setting. It is important that Ms. Telafero understand that Ralphaela is a child who is hurting, and Ms. Telafero needs to demonstrate patience and consistency in caring for Ralphaela as she heals.

Attachment Issues

The hope with all adoptions is "that love and affection will overcome all" (Carnochan, 2006, p. 34). Unfortunately, this is rarely the case with older children. The older child comes into an adoptive arrangement with years of memories and experiences. Therefore, it is important to understand the child's role in the adoption process. For instance, did Ralphaela know that Ms. Telafero's home was a foster–adopt home? The other reality is that Ralphaela has a birth mother who has been a part of her life since birth. Sophia did not provide safety, stability, or maternal care, but she was still in the picture. It seems that this connection with her birth mother was very disruptive; Ralphaela's mother would drop by unexpectedly, or Ralphaela and her grandmother would hide out to avoid her. It is important to assess how this interaction with her birth mother affected her ability to trust her environment.

In adoption scenarios, there are often references to the adoption triad or adoption triangle. These terms refer to the silent or unspoken third party presence in the adoptive relationship—the birth parents. The counselor's ability to address substance abuse issues was important in helping Ralphaela understand her mother's inability to care for her. Nonetheless, this may not be the end of the discussion. At some point, Ralphaela may want contact with her mother to maintain some semblance of relationship. It is not uncommon for a child to hope that the troubled parent will get better and be able to care for him or her. It is important to address Sophia's mental health issues with Ralphaela because children often wonder whether they will have the same disorders. The counselor can bring these issues to the surface with Ralphaela and Ms. Telafero. Often in adoptive arrangements there is a belief that if no one talks about the problem, it will go away. In Ralphaela's case the problem is the memory of her grandmother and her ever-present birth mother. Secrecy can thwart attachment (Schooler & Norris, 2002).

One of the tools available to counselors in helping children through the foster care and adoption process is helping the child create a *life book*. A life book is a compilation of memories, pictures, words, feelings, drawings, report cards, letters, and anything else the child has collected throughout childhood. The book can be a creative process between the counselor and child. A life book is especially beneficial for older children during preparation for adoption (Backhaus, 1984). It serves as a symbolic process of honoring the child's background and culture as it helps to minimize the child's distress, answer questions, reframe memories, and present the past in an understandable and memorable way (Backhaus, 1984).

One of the goals of adoption counseling is helping to foster a strong, positive, and loving attachment between the adoptive parents and the child. Like any new relationship, this takes time. Ralphaela needs time to adjust to her life circumstances without her birth family. Individual and family therapy provides a place where these difficult issues can be disclosed and discussed. Counseling also provides an opportunity to build trust and respect, clarify boundaries and household expectations, and encourage closeness through communicating and identifying mutual interests.

When adoption occurs, one hopes for a smooth and conflict-free process. Unfortunately, children adopted at an older age are at risk for exhibiting behavioral problems, often because they have the inability to process the depths of their emotions or make rational sense out of what is happening to them. There are a number of resources available for adoptive parents: books, support groups, and Web sites. I would encourage Ms. Telafero to read and learn what this experience is like for Ralphaela so that she can begin to have the compassion and patience to respond to Ralphaela's emotional outbursts, which can be expressions of gratitude or anger (Carnochan, 2006).

Attachment and bonding difficulties realistically can be anticipated. These difficulties can manifest in a number ways toward the adoptive parent; for instance, children might show little to no interest in attaching, lack of affection, and increasingly destructive behaviors. Howe (1998) found that some older children exhibited the following behavioral and personality traits: insecurity and anxiety, attention seeking and demandingness, restlessness, poor concentration skills, and difficulty with peers.

Clearly, risk factors are present in older child adoptions, and, for Ralphaela, the risk factors pertain to the traumatic events she has endured. The two most important protective factors for Ralphaela, as identified in the case study, include her ability to do well in school and her normal development despite perinatal addiction. The additional protections for Ralphaela are individual and family counseling. Ralphaela, like many other foster and adopted children, has the opportunity to lead a happy, healthy, and full life. Ralphaela's ability to work in counseling to address grief and loss issues and begin to heal from the various traumatic events will increase her chances for attachment and intimacy in future relationships.

References

Backhaus, K. (1984). Life books: Tools for working with children in placement. *Social Work, 12*, 551–554.

Barth, R., & Berry, M. (1988). *Adoption & disruption: Rates, risks, and responses.* New York: Aldine DeGruyter.

Black, S. (2005). When children grieve. *American School Board Journal, 192*(8), 28–30.

Bradshaw, J. E. (1990). *Bradshaw on the family: A new way of creating solid self esteem.* Deerfield Beach, FL: Health Communications, Inc.

Carnochan, P. (2006). Walking through walls: The mind of a foster child. In T. Heineman & D. Ehrensaft (Eds.), *Building a home within: Meeting the emotional needs of children and youth in foster care* (pp. 23–42). Baltimore: Brooks.

Casey Family Programs. (2005). *Former foster children in Washington and Oregon suffer post traumatic stress disorder at twice the rate of U.S. war veterans, according to new study.* Retrieved November 21, 2005, from http://www.casey.org/MediaCenter/PressReleasesAndAnnouncements/NWAlumniStudy.htm

Flach, F. F. (1988). *Resilience: Discovering a new strength at times of stress.* New York: Fawcett Columbine.

Howe, D. (1998). *Patterns of adoption.* Malden, MA: Blackwell Science.

National Adoption Information Clearinghouse. (1994). *Single parent adoption: What you need to know.* Retrieved January 18, 2006, from http://naic.acf.hhs.gov/pubs/f_single/f_single.pdf

Schooler, J., & Norris, B. (2002). *Journeys after adoption: Understanding lifelong issues.* Westport, CN: Bergin & Garber.

Smith, S., & Howard, J. (1991). A comparative study of successful and disrupted adoptions. *Social Services Review, 6*, 248–265.

22

"Misguided Attempts to Love": Intergenerational Substance Abuse

Substance abuse is a family disease. It affects all members of the family and is often sustained by family dynamics. This incident explores the complexities of substance abuse and its relationship to issues of child abuse and neglect. Included in the discussion of this incident are issues related to interpreting children's play and determining whether the play represents reality or fantasy. Additionally, the respondents address the difficulty involved in deciding whether to make reports of suspected abuse or neglect and whether foster care placement is helpful or harmful to children.

■ Critical Incident

Glenda Clare

I first met "Christie Sullivan" 2 days after her return home from the burn treatment center. Christie had suffered third degree burns to her torso, arms, and legs in a fire that started when this 5-year-old child tried to prepare a meal for herself and her mother on a gas-igniting stove. The child narrowly escaped with her life. I was told that she would need to undergo years of burn treatment, physical therapy, and counseling to get her life back on track. As I drove down the street and spotted what I thought was the Sullivan home, I was surprised. In front of the home were three large vans displaying the logos of ABC, CBS, and NBC affiliates. I wanted to turn around and leave but reminded myself why I was there. My job was to provide counseling to Christie so that she could overcome a challenging time in her life.

Thus began my work with the Sullivan family. I parked my car and slowly made my way to the house. Because this was my first visit to the home, I decided to leave my rolling cart of toys in the car. I would use them after my initial assessment with the child. I was told that Christie and her Aunt Maggie were taking the media on a tour of her grandparents' newly restored home. Clearly excited by the media attention, Christie's grandparents sat on the back porch with my clinical supervisor, who was assigned to conduct the family counseling sessions for the Sullivans. I joined them to discuss the individual play therapy I would be providing for Christie.

As we sat together on the porch, Christie's grandmother, Alice, talked about the circumstances of the fire and the trauma that ensued. Her eyes began to tear as she shared that a restraining order had been taken against the child's mother, Marilyn. When I asked about the reason for the restraining order, Alice lowered her head and quietly shared that her daughter had admitted to using crack cocaine prior to the onset of the fire. High on crack, Marilyn had been unconcerned that her 5-year-old daughter was hungry. As always, Marilyn allowed Christie to go downstairs to prepare dinner for the two of them without assistance. She had not realized that Christie could spill oil on herself and the stove and thereby create a fire.

Both grandparents were at work at the time of the fire. Nevertheless, they admitted having been somewhat aware of Marilyn's drug use. Over a series of sessions that my clinical supervisor facilitated, Alice and Thomas admitted that they had decided that if Marilyn were going to get high, it was best that she do it at home. Marilyn had lived with them all of her life. Alice felt the need to take care of Marilyn, especially because Marilyn was Alice's youngest child. Mr. and Mrs. Sullivan provided Marilyn with room, board, clothing, and whatever money she needed. When she came home pregnant and gave birth to Christie, Marilyn stayed home to raise her child. Alice would have it no other way. Occasionally, Thomas objected, but he always relented to his wife's pleas about needing to keep her family safe. Alice said that the Sullivan home was one of loving care and support. Alice explained that her own mother had overcome drug addiction without intervention and that she was sure that Marilyn would eventually do so as well.

During family counseling, Alice often verbalized resentment that she now had the responsibility to provide full-time care for Christie. There was a restraining order preventing Marilyn from entering the Sullivan home or being within 20 feet of Christie and a court order requiring Marilyn to enter drug treatment. Mrs. Sullivan complained that she never had time for herself and always needed to take Christie to an appointment, tend to the child's bandages and bathing procedures, or be available for counseling services in the home. Mrs. Sullivan reported that she wanted to spend time with her daughter Marilyn but could not because of Christie. For now, though, they needed to deal with Christie's issues that resulted from the fire.

After having a number of play therapy sessions with me in the Sullivans' home, Christie began kindergarten. To lighten the burden on Alice and lessen her resentment of Christie's needs, I decided to get permission to have Christie's play therapy sessions at her school. I was able to negotiate a schedule to facilitate play therapy between the hours of 1:00 and 2:00 every Monday and Wednesday afternoon.

Christie was a delightful child. Her teacher said that she always attempted to get along and never called any particular attention to herself. She always had a smile on her face, but if one looked deeply into her eyes, there was a seeming sadness. Although her grandparents said that Christie was slower than most children, her teacher reported that she had average capabilities.

Most of Christie's early play sessions focused on fire and medical issues. She often recreated the scene of the fire. In these scenes, a child was usually carried out of the home and taken to the hospital by firemen. Nurses and doctors cared for the child during her stay at the hospital. As time passed, a magic wizard was periodically used to change the events of the fire and return the child to her prefire (good skin) state. Eventually, Christie's play began to focus on mother–daughter relationships. Christie played out a child who was very angry at a mother who rarely paid attention to the child's needs.

Christie seemed to be more at ease with the play sessions held at her school than with those held at the Sullivan home. In the home, there never seemed to be enough privacy for our sessions. Thomas often "needed" to be in the adjoining kitchen during play sessions, and I suspected that he listened to our sessions as he spent 45–50 minutes allegedly cleaning the kitchen area. Once, after he entered the playroom uninvited, I confronted him. In contrast, the sessions at the school were strictly confidential. There, grandma and grandpa were unable to sneak a peek or enter play sessions unexpectedly.

After about 3 weeks of play sessions at school, Christie's play began to center on time spent with her mother. These scenes depicted Christie and her mother playing games. I initially thought these were positive memories of the past. As time went on, however, I began to wonder whether Christie was actually seeing her mother in spite of the restraining order. Although Marilyn had been court ordered to drug treatment, she had not completed her program. In fact, Marilyn had been missing for weeks. No one seemed to know where she was. Christie, however, talked and played out vivid scenes with her mother. I became perplexed and brought this matter up in clinical supervision.

My clinical supervisor invited me to attend the Sullivans' next family session, and we agreed that the two of us would then confront Mr. and Mrs. Sullivan about our suspicions. During this session, I reminded the grandparents of the restraining order and the necessity that Marilyn complete drug treatment. I shared that Child Protective Services (CPS) could remove Christie from their care if it was found that Marilyn was visiting the Sullivan home. Alice seemed appalled at the suggestion and vehemently denied that this had happened. Thomas, however, sat quietly listening to the information that was shared.

Within a week, Christie was removed from the Sullivan home and placed with a foster care family. Apparently, a well-meaning neighbor had called the police on seeing what appeared to be a prowler creeping around the house. One of the officers familiar with the family's situation immediately called CPS when the creeper was discovered to be Marilyn.

This was a hard case for me. So many things transpired during this case, and Christie's needs seemed to be so very unimportant to all the adults in her family. Her needs were either neglected or resented by her mother and grandmother. As her teacher described, Christie seemed to try so hard to get along and not draw any attention to herself. I was actually happy to see Christie removed from the Sullivan household. I thought her needs could be better met with a foster family who might want to adopt this very loving child.

In thinking back to the day I first met the Sullivan family, I knew that something was wrong the minute I came to the house and saw all the media vans. Christie's grandparents seemed to need and want attention and seemed totally unaware of the possible impact this could have on Christie. I remember feeling irritated when Alice complained about having to care for Christie and talked about how very much she wanted to spend time with her daughter instead. I always hoped that Mrs. Sullivan would show more caring and concern for her granddaughter. Finally, because Thomas made so many attempts to violate the privacy of our play therapy sessions, I always wondered what he feared. His lurking behaviors made it seem as though he thought his granddaughter might accidentally share some family secrets.

In the end, the Sullivan family was not meeting the needs of this child. There was a generational history of accepted substance abuse (Christie's great-grandmother and her mother), and there was a clear pattern of enabling. Although ordered to attend 12-step meetings, Mr. and Mrs. Sullivan did not seem interested in learning more about this family disease. Despite Christie's traumatic experience, they continued to be codependent and supported Marilyn's drug-related activities. I felt that it was in Christie's long-term best interest that she be removed from the home of her biological family.

Questions

1. Could I have been reasonably sure that Christie's play signified Marilyn's actual return to the Sullivan home? Should I have called CPS rather than waiting for a neighbor to report someone creeping around the Sullivan house?
2. At what point should a counselor report to CPS a belief that caretakers are neglectful?
3. Was it really in Christie's long-term best interest to be removed from the home of her biological family?

■ Response

Katrina Cook

The American Counseling Association's (2005) *Code of Ethics* specifies that "the primary responsibility of counselors is to respect the dignity and to promote the welfare of clients" (p. 4). Because children are dependent on their parents or guardians, their welfare is vulnerable to the choices and actions of those caregivers (Remley & Herlihy, 2005). When dependent clients, such as children, are potentially harmed by the actions of their caregivers, counselors have a duty to protect those children and must intervene on their behalf (Remley & Herlihy, 2005).

In this case, Christie's mother was incapacitated by drug addiction, and this had already resulted in tragic and severe consequences for Christie. Any counselor working with Christie would understandably have a heightened sense of awareness regarding indications of further abuse. Even with a heightened awareness, however, identifying signs that a young child is experiencing abuse can be a most challenging task for counselors. Whereas some signs of physical abuse—such as bruises, welts, or, as in Christie's case, severe burns—may be obvious, others are much more subtle. At stake, of course, is the safety of the child.

Christie's counselor clearly understood her responsibility not only to assist her young client with emotional healing from the trauma of the burns but also to attend to her client's overall well-being in the Sullivan home. I agree with the counselor's decision to use a play therapy approach with Christie, given that it is recognized as an appropriate and effective approach to work with young children who have experienced trauma (Kanters, 2002). In this case, play therapy gave Christie the opportunity to reenact the fire while also creating more preferred outcomes, such as the wizard who magically cured her injuries. Christie's initial play therapy themes also focused on expressing angry feelings toward her mother.

Eventually, the counselor noted a shift in Christie's play themes, as she began acting out positive interactions with her mother. This shift led the counselor to suspect clandestine visits from Marilyn. Although play therapy does allow children the opportunity to express feelings and experiences they are not developmentally able to verbalize, I caution against assuming that the play always represents actual or current events. Axline (1947) indicated that children's play symbolizes their feelings. Christie's play reflecting positive interactions with her mother might have been more indicative of what Christie hoped would happen rather than of what she was actually experiencing. Using Christie's play as evidence that Marilyn was defying the restraining order and visiting the Sullivan home could be an overinterpretation on the counselor's part. In fact, even though Marilyn was later caught at the Sullivan residence, there was no indication that she had made previous visits. The neighbor's description of Marilyn as creeping seems to imply that Alice, Thomas, and Christie were not even aware of or expecting Marilyn's presence on this occasion.

Although the counselor should not have automatically concluded, on the basis of themes in Christie's play, that Marilyn was, in fact, visiting Christie, it is possible that these themes could reasonably lead to suspicions of such visits. If this were the case, the counselor should have contacted CPS and reported her suspicions. Although the specific regulations may vary, all states have mandatory child abuse reporting laws requiring counselors to report suspected abuse (National Clearinghouse on Child Abuse and Neglect [NCCAN], 2004a). Certainty of the occurrence of abuse is not a prerequisite for reporting child abuse. In fact, counselors should be clear that it is not incumbent on them to prove the existence of abuse before making a report. The CPS office, not the counselor or other mandated reporter, is responsible for the investigation and substantiation of abuse.

That being said, I also caution against automatically picking up the phone to call CPS. Counselors should consult with other professionals and use professional judgment before taking such a step. Consultations are especially helpful for clarifying whether there is reasonable cause for suspicion or whether the counselor may be projecting onto the client or overinterpreting ambiguous communications. In this case, the counselor very appropriately consulted with her supervisor, and together they developed a course of action to confront Thomas and Alice with their suspicions about covert visits from Marilyn. Given the ambiguity of the information that led to this suspicion, I agree that this was a more appropriate approach than an automatic call to CPS.

The next question posed by the counselor in this incident is also related to the issue of making referrals to CPS. When should a counselor report to CPS a belief that caretakers are neglectful? The NCCAN (2004b) defined neglect as "a failure to provide for a child's basic needs" (p. 1). These needs could include physical, medical, educational, or emotional needs (NCCAN, 2004b). Again, counselors need to exercise careful deliberation and consultation before determining the possibility of neglect.

When reviewing Christie's case, the counselor identified several concerns that may indicate possible neglect. First, she noted that Thomas and Alice did not seem particularly interested in Christie. Alice reported that she missed her daughter and seemed to resent Christie's presence. Alice viewed Christie's need for intensive medical care as a burden. Neither Alice nor Thomas acknowledged a need to become educated about substance abuse or enabling behaviors. Thomas violated Christie's boundaries by interrupting her home counseling sessions. When the counselor noted that Christie seemed to feel more comfortable during the school counseling sessions than the home sessions, she attributed this to the family's blurred boundaries, as evidenced by

Thomas's intrusions into Christie's home counseling sessions. Confronting Thomas and reminding him of confidentiality issues seemed to redirect his behavior.

These attitudes and behaviors might not necessarily indicate abuse. Nevertheless, the counselor expressed a belief that neglect was occurring. Her conviction about the presence of neglect required her to make a report to CPS. Once again, careful deliberation and consultation with her supervisor could help clarify the counselor's concerns. At this point, I would ask the counselor to examine her objectivity in this case. Christie had already suffered a great deal, and it is understandable that a counselor would want to nurture and rescue such an engaging and resilient child. The counselor described feeling irritated by Alice's complaints about caring for Christie. She assumed that Thomas's violations of Christie's counseling sessions were motivated by a fear that Christie would reveal family secrets. She described his behavior as lurking.

The counselor's perceptions of the Sullivans may be accurate. Nonetheless, there may be many other explanations for their behavior as well. Any grandparent might reasonably feel overwhelmed by the task of providing prolonged and intense medical care for a child. Was Thomas fully informed about the importance of confidentiality before he consented to Christie's sessions? His intrusions might simply have been a result of his lack of experience and knowledge about the counseling process.

Furthermore, Alice and Thomas's resentful attitudes toward Christie may indicate a less than caring and nurturing environment. Nevertheless, her grandparents do seem to have minimally met Christie's immediate needs. Even though they viewed Christie's frequent doctor appointments as an inconvenience, there is no indication that they skipped these appointments. Although they were not open to receiving education about substance abuse and enabling behavior or counseling, they did comply with the court order to continue counseling with the supervisor. They also allowed Christie to attend her counseling sessions on a regular basis.

In expressing this, I do not wish to minimize the importance of the counselor's observations and reactions to the Sullivan family. Vigilance about the quality of Christie's care was essential. The severe trauma that Christie had already experienced from her biological family highlighted the urgency of securing her safety. Although there does not seem to be any concrete evidence of neglect from Alice and Thomas, that does not mean that neglect did not occur. Intuition is often a valuable and indispensable tool for counselors. Nevertheless, counselors must carefully explore whether they are experiencing intuition or making subjective judgments. I would encourage the counselor to balance her intuitiveness with her counseling skills and knowledge. Exploring her emotional reactions toward clients through self-reflection, consultation, and supervision can help her approach clients and their experiences more objectively.

In this case, however, a neighbor's report rather than the counselor's report led to the CPS decision to remove Christie from the Sullivan home. When Christie's mother was caught at the home in violation of the restraining order and questions were raised about the Sullivans' compliance with the court order, Christie was placed in foster care. This placement apparently also resulted in the counselor being unable to continue counseling Christie.

It can be extremely frustrating when a counseling relationship is severed so abruptly. When advocating for their more vulnerable clients, counselors can sometimes come to believe that they are the only ones who can help those clients. Letting go of clients such as Christie and trusting that other caring professionals and adults will provide for them can be difficult, especially when there is no guarantee that this will happen. Even though the counselor seems to believe that Christie was now in a place where she would be better loved, she still questions the long-term consequences of removing Christie from her home.

Removing children from their home and placing them in foster care remains a controversial subject. Research conducted about the long-term effects of foster care has produced contradictory results (McDonald, Allen, Westerfelt, & Piliavin, 1996). Although the quality of care that Christie received in the foster care system is unknown and more research needs to be conducted in this area, there is evidence that placement with a stable foster family increases the possibility of positive outcomes (McDonald et al., 1996). It is my hope that such will be the case for Christie.

Response

Christina Rosen Galvin

In reading this critical incident about Christie Sullivan, I was not surprised that the counselor in this case had questions. This case was difficult, and I believe that it is healthy, natural, and insightful to be asking these kinds of questions. It is admirable that the counselor has taken the time to reflect on the decisions she made and the impact this case had on her. I can only imagine her feelings and reactions when she arrived at Christie's house and found her traumatized client amidst a swarm of media. Later, the counselor was also confronted with the grandmother's negative attitude toward caring for her granddaughter and the grandfather's violation of Christie's privacy and lack of trust during home counseling sessions. Further into the counseling process, the counselor also discovered that the grandparents continued to put their daughter's needs ahead of the more pressing needs of their granddaughter. Obviously, the actions of the grandparents were not ideal, in that they chose to ignore the restraining order, the court order to attend the 12-step groups, and the needs of their traumatized granddaughter.

Although counselors can expect these behaviors from an individual who has active substance dependency issues, it is still a difficult and challenging situation. The situation becomes particularly difficult if the counselor forgets that the entire family is operating from an intergenerational substance abuse or dependency system and instead believes that the family is unaffected by the member who is chemically dependent. To the contrary, it has been my experience that such families are indeed affected by a family member's chemical dependency. These families may fail to engage in appropriate behaviors, such as (a) setting appropriate priorities, (b) nurturing the person who is in immediate need, (c) protecting vulnerable family members, and (d) setting boundaries with the person who is inflicting harm.

In addition to dealing with these issues, Christie's counselor must also collaborate with the Sullivans' family counselor and CPS while balancing the heavy caseload, productivity requirements, and administrative tasks so common for agency counselors. It is my hope that, in responding to this critical incident, I will (a) normalize and validate the counselor's process, (b) discuss issues and dynamics related to intergenerational substance dependency in families, (c) answer her questions about interpreting Christie's play and about contacting CPS, and (d) discuss the importance of supervision in these cases.

To preface my comments, I note that I think this would be a difficult case for any counselor. The counselor demonstrated an ability to encourage, assess, and then advocate for her client. For example, the counselor effectively advocated for Christie by arranging to meet her during school hours, thus building trust and ensuring her client's privacy. This arrangement also provided a respite for the grandparents from having to be at home for their granddaughter's counseling sessions and avoided any burden related to transporting Christie to and from counseling sessions. Furthermore, the counselor continued assessment during play therapy and advocated for her client by speaking to her supervisor about Christie's emphasis on playing games with her mother. This led to the counselor being able to confront the grandparents and to observe the inconsistencies in their reactions to her confrontation. To help prevent potential manipulation and missing information, I have found it important for both the child and the family counselor to have joint sessions with the family as often as possible or, at a minimum, have weekly consultations with one another.

Dynamics in Families With Chemical Dependence

As I explore this case, it is important to consider some dynamics that could be playing out in this family. As a counselor experienced in working with families, I am aware that certain roles, rules, and expectations are passed down from generation to generation. Dynamics such as enabling, denial, inappropriate boundaries, and the creation of chaos or confusion are common in families with a member who is substance dependent. When someone in the family is struggling with substance dependency, particularly intergenerational substance dependency, there are often certain rules, roles, and values the family follows, such as the "don't talk" rule (Black, 1981; Satir, 1972). The family keeps secrets to prevent the outside world from learning what is really going on (Black, 1981; Satir, 1972). Another rule is "don't rock the boat," which has the underlying messages of "don't create or confront problems" and "keep peace in the family at all costs" (Black, 1981; Satir, 1972).

An example of such dynamics evident in this case is the counselor's observation that Christie's grandmother was enabling her daughter and that there was a family history of enabling behavior. It does not surprise me that the grandparents in this case did not follow up on court recommendations for them to attend a 12-step program. This is consistent with my own clinical experience. Clients often struggle with denial and continue to believe that no problem exists despite clear evidence indicating otherwise.

As a family counselor, I have had the opportunity to broach the topic of denial, educate the family from a systems perspective, and assist the family in making appropriate changes. Rarely have I been able to influence the family system enough to make dramatic changes simply by working with a young child. More comprehensive action is typically needed, such as family counseling and family involvement in a 12-step program. As a family counselor, I can work with the family and encourage them to attend 12-step meetings. Nevertheless, first I have to work with their current motivations and desires. In my experience, it often takes a significant negative life event, such as loss of custody, to prompt a family to become willing to make dramatic changes. Sometimes even this event is not enough to change the family's generational patterns.

In my work with children and families, I have also had to remember that what seems reasonable to me, in terms of boundaries, priorities, and appropriate behaviors, may be very unfamiliar to the child or family. Therefore, it is up to the counselor to ensure that counseling focuses on the best interest of the client rather than reflecting the counselor's own needs or background. For me, this is part of what makes working with children and families both challenging and interesting. When a counselor carefully observes his or her own reactions, it can serve as a guide for effectively exploring issues with clients and families. Rather than making quick assumptions or forcing insights, I instead use my own reactions to further guide questions and exploration. This occurred for the counselor in this scenario; she began to see a common theme in Christie's play, which ultimately led to a suspicion that Christie was seeing her mother against the court order and CPS's mandate. When faced with this suspicion, the counselor then sought supervision to determine the appropriate response.

Using Supervision to Make Decisions About Reporting Suspected Abuse or Neglect

The counselor posed a question about how to decide at what point to notify CPS of the situation. Although it is not a counselor's responsibility to investigate allegations or suspicions of court order violations, counselors are mandated reporters in all states and, as such, are legally obligated to report suspicions of child abuse or neglect. One of counselors' ethical duties is to advocate for the client and to do no harm (American Counseling Association, 2005). The counselor's role as advocate includes speaking for clients when they cannot speak for themselves and protecting them when they are unable to protect themselves (American Counseling Association, 2005).

Nonetheless, knowing when to notify CPS and whether such a call is in the best interest of the child is sometimes difficult. In Christie's case, there were a number of unclear issues. To begin with, it was unclear whether the shift in her play toward playing games with her mother meant that Christie's mother was currently visiting her. An alternative explanation is that Christie had moved through part of the healing process and was actively engaging in wishful thinking. Given this ambiguity, the counselor wisely sought supervision to discuss the shift in Christie's play. This was an important step in the decision-making process (Bernard & Goodyear, 1992; Holloway, 1995; Meier & Davis, 2001).

As a result of this consultation, the counselor decided to confront the grandparents in a manner that did not break Christie's confidentiality. This gave the counselor a chance to explore whether the grandparents were allowing their daughter Marilyn to visit Christie. It is important to remember that, on the basis of the grandfather's close oversight of her sessions with Christie, the counselor suspected there was something this family might be trying to hide. When the counselor confronted the Sullivans, the grandfather remained silent and made no eye contact, whereas the grandmother adamantly denied that Marilyn was coming to the house.

Another question is whether the counselor next should have asked Christie directly, potentially placing her in the awkward position of betraying a family secret (Black, 1981; Satir, 1972). Confronting Christie directly could leave her feeling guilty about her mother's trouble with the law. It is also possible the grandparents would be angry with Christie for betraying a family secret.

Yet another question for discussion in supervision is whether the mother's visits to Christie would constitute abuse or neglect or whether they would more accurately be viewed as simply a probation violation. I argue that—if the play did not present signs of neglect, the grandparents' absence, or the mother's substance use—the mother's actions would probably not be considered neglectful. Therefore, if there are no signs of current harm to the child, is it a counselor's duty to report violations of court order, particularly when there is no felony charge? My response to this question is that there is simply not a right or wrong answer. Again, in situations such as these, it is important to use sound, careful judgment and to seek supervision.

Unfortunately, in my years of working at mental health agencies, I have come to understand that there is often little time in supervision for in-depth discussions of issues such as when to contact CPS. Because of the great demands on the counseling supervisor, supervisory sessions often pass quickly, focusing on immediate crises, administrative needs, and productivity issues. Also, even though a supervisor may be competent, decisions related to contacting CPS can be difficult for even the most seasoned professional. Given that such decisions as these are not absolute, it is ultimately the counselor's responsibility to seek supervision and to use sound judgment when deciding whether a CPS report is warranted.

Christie's Best Interests

I have found it is often difficult to determine what actions are in the best interest of clients, particularly when one is dealing with the custodial rights of biological parents. In this particular case, it is clear to me that Christie's grandparents were unable or unwilling to protect Christie from her mother. The grandparents' main concern seemed to be protecting their daughter Marilyn and having her in their life. When there is clear indication that a child is not being protected, the child needs to be removed from the biological family. In my opinion, every child deserves to be safe and to have the opportunity to bond, trust, love, express feelings, and learn about boundaries.

Keeping this in mind, one also needs to recognize that attachment occurs very early in a child's life and that, despite the problems leading to a child's removal, the child is still likely to have a bond with the biological family. There are no guarantees that adoption or foster care will be better for a child in the long term. Adoption and foster care relationships can be just as difficult as those in the biological family, simply because all families are still human families. There is also no guarantee that the child will be able or willing to attach to an adoptive or foster family.

Knowing this, I am never quick to suggest removing a child from the care of a biological family. Conversely, I do not want to allow a child to stay in a family that is neglectful or abusive. If Christie is fortunate enough to be adopted quickly rather than being moved from one foster care home to another, then there is a good chance she will develop healthy attachments to the adoptive family and lead a very productive life. I do not believe anyone can ever predict the exact effect of the adoption or foster care process or whether attachment issues will present themselves later in life. Conversely, leaving a child neglected, abused, or unprotected in the biological home can predictably create significant mental health problems.

Collaboration Between Counselors and CPS Workers

Another topic I would like to discuss is the counselor's role in relation to third party involvement with clients. When CPS is already involved in a case, I believe it is important for the counselor and the CPS worker to collaborate closely to prevent either party from being manipulated. Such collaboration ensures that information is not overlooked and provides continuity of care for the client. Nonetheless, it is vital that confidentiality be maintained and protected.

In this incident, the counselor actually might have had two clients: Christie, who was the primary client, and the court system or CPS. I note this because my suspicion is that the counselor was responsible for sending reports to both CPS and the court regarding Christie's progress and welfare. I have found that this process is more efficient when I establish a collaborative relationship with CPS in which there is a clear understanding of the rules of confidentiality and a signed authorization to release information. With such a collaborative relationship in this case, Christie's counselor could have notified her CPS contact about her concerns, and this might have resulted in the CPS worker's decision to visit the grandparents' house at different times during the day or night. This type of collaboration only works if the counselor can rely on the CPS worker to carry out the investigation without creating suspicion by pointing to the child's counseling session as the source of information. Remember that, as counselors, our ethics tell us to first do no harm.

Although it is not easy for counselors at mental health agencies to collaborate with CPS and the court system because of heavy caseload demands for all involved, it is still in the best interest of the child to maintain a cooperative professional relationship. Given that, I must admit that I have had experiences in which CPS workers did not always protect the child. Because of overwhelming caseloads, it has often been difficult for CPS to take action, particularly when allegations are not supported by hard evidence or when the workers' caseloads are so heavy that they do not allow time to uncover such evidence. There have also been instances in which I have reported my suspicions only to later discover that the CPS worker had confronted the parents without removing the child from the home, which ultimately increased the danger to the child. Finally, there have been instances in which the child has been removed too quickly from the home, without adequate information. Even so, more often than not, CPS has actively investigated reports and has handled situations in a manner that prevented additional harm to the child.

In closing, I note that the questions that the counselor asked in this case were very important. I hope that my difficulty giving clear and concise answers to these questions demonstrates the complexity of the case. In my response, I have attempted to provide some basis for discussion of ethical considerations and the opportunity to see this case and others from different points of view. Cases such as these call for the wisdom of clinical experience, the use of sound judgment, the review of ethical guidelines, supervisory consultation, and the ability to see the complexity of the case to make the best possible decisions.

References

American Counseling Association. (2005). *ACA code of ethics*. Alexandria, VA: Author.

Axline, V. M. (1947). *Play therapy*. New York: Ballantine.

Bernard, J. M., & Goodyear, R. K. (1992). *Fundamentals of clinical supervision* (2nd ed.). Boston: Allyn & Bacon.

Black, C. (1981). *It will never happen to me!* Denver, CO: M.A.C.

Holloway, E. (1995). *Clinical supervision: A systems approach*. London: Sage.

Kanters, A. L. (2002). Resolution of symbolic play therapy narratives of traumatic events: Exposure. *Dissertation Abstracts International, 62*(10-B).

McDonald, T. P., Allen, R. I., Westerfelt, A., & Piliavin, I. (1996). *Assessing the long-term effects of foster care: A research synthesis*. Washington, DC: Welfare League of America Press.

Meier, S. T., & Davis, S. R. (2001). *The elements of counseling* (4th ed.). Belmont, CA: Brooks/Cole.

National Clearinghouse on Child Abuse and Neglect. (2004a). *Mandatory reporters of child abuse and neglect*. Retrieved January 21, 2005, from http://nccanch.acf.hhs.gov/general/legal/statutes/manda.cfm

National Clearinghouse on Child Abuse and Neglect. (2004b). *What is child abuse and neglect?* Retrieved January 21, 2005, from http://nccanch.acf.hhs.gov/pubs/factsheets/whatiscan.pdf

Remley, T. P., & Herlihy, B. (2005). *Ethical, legal, and professional issues in counseling.* Upper Saddle River, NJ: Pearson.

Satir, V. (1972). *Peoplemaking.* Palo Alto, CA: Science & Behavior.

Part

 V

Grief and Loss

23

"I Never Got to Say Good-Bye": Death of a Sibling

The incident explores issues related to the sudden death of a sibling and use of the combination of individual and family counseling provided by a husband and wife team. Structural family changes and conjoint family therapy are of primary focus in this incident and the accompanying responses.

■ Critical Incident

Shawn Patrick and John Beckenbach

Sometimes a case stands out not so much because of its textbook elements as because of its pure impact on the counselor. When my husband and I were working as family counselors at a community agency many years ago, we were presented with a family who left us with a resonating image that remains with us today. This family gave us an opportunity to use different methods of therapy, including a sort of conjoint family therapy, and also touched us on a very personal, human level.

The family was composed of "Mr. and Mrs. Mort Thompson" and their three children, "Mark," "Matt," and "Missy." The oldest child, Mark, had recently entered the teenage world, was popular in school, was an honor roll student, and helped his mom often at home. Matt, the middle child and in middle school, wanted to follow in Mark's shoes, yet he preferred playing the class clown and teasing his younger sister. Missy, the youngest and in third grade, enjoyed drawing and dancing more than reading and studying and found the most fun in playing with her oldest brother, Mark. Mr. Thompson frequently found himself between jobs, and Mrs. Thompson worked as a clerk at the local retail store. Economically, the family barely survived on a daily basis and was squished into a claustrophobic apartment without extravagances. Mrs.

Thompson's goal for the summer was to save enough so the kids could join a community sports league.

Unfortunately, the Thompson family was characterized more by conflict than by laughs. Mr. and Mrs. Thompson acknowledged that they frequently argued about finances and parenting. Missy and Matt antagonized each other daily, escalating the dissension during parental arguments. Mr. Thompson spent much time away from home, but when he was around, his anger often spilled onto all of the children. Mark often stood at the center of the storm, helping to soothe the arguments between Mom and Dad while protecting his younger siblings from his father's wrath.

Mr. Thompson eventually became fed up with the family situation and disappeared, leaving the family with no financial support. Although the family was financially burdened, Dad's permanent absence provided a welcome relief from the constant arguing. Mark stepped into a fatherly role to help his mom take care of the others and build a happier family. Mrs. Thompson wanted to give her family a new start, something to help them heal from all the wounds of the past. After scrimping and saving for some time, she surprised her kids with a trip to that magical kingdom, Disney World. The trip started as wonderfully as they had expected, and the family delighted in the roller coasters, ice cream, and Mickey Mouse. It was more fun than they had experienced in a long time. Nevertheless, by the 3rd day, something seemed different. Mark was running a high fever and was too weak to go to the park. He had been coughing for a couple of days, and the family initially assumed it was a cold or allergies. At this point, though, Mrs. Thompson decided to take him to the hospital because he had deteriorated so quickly. By the time Mark was admitted, he was losing consciousness. It was soon determined that Mark had a viral infection that had entered his nervous system. Twelve hours later, Mark died. The last image of Mark the family had was of him consumed by alien-like machines in a sterile, white room.

The family came to us approximately 2 months after Mark's death on recommendation from the children's school. In the time between Mark's death and the beginning of counseling, Matt had gained 30 pounds, and his grades had dropped significantly. He no longer played the role of class clown and instead withdrew from his peers. Missy had begun arguing with her classmates and was having difficulty paying attention in class. At home, Missy's behaviors regressed significantly, and she even had problems taking care of herself. The teasing between Matt and Missy had escalated into arguments and occasional physical fights. Mrs. Thompson was at a loss for how to care for either of them while trying to reconcile her own grief.

When the family first sought counseling, my husband and I met with them as a group. After hearing their history and current situation, however, we decided that individual and family work were necessary. One of us met regularly with each child, and together we met with the family. This format allowed us to assess and work with the individual needs of the children while restructuring the family system.

When Matt entered counseling with my husband, he appeared frightened, confused, and lost. Why would he be otherwise? In many ways, his older brother had provided guidance and security. Mark had given Matt protection from his father's anger, took him places, showed him how to be cool, and was his best ally in life. Matt looked up to his older brother, and now Mark was gone. This left a very large void in Matt's life, and Matt was withdrawn, lonely, and, above all, sad.

Counselors spend a lot of time emphasizing the importance of a therapeutic relationship to facilitate growth in clients. This seemed to be even more critical with Matt. The problems in his life were directly connected to the loss of his brother. Matt had lost the anchor in his life and was adrift. He needed someone to care about him and to be his fill-in brother while he worked toward greater acceptance of his loss.

Tending to the relationship held the majority of my husband's attention while he was working with Matt. He tried to offer himself as a big brother figure to provide the vehicle for counseling to occur. He used play, art, music, and talk therapies to promote connection, empathy, and positive regard. This relationship grew for some time, and, as the weeks went by, Matt began to express himself more and more. At first he was unable to discuss what had happened to his brother, much less his feelings about the loss, but in time he began to open up.

More grief-oriented counseling then began to take place with Matt. One recurrent theme for Matt was the sense of unfinished business. He had been unable to speak with Mark at the end of Mark's life. Mark's illness developed so quickly that he and Matt were unable to say "good-bye" or "I love you." Matt carried tremendous pain about this. Various techniques were used to promote a sense of resolution and acceptance of the loss. These techniques included writing letters to Mark, listening to Mark's favorite songs, and discussing what Matt missed about his brother. It was at this time that other issues began to emerge. Not only was Matt struggling with the loss of Mark, he was also finding himself in a new role as oldest child in his family. The counseling relationship helped to facilitate Matt's transition into this role.

Success of this therapeutic process became measured by creative adaptation of a genogram. Early in the therapy process, my husband had used genogram symbols to get an idea of how Matt viewed the structure of his current family. Matt frequently referred to Mark in the present tense, which suggested that he was unwilling or unable to let him go. In constructing his genogram, Matt also positioned Mark as the center of the family, with the rest of the members stemming from him. Later in counseling, Matt's greater acceptance of both the loss of his brother and his new role became apparent when he created a new genogram. His new picture portrayed a circle of himself, Missy, and his mother tightly connected, with Mark's symbol extending out from the circle toward Heaven.

While my husband was working with Matt, I was providing individual counseling for Missy. She welcomed the process and seemed very excited to have her own special hour to meet with someone. Her interests immediately turned toward drawing, painting, and anything else related to creating art. At first, she could say that her brother had died but was unable to discuss any details related to the events of his death. In fact, at the mere mention of the hospital where Mark died, Missy would immediately start humming to herself while staring off into some corner of the room. Play therapy became the mode for engaging Missy and creating a therapeutic relationship.

Missy's play revealed themes of feeling isolated and lost. Rather than talking about what had happened, Missy communicated by bringing in her favorite toys, drawings, and pictures from the Disney World trip. Her play was often scattered in that she would quickly jump from activity to activity with little to no transition. In the midst of creating some new picture out of glitter and clay, she would tell a story that generally featured Mark as her best friend and the hero who "built me castles and made banana splits for dinner." Anyone else was described as "annoying and stupid," and she felt like no one at home ever wanted to do what she liked to do.

Work with Missy seemed characterized by intermittent sprinkles of observable therapy with a general atmosphere of positive regard. Our play sessions provided Missy with a time and place where she could just simply be herself, in all her quirky ways, and have complete control over everything around her. Her stories, although based on small pieces of real events, were actually fantasies that allowed her to describe fear, anger, and sadness from a distance. I became the consistent figure for her to bounce around as she probed the scary places in her imagination. Eventually, Missy was even able to explore the last nightmare image of her dying brother.

What seemed to facilitate Missy's transition out of complicated grief was a particular story she began repeating week after week. It began as a series of hypotheticals in which she would ask me questions such as, "What if a man broke into your house and pulled out a gun?" Each question would build on the previous one, with growing themes of violence. I would respond to these by pointing out that such a situation might make me feel scared, lost, or out of control. Every week the process and outcome of the story remained the same, until at one point she began to provide her own responses to the questions. In time, even though the story still featured fear or perceived threat, Missy began to tell it with greater mastery and less reliance on me to fill in the blanks. Then she stopped telling the story altogether, and she started talking about creating a good-bye ritual for Mark.

As my husband and I concluded our work with the Thompson family, we felt deeply gratified by the opportunity assist them with their journey through grief after Mark's tragic death. Mrs. Thompson, Matt, and Missy clearly benefited from counseling and were able to move on to better times. As we said our good-byes, though, my husband and I were also aware that the impact of the counseling experience had been mutually beneficial. We knew that this was a case we would always remember and from which we had learned a great deal. Relatively novice counselors at the time, we were faced with many questions as we began our work with the Thompson family.

Questions

1. What factors may counselors need to consider when dealing specifically with loss of a sibling?
2. How else can counselors address the structural change created by the sudden death of a sibling?
3. What strengths and weaknesses are present when counselors use conjoint family counseling in cases like this?
4. Is the creation of a stable, therapeutic relationship sufficient to help children resolve issues such as grief?

■ Response

Nancy Boyd Webb

This incident deals with the family tragedy caused by the sudden death of a beloved teenage eldest son and brother shortly after the father had abandoned the family and the teen, Mark, had begun to take over the parental role. Thus, the terrible loss of the idealized brother and son was greatly compounded by the earlier loss of the adult father figure, who seemed to be cast in the bad guy role. Clearly, this family needed help not only with their grief but also in coping with the void created by the sudden absence of the two eldest men in their family unit.

The therapists, who worked as a husband–wife team, provided the Thompson family with an example of effective collaborative intervention addressing the needs of the family as a whole as well as the individual concerns of the two surviving children. Whereas the account presents only summarized highlights of the treatment, it is quite evident that the therapy with both children was based on positive therapeutic relationships in which the male therapist deliberately attempted to "offer himself as a big brother figure" to Matt and the female therapist used play therapy to engage and work with Missy. Therapy or counseling with the mother is not addressed, but this clearly would have been essential for the children to achieve the gains reported in this incident.

Important Considerations in Sibling Bereavement

In my book *Helping Bereaved Children: A Handbook for Practitioners* (Webb, 2002), I presented a tripartite assessment conceptualization that guides therapists in evaluating the three groups of interacting factors that contribute to the nature of a particular bereavement response. These are

- factors related to the individual,
- factors related to the death, and
- factors in the support environment.

The individual factors relevant in this case example include the child's past history of losses and his or her perception of the meaning of this particular death. In this instance, we do not have information regarding the children's past history of losses, but we do know that the father abandoned the family and that Mark had stepped into the paternal role. Because of this fact, Mark's sudden death took on special meaning. Matt and Missy had twice lost a protector. All the family members would certainly wonder why this had happened to them, and the abrupt nature of the death in a strange location probably tended to magnify their sense of bewilderment. Missy's hypothetical questioning in play therapy sessions about possible violent occurrences seemed to reflect her fear that terrible events would continue to happen. She was not feeling safe. The therapist appropriately tried to normalize the child's feelings of fear and loss of control, without making a direct connection to Missy's personal losses. The girl used these hypothetical scenes to gradually assume some mastery over her life, and this permitted her to deal more openly with her grief and her need to say good-bye to her dead brother.

In considering the impact of the loss of a sibling, counselors must evaluate the role of the deceased in the family, which, in this instance, was that of protector. Mark's death not only was a personal loss for each family member but also was a threat to the family's sense of security. Play therapy can offer symbolic help when the therapist brings in protective figures, such as extended family members, neighbors, or police, who would be available to help the child's fictional family figures. For example, the therapist might have suggested that the mother would know how to protect her family in this symbolic play. Therapists must always consider the nature of the parent's bereavement response after the death of a child because the surviving children will take their cues from the parent. When the parent conveys a sense of control and stability (despite the bereavement), the children will feel safe and less vulnerable to possible future danger.

Dealing With Structural Changes Created by Sudden Sibling Death

In this family, Mark's role as protector must be filled for the children to feel safe. Use of the genogram to convey the family structure before and after the death served as a helpful tool. This would have been even more effective, in my opinion, if other extended family and community resources had been included in the genogram. Mrs.

Thompson, a single, grieving mother, clearly needs and deserves support, and it would be appropriate and helpful for the therapist to inquire about the presence of any uncles, scout leaders, coaches, or religious counselors who could serve as an important adult male presence in this family and include their names on the genogram. I am concerned about the apparent tendency in this family to move the next youngest boy into the missing parental role because this is unfair to Matt, who needs to pursue his own age-appropriate interests and activities. The fighting between Matt and Missy seems to reflect the absence of rules and boundaries and possibly also reveals the mother's inability to maintain control. This could have been addressed in family therapy, but, in addition, the mother needed a place to grieve her losses apart from her children.

Conjoint Family Counseling

The use of conjoint family counseling was extremely helpful in this situation because of its potential for setting up family rules, as just discussed. It also permits the shared grief process of reviewing the life of the dead family member, including the recall of both happy and negative memories. Furthermore, it can facilitate the planning of a good-bye ritual and the decision about whether to include extended family members in this process. There was no mention in the case description about whether the father had been notified about Mark's death and whether he had attended the funeral. Regardless of the mother's negative feelings about her husband, his role as father remains significant for the children. The family would benefit from help in dealing with their conflicted feelings if Mr. Thompson were to return for the funeral or after. In my opinion, this should be dealt with in individual counseling, in addition to family counseling, because of the complicated nature of each person's relationship with this significant family member. It has been said that it is more difficult to deal with feelings of anger and loss after a marital breakup than after a death because marital splits are, in essence, intentional. This family was faced with having to cope with both losses simultaneously.

Impact of the Therapeutic Relationship on Grief Resolution

What is meant by the term *grief resolution?* Experts in thanatology emphasize the concept of continuing bonds to the deceased, thereby inferring that the memory of the deceased remains with the living relatives forever. This view expects that Mark's absence will be keenly felt by his brother, sister, and mother at certain times when specific circumstances cause them to remember him. For example, when Matt graduates from middle school and enters high school, he may long for his older brother's presence, both to admire his achievements and to mentor him in the new school environment. This does not imply that Matt has not resolved his grief but expresses that he misses his brother's presence.

In this family, both children had regressed significantly after Mark's death. The therapeutic relationship helped both of them to navigate and survive the strong currents of their grief. Clearly, their mother could not effectively focus on each of them individually because of her own grieving. The therapy definitely seemed to assist each child to regain his or her developmental course and to halt the regressive behaviors that were interfering with school, peer, and family interactions. In my opinion, it was very beneficial, and it seems that, without this assistance, the children and the family as a whole were heading for a future of difficulties. I also believe that future counseling and therapy will be needed by various family members regarding the absent father–husband. Because of the family's very positive experience in therapy, it is likely that they will be open to future counseling when the need arises.

Response

Jolie Ziomek-Daigle

The experience of loss can permeate most aspects of one's life. When a loss occurs, normalcy simply does not exist. Daily routines that once seemed familiar and ordinary become difficult and foreign. There are many factors that counselors need to consider when counseling a child who has lost a sibling. First and foremost, are the basic needs of the child being met? Is the child receiving food and shelter? Is the parent in need of monetary support? In this case, Mr. Thompson disappeared, leaving the family with few financial resources. Although Mr. Thompson's disappearance might have been welcomed, it left the family solely dependent on Mrs. Thompson's salary. The initial session can be used to assess the basic needs of the family and to recommend resources available to the family. These resources may include hospice and, farther down the road, perhaps a nutritionist for Matt.

Another basic need worth considering is safety. Obviously, the Thompson family unit has been disrupted and turned chaotic. Mark, who acted as a protector and provider for Matt and Missy, is gone. In addition, Mark served as a confidant and helper to Mrs. Thompson. It is imperative that each family member identify both members of the family and individuals outside of the family who are available for support. The school atmosphere is another major factor to consider when one is counseling children who have lost a sibling. The school, as an institution, offers many potential benefits to its students. Besides being a place of learning, it also provides security, structure, routine, and relationships. Therefore, it is important that counselors assess the school situation. Has the school been notified? Who was notified, and when? Has the school notified the child's teachers? Has the parent met with the school counselor or social worker?

This is a time when it is particularly important that parents remain in constant contact with the school to provide the child with consistency. Both Matt's and Missy's grades had dropped considerably after Mark's death. Mrs. Thompson could work in conjunction with the teachers to use a daily and weekly progress report system. Progress reports offer a two-way communication between teachers and parents and help students to organize and plan in advance. Counselors can encourage parents to communicate consistently with school agents to provide a stable environment of familiar faces for grieving children.

Disruption of homeostasis is another loss that often accompanies the death of a family member. The family system has been scattered like pieces of a puzzle, and the once familiar structure no longer exists. Matt and Missy have new roles; their old ones passed with Mark. Although the loss and grief are difficult, this is also a time of new beginnings and new roles. Creative activities for all family members addressing the loss of the old roles and introducing the excitement of the new are imperative. If appropriate, these activities should be shared among family members so that the new expectations are understood by all.

The conjoint family counseling approach used by the counselors exhibited many strengths. First, both children received individual counseling, and the family also received counseling as a unit. This allowed the needs of all family members to be met while the family system was restructured. Second, Matt was able to work individually with another man. Because a male figure was available to Matt, the therapeutic relationship echoed some aspects of Matt's relationship with his brother. Additionally, Missy benefited from her sessions as she fostered a relationship with her counselor through play and the creative arts, gaining confidence and control over her situation.

My concerns about using conjoint family counseling are quite minor. I wondered whether Mrs. Thompson also would have benefited from individual counseling. It seemed like the focus and energy expenditure were almost exclusively on the two children and the family unit as a whole. What about Mrs. Thompson's grief and the change in her role? I also reflected on the potential for Matt to become dependent on his counselor, given that his father and brother no longer existed in his world. Finally, I was curious to know more about Mr. Thompson. Could he have participated in the family counseling sessions? Might the change in the family structure solicit responsibility and commitment to his children?

The creation of a stable, therapeutic environment is an important starting point and should remain a constant throughout a counseling relationship. Very often, life's changes are not welcomed, but they occur. When children experience a loss of this magnitude, their world is turned upside down, and old routines no longer exist. Consistently and intentionally, these counselors provided the Thompson family with individual and family counseling services, meeting their individual needs while the family as a unit was being restructured. With the creation of a stable, therapeutic environment that allowed creativity and risks, the Thompson family eventually moved from grief to acceptance.

Reference

Webb, N. B. (2002). *Helping bereaved children: A handbook for practitioners* (2nd ed.). New York: Guilford Press.

24

"But All My Friends Are Here!": Minimizing and Managing the Effects of Relocation

This incident explores the use of child-centered play therapy and creative counseling with young people facing transitions as a result of relocation in middle childhood. Research on the impact of moving on children is presented, recommendations for effectively addressing issues related to relocation are offered, and multicultural considerations are discussed.

■ Critical Incident

Jodi Ann Mullen

"Anastasia (Ana) Cassopolis's" parents were successful restaurant owners who, after 8 years of countless hours, energy, and sacrifices, had finally attained their financial goals. The family of five had been living in a modest three-bedroom home in a nice suburban neighborhood. Mr. and Mrs. Cassopolis had long considered their home too small and had been dreaming of purchasing a larger home to better accommodate their family. The success of the restaurant had finally made purchasing another home, one that would allow the children to have their own bedrooms and a pool in the backyard, a feasible dream.

After some thoughtful searching, Ana's parents found exactly what they were looking for in a home. The neighborhood was safe, and the house was clean and spacious. Even better, the prospective new home was only a few minutes from the restaurant, and the shorter commute would allow for more family time. Mr. and Mrs. Cassopolis could hardly wait to share the news with their children. Ana, Damian, and Megan were all very excited when they heard the news. When the family drove by the new house, it occurred to Ana that this house was in the opposite direction from her school. She asked, "Will I still take the bus?" Her parents then shared with the children that they would be changing schools. Megan and Damian (twin kindergarteners) could not have cared less. Ana, however, was angry and sad. This mood, which was uncharacteristic of Ana, persisted for 3 weeks. Because her mood was now interfering with her academic performance and friendships, Ana's parents brought her to counseling.

Ana was a 9-year-old Caucasian girl of Greek descent. Her family spoke both Greek and English at home. She was a third grader and had always been a fine student and a respectful child. Ana had many friends, and her teacher described her as a quiet leader. She participated in dance and gymnastics outside of school. Ana had never been to a counselor before, but her aunt was a counselor and play therapist, and Ana said she liked visiting her office.

Prior to meeting with Ana, I chose to speak with her parents on the phone to gather demographic information and get a sense of what they believed was going on for Ana. I could hear in Mrs. Cassopolis's voice her disappointment at her daughter's reaction to the move as well as a sense of guilt about "making her leave her friends and school." As a practitioner in private practice, I had some latitude regarding how to proceed. I wanted to create an atmosphere of trust with Ana's parents and invited them in to meet with me so that I could get more information about Ana. They were so distressed about her attitude and new difficulties in school, however, that they expressed a preference that I get started with Ana immediately rather than meet with them first. Ana's mom noted that she was very familiar with child counseling and play therapy because of her sister-in-law.

Because 9-year-old children can be so different in terms of their development, I wanted to be sensitive to how Ana perceived herself developmentally. I therefore decided to use an office set up for play therapy but also included many arts and crafts supplies with the hypothesis that a mature 9-year-old might interpret the playroom as babyish. Although I knew that Ana and her family already had some sense of what a counselor and play therapist does, I did not want to assume that they knew what this counselor and play therapist would be like.

On Ana's arrival, I greeted her and her mother warmly. I gave her mom the requisite paperwork to complete, and, because the twins were with her, I let her know I would phone her later to schedule the next appointment. When I asked Ana whether she was ready to get started, she shrugged and started to cry. Her mother said, "Ana, she's a nice lady. Just go with her and please stop sulking." Although Ana complied with this instruction, it was important to recognize her feelings, and I did so as we slowly walked to the playroom.

I use a child-centered approach and therefore introduced the playroom to Ana by suggesting that it was a special place where she could say anything and do almost anything (Landreth, 2002). Ana slowly explored the room and asked a lot of questions. I accurately reflected her feelings and followed her lead. She mentioned that her aunt had a room that looked like this and that she liked it. Near the end of our session, she said, "I want to come back here again, but I'm not sure I can because I am moving."

In contemplating a child's diagnosis, I believe it is imperative to balance accuracy with stigmatization. I would rather err by underdiagnosing a child than by overdiagnosing a child. That being said, I felt confident that a diagnosis of adjustment disorder with mixed anxiety and depressed mood was the most consistent with Ana's presentation. Of course, I continued to assess her anxiety and depression throughout the counseling process and also thoughtfully considered other possible mental health diagnoses that might have been better suited to her clinical presentation and subsequent treatment.

I decided to continue using the child-centered play therapy approach with Ana because it seemed to me that she was overwhelmed with strong and conflicting feelings about her move. Using this treatment approach, I was able to highlight her confusion, anger, sadness, loss, excitement, and fear. After several sessions, Ana remarked that she wanted to make something for her teacher and friends. I followed her lead as she created good-bye pictures for everyone in her class. The following session, she brought a class list that she had obtained from her teacher because she "didn't want to forget anyone."

When I spoke with Ana's parents, they informed me that they now had a closing date and would be moving into their new home in 4 weeks. Ana's mother reported that Ana had become less moody but indicated that she still got angry and had even said, "You can move without me!" On a positive note, Ana's mother also shared that Ana was not having as many problems with her friends as she had been a month ago and that her academic performance was once again high.

I wanted to continue my work with Ana, but I also felt it important to involve her parents more. Ana's mother was in agreement, and we set up a meeting. At this meeting, I explained that Ana had many feelings about the move and that her feelings of loss and grief were the most salient. I suggested that Mr. and Mrs. Cassopolis help Ana say good-bye to all the people, places, and things that were important to her. I also encouraged them to help her to say hello to her new room, school, pool, and so forth in their new location. Ana's parents said that they had never thought of moving to a better and bigger house as a loss, but they agreed to do as I suggested. This was when I felt worried. Would they really follow through? Did they truly grasp that this move represented a significant loss for Ana?

To my relief, Ana shared in our subsequent sessions that she had been saying good-bye to things in her neighborhood and wondered aloud when she would say good-bye to me and the playroom. I reflected that maybe she wanted to decide about this good-bye. She confirmed this and said, "I want to come five more times."

After five more sessions, Ana did say good-bye. She had moved into her new house and started in her new school the week prior. Her mother indicated that she and Ana's father were very pleased to see Ana feeling better, "like her old self." They remarked that they also felt sad about the move as it got closer and that they had made a family good-bye and hello project. I was pleased with their follow through and recognized how their support helped Ana move quickly through the process of therapy.

Questions

1. Did I end the intervention too early? Should I have waited until Ana was settled in her new home and school? In what ways could further counseling interventions have benefited Ana?
2. Were there other ways I could have (or should have) involved Ana's parents?
3. Were there issues that I should have addressed directly with Ana or her parents, such as her ethnicity?
4. What other supports, in addition to counseling, might help a child through the multiple and intangible losses that are connected with moving?

Grief and Loss

■Response

Diana H. Gruman

As one can see in this case study of Ana Cassopolis, moving can cause tremendous stress for children. In oft-cited surveys of children's worries, moving typically ranks among the top responses. Yet, in America, changing residences is a fairly common occurrence. On average, 15.1% of people over the age of 1 year changed residences in 2003, with the highest percentage of mobility in Nevada (21.3%) and the lowest percentage in New Jersey (10.8%; U.S. Bureau of the Census, 2004).

For some military or migrant families, changing residences and schools is a challenge faced on a yearly basis. Furthermore, lower income families tend to move more frequently than their more privileged counterparts (Alexander, Entwisle, & Dauber, 1996; Rumberger, Larson, Ream, & Palardy, 1999). Adults such as Mr. and Mrs. Cassopolis may see moving as a commonplace, easily surmountable challenge, but for children like Ana, the pain and trauma caused by the disruption may be overwhelming. It is therefore important for counselors to be aware of the typical effects of moving on children to better address the unique needs of children such as Ana.

In this piece, I respond to the counselor's questions by placing Ana's experience in the larger context of children's adjustment processes following a move. In this way, I hope to describe how a counselor might best assess the risk level of young clients facing a residential move. As a former elementary school counselor, I also show how one might take a more systems-based approach to broaden the interventions for young clients such as Ana.

First, to address the counselor's questions regarding her treatment approach, I note that it seems that the play therapy process was quite successful in meeting Ana's immediate needs. The counselor's open style and empathetic approach were very appropriate given the combination of grief and anger that Ana presented. Ana found an accepting place to express her feelings and to work out a strategy for saying good-bye to familiar people and surroundings at a time when her parents were unable to provide the support she needed. The therapeutic process provided a bridge so that Ana could travel the emotional road between the two locations, from her old home and school to her new home and school. After the move, all signs indicated that Ana had made a successful transition to the new school. It is remarkable that, after only 1 week in the new school, her parents expressed that Ana was "like her old self."

Despite this immediate success, the counselor questioned whether termination came too early and whether there were other interventions that might have helped a child like Ana. To answer these questions, one has to consider the potential long-term consequences of moving for Ana and other children. Research indicates that it is common for children to experience short-term academic or social problems after a move. Most children who move infrequently, however, are able to bounce back and do not face long-term consequences (Simpson & Fowler, 1994; Tucker, Marx, & Long, 1998). In fact, for socially astute and academically talented children, the challenges presented by one school change may lead to positive growth.

If Ana were to move numerous times over the course of her school years, however, the risk of school problems would increase (Nelson, Simoni, & Adelman, 1996). Frequent mobility, often defined as three or more moves, has been correlated with an increased risk of developing emotional and behavioral problems as well as school problems, such as increased suspension, expulsion, and retention rates (Simpson & Fowler, 1994; Tucker et al., 1998). In terms of academic deficits, one study found that children who moved several times during their elementary school years were a full year behind their more stable peers on standardized math tests by the sixth grade (Kerbow, 1996). Because Ana was experiencing her first move and did not have prior academic or social problems, she was likely to fully recover after some initial setbacks.

In addition to prior residential stability and personal strengths, Ana also had some other protective factors working in her favor. First, Ana was living in a stable family unit. Studies show that children who live in an intact family are protected even when they are hypermobile—moving more than six times during their school career (Tucker et al., 1998). The theory is that two-parent households like that of the Cassopolis family often have more social capital to cope with the stress of moving while simultaneously supporting the emotional needs of their children. Second, Ana was not experiencing other stressful life events at the time of the move. Researchers have found that when children face multiple sources of stress, such as a family breakup, a death or illness, or low socioeconomic status, the risk of school problems increases (Simmons, Burgeson, Carleton-Ford, & Blyth, 1987; Wood, Halfon, Scarlata, Newacheck, & Nessim, 1993). Because Ana was not coping with other significant family traumas, one could expect that, with some support, she would not suffer significant long-term consequences. Finally, Ana's gender may provide some measure of protection, because research suggests that boys may suffer more than girls from school changes (Ellickson & McGuigan, 2000; Vernberg, 1990).

Even though Ana was protected from long-term negative consequences by a number of factors, I can suggest additional ways that the counselor might have intervened on her behalf. First, the exact location for the move had already been determined when therapy began. Knowing the end point is an advantage in that it allows the family and support workers to draw on resources in the new community to ease the transition. Most important, the family or counselor could have contacted the new school to learn more about the school environment and the reception that Ana was likely to experience on her arrival. Several questions could be asked. Is there a school counselor in the building? Would Ana have an orientation? Could the family meet with the new teacher prior to the first day? Does the school offer the same services (English language learning, special education, or gifted programs) as the old school? Can the school expedite the transfer of Ana's student file to facilitate her placement in a particular program or classroom?

Second, time was on the family's side. Many mobile families are forced to move on short notice because of domestic violence or financial instability. Ana's family had weeks to gather information and make plans for the move. Perhaps Ana's old school was concluding a key curricular project or her new school was holding tryouts for her favorite team sport on a particular day. If Ana's parents had some flexibility, they could select Ana's school end and start dates to take into account these factors. Such flexibility on her parents' part would allow Ana to feel some sense of closure at her old school and the anticipation of new beginnings at her new school.

The counselor also asked questions about involving Ana's parents in therapy and locating other sources of support. In keeping with a systems approach, I would recommend that the counselor increase contact and teamwork with both the family and the schools. By communicating with the parents and school personnel, the counselor could better determine whether family problems or specific school factors were contributing to Ana's reluctance to change schools. For example, were Ana's parents so involved in running the business that they regularly failed to acknowledge and meet Ana's emotional needs? Were there signs of marital discord? In such cases, family therapy might resolve Ana's problems more comprehensively than individual counseling. In terms of school system issues, there could be a number of factors that raise the stakes of moving for Ana. For example, was Ana resisting the move because she had recently developed a special bond with a particular teacher? Was she particularly distressed about losing track of friends in the old school who shared her ethnic heritage and first language? Many times, counselors do not have the luxury of addressing these types of questions. In Ana's case, however, the family had the financial resources for counseling and the time to create optimal conditions for Ana's transition to the new neighborhood and school. Lack of involvement with the old and new school prevented the counselor from answering many of these questions and from building supportive structures that would nurture Ana's development long after the termination of individual counseling.

In conclusion, children who change schools benefit from the kind of support and acknowledgment that Ana received in the play therapy sessions with the counselor. In my own experience in the schools, I tried to meet with each transfer student to allow the child to share his or her story and, when necessary, intervene to help his or her transition. Research indicates that support from parents, teachers, and others can make a critical difference in the long-term success rates of mobile children (Dubois, Felner, Brand, Adan, & Evans, 1992; Jason et al., 1992). For children with multiple risk factors and frequent mobility, the prospects for school success grow increasingly dim with each additional stressor and school change. If Ana needed and benefited from counseling, imagine the personal and educational support that these children require when faced with a move. As the author of the critical incident suggests, the losses children suffer with a move are intangible. No matter what professional role one plays (e.g., school counselor, social worker, or psychologist), one needs to assess the risk factors that affect each mobile child, determine what resources are available in the systems surrounding the child, and match one's interventions accordingly.

Response

Michelle R. Holcomb

In considering this case overall, I estimate that Ana's basic therapeutic needs were met, as evidenced by her improved grades and behavior at school. Her parents also remarked on this noticeable improvement on her completion of the therapeutic intervention. The questions that come to my mind when I conceptualize this case include the following:

- Will Ana have continued difficulty with loss issues in the future?
- If so, how will her family support her struggle?
- What are the multicultural issues in this case, and how might the therapeutic interventions change as a result of multicultural considerations?

When a counselor is saying good-bye to clients, he or she must take many considerations into account. One such consideration relates to treatment goals. Did Ana reach treatment goals? The counselor used a child-centered approach to play therapy, addressing adjustment issues related to feelings of confusion, anger, sadness, loss, excitement, and fear of relocating. In the play sessions, the counselor found that Ana's need to control her next good-bye was evident. The counselor responded to this need by allowing Ana to take the lead in determining the pace, structure, and duration of counseling. Later in therapy, a strong therapeutic relationship was evident, and Ana became responsible for determining her own continued need for therapy. The counselor's intuition led her to facilitate the opportunity for Ana to say good-bye on her own terms. This moment was pivotal therapeutically, as evidenced by Ana's firm statement that she needed five more sessions, a sign that Ana was capable of recognizing her needs and asserting herself well enough to get these needs met.

A second consideration involves the client's posttermination success. Did Ana have a support system to help her maintain treatment goals after termination? At the onset of therapy, the counselor recognized possible resistance from the parents and determined that engaging them in Ana's treatment was critical. The counselor involved Ana's parents in homework activities and continually requested feedback regarding Ana's behavior at home and at school. By participating in Ana's healing, Mr. and Mrs. Cassopolis were able to recognize the impact moving had on Ana and reflect on their own feelings regarding the move.

A third consideration to take into account prior to termination is whether the client will be able to take the skills learned in therapy and apply them to the real world. With children, it is likely that they may have difficulty maintaining treatment goals, simply because they experience so much growth and change through the developmental process. In Ana's case, I would recommend that the counselor have a frank discussion with her regarding grief and loss prior to the final session. In the discussion, the counselor should review with Ana how she was able to successfully grieve the loss of her old home and school. Furthermore, the discussion should include sharing with Ana that she will experience grief and loss throughout her life and exploring with Ana how she will she cope with future loss. Such a discussion regarding future loss may help Ana explore healthy coping strategies and make her mindful that loss is a normal part of life. In addition to this direct work with Ana, I would recommend providing her parents with psychoeducational sessions addressing issues related to developmental stages of loss with children and adolescents, recognizing signs and symptoms of anxiety and depression in children, and understanding the importance of modeling appropriate coping skills for children.

In reading this case, I was surprised by the limited focus on multicultural considerations as they pertain to the therapeutic relationship. According to the American Counseling Association's (2005) *Code of Ethics*, "counselors recognize that culture affects the manner in which clients' problems are defined" (p. 12). Similarly, Hays (2001) stated "that a knowledge of the clients' salient identities gives the counselor clues about how clients see the world, what they value, how they may behave in certain situations, and how they are treated by others" (p. 58). Multicultural considerations are fundamental in conceptualizing a client, determining treatment goals, and making a diagnosis. Without these considerations, many counselors are likely to misdiagnose and mistreat clients.

At the onset of counseling, a comprehensive psychosocial assessment should have been conducted with Ana and her family and should have included questions addressing issues of age, generational influences, developmental or acquired disabilities, religion and spiritual orientation, ethnicity, socioeconomic status, sexual orientation, indigenous heritage, national origin, and gender (Hays, 2001). The counselor missed a great opportunity to explore multicultural issues when Ana's mother indicated use of both Greek and English languages at home. I would recommend an ethnographic approach, allowing Ana's mother to be the expert and teach the counselor about her Greek heritage. I would begin studying the Greek culture as it relates to participation and perception of counseling and determine where on the spectrum Ana's family falls as a traditional or nontraditional Greek family.

Through my own study of the Greek culture, I found one aspect critical in considering treatment goals for Ana and her family. In Greek culture, there is an overarching emphasis on family. According to McGoldrick, Giordano, and Pearce (1996), "because the family is the central social unit, needs of the individual are not focused on in the same way as they are in American families, and every member is expected to defer to the greater needs of the family" (p. 518). Because of this emphasis on family over the individual, counselors working with Greek families frequently encounter concerns about separation and boundaries (McGoldrick et al., 1996). How would this knowledge of traditional Greek culture affect counseling with Ana? Is it possible that Ana's struggle with relocation was overlooked because of the greater needs of the family?

Additional multicultural issues to consider in Ana's case include spiritual needs, parental roles, Ana's role in the family, parental expectations of Ana at home and at school, and conflict resolution among family members. In addition, the family's perception and valuing of counseling should be noted. In a study among Greek Americans, Barlow (2000) found strong ties between acculturation and the client's perception of counseling. Greater client acculturation tends to correlate with more positive views of counseling interventions. Would these considerations provide insight into Ana's struggle? Did the family's level of acculturation affect their participation in counseling?

Again, I would caution the counselor in assuming that Ana's family ascribes to the traditional Greek culture, but I would recommend that the counselor explore how these traditional Greek roles mirror the Cassopolis family's worldview. I would examine how the family's worldview affected Ana's presentation and would develop treatment goals accordingly.

The counselor in this case also inquired about whether there are other supports that might help a child through multiple and intangible losses connected with moving. Research supporting best practices for counselors working with relocation issues is limited and tends to focus on the relocation of military families. Nonetheless, symptoms such as sleep difficulties, unexplained crying, eating or appetite changes, complaints of stomachaches or headaches, lower grades, increased irritability, and changes in behavior at home and school are recognized as basic indicators of adjustment difficulties. In addition, it is critical that anxiety and depression are assessed and monitored throughout the counseling relationship.

When working with relocation issues, I have had success in using activities such as writing letters, creating change-of-address cards or an autograph book, taking pictures of favorite places, and buying an address book for e-mail addresses. I also encourage parents to prepare children for relocation using children's books such as *We Are Moving: Let's Make a Book About It* (Biale, 1996). In addition, I assist parents in finding community resources that connect children to the new community as soon as possible. Involvement in after-school activities, such as Boy Scouts, Girl Scouts, sports programs, and church, can prove invaluable to a child's transition.

References

Alexander, K. L., Entwisle, D. R., & Dauber, S. L. (1996). Children in motion: School transfers and elementary school performance. *Journal of Educational Research, 90*(1), 3–12.

American Counseling Association. (2005). *ACA code of ethics.* Alexandria, VA: Author.

Barlow, T. (2000). *Greek-Americans: Acculturation and attitudes toward psychological/counseling services.* Unpublished doctoral dissertation, Cleveland State University.

Biale, R. (1996). *We are moving: Lets make a book about it.* Berkeley, CA: Tricycle Press.

Dubois, D. L., Felner, R. D., Brand, S., Adan, A. M., & Evans, E. G. (1992). A prospective study of life stress, social support, and adaptation in early adolescence. *Child Development, 63,* 542–557.

Ellickson, P. L., & McGuigan, K. A. (2000). Early predictors of adolescent violence. *American Journal of Public Health, 90,* 566–572.

Hays, P. (2001). *Addressing cultural complexities in practice: A framework for clinicians and counselors.* Washington, DC: American Psychological Association.

Jason, L. A., Weine, A. M., Johnson, J. H., Warren-Sohlberg, L., Filippelli, L. A., Turner, E. Y., & Lardon, C. (1992). *Helping transfer students: Strategies for educational and social readjustment.* San Francisco: Jossey-Bass.

Kerbow, D. (1996). Patterns of urban mobility and school reform. *Journal of Education for Students Placed at Risk, 1,* 147–169.

Landreth, G. L. (2002). *Play therapy: The art of the relationship* (2nd ed.). New York: Brunner-Routledge.

McGoldrick, M., Giordano, J., & Pearce, J. (Eds.). (1996). *Ethnicity and family therapy.* New York: Guilford Press.

Nelson, P. S., Simoni, J. M., & Adelman, H. S. (1996). Mobility and school functioning in the early grades. *Journal of Educational Research, 89,* 365–369.

Rumberger, R. W., Larson, K. A., Ream, R. K., & Palardy, G. J. (1999). *The educational consequences of mobility for California students and schools* (PACE Policy Brief, Vol. 1, No. 1). Berkeley: University of California.

Simmons, R. G., Burgeson, R., Carlton-Ford, S., & Blyth, D. A. (1987). The impact of cumulative change in early adolescence. *Child Development, 58,* 1220–1234.

Simpson, G. A., & Fowler, G. A. (1994). Geographic mobility and children's emotional/behavioral adjustment and school functioning. *Pediatrics, 93,* 303–309.

Tucker, C. J., Marx, J., & Long, L. (1998). "Moving on": Residential mobility and children's school lives. *Sociology of Education, 71,* 111–129.

U.S. Bureau of the Census. (2004). *Data set: 2004 American community survey. Ranking Table R0701: United States and states: Percentage of people 1 year and over who lived in a different house in the United States 1 year ago.* Retrieved March 2, 2006, from http://tinyurl.com/h98we

Vernberg, E. M. (1990). Experiences with peers following relocation during early adolescence. *American Journal of Orthopsychiatry, 60,* 466–472.

Wood, D., Halfon, N., Scarlata, D., Newacheck, P., & Nessim, S. (1993). Impact of family relocation on children's growth, development, school function, and behavior. *Journal of the American Medical Association, 270,* 1334–1338.

25

"We Can't Believe It Happened": Crisis Consultation

This incident focuses on ways counselors may serve as consultants to assist schools in responding to tragic loss. The critical incident involves the murder of a child and her mother, a long-time staff member at her daughter's school. The respondents address the importance of formal crisis plans and the role of the outside consultant.

■ Critical Incident

Susan A. Adams

During my first semester as a counselor educator at a small, southern regional university, I received a call from the principal of an elementary school, about an hour away, requesting consultation and some crisis intervention assistance. It was a Monday morning, and the principal had just learned that Alicia Li, a fifth grade student, and her mother had been found murdered at their home that morning at about 9:00 a.m. The police had apparently arrested the father–husband for the murders, but very little other information was available at the time. The principal explained that the Li's were an Asian American family who were active and fairly well known in the town and that Mrs. Li had worked in the school's cafeteria for over 10 years. He voiced concern about how to manage the grief responses of the school community and expressed hope that I might be able to assist.

In addition to having worked in the school's cafeteria for the past decade, Mrs. Li was well known in the community as a genuine caregiver. She was active in her church and held a leadership role. Although the townspeople remained socially separated according to race, many of the Caucasian population knew Mrs. Li because she had also worked as a cook and catered many community social events through the years to supplement her income. She was well liked and respected as an honest, hard-working woman who did a wonderful job caring and providing for her only child, Alicia. The principal shared that Alicia was a quiet girl who did well in school but said that she had no particularly strong connections with her teachers. Alicia did, however, have several friends with whom she had attended school for the past 6 years.

To complicate matters, the principal also explained that his school counselor was out of town at a professional conference for the remainder of the week. He indicated that there was no one else available to deal with the situation at the school and expressed immense gratitude when I indicated my willingness to assist the school with this crisis. He said that he had already prepared a statement to be read to the teachers and students that afternoon and asked me to be on hand the following morning to help develop a plan for the week and to deal with whatever emotional problems might arise among the students, teachers, or staff.

The following morning, I met with the principal and several teachers and support staff to discuss how my presence could be beneficial. The principal indicated that he had made the announcement to inform the school community about Alicia's and Mrs. Li's death the prior afternoon but was unsure of how the students and staff were reacting. He noted that there were more students absent than usual but that he was unaware of any specific student reactions. He also reported that the cafeteria workers were visibly distressed but seemed to be hanging in there and that he had called in a substitute who often filled in for absent cafeteria personnel for the remainder of the week. He indicated that no attempts at any kind of informal assessment of the students' or teachers' reactions had been done and that classes were being conducted as usual, without discussion of the previous day's murders.

As the consultant, I suggested that, initially, the best use of my presence might be to assess the school situation in terms of what potential issues might need to be addressed. Once this assessment was complete, a plan could be created about how to proceed. We agreed that, while I was in the process of conducting the assessment, the principal would contact the school counselor to make sure she had heard the news and to discuss potential counseling issues. He also expressed a willingness to be as flexible as necessary with the school schedule and teachers' schedules.

In preparing to conduct the assessment, I identified three groups of stakeholders likely to be most deeply affected by the tragedy: students who knew Alicia or Mrs. Li, Alicia's fifth grade teachers, and Mrs. Li's coworkers in the cafeteria. With regard to assessing student needs, I recognized that the entire staff of teachers was in a unique position to observe and report student needs. To equip them to do so, I needed to inform them as quickly as possible about potential crisis symptoms. In doing so, I would explain that students experience many different feelings and reactions to crisis situations and that teachers were the experts and needed to be looking for behavioral changes indicative of a need for intervention. These needed to be noted and reported to the principal, who was acting as the school coordinator. In particular, any immediate needs or concerns would be communicated to the principal as needed. A meeting was set for the end of the school day to discuss the teachers' observations and concerns regarding the students throughout the day.

In addition to reliance on the observations of the entire teaching staff for reports of student reactions, another key component of my assessment was to directly evaluate the students of the fifth grade. Those most significantly affected would be the children in Alicia's classes and those who were among her closest friends. Classroom visits and focus groups would be used to facilitate discussion with the students.

Parents would also receive a written communication inviting them to report reactions of their children.

Another group likely affected by the murder of Alicia and Mrs. Li was Alicia's three fifth grade teachers, all of whom taught Alicia for some part of her school day. Her homeroom teacher was Caucasian and indicated that she had only been teaching 1 year prior to this incident. She had not personally experienced a significant death in her family. The second teacher was African American and reported that she had been teaching for over 20 years. She had known many who had died during her lifetime. The third teacher was Native American, had been at the school for 5 years, and had experienced the death of several significant family members. She said that she was sad about the situation but indicated that, according to her belief, death was a natural part of life.

The third group of stakeholders was the cafeteria personnel. Mrs. Li had been a long-time coworker, friend, and neighbor to many of these people. To assess their needs, I would meet with them and facilitate discussion of their concerns.

Questions

1. The lack of a crisis intervention plan left no clear instructions related to the necessary steps to be taken to stabilize the situation. What roles should I have taken as the consultant in this situation?
2. How could I best assess the most critical needs and determine who should be my main focal point, at least initially?
3. This case was complex in that it involved several diverse populations with different needs and different ethnic beliefs and values. What specific needs and issues might you anticipate for each of these diverse groups?
4. The absence of the school counselor further complicated the situation because she had some history with the faculty, staff, students, principal, and community. Did I have an ongoing role until the school counselor returned? How might we best transition the intervention process on the school counselor's return?

■ Response

Kathleen (Ky) T. Heinlen

Responding to trauma has become a more central aspect in the work of counselors in recent years. This incident focuses on managing a crisis in a school setting in a small, southern town. Because this case is centered in the school environment, it is important for the counselor, at the very least, to be familiar with the unique needs and dynamics inherent in the school setting. As Oates (1993) pointed out, death in a school community is not a new phenomenon; nevertheless, two relatively new factors have affected children's understanding of death and dying. Because individuals and families are more mobile, they frequently move away from extended family, and, when a crisis occurs, their support network may be limited. Modern medical technology has also changed the context in which people die. Whereas it used to be common for children to see people in declining health and dying in the home, today most people die in a hospital. This is significant because children and even adults have become inoculated from the experience of death, and therefore when it occurs they may need more assistance in processing their thoughts and feelings regarding the event. Counselors also have to consider the context—in this case, a small, southern town—in determining the most appropriate approach in working with individuals. In a small, rural community, death and acts of violence are less commonplace than in big cities such as New York or Los Angeles. Being sensitive to these needs as well as the needs of this diverse population, I would want to clearly define my role as a consultant, assess the needs of the community, and work to transition services back to the school counselor on her return.

In my role as a consultant, I would have two tasks at hand. First, I would need to address the short-term crisis needs relative to this incident, which would include determining the degree of trauma and identifying the most appropriate interventions to use. Second, I think it would be important to work with the school community to develop a plan for crisis management to address future incidents. The roles I would want to take in this situation would include that of a counselor as well as an adviser.

In reviewing the crisis protocols recommended by the National Organization for Victim Assistance, Bauer (2001) identified the goals of responding in times of crisis as to "diffuse emotions and re-engage the cognitive process, help to organize and interpret the cognitive process, integrate the traumatic event in to the life story, and interpret the traumatic event to derive meaning" (pp. 239–240). As a counselor, my first response in this incident would be to work with individuals, helping them tell their stories about this event and make sense of how this has affected their life. To do that, I would need to assess the most critical needs and determine who should be my main focal point.

Addressing Individual Grief

There are several models for triaging individuals in a crisis, and I would want to use two different methods of assessing who was most in need of services. Oates (1993) delineated a scoring schema for determining the degree of trauma on the basis of the individuals involved in the incident, what happened, and where the tragedy occurred. In this incident, Mrs. Li and her daughter Alicia were affiliated with the school, and both were popular and well liked. The violent manner in which they died increases the degree of trauma; conversely, the fact that the murders occurred in their home as opposed to the school mediates the overall score. On the basis of this rating system, it is clear that there is a high degree of trauma present in this incident. Although this schema is used to assess the situation, it can also be useful for reflection by the individual about why this tragedy is so difficult to deal with. As a general rule, those who are closest to the crisis are most at risk for having difficulties dealing with the trauma. As the author pointed out, those most likely to be significantly affected are the children in Alicia's classes as well as those who were among her closest friends.

Using the teachers as first-line observers for signs of difficulty was an important first step in identifying others who might be struggling. Responses to trauma vary greatly on the basis of a number of factors, including personality, stress levels, and resilience. As Nader (2004) pointed out, it is particularly important in assessing children to get input from multiple sources. Although classroom observations are certainly important, it is equally important to connect with parents and family members to assess how the children are doing at home. Therefore, in addition to relying on teacher observations, I would also want to connect with parents in the school community to assess the extent that any of the children were struggling with difficulties at home. I would also want to assess how the children as well as the adults were doing across several domains, including physiological, emotional, and cognitive (Bauer, 2001). The physiological symptoms I might expect to see include confused thinking, a feeling of being frozen, and a sense of disconnectedness. Emotional responses of fear and anger are common in times of crisis, as are disbelief and denial. I would pay particular attention to statements made by individuals that reflected cognitive distortions about the incident. These statements might include things like, "If only I had offered to have Alicia come over to my house and play," or, "I knew her husband seemed like the violent sort, and I should have warned her." Last, I would want to spend the day on site so that I could personally observe and talk with students and staff to discern any individuals I thought were exhibiting signs of difficulty.

Grief in a Cultural Context

Understanding these grief reactions in the context of the variety of cultural perspectives present at the school is important. In this incident, not only different populations (students and adults) but also a variety of ethnic groups in both populations are affected. Although I think it would be very important to be sensitive to each particular variable of diversity, I believe the most important piece is to be comfortable talking about death and encouraging individuals to reflect on how their own cultural perspective helps them deal with integrating this event into their life. There are, however, a few specific needs and issues I might anticipate for these diverse groups.

For the children, it is important to consider the impact of this event in light of their developmental process, in particular how they are working to develop peer relationships. Silverman (2000) captured this in her discussion about the struggles of losing a friend in adolescence in her statement, "To understand what is lost, it is helpful to define what we mean by a friend and friends bring out parts of ourselves that family may not know or see" (p. 168). One specific need I would anticipate is to address how the death of Alicia fits into having and developing friends for her classmates.

Because it is clear that the Li's were a part of the Asian community, I would make sure I understood what death means to that community and what rituals might be most helpful in processing this loss. In addition, given that there is a gap between the Caucasian townspeople and the Asian community, it would be important to be respectful of individual differences and work to create a means of coming together in this time of crisis.

A final issue I might anticipate regarding the diversity present in this incident relates to the teachers and staff. Among Alicia's teachers are individuals who not only have varying experiences with death but also have different depths of experience in the classroom. Individuals who have had little personal experience in losing someone can be expected to have greater difficulty in dealing with this loss. In addition, because this is a school crisis, the teachers who have had many years of experience in the classroom might be better able to manage the additional tasks of monitoring students for signs of distress than their early-career counterparts.

Intervention Strategies

In my role as a counselor, I would need to address the short-term needs arising from this critical incident. This would include assessing the individuals in the school community for signs of difficulty in dealing with this trauma and identifying appropriate intervention strategies. All of this would be completed in the multicultural context of this diverse population. The second task I would have as a consultant would be to help the school community develop a crisis management plan so that, in the future, there would be a clear protocol for dealing with critical incidents of this nature. On the return of the school counselor, my role might be, assuming the school community requested the assistance, to work with key stakeholders in developing this plan.

To transition the intervention process on the school counselor's return, I would prefer to have direct contact with the counselor throughout the week as opposed to having the principal serve as an intermediary. In this manner, the school counselor and I could collaborate regarding various individual responses as well as plan for intervention strategies. My experience has been that although it is sometimes more efficient to let others handle communication with key individuals, in the long run it is more time effective to have direct communication. There would be several key points in the transition process, and two of the intervention strategies would actually occur once the school counselor returned. First, I would recommend grief groups for a period of a few weeks after the incident, with the structure and format of those groups determined in large part by the school counselor. In addition, creating some kind of memorial or closure ceremony would be critical to helping individuals come together and deal with this loss. I would ordinarily recommend that this be done within a few days of the incident, but in this case it would be very important for the school counselor to be a part of that experience. Therefore, working with her to determine how this could best be accomplished in her school would be important. Finally, in terms of planning for future crisis management, I would want to work with the school counselor as one of the key stakeholders in the school community.

My role as a counselor and adviser would involve assisting this school community in dealing with the acute short-term effects of this critical incident as well as planning for future crisis management. As a counselor, I would work to assess individuals and anticipate a variety of specific needs and issues relevant to this diverse population. As a consultant and adviser, I would help the school plan for the future and map out strategies for dealing with crises in the future. I would see myself not as a temporary fix for this current incident but rather as a partner in dealing with the mental health needs of this community. This incident, however traumatic, would be an opportunity for me to work as a liaison in the school and develop a working partnership that could benefit the school and the community at large.

Response

S. Kent Butler

In this day and age, it seems negligent and possibly even unethical that a school system would not have a crisis intervention team or plan in place. Because of this lack of planning, the first order of business for the consultant should have been ensuring that the needs of the students, faculty, administrators, staff, and local community were being addressed. The American School Counselor Association (2004) addressed the fact that school counselors need to be continually engaged in responsive services. Responsive services are comprehensive activities that are preventative or interventive and meet the urgent and prospective needs of students.

Crisis Planning

The immediate creation of a crisis team is crucial. The crisis team, depending on the staff configuration, would likely consist of the principal, school counselor, school social worker, school psychologist, school nurse, secretary, and two teacher representatives (Emergency Evacuation Committee, Hamden Public Schools, 2003). All of these individuals would have specific roles assigned to them. The principal would be responsible for handling all communications with the superintendent, parents, news media, and so on. The secretary would field all questions and direct calls to the appropriate team member. The school counselor, nurse, psychologist, and social worker would address all concerns of students, teachers, staff, and the local community.

The specifics of the crisis team and the role of each member can be catered to once the situation has calmed down sufficiently. The prompt return of the counselor, because of her history at the school, seems appropriate and should supersede the conference. Once she is on board, the counselor and the crisis team, along with the consultant, should sit down and create a comprehensive crisis intervention plan. This should be a global plan that has at its core a plan of action, flexible in nature, mapped out as to how the school is to react in times of crisis.

Immediate Response

Even in the absence of the school counselor, a temporary crisis team should have convened on Monday morning or afternoon before the principal made the announcement to the school. After dismissing the students for the day, the first order of business for the crisis team would be to debrief the teachers and staff and make them cognizant of potential behavioral cues or warning signs students or anyone else affected by the deaths might show. Even though the principal requested services for the next morning, the consultant should have availed herself as soon as possible on the day of the tragedy. It seems careless to wait a full day before setting an action plan into motion. It also seems important that the consultant be witness to the emotional and behavioral states of mind of the entire school community following the announcement of the misfortune. Attending this meeting, along with being on hand during the initial announcement of the tragedy, would greatly benefit the consultant as she ascertained the most critical needs of the school and prioritized areas worthy of preliminary concentration.

The debriefing period is also a time to check in on the well-being of the teachers and staff. Although Alicia Li was presently in the fifth grade, one should assume that she had contact with a majority of the school's teachers during her kindergarten through fourth grade matriculation and that these teachers may be affected by her passing. Furthermore, it is plausible that Mrs. Li might have had extensive contact with teachers, students, and staff (including coworkers) at the school.

It is likely that parents and community members would be in need of grief counseling, advice, and so forth for themselves or their children. Sending students home with a letter from the principal is simply not enough. The crisis intervention team, along with the consultant, should be available at the school for a portion of Monday evening to meet personally with students, parents, cafeteria staff, and other community members and to act as a referral agent for those in need of continued services.

Ongoing Response

Tuesday morning poses a different dilemma—how does one go about the day? The plan of action mapped out in the critical incident is a very good one. It is important, however, that the school schedule remain as relatively unaffected as possible. The students need to follow a normal routine, inclusive of lunch in the cafeteria. This is the day when teachers, who were debriefed on Monday, play a very important role. It is their responsibility to pay particular attention to their students and refer concerns to the appropriate crisis team member. As spokesperson for the school, the principal would most likely be handling other important matters and would not be able to be school coordinator, as mentioned in the incident. That task would have to be the responsibility of one of the other crisis team members, who would consult with the school principal only on extreme cases or in cases of emergency. Depending on the school counselor's return, the consultant might be best suited for this coordinating position.

Issues of Diversity

A final area to discuss is issues pertaining to diverse groups. Although complex, the situation was not made more so by the inclusion of diverse populations. Multiculturally competent counselors should be able to work with each individual on the basis of what he or she brings to the table. With the exception of Alicia and her mother, the only other ethnicities spoken of were those of Alicia's present teachers, coupled with their experiences with death and number of years on the job. Nothing abnormal stands out from the information provided.

"Counseling and consultation in the schools is embedded in a social relational process—that is, in processes of gaining self-awareness through experiencing one's self and experiencing others" (Butler, 2003, p. 129). The appropriate thing to do in this case would be to work with clients individually, assessing where they were presently and helping them to work through their issues. A multiculturally competent counselor would do this whether the client was Caucasian or a person of color. Multicultural competency and sensitivity should inform counselors' work with clients in a cultural context. Understanding a client's cultural background is important but does not supersede individual worldviews; differently stated, the fact that a person is from a specific cultural heritage does not mean he or she subscribes fully to that particular culture's beliefs and practices.

References

American School Counselor Association. (2004). *The role of the professional school counselor.* Retrieved December 22, 2005, from http://www.schoolcounselor.org/content.asp?pl=325&sl=133&contentid=240

Bauer, A. (2001). Responding to a community crisis. In E. R. Welfel & R. E. Ingersoll (Eds.), *The mental health desk reference: A practice-based guide to diagnosis, treatment, and professional ethics* (pp. 239–245). New York: Wiley.

Butler, S. K. (2003). Multicultural sensitivity and competence in the clinical supervision of school counselors and school psychologists: A context for providing competent services in a multicultural society. *Clinical Supervisor, 22,* 125–141.

Emergency Evacuation Committee, Hamden Public Schools. (2003). *Hamden Public Schools emergency operations plan, Hamden, CT.* (Available from Hamden Public Schools, 60 Putnam Avenue, Hamden, CT 06517)

Nader, K. O. (2004). Assessing traumatic experiences in children and adolescents: Self-reports of *DSM* PTSD criteria B-D symptoms. In J. P. Wilson & T. M. Keane (Eds.), *Assessing psychological trauma and PTSD* (pp. 513–537). New York: Guilford Press.

Oates, M. D. (1993). *Death in the school community: A handbook for counselors, teachers, and administrators.* Alexandria, VA: American Counseling Association.

Silverman, P. R. (2000). *Never too young to know.* New York: Oxford University Press.

Part

VI

Physical Ailments

26

"But He Needs Me": Responding to a Child's Catastrophic Illness

This incident explores the difficulties that families address when a child is diagnosed with a terminal or catastrophic illness. The incident is descriptive of a gross maladaptive control response of a family to the terminal illness of one of the children. Respondents explore dynamics underlying an overly controlling mother's failure to comply with treatment recommendations and provide suggestions regarding best practices for counseling catastrophically ill children.

Critical Incident

LeAnne Steen

I first met "Benji Dulaney" while volunteering as a play therapist through the pediatric oncology child-life department of a local metropolitan children's hospital. Benji was 5 years old and had been diagnosed with congenital heart defects while still in the womb. Because of the severity of these defects, the doctors strongly recommended an abortion. Benji's mother determinedly declined. When Benji was born, doctors predicted a life expectancy for him of no more than a year.

Although he had beaten the odds by surviving 5 years, Benji was faced with continual catastrophic illness and ongoing medical interventions. His nightmare of chronic hospitalization began immediately after birth. He required several open-heart surgeries in his 1st year of life, and the doctors managed to heal his heart enough to sustain him for 3 years.

When he was 3, Benji's mother took him to another state, where he successfully underwent a complete heart transplant. Mrs. Dulaney explained, however, that two to three additional transplants would be needed to take Benji into adulthood, as he would outgrow each child-size heart. She reported that very few children survive a second transplant and that, to date, none had survived a third. After the heart transplant, Benji continued to gain strength and mobility over the next year but then suddenly developed a form of lymphoma, presumably from the intensive heart medication. Because of his precarious heart condition, the cancer treatment was reportedly nonaggressive and primarily consisted of lowering his dosage of heart medication. By the time I met Benji, he had become less cooperative with the doctors and combative when faced with medical procedures. For example, Benji became so combative during simple blood analysis tests that he had to be held down by several adults to complete the procedure. This experience was obviously very painful for everyone involved.

At this point, one of the child-life specialists recommended that I begin working with Benji and his family. I was asked to intervene especially because the family seemed to be displaying a variety of maladaptive strategies in an attempt to cope with Benji's illness. On meeting with Mrs. Dulaney, Benji's mother and primary caretaker, I immediately understood the intensity of the difficulty with which the specialists were faced.

Mrs. Dulaney was a 35-year-old Caucasian woman who lived at home with her 36-year-old husband and their three children: Benji, age 5, and two physically healthy sons, ages 14 and 8. Mrs. Dulaney described the home family life as rather dismal and painful. A former teacher, Mrs. Dulaney had quit her job to take care of Benji full time. The loss of income, in conjunction with the catastrophic illness of their youngest child, was the minimal family problem. Mrs. Dulaney reported that her relationship with her husband had become distant and disconnected and lamented that she received very little emotional support from him for her sacrifices.

Mrs. Dulaney explained that these sacrifices surrounded her role as Benji's primary caretaker. In fact, she explained, her focus had been completely dominated by Benji for the last 5 years. Although she was clearly overwhelmed by Benji's medical needs, Mrs. Dulaney repeated several times that he had not been expected to live for a day and that she had been able to have him for 5 years. She described a detailed process of continually exploring possible medical options to help Benji. There were periods when she and Benji were away from the household for months at a time while seeking treatments out of state.

In describing Benji's needs and her role in his life, Mrs. Dulaney seemed to be completely entrenched in her role as his caretaker. At times, she was overly focused on her role as a caretaker and provided more assistance than Benji actually needed. For example, she reported that Benji could not do simple things, such as feed and dress himself, without her assistance, in spite of the fact that he could maneuver with ease around the entire hospital and clinic carting the large IV rolling trammel.

Mrs. Dulaney had become overly indulgent of Benji and almost completely emotionally unavailable to her other two children. She complained that her other children had become sullen and agitated. The oldest child was displaying severe emotional problems and had become physically aggressive toward his father several times in the past few months. The middle son was disconnected and apathetic, and this so-called coping ability gained him the status of the good child in the family.

As a counselor, my concerns were that Benji's family was obviously having significant difficulty in reaction to his illness and that the family was manifesting a serious maladaptive coping reaction. In addition to being concerned about the entire family's welfare, I was also specifically concerned about the impact of the family's coping style on Benji's health. The literature indicates that children with catastrophic illnesses may sense the anxiety of parents and siblings and try to protect the family by avoiding communication about the prognosis, the illness, their personal concerns and questions, and anything that they perceive as potentially anxiety provoking for the family (Blake & Paulsen, 1981; Goodman, 1999; Gray, 1989; Kaplan, 1999; Le Vieux, 1990; VanFleet, 1992; J. R. Webb, 1995).

I decided that the best way to help Benji and the family would be through filial therapy. Filial therapy is the method developed by Bernard and Louise Guerney (e.g., B. Guerney, Guerney, & Andronico, 1970; L. Guerney, 1980) whereby parents learn the basic skills of child-centered play therapy and have play sessions at home. Filial therapy has been shown to be useful for general relationship enhancement as well as a positive intervention for children experiencing emotional and psychological problems (Ginsberg, 1997; Jones, 2001; Kraft & Landreth, 1998; Lahti, 1993; VanFleet, 1992). My intention in selecting filial therapy as the treatment approach was to facilitate communication between Mrs. Dulaney and Benji to alleviate some anxiety and tension.

Parents of children with life-threatening illnesses often feel a sense of denial, a loss of control, and uncertainty as to how to care for the child (Yiu & Twinn, 2001). Filial therapy facilitates a sense of parental mastery in that parents learn skills that increase sensitivity and empathy to their children (Ginsberg, 1997; L. Guerney, 1980; Lahti, 1993; Rennie & Landreth, 2000). As the child communicates perceptions and experiences through the parent–child play sessions, the parent gains more acceptance of the child's disorder and the uncertainty of the future, and this increases the potential for family cohesion (Blake & Paulsen, 1981; Glazer-Waldman, Zimmerman, Landreth, & Norton, 1992; Kaplan, 1999). My hope was that as Mr. and Mrs. Dulaney began to learn the basic skills of child-centered play therapy, they would begin to develop more positive communication cycles throughout the entire family, including communication between them as parents and spouses and between them and their other two children.

I therefore invited both Mr. and Mrs. Dulaney to participate in filial therapy. Mr. Dulaney, however, indicated that he was too busy working to come to the appointments. Because Mrs. Dulaney was Benji's primary caregiver and brought him to all appointments, I began by seeing her in filial therapy for several weeks. During our sessions, we spent half of the time in traditional filial therapy learning the skills of play therapy and half of the time in traditional talk therapy to provide a venue in which she could verbalize her pain and frustration with the entire experience.

I felt I was able to develop a genuine and strong relationship with Mrs. Dulaney. Despite the rapport we developed, however, Mrs. Dulaney seemed to be highly resistant to most of the recommendations of filial therapy. Although she was able to successfully complete tasks such as practicing reflective listening and setting limits in the filial therapy sessions, Mrs. Dulaney was rigidly invested in her roles of caretaker and mother of a catastrophically ill child. Although she reported some changes in her language, such as reflecting some of Benji's feelings at home, Mrs. Dulaney was either unable or unwilling to implement the majority of my treatment recommendations in her household.

Although she continually complained about how stressed she was and how stressful the household was, Mrs. Dulaney seemed incapable of making any changes that would help alleviate her stress. She refused to have play sessions between our visits and explained that she did not have time for them. This unwillingness to surrender (part of) the caretaking role and implement treatment recommendations was not specific to filial therapy. Indeed, Mrs. Dulaney seemed to resist other recommendations as well. For instance, she took Benji to see a specialist to help him learn how to eat on his own, and they spent 2 weeks with the specialist having several meals a day. Although Benji was able to begin to learn to feed himself as a result of this training, Mrs. Dulaney refused to follow through with the regimen once she returned home. Instead, she continued to get up every 3 hours at night to feed him with the feeding machine. I tried, repeatedly and unsuccessfully, to help Mrs. Dulaney realize that implementing the recommendations of the specialists (me, the eating specialist, doctors, etc.) would be initially difficult but would ultimately help alleviate household stress.

Eventually, we completed all the filial therapy sessions, and she chose to terminate her meetings with me. I offered to provide play therapy for Benji as well as his oldest brother, who was rapidly becoming suicidal and was being temporarily hospitalized. I offered to see the family. I even offered to see the couple in an attempt to maintain contact and try to alleviate the stress in the household. Mrs. Dulaney refused my offers of further treatment and maintained that she was too "stressed out" to meet with me while she was at the hospital. She reported that she wanted to use that time to "relax in the waiting room and talk to other parents." Although the extenuating circumstances facing the Dulaneys were severe enough that it would have been difficult to engage them in any form of family therapy at that time, I often wonder whether I could have done something different to more effectively help Mrs. Dulaney with the psychoemotional healing of herself, her family, and her ill child.

Questions

1. How can a counselor engage a parent of a catastrophically ill child in filial therapy?
2. What other approaches to the problem might have been more effective?
3. What treatment strategies have been demonstrated to be useful with the population of families who have a child with a terminal or catastrophic illness?

■ Response

Heather M. Helm

Facing the profound effect of catastrophic illness on individuals and families is often daunting at best. The complexities of what these families must face while attempting to maintain some semblance of normalcy can leave the family and any helpers involved feeling helpless and perhaps hopeless. It is hard to imagine the depth and breadth of emotion that Mrs. Dulaney is feeling. It is clearly indicated in the incident that she feels joy and perhaps relief over having had Benji in her life for the past 5 years. Nevertheless, these feelings are obviously mixed with fear, anxiety, grief, loss, and, clearly, a resulting need for control.

The counselor in this incident indicated that she often wonders whether she could have done anything different to engage this family in any form of therapy. My response to that is, unfortunately, perhaps not. As counselors know and are frequently reminded in the helping profession, one cannot force anyone to want or to receive help. Nevertheless, I do want to emphasize that the counselor's questioning of herself is understandable given the difficult position of believing that, if the family had only complied with any treatment recommendations, a profound difference could have been made in the health and well-being of Benji, the functioning of the marital dyad, and the well-being of the other children. In this response, I focus on (a) ideas for engaging Mr. and Mrs. Dulaney in filial play therapy, (b) suggestions for other approaches that might have been effective, and (c) useful strategies for working with parents of chronically ill children.

Mrs. Dulaney is clearly a frightened woman. Many parents of catastrophically ill children struggle with change. Often, they fear that if they change any aspect of their life, it might negatively affect everything else, including the health of the child. It is understandable that this contributes to the parents' feeling that they need to maintain ultimate control even when they see that other family members are suffering or that change may be beneficial. Mrs. Dulaney may not be blind to the situation at home; in fact, she may be keenly aware of how dire the situation is becoming. Nevertheless, she may also fear that change may result in intolerable consequences. She may certainly fear that initiating therapy could be threatening, and this fear would lead to resistance. In addition, it appears that Mrs. Dulaney has formed her identity not only around being Benji's caretaker but also around being the only person capable of caring for him. Certainly, chronic illness in young children can result in parents feeling a strong need for control in the life of their children. They often feel as if they are the only ones who understand their child and therefore the only ones keeping him or her alive.

My first thought as I read about Benji and his mother was that filial therapy could benefit the entire family. Nevertheless, as the counselor in this incident indicated, Mrs. Dulaney was clearly resistant to incorporating filial therapy techniques at the time. I wonder whether initiating a referral for filial therapy in the home might decrease Mrs. Dulaney's resistance and facilitate change. Gaining consent for entry into the home would likely be a challenge given the level of resistance demonstrated by Mrs. Dulaney, but if entry could be gained, the counselor would stand a chance of reaching the family. If home treatment could be initiated, allowing the rest of the family to also receive services, Mrs. Dulaney would perhaps relinquish some control, and the counselor might be able to gain a broader perspective on the functioning of the family. Of course, this would only be a start, and it would provide no guarantee of success. Additionally, if entry could be gained into the home, Mrs. Dulaney would not have to divert her attention from Benji during times of perhaps intense stress while Benji received treatment.

If home treatment were not an option, I would suggest putting together a filial group at the hospital for parents dealing with stressors related to their chronically ill children. The group format not only would serve to normalize the experiences of each of the families but also could help Mrs. Dulaney see how other parents are coping and hear about strategies they are using to cope. It would also provide role models of other parents who are going through similar struggles. Additionally, having Mrs. Dulaney participate in a group would allow her access to the support of other parents, which she so clearly desires when she is at the hospital. It seems that Mrs. Dulaney finds tremendous comfort in being around others who understand her experience. Such a combination of filial play therapy groups mixed with the support of other parents might also eliminate or at least reduce Mrs. Dulaney's resistance to complying with treatment recommendations and ultimately making changes.

Finally, information seminars provided by hospital caregivers, including mental health professionals, could be a powerful way to disseminate information. Similar to a filial support group, information seminars can reduce resistance, provide a community of support, and provide a forum for information dissemination. Informational seminars provide a nonthreatening intervention that may be ideal for parents of catastrophically ill children. This is important because it is difficult for many parents of a catastrophically ill child to admit their sense of powerlessness and ineffectiveness. For a parent to change, such an admission is often necessary. An informational seminar on the uses of filial therapy, of course, would not provide Mrs. Dulaney with a sufficient level of training in the practice of filial therapy (as such training requires education, observation, and follow-up), but hearing the stories of other parents' success in using parenting techniques might convince Mrs. Dulaney to allow the counselor access to her family.

Regarding other approaches, bibliotherapy might be another way to reach Mrs. Dulaney. There are a number of books on the market designed to assist parents in facing the emotional challenges of raising a child with a chronic illness (e.g., Marsh, 1995). Some of these books seek to help parents better balance the demands of a sick child with the demands of raising children who are not sick. Clearly, Mrs. Dulaney was trying her best to resist relinquishing any aspect of her control over Benji's daily life and was doing so to the point that she would not allow him his independence even when all the health professionals in his life were indicating that increased independence was in his best interest. Bibliotherapy might also provide some normalization of these feelings and ultimately allow Mrs. Dulaney to assist Benji in living more independently by giving him some choices; perhaps it would also assist Mrs. Dulaney in remaining consistent and using discipline with Benji. With regard to giving Benji choices, even allowing small choices during treatment can reduce the child's degree of fear and thereby increase treatment compliance. Additionally, bibliotherapy can be a nonthreatening medium with which the counselor can build trust and, ultimately, a collaborative relationship with the parent.

Because the parents of catastrophically ill children have so many demands placed on them and are facing unknowns on a daily basis, it is absolutely necessary to figure out how to make change important. When I consider Mrs. Dulaney according to Maslow's (1954) hierarchy of needs, I find that she is often functioning only on the safety level and is specifically focused on maintaining Benji's safety. Therefore, some of her own needs as well as the needs of her family have become secondary. In particular, she seems to have put needs for love, esteem, and self-actualization out of her focus as she cares solely for Benji and acts at times in ways that are not in his best interest. Unfortunately, the rest of the Dulaney family members may be at a different level of need (this seems to be the case), and all are therefore struggling. Nevertheless, according to Maslow, one cannot fulfill needs at levels higher on the hierarchy (or even aspire to fulfill them) when the focus is on safety and survival.

Ultimately, change may not be important to Mrs. Dulaney, and, as I have stated and as Swanston, Williams, and Nunn (2000) reinforced, "it is important to empower health care consumers by giving them information and the opportunity to make choices about treatment and their sources of support" (p. 13). Benji should be given as many opportunities as possible for power and choices regarding his treatment, as should Mrs. Dulaney over her own, specifically related to mental health and support services.

Finally, I wonder whether the provision of case management services may best serve the Dulaney family. For example, there may be some services available that could reduce the pressure on the family in tangible ways and thereby allow them the time and perhaps the luxury of attending to some of the emotional needs of the family as a unit and of each individual in the family. Regardless of the financial situation of the Dulaney family, catastrophic illness typically generates great financial stress; therefore, there may be financial resources available. Additional services—such as respite care, transportation, and assistance with home modifications to accommodate treatment at home—can make a major impact on the family and their level of stress.

In my response to this critical incident, I have focused primarily on interventions that may succeed in engaging Mrs. Dulaney. I have done so because it is imperative that she remain an ally throughout the course of any type of therapy. The literature is varied, to say the least, regarding treatment efficacy for families with catastrophically ill children. Many of the studies fall short because of small sample sizes (Swanston et al., 2000) and because the use of true experimental design is challenging at best when one is studying the effects of mental health treatment. Although research on best practices is inconclusive, there are some themes specifically related to how parents respond to their chronically ill children that are present throughout the literature. In particular, giving the child control over his or her treatment is essential. Allowing children to have the right and ability to fight for their own survival, as opposed to relying on another person, is essential for healing and survival. Benji may need to feel that he is able to fight for himself and not rely completely on his mother.

Additionally, the healthy children in a family with a catastrophically ill child may resent the time spent with the sick child and the special status of the sick child. Parents with catastrophically ill children should not be afraid to discipline their healthy or their sick children. Parental reluctance to set limits is understandable; nonetheless, limit setting and discipline are helpful because they provide children with structure and, perhaps most important, security. Along with this, the chronically ill child needs some responsibility and routine. As the author of the critical incident indicated, the catastrophically ill child often feels responsible for the struggles of the family and will attempt to protect the family. If catastrophically ill children are provided with responsibilities, they are more likely to feel like contributing members of the family, and they may feel a greater sense of normalcy and routine in a typically unpredictable situation. Essentially, the family needs to work together to create a sense of the new normal, given that their situation will never return to life as it was before the illness. Although all of these recommendations could be used with the Dulaney family, the effectiveness of such interventions assumes compliance and desire for change on the part of the parents. Perhaps there will be a time when Mr. and Mrs. Dulaney feel that change is necessary and the effort worthwhile.

In closing, I applaud the efforts of the counselor in this case. As I wrote this response, I felt overwhelmed by the complexity and gravity of the Dulaneys' situation. Although there are many options for treatment, the key is to reduce resistance, and this may take time. Essentially, it may be necessary to frame counseling as a way to equip Mrs. Dulaney with more effective coping skills (rather than as a way to reduce the degree of control she asserts over Benji's life) so that she does not have to view herself as lacking or as having done something wrong to comply with treatment recommendations. It seems that the ultimate goal for treatment with the Dulaney family is to develop coping strategies for each family member, with specific attention to balancing the medical and emotional needs of the catastrophically ill child with the physical and mental health of the parents and the other children and with the demands of other roles and responsibilities.

Response

Laurie Shepherd Johnson

Catastrophic illness diagnosed on the part of one family member affects all members of the family and generates a crisis that creates disequilibrium for the whole family system. This is particularly true when a child in the family is seriously ill. When a child is diagnosed and treated for life-threatening conditions, there are medical, psychological, financial, and spiritual issues that affect the integrity of the family fabric and create a multidimensional context for treatment consideration. Any treatment plan must address not only the emotional and psychosocial needs of the sick child as patient but also the needs of the parental caregivers and the siblings who are well. Indeed, an effective counseling treatment plan for the critically ill child must address the relationships in the family as a whole system.

In considering the case of Benji Dulaney, I am struck by the complexity of elements affecting this young child's chances for well-being. As a bereavement counselor who specializes in supporting clients through issues of loss and grief, I am naturally inclined to understand the dynamics of this case and its treatment indications through the perspective of loss. Little Benji Dulaney has experienced many losses in his short life. He was diagnosed before birth with a catastrophic heart condition and given a limited prognosis. At age 3, he had to have a heart transplant, and there are indications that he will need additional transplant surgery in the future. Now, at the age of 5, he is being treated for the additional diagnosis of lymphoma (blood cancer). Predictably, these many challenges have kept him from developing normal bonds with his parents, siblings, and friends. Finally, he has lost out on normal childhood pleasures and experiences that help to develop a sense of competence and industry in a child (Erikson, 1963). When considered in these terms, Benji Dulaney's life represents a landscape of loss.

Part of the loss landscape is reflected in Mrs. Dulaney's unconscious and maladaptive anticipatory grief. This is seen not only in her singularly controlling relations with Benji but also in her treatment of her husband and other sons, with whom she has avoided attachment relationships. Another part of the loss landscape is evidenced in how Mr. Dulaney seems to have surrendered his parental role in the care of Benji, his seeming disengagement from a healthy relationship with his other sons, and his detachment from his wife. For Mr. and Mrs. Dulaney, the standard parental role of protecting one's children from harm has been lost to an illness they have virtually no control over. As is commonly the case, these losses have led to feelings of helplessness, hopelessness, anger, and guilt, each of which is being played out in different ways by Mr. and Mrs. Dulaney.

Benji's siblings have also been affected by his catastrophic illness and are similarly subject to the loss landscape. Since he was 9 years old, the oldest child—now a teenager of 14—has experienced a loss of maternal care and investment and the absence of healthy paternal engagement and, due to circumstances beyond his control, has lost out on a healthy fraternal relationship with his ill brother. The middle sibling, at age 8—who was only 3 when Benji was born—is virtually lost in space in a family system in which the foundations for identity, integration, and belonging have been eroded.

This family crisis is harvesting dramatic loss that is being masked in maladaptive grieving behaviors on the part of each member. Until now, loss has sidelined the potential for the nurturing support that adaptive family systems typically offer the child in crisis. These losses compound Benji's already dramatic challenge of living with a life-threatening disease. Now, the hope is that Benji and his family can develop some resilience with the support of counseling. With this in mind, I would suggest the following treatment goals and strategies.

Holistic Treatment Plan Goals

Given the multidimensional context of this case, the treatment approach needs to be multidimensional as well. In working to support Benji and his family, I would develop a holistic treatment plan informed by developmental, integrative, and collaborative principles. The treatment goals would be

- to promote Benji's expression of feelings, sense of mastery, and coping skills;
- to decrease anxiety on the part of Benji and promote his quality of life;
- to strengthen the Dulaney family system; and
- to address the loss dynamics affecting each family member, especially Mrs. Dulaney as primary caretaker.

Treatment Strategies

In counseling Benji, I would use a team approach and work in cooperation with the medical and health care professionals involved in the case as well as with relevant school personnel when Benji begins school. As part of this treatment approach, I would make every effort to identify, refer, and liaise with the other mental health treatment services that are needed to assist the other family members with issues related to or stemming from Benji's medical condition.

Although Benji's illnesses are indeed life threatening, both his heart and his blood cancer conditions would be treated as chronic rather than terminal today because of the longer prospects for survival offered by advanced medical treatments. As such, counseling treatment emphasis should be placed on improving the quality of Benji's life rather than on addressing his impending death. This would involve working with the entire family. In discussing treatment strategies, I would recommend individual counseling for Benji, family counseling, and individual counseling for Mrs. Dulaney.

Individual Counseling

In counseling Benji, I would want to learn more about his conception of his disease as well as assess his developmental understanding of death. Children conceive of death differentially according to their developmental age. For example, because their intellectual capacity to understand death fully is not yet formed, preschoolers do not commonly perceive death as final but rather believe it is a reversible state. As a 5-year-old, Benji is likely to engage in magical thinking, whereby the cause and effect of things (e.g., his illness and treatment) are highly personalized. As such, he could be seeing his illness and the hospitalized separations involved as punishment for his imagined wrongdoings. Rando (1984) pointed out that "guilt and feelings of rejection are common in sick children at this age, and there might be feelings of anger or resentment directed towards the self and significant others" (p. 387). Researchers now know that children with catastrophic illness are able to understand the seriousness of their own condition and that they consequently experience grief related to their illness. They should therefore be provided support and help in coping with these feelings (Sourkes, 1995). Toward this end, the child's expression of fears and grief feelings should be fostered on an age-appropriate basis (Spinetta & Deasey-Spinetta, 1981). The counselor should seek team consensus from all parties—including the parents and medical personnel—in determining how much and in what terms this communication should take place, and this communication should be thoughtfully guided by best practice knowledge in the field (see Bluebond-Langner, 1996; Deasey-Spinetta, Spinetta, & Hung, 2003).

Because young children are developmentally limited in their intellectual and cognitive capabilities, counselors recognize that standard talk therapy methods do not apply to work with this age group. The application of play therapy techniques rather than talk methods is clearly indicated as the primary treatment mode with this 5-year-old boy. The use of play therapy as the primary therapeutic modality would offer Benji a safe and open opportunity to act out feelings, explore troublesome emotions, reduce anxiety, problem solve, and develop new behaviors (Sweeney, 1997). Through the use of puppets, for example, Benji would be enabled to dramatize his feelings of guilt and anger and reduce the sense of tension that is now being manifested in his combative ways during treatment. In discussing treatment of the seriously ill child, Eng (1999) described puppet play as "an unstructured, nondirective form of therapeutic play which allows the caregiver to help the child communicate in a nonthreatening way" (p. 129). Knowing that play is a child's medium for expression, I would provide Benji with a wide range of toys, games, and creative objects and activities as nondirective means for working out his feelings. (Although it is perhaps obvious, it bears stating that the counselor must take particular caution to ensure the sanitation of all play objects when conducting play therapy with an ill child.) I would expect that this type of nondirective individual play therapy would facilitate the safe expression of Benji's emotions, which otherwise he cannot readily articulate.

As a means of further decreasing Benji's anxiety, I would also incorporate psychoeducational activities, commonly offered at hospitals and treatment centers serving children, to help him learn about the hospital, his medicine, and surgical procedures in order to help demystify his illness and treatments. Bibliotherapy is also an excellent way to provide psychoeducational and therapeutic support to children who are seriously ill. There is a growing body of relevant bibliotherapeutic resources geared for this population. In this vein, I have recently used a great little book titled *Henry & the White Wolf* (Karu & Karu, 2000). This is the story of Henry, a sick hedgehog, who holds onto a stone for courage when the white wolf forces difficult treatment on him, which, in the end, helps him to get better. This book also comes with a small round stone for the sick child undergoing treatment to hold onto for strength. Other books relevant to children with serious or catastrophic illness are identified by sources such as http://www.cshcn.org/palliativecare/resources.html.

Family Involvement

Beyond working with Benji on an individual basis, I would clearly incorporate systems work as a means of further fortifying the family system, which has been so dramatically affected by (and is recursively affecting) Benji's illness. Given the broken family dynamic here, in which the controlling and anxious ways of the mother and the disengagement of the father have prevented meaningful family communication and have exacerbated Benji's and his siblings' sense of isolation, family play therapy methods can help address the family communication and relational problems that directly impinge on Benji's emotional welfare and ability to succeed in treatment.

Family play therapy has been found effective in the treatment of children undergoing medical treatment for serious and chronic illness (Jones, 2001; N. B. Webb, 1999).

The goals of such treatment include promoting integration in the family system and increasing healthy communications between and among members. As indicated in the case description, filial therapy is a form of family play therapy that can be applied when a problematic parent–child relationship dynamic is at work. Filial therapy was developed as a combination of family therapy and play therapy that would strategically engage the parents directly in the child's treatment (B. Guerney et al., 1970). In filial therapy, parents learn child-centered play therapy skills (which foster empathy, unconditional regard, acceptance, and encouragement) to use with their own children. Through this approach, parents have been helped to better understand and communicate with their chronically ill child while confronting the hardship of prolonged illness (Glazer-Waldman et al., 1992; VanFleet, 1992). Research has further validated filial play therapy as a psychotherapeutic approach that can help young children by increasing the parents' level of empathy with their child and decreasing their parenting stress (Chau & Landreth, 1997).

Nevertheless, some parents of seriously ill children are unable to fully accept their child's illness (and impending mortality) and consequently act in self-protecting ways that inadvertently deny the psychological experience of the child. In these cases, it is essential to work toward promoting parental empathy. Mrs. Dulaney seems to be locked into her own loss anxiety, failing to understand Benji's emotional plight as a result of his disconnection from his father and brothers. In this case, filial therapy can potentially help her (and Mr. Dulaney) develop empathy and improve communications with her child. Filial therapy can be particularly helpful in empowering the parents as a subsystem and in identifying issues that need to be addressed in the family for further care (Johnson, Bruhn, Winek, Krepps, & Wiley, 1999). Because filial therapy trains the parents to conduct child-centered play sessions at home, it is particularly empowering for those families in which the sick child is well enough to be at home. Filial therapy can help to strengthen family relationships that have been stressed by long-term illness and can offer a framework for spending quality time together under otherwise fractious conditions. Although using filial play therapy in Benji's treatment plan would clearly be supported by the research literature, its actual efficacy, as with all practice approaches, is determined in the end by the child's particular family context. In Benji's case, the parents' emotional and physical availability is a point of concern.

Given the significant role taken on by the parent in filial play therapy, Reynolds and Schwartz (2003) emphasized the necessity for the physical and psychological availability of the parents in this treatment approach; if such full-fledged availability is not apparent, then "an alternate approach should be sought" (p. 24). This criterion raises some questions with respect to Benji's current family scenario. Given the discordant stances of an overly controlling mother and a virtually absent father, will the necessary physical and psychological availability be there to successfully use filial therapy with Benji and his parents?

The first few sessions in filial play therapy (usually 10 to 12 sessions overall) entail engaging the parents in the process by explaining the method's rationale. At this stage, it would be important to stress with the Dulaneys that filial therapy makes particular sense to use with Benji given its established success as an approach for addressing issues surrounding a child with catastrophic illness. In trying to further engage the Dulaneys in committing to this approach (or any other family-based strategy, for that matter), it would be critical to address the resistance manifested in the father's absence and the mother's anxiety-based control behaviors. This resistance might first be addressed through individual psychodynamic counseling or even through some conjoint family work, in which the therapist could use methods such as sculpting and systems games (Satir, 1984) to help the family assess their relational problems (e.g., the triangulation dynamic that seems to be at play here) through physical enactments. In the end, if questions remain as to both parents' commitment to this intervention, filial therapy would not represent an effective treatment strategy.

In trying to help Benji's family better address the relational issues that are affecting their ability to cope adaptively in these circumstances, I would look to engage his brothers as well as his parents in the play therapy procedures. Strategic family play therapy (Ariel, 1992, 1997) is closely aligned with filial play therapy but specifically involves the whole family and does not rest on the parents' ability to carry out the play therapy protocol at home. In this method, free, imaginative play is fostered among all family members. In this approach, make-believe play helps family members work through their conflicts in nonthreatening ways. Through imaginative play, the family invokes their own themes, which are observed by the counselor and assessed for points of tension and maladaptive coping behaviors. The counselor then joins in the play by tapping into the observed tension points and carefully directing the play in gentle ways. The goal is to provide a safe forum for the expression and exploration of family relational problems that affect the child client. The disengagement of Benji's father and brothers (not to mention the significant emotional problems emerging in the eldest sibling) could be addressed through the strategic family play therapy approach if all members were willing to commit to the process. In the end, if the family system could be organically strengthened, Benji's emotional and physical welfare would also be strengthened.

Additionally, it would be useful for Benji to participate in group play therapy during hospitalization periods. Group play therapy has been found to be effective in treating children who are experiencing chronic illness or in need of anger control and reempowerment (Homeyer, 2000). As a child who has been dealing with the implications of critical illness throughout his short life, Benji could benefit from the decreased anxiety and increased sense of mastery provided through group play methods. His recent combative behaviors shown at medication and testing times reflect his sense of loss of control and anger, if not anxiety, over all that is required in his daily life to survive. Group play therapy can be instrumental in allowing the angry, disempowered child to work through those issues (Sweeney & Homeyer, 1999). For the sick child who has experienced the loss of normal peer relations because of continued hospitalizations and medical treatment, group play with other children can establish social context and promote a sense of freedom, offering a harbor from the tides of continual adult encroachment.

Following a holistic approach in helping Benji, I would want to provide (or make a referral for) individual counseling support to other family members, including the siblings, to assist each of them in dealing with the emotional issues, such as anger, resentment, anxiety, guilt, and anticipatory grief generated by living in a family with catastrophic illness. The well siblings of a critically ill child experience significant burdens (emotional and social) that are oftentimes not understood by others; as such, they can easily become the forgotten children in these crises. Although space does not permit detail here, I encourage counselors working with this population to educate themselves on the relevant issues and use of age-differentiated therapeutic and psychoeducational techniques when counseling children who have a parent or sibling with cancer (see Johnson, 1997).

Engaging the Primary Caretaker

Although much of what ails this family can be addressed through systemic methods, as I have described, Mrs. Dulaney's controlling and isolationist behaviors in relation to Benji are highly problematic and generate multiple layers of difficulty for all members of the family. A holistic treatment plan for Benji would include seeing to it that Mrs. Dulaney engages in individual counseling with a competent practitioner who has experience in dealing with loss and illness issues. This would be indicated in addition to any family counseling to be done. Mrs. Dulaney needs to be helped to see that, through her self-claimed identity as sacrificial mother, her overprotecting ways (in reaction to loss anxiety) are cutting off a necessary support network for Benji, increasing his separation anxiety (if not death anxiety), and contributing to his personal disempowerment—all antithetical to his well-being. Ever since her pregnancy with Benji, Mrs. Dulaney's shattered dreams and intrapsychic loss (in not having a healthy child) have been masked by her dogged need to control Benji's life. In this way, her sorrow remains hidden and her grief disenfranchised (Doka, 1989). Helping Mrs. Dulaney to acknowledge and discuss her shattered dreams will speed the healing process (Bowman, 1999). Toward this end, the counselor working with Mrs. Dulaney could incorporate narrative therapy methods that have been found useful in freeing people from the stories that imprison them (Neimeyer, 2000; White, 1995; White & Epston, 1990). By helping her to deconstruct the restrictive vision she has authored for herself, her family, and the world, the counselor could help Mrs. Dulaney to reauthor her shattered dreams and make new meaning of her role in the family and in the oversight of Benji's illness. Narrative therapeutic methods, including guided imagery and the use of metaphors, could also be used with Mr. Dulaney to help him acknowledge his own shattered dreams and reauthor his (disengaged) role in the family.

Conclusion

My conceptualization of this case emanates from both intrapsychic and systems models of counseling, and my proposed approach in working with Benji is informed by developmental, integrative, and constructivist principles. To consider supporting Benji, a young child stricken with catastrophic illness, the counselor needs to assess him in context and seek to incorporate the family (individual members and the family as a whole) in the treatment plan. In this process, developmental considerations of where the child is and where the family is (collectively as well as in relation to the individual members) will be most critical in determining intervention strategies. The technical eclecticism counselors are taught in professional training becomes the working paradigm in cases such as these. Indeed, there is no singular theoretical approach that can be considered sufficient for understanding or treating the multidimensional issues affecting Benji's emotional well-being. When constructivist principles inform my consideration of what might be most effective to address Mr. and Mrs. Dulaney's grief, I am guided by the child-centered principles of therapeutic play and by family systems models when determining interventions directly for Benji. Although it is not always tenable in today's world of managed care, the holistic approach I have described would be, I believe, well advised. Its overarching goal would be to cultivate resiliency in this family in an effort to support Benji and enhance the quality of his life as he continues to live, day by day, for, I hope, years to come.

References

Ariel, S. (1992). *Strategic family play therapy.* New York: Wiley.

Ariel, S. (1997). Strategic family play therapy. In K. O'Connor & L. M. Braverman (Eds.), *Play therapy theory and practice: A comparative presentation* (pp. 358–395). New York: Wiley.

Blake, S., & Paulsen, K. (1981). Therapeutic interventions with terminally ill children: A review. *Professional Psychology, 12,* 655–663.

Bluebond-Langner, M. (1996). *In the shadows of illness.* Princeton, NJ: Princeton University Press.

Bowman, T. (1999). Shattered dreams, resiliency, and hope: "Restorying" after loss. *Journal of Personal and Interpersonal Loss, 4,* 179–193.

Chau, I. Y. E. F., & Landreth, G. L. (1997). Filial therapy with Chinese parents: Effects on parental empathetic interactions, parental acceptance of child and parental stress. *International Journal of Play Therapy, 6,* 75–92.

Deasey-Spinetta, P., Spinetta, J. J., & Hung, F. (2003) *Emotional aspects of childhood blood cancers: Handbook for parents.* Retrieved August 20, 2005, from www.leukemia-lymphoma.org/attachments/National/br_1087232555.pdf

Doka, K. (1989). *Disenfranchised grief: Recognizing hidden sorrow.* New York: Lexington Books.

Eng, B. (1999). Puppets: Bridging the communication gap between caregivers and children about death and dying. In S. L. Bertman (Ed.), *Grief and the healing arts: Creativity as therapy* (pp. 127–137). Amityville, NY: Baywood Publishing Company.

Erikson, E. (1963). *Childhood and society.* New York: Norton.

Ginsberg, B. (1997). *Relationship enhancement family therapy.* New York: Wiley.

Glazer-Waldman, H., Zimmerman, J., Landreth, G., & Norton, D. (1992). Filial therapy: An intervention for parents of children with chronic illness. *International Journal of Play Therapy, 1,* 31–42.

Goodman, R. F. (1999). Childhood cancer and the family: Case of Tim, age 6; and follow up at 15. In N. B. Webb (Ed.), *Play therapy with children in crisis: Individual, group, and family treatment* (2nd ed., pp. 380–406). New York: Guilford Press.

Gray, E. (1989). The emotional and play needs of the dying child. *Issues in Comprehensive Pediatric Nursing, 12,* 207–224.

Guerney, B., Guerney, L., & Andronico, M. (1970). Filial therapy. In J. Hart & T. M. Tomlinson (Eds.), *New directions in client-centered therapy* (pp. 373–386). Boston: Houghton Mifflin.

Guerney, L. (1980). Filial therapy. In R. Herink (Ed.), *The psychotherapy handbook* (pp. 227–229). New York: New American Library.

Homeyer, L. E. (2000). When is group play therapy appropriate? *Psychiatric Times, 17.* Retrieved August 20, 2005, from www.psychiatrictimes.com/p000949.html

Johnson, L. (1997). Developmental strategies for counseling the child who has a parent or sibling with cancer. *Journal of Counseling and Development, 75,* 417–427.

Johnson, L., Bruhn, R., Winek, J., Krepps, J., & Wiley, K. (1999). The use of child centered play therapy and filial therapy with Head Start families: A brief report. *Journal of Marriage & Family Counseling, 25,* 169–176.

Jones, E. M. (2001). Play therapy for children with chronic illness. In G. Landreth (Ed.), *Innovations in play therapy: Issues, process, and special populations* (pp. 271–288). Philadelphia: Brunner-Routledge.

Kaplan, C. P. (1999). Life-threatening blood disorder: Case of Daniel, age 11, and his mother. In N. B. Webb (Ed.), *Play therapy with children in crisis: Individual, group, and family treatment* (2nd ed., pp. 356–379). New York: Guilford Press.

Karu, T., & Karu, T. (2000). *Henry & the white wolf.* New York: Workman Publishing Company.

Kraft, A., & Landreth, G. (1998). *Parents as therapeutic partners.* Northvale, NJ: Jason Aronson.

Lahti, S. L. (1993). An ethnographic study of the filial therapy process (Doctoral dissertation, University of North Texas, Denton, 1992). *Dissertation Abstracts International, 53,* 2691.

Le Vieux, J. (1990). Issues in play therapy: The dying child. *Association of Play Therapy Newsletter, 9*(4), 4–5.

Marsh, J. D. B. (Ed.). (1995). *From the heart: On being the mother of a child with special needs.* Bethesda, MD: Woodbine.

Maslow, A. (1954). *Motivation and personality.* New York: Harper.

Neimeyer, R. (2000). *Lessons of life: A guide to coping.* Memphis, TN: Center for Loss and Transition.

Rando, T. (1984). *Grief, dying and death: Clinical interventions for caregivers.* Champaign, IL: Research Press.

Rennie, R., & Landreth, G. (2000). Effects of filial therapy on parent and child behaviors. *International Journal of Play Therapy, 2*(2), 19–37.

Reynolds, C., & Schwartz, R. C. (2003). Filial therapy: An introduction for psychotherapists. *Annals of the American Psychotherapy Association, 6,* 22–26.

Satir, V. (1984). *Satir step by step: A guide to creating change in families.* Palo Alto, CA: Science and Behavior Books.

Sourkes, B. M. (1995). *Armfuls of time: The psychological experience of the child with a life-threatening illness.* Pittsburgh: University of Pittsburgh Press.

Spinetta, J. J., & Deasey-Spinetta, P. (1981). Talking with children who have a life-threatening illness. In J. J. Spinetta & P. Deasey-Spinetta (Eds.), *Living with childhood cancer* (pp. 234–252). St. Louis, MO: C.V. Mosby.

Swanston, H., Williams, K., & Nunn, K. (2000). The psychological adjustment of children with chronic conditions. *Clinical Approaches to Early Intervention in Child and Adolescent Mental Health, 5,* 1–45.

Sweeney, D. S. (1997). *Counseling children through the world of play.* Wheaton, IL: Tyndale House Publishers.

Sweeney, D. S., & Homeyer, L. E. (1999). *The handbook of group play therapy: How to do it, how it works, whom it's best for.* San Francisco: Jossey-Bass.

VanFleet, R. (1992). Using filial therapy to strengthen families with chronically ill children. In L. Vandecreek, S. Knapp, & T. Jackson (Eds.), *Innovations in clinical practice: A sourcebook* (Vol. 11, pp. 87–97). Sarasota, FL: Professional Resource Press.

Webb, J. R. (1995). Play therapy with hospitalized children. *International Journal of Play Therapy, 4*(1), 51–59.

Webb, N. B. (Ed.). (1999). *Play therapy with children in crisis: Individual, group, and family treatment* (2nd. ed.). New York: Guilford Press.

White, M. (1995). *Reauthoring lives: Interviews and essays.* Adelaide, Australia: Dulwich Centre Publications.

White, M., & Epston, D. (1990). *Narrative means to therapeutic ends.* New York: Norton.

Yiu, J., & Twinn, S. (2001). Determining the needs of Chinese parents during the hospitalization of their child diagnosed with cancer: An exploratory study. *Cancer Nursing, 24,* 483–489.

27

"My Head Hurts—Come Pick Me Up From School, Gramma!": Somatization

This incident focuses on the role of counselors in assisting child clients whose physical symptoms may have psychological causes. This particular case underscores the importance of holistic intervention with children presenting somatic symptoms. Respondents discuss the efficacy of multiple intervention techniques, including journaling and play therapy.

■ Critical Incident

Suzanne E. Degges-White

As a counselor, I work on staff with a group of neurologists who specialize in headache treatment. In this capacity, I have seen a fair number of adolescents who were dealing with headaches brought on by academic or sports-related stress—placed on them either by themselves or, too often, by their parents. I have also, on occasion, seen children as clients.

Nevertheless, I was a bit surprised when Dr. Adler, the chief neurologist, met with me to discuss a client he was referring to me and shared that the new client, "Sue Ellen," was only 9 years old. Dr. Adler explained that Sue Ellen's maternal grandmother, Mrs. Gayle, had brought her to the clinic because the young girl had been complaining of severe headaches for a period of approximately 6 weeks. The neurologist had examined Sue Ellen and listened carefully to her description of the headaches, which reflected some of the symptoms typical of migraine headaches. When asked about any other physiological problems, Sue Ellen also described a series of stomachaches. Sue Ellen noted that she often woke up with the headache or the stomachache and said that if it began later in the day, the pain was likely to become severe quite rapidly.

Abdominal migraines, also known as headache-free migraines, are episodes that produce many symptoms similar to those of migraine (blurred vision, aura, etc.), except that there is an absence of headache. They are most often diagnosed in children and generally cause abdominal pain, nausea, constipation, or diarrhea. Dr. Adler was considering both types of migraines as possible diagnoses for Sue Ellen and had not prescribed any medications other than over-the-counter analgesics and antinausea products for treatment. Dr. Adler believed that there might be more to the picture and therefore referred Sue Ellen to me for counseling. Sue Ellen was scheduled to see him again in 4 weeks, and he was hoping that I would be able to see her for two or three sessions prior to their next appointment.

Less than a week later, I had an appointment scheduled with Sue Ellen. On the afternoon of the first counseling session, I went to the lobby to collect Sue Ellen and her grandmother so that I could initially meet with both of them to learn as much as possible about the presenting issues. As Sue Ellen and Mrs. Gayle entered my office, Sue Ellen took a quick look around the room at the various seating options and then hopped up onto the chaise that was typically used by clients with whom I was implementing relaxation therapy. Sue Ellen stretched out and firmly noted, "I bet this is where you shrink people's heads, isn't it?" I smiled and responded, "Clients may choose to sit in any of the seats here, and sometimes clients find that chair particularly relaxing." Sue Ellen's grandmother admonished her to "stop fooling around and sit up like a lady should!" I reassured her grandmother that Sue Ellen was fine where she was and that it was important that clients feel comfortable to benefit the most from our work together.

As Sue Ellen began to tell the story of her aches and pains, she adamantly stated that she "knew" she was suffering from some terrible terminal illness, which she supposed was a rare brain tumor that also caused severe pains in her stomach. She also asked why the doctors were not performing more tests on her and asked me to help convince the doctors of how serious her sickness really was. As Sue Ellen poured out her concerns, Mrs. Gayle kept trying to quiet the child so that she could talk to me about Sue Ellen's various episodes and symptoms. Eventually, Mrs. Gayle was able to share that the symptoms had begun around the time of Sue Ellen's return to school after the winter break (it was now late February) and that she was most concerned because Sue Ellen had missed 8 full days of school and had called for early pick-up on at least a half a dozen more. Mrs. Gayle expressed worry about Sue Ellen's grades and about determining the source of her physical complaints.

I asked whether there was anything else that she thought I needed to know about Sue Ellen's situation, and she responded in the negative. When I asked about how a typical day without a headache or stomachache might go, Sue Ellen smiled and said, "Those days are wonderful! They are usually weekend days, so I can have a lot of fun on those days!" I then asked about the typical headache day, and Sue Ellen replied, "If I'm at school already, they're horrible days—I feel like crying when the headache starts and I have to go to the nurse's office so that I can call Gramma to come pick me up."

The approach of the physicians at the medical center is that children's complaints should be taken seriously and that children should be empowered to take action at the onset of a headache. They encourage children and their parents to talk with the teachers and administrators and ask that the child be permitted to find a quiet place to rest when a headache is coming on. This is good advice, and much of the work I do with patients is helping them learn to implement relaxation exercises and techniques to ward off impending headaches. I therefore decided that this would be where I would start with Sue Ellen.

A week later, Sue Ellen came back to my office alone and, as expected, threw herself across the chaise. I noted aloud that this was a good choice, not because we were going to "shrink her head" but because we were going to help her learn how to relax. After Sue Ellen shared that she had missed another day of school, we talked about how relaxation exercises might help her hold a headache at bay so that it did not get so big that it interrupted the entire day. We also talked about how learning to keep calm might help with her stomachaches too. Age-appropriate relaxation techniques included deep breathing, progressive relaxation, and guided meditations that focused specifically on headache relief. Sue Ellen was a good patient in that she closed her eyes and really tried to relax in the office. She admitted that she was not sure she would be able to do the exercises all the time but assured me that she would try. I provided her with a tape of a couple of child-friendly guided meditations (Curran, 2001; Klein & Holden, 2001; Lusk, 1992; Olness & Kohen, 1996) and suggested that she practice, on a daily basis, the different techniques she had learned.

Mrs. Gayle was half an hour late with Sue Ellen for our next appointment, so we only had a few minutes to meet and discuss progress. Sue Ellen said that she needed a note from me or the doctor for her school. She said that she thought the relaxation exercises were really helpful but that she needed to be by herself in the nurse's office, rather than the classroom, for the techniques to be successful. I encouraged her to really try hard and train herself to relax in her classroom because that would give her more power over the headaches and stomachaches. Sue Ellen said she wanted to but that she really needed the note "now." I picked up on her urgent use of the word *now* and asked her whether something had changed at school. Sue Ellen revealed that she had been getting the start of headaches several times a day and that the teacher and nurse would only let her take two breaks each day. Feeling that this was a generous amount, I asked how many times she felt headaches starting. Sue Ellen replied with a straight face, "Sometimes I get five headaches a day! I probably have a brain tumor, not just headaches, and the doctor should really run some kind of tests on me soon." After this statement, she asked me to read one of the guided meditations to her during the remaining few minutes of the session.

I made a phone call to Mrs. Gayle later that day to discuss her granddaughter. Mrs. Gayle revealed that Sue Ellen was being picked on and bullied by a group of girls in her classroom who made fun of Sue Ellen for being somewhat overweight and for having few friends. These girls were surreptitious in their teasing and taunting and did not raise the attention or ire of the teacher. Sue Ellen was afraid of the consequences she would suffer if she tattled on them.

This information, of course, was important and would have benefited me had I been aware of it earlier. It was then that several questions formed in my mind: Are Sue Ellen's headaches and stomachaches fictitious or genuine? Is she suffering from school phobia? Are her headaches due to psychological factors affecting her general medical condition? Is Sue Ellen a budding hypochondriac?

The next day, I met with Dr. Adler for our weekly consultation and shared the new information regarding Sue Ellen's case. We discussed Sue Ellen's earlier descriptions of her symptoms and the ways they closely paralleled actual migraine episodes. Nevertheless, we both noted that she seemed more affected by the attention than truly bothered by the accompanying alleged pain. We also noted that some of the typical telltale signs of migraine were absent. Dr. Adler's next appointment with Sue Ellen was the following week. Because she had an appointment with me immediately afterward, we decided that I would also be present while he met with Sue Ellen and Mrs. Gayle. This way, I would be up to date on the medical side of things before the counseling session began.

A week later, I was sitting in with Sue Ellen, Mrs. Gayle, and the neurologist. Mrs. Gayle was complaining that Sue Ellen's physical problems were still out of hand; Sue Ellen was declaring that she knew something terrible must be wrong with her. The doctor was trying to reassure the child while attending to the grandmother's report of Sue Ellen's behavior. Dr. Adler gently told Sue Ellen and her grandmother that it seemed that Sue Ellen's headaches and stomachaches were not migraine related and that the best course of action would be continued treatment with the previously suggested over-the-counter products. Dr. Adler also recommended that Sue Ellen continue to meet with me for counseling on a weekly or biweekly basis so that she could find better ways to deal with the stressors that were contributing to her physical symptoms.

Unfortunately, once Mrs. Gayle heard that there were no serious physical problems with her granddaughter, she also decided that further counseling was not necessary. Although we had a session scheduled for that afternoon, Mrs. Gayle only allowed Sue Ellen to stay for half an hour. During this time, I suggested that we do a guided relaxation exercise, and I decided to use a visualization exercise with Sue Ellen that would encourage her to feel strong and safe by incorporating positive affirmations related to increased self-esteem and personal strength. I was worried about how the situation with the teasing would turn out.

After Sue Ellen left my office that day, I tried to reflect on how I could have changed the course of treatment so that she would have been able to reap the greatest benefits from the sessions we had. Although I did serve in an adjunctive capacity to the neurologists, I wondered whether I should have been less medically oriented in our early sessions. I wondered whether I should have been more persistent in finding out more about Sue Ellen's life than just about the aches and pains. I felt good about having focused on relaxation strategies with Sue Ellen because she could benefit from them throughout her life and because learning how to handle stress improves both mental and physical well-being. Nonetheless, the experience left me feeling that I had underserved a client, yet I was unsure of exactly how I could have managed a more effective overall outcome for Sue Ellen.

Questions

1. When working as an adjunctive therapist in a medical setting, how can counselors best sell their services as legitimate and valuable to their clients, even beyond a focus on medical concerns?
2. What is the best way to get the whole story when working with young clients who may not be able to articulate it and who have parents or guardians who do not know what is truly relevant to the situation at hand?
3. What are some good approaches to working with children who present with "schoolitis" or mild forms of hypochondriasis?

Response

JoLynn V. Carney

It is easy to imagine how distressed this counselor might be when thinking that the client, Sue Ellen, had been underserved. This is a core fear for many counselors, who strive daily to use all available resources to facilitate client functioning. Sue Ellen is definitely struggling with pain and anxiety while maintaining the age-appropriate work of going to school. I focus my response on (a) a perspective validating the value of the counselor's role with Sue Ellen, (b) an approach for gathering the context of the client's presenting issues, and (c) some intervention strategies for working with children who present with schoolitis.

Counselors working as part of a medical professional team can sometimes be seen as tangential to the process of diagnosis and treatment. Although chronic pain is typically considered a medical issue, counselors clearly have an integral role in discussions regarding management. Proven techniques of relaxation, guided imagery, biofeedback, aromatherapy, and so forth are used to empower clients dealing with constant pain. Yet, even in this environment, counselors like the one in this case study need to reinforce the skills they offer as valuable to overall client treatment.

I often find it important to begin counseling by discussing with clients and their family the mind–body connection (Pert, 1999) so that clients understand the need to enhance the mind's function as a support to the body's function. Helping Sue Ellen and her grandmother understand the interactive dynamic among Sue Ellen's thinking, emotions, and physical symptomatology could empower both of them. This is especially true given that Sue Ellen's thoughts of her pain probably center on catastrophic words such as *terrible* or *uncontrollable* and given that her affect is highly anxious. Clients come to see the need for counseling as an adjunct to medical treatment when they come to understand the delicate interplay among their thinking, emotions, and experiences of pain.

Early in treatment, I make a point of acknowledging the expertise of everyone involved in treating the client. I work to create a holistic perspective that interweaves the expertise of each member of the treatment team to help the client toward fuller functioning. I would identify the expert roles of Sue Ellen and her grandmother just as clearly as my own and Dr. Adler's. This important interweaving of our various kinds of expertise and roles strengthens my own credibility in the medical setting along with the credibility of the client and family. Enhancing client and family credibility is vitally important to overall treatment outcome. Emphasizing each member's importance and potential tasks creates a sense of empowerment, and trust in the treatment process is more likely to develop.

The first session is when I would explore what supports are in place to assist the client and family. I would be looking to identify what Sue Ellen and her grandmother define as supports so they can see positives in addition to problems. Once some supports were established, we would seek ways to consistently implement those supports. We would all be helping from Sue Ellen's frame of reference, with Mrs. Gayle and me being primary to the role of supporter.

I approach clients from the viewpoint that I am not there to force therapy on the basis of my perceptions but that I am seeking an alliance in which we will all work as a team. Using some time in the initial session with Sue Ellen and Mrs. Gayle to establish an understanding of interconnecting roles and developing the essential alliance could have changed the course of treatment outcome experienced by the counselor in this scenario. Mrs. Gayle might have been less apt to withdraw Sue Ellen from treatment if she had gained more of an alliance with the counselor in the first session. I might ask Mrs. Gayle to engage in a dialogue that would bring into play her personal experiences that could be related to Sue Ellen's: "Mrs. Gayle, please think about a time when you are feeling anxious. What signs might I see that tell me you're anxious? What impact do these feelings of anxiety have on the way you look, feel, and act?" A follow-up question might be, "What type of support have you experienced when you were struggling?"

I would follow up Mrs. Gale's personal experiences with a discussion on how they might parallel those of her granddaughter. I would share that it is normal to have times in one's life when one feels anxious, sad, or overwhelmed. People get through these times more productively if they can find and use available support to cope with the stressors. This is the beginning of a brief introduction to a wellness versus a deficit model. Throughout this dialogue, my goal would be to create a more significant treatment alliance among Mrs. Gayle, Sue Ellen, and myself.

Sue Ellen's anxiety seems closely tied to her fears about her headaches and stomachaches. She "knows" this is a terrible illness and asks her counselor to help convince the doctors about her sickness. The client's story focuses totally on the illness aspect of her life, which is reinforced by Mrs. Gayle, who wants medical treatment for Sue Ellen's illness to reduce symptoms and school absences. Sue Ellen's anxiety and fears are left virtually unattended.

Sue Ellen seems to be quite articulate for a 9-year-old, given that she is able to express clearly her distress, yet she and her grandmother do not report the whole story to the counselor. Gaining a fuller understanding will require expanding the sickness focus to encompass not only the physical symptoms but also the psychological and social aspects of Sue Ellen's life. To capitalize on the expressive talk of Sue Ellen and other young, female clients, a counselor could suggest journaling as one vehicle for gaining additional information. Creating a diary of sorts allows clients to freely express their thoughts, feelings, and accompanying actions. Sue Ellen's writing between sessions would have helped fill in the picture and provide greater context for her somatic complaints. Being allowed into this aspect of Sue Ellen's life (her life between sessions and her inner thinking) would have provided a personal perspective of gains received through her sick-role behaviors. The counselor could have come to understand the special attention Sue Ellen gains from family, school personnel, and friends or even recognize in Sue Ellen's writing her sense of decreased responsibility in her roles at school or home. The counselor might have identified emotions, such as anxiety, depression, and even anger, that underlie the pain. Reading the journal would take the counselor out of the verbal detective role of asking questions and allow for a more genuine responding based on the client's written expressions.

Engaging Sue Ellen in play therapy could also have been helpful as a nonverbal tool for gaining additional insight. Play therapy is invaluable for dealing with younger clients, whether in the form of drawing and art, sand tray therapy, or various other techniques. These vehicles allow the counselor to view the world from the young person's point of view, in which verbal interaction is less significant and creativity is greater. What might arise from watching, playing with, and perhaps talking about toys that children play with in the sand or puppets they engage in conversation with can be very different from what one can learn from asking questions or trying to directly discuss issues with a child. Creative use of toys, games, drawings, and books almost always leads to more information from children than discussion alone.

It behooves counselors working with young children to use alternative sources of information to supplement the information provided by the client. Mrs. Gayle, for example, supplied additional data about peer abuse at school, although such information was not volunteered early in the treatment course. Other family members' perspectives (if available; e.g., siblings and parents) would also be valuable sources. The school is another important source of information, given that many of Sue Ellen's pain episodes occurred there, whereas many pain-free days were on weekends. A signed release of information form to contact school personnel (e.g., teacher and school counselor) would have provided context for the role of the school environment in Sue Ellen's pain. Ecological contexts such as these are vitally important to understand what triggers and reinforcers exist in the environment. These additional ways of gaining information from the client, from family members about their dynamics, and from the school context would provide a much more comprehensive conceptualization of Sue Ellen's life. Such information would be crucial to diagnosing and treating her presenting medical issue in its psychological and social context of peer abuse in school.

A more holistic evaluation of Sue Ellen's medical complaints could be viewed by Sue Ellen and others as a coping mechanism to survive the abuse at school. Sue Ellen is among many children whose somatic complaints (headache, stomachaches), affective distress (anxiety, depression), revenge drive (suicidal or homicidal ideation), and school truancy are symptomatic of peer-abused youths in schools (Rigby, 2002). Referral to appropriate treatment sources and modalities for Sue Ellen would have lessened her counselor's sense that Sue Ellen might have been underserved in the neurologists' group practice.

My strategies for working with Sue Ellen would definitely begin with individual and family empowerment counseling, whereby I would work from a strength-based versus deficit model. We would collectively identify available resources as supports for good treatment outcomes. Positive relationships with others would be established, especially with individuals who could act as advocates for Sue Ellen. One excellent advocate for Sue Ellen in light of the peer abuse would be the school counselor, who, along with Sue Ellen's teacher, could help create an atmosphere of empowerment. Empowerment is an optimal term; I have seen very well-meaning school counselors, teachers, administrators, and even office staff unintentionally create an environment of learned helplessness in which targeted students believe they do not have the personal resources to deal with the abuse but must rely on the adults in the situation to keep them safe.

Working to help Sue Ellen develop an accurate self-concept would be crucial to this empowerment process. She needs to understand her personal qualities (productive and unproductive) that are important in producing successful versus unsuccessful social interactions. Especially in cases of chronic peer abuse, friends, even one friend, can be a tremendous protective factor, so identifying any positive relationships that could offer acceptance and friendship would be important. The ultimate goal is to promote a sense of belonging to reduce the schoolitis. The classroom teacher could facilitate this process by developing activities that involved the student in give-and-take activities, which could be as simple as daily greetings and reciprocal smiles among the students.

I use desensitization techniques with children to help them better understand their situation and as a means of treatment for pain and other issues. One technique might be to have Sue Ellen visualize successfully participating in a school day. We could explore what the successful school day would look, feel, smell, and sound like. This would allow for a comparison of what the perfect day looks like in relation to Sue Ellen's actual experiences. The additional information gained could lead to brainstorming ways to improve the school day.

Relaxation and guided imagery can reduce the stress surrounding school and, in Sue Ellen's case, the peer abuse. Bibliotherapy, as implemented by the counselor, family, or teachers, can provide a useful vehicle for teaching and exploring the feelings surrounding schoolitis (e.g., Darcey, Fiore, & Ladd 2000; Moser & Pilkey, 1988). Therapeutic counseling groups are another means of acquiring good outcomes for many children who suffer from schoolitis. Throughout the treatment process, the counselor can join with clients and their family in acknowledging any personal progress toward the development of an accurate self-concept and individual responsible behavior that capitalizes on the empowered sense of self (Knapp & Jongsma, 2002).

Response

Constance J. Deuschle

This case scenario, somatic distress and pain, presents a complex situation requiring attention to all of the details that are pertinent to the development and implementation of a positive intervention plan. It was not difficult for me to identify with the questions asked by the counselor as she questioned whether she could have served her client, Sue Ellen, more effectively, thus eliciting a different outcome. Although I do not have a definitive answer to her questions, the situation does offer a learning opportunity to all counselors. One indicator of an effective counselor should be the ability to continue to reflect on the counseling process with clients who are no longer part of one's daily and weekly caseload.

In response to the question about the best way to get the whole story when working with young clients and families, there may not be a single answer. This is especially true when the client or family may not articulate or even understand all of the variables needed to offer effective counseling intervention. The presenting problems with Sue Ellen focused on physical symptoms, yet a physical report is not included with the case. Except for the information provided by the neurologist, one could assume that, with normal development, Sue Ellen is like most 9-year-olds who are prepubescent. Young people this age may have growth spurts that could result in weight gain and muscle growth, changes in body proportions, increased gender development, and sexual fantasies about themselves and others (Davies, 1999). Is there a way to create a more comprehensive understanding of Sue Ellen's experience?

Erikson's (1968) human development theory could help the counselor consider a comprehensive approach to working with Sue Ellen. Erikson's industry versus inferiority stage presents the 9-year-old child as progressing through social skill development (Berk, 2004). By relating more with peers, moving from free play to more structured play and teamwork, and mastering the core academic disciplines, the child is able to resolve the crisis and to feel a sense of competence and confidence. Attending school is emphasized at this stage of development. The child also becomes more accomplished in building and creating and begins making more difficult decisions (Berk, 2004). The child becomes more independent, can engage in abstract thinking, and takes on increased responsibilities at school and home. At this age, young people would rather blend in with peers as they become more self-conscious, self-doubting, and self-critical. During this stage, mood swings may increase.

Unsuccessful accomplishment of tasks inherent in this stage may result in the child becoming self-critical and possibly experiencing feelings of shame or guilt.

It is helpful to use a comprehensive approach with young clients to reduce the possibility of missing a part of the whole story that could contribute to a positive long-term outcome. It is also important not to rush into unsubstantiated conclusions without all of the information necessary for a competent assessment. The neurologist was able to provide some information about Sue Ellen and to eliminate some of the identified physical concerns. For the counselor to determine a final diagnosis of somatoform disorder specified according to the *Diagnostic and Statistical Manual of Mental Disorders* (4th ed., text rev.; American Psychiatric Association, 2000), Sue Ellen must have had the presenting symptoms for a period of at least 6 months.

Along with physical and psychological symptoms, temperament traits would be helpful in the assessment of the young client. The understanding of how a child responds to certain situations is a guide in preparing the child for more challenging situations. On the basis of research by Thomas and Chess (1977, cited in Berk, 2004), several areas of development could be considered to better assess the temperament style. These include how the child relates to eating and sleeping, transitions and changes, physical stimuli, new situations or strangers, and working through obstacles; whether the child has high or low energy levels; and the degree of concentration and distractibility. The counselor was able to assess the increased stress Sue Ellen felt when she was in the school setting and at times when she was at home. The connection between increased stress and physical pain was established during the last visit with the neurologist, Sue Ellen, her grandmother, and the counselor. With this understanding, the counselor taught stress identification and management techniques to Sue Ellen with the hope of reducing the painful headaches and stomachaches. Nevertheless, unanswered questions and concerns still remained in the assessment of Sue Ellen.

Temperament evaluation might also be part of a comprehensive assessment to better appreciate the impact of Sue Ellen's sensitivity and coping abilities. Studies indicate that the prevalence of somatoform disorders in children range from 1.3% to 5% of the general child population, with a higher percentage in girls. Research supports the role of stress in the course of some illnesses. Stress may be exacerbated in some children who have more difficulty in the expression of emotions at school, with family, and in other situations (Oatis, 2002). Specific origins of somatoform disorder are not clearly understood. Understanding family history regarding anxiety and depression would be a valuable part of a comprehensive assessment, given that there is evidence of a predisposition for somatization in children from families with a history of anxiety and depression (Oatis, 2002).

Sue Ellen's presenting physical complaints and her catastrophizing of the situation were the initial impetus for seeking help. Although the presenting problems provided a beginning for the counselor and although the information was given to her directly from the neurologist, it is recommended to obtain information firsthand from the client (Hersen & Van Hasselt, 1998). This provides a foundation for understanding the problem from the perspective of the client and may encourage the client to provide information that he or she might not have previously disclosed. The medical history of the family would be pertinent to clearly understanding Sue Ellen's somatic illnesses. Activities or situations occurring during the winter break might help establish the circumstances that led to Sue Ellen's headaches and stomachaches. The reasons Sue Ellen lives with her grandmother and the expectations about this living arrangement would be helpful in better understanding their relationship. Furthermore, negative school experiences, including information about bullying at school, could be gathered through individual counseling sessions.

Through the utility of their counseling skills, counselors are taught to work effectively with other professionals and to practice their abilities to work collaboratively with others as team members. Providing ongoing information to the neurologist could offer further education about how the mental health and the medical fields can work together to provide a comprehensive and professional approach to working with school-aged children. Nevertheless, there remains the professional obligation to the child, the duty to do what is right for each client and to be willing to stay the course through the patience and perseverance required in challenging circumstances. Sue Ellen might have given more clues about the etiology of her headaches and stomachaches given more time alone with the counselor and without the presence of her grandmother (Davis, 2005). If the grandmother would reconsider and allow Sue Ellen to have more counseling sessions with the counselor, various play therapy techniques (e.g., sand play, bibliotherapy) would be helpful in soliciting thoughts and feelings from the child.

In addition to addressing client-articulated concerns, it is imperative to rule out other causes of Sue Ellen's physical symptoms and determination not to attend or stay in school. Somatic symptoms may be reflective of child abuse or school phobia. Both of these concerns must be assessed and eliminated or other appropriate actions taken. One behavioral indicator for abuse is low self-esteem, not only at home but also in the school setting (Tower, 1996). School phobia literature addresses children who refuse to go to school and articulates how their behaviors reflect anxiety about separating from home and spending the day in school. Children may fear something unexpected could happen at home while they are away at school (American Academy of Pediatrics, 2001). Older students may fear their school performance is below expectations, feel insecure on the bus, or be troubled by bullying or other conflicts at school (American Academy of Pediatrics, 2001).

When counselors encourage students and family members to continue counseling and they refuse or resist following through with counseling appointments, it can be disheartening. Engagement of clients and family members may be impossible to guarantee, but there may be some factors that encourage client engagement. Tryon (2002) suggested that factors such as client and counselor characteristics and attitudes about counseling benefits may contribute to client engagement. In addition, a prior history of positive counseling experiences and client readiness increase the possibilities of client engagement. Many of these factors are not in the control of the counselor, and it may be understandable that Sue Ellen's grandmother chose to discontinue counseling after the neurologist affirmed the absence of a medical diagnosis. The counselor then had the opportunity to initiate further dialogue with the grandmother for ways of staying in contact regarding Sue Ellen's behavioral progress. It is important to remember that there are times when families need to think through options and choices, and they may later reconsider decisions such as discontinuation of counseling.

Sue Ellen's complaints may continue and may escalate, propelling her grandmother to again seek the help of a counselor. This counselor could provide materials for the grandmother to further explain somatoform disorder and to emphasize the connection between early somatoform disorder and hypochondriasis in adults (Oatis, 2002). To reduce the possibility of Sue Ellen's misinterpretation of her bodily symptoms, which could lead to hypochondriasis, it is imperative that the counselor makes every effort to educate the grandmother and to continue communicating with her in some way.

Ongoing intervention will likely look different than that articulated as part of this case study. Fortunately, 9-year-old students are required to attend school. The pattern of school absences and partially attended school days promotes school involvement and may provide an opportunity for continued intervention beyond the services of this counselor. How the school continues involvement with Sue Ellen's grandmother is vital in determining how the school can remain connected with Sue Ellen. A school with a student assistance team or other intervention team is well equipped to develop individual student intervention plans and to follow up with the plan's goals (Wittmer, 2000). A team would likely be composed of the school counselor and the school nurse, who see Sue Ellen frequently, and would promote the brainstorming of supportive strategies for Sue Ellen and her grandmother. The team could also invite the neurologist or other medical professionals to a meeting to demonstrate the school's systematic approach to supporting all students. Even further medical testing cannot be ruled out and may be indicated at a later time. What is important is to attempt to unlock the fears expressed by Sue Ellen and to help her find peace of mind at home and school.

References

American Academy of Pediatrics. (2001). Policy statement: The assessment and management of acute pain in infants, children, and adolescents. *Pediatrics, 108,* 793–797.

American Psychiatric Association. (2000). *Diagnostic and statistical manual of mental disorders* (4th ed., text rev.). Washington, DC: Author.

Berk, L. (2004). *Development through the lifespan* (3rd ed.). Boston: Allyn & Bacon.

Curran, E. (2001). *Guided imagery for healing children and teens: Wellness through visualization.* Hillsboro, OR: Beyond Words Publishing.

Darcey, J., Fiore, L., & Ladd, G. (2000). *Your anxious child: How parents and teachers can relieve anxiety in children.* San Francisco: Jossey-Bass.

Davies, D. (1999). *Child development: A practitioner's guide.* New York: Guilford Press.

Davis, T. (2005). *Exploring school counseling: Professional practices and perspectives.* Boston: Lahaska Press.

Erikson, E. H. (1968). *Identity: Youth and crisis.* New York: Norton.

Hersen, M., & Van Hasselt, V. (1998). *Basic interviewing: A practical guide for counselors and clinicians.* Mahwah, NJ: Erlbaum.

Klein, N. C., & Holden, M. (2001). *Healing images for children: Teaching relaxation and guided imagery to children facing cancer and other serious illnesses.* Watertown, WI: Inner Coaching.

Knapp S. E., & Jongsma, A. E. (2002). *The school counseling and school social work treatment planner.* Hoboken, NJ: Wiley.

Lusk, J. T. (1992). *Thirty scripts for relaxation imagery and inner healing.* Duluth, MN: Whole Person Associates.

Moser, A., & Pilkey, D. (1988). *Don't pop your cork on Mondays!* Kansas City, MO: Landmark Editions.

Oatis, M. (2002, January–February). Psychosomatic illness in children and adolescents: Somatoform disorders. *Child Study Center Newsletter, 6*(3), 1–4.

Olness, K., & Kohen, D. P. (1996). *Hypnosis and hypnotherapy with children* (3rd ed.). New York: Guilford Press.

Pert, C. B. (1999). *Molecules of emotion: The science behind mind–body medicine.* New York: Simon and Schuster.

Rigby, K. (2002). *New perspectives on bullying.* Philadelphia: Jessica Kingsley.

Tower, C. (1996). *Child abuse and neglect* (3rd ed.). Boston: Allyn & Bacon.

Tryon, G. (2002). *Counseling based on process research: Applying what we know.* Boston: Allyn & Bacon.

Wittmer, J. (2000). *Managing your school counseling program: K–12 developmental strategies* (2nd ed.). Minneapolis, MN: Educational Media Corporation.

Part

VII

Protecting Children From Themselves

28

"Why Didn't You Tell Me?": School Responsibilities in the Wake of Death by Autoerotic Asphyxiation

This incident focuses on the practice of autoerotic asphyxiation and discusses the role of the school in responding to deaths that result from this practice.

Critical Incident

Susan A. Adams

When I accepted a new school counseling position in a southern, rural middle school after working for 4 years as a school counselor in the inner city, I felt fairly confident in my skills and knowledge base. The inner city job had been my first school counseling position after I completed my master's degree, and I had learned an immense amount on the job. I found myself at a loss, though, when faced with responding to the death of "Paul Keating" just 2 weeks into the school year. Paul was a handsome and popular 13-year-old who was well liked by nearly everyone. He was an eighth grader with younger siblings also enrolled in the middle school, and almost everyone knew him. As a result, nearly everyone was affected by his death.

Although I had certainly been schooled in issues related to grief, suicide, and trauma and had unfortunately been faced with helping a school overcome a student's death in my former district, I found myself feeling like a complete novice with regard to Paul's death. I learned that Paul had died as a result of autoerotic asphyxiation (AEA; Blanchard & Hucker, 1991; Garos, 1993–1994; Jenkins, 2000). AEA? I had never heard of it. More on-the-job training was certainly in my future.

I quickly contacted my adviser from my master's degree program to consult with her about AEA. Although my adviser indicated that she did not have expertise on AEA, she referred me to another faculty member who did. To my relief, "Dr. Ames" had a special interest in grief and loss issues, had received training in addressing AEA prevention, and was available to consult with me immediately.

Dr. Ames explained that AEA is a practice intended to heighten the pleasure experienced during masturbation. She indicated that it involves intentionally reducing the blood flow in the neck's carotid arteries by using some type of restriction (e.g., rope, necktie, cord, chain, scarf). Dr. Ames said that this results in the disequilibrium of oxygen and carbon dioxide in the brain and contributes to an enhanced euphoric feeling while the person engages in masturbation. The person's intention is to then use an escape plan to eliminate the restriction of blood flow to the brain and to restore the brain's access to oxygen.

Unfortunately, many things can and do go wrong when AEA is used. Frequently, the escape plan does not work, and the person is not able to disengage the restrictive device. This might occur, for example, if the restrictive device becomes tangled in one's hair, if one uses a chair to create the restriction and accidentally kicks it over, or if one loses consciousness before using the escape plan. When things go wrong during AEA, young, healthy people can suffer a heart attack, metabolic acidosis, or aspiration of vomit. As such, AEA can result in long-term consequences, such as permanent brain damage, rupture of the windpipe, fracture of the larynx, stroke, seizures, and death. In the event of death, it is considered an accidental death, not a suicide. Although this practice involves intentional restriction of blood to the brain, the goal of AEA is not to die but rather to enhance sexual pleasure.

Although the district was located in a rural area, most of the parents in this district were affluent and highly educated. The majority of parents worked in a nearby city and commuted a minimum of 1 hour each day. Even though there was a strong, organized community sports system as well as after-school activities offered by various churches and social organizations, most students had at least 1 day a week when they were not involved in any extracurricular activities. Apparently, the practice of AEA had become rather popular among the older middle school and high school students during their unsupervised time at home.

As news spread about Paul's death and the school staff met to discuss our next steps, I learned that Paul was the third boy to die of AEA in the past 3 years and that seven other boys had also died from hanging but that their deaths had not officially been attributed to AEA. I also learned that the school had not responded in any way to these deaths, allegedly because they did not occur at school.

Paul's mother, Mrs. Keating, was devastated by her son's death, and this pain was exacerbated when she discovered that his death had resulted from AEA, that at least 3 and possibly 10 boys had died from it in the past 3 years, and that the school had never provided any public education about it. "Why didn't you tell me this was going on?" she sobbed. She argued that, had she known that so many children were engaging in such a dangerous practice, she would have talked to her son about it, and perhaps he would not have died. She argued that, because all these boys were students at the same school and because the stakes were so high, the school should have addressed it.

Although the school's principal publicly insisted that the school had no obligation to address AEA because the deaths did not occur at school or involve any school personnel, he privately came to me to consult about the issue. After I had several lengthy conversations with my principal and other school personnel, they agreed that I could ask Dr. Ames to serve in a more formal consultation role. My hope was that Dr. Ames could visit our school, provide an in-service training for school staff, and do a presentation about AEA for the students and parents. I also hoped that she would help me develop a strategic plan to deal with some of the grief reactions evident among the student body. The grief reactions being exhibited by students included a significant increase in fighting on the school grounds, large numbers of absences, and an increase in students seeking appointments with me. During sessions I had with these students, the most common presenting issues were feeling out of control, experiencing disturbed sleep patterns, and feeling apathy.

Dr. Ames did consult with me about ways I could assist grieving students and provided an in-service training to school staff about AEA. To my dismay, though, the district was extremely reluctant to provide education for students about AEA. District personnel expressed fear that this education might increase the behavior rather than eliminate it. Only after lengthy discussions was it decided that Dr. Ames could make a presentation to the student body, and she was instructed that she could only address suicide prevention and could not even mention AEA. Although she was allowed to hold additional meetings in the school building to present information to community leaders and parents, Dr. Ames was unable to address AEA directly with the students.

As a school counselor, I had some significant concerns with this decision. I recognized that there might be many reasons not to address this topic, but I also worried that the shroud of secrecy would allow the practice of AEA to continue and spread. Although I firmly believe my new colleagues were clearly well intentioned and made decisions that they thought would best meet the needs of the students, I also wonder whether their fear of legal responsibilities contributed to their unwillingness to have the school actively work to educate students about the dangers of AEA.

Questions

1. What were the specific issues that needed to be addressed with each of these groups (i.e., students, school personnel, parents, community leaders, churches)?
2. How much information did the students need to know, and who should have provided that information?
3. What are the consultant's ethical, legal, and professional responsibilities to the school when she accepts this assignment? What are her responsibilities to the students and to the school counselor?
4. What other thoughts do you have about this scenario and its ethical, legal, or clinical issues?

■ Response

Constance J. Deuschle

Many school counselors would agree with the counselor presenting this case that 4 years of inner city counseling would provide a solid and rather extensive education in issues faced by school counselors. The occurrence of an incident such as AEA to enhance sexual gratification in young men continues to remain one of the serious risk behaviors that may seduce adolescents (Ueno et al., 2003). The handling of delicate situations such as AEA (Silentvictims.Org, 1996) is not foreign to most school counselors. School counselors are prepared to handle many issues that result in strong emotional responses by students, parents, and school administrators. Because this activity is solitary and secretive in nature, the importance of handling Paul's death with great sensitivity for everyone affected by this loss requires the school counselor to make the best possible decisions in the midst of daily ethical dilemmas and controversial circumstances.

The education of others begins with the school counselor reading about AEA and preparing to answer questions that will be asked about this behavior. AEA syndrome dates back several hundred years, yet it continues to be misunderstood and misinterpreted by many of the people directly involved in the identification, diagnosis, and treatment of this high-risk sexual activity (Rosenblum & Faber, 1979; Ueno et al., 2003). AEA involves the deliberate induction of cerebral hypoxia for the purpose of sexual arousal (Erman, 2005; Hucker & Blanchard, 1992; Ueno et al., 2003). Usually men, both young and more mature, are involved; only a small number of women have been identified as using AEA. Presently, the research has identified a higher incidence of sexual asphyxia in Anglo-Saxon and Germanic populations and a lower incidence in Latinos and non-Caucasians (Ueno et al., 2003). It is necessary to differentiate between AEA and suicidal behaviors to focus on appropriate educational opportunities and interventions. Nevertheless, there may be some overlap in the prevention and treatment of both.

On the basis of studies of deaths from suicide and AEA, there are defining indicators that can provide some answers and, possibly, some relief for grieving family members. A significant responsibility of the school counselor is to provide information substantiated by research. Researchers have identified a number of elements that can differentiate suicidal deaths from AEA (Hucker & Blanchard, 1992; Ueno et al., 2003). According to Ueno et al. (2003), deaths that result from AEA generally have the following elements:

1. an adolescent or young adult man;
2. ropes, belts, or other binding materials that allow for voluntary compression and release of the neck and that may be padded to prevent markings;
3. evidence of masturbation or attire that exposes the genitals;
4. a solitary act;
5. no apparent wish to die or suicide note;
6. may have erotic pictures or literature present;
7. body found in bedroom or bathroom.

Hucker and Blanchard (1992) reported that suicide deaths resulting from asphyxiation might have similarities to AEA, with the following differences:

1. may be an adolescent or young man or a person of any gender or age;
2. means of escape are not planned or implemented;
3. clothing may not expose the penis or genitals;
4. may be a solitary act;
5. a suicide note or evidence of suicidal ideation may be left behind;
6. pornographic or erotic literature may not be present;
7. body is found in home, jail, psychiatric ward or hospital, or nursing home.

Given the history of deaths in this school community directly related to AEA, what are the specific issues that need to be addressed with the student body about the death of Paul Keating, and how and by whom should the information be provided? It is important to review the circumstances surrounding this 13-year-old boy and to identify any factors that might have alerted the school counselor, school staff, or family to Paul's risky behavior or AEA.

Paul was a well-liked eighth grade student. Thus, this case does not suggest that Paul was an isolate in school. The community was described as offering multiple activities for students and families. People were busy with their own lives, and attention to unfamiliar or unpopular adolescent concerns, such as AEA, might have been limited.

With a history of accidental deaths and possibly suicides among young boys in the community, there continued to be a veil of secrecy about the cause of the deaths and reluctance to directly discuss the issues surrounding the tragedies. The directive by the school district that students could only be given information about suicide prevention also challenged the school counselor. The *Ethical Standards for School Counselors* (American School Counselor Association, 2004), which emphasizes that the primary responsibility of the professional counselor is to the client (student), further complicates the delivery of information to the students. All of this information helps determine the actions of the school counselor. Upholding the request of the school district that employs the school counselor and providing the highest standards of best practice to students need not be opposing positions. School counselors are equipped to work in the school environment and with respect for the political constraints that may be requested. Paul's death provides the school counselor with an opportunity to educate the school staff, students, and community about the normal developmental stages and tasks of adolescence and the at-risk behaviors that accompany this difficult transition through autonomy, self-awareness, and personal identity. It is imperative for school counselors to inform students, parents, and the school staff in regard to dangerous adolescent behaviors to help identify and prevent accidental death.

Although she was restricted from speaking directly to students, Dr. Ames, an accepted expert in the area of AEA, could speak to the community about the practice of AEA, the materials used in this practice of sexual hanging, and the reasons why predominately young men participate in the activity (Silentvictim.Org, 1996). Dr. Ames could present material that discussed suicide identification and prevention as well as AEA and other risk behaviors that adolescents may choose. The presence of the school counselor during Dr. Ames's presentation is important. This provides continuity of information and encourages parents to continue to talk with the counselor or to have students talk with the counselor when Dr. Ames is not available. As a consultant, Dr. Ames's contributions are invaluable and offer a bridge between the community and the school. The school counselor remains available for further dialogue with the students, school staff, and community.

Given the lethality of AEA and the history of this practice among the youths of the community, as the school counselor, I would immediately plan for a community night at the school. Representatives from multiple community resources could be invited to present informational sessions throughout the evening, and parents, guardians, clergy, and other community agencies could be encouraged to attend. Police and drug task force personnel and mental health providers could offer workshops and training sessions. Individual speakers or panels could provide sessions on parenting and stress management, adolescent development information, and other identified needs of the school and community.

As a consultant, Dr. Ames could contribute significantly to the understanding of AEA as a presenter at the community night. The consultation process with this case, albeit prescribed and fragile because of different needs and perceptions, could still fulfill the collaborative problem-solving process that is instrumental in consultant practices (Brown, Pryzwansky, & Schulte, 2006). Defining the topic of AEA would be important to determine achievable goals and appropriate intervention strategies.

Before the initial meeting of Dr. Ames and others, those leading the community night must discuss and resolve the question of how to educate the students and entire school community about AEA without betraying the responsibilities of the school counselor to the students and parents, without offending the populations involved, and without causing administrative conflict that could result in serious repercussions for the school counselor. Collaboration among all of the community stakeholders would help promote open and honest discussion with all of the community representatives and encourage continued dialogue with families and their children.

Nevertheless, there are remaining problems that must be addressed: how to deal with the grief and loss issues of the students and school community, the denial of the risky behavior that contributed to Paul's death and the deaths of other students, the legal and ethical implications, and future consequences from enabling the school's refusal to openly discuss AEA and other self-defeating and risky behaviors. School counselors know from the reality of working in a diverse school culture that timing is important and that change takes an insufferable amount of time. Even when life and death issues need to be identified and prevented, the steps taken to work in the current school framework must be judiciously considered. There may be multiple strategies that can be developed to address these concerns; nevertheless, there are professional responsibilities that must be upheld by the school counselor.

Paul was well known throughout the school, and the students need an opportunity to express their thoughts and feelings about his death. I would encourage the school counselor to lead staff and students through the grief process without full disclosure of the details of Paul's death. The school counselor could also discuss grief issues that might emerge, either individually or in small groups. Dr. Ames could be consulted to assist with the development of policies and procedures, including prevention, identification, and interventions for students who are working through grief issues that interfere with learning. Together, Dr. Ames and the school counselor could provide school staff, students, and the community with resources to explain the grief process and to encourage students to seek help in and outside of school. Phone calls may be necessary to speak with families of students who are experiencing a higher level of grief, which could become more serious without further counseling services.

Most crisis plans in schools emphasize the importance of knowing factual information that can be shared with students, and many school counselors are guided by the wishes of the parents about what could be shared and what should be withheld. Paul's mother expressed her feelings regarding the school's withholding of information about AEA and prior deaths that resulted from AEA. The school counselor should meet with Paul's family to determine what could be shared with students within the confines of the school's limitations. Explanations to the family of how school counselors can work with students individually and in small and large groups might be helpful to Paul's family, with the understanding that AEA may not be addressed directly with students. Families and community resources should be informed about prevention and intervention strategies implemented in and beyond the school setting. Paul's family may choose to help in the efforts to educate the community about AEA and to assist in communicating normal developmental challenges faced by adolescents. Churches may be asked to provide current literature about AEA and other high-risk behaviors along with helpful Web sites or local contacts.

Trust issues among adolescents are critical, and once the trust is broken or jeopardized in any way, adolescents are often reluctant to reestablish the trustworthy relationship. Students who choose to share their own practices of AEA or other harmful behaviors with the school counselor may need assistance in accepting the help necessary to keep them safe. The school counselor has the skills and knowledge to normalize many of the developmental concerns expressed by students. Students need to be reminded that during puberty, the primary and secondary sexual characteristics appear and the corresponding hormonal changes are responsible for some of the emotional and social experiences that may cause individuals to experience sexual urges and desires (Berk, 2004). As with other high-risk behaviors, school counselors can work with individuals involved in AEA to teach them about their emotional and sexual desires and ways to control those desires without acting on them. In developmental guidance activities, students should be taught to report peers who may be engaging in AEA, just as they are encouraged to report other at-risk behaviors, such as substance abuse, self-injury, and suicidal ideation.

The school counselor's role is multifaceted in dealing with complicated ethical issues. The decision of the school district to withhold direct discussions with the students regarding AEA cannot be ignored, and the school counselor should not attempt to change the district's perspective by the use of confrontational dialogue. Rather, by listening to the district leaders' fears and perceptions and providing accurate and relevant information, the school counselor may be able to raise their awareness with regard to the need to educate all people about AEA to reduce the pain, confusion, embarrassment, and psychological trauma to all of the families who experience a death from AEA. These attempts to help in the understanding of the normal developmental needs of young people and the physical and emotional changes adolescents experience as they seek to move through developmental stages can help in the understanding of why and how youths become involved in AEA.

This incident highlights the importance of ongoing professional development. School counselors have a responsibility to stay involved in professional development and to participate in ongoing opportunities for learning to expand their professional knowledge. School counselors should be encouraged to be involved in professional networking as a means of remaining informed and prepared for dealing with the critical incidents they face daily. As described in this critical incident response, the school counselor can be a significant resource in the prevention, identification, referral, and treatment of AEA and other high-risk behaviors.

Response

G. Kurt Moore

In response to the school counselor's first question, regarding the specific issues that need to be addressed with each group of stakeholders, I begin by discussing the students. In my opinion, there are two primary issues that need to be addressed with the students: first, their grief reactions, and second, AEA. For both issues, I strongly advocate that counselors normalize, normalize, normalize. With regard to AEA, I also caution that education efforts should not be restricted to boys. AEA has been documented in women (Martz, 2003); teenage girls will certainly hear of it, and many will no doubt try it.

Increased aggression is a normal adolescent response to sorrow. Somatic symptoms, especially stomach trouble, headaches, and lowered immune responses, are also entirely normal, as are sleep disruption, emotional lability, and feelings of anxiety and apathy. These grief reactions are expected responses to the death of a student, regardless of the cause. Sufferers of loss and trauma usually benefit from empathetic education about their symptoms. The knowledge that one's symptoms are a natural response to an unnatural event (Thompson, 2004) better empowers one to manage them.

There is scant evidence to support the idea that ignorance creates safety. Although it is understandable to worry that education about AEA might increase its incidence, the school counselor could argue the point by using the example of STD prevention efforts. By normalizing the facts that most people have sex and that sexual activity can transmit disease, Canada and Western Europe have managed to achieve much lower rates of adolescent STD infection than has the United States. The school counselor could reframe her argument in favor of AEA education: "We teach about the dangers of STDs—why not about the dangers of AEA?" In my experience, middle school students discuss sexual matters constantly. Parents and teachers are usually far too naive about eighth graders' level of knowledge.

Another important group of stakeholders affected by Paul's death is the school personnel. The adults working in the school are probably grief stricken, guilt ridden, and confused. It sounds as though they are indulging in a hearty dose of denial as well. They have the same needs as the students. I hope that the counselor will be able to share adult-level facts about AEA with a minimum of political trouble. School personnel can be extremely effective allies in both grief work and prevention. This may be an opportunity for the counselor to create stronger working relationships with the other adults in the building. When I worked at an excellent alternative high school, one of our mottos was "Every adult in the building is a counselor." This did not mean that everyone tried to do untrained and unsupervised counseling but rather expressed that every adult worked to be a trustable source of help for our students.

I also believe it is essential that, after Paul's death, communication be made with the parents. I would advocate for a districtwide mailing to all parents, from Grade 6 through high school. This mailing should speak directly to the practice of AEA, describing its popularity and dangers. The mailing should provide Web addresses for information sites, such as www.silentvictims.org. This information will arm parents (if they are willing) to discuss AEA with their children. The counselor must be prepared to answer calls from concerned and outraged parents; if the consultant is willing to accept these calls, she can be an additional resource.

The next question posed by the school counselor was in regard to how much information the students need to know and who should have provided that information. The students need to know that any efforts to decrease oxygen supply to the brain can be deadly, whether the goal is to increase sexual pleasure or to achieve a temporary high. They need to know that AEA can cause brain damage, as can the use of inhalants. When AEA is reframed from a dirty little (open) secret to a somewhat dreary health threat, the practice loses some of its erotic power.

Most parents want the opportunity to address these issues with their children. Many parents never get around to it because of embarrassment, ignorance, or apathy. The mailing to parents that I have described could include some suggestions for ways for parents to broach the subject with their children and a list of talking points. Again, if the community normalizes AEA and categorizes it as a health hazard, the practice will lose the power of secrecy.

Because many parents will choose not to discuss AEA with their children, the school has to do the job as well. I view the school district's decision to transform AEA into suicide as distressing, dishonest, and dangerous. A much better approach would have been to initiate small-group interventions about sexual health, possibly as part of physical education, health, or life skills courses. (This assumes, of course, that the school is not in an abstinence-only state; e.g., Texas.) This touches on some large issues about education and sexuality that are best addressed elsewhere. The point, I believe, is that AEA is an act not of suicide but of stimulation and should be treated as such. It occupies the uneasy ground between sex and drugs.

With regard to the consultant's ethical, legal, and professional responsibilities (to the school, students, and school counselor) by accepting this assignment, I believe that the consultant has a primary responsibility to share accurate information with everyone possible. If the school district refuses to allow the consultant to do so, then the consultant has an ethical responsibility to terminate the relationship.

I close by sharing other thoughts I have about this scenario and its ethical, legal, and clinical issues. AEA is not new; it has been a documented practice since at least the time of the Marquis de Sade, who described it in *Justine; Or, the Misfortunes of Virtue* (Sade, 1791/1966). Sigmund Freud (1905/1953) asserted the existence of children's sexuality 100 years ago. Why do we still struggle with this issue? Children are complex creatures with a full complement of sensations and desires. As parents and educators, we have an ethical responsibility to address this reality. Denial and ignorance have not protected children from pregnancy, STDs, suicide, or violence. There is no reason to suppose that denial and ignorance will protect anyone from AEA either.

References

American School Counselor Association. (2004). *Ethical standards for school counselors.* Alexandria, VA: Author.

Berk, L. (2004). *Development through the lifespan* (3rd ed.). Boston: Allyn & Bacon.

Blanchard, R., & Hucker, S. J. (1991). Age, transvestism, bondage, and concurrent paraphilic activities in 117 fatal cases of autoerotic asphyxia. *British Journal of Psychiatry, 159,* 371–377.

Brown, D., Pryzwansky, W., & Schulte, A. (2006). *Psychological consultation and collaboration* (6th ed.). Boston: Allyn & Bacon.

de Sade, D.-A.-F. (1966). *Justine; Or, the misfortunes of virtue* (H. Weaver, Trans.). New York: Putnam. (Original work published 1791)

Erman, S. (2005). Word games: Raising and resolving the shortcomings in accident-insurance doctrine that autoerotic-asphyxiation cases reveal. *Michigan Law Review, 103,* 2172–2208.

Freud, S. (1953). Three essays on the theory of sexuality. In J. Strachey (Ed. and Trans.), *The standard edition of the complete psychological works of Sigmund Freud* (Vol. 7, pp. 135–243). London: Hogarth Press. (Original work published 1905)

Garos, S. (1993–1994). Autoerotic asphyxiation: A challenge to death educators and counselors. *Omega, 28,* 85–99.

Hucker, S., & Blanchard, R. (1992). Death scene characteristics in 118 fatal cases of autoerotic asphyxia compared with suicidal asphyxia. *Behavioral Sciences and the Law, 10,* 509–523.

Jenkins, A. P. (2000, March). *When self-pleasuring becomes self-destruction: Autoerotic asphyxiation.* Paper presented at the meeting of the American Alliance for Health, Physical Education, Recreation and Dance, Orlando, FL.

Martz, D. (2003). Behavioral treatment for a female engaging in autoerotic asphyxiation. *Clinical Case Studies, 2,* 236–242.

Rosenblum, S., & Faber, M. (1979). The adolescent asphyxia syndrome. *American Journal of Child Psychiatry, 18,* 546.

Silentvictim.Org. (1996). *Autoerotic asphyxiation syndrome in adolescent and young adult males.* Retrieved November 17, 2005, from http://www.silentvictims.org/aea.pdf

Thompson, R. A. (2004). *Crisis intervention and crisis management: Strategies that work in schools and communities.* New York: Brunner-Routledge.

Ueno, Y., Migiwa, A., Nushida, H., Nakagawa, K., Adachi, J., & Nagasaki, Y. (2003). Sexual asphyxia by hanging—a case report and a review of the literature. *Legal Medicine, 5,* 175–180.

29

"I'm Too Fat": Body Images in Childhood

This incident demonstrates the complex social, cultural, systemic, and physical concerns present when counselors are assessing and addressing eating disorders in childhood. Respondents to this incident reflect on the effectiveness of Adlerian and family systems interventions.

■ Critical Incident

Jan R. Bartlett

On a chilly January afternoon, I was enjoying the snowy view from my rural school counseling office window as I sat sorting mail on my desk. I remember the unnatural quiet of the school that day; only the principal and I were there. I was the only school counselor for the district's 500 students, and the building was usually noisy, even with my door shut. Around 5 o'clock I looked up to see "Mrs. Jensen" at my door; she had just gotten off work and needed to talk. Her son, "Mark," and daughter, "Angela," had just transferred to our school over the holiday break. Mark Richards was in eighth grade, and Angela Richards was in sixth grade. Mrs. Jensen had recently married, and the family had moved with the children's new stepfather to our state. Their stepfather was disabled, and Mrs. Jensen was a nurse who worked in a local nursing home.

Further background information is pertinent to case conceptualization. The family had moved into an alternative community of several hundred acres that was located in an isolated valley on private property. The landowners maintained their own dirt roads and built structures however it suited them because no codes were enforceable in this rural area. I was aware that several drug arrests had occurred in the vicinity, a fire had recently destroyed one family's home, and several instances of domestic violence had been reported. The land was very affordable, and most of the children from this community qualified for the free and reduced-price lunch program. The Jensen family lived in an older, single-wide mobile home that was on the property they had bought. Angela was sharing a room with her brother until they could purchase a larger mobile home. I never met Mr. Jensen, the children's stepfather, but saw him several times from a distance picking up the children. The children's biological father was never mentioned, and when I inquired about him, Mrs. Jensen said they had no contact with him and wished for none.

Mrs. Jensen was concerned about Angela, who was 11 years old, and was not sure what to do. During the previous year, while the family was still living in the Southwest, Angela had begun to restrict her food intake and to run all the time. Mrs. Jensen said that, since moving, she had become increasingly concerned that Angela was not eating enough to be able to have the energy to run. Angela would run several miles a day if weather permitted, and she ran primarily on the dirt roads in their community, with her mother driving behind her. Sometimes Mrs. Jensen would take Angela to the local football field, where she ran laps. If Angela were unable to run because the family had an appointment or the weather was too cold, she would get very agitated, saying that she "needed" to run. I assured Mrs. Jensen that I would meet with Angela the next day and begin to build a relationship with her. We agreed that I would meet with Angela weekly for a while, and Mrs. Jensen seemed relieved to have support and help for her daughter. Furthermore, Mrs. Jensen said that Angela did not consider herself to have a problem but thought that she was attempting to be healthy and athletic. I knew it would be fairly easy to check in with Angela because she was a new student.

After Mrs. Jensen left my office, I reflected on my first meeting with the family. Mrs. Jensen and her two children had entered my office about 30 minutes before school started on the 1st day after the break, and they brought recent report cards as well as Mrs. Jensen's paperwork to have records sent from their previous school. Mrs. Jensen wanted to make sure that the children were in the appropriate classes. Mark was an average student and not thrilled with school in general, although he liked computers a lot. Angela had been in accelerated classes in her former school and loved school. In fact, when she shared with me about her math class, it was the only time I saw a hint of enthusiasm, a light in her eyes.

My memory of Angela was that she was not thin but appeared to be of normal weight. Her mother said that Angela had never been overweight. Angela was of medium height and had a pale complexion and long, almost platinum blonde hair. In truth, she was very striking and would qualify as beautiful to many people, but her hunched shoulders and quiet persona led me to believe she did not see herself the same way. Later, she told me that she considered herself to be ugly and, indeed, fat. Angela's speech was barely audible, and she rarely made eye contact. Angela did not resemble her mother or brother, given that both of them were dark blonde, and even their facial features were different from Angela's. Not only did mother and son resemble each other physically, they seemed incredibly emotionally connected as well. I remember them joking together and laughing in my office while Angela remained distant, rolling her eyes during this time. Another difference that I noticed was that Mrs. Jensen and her son Mark were extremely obese. I began to wonder whether Angela's refusal to eat and excessive running were tied in any way to the weight of her mother and brother.

With respect to theory, I approached our work from a relational and person-centered model. I believe that, in many cases, the problems of clients or students stem from emotional disconnections and the absence of healthy, sustaining relationships. The challenge of body image issues and eating disorders is that they are complicated, given the societal pressures and messages valuing thinness. Cultural, peer, and media messages stress that thin is beautiful. I have long been of the opinion that perhaps healthy relationships and connections could provide a sense of resiliency and empower people to be comfortable and happy in the unique body that each inhabits. I was not yet convinced that Angela had a problem with food and exercise, although her mother was certain this was the case. At another level, Angela concerned me in her physical posture and manner of communication; she definitely seemed wounded at some level.

In our first meeting, I inquired into Angela's classes and asked how everything was going. Her standard response was, "Fine." Her teachers said that she was an excellent student but that Angela did not participate in activities and tended to stay by herself. I did not bring up the eating and exercise issue until our second meeting. During our second session, I told her that her mother was concerned about Angela's restricted eating and passion for exercise. Angela's response was that she ate enough, although not the quantity that the rest of her family consumed. Angela said only that she was fat, and that was the reason she wanted to exercise and eat small portions. From a psychoeducational standpoint, I mentioned that a child's body needs calories to grow and develop, especially if he or she is exercising regularly. I asked where she got the message that she was fat. Angela said, "I am not blind. I can see in the mirror." Clearly, she saw something different than I did. She hinted at teasing at her previous school but would not go into details. She spoke in broad, sweeping terms, and when I asked for more detail she became short and agitated. I perceived this as a trust issue and understood that I would need to gain her trust before she would open herself emotionally.

Angela would not talk about her family other than saying they got along fine. When asked specifically about her brother, she said that he was gross and annoying, because Mark thought everything was funny, and it was not all funny. Angela clearly did not like her stepfather. When I mentioned him, she sneered and said, "We had to move because of him; he does nothing all day and my mother supports all of us." Angela went on to say, "We live far from everyone. I will never have a friend over to my house; we don't even have a phone." I began to wonder whether the family was hiding; the family was mysterious, and the only phone number listed was Mrs. Jensen's work number. Conversely, Mrs. Jensen seemed very cooperative and concerned about her children; after all, she had sought my help.

After several sessions, I found that humor worked well with Angela. I stayed in the here and now and away from the food and exercise topic. We went outside, and I showed her some of the projects going on in the high school; these included the greenhouse, where flowers were blooming in the winter. As Angela stood looking at an orchid, she said, "I love beautiful things, but we don't have any." She had begun to share her thoughts, and I sensed movement; I hoped that we could reach a place of meaningful dialogue and explore more of her feelings.

Later that month, I spoke with our new secondary math teacher, Mr. Edwards, who wanted to start a track team for the school. I spoke to him about our new student and her passion for distance running. Mr. Edwards put a great deal of emphasis on health and fitness, which included appropriate fuel: lean meats, fruits, grains, and vegetables. Angela and I went to speak with Mr. Edwards, and she seemed very pleased that he might let her train with the other students, who were a bit older. I was concerned that Angela was, in a sense, running away from her deeper issues and thought that working with other students and a coach might help. It seemed like a win–win situation because Angela had never been on any kind of team before and there would be no financial cost to the family. Coach Edwards stressed to Angela that he had rules that had to be followed and that students needed to be physically fit and eat a healthy diet. Several weeks later, Angela's mother said she had been eating better since she began running with the coach and other students. Angela stood a bit straighter, and I noticed that she would look me in the eye on occasion and smile. The thing that continued to trouble me, however, was that she still seemed to want to be invisible. She wore sweats most of the time, and when students gave her a compliment, she could neither hear it nor believe it.

As the months passed, I noticed that the family seemed constantly engaged in one crisis or another—health issues for the mother and the stepfather, finances, vehicle problems, or work issues. Mrs. Jensen always came to me seeking assistance and guidance for resources to help them. Angela's eating behaviors seemed to coincide with the family crises, and at times she would refuse to eat at all. Coach Edwards told her that she could not practice with the team unless she was eating well-balanced meals, and, when challenged with not being able to run with the team, she began to eat better again.

As time went by, our connection grew, and Angela came to trust me more, although she still withheld significant emotion. She would not talk about past events or her family, and she seemed to enjoy being mysterious. I grew frustrated with our sessions because I had come to suspect that she had experienced some trauma or abuse, yet she never shared any facts or stories to indicate this. She preferred to discuss the future: running on the varsity team, going to college, and one day moving away and having her own beautiful house and things. To me, these dreams all indicated a desire for control of her future, and I sensed that control was the main principle behind her eating or not eating. I tried to help Angela create more areas of her life in which she had a voice and an ability to influence outcome. She was already running with the team, and I decided to also put her math skills to work. I helped Angela begin mentoring lower elementary students using creative games she had developed to help with their multiplication and division skills. She was held in esteem by both her teammates and those in the elementary school for her hard work and talent. We worked together for a year and a half, and then I moved on to work full time on my doctorate the following school year. I heard that Angela eventually became a member of the eighth grade track team and continued to excel in school. I always felt there was something important just below the surface that she needed to tell me but would not or could not share.

Questions

1. What other approaches would have been helpful in working with Angela?
2. I felt and thought that Angela was not sharing something important with me. Was this her way of controlling me as well? Maybe the suspected trauma was repressed and she was unaware of it. Alternatively, was I merely imagining things?
3. Angela was not like other students I had with eating and body image issues. Those students wanted to look older, often dressed inappropriately, and engaged in risky behavior to attract attention. Angela wanted to draw no attention to herself and did not seem to want to be considered attractive, yet she clearly did not want to be considered fat but wished to be seen as fit and healthy. Is it plausible that the health issues in her family were driving her fear of being fat more than compliance with cultural and media expectations?

Response

Nicole R. Hill

One issue that emerges when I consider the case of Angela is the importance of engaging in a systems perspective because it places the client in the context in which he or she lives. Such a perspective is especially critical when one is working with adolescents because their decision making and ability to exert influence are dictated on some levels by the adults in their family, school, and community. Given the school counselor's description of the chaos in the family and the apparent correlation between Angela's eating behaviors and the existence of family crises, it is critical that the counselor explores and acknowledges the familial and social influences on the client. The school counselor recognizes how media messages about young girls and attractiveness influence Angela's body image, yet an even more powerful influence seems to be Angela's family of origin. Embracing a systems perspective requires a conceptualization that focuses on the family as the client's first social microcosm and an intervention that mitigates any potential negative impact of the family.

Another approach to working with Angela that integrates a systems perspective and focuses on strengths is Adlerian counseling (Adler, 1959). Angela could benefit from the empowering and encouraging orientation that is present in Adlerian counseling. Additionally, Adlerian counseling highlights the importance of social connectedness. Angela is isolated in her family, in her community, and at school. Her feelings of low self-worth and her seeming desire to be invisible stem from this social isolation. Adlerian counseling highlights the role of encouragement in shifting the disempowering experience of clients to one of success and empowerment. Given the immediate behavioral changes that Angela exhibited when the school counselor facilitated her participation on the track team, I am convinced that Angela had minimal experience with and awareness of her own strengths. Her interaction with positive role models and the encouragement she received in building on her success, namely the distance running, engendered an improvement in her self-worth. Social relationships were also developed in that Angela was "held in esteem" by her teammates and by her coach. Such changes suggest that Angela's introduction to different opportunities for success created the environment necessary for her to grow and to realize her potential.

Adlerian counseling emphasizes that the family constellation functions as the initial social comparison group in which one's lifestyle develops (Adler, 1959). Angela's lifestyle includes her perceptions of herself, her beliefs about her relationships with others, and her view of the world. It is evident that Angela perceives herself as not worthy in that she values being active and fit yet perceives herself to be fat. I also think that Angela is discouraged about her relationships with others. She seems disconnected from her mother, brother, biological father, and stepfather. In the family constellation, her biological father is absent; her mother and brother are very emotionally connected and similar in humor, personality, and physical appearance; and her stepfather is ostracized. This leads me to wonder whether Angela engages in the running and eating behaviors to differentiate herself from those in her family. From an Adlerian perspective, siblings tend to compete with each other and to achieve in areas that are different from each other. Because Mark is funny, extremely obese, and close with the children's mom, Angela works to be successful by being the opposite: reserved, fit, and distant from their mom. She is occupying a different niche in the family, which affords her attention and a specific role.

In the lifestyle of the client, private logic exists that tends to dictate how he or she perceives experiences and makes meaning of life (Adler, 1959). I wonder whether Angela's private logic is "I only belong when I am different" or "I count when I control myself (i.e., eating) and my role in the family." Such cognitive assumptions would contribute to Angela's behaviors of monitoring food intake, engaging in physical activity, resisting eye contact, dressing in baggy clothes, and not engaging peers. From an Adlerian perspective, behavior is purposeful (Adler, 1959), so Angela's behaviors function to create control and to generate attention. These goals of her behavior are even more apparent when one considers the effectiveness of the school counselor's intervention related to the track team. As soon as Angela could pursue the goals of attention and control through joining the track team, she chose to do so, with much success.

Subsequently, a counselor working with Angela could continue to build on the efforts of the school counselor by helping Angela experience attention and control in healthy ways that highlight her strengths. Mentoring younger students and running on the track team are excellent examples of how to shift behaviors that are generating the same outcome: attention and control. A counselor could also intervene with Angela's teachers and family members to find strategies for providing reinforcement in terms of attention and control in response to healthy behaviors. Any counselor working with Angela needs to actively encourage her as she gains insight into herself and as she works to gain attention and control by being successful and by counting, or feeling worthwhile, through her strengths as a person.

For an approach to be successful, a counselor also needs to recognize Angela's developmental level. Angela is in early adolescence, which is paradoxically characterized by a push for autonomy coupled with increased dependency. It has been my experience with clients at this age that there is a strong desire to self-define and to differentiate; in addition, there is a continued dependence on the family for stability and for a definition of who the client is as a person. A developmental perspective recognizes that emotions during early adolescence tend to be overwhelming and expressed in action. I believe that for a counselor to be successful with Angela, it is critical that he or she normalize some of the developmental issues. I would reframe some of Angela's actions as expressions of her emotions. I would provide opportunities for her to express her emotions through expressive arts and by allowing her to make meaning out of her actions. Also, a counselor could reflect the push and pull of individuation–differentiation and belonging–dependency. This developmental perspective fits well with the Adlerian notions of encouragement and empowerment (Adler, 1959).

The school counselor who has been working with Angela wonders whether Angela's focus on the future and her reluctance to express intense emotion mean that she is not sharing something important with the counselor. I believe that Angela's future orientation is a positive aspect that speaks to her resiliency. Her plans for her future suggest a few things: her level of optimism, her belief in her ability to create something different for herself, and her commitment to being successful. From an Adlerian perspective, it is most important to focus on what clients are striving for in their future (Adler, 1959). Angela clearly expresses her strivings and thus places herself in the role of crafting and shaping her own experience. I would highlight this as a strength for Angela. Similar to the school counselor in the case, I believe in the power of individuals to thrive in the presence of healthy relationships. Angela's decisions about how much she discloses and the nature of her sharing are her choices. As a counselor, I would emphasize this choice and focus on it as a source of empowerment rather than as a source of shame and repression.

Overall, I concur with the school counselor in my conceptualization of Angela's fear of fat as being in response to family dynamics as opposed to a clinical eating disorder. To be ethically competent, it is necessary for the counselor to refer Angela to a physician so that a medical evaluation can be conducted. Such information is imperative so the counselor can be certain to rule out anorexia. If the medical evaluation suggested none of the physical correlates of an eating disorder, then I would pursue a counseling approach that involved the family in counseling. In individual counseling I would continue to focus on Angela's strengths, encourage her development of relationships, normalize her experiences, support her efforts to differentiate from her family, and increase her ability to experience attention and power in positive and healthy ways.

■Response

Torey L. Portrie Bethke

My first impression of the counselor's conceptualization of this case is the opportunity for a family counseling approach. Such a family-based approach would highlight how Angela's family may affect her health, development, and personal wellness. A systems perspective that explores family dynamics, including beliefs, values, perceptions, and how these affect the family system could be used to help the family better cope. A systems perspective also acknowledges the greater societal system and how it influences the family. The systems affecting Angela and her family include society as a whole; the community; the school, including Angela's relationships with peers; and the influence of societal media. The American media, which tend to portray natural beauty as flaws and imperfections, influence people across all stages of development. Angela's family system seems to be struggling to find a healthy balance regarding nutritional consumption, exercise, work, and leisure activities. The family experience is further complicated by seemingly ineffective communication patterns. The family's familiar way of living is described as crisis oriented, and Angela's coping strategies are described as restriction of food and an extreme need for exercise.

Angela is considered to be at a vulnerable age, with the potential onset of menstruation and the desire to fit into the media's conception of beauty. Angela's perception of her family's dysfunction and lack of a healthy lifestyle may lead her to rely more heavily on the media's image of health and optimal physical appearance. It is also plausible that desire to meet the media's perception of body image influences Angela's response to crises in her family. Providing family counseling would expand the family's coping skills and might help to reduce the family's pattern of using food as a coping mechanism. Family counseling would also highlight the interrelation of other societal systems, including the school community.

A healthy family system is one willing to try new behaviors that may be more uncomfortable and less familiar and to relinquish behaviors and communication styles that no longer fit. Angela's family members need to engage with the counselor to identify areas in which their communication is impaired and affecting their efficacy. The goal is to help family members feel better about themselves and their ability to communicate with each other. The family seems to work hard to help each other; nevertheless, there seem to be challenges for Angela with her new stepfather. Therefore, engaging the family in a discussion regarding the blending of their family is also an important step. Satir's (e.g., Satir & Baldwin, 1983) experiential counseling assumes all human beings carry with them all the resources they need to flourish and grow as a family and as individuals. Given this assumption, the approach provides the family an opportunity to learn how to use their own resources and cope with situations differently. Satir and Baldwin (1983) encouraged families to live in the moment and be willing to sit with ambiguity to recognize feelings and cope with uncontrolled situations rather than turning events into crises and controlling them through eating or restricting food. Using this as a framework, I would address additional concerns regarding the family system and the school counselor's role.

Satir's (e.g., Satir & Baldwin, 1983) experiential humanistic family counseling philosophy states that mentally healthy families strive for *wholism*—a balance among physical, mental, emotional, and spiritual development that serves to maintain a positive self-image. Implementing Satir's experiential counseling approach requires counselor awareness and knowledge of family systems, including how the school children are affected by environmental conditions in the family, school system, community, and society. Developing a collaborative approach that includes Angela, her family, and the school counselor is integral to providing a supportive system and is considered an ethically mandated function of the school counselor (Bodenhorn, 2005). Involving Angela's mother, brother, and stepfather would increase the family's ability to work through the dynamics that seem to be perpetuating the family crises and Angela's restrictive eating behaviors.

The counselor described Angela's perceptions of her family as dysfunctional; therefore, it is likely that she may seek other stable role models. It is possible that Angela may rely even more than her peers on the media's inappropriate perceptions of health and wellness. Angela articulates her perception of a healthy person as not being fat and being physically fit—the opposite of her family system. Angela may perceive her mother as struggling to support the family, and this may lead Angela to interpret her own role as placating: to please her mother by earning excellent grades, taking up few resources and little space in their small house, and eating small portions. Angela's restriction of food seems to follow family crises that Angela has no control over. Considering her age and lack of resources, Angela may perceive her food intake as the one thing she can control. One might conceptualize Angela's behavior as her desire to give back to the family, providing others with more resources. She may believe that if she eats less, the family will spend less money and the portions she restricts will be available to other family members.

Additionally, Angela may recognize that she lacks the close connection that her brother and mother experience and, as a result, may be experiencing low self-worth and self-esteem. This seems to be evident in her slouching shoulders, rare eye contact, and barely audible speech. Angela's restriction of food and preference for dressing in baggy clothing may also illustrate her desire to be invisible, to disappear. Furthermore, Angela isolates herself from activities with other classmates, seeming to avoid attention and eating less in an effort to be smaller and smaller, to wither away. These behaviors speak loudly to Angela's emotional pain and hurt. They communicate, "I am hurting." Satir and Baldwin's (1983) experiential counseling collaboratively helps the family develop coping skills and handle perceived fearful situations, including limited resources and security. The goal is that future situations will be handled differently and may not be perceived as problems (Satir & Baldwin, 1983).

Angela's system seems to be a closed system in which family members protect themselves by fixed rules, obedience, conformity, and rigidity. The family essentially restricts allowance of the outside world into their system by living far out of town in an isolated community. Angela's communication style, seemingly lacking in openness, is indicative of protective behavior. This strategy is consistent with Angela's restriction of food (i.e., not letting too much into her world).

Not sharing information, as perceived by the counselor, may be conceptualized from Satir's (e.g., Satir & Baldwin, 1983) humanistic perspective as Angela's way of protecting herself and her family. Humanistic philosophy assumes that the family is capable of growth and change, that the family members have in themselves the resources and ability they need to become aware of their problems and to solve them (Satir & Baldwin, 1983). In this context, sharing a secret may not be considered the goal of counseling; nevertheless, the counselor's role of providing a nonjudgmental and safe environment in which the client can grow and replace dysfunctional behaviors with different coping strategies is important from a humanistic view. Angela's reluctance to share information is not necessarily an issue of control but can more appropriately be viewed as a personal choice for protection. I consider Angela's living situation challenging because of the community characteristics and the rooming arrangement with her older brother. An experiential counselor might want to implement metaphors to help break through the protective barrier of silence and to further explore likely hidden issues. Possible metaphors include, "You seem to be running away from deeper issues," and, "Angela, I wonder whether your need to run is your way of running from the emotional pain you feel inside?" These particular metaphors highlight connections among Angela's need to run, her restriction of food as a way to ask for help, and the emotional impact of feeling disconnected from her family and peers. The therapeutic opportunity provided by metaphor use may be to connect events, ideas, personal characteristics, or existential meanings in a way that is perceived as more distant from the actual situation and is thus less threatening for Angela. Highlighting family strengths will increase self-esteem and encourage the maintenance of new coping strategies.

Angela seems to demonstrate several strengths; she is internally motivated to perform well in school, applies her academic skills to help younger children, is self-disciplined (as demonstrated by her commitment to exercise and a healthy diet), and has a mother who seems to be motivated to help her daughter and the other family members. An additional strength is her ability to be considerate and helpful toward others. This characteristic may ultimately empower Angela to help herself develop a healthy balance. Angela stated she wants to maintain a healthy lifestyle; therefore, it is imperative that Angela and her family are provided with professional services from a dietitian to develop an appropriate balance between eating and exercise. A healthy balance may help the family better cope with life stressors and crises instead of coping by restricting food or overeating. Referring the family to a dietitian is also a tertiary prevention strategy to prevent further eating issues in the family.

The counselor described Angela's family as obese, and Angela's desire to be thin may be a result of her dissatisfaction with her family's food struggles. Providing education from a licensed dietitian may help prevent further eating problems for Angela and her family. The counselor stated that Angela is of normal body weight; nonetheless, she seems to hide her body in oversized, baggy clothing. The counselor offers that Angela engages in this behavior to draw no attention to herself, desiring to be invisible. It is my professional position that all clients who struggle with eating and a desire to be invisible need to be formally assessed for an eating disorder. The counselor's perception of Angela may not be accurate enough to determine whether Angela is suffering from an eating disorder. Normal body size and a perception of being fat may be indicative of bulimia nervosa; nonetheless, Angela's desire to be invisible, her restriction of food, and her excessive exercise are more indicative of anorexia nervosa. It is important that the counselor use the *Diagnostic and Statistical Manual of Mental Disorders* (4th ed., text rev.; *DSM–IV–TR*; American Psychiatric Association, 2000) to fully conceptualize the client and holistically view all areas of her health. In addition, all clients who restrict food and nutrition need to be referred for a medical evaluation, regardless of body size. As a licensed counselor, I am not practicing within my professional boundaries when I guess whether a body size is normal or whether a person is healthy when he or she is restricting food. Therefore, further professional consultation with a physician is warranted.

Using the *DSM–IV–TR* in counseling practice is essential for conceptualizing and assessing clients. With regard to Angela, further information is needed to determine the extent of her exercise history and nutritional restriction. If a counselor is not familiar with the diagnostic criteria in the *DSM–IV–TR*, then he or she will not conduct a proper assessment. This proper assessment is needed to ensure the client's safety and overall well-being as well as to inform the necessary preventative measures. Understanding eating disorders and their long-term, devastating effects is an important step to helping clients receive proper referrals, appropriate medical treatment, and positive life-long outcomes. Eating disorders such as anorexia nervosa are reported by the *DSM–IV–TR* to begin in middle to late adolescence (ages 14–18). Given Angela's development, there may be time to intervene and educate her and her family regarding healthy eating, appropriate exercise, and the long-term impact of eating disorders. The ultimate therapeutic goal is that Angela will learn to redirect and reshape her ways of coping with her family and herself to more healthy behaviors (Satir & Baldwin, 1983). One must further consider Angela's fear that she is fat and how this fear exacerbates her desire to be thin. Angela may be experiencing the onset of menstruation, and her attempt to restrict food may be her way of controlling the physical changes her body is experiencing. If an eating disorder is not diagnosable at this time, the counselor's role is to prevent Angela from continuing unhealthy coping skills, including food restriction.

In conclusion, experiential counseling interventions that raise self-esteem, develop congruent communication, and provide useful guides (e.g., a dietitian) will likely be effective in helping the family develop new coping skills. Satir and Baldwin (1983) stated that raising the family's esteem is a process that takes place across many counseling sessions. Five freedoms are recognized in experiential family counseling:

(a) To see and hear what is here, instead of what should be, was, or will be.
(b) To say what one feels and thinks instead of what one should.
(c) To feel what one feels, instead of what one ought.
(d) To ask for what one wants, instead of always waiting for permission.
(e) To take risks in one's own behalf, instead of choosing to be only "secure" and not rocking the boat. (Satir & Baldwin, 1983, p. 169)

Angela and her family seem to have the potential to work together and gain the esteem necessary to improve their lifestyle.

References

Adler, A. (1959). *Understanding human nature.* New York: Premier Books.

American Psychiatric Association. (2000). *Diagnostic and statistical manual of mental disorders* (4th ed., text rev.). Washington, DC: Author.

Bodenhorn, N. (2005). American School Counselor Association ethical code changes relevant to family work. *Family Journal: Counseling and Therapy for Couples and Families, 13*, 316–320.

Satir, V., & Baldwin, M. (1983). *Satir step by step: A guide to creating change in families.* Palo Alto, CA: Science and Behavior Books.

30

Self-Injury: "Cutting the Crazy Out of Me"

This incident explores the unique challenges of counseling with children who self-injure. The chapter focuses on understanding the purposes of self-injury and on assessment and treatment considerations.

Critical Incident

Heather C. Trepal

"Kizzy" was an 11-year-old African-American girl who was an early client in my child and family practicum at a family clinic. She presented at the intake with her foster mother, to whom she lovingly referred as Grandma. During the intake, Grandma explained that the counselor from Kizzy's middle school had called her into the office earlier in the week and revealed that Kizzy had been self-injuring. It seems that some of the other girls in her class noticed the marks and keloid scars on Kizzy's forearms and cornered her in the bathroom until she confessed that she had been cutting herself with razor blades on a weekly basis. Both fascinated and shocked, a few of the girls went to the school counselor, who then talked with Kizzy.

Kizzy was a quiet child and refused to say much to the school counselor except that the girls had pushed and shoved her and called her names. She said that she was scared they were going to beat her up, so she gave up her secret about cutting. Kizzy indicated that she had not told anyone until this point. The school counselor was understandably concerned about the dangers of cutting and recognized the need for therapeutic intervention. She therefore contacted Kizzy's foster parent and strongly suggested that they seek professional counseling services at our clinic.

I sat quietly during the intake and mostly listened to Grandma tell Kizzy's life story. For an 11-year-old, Kizzy had been through some tough times. Her biological mother and father, both drug addicts, had a tumultuous on-and-off relationship, and they had six children between them. Kizzy had been sexually abused by one of her mother's boyfriends when she was 7 and again by a relative around the age of 9. Last year, both of her parents were arrested during a drug bust, and five of the six children were adopted by a family in the northern part of the state. Kizzy, the oldest, was the only one who was not adopted, and the adoptive parents made no secret that they felt she was different from the other siblings. Kizzy bounced around from one foster home to another until she wound up with Grandma, roughly 60 miles from the rest of her siblings, with whom she had monthly visitations.

One of my first imperatives was to assess the self-injury with regard to lethality. Being a novice counselor, I was under the impression that self-injury was necessarily a suicidal gesture, and I treated it as such. I had Kizzy and Grandma sign a no-harm contract and had them identify resources they could put in place should they need them. I was unaware of any way to assess the self-injury, so I just joined with the client and tried to get more information while continuing to assess for risk.

Kizzy said little to me in the intake session, but I noticed that she was observing me with keen interest. Recognizing that Kizzy was not very verbal, I decided to try different ways of getting her to interact during our individual sessions. We played games, played with dolls, listened to music, and drew while I tried to get to know her. Finally, during our fourth session, Kizzy drew a body and aggressively detailed red lines across its arms and chest. She said, "Sometimes it feels like I am cutting the crazy out of me!"

From that point on, Kizzy began to tell me about her cutting. She said that she started to self-injure after the first sexual assault, when she was 7. After a flashback, Kizzy reported feeling like she "just wasn't there," and, in a moment of desperation, she grabbed a pencil and started stabbing her arm with it. The physical sensation of the pencil piercing her skin snapped her back into the present moment, and she was able to disrupt the flashback and temporarily forget the sexual assault. Kizzy reported that, soon thereafter, she began stabbing herself with objects whenever she got upset about the sexual assault or when she did not want to think about the problems in her life, such as her parents, their drug use, and the people who used drugs with them in her presence.

After the second sexual assault, Kizzy reported feeling like there was something wrong with her, making her an easy target, and that people could see this. She progressed to cutting the skin on her upper and lower arms with glass and razor blades whenever she had flashbacks, was under stress, or wanted an emotional escape from her present physical situation. After the recent incident at school, she reported that she had started cutting herself on her upper chest because her arms were starting to show raised scars, thus making them more noticeable. I continued to ask her about suicide, and eventually Kizzy informed me that she was not cutting herself to die but instead to make her want to live.

Soon after our fourth session, I was informed by Grandma that Kizzy was being relocated to another foster home in a different state. Grandma said she found herself unable to handle Kizzy's self-injuring and called her "a crazy child." Grandma expressed a belief that Kizzy needed a foster family who could provide more intense supervision. I sometimes wonder what happened to Kizzy and about her use of self-injury.

Questions

1. What purposes are served by self-injurious behaviors, such as cutting?
2. What are important things to consider with regard to the assessment of self-injurious behavior?
3. Are there evidence-based treatment strategies that can be used with clients who present with self-injury?
4. What are some diagnostic considerations?

■ Response

Elizabeth E. Shanahan and Emily Phillips

Kizzy's story is similar to several case studies in the professional literature on the topic of adolescent self-mutilation. Several studies indicate that there is a common trend among self-injuring adolescent girls who want a deep emotional pain to go away; to get rid of those negative feelings, the girls use different techniques to self-injure (e.g., cutting their wrists until blood rushes out; Clarke, 1999; Conterio, Lader, & Bloom, 1998; Holmes, 2000; Shandler, 1999; Strong, 1998). Throughout each of their respective books, all of these authors presented descriptive case studies surrounding the issue of adolescent self-injury. Many students who self-injure feel as though their life is out of control because of negative current or past events. One way to feel or regain control is to physically self-mutilate and cut one's skin. The majority of young people who self-injure are not attempting to end their life; they are instead trying to feel alive or to control overwhelming feelings of stress. For most individuals who self-injure, especially for adolescents, self-mutilation is not considered a way to commit suicide but is an effort to take control of their body (Clarke, 1999).

When someone self-injures, the rush of blood is a symbolic sign that the internal turmoil is being released. This has the potential to create a calming effect and help to alleviate the adolescent's emotional pain. Zila and Kiselica (2001) described that individuals who self-mutilate often feel "a sense of relief" (p. 47) after the self-injury has taken place; Pipher (1994) referred to it as a "cathartic" (p. 158) experience. If a person feels better about a problem after cutting his or her wrist to the point of bleeding, the act of cutting becomes self-reinforcing and is therefore difficult to stop repeating.

Although most self-mutilators do not want others to know they are self-injuring and hide their scars by wearing long-sleeved shirts and pants, some adolescents might be trying to communicate through the violence they are inflicting on their skin. McLane (1996) described that "when trauma cannot be expressed, other forms of communication become necessary" (p. 107). Trauma might be anything from physical or sexual abuse to the breakup of a relationship. It seems as though the important message is that adolescents who are self-mutilating might be trying to communicate messages to the outside world through their self-injuring.

There are also students who see self-injuring as a popular way to gain attention from peers. For example, while speaking at an adolescent self-mutilation workshop in a school setting with seventh and eighth grade students, Elizabeth E. Shanahan was told by several students that some girls self-injure to get attention from boys who have ended dating relationships. The girls in these situations apparently believed that if they harmed themselves and made the injuries noticeable to other students, the boys would want or feel obligated to date them again. These students also suggested that we view the movie *Thirteen* (Hardwicke, Levy-Hinte, London, & Reed, 2003) and indicated that this movie deals with several adolescent issues, including self-injuring. This movie is particularly useful for learning about self-injury through popular films.

One of the most important things to consider when assessing self-injury is to determine whether it is self-mutilation or a suicide attempt. Students, like Kizzy, may actually disclose to school counselors that their intent in cutting their skin is not to commit suicide but to actually feel something, such as the pain that comes with self-injuring. There are also differences between how girls and boys use self-mutilation. Brumberg (1997) commented, "The body is a consuming project for contemporary girls because it provides an important means of self-definition, a way to visibly announce who you are to the world" (p. 97). This statement seems to show the importance adolescent girls place on their body and the way they are viewed by the rest of the world. Self-mutilation of the body might be one of the only ways to show the outside world the pain one is feeling on the inside. According to Ng (1998), men more typically show anger outwardly, whereas women turn negative emotions inward. Therefore, it could be possible that men engage in more outward forms of self-mutilation, such as hitting or throwing themselves into walls, whereas women may tend to a more inwardly focused behavior, such as cutting their body.

A national treatment program designed to help individuals who self-mutilate, S.A.F.E. Alternatives (the abbreviation stands for "Self-Abuse Finally Ends"), provides information and resources for help with self-injury. Counselors who are interested in learning more about this nationally recognized self-injury treatment program may wish to visit the Web site at http://www.selfinjury.com. On request, this organization will also send a helpful informational packet. An activity book has recently been published for counselors who work with adolescents who self-mutilate. This book provides information about different ways of interacting with individuals who self-injure (Bowman & Randall, 2004).

Because of their frequent contact with adolescents, school counselors have a unique opportunity to identify self-injuring students and to help them find more positive ways to cope with internal problems. Awareness of adolescent self-mutilation is only the beginning for counselors confronted with adolescents who self-injure. In the school setting, school counselors can also respond to the self-mutilation phenomenon proactively by incorporating current resources about this issue into existing comprehensive counseling programs. Adolescents may find it difficult to admit to engaging in self-mutilation or to talk about it in general, so it may be especially helpful to provide psychoeducation about self-injury in the context of classroom guidance lessons. It is essential for all adolescents to know to whom they can speak about their problems.

Once self-mutilating students are able to communicate about their practice of self-mutilation, they may find they are better able to cope with problems without self-injuring. Because these children need to know they are not alone and that other individuals also self-injure, group counseling activities might work best for adolescent students who have already been involved with individual counseling and who seem to require the support of fellow peers who are experiencing similar issues with self-mutilation.

Response

Ann Vernon

Although self-injury is not a new phenomenon, it is becoming increasingly common among adolescents. In this response, I address the purposes of self-injury as well as assessment and treatment considerations for counselors working with clients who self-injure. Before I do so, it is prudent to briefly address what self-injury is and is not.

Although it is often assumed to be a suicidal gesture, self-injury is not synonymous with suicide. According to Zila and Kiselica (2001), self-mutilators do not intend to destroy themselves. Rather, they are using physical pain to mask or cope with emotional pain. Self-injury also should not to be confused with self-mutilations such as tattoos or body piercings, which are more of a fashion statement, given that the intent of these latter activities is not to inflict pain in an attempt to deal with pain. According to my clients who engage in various forms of self-injury, activities such as cutting get the pain from the inside to the outside. Self-injury provides temporary relief from sadness, anger, loneliness, hopelessness, and depression. Self-injury is an addictive, compulsive behavior in that the calm people experience after the self-mutilation is self-soothing, so it is difficult to discontinue.

Purposes of Self-Injury

Self-injury typically begins during adolescence and is more prevalent in young girls (Nock & Prinstein, 2004). As in Kizzy's case, self-injurers often have a history of abuse. Self-injurers engage in this self-destructive behavior when overcome with intense feelings, such as guilt, shame, anger, hurt, or rejection as they recall painful events from the past. In abuse cases in which the survivor does not tell others about the abuse, he or she eventually experiences such tension that he or she has to do something to relieve it. Self-mutilation also serves this purpose; it helps abuse survivors feel more empowered and in control. As paradoxical as it may seem, inflicting more pain results in relief; clients report feeling more relaxed after they hurt themselves.

In addition to her history of abuse, Kizzy has had to deal with rejection from her parents, her foster families, and her classmates, which has no doubt had a negative impact on her self-esteem. Having been rejected, Kizzy probably assumes that no one is there for her; as she sees it, she has to cope with her problems by herself. As an 11-year-old who is still probably in the concrete thinking stage with regard to cognitive development, she is not very good at generating constructive solutions to problems, particularly when hers seem so overwhelming. Not having been used to asking for or receiving much support, Kizzy resorts to self-injury.

Diagnostic and Assessment Considerations

Self-injury is difficult to assess because self-injurers generally do not want to call attention to themselves; they usually perform their rituals in private and cover their scars because they are humiliated. In Kizzy's case, other classmates discovered her scars and reported them to the school counselor, who, in turn, referred her to a therapist. Mental health professionals, of course, cannot rely on peers to report a client's self-injurious behaviors and must therefore engage in additional assessment strategies. Self-mutilation is generally comorbid with other disorders: eating disorders, depression, anxiety, posttraumatic stress, and borderline personality disorder (Conterio et al., 1998). As such, it is important to incorporate assessment for self-injury whenever one is treating clients with these disorders.

For example, when adolescents are depressed or withdrawn, professionals as well as parents need to consider the possibility of self-mutilation. In my experience, clients are seldom referred because of self-injurious behavior because others are not generally aware of it. They are typically referred (or self-referred) for depression, so when this is the case, counselors should always inquire in a routine assessment of the frequency, intensity, and duration of the depression whether clients are suicidal or have ever hurt themselves. My experience is that they typically do not deny this because, at some level, they want others to know. Although they are not good at asking for or receiving help, they do want someone to help them deal with their pain.

A counselor should also consider the possibility of self-injury when a client has a history of abuse. Alienation can also lead to self-injury. I think it is significant that Kizzy reported being pushed, shoved, and called names by other girls. Given that she is a young adolescent, peer relationships are of utmost importance. If she is being bullied and rejected, self-injury may seem to her to be her best way of coping.

Treatment Strategies

Because self-mutilators have relied on themselves and their own methods of coping, it is imperative that counselors create a supportive environment for the clients to share their negative emotions. This is also important because as in Kizzy's case, these clients often feel like no one is there to listen to them. It is also helpful for the counselor to matter of factly ask clients to show the scars. As counterintuitive as it may seem, it is important to avoid pathologizing the self-injurious behavior because this risks increasing the client's shame. In my clinical experience, clients seem relieved that someone is paying attention to the hurt that is manifested in this self-destruction. This sense of relief and sincere attention helps the client gain control over the impulse to engage in self-injury.

Family counseling is highly recommended because communication and attachment issues are generally present with self-mutilators. Educating parents about self-mutilation is important to help them learn to see it as a way children express pain rather than as bizarre behavior. Teaching all family members how to communicate openly, respectfully, and assertively is imperative.

Because there is so much pent-up emotion associated with self-mutilation, journaling can be an excellent form of catharsis. Having clients write letters to persons who have hurt them (not necessarily sending them) can be beneficial as well. I do not use behavioral techniques, such as snapping a rubber band, as a reminder not to self-mutilate because this in itself is a form of mutilation, but I have used other behavior modification techniques. For example, I have asked clients to make a list of pleasurable activities and to reward themselves with one of these activities when they were able to substitute a more self-enhancing way of reducing pain and tension for the self-destructive approach.

I have found success with several cognitive-behavioral strategies. I ask clients to draw a picture of their head with thought bubbles. In each bubble, they identify thoughts that they have that trigger their need to self-mutilate. I then help them identify irrational thinking and cognitive distortions that lead them to their self-destructive behavior and help them modify the thinking so they can, in turn, change the behavior. Another way of doing this is to have them draw around their hand and, on each finger, identify their self-destructive thoughts (Vernon, 2004). In between the fingers, they are to identify something they could think to themselves to avoid engaging in the self-destructive behavior. I have also had clients keep a "toolbox"; they make a list of things they could do to substitute for the self-injurious behavior, such as go for a walk, draw, journal, talk to someone, or listen to soothing music. Then they put things inside their toolbox to represent these alternative behaviors—a CD, drawing paper and markers, phone numbers of people they can rely on, or a city map with walking trails identified. This concrete strategy is helpful because when the tension builds up, clients are unable to think constructively about what to do and instead rely on their impulses and what is familiar. The toolbox full of constructive suggestions makes it easier to substitute a less self-destructive approach.

Conterio et al. (1998) developed the successful S.A.F.E. Alternatives Program (see www.selfinjury.com). This program relies extensively on writing assignments to help clients deal with their conflicted feelings and to keep an impulse control log in which they record their urges to self-injure and what triggered the urges. The program also helps clients look at the underlying dynamics of their behavior and what compels them to do this. It helps clients move beyond the simplistic connection that they were rejected or abused and to look at clues as to why people behaved as they did. The goal is to empower clients so they no longer feel helpless and victimized. In this program, counselors do not view the behavior as crazy; rather, they acknowledge that self-injury served the clients well during difficult times and work to teach the clients that there are other, more self-enhancing approaches to managing their problems.

Ultimately, the treatment approach should be tailored to the client's developmental level and should address the specific presenting issues. In Kizzy's case, dealing with the trauma of abuse and dysfunctional family issues would be a major focus, and the counselor could eventually move into the cognitive-behavioral strategies to help Kizzy identify more appropriate ways to deal with her feelings. Overcoming self-injury is difficult but possible. The earlier it is detected, the better.

References

Bowman, S., & Randall, K. (2004). *See my pain! Creative strategies and activities for helping young people who self-injure.* Chapin, SC: Youth Light, Inc.

Brumberg, J. J. (1997). *The body project: An intimate history of American girls.* New York: Random House.

Clarke, A. (1999). *Self-mutilation: A helping book for teens who hurt themselves.* New York: Rosen Publishing.

Conterio, K., Lader, W., & Bloom, J. K. (1998). *Bodily harm: The breakthrough healing program for self-injurers.* New York: Hyperion.

Hardwicke, C. (Writer/Director), Levy-Hinte, J. (Producer), London, M. (Producer), & Reed, N. (Writer). (2003). *Thirteen* [Motion picture]. United States: Fox Searchlight Pictures.

Holmes, A. (2000). *Cutting the pain away: Understanding self-mutilation.* Philadelphia: Chelsea House Publishers.

McLane, J. (1996). The voice on the skin: Self-mutilation and Merleau-Ponty's theory of language. *Hypatia, 11*(4), 107–118.

Ng, G. (1998). *Everything you need to know about self-mutilation: A helping book for teens who hurt themselves.* New York: Rosen Publishing.

Nock, M. K., & Prinstein, M. J. (2004). A functional approach to the assessment of self-mutilative behavior. *Journal of Consulting and Clinical Psychology, 72,* 885–890.

Pipher, M. (1994). *Reviving Ophelia: Saving the selves of adolescent girls.* New York: Grosset/Putnam.

Shandler, S. (1999). *Ophelia speaks.* New York: Harper Perennial.

Strong, M. (1998). *A bright red scream: Self-mutilation and the language of pain.* New York: Penguin.

Vernon, A. (2004). *What works when with children and adolescents.* Champaign, IL: Research Press.

Zila, L. M., & Kiselica, M. S. (2001). Understanding and counseling self-mutilation in female adolescents and young adults. *Journal of Counseling & Development, 79,* 46–52.

31

"Are You Saying Corey Is an Addict?": Childhood Substance Abuse

This incident explores the complexities of identifying substance use, abuse, and dependency in preteenage children and distinguishing them from other disorders. This incident examines possible diagnostic comorbidity and collaborative, multifaceted treatment options.

Critical Incident

Christina Rosen Galvin

"Corey Kramer" was a 12-year-old Caucasian boy in the sixth grade when he was referred to me for counseling. He was the second oldest of four children. Corey's older sister, Tracy, was 14 years old, and his younger siblings, Susan and John, were 10 and 8 years old, respectively. His parents were Mary (32 years old) and George (35 years old), both of whom worked blue-collar jobs. Corey was referred to our community mental health agency by his school principal and school counselor. As part of the referral process, I learned that the school was not sure what was going on with Corey. During the last year, teachers and staff had noticed his behavior and attitudes changing and, in the past several months, becoming markedly different. Corey continued to maintain good grades, but he seldom finished his homework on time. When changing classes, he was now rarely on time for the next class and would explain only by saying that he lost track of time. He had been seen talking with kids from the high school before and after school. He was disciplined for this and reminded that he was breaking the rules by meeting with high school kids. The high school students were also disciplined. Although there was no evidence that drugs were being sold or received, school administrators were concerned about the possibility.

Corey was also late for school at least two or three times per week. Some days he seemed melancholic, and other days he seemed overenergized. Similarly, some days his attitude was positive, and other days his attitude was extremely negative, especially toward authority figures. Corey had a tendency to overreact whenever he was corrected by someone in authority. Although he had not cursed at anyone, he had walked away from teachers when being reprimanded and had demonstrated an "I don't care" attitude. Corey continued to participate in class, but his teachers stated that he was unpredictable. Some days, he did not create any problems but instead just seemed very mellow and joked around. However, if the teacher attempted to correct him or called on him to answer questions, he might withdraw or become irate. On other days, he would fall asleep in class. Conversely, he could be very hyper and easy to anger. Corey had received detentions and had been suspended twice because of his behavior, but he had not been expelled until recently.

Prior to the expulsion, the school counselor met with Corey at least six times in an attempt to discover what the problem might be. Out of their six sessions together, Corey nearly fell asleep in two sessions; became so enraged that he began yelling and slammed the door in another two sessions; and was bouncing off the wall, joking, and being very jovial in the other two sessions. At Corey's last session with the school counselor, his eyes were glassy, his breath had an odor, and he cursed and verbally threatened the counselor. One other time, he attended a session with glassy eyes and an odor. It was hard to distinguish the odor, however, because he was chewing gum and had just finished a bag of Doritos. The school counselor suspected that he was using marijuana, alcohol, and possibly "skittles" (the street name for Dextromethorphan, an over-the-counter cough suppressant chemically related to codeine and used as a recreational drug) but did not have any proof. Nonetheless, the school counselor also wondered whether Corey could have another mental health diagnosis.

Because of Corey's seeming lack of progress with his school counselor and his continued troublesome behavior, the principal in the school called an expulsion hearing for Corey and his parents. To avoid Corey's expulsion, Mr. and Mrs. Kramer consented to a mental health and substance abuse evaluation and agreed to follow all treatment recommendations. It was at this point that the school referred Corey to the community mental health agency where I work because our specialty is chemical dependency and dual diagnosis.

During the initial intake with Corey and his family, I asked about his behavior and attitude at home. Mary and George expressed a sense that Corey was "just struggling with becoming a teenager." They said that it was often difficult to awaken Corey for school and talked about his unpredictability, complaining that he was more hostile toward his siblings on some days, that other days he was "bouncing off the walls," and that there were times when he just slept all day. Mr. and Mrs. Kramer reported that there seemed to be no pattern to his moods and behaviors and complained that Corey never did his chores. They indicated that discipline no longer work and stated, "We have removed everything from his room—TV, play station, and his boom box. He has started hitting his older sister even though he knows this is against the rules of the house. We never know what mood he will be in! One minute he has the 'I don't care' attitude and the next minute he is happy. Then suddenly, for no reason, he is angry. We can't wait until his hormones settle in!" When grounded, Corey would not come home as instructed, nor would he stop watching TV with the family and go to his room. Mr. and Mrs. Kramer said that their attempts to discipline him often ended up in an argument, with Corey typically storming out of the house and not returning for hours.

I asked about Corey's friends, and his parents said, "Nothing has changed." His older sister, Tracy, commented sarcastically, "That's because you don't know about *all* his friends." Corey then shot her a dirty look and barked, "You don't know what you're talking about! What other friends?" His sister became very quiet. I encouraged her to tell me what she knew and explained that it could help me in counseling the family. She began to cry and said, "He is hanging out with some older kids from high school. They are meeting him at school and then he leaves with them. Sometimes they pick him up during school or after school." Corey began to yell, "You are stupid and crazy!" and proceeded to curse at everyone. I managed to calm Corey by stating, "I hear that you are angry at your sister. Do you want to tell me what is going on?" He angrily insisted, "I don't know what the big deal is or why she is telling these stories."

I then asked Corey, "Given that you don't work, how are you getting money to hang out with these friends?" He responded, "I get an allowance." Then, all of Corey's siblings exclaimed, "You take our allowance, too!" His parents looked surprised. Mrs. Kramer then said, "Corey, I've also been giving you extra money for after-school activities. What exactly are your after-school activities?" Corey's anger flared again. I asked, "Corey, have you been using drugs and alcohol?" He responded with an emphatic, "No!" Tracy started crying and stated, "I saw you smoking something and drinking with your new friends. I saw you take some pills, too!" Corey started yelling again and stated, "I only drank once, and I was smoking a cigarette, not pot. And it was candy, not pills! Do you think I'm a druggy or something?" His mom starting crying and confessed, "Six months ago when I was doing laundry, I found colored pills and a baggy that had something in it. Corey, you told me the baggy and the pills belonged to your friends. You lied to me!" George then put his hands in his face and, while shaking his head, stated, "This past summer I confronted you, Corey. You told me that you were only trying it and you would never use pot. You said that you would not drink again until you were an adult. You lied!" George continued, "Mary, I am so sorry. Last summer I caught Corey drinking beer and one day, when I came home early, his room smelled like pot. I didn't say anything to you because I thought Corey and I had an agreement. He assured me that he would not drink anymore and that he wasn't smoking weed." Mary looked at George and said, "I didn't tell you about the drugs I found in the laundry because I didn't want you to get mad. How could we let this happen?" Both parents looked at me and lamented, "We don't know who Corey is anymore. This is not like him. He never lied before, and we never had trouble with him. He was such a good kid, and we were so close."

When I subsequently conducted a complete substance abuse evaluation with Corey, I diagnosed him with alcohol abuse, marijuana abuse, and amphetamine abuse. He was close to dependency, but there were no signs of physiological dependence. Corey attended counseling twice a week for 12 weeks. The first 6 weeks involved an educational group, a combination of individual and family counseling, and random urinalyses. Individual counseling occurred with the school counselor, and I conducted the family counseling and substance abuse education. In individual counseling, Corey's goals included appropriate expression of feelings, development of coping skills and constructive activities, and separation from his high school friends. In family counseling, we worked on codependency and enabling dynamics, sobriety, communication skills, discipline, and boundary setting. Corey's urinalyses were dirty for the first 3 weeks, and then they were clean thereafter. His behavior at school improved, but he was still moody at home.

During the last 6 weeks, individual counseling ended because school was out for the summer. Corey then participated in relapse prevention group counseling and continued in family counseling, both conducted by me. All counseling interventions ended after the 12 weeks because his family did not have insurance and could no longer afford the sliding fee scale. During the summer months, his parents agreed to periodic urinalyses for Corey. Corey also obtained a volunteer position for the summer months to keep him busy for 3 days a week while his parents were working. Nevertheless, I was worried that Corey would return to using once he was back in school. Corey did not return for counseling while I worked at the agency. About 1 year after working with Corey and his family, I left the agency. I have the following questions about this scenario.

Questions

1. What methods of treatment have been found to be most effective with young substance-abusing or -dependent clients?
2. What additional counseling resources might exist for families with limited income?
3. I hypothesized that Corey's unpredictable behavior and extreme mood swings were the result of his drug and alcohol abuse. On the basis of current research, though, some counselors might suggest that Corey actually had bipolar disorder. Is it possible that I missed this diagnosis? How could I have ruled it out?

◼ Response

John Sommers-Flanagan

Before responding to the three specific questions posed at the conclusion of this incident, I want to make several comments about my personal reaction to this case and this approach to treatment. My first reaction is that Corey was lucky to have this therapist; he was also fortunate to have been enrolled in a school district that acted relatively quickly and decisively when his behavior began to deteriorate. Also, after a brief initial period of denial, it was very beneficial that Corey's family members, in particular his parents, were able to reflect on and acknowledge clear signs of substance abuse as well as mistakes they made in failing to confront the situation earlier. Overall, my sense is that many people in Corey's life quickly began to address his problems and to set important limits on his misbehavior, both of which are critical for a successful substance abuse intervention. Without the concrete assistance and limit setting from his school, family, and counselor, Corey undoubtedly would have continued on a negative trajectory and deteriorated into a worse physical, emotional, and mental condition on entering treatment.

Corey presented with a wide range of complex and fluctuating symptoms. This puzzling diagnostic picture among youths referred for counseling is common. The tendency for young clients to present with a smorgasbord of symptoms can be found across diagnoses (e.g., substance abuse, attention-deficit/hyperactivity disorder, oppositional defiant disorder, conduct disorder, eating disorders, learning disorders). Because of the tendency toward multisymptom pictures in children and adolescents who come to counseling, I am not at all surprised that his counselor had concerns about Corey's definitive diagnosis. Although I offer my thoughts about this issue later, for now I want to emphasize that accurate psychiatric diagnosis with 12-year-olds is extremely difficult. Consequently, I recommend beginning treatment by offering the least pathological diagnosis possible (Sommers-Flanagan & Sommers-Flanagan, 2003).

The treatment provided to Corey was highly commendable for many reasons, but one particular aspect of the treatment stands out to me. His treatment included effective school and mental health agency communication and collaboration. This general model of service delivery represents state-of-the-art mental health services. Although many contemporary school counselors do not see themselves as providing mental health services, in this case, with the appropriate support of a mental health agency and a competent professional counselor, the school counselor functioned as a crucial part of the mental health treatment team. Although there are no empirical data to support this claim, I am confident that the kind of treatment described, which allows no chance for Corey to fall through the cracks between the school and the mental health agency, is the most effective general treatment model possible.

Effective Methods of Treatment

Several professional groups have published formal lists of empirically supported psychotherapies. These lists do not include any specific treatments for 12-year-old boys who carry a polysubstance abuse diagnosis. Therefore, my initial response to the first question is to emphasize that effective treatments for this population are defined more by a rational analysis of existing research and practice than by any clear-cut, research-mandated guidelines. Nevertheless, there is a substantial body of research and practice relevant to counseling polysubstance abusing youths. This research includes (a) a limited number of treatment studies with youths who are abusing substances, (b) outcome studies with adults who are abusing substances, (c) articles and books that make recommendations for working with difficult youths on the basis of clinical experience rather than empirical research, and (d) research reviews focusing on empirically supported relationship factors. Overall, on the basis of this information, there is a general consensus regarding what kinds of treatment approaches are most likely to be effective. This consensus includes the following principles or guidelines.

Family therapy. Family therapy is strongly recommended, especially if the parents, like Corey's, are cooperative and bring positive resources to counseling. In particular, there is positive research support for functional family therapy (Sexton & Alexander, 1999) and multisystemic family therapy (Swenson, Henggeler, Taylor, & Addison, 2004). These two research-based approaches require fairly extensive and specific training and therefore may not be a practical choice for many professional counselors. (This is one reason narrow research-based or manualized treatments are often impractical in real-life situations, but I will avoid my typical rant about the lack of external validity of tightly controlled research studies.)

In the absence of specific training in one of these research-based approaches, family therapy is appropriate as long as the counselor has substantial family therapy training. Extensive training is needed because, as reported in this case summary, family dynamics and interactions in these cases are complex and intense, and they emerge quickly and sometimes explosively. Obviously, it would be a bad idea (both for the counselor and for the family) to put a novice therapist in charge of family therapy with a boy like Corey. One very important issue to address in both individual and family therapy with Corey is his use of negative affect and intimidation to manipulate family members. I like to point out to challenging youths and their parents that the family needs to have a respect rule, which translates into the following family policy: "Whenever someone is yelling, acting obnoxious, or being disrespectful, the consequence is that that person always gets less freedom." To enforce this family policy, sometimes parents need to be coached on how and when to contact law enforcement for support of their family rules.

Psychoeducation. On the basis of both intervention and prevention research, I strongly recommend that Corey's treatment include a psychoeducational component. The educational component may be delivered individually to Corey, separately to Corey's parents, or in the context of family therapy. In particular, because there is substantial research regarding risk factors leading toward juvenile delinquency, Corey's parents should be trained in specific skills for providing adequate parental supervision, close monitoring of social behavior, positive reinforcement for prosocial behavior, and limit setting (Reid, Patterson, & Snyder, 2002). I also recommend additional education about typical substance abuse warning signs.

In my private work with difficult preadolescents and adolescents, I have found that it is especially important to help parents reduce their reactivity to their child's misbehavior by framing their child's negative behaviors in positive or neutral ways. For example, when parents react to their child's lying behavior, I generally coach them in using a process of "getting curious, not furious." This process helps parents to step away from their emotional reactions. Furthermore, I often explain to parents (even in front of their child) that many of the most difficult youths with whom I have worked love it when their parents get so upset with them that the veins in the parents' neck begin bulging and pulsating. My point is to help parents understand in a somewhat humorous way that using boring consequences in combination with exciting reinforcement is much more effective than exciting (angry) consequences in combination with boring reinforcement.

It is also crucial for Corey's parents to understand more about the reasons why he has lied. Therefore, in family therapy I would likely provide the following explanation: "I hear that you both, Mary and George, are very angry about the fact that Corey has been lying to you. I don't blame you . . . I would be angry too. But, if we can step back for a moment, I want to offer up some reasons why Corey has been lying. First, he's obviously lying because he wants to keep getting away with his drug use and he knows you love him too much to let him get away with it if he's truthful. Second, he's also lying because somewhere inside he's feeling pretty ashamed about what he's been doing. And that's probably why he's so defensive right now too. Think about it; it's really hard to admit that you're doing something shameful, illegal, and embarrassing. Third, Corey is also lying because he is becoming psychologically addicted to these dangerous substances. When this happens, it's not unusual for people—even boys Corey's age—to betray the trust of their parents and to use and abuse their siblings. Even when Corey is not drinking or smoking or using, he is still somewhat under the influence of the drugs." Note that I use this sort of direct educational intervention only if there is substantial assessment information affirming the existence of substance abuse and that I recommend the word *addiction* for use even if the client does not meet the *Diagnostic and Statistical Manual of Mental Disorders* (4th ed., text rev.; American Psychiatric Association, 2000) diagnostic criteria for substance dependence.

Individual counseling. Individual counseling is always strongly recommended for youths who are abusing substances. This is primarily because of the powerful emotional effects of substances. Most youths need specific help dealing with the strong emotions that rise to the surface when they are abstaining from drugs and alcohol. Additionally, they need help finding enjoyable alternative social and personal activities. Finally, individual counseling focuses on cognitive components, such as the thinking errors associated with the temptation of drug and alcohol use and with relapse prevention strategies. Overall, rather than using a confrontational approach with individual youths, I believe a user-friendly approach, such as motivational interviewing, is much more effective—and youths are then more likely to want to return for counseling (Miller & Rollnick, 2002; Sommers-Flanagan & Sommers-Flanagan, 2007.

Group counseling. Group counseling is an important part of substance abuse treatment. It offers social support for abstinence, and if the group is in a positive working stage, the group members are able to confront each other in important and productive ways.

Additional Counseling Resources for Limited-Income Families

With regard to this particular question, I am afraid I do not have much to offer. Because finding counseling resources for limited-income families tends to be a very localized phenomenon, my main recommendation is for counselors in this situation to systematically explore the availability of local resources. There are often individual counselors or clinics that provide counseling services to limited-income families on a low- or no-fee basis. In addition to school counseling services and state-facilitated local insurance programs for un- or underinsured children (e.g., Blue Chip), I am often surprised to find that parents are unaware that they may qualify for some of the following resources:

- Medicaid,
- employee assistance programs, and
- community-based parent education or consultation services.

Ruling Out Bipolar Disorder

For this last question, I have decided to be completely straightforward, despite the fact that I may offend some readers. The counselor notes, "On the basis of current research . . . some counselors might suggest that Corey actually had bipolar disorder." On the basis of the information provided, however, those counselors would simply be wrong. I believe the current pandemic of juvenile bipolar disorder in this country is completely unwarranted. This is especially true in cases like Corey's, in which a youth is actively using drugs.

It is the responsibility of the treating mental health professional to provide a diagnosis based on facts and not fashion. Although it is currently fashionable to diagnose young clients with bipolar disorder, in my experience, it is almost always inappropriate and deleterious to the youths. I say this primarily because the main treatment option for children diagnosed with bipolar disorder is medication and because there are no proven safe and effective medications available for youths with this diagnostic label. Similar to the recent debacle with serotonin-specific reuptake inhibitor antidepressants, whereby the Food and Drug Administration determined that selective serotonin reuptake inhibitors may contribute to suicidality, the medications used for treating youths labeled as bipolar have not been adequately researched with this population. In particular, I am referring to the inappropriate use of lithium carbonate, antipsychotic medications, and antiseizure medications with young clients who have been assigned the trendy bipolar label.

Now, having finished my bipolar rant (which may indicate, in some practitioners' eyes, that I am the one in need of medication), I have a few important comments about efficiently ruling out the bipolar diagnosis in youths. First, it is important to follow the guideline mentioned previously of always assigning the least restrictive or least pathologizing diagnosis. This is especially important when the counselor has a clear and present explanation for the symptoms (i.e., substance abuse). Second, counselors should follow the guideline of automatically ruling out bipolar disorder in youths unless and until they have clear evidence to rule it in. Third, when counselors are ruling in bipolar disorder, they should strictly adhere to the *Diagnostic and Statistical Manual of Mental Disorders* criteria rather than using modified criteria published in popular books and on the Internet. Additionally, because bipolar disorder has substantial biogenetic components, counselors should always lean away from it as an explanation for psychiatric symptoms unless they have firm evidence of bipolar disorder in a biological parent or grandparent. Fourth, because bipolar disorder is generally a chronic condition, counselors must remember that it is inappropriate to provide it as a diagnosis until they have had a substantial period of observation. In my practice as a mental health consultant for a residential educational and vocational center for 16–24-year-olds in Montana, the attending physician and I frequently have the pleasant surprise of watching youths diagnosed with bipolar disorder suddenly "recover" and not need medication treatment shortly after their arrival. Our leading hypothesis for this recovery is the healing quality of a drug-free period and separation from destructive family systems. Fifth, my cynical response to this issue is that the diagnosis assigned by the professional counselor or psychologist carries much less treatment relevance than the diagnosis assigned by the psychiatrist or physician. If a counselor thinks, in his or her professional opinion, that a child he or she is working with may have bipolar disorder, it is fairly simple to find out which physicians in the community are inclined toward this diagnosis. The counselor may then refer the child to a physician who will make his or her definitive diagnosis without much concern about the counselor's previous diagnostic musings.

Concluding Comments

Reading through my comments, I recognize two main themes: (a) I have grown a bit cynical (and perhaps outspoken) about what I consider silly and inappropriate trends in mental health diagnosis and treatment, and (b) I still feel a twinge of excitement when I get to read (and comment on) an excellent example of clinical counseling, such as the case described. In conclusion, despite the passion and attachment I feel about my preceding comments, I believe it is very important to express with complete humility that my thoughts on this case in general and on bipolar disorder in particular could, of course, be completely wrong.

Response

Linwood G. Vereen

The practicing counselor must take into account a number of variables when considering which treatment methods work best with dependent or substance-abusing clients. One must first look at theory of orientation and make comparisons on the basis of previous experience and practice. For example, one counselor may propose a behavior modification program for Corey on the basis of past experience and success in its use with preadolescents. Conversely, another counselor may find value in providing a small-group experience for Corey. In addition, counselors may find themselves in a working environment or facility in which there are preferred methods of treatment, and this, too, will affect their choice of method.

What remains important is that the onus is on the counselor to continue to explore new ways of finding counseling success through continued education, study, and practice. Personally, I have found that success with preadolescents comes when I allow them to assume responsibility for their own well-being, mirroring their desire to exert developmental independence from their parents or caregivers. It is critical that Corey be allowed to have ownership and to assume an active role in his own success as well as to assume the role of expert on himself in many areas. I would work with Corey to develop strength-based goals, treatment plans, and interventions because these have proven helpful in my work with clients in similar situations. I would also work with Corey to develop an integrative approach that fosters and enhances his growth and development by allowing him to assume leadership and ownership of his own identity development, prosocial skills, stress management, and psychoeducation.

In work with adolescents, the literature stresses the importance of building a therapeutic relationship as a catalyst for change. To foster this therapeutic relationship, it is important to avoid assigning clinical labels, playing the role of expert, or asserting education credentials and to instead emphasize commonalities between counselor and client (Hanna, Hanna, & Keys, 1999). Counselors should also be cognizant that the relationship-building process may take more energy and time with adolescents than with other clients. Patience and ongoing intentionality are necessary to engage adolescent clients, such as Corey, who may initially categorize the counselor as "one of them" or as a representative of the authoritative system.

When working with a client such as Corey, the counselor can look to creative and developmentally appropriate interventions to assist in client personal growth and development. For example, if I am flexible and patient, use interventions such as joining, and exhibit a willingness to work out of the office, I may find success with clients like Corey. Another creative intervention could include the use of adventure-based counseling as a means to help Corey connect with his feelings and thoughts about his life situation. In addition, the use of empowerment strategies and interventions might help Corey assume responsibility for his personal growth and well-being. It would also be helpful to Corey to have a counselor who is accepting of him, believes in him, and is willing to risk self-disclosure to further the therapeutic connection.

Prior to the development of goals, treatment planning, and the implementation of interventions, it is critical to investigate factors in Corey's life that have influenced his substance use. For example, I would explore family attitude, parental management and permissiveness, sibling relationships, and level of conflict in the home. I would also explore Corey's significant peer relationships in connection to use of substances, extracurricular activities and sports, and social involvement in and out of school. All of these variables tend to be related to substance use in preadolescence, and thus they are important factors for counselors to assess and address.

The question of what additional counseling resources might exist for families with limited income is situationally based. For example, is Corey living within city limits or in a rural area? Such a question is critical because there are marked differences in availability of services on the basis of location and setting. Given this fact, in my current community in Idaho, there are many kinds of resources available to families in need. Many agencies offer psychosocial rehabilitation services to needy families. Psychosocial rehabilitation enhances counseling services by providing an additional resource of case management to families with a limited income. Another resource that comes to mind is the family counseling services offered through my university's counseling department. The psychology department offers family counseling on a sliding fee scale as well. In addition, Idaho's Department of Health and Welfare is instrumental in providing wraparound services for families in need. Local agencies, such as the community recreation center, Family Service Alliance, and local churches or youth groups, may also provide support groups as well as individual, group, and family counseling. These are but a few additional resources that may be available to families in financial need. Finally, there is also the need for counselors to take it on themselves to provide pro bono services to families with limited income.

This question should also serve to remind counselors and educators of their obligation and duty to be aware of and have information to provide to their clients about additional services that are available in their own community. It is each counselor's responsibility to keep an updated referral list of area counselors and service providers for those in need. Taking these steps ensures that the counselor is practicing ethically and that he or she is keeping the welfare of Corey and others like him in the forefront of his or her mind.

It is very possible to miss a diagnosis of bipolar disorder in clients like Corey. Counselors must be cognizant and intentional in their differential diagnosing of clients when the potential for dual diagnosis exists. When working with such clients, I am challenged to be intentional in my work and in my diagnosis of the client's presenting and underlying concerns. I am also reminded of the value and benefits of consultation and supervision to assist me in overcoming my own blind spots as a counselor. There are a few other issues to consider.

First, there is a need to continually look at Corey's individual growth and development as a catalyst for his change in mood and affect. For example, his search for the approval and companionship of older students is a developmental growth issue that many have experienced. Second, it is necessary to look at Corey's development into adolescence over time to assist in the conceptualization of his presenting and underlying concerns. As a counselor, it would be my obligation to engage in an ongoing evaluation of Corey's mood and affect to aid in further diagnosis as well as to explore the need for a medical evaluation to rule out any alternative diagnosis. Third, there is a need for ongoing monitoring of Corey's moods as they manifested in different settings. Mood fluctuations that are evident in school, at home, and in Corey's peer relations would be more indicative of a mood disorder than would a situation-based manifestation of mood change. Finally, it is important to take into consideration the symptoms that Corey may experience as his system works to cleanse itself of toxins. The counselor must take into consideration all of these issues to provide a diagnosis and treatment approach with Corey that is thorough, multifaceted, and effective.

References

American Psychiatric Association. (2000). *Diagnostic and statistical manual of mental disorders* (4th ed., text rev.). Washington, DC: Author.

Hanna, F. J., Hanna, C. A., & Keys, S. G. (1999). Fifty strategies for counseling defiant, aggressive adolescents: Reaching, accepting, and relating. *Journal of Counseling and Development, 77,* 395–404.

Miller, W. R., & Rollnick, S. (2002). *Motivational interviewing: Preparing people for change* (2nd ed.). New York: Guilford Press.

Reid, J. B., Patterson, G. P., & Snyder, J. J. (2002). *Antisocial behavior in children and adolescents.* Washington, DC: American Psychological Association.

Sexton, T. L., & Alexander, J. (1999). *Functional family therapy: Principles of clinical intervention, assessment, and implementation.* Henderson, NV: RCH Enterprises.

Sommers-Flanagan, J., & Sommers-Flanagan, R. (2003). *Clinical interviewing* (3rd ed.). New York: Wiley.

Sommers-Flanagan, J., & Sommers-Flanagan, R. (2004). *The challenge of counseling teens: Counselor behaviors that reduce resistance and facilitate connection* [Videotape]. North Amherst, MA: Microtraining Associates.

Sommers-Flanagan, J., & Sommers-Flanagan, R. (2007). *Tough kids, cool counseling* (2nd ed.). Alexandria, VA: American Counseling Association.

Swenson, C. C., Henggeler, W. W., Taylor, I. S., & Addison, O. W. (2004). *Multisystemic therapy and neighborhood partnerships: Reducing adolescent violence and substance abuse.* New York: Guilford Press.

Part

VIII

School-Based Counseling

32

Academic Difficulties: "The Boy's Just Lazy!"

This incident focuses on working with families in which a child struggles academically. Respondents discuss the impact of developmental milestones, cultural tasks, and family dynamics on a student's transition to middle school and explore the decision-making process about whether to do formal testing and evaluation when the parents disagree about the reasons for these academic struggles.

◼ Critical Incident

Jody J. Fiorini

"Nathan Washington" was an 11-year-old biracial sixth grader who lived in a wealthy suburban neighborhood in upstate New York with his parents, Ed and Elena Washington, and one of his two older sisters. His mother brought him to be evaluated for possible learning disabilities. I work as an independent counselor with several professional colleagues in an agency that specializes in working with children and adolescents. The agency employs several registered play therapists and a variety of other counselors who have experience and training in counseling children. My expertise is working with special needs children, particularly those with learning disabilities, and their family members.

Before meeting with Nathan, I first met with his mother, Elena Washington. Mrs. Washington, an Italian American who worked as a successful attorney, explained that Nathan's school counselor had referred the family to me to determine whether an undiagnosed learning disability might be contributing to Nathan's difficulties. She expressed a great deal of concern about Nathan's academic performance as well as his attitude and behavior problems in school. Mrs. Washington indicated that Nathan's grades had dropped drastically since last year, that he had been close to failing several courses in the last marking period, and that he was currently failing two classes this marking period. When asked to clarify her concerns about her son's behaviors, Mrs. Washington stated, "Nathan gets into trouble a lot at school. He talks all the time, acts like a smart aleck, and practically lives at the principal's office." She stated that she had noticed a distinct change in Nathan's behaviors during the end of the previous school year but that his acting-out behaviors had escalated and his grades had declined further during this academic year.

Mrs. Washington expressed confusion about her son's academic struggles and explained that, in contrast, his two older sisters were "star students." She indicated that Jessica, a 16-year-old 10th grader, was already looking into colleges and had her sights set on majoring in international relations at an Ivy League college. Her grades were outstanding, and she was very involved in clubs and organizations and was an officer in her sophomore class. I also learned that Nathan's oldest sister, Vanessa, was a 19-year-old sophomore in college who was majoring in premed, with the goal of applying to Johns Hopkins University to begin her medical training after graduation. She was currently maintaining a 4.0 grade point average.

When asked about her feelings about Nathan's difficulties, Mrs. Washington sighed and leaned forward. "I've always known there was something different about Nathan," she reported. "Everything came easily for his sisters, but reading and learning have always been a struggle for Nathan. He spends so much time trying to understand what he reads. He tries, well, he used to try, to do his homework . . . but he gets so frustrated! He doesn't know it, but I once saw him throw his books across the room before when he thought no one was looking."

When asked about her husband's reaction to their son's difficulties, Mrs. Washington frowned. "He thinks Nathan's just lazy. The school suggested that we get Nathan tested for a learning disability, but Ed doesn't believe in learning disabilities. He thinks this is just an excuse for poor behavior." She explained that her husband, an African American, had a strong work ethic and greatly valued education. She indicated that he worked on the assembly line at a major car company and that, although he earned a very good income, he wanted "something better" for his children.

After this initial meeting with Mrs. Washington, I made an appointment to meet individually with Nathan. Nathan walked confidently into the counseling office and chose the chair farthest from me. He was tall for his age, with a thin, athletic build. After covering informed consent, I started the session by asking Nathan to tell me about himself. He told me that he was on the cross-country and track teams, that he loved to draw, and that he played the drums in the school band. He reported having "lots of friends" who liked him because he was "so freakin' funny." "I love to make people laugh," he said. Nathan stated that he liked his teachers but hated school. I asked him to elaborate. Nathan expressed feeling like he had let his parents down. "My mom and dad really care and they want me to do well. But even though I really try, I just can't do it. I'm not like Jessie and Vanessa. I'm a loser. My dad is right."

On the basis of my meetings with Nathan and his mother, an evaluation for possible learning disabilities certainly seemed warranted. To begin the evaluation, however, I also needed to gain the support of Nathan's father. In preparing to discuss my recommendations with Mr. and Mrs. Washington, I found myself thinking about the possible reasons for Mr. Washington's apparent resistance to the concept of learning disabilities, about the impact of family dynamics on Nathan, and about ways to possibly assist Nathan.

Questions

1. Do you believe that it would be beneficial for Nathan to be tested for learning disabilities? If so, how would you address Mr. Washington's resistance considering that cultural issues might be at play?
2. How might Nathan's difficulties be affected by the high performance of his sisters? What interventions might help address this?
3. How might the transition from elementary school to middle school have influenced Nathan's difficulties?
4. What strengths do you see in Nathan that could be used to help him become more successful? What techniques or strategies would you use to increase both his self-esteem and his self-efficacy?

■Response

Rhonda M. Bryant

As I consider the situation of Nathan Washington and his family, I know I would welcome the opportunity to assist this student in his academic, social, and intrapersonal development. Nathan is an energetic yet seemingly distracted young man who is facing three serious challenges in his academic and home environments. First, it seems that he has developed a reputation among his family and some school staff as having attitude and behavior problems. Second, although Nathan feels that he is popular with his peers, numerous referrals to the principal's office may preclude friendships with students who would be a positive influence because they perceive Nathan's behavior as unconstructive and distracting. Third, Nathan's gregarious behavior may belie his disappointment that he has not met the expectations of his parents, his teachers, his peers, and himself.

Despite these challenges, Nathan has ample available resources that could assist him. Nathan is able to identify and articulate his concerns about meeting his parents' expectations. His uneasiness about disappointing them suggests that he is able to understand how his behavior affects others. In addition, because Nathan experienced success in elementary school, it seems likely that he does possess core academic and interpersonal skills that he can tap as he moves into middle school. Nathan also enjoys the support of his parents, who wish to help him overcome his difficulties. Finally, Nathan has cooperated with counseling thus far. This may indicate that he desires a change in his present circumstances.

My training as a counselor and mental health service provider leads me to consider Nathan and his family's situation from a comprehensive developmental perspective. I am concerned about how Nathan is meeting psychosocial and cultural milestones and managing family dynamics now that one sister has left home and another is preparing to leave. Finally, I wonder how the family is coping with the stress caused by Nathan's behavior.

Meeting Developmental Milestones

Psychosocial tasks. Erikson (1963) stated that children ages 6 to 12 must learn how to achieve success in school by acquiring the skills to plan, implement, and complete projects. During this 6-year period, children choose friends and sustain friendships and they move from the home as a primary focus and expand their world to include peers. Erikson maintained that if children do not perceive success in school and social areas, feelings of inferiority and incompetence can result. Nathan, an 11-year-old enrolled in the sixth grade, is trying to become skilled at passing his courses and getting along with others. In addition to these tasks, Nathan has to learn how to follow rules and negotiate with authority figures when appropriate. Because Nathan's mother has said that his grades and behavior were better in elementary school, I believe that Nathan can reference feelings of competence in academic and social settings. Nevertheless, Nathan's description of himself as a loser indicates his current frustration and lack of confidence in his abilities in spite of his past success in elementary school.

Nathan is the youngest child of three. His two older sisters have established legacies as high academic achievers and do not seem to have struggled academically or socially. Given his sisters' accomplishments and their ability to excel in school and with peers, it would not be surprising if Nathan's parents were overwhelmed by his behavior. The Washingtons value education as a means of attaining social and financial security and take pride in their daughters' goals and achievements. Thus, it is not surprising that Nathan's behavior is unacceptable to them because it is inconsistent with the value the family places on education. The parents' pursuit of counseling suggests that they are willing to explore new avenues to assist Nathan.

Cultural tasks. Nathan is a biracial child who enjoys a supportive mother and father. His mother, an Italian American, believes that Nathan may have an undiagnosed learning disability. His father, an African American, believes that Nathan is being lazy and needs to focus on his work. I believe that it would benefit Nathan if both his parents supported educational testing. Their support would be helpful in that it would give them a context for Nathan's behaviors and provide effective ways to address his studies and behavior. Therefore, I would like to talk with both of them about the implications of testing and a possible diagnosis of specific learning disabilities.

At first glance, the disparity between the parents' perceptions of the problem seems to have nothing to do with race or culture. Yet African Americans can hold broader parameters of normal behaviors than those provided for in clinical assessments of disability (Harry, 2003). This could mean that it is culturally unacceptable for Mr. Washington to believe that Nathan has a disability. Instead, Mr. Washington may find it more culturally acceptable to encourage his son to work hard and to take full advantage of educational opportunities rather than to squander them by failing and getting into trouble. Mr. Washington could be wary of entering the special education process because African American children continue to be overrepresented in special education programs in America's schools (Office of Special Education Programs, 2000). Mrs. Washington's success in her educational pursuits (as evidenced by her accomplishments in college and her subsequent graduation from law school) might have engendered implicit trust in the educational process.

The development of a racial identity is a key component throughout the life span, but it is particularly critical in childhood because children define themselves through seeking friends and their peer experiences shape their values. Racial identity is the degree to which a person can relate to and identify with a racial group in society (Cross, 1991). The development of racial identity provides a framework for children to define their values, beliefs, and goals. Nathan's mother is Italian American, and his father is African American. People may try to categorize Nathan on the basis of preconceived ideas about what Black people look like or what White people look like and treat him on the basis of racial stereotypes. Alternatively, he may feel pressured to choose between two heritages. Children of White and Black parents may face additional challenges because of the long-standing difficulties that these racial groups have had in America (Chiong, 1998).

I would be interested in how Nathan's parents help him address racial identity development. Is he encouraged to explore both his heritages? Do his parents believe that race is not important and encourage Nathan to adopt a race-blind approach to his heritage? The possibilities are numerous, but it is important to determine the cultural values and strengths that the family and Nathan can use during this time of adjustment.

Family dynamics. Nathan's family consists of his two older sisters and his parents. At this time, I do not have any knowledge of extended family members. Nathan seems to want to please his parents and expresses regret that his father thinks he is a loser. With the success of his sisters, Nathan may want the accolades and attention that his sisters enjoy. I know that Nathan compares himself with his sisters and may feel that his parents expect him to perform like they have. The critical incident does not clarify what the Washingtons expect of Nathan and to what extent Nathan's motivation and abilities will allow him to reconcile his parents' expectations with his own. Currently, Nathan does not feel that he has his father's approval, and this undoubtedly hinders their relationship.

Strategies and Techniques

My work with the Washington family would underscore the following:

- Nathan has had success in previous academic settings, and it is normal for students to feel challenged and even overwhelmed when they move to middle school. My job would be to reframe his current functioning in the context of psychosocial task accomplishment and developmental transitions.
- Nathan is developing a racial identity as a normal part of his maturation. Social and intrapersonal implications of a diagnosis of disability may be complex given his dual heritage. I believe that Nathan's parents are the role models who will assist him in determining his values and beliefs about race and ability.

On the basis of the information provided by Nathan, his mother, and the school counselor, it seems that Nathan may have some kind of learning disability. I would like to meet with just the parents to find out what courses of action they would like to take to assist Nathan. In particular, I would use the core counseling skills of empathy, unconditional positive regard, and genuineness to let the Washingtons know that they have a tough but addressable situation with Nathan. In particular,

- I would invite both parents to discuss Nathan's strengths and to identify what skills have helped him during his transition to middle school.
- I would avoid seeing Mr. Washington as resistant to counseling or testing because he does not believe Nathan's situation warrants testing. He has the right to make educational decisions for his son, and, if testing is not completed, it is my ethical responsibility to assist the family even if I believe that testing would help Nathan.
- I would give both parents the opportunity to express any concerns about the testing process.

- because Mr. Washington has expressed doubt about Nathan having a learning disability, I would provide written information about learning disabilities, parental rights under the Individuals With Disabilities Education Act, and the testing program in the school's jurisdiction.
- I would ask the parents to consider getting Nathan a complete medical evaluation to rule out physiological reasons for Nathan's behavior changes.
- I would provide information about parent organizations that provide in-school advocates for students with academic difficulties.
- I would provide written information that discusses alternatives to testing and behavioral strategies. The family has the right to make an informed decision about interventions for Nathan.

Nathan has experienced a decrease in his self-esteem and self-efficacy during his transition to middle school. I would attempt to assist him in these areas by

- using solution-focused counseling to help him recognize that he is not always in the principal's office and that he is not failing every class. For example, what happens when he makes choices that allow him to stay in the classroom? What makes the classes he is passing different from the ones he is not? Helping him discover that he makes good choices every day might boost his self-esteem and his feelings of effectiveness and lead him to make better decisions in the classroom.
- using expressive therapies to assist Nathan in recognizing that transition is hard but possible. Music, poetry, journaling, or bibliotherapy might be useful tools in working with Nathan.
- using school resources to assist Nathan with the transition to middle school. Peer tutoring programs or teacher assistance programs would provide Nathan a broader support network in addition to his classroom teachers and peers.
- teaching Nathan about Ellis's (see Ellis & MacLaren, 1998; Thompson, Rudolph, & Henderson, 2004) rational emotive therapy/ABC model (where *A* refers to the activating event, *B* refers to the beliefs and meaning that an individual attaches to the event, and *C* refers to the consequences of the beliefs on the individual's behavior and emotions) to help him manage school-related stress. I would also teach him strategies to manage anger and frustration.

Conclusion

Nathan and his family have a number of resources to assist him as he attempts to get back on track with his academic and social development. Nathan is a perceptive child who has had previous success in school, has parents who commit their time and efforts to assist him, and has the assistance of the school counselor, who has been instrumental in creating a support system for him in and outside of school. I would hope to facilitate Nathan's development by teaching age-appropriate coping strategies, helping him identify positive exceptions to his problematic behaviors, and instructing him how to identify and appreciate his uniqueness and abilities. Although I believe that Nathan could benefit from educational testing, my affirmation of his parents' right to choose would undergird my interventions with them. It is my hope that Nathan and the Washingtons will come to understand his abilities in various psychosocial, cultural, and familial contexts and that this process will help Nathan flourish as he grows into manhood.

Response

Carol A. Dahir

Adolescents often take the first steps toward separating from their parents during the middle school years. In exploring and defining their independence, these youngsters struggle with figuring out who they are, what they do well, and how to form new social affiliations. During these adolescent and preteen years, children are evaluating their interests, social skills, and abilities. They struggle with behavioral reconciliation, whether challenged by peers, parents, teachers, or other authority figures. The strongest influence on middle school youths is peer group affiliation, as they search for a place to belong and rely on peer acceptance and feedback. As youths explore the boundaries of acceptable behavior and attempt to understand mature, meaningful relationships, they face increased pressures regarding sex, alcohol, drugs, and other risky behaviors. Compounding these pressures are academic stresses related to high-stakes testing, more challenging course work, and high expectations on the part of teachers and parents to assume and accept responsibility, both academically and socially. It is no wonder, then, that middle school youths find themselves caught in situations unlike those they have faced before (Dahir & Eby, 2002).

Mrs. Washington had noticed a change in Nathan's work at the end of fifth grade and called immediately after receiving his first sixth grade report card. She asked to see the school counselor, expressing her concern that her son was doing poorly and that his grades had dropped dramatically. As a former middle school counselor with 10 years' experience, I have personally worked with a number of parents and students to address issues related to dramatic drops in student performance. In responding to this critical incident, I draw on my own experiences in working with students like Nathan and offer suggestions in accordance with how I might have proceeded with Mrs. Washington and her son. My recommendations focus on the importance of implementing a prereferral plan prior to determining whether an assessment for learning disabilities is warranted. The prereferral plan should consist of a multidimensional approach to understanding Nathan's strengths and difficulties and of intervention plans involving Nathan's parents, teachers, and school counselor.

I support the school counselor's decision to first meet with Nathan's mother and would have done so myself. In addition, I would inform Nathan that I would be meeting first with his mom and that I would ask him to join us a little bit later. At the meeting described, Mrs. Washington communicated her confusion about the cause of Nathan's poor performance and expressed an interest in evaluating Nathan for learning disability despite her husband's strong opposition. According to Mrs. Washington, her husband did not believe that his son had any disability and felt the boy was just plain lazy. When the school counselor met with Nathan, he seemed very disheartened. He indicated that he found the work much harder than in elementary school and that he was having much more trouble than his sisters had at his age. He also admitted that his classroom behavior had not been the best. He spent a considerable amount of time fooling around and then getting lost in the lessons.

On hearing this, I would want to further discuss Nathan's previous academic performance and would wonder about whether his current academic performance might be most accurately viewed as caused by adjustment issues, behavioral and socialization problems, academic difficulties, or, perhaps, a combination of all three. In addition, the school counselor raised the issue of whether cultural issues might be at play in Nathan's case. Research has revealed that Black students are often overrepresented in special education classrooms (Zehr, 2004). Although Nathan is biracial, it is essential to recognize that bias may exist and address any concerns expressed by his mother and father, his school counselor, and his teachers. It will be several weeks before the school counselor will be able to confidently determine whether Nathan truly needs an evaluation for learning disabilities or whether other sources of structure, support, and counseling would be sufficient to help him to succeed at an expected level of accomplishment.

There are many variables at play; I would not want to quickly resort to recommending testing for classification without exploring all of the possibilities through a comprehensive assessment. The middle school years often reveal students' shortcomings that might not have surfaced in a less-pressured elementary school environment. The expectations of multiple teachers can be confusing for students who have had a primary dependence on one or two instructors. Students often find themselves overwhelmed organizationally, distracted by socializing at their lockers, and frantic to remember what they studied the night before for a test that will be given at the end of the school day.

Developing a Prereferral and Intervention Plan

To begin determining the root cause of Nathan's poor performance, I would ask Mrs. Washington to give me an opportunity to work with Nathan and to explore a series of strategies involving both of his parents, his school counselor, and his teachers. Part of my goal would be to better understand Nathan's interactions in his school world and his world outside of the school. School counselors and many educators subscribe to the belief that all children can learn and all children can achieve (Stone & Dahir, 2006). All school personnel should be sensitive to the time students need to understand and learn, even at a level of minimum proficiency. School counselors are in a unique position to collaborate with faculty and to identify the essential resources and support systems that each student needs to be successful (Stone & Dahir, 2007). Nathan's school counselor should be a key facilitator to monitor his success.

I might offer Nathan and his parents a prereferral plan that would involve counseling, academic support, and parental involvement in an attempt to improve Nathan's academic performance. The three of us would agree to carefully monitor Nathan's progress. As part of this plan, I would ask Mr. and Mrs. Washington to formally structure Nathan's homework and study time. Although Nathan was apparently conscientious about doing his homework, his parents might not have been checking whether it was done properly or thoroughly. Because homework is a key factor in understanding the assignments and daily class work, it would be important to determine whether this intervention might be sufficient to remedy Nathan's academic difficulties. After using prereferral strategies, we could analyze Nathan's progress and determine whether we should proceed with the learning disabilities evaluation. In the event that a learning disabilities evaluation seemed warranted at that time, it would be necessary to assess Nathan's ability and to compare it with his achievement levels.

Assessing Nathan's Ability and Achievement

What is Nathan capable of accomplishing? Nathan himself could not articulate this and, in his meeting with the school counselor, expressed confusion and defeat when it came to academics. Nathan revealed that he has a good sense of humor; his friends love his joking around, but he often gets into trouble with his teachers. Sometimes he is not sure whether he could do better if he did not let other things get in the way. He indicated that school used to be fun and easy for him, but now it is a stressor. He is talented and accomplished in athletics, art, and music; nevertheless, this has not been enough to boost his self-esteem and help him find balance in his school accomplishments. Although Nathan is engaged in school through socialization and activities, he is disengaged from academics and his studies. Nathan is unable to pinpoint his academic abilities.

Ability is a student's capacity or aptitude to master a skill, task, or concept; the term *disability* describes a student's incapability to accomplish or acquire the same skill, task, or concept in certain situations (Woolfolk, 2004). A learning disability can be defined as a deficit in one or more cognitive processes or a problem with the acquisition and use of language (McDevitt & Ormond, 2002). Students who are learning disabled may have difficulty with reading, writing, reasoning, or mathematics, and special education services may be required (Woolfolk, 2004). For some educators, the designation of learning disabled helps to explain why and how some students struggle with language, communication arts, and math without other apparent signs of impairment. Labels can simultaneously stigmatize and provide opportunity for students (Keogh & MacMillan, 1996).

It is not uncommon for counselors to find themselves involved in complex situations, such as Nathan's, that require different levels of assessment. As advocates for students and their families, counselors must also have the competence to interpret the data that are used for placements, classification, or assignment of services (Guindon, 2003). In assessing Nathan's ability and achievement, the school counselor can gather data and information from his teachers, research and interview, look for patterns, and organize the results in a way that has meaning for decision making and problem solving. Learning ability is distinct to the individual; each child has unique talents, skills, and limitations (McDevitt & Ormond, 2002). Perhaps more important than understanding his ability level, Nathan needs to understand how he learns and his preferred style for learning.

According to Woolfolk (2004), learning preferences are individual inclinations for a particular modality or environment. For some students, the traditional lecture format does not spark a deeper level of understanding; for others, a kinesthetic approach involving an active, hands-on experience is the most meaningful method of learning. It is difficult, perhaps almost impossible, for a classroom teacher to address the dominant learning style of every student that he or she comes into contact with on a daily basis. Nevertheless, each student can benefit from understanding her or his individual learning preference and learn to adapt to different instructional situations and different styles of teaching (Dunn & Dunn, 1987). School counselors who are knowledgeable about learning preferences and learning styles can help individuals and groups of students explore an important dimension of self-knowledge and adapt that understanding to the teaching and learning environment (Dunn & Dunn, 1987). I recommend that Nathan's school counselor share Nathan's dominant learning style with his teachers.

Simultaneously, the school counselor should also investigate Nathan's classroom work, progress on tests, and quality of homework and consult with his teachers to see whether there are learning issues that may be contributing to the behavioral problem. Some students need additional tools, time, and specialized instruction to achieve at a minimum proficiency. As part of the prereferral intervention plan, I would work with school personnel to connect Nathan to academic support services, such as the academic center or tutoring, to help him better understand how to organize his day and develop study skills. I would ask his teachers to closely monitor where he is having difficulty. It is equally important that all school personnel stay in close communication with Nathan's parents.

Using Counseling Theory and Techniques

According to Cobia and Henderson (2003), counselors are ethically obligated to help each student accept and respect his or her uniqueness. It is a duty of the counselor to develop services and strategies that support educational and career needs and emotional and behavioral growth (Cobia & Henderson, 2003). As the school counselor, I would assure Mrs. Washington that Nathan would benefit from a weekly counseling session as we implemented the prereferral intervention plan and sought to explore, investigate, and monitor the supports needed for success.

To establish a counseling relationship, the school counselor must actively listen and pay close attention to everything that she is sharing in the counseling session. The school counselor's body position, eye contact, nonverbal encouragement, and relaxed and open posture will all contribute to Nathan's perception of the counselor's involvement. Most important, Nathan will feel secure and experience empathy as the counselor responds in a way that communicates an understanding of Nathan's frame of reference and point of view (Egan, 2001). A skilled counselor can perceive the world as the student sees it and has the ability to communicate that understanding.

The counselor must establish a relationship of trust to reassure Nathan that s/he is there to help him discover his strengths, overcome obstacles, and make choices to have a more successful year in sixth grade. Through relationship building, the counselor can observe and understand Nathan's perspective on his ethnic and cultural heritage, his social and economic status, his parents' education and career positions, and his relationships with his siblings. Some or all of these factors may influence Nathan's perception of himself and his view of the world.

Reality therapy seems most appropriate as a primary way of working with Nathan. Reality therapy helps children understand the need to be psychologically strong and make healthy, productive choices in their interpersonal and intrapersonal relationships (Glasser, 2000). The ultimate goal is for the client to develop autonomy and take responsibility for the behaviors that affect him or her and others. I would use humor, role play, confrontation, feedback, goal setting, and planning to help Nathan explore options, encourage him to learn how to make more effective choices, and develop the skills to cope with daily stresses and problems. Self-exploration would help Nathan to dig deep into who he is and explore his feelings about his high-achieving siblings, his biracial background, and the influence of his parents' expectations.

My goal would be to teach Nathan how to become responsible for his actions through the use of positive planning and action steps. Nathan could then explore how his behavior is inappropriate and sometimes negative and would begin to understand that he is in control of the desired changes. Reviewing past behaviors helps the student take charge in the present and plan for the future, and establishing realistic goals influences changes in behaviors. Humor is one of the techniques that must be used respectfully. Middle school students have fragile egos; Nathan cannot think that the counselor is making fun of him. If used sensitively, however, humor may help him to look at the situation differently and see how unrealistic it was. Children learn to evaluate their behaviors and begin to recognize which behaviors are unproductive.

Children take action to create a plan for changing behaviors. Reality therapy places the responsibility on the student to accomplish the goals set forth in the plan of action (Glasser, 2000). The counselor never gives up on the child, and the child assumes responsibility to break the cycle of failure.

Engaging in reality therapy would require Nathan to accept responsibility for determining the course of action he would follow. Reality therapy does not dwell on the past but rather focuses the student on present difficulties and on future changes in action and behavior. Children may experience reality therapy as empowering because it helps them realize that they have choices and that there are alternative ways to resolve a situation or problem. It keeps the child focused on dealing with the here and now to gain self-confidence and assurance. Nathan is old enough to understand choice and demonstrate the desire to change his behavior. The use of reality therapy would also help us to determine whether wiser choices might have an influence not only on behavioral issues in school but also on his academic success.

Counseling can help children realize what their dreams are, what they need to do to achieve them, and how this will assist them in enjoying success in their school and home life. Adolescents and preteens need a sense of where they are going and what the outcome of their labors will be. What is Nathan's dream? I would ask him to talk about his future goals and to see whether he can visualize himself succeeding, not failing, at something he wants badly.

The prereferral plan involves all who interact with Nathan each day and can lend support. Placement into special education is a complex process involving many school professionals in addition to parents, guardians, or caregivers, and the need for services requires a comprehensive assessment. Most important, Nathan knows he has a team of family, school professionals, and his school counselor working collaboratively to help him find success.

References

Chiong, J. (1998). *Racial categorization of multiracial children in schools*. Westport, CT: Bergin and Garvey.

Cobia, D., & Henderson, D. (2003). *Handbook of school counseling*. Upper Saddle River, NJ: Pearson Education.

Cross, W. E., Jr. (1991). *Shades of black: Diversion in African American identity*. Philadelphia: Temple University Press.

Dahir, C., & Eby, L. (2002, Winter). *Building resiliency: The role of the school counselor. Middle matters*. Alexandria, VA: National Association of Elementary School Principals.

Dunn, K., & Dunn, R. (1987). Dispelling outmoded beliefs about student learning. *Educational Leadership, 45*, 55–63.

Egan, G. (2001). *The skilled helper* (7th ed.). Monterey, CA: Brooks/Cole.

Erikson, E. (1963). *Childhood and society*. New York: Norton.

Ellis, A. N., & MacLaren, C. (1998). *Rational emotive behavior therapy: A therapist's guide*. San Luis Obispo, CA: Impact Publishers.

Glasser, W. (2000). *Reality therapy in action*. New York: HarperCollins.

Guindon, M. H. (2003). Assessment. In B. T. Erford (Ed.), *Transforming the school counseling profession* (pp. 331–356). Upper Saddle River, NJ: Merrill Prentice Hall.

Harry, B. (2003). Trends and issues in serving culturally diverse families of children with disabilities. *Journal of Special Education, 36*, 132–140.

Keogh, B. K., & MacMillan, D. L. (1996). Exceptionality. In D. Berliner & R. Calfee (Eds.), *Handbook of educational psychology* (pp. 311–330). New York: Macmillan Library Reference.

McDevitt, T., & Ormond, J. (2002). *Child development and education.* Upper Saddle River, NJ: Merrill Prentice Hall.

Office of Special Education Programs. (2000). *Twenty-second annual report to Congress on the implementation of the Individuals With Disabilities Act.* Retrieved July 11, 2002, from http://www.ed.gov/about/reports/annual/osep/2000/preface.pdf

Stone, C., & Dahir, C. (2007). *School counselor accountability: A measure of student success* (2nd ed.). Upper Saddle River, NJ: Pearson Education.

Stone, C., & Dahir, C. (2006). *The transformed school counselor.* Boston: Houghton Mifflin/Lahaska Press.

Thompson, C. L., Rudolph, L. B., & Henderson, D. (2004). *Counseling children.* Belmont, CA: Thomson Brooks/Cole.

Woolfolk, A. (2004). *Educational psychology* (9th ed.). Boston: Allyn & Bacon.

Zehr, M. (2004, January 14). Report updates portrait of LEP students 2004. *Education Week, 23*(18), 3.

"Stan Is Driving Me Crazy!":
Behavior Problems

This incident explores a classroom teacher's yearlong struggles to manage the behavior problems and address the issues affecting a challenging first grader. The authors consider attention-deficit/hyperactivity disorder as a possible factor in this student's misbehavior and explore treatment options, including medication and systemic consultation.

■ Critical Incident

Jill Bills

As a first grade teacher, I am always a little sad to see my students leave for the summer yet excited to see my new class roster and discover who I will have in the fall. I vividly recall scanning my new class list for familiar names 4 years ago. One name in particular stuck out: "Stan Barnes." I pondered his name and wondered why I recognized it.

Then it hit me like a ton of bricks. That was the name I had been hearing almost every day in the teacher's lounge. "Stan did this, Stan did that. Stan is driving me crazy!" his kindergarten teacher would say. I am a person who likes challenges, so I confidently thought, "I can do a better job with ol' Stan, and you won't hear me complaining in the teachers lounge. Nosiree! I'm going to take a positive approach." In retrospect, though, my year with Stan turned out to be one of the most challenging of my 17 years as an early elementary teacher.

When fall arrived, Stan entered the building on the 1st day of school with a bang. He was loud, physically pushing other students and making goo-goo eyes at the girls while whistling at them. "Yikes," I thought, "What kind of home life could this little boy have?" Because Stan came to school well groomed and dressed in designer clothes every day, if one did not know about him, one might have thought, "What a cute boy, and look how well he is taken care of." As the saying goes, however, looks are deceiving.

Stan's behavior in my classroom ranged from mildly annoying to overwhelmingly scary. He displayed impulsiveness, restlessness, a short attention span, distractibility, and learning problems. Stan also physically intimidated other students to get his way. My impression was that these behaviors were classic symptoms of attention-deficit/hyperactivity disorder (ADHD).

At first, I was confident that I could manage Stan and his behaviors through tried and true classroom interventions. I tried seating him with a group of hard-working, mild-mannered students so that they could serve as role models. I tried seating him close to the front of the classroom so that I could more easily redirect his attention to appropriate tasks. I tried allowing him to be active at his seat and while moving to other areas in the classroom, but his karate kicks were dangerous to the other students. I tried reading books to the class about self-esteem, kindness, consideration of others, social skills, and diversity, but it seemed that only the other children in the class were learning from the bibliotherapy. I tried helping Stan recognize his role in classroom problems, but he would deny any responsibility and proceed to argue with me about classroom procedures.

I knew I needed help when I realized that I was complaining practically every waking hour to my husband, also an educator, about Stan. "Stan did this, Stan did that. Stan is driving me crazy!" Oh, no! It was becoming a pattern for Stan's teachers, who were responsible for educating him, to become so frustrated that they could no longer truly feel a positive regard for him. On reaching this realization, I talked to the school counselor and asked for his help.

After patiently listening to my whining, he suggested that I might benefit from the assistance of our intermediate school district's behavioral consultant. I left this meeting with renewed hope and quickly contacted the behavioral consultant. A few days later, we met for about an hour. After we discussed my struggles with Stan, she shared some strategies from a program called Love and Logic (Fay & Funk, 1995). She explained that instead of reacting to Stan's impulsiveness with anger, confrontation, or resentment, I was to use empathy. Although my initial reaction was, "Yeah, like this is going to work," I was out of ideas and desperate for something that would work better with Stan.

I decided to give it a try and was pleasantly surprised by how quickly Stan's behavior issues de-escalated. Stan continued to have outbursts in the classroom and the playground, but I felt more in control of my feelings and behavior. My empathetic phrase was, "Hmm, this is so sad. What are you going to do about your problem with _____?" Stan was clearly confused by the change in my reactions and asked, "Why do you keep asking me what I'm going to do about my problem?" I explained to him that people cannot fix a problem if they do not think they have a problem, so he needed to own his behavior.

Although my days with Stan clearly improved, something kept nagging me about his behavior toward little girls. I considered his behavior as overly sexual and developmentally inappropriate for a 6-year-old. For example, Stan would lean against the lockers while we were lining up for recess and whistle at girls as they passed by, saying things like, "What's up, good looking?" and, "Hey, baby." Once, Stan was sent to the principal's office for squeezing a female classmate's bottom. Finally, I noticed that the good-bye kisses he exchanged with his teenage stepsister each morning were much more than a little peck on the cheek.

I visited the school counselor again with these new issues. We both agreed it was time to involve Stan's parents, given that the most successful counseling with children includes individual, classroom, and home interventions. In preparing to meet with Stan's parents, we researched available community supports and discovered that Stan qualified for a home–school intervention serviced by a local mental health agency called Kids in New Directions. This agency was created by a local family court judge and was designed to intervene while children are young to prevent them from entering the judicial system at an older age because of illegal behavior.

Stan was assigned a wonderful caseworker named Molly. Molly did home visits to work with Stan's custodial mother and stepfather and his noncustodial father, who had visitation with Stan every other weekend. She also visited our school to work with Stan individually and to offer assistance to me. I thought, "Now we will see some more positive changes in Stan!"

When Molly met with Stan's parents and suggested that they use Love and Logic (Fay & Funk, 1995) strategies so that their method of disciplining Stan would be consistent with the school's approach, she was met with great resistance. In fact, Stan's parents denied that he even had behavior problems and instead blamed the school and me for not working hard enough for Stan. When Molly communicated this to me, I became incredibly frustrated, given that I had spent so much time trying to manage Stan at school. I was trying more than hard enough, and it was draining my energy. He was not progressing in the academic areas and was not learning to read, as his classmates were at the time.

Molly finally referred Stan and his family to a local psychologist for further assistance. The psychologist met with Stan and his mother individually. In a phone conversation with me, the psychologist told me she had suggested ADHD medication for Stan and several more counseling sessions for the mother. The mother opted out of the medication suggestion for Stan but attended two of the counseling sessions. I questioned whether these sessions could possibly be the magic solution for Stan and became even more discouraged when his mother told me that she had quit counseling because the psychologist wanted her to change and that was too hard. In April, Stan's mother began visiting the school more frequently, and I became so intimidated by the aggressive nature of her personality during these visits that I requested that the principal be present whenever she paid me a visit. I later found out she had an alcohol abuse problem.

Molly continued to work with Stan until the end of the school year, and, although we saw little additional improvement with Stan, she really encouraged me and complimented me on my efforts. Such difficult students often feel very alone and are sometimes even ostracized by school staff members. I kept thinking that Stan needed a fresh start at a different school. His name was so well known among staff members in a negative light that even if he made improvements, they might not be noticed.

I was therefore pleased to learn that Stan and his mother did move to a neighboring school district. In addition to seeing this as a fresh start for Stan, I was also relieved that I would no longer have to deal with him and his antics. Unfortunately, when I asked a the teacher's assistant from Stan's new school whether she knew of Stan Barnes, she responded, "I do not have him in any of the classrooms I help in, but I do hear his name mentioned in the teachers' lounge a lot." So, just like the old country song by Clint Black says, "Wherever you go, there you are" (Black & Nicholas, 1996).

This incident happened 4 years ago but is still quite memorable to me. Did I feel successful with Stan? The answer is yes and no, but mostly no. I did grow and learn as a result of my struggles with Stan. I really reached out for help from other professionals that year, more so than I had in the past. I enrolled in the Love and Logic training program (Fay & Funk, 1995) and now regularly use these strategies in my classroom. I learned firsthand that the emotional and social development of a child is as important as the cognitive development. In addition, my struggles with Stan inspired me to pursue a master's degree in counseling. I want to be a positive influence on children and their caretakers.

Questions

1. What else could I have done as Stan's classroom teacher?
2. What type of support structure could be developed in the school setting to help school personnel better manage Stan's behavior and address his problems?
3. Do you believe an ADHD medication would have been beneficial to Stan, as suggested by the psychologist?
4. If you were the counselor working with Stan (in either the school or the community setting), how would you have proceeded? What evaluations and interventions might have been helpful?

■ Response

Larry Golden

I have never met the author of this critical incident, but I am sure that I would like her. Her enthusiasm, resourcefulness, and sense of humor while taking on such a challenging kid as Stan are qualities that I look for in teachers, counselors, and friends. Jill could have chosen to present a nice, neatly packaged success story; instead, she offers us an open-ended, troubling experience with an ambivalent outcome. I admire her honesty, and I appreciate the chance to struggle with this tough as nails situation.

I have decided to organize my response around the questions. First, the author asks, "What else could I have done as Stan's classroom teacher?" I look first at what strategies were used. The teacher used tried and true classroom strategies to manage Stan's behaviors. She seated him near good role models and in the front, where she could keep an eye on him. She bent over backwards to allow Stan to be active, until his karate kicks became dangerous. She read books to the class that taught lessons regarding social skills. This teacher complained during "every waking hour" to her long-suffering spouse. She confronted Stan directly, but he denied responsibility. She used love and logic. She further consulted with Stan's rather unpleasant mother. She recruited the school counselor, the principal, a court-appointed caseworker, and a psychologist. I believe that the array and scope of strategies are indicative of a hugely resourceful teacher, and I cannot think of even one more thing she could have done. What was the outcome of this extraordinary effort? This compassionate and resourceful teacher was thwarted at every turn. I deeply empathize with her. I once taught fifth grade, and it was the best job I have ever had. Every morning, I knew that this was the most important work I could possibly be doing, and then there were the kids like Stan, the troubled little souls I cannot forget. What on God's earth has become of them?

The second question is "What type of support structure could be developed in the school setting to help school personnel better manage Stan's behavior and address his problems?" Is the nation ready to invest in one-on-one classroom supervision for kids like Stan? Perhaps a teacher's aide could be enlisted to work one on one with Stan, freeing the classroom teacher to teach. If this sounds like an expensive solution, consider what the schools and community will face as Stan grows up, assuming that no one has helped him control his behavior. Availability of student support professionals is the key to an effective intervention.

I was also impressed by the interventions of the court-appointed caseworker. She did home visits to work with Stan's custodial mother and stepfather and came to the school to work with Stan individually and to assist the teacher. The schools need more professionals like her.

This case demonstrates the importance of administrative support and involvement. The teacher wrote that she felt intimidated by Stan's aggressive mother and that she requested that the principal be present at their conferences. This kind of situation is scary. The problem of parents and students "going off" on school personnel is becoming an occupational hazard. Many middle schools and high schools already station police in the halls. In our miserably uncivil society, we must first ensure that our schools are safe and orderly. This is perhaps the most important school mandate of all when one is serving students who demonstrate such severe dysfunctional behaviors.

Next, the author raises a question regarding the possible benefit of ADHD medication. During 25 years of private practice as a psychologist specializing in children and families, I have seen a lot of ADHD. Whether or not I thought ADHD was a factor, I would work with the teacher and the parents to modify the problematic behavior. If that failed, I would talk with the parents about a referral to a psychiatrist and an evaluation for medication. I worked with a competent child psychiatrist who helped parents understand both the benefits and the dangers of medication. Until very recently, there was no biological test for ADHD. If the medication brought the hyperactivity under control, ergo, the child had ADHD. Sometimes medication really does help; nonetheless, considering Stan's case, I would hate to see a 6-year-old on psychotropic medication.

Stan's case is complicated by overwhelming systemic problems, possible sexual abuse, and alcohol abuse. This family is falling into chaos, and it is hard for me to picture any effective follow-through with psychotherapy or medication. In fact, the mother has a history of opting out of treatment. Although it is probably not true in this case, it would not be the first time that a frustrated therapist referred a difficult family to a psychiatrist just to be rid of them.

Finally, the author wants to know what I would have done if I were a counselor working with Stan. I think that she is right to suspect sexual abuse, and a call to Child Protective Services would be in order. Given his age, the talking cure has little to offer Stan. Play therapy, however, would be a good bet because, at the very least, it is likely to uncover any sexual abuse that might be present.

Additionally, I have a strong bias in favor of family therapy. I have never believed that my counseling skills are so magical that I can help a child in an individual weekly session. Children live with their family. If counselors want to make a difference in children's life, they must engage the family. Unfortunately, in Stan's case, his mother wanted no part of counseling. Why was this so? Was she a mother who did not care about her own child's welfare? I doubt that. I suspect that alcohol is the real culprit. If Stan's mother commits to counseling, sooner or later she will have to confront her alcohol abuse. The only hope that I see is if the authorities—the courts, child welfare workers, and school administrators—can apply sufficient pressure to force this mother to face up to her alcohol problem.

My 25 years of practice have humbled me. No one has the answers for every child's problem. Interventions can help, but there are limits. As I think back on this difficult case, what gives me the most hope is that this teacher's intense experience with Stan inspired her to go into school counseling. We need such gifted and caring people in our profession.

Response

Marie A. Wakefield

Using effective management strategies that will result in an optimal learning environment is a relentless challenge for any classroom teacher. Regardless of age, gender, ethnicity, or socioeconomic status, classroom rosters inevitably include students whose behavior may test the very fibers of one's ability to maintain sanity.

Stan's teacher already had an opinion of what he was like before she met him. The teacher's lounge is not the best place to collect information that will affirm an insightful approach to a student's problem behavior. Reading files or talking to previous teachers prior to meeting students often taints the teacher's opportunity to establish a positive rapport. After she heard Stan's name repeatedly, the classroom teacher's definitive positive approach plan lost steam early in the school year. A good beginning would include strategies that have worked successfully during the 17 years of her experience. Calling his home and welcoming him to the classroom, learning about his interests, and building a relationship with his parents before Stan started the school year are some suggestions for a proactive approach.

Classroom teachers, school counselors, and psychologists cannot adequately make diagnoses without consultation with parents and significant family members. One can only determine what support Stan needs by the results of an accurate assessment performed by a qualified person. One evident factor is that he lives with his mother and stepfather. Children who have experienced a divorce, a move, a change in school, or other significant events may act out. Examining how Stan has changed since the divorce is critical. If, in fact, it was established that ADHD was Stan's diagnosis, other strategies might have included a specific behavior contract, documented and well-communicated consequences and rewards, variations in his work schedule, an assigned work environment, and tasks tailored to his academic level. Additionally, Stan may need some assistance in organizing his day through established routines, work folders, concise directions on shorter assignments for the completion of tasks, limited choices, frequent conference checks by the teacher or a buddy for task completion, and daily parent–teacher logs to track accomplishments. In addition, Stan could be evaluated for possible sexual abuse, family trauma, or bipolar conditions. If another close family relative were diagnosed with ADHD, it would be important to determine where Stan fits in relation to the heredity of this disorder.

Calling on the System

The management of a student who displays disruptive behavior requires a team approach from all school personnel. One effective structure in a school setting is the use of a behavior team, whose responsibility is to examine the teacher's documentation of behavioral concerns and make appropriate suggestions and referrals. The team usually includes the psychologist, a special education representative, the school nurse, the classroom teacher, the school counselor, other classroom teachers, the administration, and perhaps even a behavior specialist. The team is charged with responsibility for ensuring complete documentation from the teacher and implementation of the recommended interventions. It is important to know what interventions were tried, how often they were tried, and the length of time they were used. For a collaborative team, expanded options become available. Suggestions include building a flexible schedule in which Stan reports to a buddy in the classroom when he is too disruptive, establishing daily short visits with the school counselor, assigning an adult mentor as another significant person for Stan to communicate with, using consistent language among all staff throughout the school as a way of redirecting inappropriate behavior from all students, and having the teacher meet daily with Stan to share any classroom or schoolwide goals he has successfully achieved. Even the smallest of steps toward progress must be recognized and reinforced. If he regresses, someone needs to be available to discuss the causes and encourage him to try harder the next day.

Considering Medication

Stan may be displaying a number of inappropriate behaviors that are very related to symptoms of other disorders. Establishing an accurate diagnosis is the first step. Second, giving Stan medication without his parents' supportive approval and willingness to be partners in changing his behavior is a serious roadblock. If Stan truly has ADHD, behavioral changes can successfully occur in combination with medication and therapy. Nevertheless, in this scenario, there is not enough information to draw this conclusion. If the parents do not see his behavior as a problem or are too distracted by the chaos in their life, the argument would be a waste of time. Because the mother is having some difficulty in her life with alcohol, she may not be able to manage something else.

Experts place a great amount of significance on the need to have a structured learning environment to inculcate various coping skills, good study habits, responsibility, and a sense of discipline. I support the use of medication only if parents actively participate in monitoring its dosage and effectiveness. Many times, parents have displayed an attitude of complacency, as if the drug is the cure to the problem. The home and school, as a collaborative team, can provide more stability and consistency for the foundation of a win–win situation. Beneficial results for students that I have experienced include a better focus on academics, the ability to problem solve productively, and a display of appropriate social skills over a period of time.

Expanding Evaluation and Treatment Options

To adequately provide service to Stan, I would recommend that he be seen by a physician to rule out a physical problem, determine an accurate diagnosis, and gather any pertinent family history. Stan may very well be reacting to a chaotic home situation. Because the involvement of the parents is so critical, I would think of creative ways to develop a working relationship with them. One way to draw parents in when they are experiencing difficulty or change is to hold parent meetings related to topics of interest. Invite them to the classroom for special events or times when adult volunteers are needed. These strategies provide the venue for parents to establish a support group and share valuable information in a nonthreatening way, and they give the school an opportunity to reach out and establish open communication on an issue that is a concern for the family and the school. I would like to know Stan's instructional levels in the core subject areas. This information should be consistently available from the classroom teacher. As data become available, the school district's behavioral consultant could assist with Stan's evaluation and possible eligibility for a 504 Plan as an intervention strategy. Under Section 504 of the Rehabilitation Act of 1973 (Council of Administrators of Special Education, 1991), Stan's school has a legal obligation to provide modifications and adaptations for students with a handicapping condition. Conversely, testing results may determine whether Stan qualifies as a special education student to receive additional supportive services through the Individuals With Disabilities Act. One can examine the overlap and disparity between these legal mandates by visiting the Web site of the U.S. Department of Education Office for Civil Rights (http://www.ed.gov/about/offices/list/ocr/504faq.html). During related evaluation, learning needs and other impairments affecting Stan's progress would be addressed. If Stan works with any other teachers—for example, the physical education or music teachers—I would conference with them to evaluate his level of participation, ability to follow directions, compliance with rules, and any other information that gives a clearer picture of Stan's progress.

If a behavior team does not exist in the school, I would establish one that included people who might have the most contact with Stan to develop a contract with him. The written contract might include three or four objectives—behavioral and academic goals, consequences, and rewards. As a school counselor, I would work closely with the teacher to ensure consistency and encourage her to identify Stan's strengths and to send a note or make a phone call to share something positive about Stan with his parents. Interactions with Stan, focused on his strengths, could be very beneficial to the effective development and implementation of the components of his educational contract as well as the rewards that elevate his self-esteem. Areas to explore include his interests, his pets, his hobbies, his favorite things, his friends at home, students he might want to become friends with at school, and a job or task at the school that could help him feel like he belonged.

References

Black, C., & Nicholas, H. (1996). Wherever you go. *The greatest hits* [CD]. New York: RCA Records.

Council of Administrators of Special Education. (1991). *Student access: A resource guide for educators, Section 504 of the Rehabilitation Act of 1973.* Albuquerque, NM: Author.

Fay, J., & Funk, D. (1995). *Teaching with love and logic.* Golden, CO: Love and Logic Press.

34

The Systemic Nature of Bullying:
"Handle Your Own Business, Punk!"

This incident articulates the reality that when systemic characteristics support tolerance for bullying behavior, the issues of intervention become wide ranging and complex.

◼ Critical Incident

Teah L. Moore

I was completing a school counseling internship in an urban middle school while working toward my master's degree when I first met "Yanna Wilkins" and "Beth Smith." These girls, both of whom were African American, had been involved in a physical altercation in which Yanna had threatened Beth with a knife. As I investigated the incident and worked with Yanna, I realized that this matter was related to bullying and that bullying existed not only among students but also among staff members working in the school. In fact, to adequately address the bullying dynamics between Yanna and Beth, it is important that I first describe the school setting and the dynamics present in the building.

This middle school served Grades 5 through 8, and the approximately 370 students ranged from 10 to 15 years of age. The student population consisted primarily of African American (92%), Caucasian (5%), and Hispanic/Latino (3%) students, and the socioeconomic status of the students' families varied from lower class to lower middle class. With regard to the staff, the administrators were all African American, and the faculty was predominately White, with only three African American teachers.

I quickly came to realize that ongoing conflict characterized the relationship between the administrators and the teachers. This was especially true of the relationship between the principal (Mr. William Smith) and the teaching staff. Mr. Smith, a former professional football player, used his size to intimidate both students and teachers. Students routinely told me about witnessing conflicts between Mr. Smith and their teachers. For example, one student told me about a time when Mr. Smith walked into a special education classroom and chastised the teacher in front of the students for her inability to control her classroom and for using him to discipline the students. As he exited the room, the principal remarked, "I wouldn't obey you either."

To be fair, one should keep in mind that the school had been on the state's accountability watch list, and standardized scores on the state test had consistently improved since Mr. Smith was hired. Strategies he used in an attempt to achieve these improvements included mandatory school uniforms, enforcement of a closed campus, and the designation of only one entrance and exit for use during the day. Lines were also painted on the floors to direct student traffic flow in the hallways, and strict regulations were instituted to prevent contact between students of different grade levels. Any student caught violating this rule was immediately sent to detention. A district police officer monitored the hallways, and school cameras were installed. As a safety protocol, an intercom system was installed in each classroom that allowed the office staff to speak schoolwide or to specific classrooms.

Although Mr. Smith had a reputation for running a tight ship and closely managing all daily operations, his attitude toward me seemed to be surprisingly laissez faire. I was a school counselor intern placed in the school by the district office through a contractual agreement between the school district and my university. On my arrival, Mr. Smith informed me that he was not interested in my presence in his school because he had not requested me to be at his school. He initially indicated that I did not need to report to him when I arrived or left, whom I saw, or what I was doing. Despite this initial communication of noninterference, however, I found the opposite to be true.

One difficulty I faced as an intern involved maintaining the privacy of individual counseling sessions. My office, which I shared with the family outreach specialist, was equipped with both a telephone and the intercom system. The telephone was useful and allowed for private contacts with parents, but the intercom system proved problematic. When conducting individual counseling sessions with students, I was frequently interrupted by Mr. Smith. He would use the intercom system in an attempt to contact me during counseling sessions. If I responded that I was with a student, he would ask me to identify the student's name, and I had to repeatedly decline to provide student names over the intercom. Although I was consistent and had clearly discussed the issue of confidentiality, this behavior persisted.

I also felt pressured by Mr. Smith to conduct evaluations that were clearly outside my competency areas. Periodically, for example, he requested that I spend time in certain classrooms for the purpose of evaluating the teacher's instructional effectiveness and ability to manage classroom behavior. I consistently declined such requests, citing both my position as an intern and my lack of training in the observation and evaluation of teachers as reasons for my refusal to conduct these evaluations.

Although I was able to avoid conducting these evaluations and to continually resist the intercom inquiries about which students I was seeing, I found Mr. Smith's managerial style to be intrusive and to reflect misunderstanding about the counseling field. Nonetheless, I was thankful for the opportunity to complete my internship in the district and was enthusiastic about helping inner city students address issues that interfered with their success at school. I had entered the internship focused on the impact of difficult family and life circumstances on the students' ability to learn. During the internship, however, I discovered that the school climate can also interfere with students' learning. My work with Yanna Wilkins and Beth Smith really brought this to light.

Approximately 3 months into the academic year, a sixth grade teacher reported to me that she had interrupted an altercation between Yanna and Beth. The teacher stated that she found Yanna, a sixth grader, wielding two knives, one in each hand, and threatening to stab Beth, a seventh grader. Yanna willingly gave the knives to the teacher, insisting that Beth and some other seventh grade girls had been physically harassing her since the beginning of the school year.

Immediately after the incident, I met with Yanna individually to allow her to share her side of the story and defuse some of the emotional tension. Yanna was emotionally bereft and had difficulty discussing the incident between sobs. I sat with her as I allowed her to cry and slowly regain her composure. Still crying, she showed me indentations in her hands where she had gripped the knives so tightly that her fingernails had dug into her palms. She was physically shaking, and she spoke no audible words as she cried. She sat crying and rubbing at the indentations in her palms. Eventually, Yanna began to talk about the incident. I assisted her in disclosing what was going on inside her. She was able to talk about her scared, sad, angry, and sometimes happy feelings.

Yanna told me that Beth and some other seventh grade girls were always "making trouble" for her and that they had threatened her physically. She explained that she was so concerned that she asked her older brother Leroy to walk her to and from school. He did so frequently, and Beth did not bother her on these days. On days when Leroy was unable to walk with her, however, Beth and the other girls would beat her up or verbally harass her. Yanna stated that the girls had come to her home the night before the incident and threatened to harm her family.

The next morning, Leroy was unable to walk her to school, so Yanna had put the knives in her book bag to protect herself. She made it to school safely but was then confronted by Beth and the other girls while at her locker. Yanna reported that Beth and the other girls began shoving her and that Beth had even slapped her in the face. Yanna indicated that it was at this point that she removed the knives from her book bag and threatened the girls. Although the other girls fled, Beth stood her ground and called Yanna's bluff.

Yanna told me that she had complained about Beth and the other girls, on numerous occasions, to teachers and to the principal but that she had been told to ignore the girls and "learn to run faster than them." Yanna had even reported the girls to the district resource officer. She said that she felt she had no other option than to find a way to protect herself and indicated that this was the first time she had ever stood up to Beth and the other girls. Yanna also expressed fear that the girls would now increase their physical assaults on her. Yanna talked about the knot in her stomach, the headache she was experiencing, and her shaking hands. Sometimes Yanna cried, and sometimes she laughed in disbelief at what she had done.

My time with Yanna was repeatedly interrupted by Mr. Smith and his administrative secretary, both of whom used the intercom system to contact my office. The principal wanted Yanna in his office and stated that he did not want me to "help her devise a story." He informed me that he planned to suspend her. Yanna heard all of this. I did convince him to allow me more time with her and agreed to walk the student to the office when we were finished.

After my conversation with Yanna, I escorted her to Mr. Smith's office and then questioned a number of other students and talked with several sixth grade teachers.

When questioned, no sixth grade girl confirmed Yanna's version of the altercation; they claimed only to have seen Yanna with the knives. Beth and the other seventh grade girls denied any wrongdoing, but two red slap marks were clearly visible on Yanna's face. Teachers described Beth as a good student who rarely caused any problems. Furthermore, Beth just happened to be the principal's cousin. Yanna, conversely, was described as a below average student who was not well liked by her classmates. Although she was a low academic performer, she had never been a problem in the classroom.

Neither Beth nor the other girls received any punishment for their actions, and all of the girls refused to participate in counseling. As per the district's policy of zero tolerance, Yanna was suspended for 2 years. While the district's decision was pending, I was able to meet with her twice more on an individual basis. During these sessions, I used art therapy to work with Yanna. During our sessions, she created a feelings booklet, explored her feelings regarding the possible outcomes of the district decision, and outlined her family's support of her. Meeting and counseling with Yanna were effective for her and created an atmosphere for other students to reach out about what was happening to them.

In the weeks that followed the incident, more students began to talk with me about being harassed by other students. One student threw a desk at a group of boys who had been teasing him about his size. Like Yanna, the students reported that they were often told by administrators and teachers to ignore the other students. They stated that Mr. Smith would call them punks for not being able to "handle their business."

As an intervention to maximize student access to counseling services, I developed counseling groups to address the bullying issue. I used a variety of treatment approaches to help students develop effective tactics to deal with the bullying, explore their emotions, and build stronger social skills. Students were exposed to expressive art therapy, aggression replacement therapy, and talk therapy. Expressive art therapy included encouraging students to express their experiences and thoughts through songwriting, dance, and art mediums. Aggression replacement therapy drew on a curriculum that explored aggression and helped students develop more socially acceptable ways of engaging with others. Talk therapies provided students an opportunity to develop assertiveness skills and listening skills and a safe forum to practice new skills.

Handling the systemic issue required more finesse, beginning with innocuous conversations with teachers. The conversations centered on the tensions and continual conflicts between the administrative staff and faculty. Faculty expressed feeling a lack of support from administration and a disrespect for various approaches to classroom management. Some felt intimidated by the students and principal, whereas others used intimidation tactics to control the students. In particular, teachers who reported shying away from interactions with the principal said that they also shied away from dealing with the bullying out of a desire to avoid administrative involvement.

This dynamic explained why Beth had rarely been in trouble and why no one supported Yanna's version of what happened. I believed that addressing the bullying issue at two levels would be a more viable approach than solely facilitating counseling groups with students. Some of the teachers were willing to participate in resolving issues among students and understood the importance of modeling appropriate behavior for the students.

On the basis of my previous experiences and interactions with Mr. Smith, I worried that the school could not address the systemic issues without creating a more adverse atmosphere. I viewed the principal as an important change agent in the school environment but was unsure of how to work with him and the other administrative staff. Clearly, efforts were needed to minimize the "us against them" mentality that permeated the interactions between the administrators and teachers as well as between the teachers and students.

Questions

1. Should I have addressed the bullying on the systemic level and the individual student level, or would I be better advised to deal only with the students?
2. How would you discuss the issue of bullying with the principal? Would you include him in addressing the systemic issues, and, if so, how?
3. What other techniques or methods would you identify as ways to address the systemic issues of bullying?
4. What individual treatment modalities would be effective in exploring bullying issues?
5. In developing counseling groups, would you consider mixing the age groups to aid in socialization and social skills?

■Response

Shannon Casey-Cannon and Hardin L. K. Coleman

Bullying is a pattern of unprovoked and deliberate negative behavior with intent to harm in the presence of a real or perceived imbalance of power (American Academy of Child and Adolescent Psychiatry, 2001; McEvoy, 2005; Smith, 1991). It cuts across social, economic, and racial lines. Examples of bullying include name calling and teasing, physical violence, damage to property, spreading rumors, and—as in the case of Yanna and Beth—threats with a weapon. Bullying negatively affects the school climate and has social, academic, and psychological consequences for both the target and the bully (Crick & Grotpeter, 1996; Hazler, Hoover, & Oliver, 1992; Shapiro, Baumeister, & Kessler, 1991; Sharp, 1996). Most middle school children report having been bullied, and bullying frequently takes the form of attacks at school or on the way to school (Clarke & Kiselica, 1997).

It is our perspective that schools and their personnel have a moral obligation to assess bullying problems, to intervene appropriately, and to be proactive in preventing this behavior. In our response to this incident, we applaud the counselor for persistence in spite of Mr. Smith's repeated attempts to thwart counseling efforts, and we fully support responding at both systemic and individual levels. This response describes strategies for ameliorating the bully-friendly environment, including individual and group treatments, structured programs for schoolwide change, and collaboration with Mr. Smith to improve interpersonal relations in the school.

Two aspects of this incident are notable in severity. First, threats with a weapon increase the potential for physical and emotional damage, necessitating an unwavering and serious consequence. Second, although the environment does not condone aggressive behavior, it does little to discourage abusive interactions, and key players rely on intimidating tactics. Mr. Smith's chastising a teacher about being out of control, given that he is unable to control his own reactions in front of students, is a particularly poignant example. The social modeling of inappropriate behavior sends mixed messages to students, who feel unprotected without clear school policy and may feel further victimized by dismissive and threatening authority figures. Issues of race or ethnicity, power, and privilege complicate this scenario.

Most bullying experts agree that primary and secondary prevention require identifying and intervening with students, teaching skills that promote positive social and emotional competence, and working to create safer, more respectful and responsive school environments (Twemlow et al., 2001). The school counselor's role is critical for (a) acknowledging and assessing the nature and extent of bullying; (b) intervening appropriately to assist targets, bullies, and bystanders; and (c) establishing programs of education and policy to promote appropriate social interaction and prevent bullying behavior.

Students often feel that adults trivialize bullying behavior, blame the target of the bullying, or respond with inaction (Casey-Cannon, Hayward, & Gowen, 2001; Clarke & Kiselica, 1997; McEvoy, 2005). This counselor was correct in her immediate response to Yanna, including her assessment of the broader context of Yanna's school experience. The counselor's patience and supportive listening helped Yanna feel safe in expressing feelings, tensions, fears, and physiological symptoms. From this report, Yanna was protecting herself in the absence of her brother. In addition, Beth upped the ante by appearing at Yanna's home, perhaps fueling Yanna's instinct to protect her family. It is consistent with research that Yanna would respond to bullying behavior with retaliation, which students often see as an inappropriate but effective response (Casey-Cannon et al., 2001).

In the absence of corroborating evidence, it was critical to carefully acknowledge Yanna's experience without expressing judgment. The counselor did well in gathering corroborating evidence, including observing marks on Yanna's cheeks and noting that Beth was the principal's cousin. Understanding why other children ostracized Yanna would also be helpful. Had she threatened other students? Did they tease her for a characteristic beyond her control, such as choice of clothes or reading ability? Typically, bullied children are those who present an easy target, are often in some way distinct or different (e.g., are perceived as being too tall), and are sensitive enough to let the bullying disturb them. Knowing how Yanna participates as an aggressor or target would help the counselor determine an appropriate response. It could be that Yanna's weak academic performance is related to marginalization in the classroom. Knowing whether Yanna's previous pleas for protection were ignored would be important for documentation if her family pursued due process or legal recourse after their daughter's suspension.

The counselor's individual meetings reduced Yanna's distress and made it easier for other students to approach her for assistance, which was extremely beneficial in this unsupportive environment. The counselor's goals mirror what has been found helpful in the research. In individual treatment, counselors address causes and consequences of bullying behaviors in supportive relationships (Nuttall & Kalesnik, 1987). They empower students to increase their sense of control over the experience, helping students become better equipped in social interactions, teaching assertiveness, and improving coping (Clarke & Kiselica, 1997; Roberts & Coursol, 1996). Some counselors find that showing antibullying videos, available at numerous Web sites (e.g., http://www.dfes.gov.uk/bullying/), is a good way to train students in appropriate responses. Antibullying videos show other typical students in conflict, helping to externalize the bullying experience for the target. That helps to minimize the target's culpability or the feeling that he or she brought the bullying on himself or herself. Finally, counselors work to improve students' sense of belonging in the overall community.

A few specific structured interventions for treatment are the "shared concern" and "no blame" approaches (Munn, 2005). Both of these tactics avoid placing blame with aggressors and instead work to support both students. The no blame approach invites students (bullied, bullies, and bystanders) to discuss the incident and provide suggestions for resolving the situation, which is helpful when circumstances are unclear. Both interventions help bullies accept responsibility for their behavior and encourage peaceful resolutions. Another treatment approach is the use of traditional solution-focused techniques that provide brief and immediate responses to resolve the situation.

Research has shown that individual interventions are most effective as part of a comprehensive school counseling program. The counselor was right to respond with small counseling groups (Nuttall & Kalesnik, 1987). Structured learning groups and interpersonal problem-solving programs can include modeling, role playing, and student-to-student feedback around social skills. Several Web sites have exercises that can be used with small groups (see http://tolerance.org/teach/activities). Exercises that promote kindness, cooperation, and communication are likely to be quite effective (Olweus, 1993). With regard to multigrade groups, the supportive mentoring of older peers could have benefits for bullied youths, although this must be weighed against the power hierarchy in mixed-grade groups. To the extent that mixing groups does not silence younger members, who may be reluctant to expose vulnerabilities in front of older students, it is likely to be beneficial. Absent research in this specific area, the counselor might be in the best position to judge the size and makeup of the group that would be most appropriate for creating a working therapy group in her school.

Instituting a schoolwide policy and antibullying program is critical for the well-being of this school, in particular on the basis of the escalation of Yanna's incident and the intimidating tactics of administration. Being "called out" by the principal likely raises confusion, self-doubt, or fear in both students and teachers alike. Teachers, for example, may be understandably concerned about how their evaluations might be affected by disclosing abuse (McEvoy, 2005). If the counselor does not address the problem systematically, she risks colluding with the intimidators in the environment. This lack of support for students could have meaningful long-term implications for the interpersonal relationships and academic performance of each student. As the counselor noted, responding without creating a more adverse atmosphere will take finesse and a collaborative, nonconfrontational approach.

Several authors have recommended schoolwide assessments, interventions, and policies that have reduced bullying behavior and increased students' feelings of safety (Clarke & Kiselica, 1997; Nuttall & Kalesnik, 1987; Olweus, Limber, & Mihalic, 1999; Roberts & Coursol, 1996). The counselor can investigate research-based programs, including Olweus et al.'s (1999) antibullying program or the Creating a Peaceful School Learning Environment program (Twemlow et al., 2001). Those interventions promote the implementation of rules and policies that prohibit bullying, encourage respect on and off campus, and identify consequences for such behaviors. Schools should send a clear message that "no bullying will be tolerated, ever" (Clarke & Kiselica, 1997, p. 318). All students should be aware of the policy, and enforcement of expectations should be consistent for all members of the community. Students can sign a no-bullying contract that formalizes their understanding of the school policy and represents a commitment to respectful behavior.

Most intervention and prevention programs include a student survey that assesses the extent of bullying problems and serves as a baseline for future assessments (Olweus, 1993; Roberts & Coursol, 1996). The survey might assess kinds of bullying, distress related to bullying, the overall school environment, and students' judgment of respect by their peers (Ray & Berg, 2000; Roberts & Coursol, 1996). Olweus et al.'s (1999) model bullying prevention program includes a specific assessment tool, the Bully/Victim Questionnaire. Even the act of conducting the assessment expresses a level of caring and concern on behalf of the administration, which would be a good first step for this school.

Multiple strategies have been suggested for antiviolence intervention and prevention programs (www.stopbullyingnow.com). Antiviolence whole school workshops help raise awareness and create commitment to and consensus around school policies and goals. Structured group interventions, such as peer counseling, peer mediation, and safe rooms, have been supported when part of a comprehensive program (Munn, 2005). Interventions also include teaching child-appropriate strategies for responding during bullying incidents, such as staying calm and looking as confident as one can when firmly asking the bully to stop. If that is not effective, students can leave the setting and approach an adult for assistance. It is important to teach bystanders to see how their silence enables bullying behavior and to be good reporters of behaviors they witness. Also, students should have ways to report incidents and be protected from reprisals for good faith reporting. Drop-in facilities can help support students at all times of day. As part of the teaching curriculum, students could create and post antiviolence banners and educational materials. Finally, increased monitoring of problem areas (e.g., locker rooms) and increased attention when the program is first implemented, when flares in behavior are to be expected, demonstrate the school's commitment to creating change at a system level.

At a staff level, the intervention program might include training faculty and administration about negative consequences of bullying and reminding them that bullying is not a toughening-up developmental task but instead a negative interpersonal experience that interferes with learning. At this school, it might be particularly helpful to work with staff to discuss which methods of discipline and student feedback are acceptable. When those standards are discussed and agreed on by the staff, adult bullies may be less likely to believe their way of operating is supported by peers or staff.

Mr. Smith's resentment and threatening disciplinary tactics are likely to interfere with a systematic program. He might believe his behavior is justified as a form of discipline or as motivation for students. He may also minimize responses to bullying in an attempt to avoid the negative attention it brings to the school or out of a fear of losing incoming students. Although we are sure the counselor considered unplugging her phone and attacking the intercom with a screwdriver, absent any institutional avenues for creating change, it is easy to see how she might join other teachers in feeling powerless. Gaining Mr. Smith's commitment as principal would be critical for successful implementation of an antibullying initiative. The situation calls for highly creative and nuanced strategies.

It is our experience that adults who are aggressive frequently are aware that their demands are outside of reason and continue to push because they can. To that end, a group of individuals talking with the principal might be more effective than an individual counselor's approach. To the extent that it is possible, it might be most important that the counselor develop allies in the environment to protect her role. For example, engaging the teachers who acknowledge the importance of modeling respectful behavior might be a good start. Other allies could include the district superintendent, parents, or grandparents. It might be that the local preacher or even another football coach would be a colleague who could talk openly with the principal and have greater influence than a counselor intern. Selecting someone with whom the principal has an existing relationship or who has more tenure in the district might be wise. The counselor would do well to consider her credibility with the larger community and how she might use it to her advantage. If she believes her credibility is low, then collaborating with someone who has more influence would be crucial.

Sidling alongside Mr. Smith to create change is likely to be more effective than confronting him directly on his behavior. The counselor might engage Mr. Smith in an antibullying program as a continuation of the meaningful change he has already brought to campus. The severity of this incident might convince him of the importance of preventing future outbursts to protect the reputation of the school. If Mr. Smith believes his motivational style is important to maintaining academic performance, perhaps the research suggesting that repeated bullying has been associated with negative school outcomes, such as absenteeism and poor academic performance, would be convincing (Roberts & Coursol, 1996). Some argue that heavy-handed approaches, rather than eliminating bullying behavior, drive the bullying underground (see www.stopbullyingnow.com). An assessment and evaluation could identify the relationship between bullying and academic performance at the school. The principal might be swayed by fewer behavioral problems in school or improved attendance rates if children are skipping school to avoid being bullied. Tactfully expressing concerns about legal ramifications should the school be approached about not protecting students might also be effective (McEvoy, 2005). Schools that receive federal funding could be held responsible for student-on-student harassment if they act with deliberate indifference to harassment that is severe enough, pervasive enough, and objectively offensive enough to prevent targets from enjoying educational opportunities (see *Davis v. Monroe County Board of Education*, 1999).

In spite of his vocalizations to the contrary, the principal seems to have a high need for control, as evidenced by numerous disruptions of the counseling process. Having external consultants deliver the message about appropriate and inappropriate behavior and its effects in the classroom is also an option. Outside consultants could also conduct in-service workshops to discuss the ongoing conflict between administrative staff and faculty. Given that ethnicity seems to be playing an active role in this setting, a diversity expert might be particularly helpful. It is important that the principal feel like a valued and key player in the decision making about his school, be engaged with the process, and get added value or acclaim from implementing successful initiatives. Providing the principal with options by suggesting a list of strategies and a procedure for experimenting with diverse strategies until the right formula is developed would allow him the most leverage for selecting options that seem most palatable for him.

In addition to recruiting other allies, the counselor might approach her internship supervisor, who could clarify misunderstandings about the counseling field (e.g., reiterate the limits of student confidentiality) and advocate for the intern. To the extent that the principal's meddling in treatment is a passive–aggressive reaction to having counselors in the school, the supervisor could evaluate and discuss subsequent placements with the principal. Placing counselors in schools that do not welcome their involvement is not conducive to a good training experience for a new counselor and has the potential of undermining the quality of the counseling performed. Loss of this placement, however, would be a horrible disservice to children in the school; the counselor's fight for inner city placements admirably represents a recent wave focusing on social justice in counseling. As standard practice, training programs could work toward placing interns in diverse communities and training the counseling students to work in systems that have diverse approaches, values, and needs.

In reviewing the literature on bullying and applying it to this case study, we find that there is clear evidence that effective interventions call for the creation of school communities that are caring toward individuals, promote respect for self and others, encourage self-regulation and the expression of feelings, and reinforce verbal mediation of conflict. It is important that schools understand that such an environment would not only serve to reduce bullying but also facilitate academic achievement. As such, it is important to make sure that every school has a developmental guidance program that facilitates the acquisition of the social skills children need to be effective members of a caring community.

It is equally important to note that such a school community might not match the experience children have in the rest of their life. Children who are poor and mobile and who live in chaotic or violent neighborhoods do not consistently experience respect for themselves and others, have models of self-regulation, or get reinforced for verbal mediation of conflict. It is very important that school professionals, as they attempt to create caring communities in schools, recognize the discontinuity for some children and include the process of bridging that gap in the design and implementation of their programming.

■ Response

Harvey Hoyo

Unfortunately, bullying incidents such as the one between Yanna and Beth occur in schools across the country. A recent survey from the University of Indiana suggested that only 55% of U.S. high school students feel safe in their school (Center for Evaluation and Education Policy, 2005). As a former school counselor and school administrator of several urban schools, I feel sympathy for the school counseling intern, who, about to enter this great profession, had to experience a school environment characterized by bullying and desperation among all the stakeholders, including administrators, teachers, support staff, and students. To provide interns with a realistic experience, many universities would not knowingly place an intern in such a dysfunctional school. Conversely, such a placement, when the intern works directly with a well-qualified university supervisor, can prove to be an excellent learning experience for the school counseling intern.

Question 1

The first question posed was whether the bullying should be addressed on both the system and the individual student levels or only on the individual student level. It is clear that the experiences presented in this vignette are complex and multifaceted. To support a learning environment that promotes both academic excellence and a positive school climate, the counselor requires a sophisticated understanding of the multiple embedded contexts that define this middle school. For example, conventional wisdom dictates that the counselor identify the problem and tackle it directly. This traditional approach would teach the intern to identify the primary client. In this vignette, however, the identity of the primary client is unclear. Is it Yanna, who threatened Beth with a knife? Is it Beth, who used her leadership skills to organize harassment parties for Yanna on days when Yanna walked home unescorted? Alternatively, is it the school principal and ex-football player, Mr. Smith, whose intimidating behavior casts a negative learning climate at the school?

The fundamental problem involves which lenses should be used to analyze the contexts at this urban middle school. Functionally, the school counselor traditionally responds directly with specific interventions aimed at targeted student problems. Organizationally, the trend is for policymakers to mandate student service solutions by seeking community partnerships. Thus, school systems often seek to develop student support systems by attacking identified problems one at a time. In my view, such thinking brings fragmentation of services with little horizontal and vertical integration of those service providers, whether they are departments in a school, divisions in a school district, individual schools, clusters of schools, districts, or public or private community agencies. There is a universal need for school districts to develop support systems that enable all students to benefit from higher standards and access to a rigorous curriculum in a safe learning environment. In other words, all reform efforts contain two basic elements: defined student results and input from all stakeholders.

In navigating through the details of this vignette, the counselor is thinking correctly as she reflects on the systemic issue. The counselor's perception of the principal as an important change agent is consistent with traditional reform research conducted by Sergiovanni (1991). There can be no excuse for Mr. Smith's pressing the counselor to conduct teacher evaluations, reprimanding adults in front of students, or breaching counselor–client confidentiality with the school's intercom. Nonetheless, having been an urban high school principal myself, I see Mr. Smith's behaviors as signaling frustrated desperation. He more than likely feels overwhelmed and sees himself as constantly battling the multiple challenges facing urban schools, including underfunding, new or unqualified teachers, lack of parental support, an old and dilapidated infrastructure, and a student population that is disengaged and ambivalent about academic achievement and school support services. Mr. Smith is frustrated at every turn, and his actions demonstrate that frustration. At an unstable urban school, the principal's plate is often overloaded.

One difficult problem is teacher attrition. According to the National Center for Education Statistics' (Provasnik & Dorfman, 2005) issue brief, half of all new teachers entering the field leave within 5 years, and most of them leave from schools that desperately need them. Teacher attrition rates are 50% higher in high-poverty and high-minority schools, where beginning teachers are twice as likely to be assigned. If Mr. Smith's school is a typical urban middle school, he must devote much of his energy—more than suburban school principals do—to creating and monitoring teacher-induction programs aimed at bringing new teachers quickly up to speed. My point is that principals, especially those at urban schools, must approach their school holistically and deal with long-term systemic reform. The one issue at a time mind-set, focused on putting out the immediate fires, often leads principals to make decisions aimed at correcting one problem while creating or exacerbating other problems. Like desperate *Titanic* passengers, many principals waste time rearranging deck chairs as they fight to save their sinking ship.

In response to the counselor's first question, therefore, I am firm in my belief that it is essential to deal with both the systemic and the individual student levels to effectively address the bullying problem. My contention is that the counselor, as a professional school counselor, needs to exert her leadership skills and become an ally with the principal in moving the school toward a coordinated, systemic, results-based solution while remaining true to the values of the American School Counselor Association's (2003) national model for school counselors. The professional school counselor should be not a lone clinician but rather an educator working alongside his or her colleagues to improve the learning environment of the school (Johnson, Johnson, & Downs, 2006).

A good university supervisor who understands the organizational dynamics of this middle school could help the counselor find her voice in its multiple contexts.

The counselor is also on target in her recognition of the need to minimize the us against them mentality held by the various stakeholders. Research confirms that professional collegiality is a fundamental source of motivation and satisfaction for teachers (McLaughlin, Talbert, & Bascica, 1990). As she begins to understand these issues, the counselor will acquire the systemic orientation of a professional school counselor.

My belief is that school counselors, much like principals, can get a birds' eye view of school operations. Unlike teachers, the bell does not regulate school counselors' daily schedule. They are partly responsible for creating their own schedule. The counselor's job description includes visiting classrooms, consulting with teachers regarding classroom behavior and learning skills, and interacting with faculty and students. Counselors can and should be prepared to work with the school leadership team to develop comprehensive, integrated action plans to resolve identified issues. It is the nature of the school counseling profession to work as part of a team, using the interests and skills of each team member to accomplish target results for various accountability reports.

Question Two

The counselor's second question was how to discuss the bullying issue with Mr. Smith and whether to also address her perceptions of systemic issues with him. Prior to discussing the issue of bullying with the school principal, the intern should first consult with her university supervisor. Most university supervisors have years of exemplary school service. In offering their insights into methods of promoting effective collaboration between stakeholders, supervisors rely on their training and experience in a variety of school settings in terms of grade level, academic achievement, and socioeconomic status. The university supervisor, especially if he or she is already familiar with this particular middle school, can best suggest ways for the counselor to approach Mr. Smith.

If I were the supervisor, my suggestion would be to first collect available data related to this bullying issue and to then involve Mr. Smith as soon as possible. Readily accessible data could include (a) suspension rates and discipline referrals related to bullying, (b) success rates and numbers of students involved in various bullying interventions, and (c) survey information related to currently used teacher strategies to address bullying. Experience tells me that, at a minimum, several teachers at this middle school already incorporate antibullying lessons as part of their classroom management systems, and they can attest that these lessons make a significant difference in encouraging a positive learning environment. The school counselor's knowledge of these data will lend her increased credibility as she meets with the principal. In a meeting with Mr. Smith, the school counselor, and a few key teachers, the intern can present a composite of this information and a tentative plan to collect more data, as recommended by Adelman and Taylor (2005).

After conducting comprehensive data collection, the intern and the school counselor could present the data to the school's advisory committee and to the faculty as a whole. It would also be important that such a presentation of data be preceded by brief, introductory remarks from the school principal to confirm his support and investment in the change process. This process of collecting and disseminating data would serve to plant the seeds of collaboration. Mr. Smith would be more likely to see the school's advisory group as an ally in his efforts to make a positive difference. From his perspective, involving the advisory group in a systemic intervention plan to address bullying would result in one less battle to fight by himself. Collective action would reinforce group camaraderie among the principal, faculty, and staff. As more people became aware of the data, further input could be solicited, and action plans could be developed over time. As the process unfolded, the us against them mentality that the counselor described would transform itself into one of collaboration.

Question Three

The counselor's third question was what techniques or methods I might identify for addressing the systemic issues of bullying. In accordance with the previously described paradigm, the school advisory committee can explore and present specific methods of addressing systemic issues, such as bullying. Schoolwide antibullying programs, such as the Ophelia Project of Erie, Pennsylvania (www.opheliaproject.org), and the Respect for All Project (www.womedia.org/respectforall.htm) are good examples of systemic measures that can be investigated and eventually integrated into classroom management systems.

With this process in place, Mr. Smith could evaluate teachers on the basis of their implementation of collaboratively adopted antibullying measures. Teacher evaluation would have a more consensual focus, and this would ensure greater compliance. Mr. Smith would then feel less need to use intimidation. Specific teachers either would implement the adopted school bullying program or would not.

Second, I would ensure that the student handbook included a list of clearly defined schoolwide rules of positive conduct. As suggested by Simmons (2002), the definition of bullying should include rumor spreading, alliance building, secret telling, and nonverbal aggression. The handbook would also include a policy acceptance form for both students and parents to sign. School counselors would present and explain these rules during induction meetings for new students and their parents. Third, many urban schools now have biannual schoolwide student disciplinary meetings, in which the principal reminds students about established behavior standards and provides reports on progress made toward reducing aggressive behaviors. In addition, many schools now use the student government organization to collect survey data from students regarding systemic issues, such as bullying.

My main point is that appropriate programs should be identified, adapted with input from all school stakeholders, and implemented systemwide. Mr. Smith should become a facilitator to develop what he sees as "our" plan, not "his plan" or "their plan." School stakeholders should feel that these programs represent their collective ideas rather than viewing them as a canned program imposed from above.

Question Four

The counselor's fourth question was what individual treatment modalities would be effective in exploring bullying issues. In terms of developing individual treatment modalities, I would first explore the books *Real Boys: Rescuing Our Sons From the Myths of Boyhood* (Pollack, 1998) and *Odd Girl Out: The Hidden Culture of Aggression in Girls* (Simmons, 2002). I became aware of these books when attending the 2004 American School Counselor National Conference in Reno, Nevada, and consider them must reads.

Simmons (2002) indicated that schools and parents tend to focus on bullying in the narrowest terms of physical acts of violence and warned about the dangers of hidden, indirect, and nonphysical bullying. Simmons contended that girls, unlike boys, who may resort to direct physical violence against their targets, often use backbiting, exclusion, rumor spreading, name calling, and manipulation to inflict psychological pain. Such behavior is, according to Simmons, equally destructive to a child, a family, and a school environment. The problem is that such behavior in girls is generally not recognized as bullying but is instead often dismissed by adults as what girls do. There were indications of this phenomenon when Beth bullied Yanna. The institution responded decisively only when a weapon appeared on campus.

Also addressing gender issues, Pollack (1998) discussed the cultural confusion about raising boys and explored the cultural push to disconnect boys from their family at an early age. He suggested that boys require more nurturing and permission to express their feelings. By extension, such insights suggest the need to create more responsive school learning communities that are sensitive to gender issues and that treat students' social–emotional health and academic achievement as equally important. Given these insights, selected treatment modalities should provide systematic ways of teaching positive communication skills and demonstrating good role modeling for students by all school stakeholders. As the counselor discovered, a negative school climate interferes with student learning.

Question Five

In her fifth and final question, the counselor asked whether I would consider mixing the age groups in developing counseling groups to aid in socialization and social skills. In the context of a developmental counseling group, I not only would mix the age groups of participants but would also seek a wide diversity of group members to provide a broad range of feedback.

That being said, it is important to explain the difference between developmental and psychotherapy group models. The developmental approach stems from the assumption that all people benefit from increased spontaneity, creativity, autonomy, and productivity. In the developmental model, participants are not viewed as sick or as requiring a remedial process. Intervention and treatment are not the focus in a developmental group; the focus is on prevention. The psychotherapy model, in contrast, involves a remedial process designed for the purpose of addressing problematic behaviors, thoughts, feelings, and even personality through intervention and treatment. Reconstructing or rehabilitating personality characteristics of individual students, of course, is not appropriate in a public school setting (Trotzer, 1999).

The self-actualizing process is key to success in a developmental group. Students are able to compare their self-perceptions with how their peers perceive them. This helps students increase their self-actualization by allowing them to confirm or modify what they thought they knew about themselves as individuals. Through a similar comparison process, participating in developmental groups allows students discover whether their expressed values are consistent with their behaviors. Thus, this model provides an effective framework for addressing academic and nonacademic concerns, such as peer pressure, decision making, and interpersonal skills (Johnson & Johnson, 1995).

In conclusion, the marginalized status and fragmentation of efforts to address student problems are not just issues in this intern's middle school but have been long-standing problems in the U.S. school system. Many planners offer simple-minded solutions to these problems by simply advocating coordination of community resources to schools, formation of community support partnerships, or coordination of psychological support services, but the problem is larger than that. For example, most urban schools need to better develop their in-service programs related to improving classroom and schoolwide approaches for dealing effectively with learning and emotional problems. Likewise, paraprofessionals and volunteers working in classrooms often receive little or no formal training or supervision before or after they are assigned duties. In addition, school environments need to be redesigned to maximize opportunities for student connectedness to value others and to minimize threats to students' feelings.

The professional school counselor has the collaborative skills to assist the school principal in making change happen. This is not to say that the school counselor should become a school administrator or an administrative assistant, but the counselor can, at minimum, serve as a catalyst to bring about needed change and ultimately to cast a wide net in positively influencing greater numbers of students. As principals have shifted their leadership focus from serving as middle managers to being instructional leaders, the professional school counselor should also shift into a leadership role by collaborating with both the internal school community and the larger external community to break down institutional barriers to promote student academic success and enhance the school's positive learning environment (Stone & Dahir, 2006). As students feel a sense of connectedness and belonging and are totally engaged in classroom learning, dealing with daily stressors becomes achievable. With great conviction, I believe such a school environment is possible at any school. In such an environment, Yanna and Beth can become friends as they continue to develop their academic and social skills. The need for finding a victim or being a victim disappears.

References

Adelman, H., & Taylor, L. (2005, Summer). Complex problems, limited solutions. *Addressing Barriers to Learning, 10*(3), 1–7. Retrieved July 6, 2006, from http://smhp.psych.ucla.edu/pdfdocs/Newsletter/summer05.pdf

American Academy of Child and Adolescent Psychiatry. (2001). *Bullying* (Facts For Families No. 80). Retrieved November 2001 from http://www.aacap.org/publications/factsfam/80.htm

American School Counselor Association. (2003). *The ASCA national model: A framework for school counseling programs.* Alexandra, VA: Author.

Casey-Cannon, S., Hayward, C., & Gowen, K. (2001). Middle-school girls' reports of peer victimization: Concerns, consequences, and implications. *Professional School Counseling, 5,* 138–144.

Center for Evaluation and Education Policy. (2005). *High school survey of student engagement 2005.* Retrieved July 6, 2006, from http://ceep.indiana.edu/hssse/pdf/hssse_2005_report.pdf

Clarke, E. A., & Kiselica, M. S. (1997). A systematic counseling approach to the problem of bullying. *Elementary School Guidance & Counseling, 31,* 310–325.

Crick, N. R., & Grotpeter, J. K. (1996). Children's treatment by peers: Victims of relational and overt aggression. *Development and Psychopathology, 8,* 367–380.

Davis v. Monroe County Board of Education, 526 U.S. 629 (1999). Retrieved December 1, 2005, from http://www.oyez.org/oyez/resource/case/474/

Hazler, R. J., Hoover, J. H., & Oliver, R. (1992). What kids say about bullying. *Executive Educator, 14,* 20–22.

Johnson, S. K., & Johnson, C. D. (1995). *Group process: A results approach.* Boston: Little, Brown.

Johnson S. K., Johnson, C. D., & Downs, L. (2006). *Building a results-based student support program.* Boston: Lahaska Press.

McEvoy, A. W. (2005, September). *Teachers who bully students: Patterns and policy implications.* Paper presented at the Hamilton Fish Institute's Persistently Safe Schools Conference, Philadelphia. Retrieved December 5, 2005, from http://www.stopbullyingnow.com/teachers%20who%20bully%20students%20McEvoy.pdf

McLaughlin, M., Talbert, J., & Bascica, N. (Eds.). (1990). *The contexts of teaching in secondary schools: Teachers' realities.* New York: Teachers College Press.

Munn, P. (2005). *Information about teachers for anti-bullying in the classroom.* Retrieved December 5, 2005, from University of Edinburgh Web site: http://www.antibullying.net/staffinfo.htm

National Center for School Counseling Outcome Research, University of Massachusetts, Amherst. www.umas.edu/schoolcounseling

Nuttall, E. V., & Kalesnik, J. (1987). Personal violence in the schools: The role of the school counselor. *Journal of Counseling and Development, 65,* 372–375.

Olweus, D. (1993). *Bullying at school: What we know and what we can do.* Oxford, England: Blackwell Publishers.

Olweus, D., Limber, S., & Mihalic, S. F. (1999). *Blueprints for violence prevention, Book Nine: Bullying prevention program.* Boulder, CO: Center for the Study and Prevention of Violence.

Pollack, W. (1998) *Real boys: Rescuing our sons from the myths of boyhood.* New York: Holt.

Provasnik, S., & Dorfman, S. (2005). *Mobility in the teacher work force: Findings from the conditions of education 2005.* Washington, DC: U.S. Department of Education, Center for Education Statistics. Retrieved July 6, 2006, from http://nces.ed.gov/pubs2005/2005114.pdf

Ray, A., & Berg, S. (2000). School safety profiler [Computer software]. San Francisco: Ripple Effects.

Roberts, W. B., & Coursol, D. H. (1996). Strategies for intervention with childhood and adolescent victims of bullying, teasing, and intimidation in school settings. *Elementary School Guidance & Counseling, 30,* 204–212.

Sergiovanni, T. J. (1991). The dark side of professionalism in educational administration, *Kaplan, 72,* 524.

Shapiro, J. P., Baumeister, R. F., & Kessler, J. W. (1991). A three-component model of children's teasing: Aggression, humor, and ambiguity. *Journal of Social and Clinical Psychology, 10,* 459–472.

Sharp, S. (1996). Self-esteem, response style, and victimization: Possible ways of preventing victimization through parenting and school based training programmes. *School Psychology International, 17,* 347–357.

Simmons, R. (2002). *Odd girl out: The hidden culture of aggression in girls.* Orlando, FL: Harcourt.

Smith, P. K. (1991). The silent nightmare: Bullying and victimization in school peer groups. *Psychologist: Bulletin of the British Psychological Society, 4,* 243–248.

Stone, C., & Dahir, C. (2006). *The transformed school counselor.* Boston: Lahaska Press.

Trotzer, J. (1999). *The counselor and the group: Integrating training and practice* (3rd ed.). Philadelphia: Taylor and Francis.

Twemlow, S. W., Fonagy, P., Sacco, F. C., Gies, M. L., Evans, R., & Ewbank, R. (2001). Creating a peaceful school learning environment: A controlled study of an elementary school intervention to reduce violence. *American Journal of Psychiatry, 158,* 808–810.

35

"And Who's Gonna Make Me?": Defiant Behavior

This incident addresses the challenges of working with children who display resistance and/or defiance and explores the dilemmas that arise when new counselors disagree with the treatment approaches recommended by their supervisor. The efficacy of Adlerian and systems-based interventions is discussed.

■ Critical Incident

Kenneth McCurdy

On graduating in May with my master's degree in community counseling, I was hired as a primary counselor in an alternative education program. The program was located in a relatively small city and was run by a residential treatment facility for delinquent and dependent youths. The program involved adherence to a strict behavior modification approach.

The professional counselor licensure requirements in my state were pretty standard. I passed the National Counselor Exam and needed to complete 3,600 hours of supervised counseling experience before receiving my full license. The staff psychologist—who had been at the agency for more than 15 years and who did all of the testing and clinical supervision—was assigned as my supervisor. I would receive 2 hours of supervision each week: 1 hour of individual supervision and 1 hour of group supervision. The group supervision sessions included the other six primary counselors and four case managers.

When the school year began in September, I was assigned to provide counseling services to 20 fourth grade students attending the alternative education program. The student population included children who were confined to the residential facility as well as students who had been expelled from the local public schools and were required to attend the alternative education day program. All of these students were in special education, so the class was a self-contained classroom staffed by the special education teacher, me, and an education aide.

I really enjoyed my job, and the first 2 months seemed to go very well. I ran two groups daily, had one or two individual counseling sessions per week with each young person, and bonded well with my student clients. In both my group and my individual sessions, I used a lot of behavior modification techniques, but I was also able to personalize my counseling sessions. At the end of October, several students with whom I had worked were able to return to their home schools, and some new students from the local public schools entered the class. "Paul Grammond" was one of these new students.

Paul was a 10-year-old, biracial young man who had been expelled from his home school and referred to our day program for severe acting-out behavior involving the use of foul language toward teachers and school personnel. Paul had been in special education since the beginning of third grade. Apparently, his behavior had become progressively worse during first and second grades, and this necessitated a review by school personnel, resulting in his eligibility for special education services, including therapeutic support services.

Paul's parents were separated. His father was a 38-year-old African American who had no contact with Paul. He was incarcerated for armed robbery, had a history of substance abuse, and had had little involvement with Paul during the past 8 years. Paul's mother, a 28-year-old Caucasian, had just completed her third outpatient substance abuse recovery program. She was unemployed and participating in a day treatment program for parenting and social skills training, run by the county's Department of Public Welfare office. Paul had three siblings: His 12-year-old sister was in residential placement, and his 7- and 9-year-old brothers lived with his mother and maternal grandmother. The state's Children and Youth Services office had removed each of the children for short periods over the years because of neglect issues.

During his 1st week in the program, Paul was reserved and kept to himself in class. He seemed to be trying to adapt to the requirements and structure of the program. I placed Paul in a group with 13 other boys, almost all of whom were from the residential program and were approximately halfway through the anger management curriculum. I also met with him individually three times during the 1st week to build rapport and establish a base from which to work. During our sessions, Paul said little and seemed to be a bit overwhelmed with the whole situation. On Friday of his 1st week, I thanked him for adjusting so well to the program and the class. As he was leaving, he said, "I can't wait 'til school on Monday."

Monday morning came, and when I saw Paul, he was smiling and looked like a new kid. He was much more talkative and was interacting with the other students. Two hours later, I received a call from the classroom teacher requesting my presence because Paul was disrupting the class. When I got to the classroom, Paul was shouting at the teacher and aide. He did not want to share his art materials with the other students and had actually taken most of the art supplies and put them in his desk. I approached Paul and asked him what was going on. He proceeded to say, "Shut up, bitch!" I was shocked. I told him that I did not appreciate him speaking to me in that manner and asked him to come with me to my office so that we could find out what was going on. He refused to go with me and scowled as he said, "You can't make me leave the class!" I therefore asked the aide to physically escort Paul to my office. On the way to my office, Paul called the aide every foul name in the book and constantly screamed at the top of his lungs, "You can't make me do anything!"

Once we got to my office, I asked Paul to sit in the chair across from my desk. I proceeded to ask him what was the matter and why was he acting like this. Paul simply put his fingers in his ears and sang, "La la la la la." I needed to get through to him and did not know what to do. I told him that if he talked with me I would give him a piece of candy. On hearing this, he stopped singing and set his hands in his lap. He asked, "Where is the candy?" I took out a small candy bar and set it on the desk between us. I asked why he was acting like this now and wondered aloud what had happened to the Paul we all saw last week. He said, "Last week I was just getting used to this place," and continued, "I don't like this place. I don't like the teacher, the aide, or you. I want you all to just leave me alone. You can't make me do anything!" He then reached for the candy bar, opened it, and ate it. After eating the candy, he said, "Are we done now? I want to go back to class." I asked him whether he was going to behave, share the supplies, and do his school work, and he replied, "Sure." I escorted Paul back to class, informed the teacher that Paul seemed to be calmed down, and asked that she keep me posted.

Fortunately, I had group supervision soon after and anxiously presented Paul's case. I had 10 minutes to present my case and began by sharing my amazement with the abrupt change in Paul from last week to this week. My supervisor said that some children go through a honeymoon period when they first come to the program. He indicated that they usually take a week or so to get to know the lay of the land, determine how they fit in the class, and figure out how to behave to get what they want. Drawing from the strict behavior modification approach used by the program, my supervisor explained that time-outs were often used to address misbehavior and that the facility had several time-out rooms. He and the others in supervision suggested that the next time Paul "went off"—and they jokingly said that children like him went off all of the time—I should instruct the aide to take him straight to the time-out room. They reiterated that because he would not want to stay in the time-out room, Paul would choose to follow the rules, do his work, and act respectfully. I inquired about what I should do in counseling to help address the true issues behind his behavior. My supervisor said to let the behavior modification techniques work and to continue to have Paul participate in the anger management curriculum because he obviously had anger issues.

As soon as I returned to my office, I was notified that Paul was disrupting the class again. I went to the class and informed both the teacher and the aide that we would be using the time-out room when Paul chose to act this way. I further clarified that each time he disrupted class, Paul was to be taken to the time-out room and instructed that he could only leave the time-out room and return to class when he chose to follow the rules, do his work, and act respectfully. Paul remained in the time-out room for the rest of the school day. When I spoke with Paul before he got on the van to go home, I told him that tomorrow was a new day and that I looked forward to seeing him and hoped that tomorrow would be a better day. He said, "It will be."

The next day, I met Paul at the door of the classroom, and he was smiling and talking with other classmates who shared the same van. I said hello to him, wished him a good day, and went to my office. Within the 1st hour of school, Paul was in the time-out room for disrupting class and throwing paper wads at other students. This pattern of disruptive behavior followed by extensive periods in the time-out room continued for the rest of his 2nd week in the program.

Questions

1. How are Paul's individual educational and treatment needs being met by the exclusive reliance on a behavior modification approach?
2. As a new counselor, I deferred to my peers and supervisor as to the best intervention to use with Paul. Where do my responsibilities lie in ensuring that I am doing what is in Paul's best interest? Do I have to perform the interventions as directed by my supervisor and routinely done at my agency?
3. I was trained in my master's program to use various approaches to work with clients. How should I proceed at this point to counsel Paul?
4. To whom and where can I turn for guidance on alternative ways to work with Paul?

■ Response

Nancy Bodenhorn

As indicated in this incident, there really are two foci here—one is Paul; the other is the counselor. Although these are, of course, intertwined, my response separates them, given that they have been separated in the questions presented. In the strictest definition of Paul's educational needs, one may argue that what he needs to be more successful is more time in class and on task. To this end, if the behavior modification techniques allow Paul to maintain the behavior required to stay in class, then the intervention is successful in meeting his educational needs. Personally, I think working with the symptoms rather than the cause may be short-sighted. I understand educational needs to include survival, systems, and generally living in the world, both as a child and as an adult. I think a critical question to which I do not know the answer is whether and how much other counseling can happen after the behavior modification (I hope) works.

More information is needed regarding Paul's special education placement and needs. It is not clear whether this alternative program meets the needs described in his Individualized Education Program. Therapeutic support services are included, but I do not know the basis for this inclusion and what Paul's specific issues and needs are. A thorough review of Paul's file, including assessments and services previously provided, is needed to determine whether his needs are being met.

I do not yet know how or even whether Paul's needs are being met by the exclusive use of behavior modification. Behavior modification works wonders with many children, but there can also be needs that are not met through this method of therapy. I would want to learn more about Paul. The relatively quick swings in his mood and behavior may indicate a chemical imbalance, possibly caused by drugs or even nutrition. I would want to know, for example, whether Paul has any breakfast at home and when and how much sugar he ingests. One concern about relying on only one mode of therapy is that simple yet powerful antecedents, such as nutrition and chemicals, may be overlooked.

I would also want to use a systems perspective to better understand the current dynamics of Paul's family. Paul has experienced much upheaval in his family life, and there may be something currently causing him concern. Someone or something in the class may remind Paul of his family or foster situations, and this may call for psychodynamic or cognitive-behavioral awareness. From what we know, Paul does not have control over many aspects of his life, and this may trigger the defiance. Person-centered counseling, possibly including play therapy or the creative arts, might allow Paul time to gain a sense of personal control. My own belief in working with children is that counselors need more flexibility than just one approach allows; children's lives are often more complex than any one theoretical perspective offers. Learning about each area of Paul's life would allow the counselor to make a more informed decision about what would be the most appropriate way to support Paul's development and would allow the counselor insight regarding how to proceed with treatment.

Paul has experienced a lot of abandonment in his life, and it is critical that his teacher and counselor help him understand the difference between abandonment and extensive time-out. Behavior reinforcement can be framed both negatively and positively. Time-out in this case is used as a negative reinforcement; Paul must do something he does not want to do when he has done something the school staff do not want him to do. I would look for positive reinforcements for Paul, allowing him to earn the privilege to do something that he wants to do when he does the things the school staff want him to do. I would also continue the group and individual sessions with him to learn more about his habits and his family situation.

I think it is important when interviewing for a professional counseling position to ask about the accepted theoretical orientation in the agency and the level of adherence to that orientation. If the agency is rigid about its expectations, I would expect the interviewer to indicate this, and the candidate should also be assertive about asking. As a new counselor and as a new employee in a setting that has (I presume) had success with the process, it is probably not a good idea to reject the history of the program and the staff. It is interesting that when the counselor had Paul in the office after the first outburst, he used a behavior reinforcement involving candy—this counselor may not be so separate from the program theory as he presents it. I would recommend that the counselor ask for an individual meeting with the supervisor to discuss concerns and options.

The incident presented is partially a supervision issue and partially an administrative issue. If the administrative requirements are that the counselor follow a path that he does not believe is in the best interest of the client, then he has an ethical responsibility to engage in a more efficacious approach or to remove himself from a practice that is not meeting the client's needs. This is, obviously, a drastic choice and not one to take lightly. Because this situation involves an issue that is both supervisory and administrative, if the assigned supervisor is also an administrator, it is important for the counselor to seek external supervision. The agency supervisor, because of allegiance to the program, may not be able to successfully supervise the counselor who carries such doubts and feelings about the program and process.

I would encourage the counselor to consult with other staff members about previous cases that were as difficult as this one. The counselor may be expecting results to happen more quickly than is realistic, and I think it would help him to have a time line of expectation. If a set of historical notes indicates that similar students spent much of their 1st month (or more) in and out of time-out but after that time were better able to be productive both in class and in counseling, then that would be an important piece of information for the counselor to know. If, alternatively, the counselor researched cases and found that a series of similar students had never adapted to the behavior modification and had left the program unsuccessfully, bringing those data to the staff's attention and suggesting an alternative approach might end up improving services provided by the agency. Individually, other counselors who had similar challenging students might indicate whether they, too, experienced frustration or doubts when they first started at the agency, how they coped with those feelings, and whether or how these feelings diminished. These reflections could serve to validate the counselor's feelings and provide some perspective regarding professional development.

My hope would be that the counselor could continue to work with the system, learn more about Paul's situation and possible causes for his behavior, allow the behavioral modification method a chance to work, continue to provide support and personal contact to Paul, continue to pursue avenues in the agency to provide alternative and appropriate services to Paul, and seek external supervision. The counselor might also choose to seek additional sources of information and support for alternative interventions. This might occur through a supervision group outside of the agency with other counselors who work with children or through more formal means, such as a class or workshop focusing on working with special needs children.

Response

Stephen E. Craig, Jennifer C. Mills, Lonnie E. Duncan

This particular incident highlights many issues, the most notable of which are the challenges of working with defiant children and the associated difficulties faced by new counselors whose treatment recommendations may be in direct conflict with those recommended by supervisors. In addition to the clear issues surrounding the counseling strategies used with Paul, there are other, more subtle, ethical issues, including the counselor's boundaries of competence and the supervisor's ethical responsibilities to the client (American Counseling Association [ACA], 2005). In our response to the questions posed, we give periodic attention to some of the ethical considerations embedded in this incident.

We hope that the counselor and supervisor have established a good supervisory relationship in which concerns are disclosed and dealt with in a collaborative manner. If they have not already done so, the supervisor and counselor should have a supervision contract that outlines, in part, expectations of the supervisee and the approaches to be used by the supervisee in his work with Paul. Initial work that includes these elements could potentially minimize confusion over what is and what is not deemed appropriate for the supervisee to do in his counseling with Paul.

It is our contention that Paul's individual and educational treatment needs are not being met adequately by a strict reliance on a behavior modification approach. One of the criticisms of a strict behavior modification approach is that it fails to consider that a child's misbehavior may be the result of internal problems (Wolfgang, 2005). Although behavior modification approaches are useful for altering some children's misbehavior, we find their exclusive use often insufficient in producing long-term behavioral change. A reinforcement program may improve Paul's school behavior but not address the underlying issue, thereby providing only temporary symptom relief. Additionally, Paul may be denied important social learning opportunities if he is treated through an exclusively behavioral therapy approach.

This incident also reflects a challenge that is frequently encountered in educational and clinical settings. Situational constraints, including the work setting's policies and procedures and the supervisor's expectations, may restrict the counselor's range of intervention options. In this case, Paul's educational environment consists largely of a behavioral modification protocol. Although advocating for something different may be ethically warranted, the ability to effect institutional change may be limited.

It is developmentally appropriate for novice counselors to question their competencies in given areas, and a natural result is to look to colleagues and supervisors to provide guidance and direction. Ongoing development as a counselor, however, requires that one move from a stage of relative dependence on the supervisor to a more autonomous but collaborative partnership with the supervisor.

Like supervisors, supervisees have ethical responsibilities to their clients. The *ACA Code of Ethics* (2005) states that "counselors and their clients work jointly in devising integrated counseling plans that offer reasonable promise of success and are consistent with abilities and circumstances of clients" (A.1.c.). The *ACA Code of Ethics* also states that counselors should advocate at "individual, group, institutional, and societal levels to examine potential barriers and obstacles that inhibit access and/or the growth and development of clients" (A.6.a.). Although the supervisor is justified in recommending that more time be given to evaluate whether the behavior modification approach is useful, the application of a standardized protocol for all children oversimplifies Paul's complex situation.

The counselor's status as a new employee under the immediate supervision of a staff psychologist is complicated. Supervisors, regardless of discipline area, have an ethical responsibility first to protect the welfare of clients with whom supervisees are working. This places a high degree of responsibility on the supervisor, and, in this instance, the more experienced supervisor might have a clear and justifiable rationale for implementing behavioral modification procedures.

Beginning counselors must learn to balance their movement toward autonomy and competence with the expertise and ethical responsibilities of supervisors. This reality does not, however, relieve the supervisee of the ethical responsibility to advocate at "individual, group, institutional, and societal levels to examine potential barriers and obstacles that inhibit access and/or the growth and development of clients" (ACA, 2005, p. 5). If a good supervisory relationship exists, the counselor may consider sharing his concern with the supervisor. Because of the inherent power differential between supervisors and supervisees, however, the supervisees should approach this topic with care. After all, the supervisor has ethical responsibilities to the supervisee's clients, so he or she has a vested interest in ensuring that clients receive a standard of care expected from a professional counselor.

A new counselor may find that his or her personal values and beliefs about human nature, change, and motivation fit well with behavior therapy assumptions, or the counselor might find that his or her values and beliefs are in conflict. For inexperienced counselors, this conflict may emerge as a quiet voice or a gnawing feeling that says, "Something is not quite right," or, "I am not sure about this." This emerging voice often conflicts with the prevailing opinions of supervisors or the institutions in which counselors work. At these crossroads, the counselor's personal autonomy is beginning to develop. Navigating this newfound tension may be difficult without good supervision.

It is important at this stage that the novice counselor not respond in a dichotomous fashion. That is, the counselor who concludes, "I don't think these people know what they are doing; I am going to just do it my way," or gives the opposite response, "I had better just go along with what they are doing here, because I feel at a loss," is not engaging in an important developmental stage of growth. Supervision can help the counselor work within the ethical, legal, and moral boundaries while developing autonomy as a professional counselor. As counselors become more experienced, confident, and competent in particular areas (e.g., ethical decision making, theoretical conceptualizations, treatment planning, multicultural competencies), they gain a more realistic view of their supervisor and find ways to integrate their personal strengths and competencies with those of their supervisor. Instead of depending on their supervisor, supervisees eventually learn to view their supervisor as a collaborative resource to be called on as a consultant (Loganbill, Hardy, & Delworth, 1982).

It seems that this counselor has been able to integrate his own theory of counseling in the past but that, in this case, the supervisor has given a directive to continue implementation of behavior modification principles. Effective supervisors respect the professional opinions of supervisees and have their supervisees' and their clients' best interests at heart. Realistically, if supervisors direct their supervisee to do something, given that the directive is legal and ethical, the supervisee should comply. There will be ample opportunities throughout one's career to assert personal autonomy without jeopardizing one's job or internship placement.

Although no single theory can explain all human behavior, theoretical orientations provide a helpful framework for counselors to understand client difficulties, determine client goals for counseling, and choose interventions that are based on some efficacious foundation. Boy and Pine (1983) suggested that theory provides the rationale for what counselors do. Nonetheless, interventions should be tailored to the unique needs of clients. In this critical incident, the problem lies not in the behaviorist tradition of conceptualizing Paul's problems but in the overreliance on behavior modification techniques to address all of his misbehavior. It may be important to revisit the foundational assumptions of the approach being used by the treatment facility—in this case, behavior modification. The developmental process of learning to critically analyze theoretical approaches as they are being used in specific treatment programs is extremely valuable. The following analysis provides a brief critique of some of the behavioral modification procedures as they are being applied to Paul.

In the case of Paul, time-outs were implemented without any explicit understanding of what parts of the environment (classroom, home life) were reinforcing his misbehaviors. Without a clear statement of the positive reinforcers in the classroom, one could assume that the counselor was not using the behavior modification approach appropriately. Additionally, the counselor stated that time-out was used for extended periods of time: "Paul remained in the time-out room for the rest of the day" and "extensive periods in the time-out room continued for the rest of his 2nd week." Time-out strategies are classified into one of three categories: (a) isolation, (b) exclusion, and (c) nonexclusion (Harris, 1985). In Paul's case, the isolation time-out was implemented, which involves physically removing a child from the reinforcing environment for a predetermined amount of time. There did not seem to be any time-specific restrictions on the isolation time-out. One could also argue that inadequate staff to monitor Paul's behavior during the time-out might minimize the effectiveness of isolation time-out procedures (Harris, 1985). Given the current pattern of misbehaviors and amount of time spent in the time-out room, it is unlikely that Paul's individual and educational treatment needs are being met. In this case, it is not only the exclusive use of behavior modification that is likely at the root of these needs not being met but also the misuse of this approach. Because the behavior modification approach is grounded in the notion that the causes are in the environment, clear and consistent observation of the environment is necessary to determine the antecedents to Paul's behavior (Harris, 1985). In other words, what conditions in the environment set off Paul's misbehavior?

If the supervisor and institution support consideration of alternative approaches to working with Paul, the counselor might consider an Adlerian approach, which, if implemented correctly, would help clarify family of origin information, the possible goals of Paul's misbehavior, and ways to encourage insight and understanding, which could lead to longer term behavior change. The counselor and supervisor did not seem to give much consideration to the uniqueness of Paul, dismissing much of the family history information, his biracial cultural background, and the potential purposes of his misbehavior. Instead of considering ways to individually tailor a therapeutic program that met Paul's needs, the supervisor and school implemented a one size fits all protocol for the students.

We recommend that the counselor obtain more input from Paul's family. Depending on who is accessible, Paul's mother, father, and grandmother could all potentially provide some helpful contextual information. From an Adlerian theoretical perspective, such information might shed light on Paul's psychological position in the family and how he gains a sense of significance and belonging. Paul's family history has played an important role in his feelings of inadequacy, and his placement in an alternative education program that focuses on time-out procedures as a means of deterring socially useless behavior seems to merely reinforce his diminished social interest.

Adlerian theorists argue that a primary motivation of children and adults is belonging. An important cognitive-developmental task for Paul is to learn to cooperate with others and find ways to belong. A strict behavior modification approach might help Paul act appropriately in class, but this would neglect the important developmental task of building a sense of connectedness with others. Adlerian approaches to working with young children argue that learning to clarify emotions, weigh alternatives, and decide on appropriate solutions are very important developmental skills that foster social interest or help children find their meaningful place in the social context. Therefore, the context cannot be separated from the behavior of the child. Further consideration of how the context may be influencing Paul's behavior would be critical to understanding his motivation.

Children who are defiant are not always motivated by externally determined, environmental conditions. Instead, children's behavior is often motivated by individually created goals. By uncovering the goals of children's misbehavior, counselors are able to more fully understand the uniqueness of children and intervene with them and their family in intentional ways. All indications suggest that the goal of Paul's misbehavior is power. Each time school personnel try to prove who is in power, Paul responds with an escalation of defiant language and resistant behavior. He acts in such a way to prove that he is the one in charge, not the school staff. The problem with physically escorting Paul to time-out or becoming personally offended by his language (e.g., "Shut up, bitch") is that it simply perpetuates the power struggle.

On considering the context, one might conclude that the history of neglect that Paul has experienced is resulting in his hoarding behavior. For example, the counselor mentioned that Paul, during art, had taken most of the art supplies to his desk and was refusing to share them. Additionally, his hoarding behavior was paired with an aggressive response: "Shut up, bitch." These behaviors may further support the hypothesis that Paul's behavior is an attempt at gaining power over his environment. This information could be used to help Paul, in individual counseling, develop more self-understanding and learn to differentiate among particular contexts. In this way, the counselor not only would be helping meet Paul's counseling needs (developing skills of differentiation, developing positive relationships with his peer group, and developing healthy coping strategies to use in his unstable family environment) but would also be helping to address important cognitive skills that are necessary for educational achievement.

In terms of intervening with Paul from an Adlerian perspective, we would seek to minimize his feelings of inadequacy, enhance his feelings of connectedness with others, and uncover the goals of his misbehavior. We would use play therapy principles and group counseling strategies, and our approach would be consistently encouraging. Much of Paul's misbehavior is reflective of a high degree of discouragement about not finding socially useful ways of connecting with others.

We would certainly continue to support Paul's inclusion in group counseling. This would provide Paul with additional opportunities for feedback from same-age peers and, with some guidance from the counselor, could further help promote social interest development. The counselor should assert considerable effort to distinguish himself from the punitive elements of the school (e.g., principals, teacher aides who escort children to time-out rooms). The counselor should also refrain from personalizing the verbal assaults from Paul, because they are likely reflective of his attempt to regain power over his situation. By eliminating the power struggle through failing to acknowledge the verbal assaults, the counselor would remove the reward that Paul has historically received. In essence, the counselor would have "spit in [Paul's] soup" (Mosak & Maniacci, 1998, pp. 55–56). This is a paradoxical intervention intended to uncover the purpose of behavior and render the symptom meaningless.

The first place to turn for guidance on alternative ways to work with Paul would be the supervisor. Because of vicarious liability issues, the supervisor should be kept abreast of all counseling plans and intervention strategies. The counselor also has ethical and legal obligations not to engage in counseling procedures for which he has not been trained. Professional association membership (e.g., ACA, American School Counselor Association, state counseling associations, divisions, and branches) might provide other helpful resources, including conference presentations, refereed journal subscriptions, and professional networks. Continued involvement with individual and group supervision is also essential. Few opportunities exist after license acquisition to receive comprehensive group supervision experiences. Of course, remaining current with the professional literature is the responsibility of any competent health provider.

In conclusion, Garry Landreth (2003) once described the uniqueness of children by saying that "some children are like popcorn and some are like molasses" (pp. 57–58). When looking at children who are defiant, we find ourselves saying, "Some children are like a river and go with the flow, and others are like fish trying to swim upstream." In both cases, movement exists, but in the latter case, children are exerting themselves in a way that might work for a while but will eventually tire them to exhaustion. Paul has endured a difficult experience, but he is surrounded by a concerned and well-intentioned counselor and school personnel. He also seems to have a grandmother who may provide some comfort for him as well as siblings who have an apparent shared experience. Helping Paul recognize his connectedness to the human condition might encourage his decision to go with the flow and ultimately overcome his circumstances. Working with children who are defiant and resistant can challenge even the most experienced counselors. Above all else, the counselor should imagine the world through Paul's eyes, remain patient with Paul's misbehavior, believe in his capacity for change, and instill in Paul the "courage to be imperfect" (Dreikurs, 1967, p. 43).

References

American Counseling Association. (2005). *ACA code of ethics.* Alexandria, VA: Author.
Boy, A. V., & Pine, G. J. (1983). Counseling: Fundamentals of theoretical renewal. *Counseling and Values, 27,* 248–255.

Dreikurs, R. (1967). *Psychodynamics, psychotherapy, and counseling.* Chicago: Alfred Adler Institute of Chicago.

Harris, K. R. (1985). Definitional, parametric, and procedural considerations in time-out interventions and research. *Exceptional Children, 51,* 279–288.

Landreth, G. L. (2003). *Play therapy: The art of the relationship* (2nd ed.). New York: Brunner-Routledge.

Loganbill, C., Hardy, E., & Delworth, U. (1982). Supervision: A conceptual model. *Counseling Psychologist, 10,* 3–42.

Mosak, H. H., & Maniacci, M. P. (1998). *Tactics in counseling and psychotherapy.* Itasca, IL: F. E. Peacock.

Wolfgang, C. H. (2005). *Solving discipline and classroom management problems: Methods and models for today's teachers* (6th ed.). New York: Wiley.

"But I Was Just Kidding!": The School Counselor's Role in Responding to Student Threats and the Potential for Violence

This incident involves a student who made threats that suggested a potential for school violence. The respondents explore the role of school counselors in assessing and treating serious mental and behavioral disorders in a school setting.

■ Critical Incident

Linda M. Fortin

"Everett Phillips," a seventh grade European American boy attending middle school in a suburban community of a medium-sized northeastern city, had been flagged by his elementary school counselor as a child in need of monitoring and counseling intervention. She reported that he showed social immaturity, had difficulty making friends, and tended to overwhelm the few friends he did make by clinging too closely. As the middle school counselor, I quickly screened Everett for possible inclusion in the comprehensive groups program as he transitioned into middle school. On the basis of this screening, Everett was placed in a group for boys and girls in need of friendship support and social skills training as they navigated the preteen years.

I noticed that Everett responded well to my offer of counseling assistance and that he seemed invested in being perceived as popular by the other students. In an apparently misguided attempt to meet this need, Everett seemed to get caught up in exaggeration and fantasy expressions that could seem odd and be frightening to other children. Everett generally did not recognize that he was scaring others with his attention-seeking behavior. In spite of this, the other students in the group seemed to feel protective of Everett, seeing him as one of them. Everett responded in kind by demonstrating a willingness to physically defend any of them who were getting picked on by older kids.

At the same time that he was having this generally positive group experience, Everett was also engaging in some behaviors that concerned his team of teachers. For example, he had told students that he had stolen pens from a teacher's desk, although he had actually brought them from home. He was observed offering some lunch change to another student and then complained to the observing teacher that the student had stolen the money from him. He regularly complained to his parents that he was bullied at school but would never reveal the names or incident details to his teachers, counselors, or administrators. The school staff interpreted most of these behaviors as part of either attention-seeking or attention-deficit/hyperactivity patterns, both of which had been positively identified in Everett's school and home histories.

An inquiry into his past difficulties revealed that his parents had long struggled with Everett. Concerned about his willful behavior and noncompliance with their expectations for toilet training and other developmental activities, Everett's parents had first requested medical and psychological evaluations for their son when he was in preschool. The psychosocial history indicated that Everett had had a difficult birth and sporadic prenatal care. Each of his parents had been married previously, and he now lived with his parents and three older male siblings from his father's first marriage. A diagnosis of attention-deficit/hyperactivity disorder (ADHD) was made at the preschool evaluation, and Everett was placed on dosages of Concerta during the day and Ritalin at night. He continued to be monitored for medication during his elementary years, and he also had some individual counseling with a child psychologist just after the evaluation period, but this had been discontinued in recent years. Although they were encouraged by the elementary school staff to resume individual counseling for their son, Everett's parents resisted. They expressed their intentions to follow through by resuming counseling for Everett when their schedule allowed, but they never seemed to get around to it.

His parents and the school staff perceived Everett as vulnerable to social problems because of his hyperactivity, anxiety, and impulsivity. He also displayed intense mannerisms, including a dramatic, seizure-like display he would invoke when frustrated. He described this as "making crazy bug eyes" while shaking, but, unlike an actual seizure, Everett could stop this behavior at will when asked to by a teacher or counselor. He commented that "people worry about me being scary" and connected his desire to be scary with his feelings of rage resulting from his sense of being bullied by peers.

Despite his difficulties, Everett was also a child with intellectual and imaginative strengths. Early in his academic career, intelligence testing identified Everett as falling in the high average range on the verbal scales and in the superior range on the performance scales. Although teachers were concerned with his willfulness and tendency to argue with adults when he was being defensive, other children admired these behaviors and described him as courageous or—in middle school parlance—cool.

The school's concerns about Everett began to mount as a result of three particular behavioral incidents that occurred within a short period of time. In addition, Everett shared with his counseling group that he had been setting fires in his driveway at home. The first behavioral incident involved Everett telling the assistant principal that he had been "jumped" by some eighth grade boys who captured him in a back hallway and reported that he had had to "fight them off." None of this, on investigation, turned out to be true. Second, other students heard Everett say that he was going to bring a gun to school. In response to this report, the school security staff conducted a 2-day investigation and interviewed all students who had reported hearing this from Everett. The investigation found nothing conclusive, however; all of the students said they had heard the rumor, but not directly from Everett. Nevertheless, a conference was held with Everett in which the principal and security director heavily emphasized the problems with his use of statements that could inflame concern throughout the school.

In the meantime, I had been in touch with Everett's parents, who continued to be concerned about potential bullying at school and who confirmed that Everett had indeed been setting fires. In fact, they indicated that his fire setting was not limited to the driveway (as Everett had indicated in his group counseling sessions) but also included fires that Everett had set inside the home. On hearing this, I made an immediate referral to a community specialist connected with the local fire department. The specialist made a home visit to help Everett and his family address this concern and prevent further incidents.

The school then had a week off for spring recess. School had only been back in session another week when the third incident of concern arose. In this instance, students reported that Everett had made out a "hit list" of people he might kill. He had not specifically shown the list to any student, but he had left it out for others to see. His list indicated three columns of potential victims—those who were marked as "yes," "no," and "maybe." When confronted about the list, Everett exclaimed, "But I was just kidding!" Even so, he was suspended from school for 5 days, and a superintendent's hearing was scheduled. The school district's intent in holding this hearing was to help Everett's parents realize that their son's rather deliberative behavior was attributable to something beyond his ADHD and that outside therapy was highly advisable. Everett's parents brought their own lawyer but, at the conclusion of the hearing, did agree to resume counseling for him with the community psychologist who had worked with them during Everett's preschool years.

After the hearing, Everett's teaching team assisted him in managing his reentry into the school and handling any student comments. At this point, his lead teacher reported to me that Everett had remarked, "My life isn't worth anything, and nothing I do is worth anything." Everett had survived the suspension, but not without an impact on his emotions and self-perception. Continued help was clearly needed. Questions that remain about Everett from my perspective as the school counselor include the following.

Questions

1. Is Everett merely a willful, highly intelligent child with ADHD, or might he qualify for another diagnosis? Could the ADHD medications be contributing to his behavioral problems?
2. What is the significance of the fire setting?
3. Should Everett be considered dangerous? How can I tell?
4. What therapeutic interventions might the school offer to really help Everett at this crucial juncture in his social development?

■ Response

JoLynn V. Carney

The evaluation of student threats and potential for violence certainly is a difficult task for counselors. Many of us can empathize with Everett's counselor, teachers, and parents as they work to assist him in his daily functioning. Everett presents to the middle school counselor with a history of treatment and complex symptomatology dating back to his preschool days, which makes a simple approach to current assessment and treatment nearly impossible. To unravel this complexity, I focus my response on (a) evaluating Everett through a medical model perspective of differential diagnosis and possible medication side effects, (b) assessing Everett's fire setting and potential for dangerousness (harming others or himself), and (c) suggesting some intervention strategies for working with Everett as he transitions from elementary to middle school.

Diagnosis and Medication

As the school counselor, I would be unwilling to simply go along with Everett's preschool diagnosis of ADHD and medication regimen as though nothing had changed for him physically, emotionally, or psychologically during the intervening years. Instead, I would want to have Everett reassessed to rule out an alternative diagnosis and determine the impact of medication at this point in his life. The current behaviors that are causing Everett the most significant impairment socially and academically (i.e., arguing with adults, fighting, setting fires, losing his temper, and creating a hit list of people to target) more closely resemble criteria of other *Diagnostic and Statistical Manual of Mental Disorders* (4th ed., text rev.; American Psychiatric Association, 2000) diagnoses, such as oppositional defiant disorder (Code 313.81 in the *Diagnostic and Statistical Manual of Mental Disorders*) and disruptive behavior disorder not otherwise specified (Code 312.9). I would therefore work closely with a mental health therapist to rule out (or confirm) the presence of these alternative or additional diagnoses. The reevaluation for these potential diagnoses would need to be conducted so that Everett could be properly diagnosed and then treated in the most appropriate manner.

Another question that begs to be answered is how much Everett's medications might be contributing to his current problems. I believe that the impact of medication on Everett's functioning should also be called into question and further evaluated. I am concerned that he has been on the current combination of medications for at least 8 years without being closely monitored by a medical or mental health professional, and I would therefore advocate for a medication recheck. Both medications being given to Everett are stimulants; Concerta (long acting) is given during the day, and Ritalin (short acting) is given at night. The labels on both of these medications mention potential side effects, including increased aggression, anxiety, and agitation. The Food and Drug Administration has recently been considering these potential negative side effects in children but as yet has not issued a formal warning statement, as it did with the use of antidepressants contributing to increased suicide risk in some children (American Academy of Child and Adolescent Psychiatry, 2002). My role with Everett would be to support him during this reevaluation and continue to work on his behaviors, cognitions, and emotions in the school context.

Potential Dangerousness

Being able to predict potential dangerousness is a difficult task for all counselors. As the school counselor, I would have a certain amount of information but not a complete picture that would allow me to know with certainty Everett's degree of dangerousness to himself and others. His fire-setting behavior is definitely one objective symptom to be explored. An important first step would be to gain an understanding of Everett's motivation for setting the small fires. Typically, counselors talk about such motivations as being nonpathological or pathological in nature, including curiosity, a cry for help, or deliberate delinquency. Everett's motivation for the fire setting is likely to be somewhere on a continuum from a cry for help to deliberate delinquency. He may be using the fire setting to consciously or subconsciously draw attention to the perceived stressors in his life. Viewing him from the deliberate delinquent frame speaks to his need to deliberately be disruptive and cause significant damage without actually causing physical harm to any person. Understanding Everett's motivation for fire setting is an important component in assessing his overall potential for dangerousness in the context of his personality characteristics and family and social circumstances.

Assessing dangerousness also requires a knowledge base of general risk and protective factors and the ability to assess the student in terms of these factors. The Secret Service National Threat Assessment Center team highlighted the difference between students who pose a threat and those who have made a threat (Fein et al., 2002). Everett made a threat against the school and his peers by saying he was going to bring a gun to school and by developing a hit list of potential people to kill. He also possibly made an indirect threat to his own life when he told a teacher that his life was not worth anything. School personnel should now be in the position of implementing a threat assessment process in which they evaluate behaviorally relevant facts rather than Everett's personality traits (Fein et al., 2002). This is an assessment of his actions in the context of posing a threat and being potentially dangerous in the school setting.

Specific questions for school personnel to investigate include the following:

- How has Everett "dealt with situations that have led him to see life as unbearably stressful" (Fein et al., 2002, p. 30)?
- What significant events or circumstances in Everett's life have been overwhelming (Fein et al., 2002)?
- "Do fellow students, friends, or others say directly or indirectly that violence is not a solution to the problems" (Fein et al., 2002, p. 30)?
- Does anyone suggest ways for Everett to get help or assistance (Fein et al., 2002)?

An integrated approach to assessment and intervention is important in Everett's case. School personnel have facts to evaluate in the context of their setting, but they have few facts from the family or community settings. Information from these settings would provide valuable data for discerning a pattern in Everett that shows whether he poses a threat of dangerousness. See http://www.secretservice.gov/ntac.shtml for specific information on the National Threat Assessment Center's School Initiative and the resources this center suggests for school personnel.

The mental health therapist, together with the school counselor, can assess risk and protective factors in terms of Everett's suicide potential. Risk factors for suicide include any behavioral components, such as personal history of previous suicide or parasuicide attempts or a family history of suicide and impulsiveness or aggressive tendencies; cognitive components, such as dichotomous thinking, restriction of thought processes, or the need for perfectionism; and psychological components, such as hopelessness, helplessness, and depression. Protective factors include family and community support, skills in problem solving and conflict resolution, support for seeking help, easy access to mental health treatment, and a lack of access to highly lethal methods for completion of suicide. See http://www.suicidology.org/ for specific information and resources provided by the American Association of Suicidology for therapists, school personnel, parents, and friends of suicidal individuals.

Therapeutic Strategies

Strategies for working with Everett include individual and family counseling. The school counselor, with a release of information and in consultation with the community mental health therapist, could provide specific interventions to reinforce and supplement the treatment plan developed by the therapist. Everett's teachers, the school counselor, and the school administrators are in a position to see him every day and would be able to provide medical and mental health professionals with important feedback regarding Everett's functioning level. Daily exposure to Everett allows school personnel to assess changes in his behaviors, cognitions, emotions, and interactions relative to medication adjustments and therapeutic interventions.

Maintaining consistency for Everett in the school setting in terms of structure, academic expectations, and continuation of social contacts is primary in providing an appropriate environment for him. Positive relationships with others would provide the social support Everett needs at this crucial juncture in his development. Continuation in his friendship support and social skills group would reduce his possible isolation and therefore reduce some of the cognitive distortions often found in students who are dangerous to themselves and others.

The school counselor can work from a strength-based (vs. deficit) model of treatment by helping Everett develop an accurate self-concept. Having an accurate self-concept would empower Everett in identifying his personal qualities (both productive and unproductive) and understanding how these qualities create successes versus problems in his life. Providing Everett with tools such as relaxation, guided imagery, and nonviolent conflict resolution would also be empowering. With these tools, Everett could view himself as able to control his behaviors instead of acting impulsively, especially at times of high stress.

In addition, the school counselor can play a crucial liaison role between the school and Everett's parents by helping each system interact productively as they assist Everett in dealing with his daily functioning. Reaching out to the family in this manner, the school counselor has the opportunity to understand what support Everett's parents might need from school personnel. This approach allows everyone to join with Everett in evaluating his current problems, including potential for dangerousness. Having Everett and his parents see the school as an ally rather than an adversary in his overall treatment process would increase the likelihood of a positive outcome for all involved.

■ Response

Maureen Finnigan Rundle and Karen Mackie

School counselors routinely encounter many students like Everett. These students fall along a continuum of more developmentally typical symptoms, such as social immaturity and "nerdiness," to more serious issues, such as homicidal and suicidal ideation. In addition to regularly dealing with students who are bullied, different, off-beat, or isolated, school personnel are often faced with the challenge of assessing the risk posed by students who make homicidal gestures. The last decade has shown that students who feel alienated from their peers are capable of inconceivable actions. Everett's symptoms, especially his hit list, are particularly alarming when looked at in the context of a school setting. Given the recent rash of school shootings throughout the country, student threats of violence are taken much more seriously than they were 20 years ago. In this culture of heightened awareness of and sensitivity to warning signs of school violence, the school counselor's task of determining where Everett falls on a continuum of differentness and of assessing Everett's potential for violence is quite challenging.

The school counselor in this incident reported that Everett is impulsive, has been diagnosed with ADHD, and is on medication. How much of his behavior can be attributed to the impulsivity connected to his attention problems? Could the type of medication or the dosage be part of the problem and be contributing to Everett's behaviors? Although these questions are beyond the capabilities of the school counselor to answer, they are important questions to ask to get a complete picture of Everett's experience. The counselor is to be commended for asking them.

The school counseling staff repeatedly advised Everett's parents to seek outside assessment and treatment, yet his parents were disinclined to follow through on this recommendation. This is a regular and frustrating occurrence for school counselors, who lack role-related responsibility to make psychiatric diagnosis or offer intensive therapy at school yet work with students in desperate need of such help every day. It was only Everett's act of creating a hit list that finally convinced his parents to seek outside assistance, as advised by school personnel, and they did so only because they faced a long-term suspension and the possibility that Everett would not be allowed to attend school for the rest of the year if they did not take action. This, too, is a familiar scenario to school staff, who often have to wait for just such a crisis to occur to be able to pull in the needed resources and supports from the mental health community or from the school system itself.

Students who are at high risk for suicidal or homicidal behaviors often exhibit warning signs like the ones Everett displays. They may tell peers what they are planning to do, or they may show patterns of angry behaviors, absenteeism, or violent drawing or writings. Usually, these behaviors are brought to the attention of parents. Yet without a crisis to compel parental action, these behaviors may be minimized or ignored. Prior to the hit list crisis, for example, Everett's parents interpreted his behaviors through the lens of bullying and blamed others for his actions. Bullying may well have been a factor, but all requests for Everett to identify and discipline the perpetrators were stymied by his inability to identity anyone by name or even by picture. This, of course, arouses suspicion, given that middle school students who are tormented by bullies are usually very willing to work with the school to make the bullying stop.

What can schools do with students like Everett? Students spend a great number of their waking hours at school, and clearly school, as a context for children's everyday experience, can be a source of much joy or a source of much torture, depending on the climate and approach of school personnel to understanding and dealing with the developmental needs of young adolescents. We have already suggested that, of necessity, clinical diagnosis and treatment issues need to be handled outside of the school setting. Even so, schools still have a great responsibility to Everett and students like him to create an environment in which they will be able to function and perhaps begin to heal.

We recommend that schools put prevention and intervention programs in place to meet the needs of young adolescents. Educational research on the middle school experience (Arhar, 1992; Eccles & Wigfield, 1997; National Middle School Association, 1995) has shown that a sense of belonging, safety, competence, and altruism are key elements to the development of young people as both learners and persons. These core needs can be incorporated into both the instructional and the counseling programs of the school. One way that Everett's school might approach this is to team students with a particular group of teachers who stay with the students throughout middle school, "looping" with them as they complete both seventh and eighth grades. This approach enables teachers to create learning communities with flexible schedules and helps students and teachers to develop better relationships with each other. The teams might also participate in such activities as field trips, community service, and competitions as well as engage in teamwide prevention efforts on social–emotional topics, such as bullying and tolerance. All of these activities are geared toward giving all students the critical sense of belonging, competence, and safety they need and constitute sufficient intervention for many students of this age.

Nevertheless, students like Everett, who are developmentally behind in socialization skills, also need more intensive interventions through the counseling department. An extensive group counseling program, such as the one in which Everett participated, can be a valuable intervention program in middle school. Students can use these groups to address common concerns, including family struggles, friendship concerns, anger management, and grief processing. According to the school counselor of this incident, Everett's group was primarily focused on developing social contacts and was targeted to creating social bonds among students who had few friends and many struggles with peer relationships. We applaud the school counselor's decision to include Everett in this group counseling experience. We might recommend that the group leaders use Yalom's (1970) process group model to create a supportive community. In doing so, the group leaders should model the curative factors of altruism, catharsis, belonging, and social practice, as identified by Yalom, and should specifically modify them for the middle school developmental level. The goal would be for the students to become focused on learning to listen to others with care and concern and on giving regular support and advice about social relationships to each peer member from the perspectives of the peers themselves.

From a school perspective, students like Everett need a comprehensive support system to make progress as learners. Everett received group and individual counseling, and the school staff communicated with his parents diligently in the hope that they might perceive the school's concern for Everett's well-being and connect to therapeutic resources outside of school without feeling blamed by the school or shamed by their child's unsuccessful social behavior. Unfortunately, schools usually cannot require parents to seek needed mental health services.

Sometimes the only option open to the school is to begin discussing with parents the need to investigate alternative placement for their children into the more reconstructive environment of the behavior management classroom. A school can force such placement, but this is rarely desirable because it sets in motion a long and litigious process between the parents and the school. For this reason, school support personnel who are aware of the mental health needs of a student or family must sometimes just stand by, often impatiently, and wait for a crisis that will afford the opportunity to reorganize the family dynamics and defense mechanisms and result in the student or parent getting needed treatment or services. Fortunately, Everett's hit list symptom was enough to get all the needed systems—home, school, and mental health—moving in a more effective way for him.

In summary, a large part of the contemporary school counselor's job is to coordinate adult communication and build a collaborative team approach toward helping students by connecting the parents, outside resources, and school staff to formulate a plan that will support the students as they experience assessment, diagnosis, and treatment. By working successfully as a team, all stakeholders develop awareness of the student's needs and provide consistency of treatment inside and outside of school. Through this collaborative effort, the student's chances of successful development and coping are improved. A school environment that has in place a comprehensive, developmental counseling program with a large variety of counseling groups, individual counseling options, and classroom interventions is also critical to serving the vast differences in social and emotional needs of young adolescents in school today.

Response

Walter B. Roberts Jr.

In the good old days of early psychotherapy, one would interpret poor Everett's behaviors as his personal, existential search for meaning. Alas, those days are gone. Actually, if one were to wait to work with the young lad with all his adolescent existential angst, one might find oneself without an office because he might well torch it before the third or fourth session.

Everett presents a tough dilemma for the professional school counselor. To what extent does one respond to a child in the school setting from what is known diagnostically as opposed to keeping the in-school response strictly in the realm of school counseling? What is the role of today's school counselor? Are we to solely stay within the bounds of educational counseling and not dare approach anything resembling therapy or a therapeutic approach while working with children who are clearly in psychological distress? Is the profession of school counseling capable of assisting the Everetts of the world?

Although I am fully able to develop diagnostic interpretations, I personally prefer to shy away from them every chance I get and focus more on the person or child within. "Label jars, not people," I tell myself. But then I always end up having to begrudgingly admit that knowing some of the classical diagnostic symptoms of a behavioral disorder might actually be useful in designing strategies for successful interventions.

Everett, however, poses particular challenges, both at home and in the school. I will throw out diagnostic jibber jabber for the moment and just note that certain behavioral manifestations demand immediate attention. Everett is a danger to both himself and others. Children and adolescents who engage in high-risk endangerment activities such as pyromaniacal exploration are screaming for help, and that help must be delivered immediately. Waiting is not an option. This brings me to the second dilemma.

In today's atmosphere, school personnel are hypervigilant for any cues possibly signaling violent activities planned by students. Sometimes such scrutiny is warranted. At other times, it is silly. What educational benefit does a 13-year-old get from being suspended from school for forgetting to remove a screwdriver from the coat he wore over the weekend while working with his father on the family car? Was Everett a real threat to the school with his hit list? Certainly, there are enough behavioral indicators to generate concern and reasonable suspicion of a potential for violence. To do nothing or ignore the connection between the hit list and Everett's past behaviors would be negligent on the part of the school and the school counselor.

School counselors are critical links in working with students like Everett, who exist—in some form, fashion, and gender—in every school. School counselors are trained to connect the dots among various, seemingly unrelated child behaviors, which are often viewed only in isolation by other personnel in the school environment. Everett's dots began, of course, immediately on his entry into formal education. He was pegged from the 1st day of school as a child in need of assistance. What type of assistance was he given, starting in preschool? He was given drugs. The thinking was, "Let's medicate the symptoms so we don't have to do the really hard work of addressing some of the root causes of Everett's behaviors. More drugs, we must have more drugs!"

Well, that is what I tell myself when I am in my "all drugs are bad; we should not give them to kids" school of thought. My more rational mind tells me that, just as there is utility in knowing the typical symptoms of a diagnostic category, medications can sometimes alleviate enough behavioral symptoms so that the clinician and child can start the process of cognitive-behavioral change. As much as I hate to admit it, Everett likely will not ever have a fighting chance to learn the rudiments of self-control and cognitive stop-gap techniques to master his impulsivity if he cannot focus for the lengths of time necessary to learn them.

Compounding this situation, of course, is Everett's chaotic home life. His parents have been inconsistent in following medical and psychological advice. His blended family undoubtedly adds additional stressors to his daily life. Additionally, he is most likely undergoing nature's own trauma for youths—puberty—and if he is not already in the depths of it, he most certainly will be soon. His parents seem defensive regarding school staff suggestions and seem to have viewed the most recent intervention over the hit list as a legal matter, as opposed to the educational and personal challenge it truly represents for Everett.

All too often, parents of children like Everett are only invited to school when there is a problem. What a welcoming place school is for those families, who need school personnel as their allies, not as agents to heap further misery and guilt on already emotionally burdened parents. It is no wonder some parents avoid school conferences like the plague. Who wants to go to a place if, whenever they leave, they feel as if their child is a screw-up and their parenting skills are the reason for their child's problems? I would not, and I dare say Everett's parents would not either.

Everett knows his more outrageous behaviors in the school setting get him attention, but the results he gets are not always exactly what he intends. He most likely did not intend to be suspended for 5 days as a result of creating the hit list. One of the markers of impulsivity is, after all, that there is usually not a lot of forethought prior to taking action. Everett's remorse and low self-esteem, as expressed in his statement that his life is not worth anything, are ripe grounds for exploration by the school counselor. In particular, the comments merit further exploration about Everett's potential for self-harm.

Everett is a child in need of both community or private and school counseling interventions. Nevertheless, in the absence of parental willingness, desire, or ability to follow a medical and behavioral intervention plan for Everett, the school counselor becomes the de facto therapeutic agent in his life. This brings me back to one of my original questions: Are school counselors to solely stay within the bounds of educational counseling and not dare approach anything resembling therapy or a therapeutic approach while working with children who are clearly in psychological distress? There are as many answers to this question as there are individuals in our profession.

The profession of school counseling has changed over the past 2 decades, as individual state legislatures widen the doors of certification and licensure for school counselors. The paradigm that one can only be a counselor if one was a teacher is a thing of the past. Although those with former teaching experience truly do have exceptional knowledge about how schools function (or how they sometimes do not function) and about how tough it is to teach children—and make no mistake about it, it is exhausting—I predict that the teacher-to-counselor paradigm will be extinct within the next decade. By 2015, no state will require an individual to have prior teaching experience before being licensed as a school counselor.

What is my point, and how does all of this relate to Everett? As more nontraditional school counselors come into the profession, they will come from more diagnostic and scientific backgrounds, such as psychology and human services. Such individuals, combined with counselor education programs (which also will be forced to meet the needs of future school counselors and their kindergarten through 12th grade clientele with a stronger emphasis on a paradigm that views the school counselor as a mental health professional), will be better equipped to provide both the educational and the therapeutic responses that students like Everett need. Some school counselors are fully capable of doing this now. Others are not so capable. Nevertheless, there is no reason the counselor in Everett's school, if qualified, should be prohibited from providing on-site, daily psychoeducational opportunities to assist Everett in developing his life skills needs and becoming successful in his educational endeavors.

Individual sessions with Everett to explore his views of school, to discuss his relationships with his peers, and to teach him additional behaviors to increase the likelihood of his success are all within the bounds of every school counselor's scope of expertise. The depth and intensity of these school counselor's interventions, however, will be determined by the level of specific expertise the school counselor holds. For instance, although every school counselor is trained to discuss with a student the merits of that student's behavior in relation to the school day, some are more capable than others (as a result of continuing education) to go a step further and intervene by teaching specific skills to decrease objectionable behaviors while increasing client assets, teaching stress reduction techniques, or using play therapy as a tool to reach those children who are less communicative.

For the immediate future, Everett must be given the chance to return to school and begin the struggle to learn new modes of behaviors that will increase his success in school. The school counselor should be able to work collaboratively with school personnel as well as with outside mental health professionals to assist in Everett's new journey. This will require that the family provide consent to his private or community counselor to share relevant pieces of information with the school counselor to assist Everett in modifying his problematic behaviors at school. A school counselor–private therapist team would increase the chances that Everett may practice any new skills taught in therapy during the school day. The school counselor, in conjunction with the special education staff, can provide additional support and advocacy for his educational goals, starting with one of the most important goals: keeping Everett in school.

Everett is a young man with educational potential but with behavioral deficits that often distract people from seeing the whole child. A school counselor in Everett's life will, among other things, be an important key to helping him stay in school, helping him navigate the world of self-esteem, and keeping his parents engaged in the total learning process.

References

Arhar, J. (1992). Interdisciplinary teaming and the social bonding of middle level students. In J. L. Irvin (Ed.), *Transforming middle level education: Perspectives and possibilities* (pp. 139–161). Boston: Allyn & Bacon.

American Academy of Child and Adolescent Psychiatry. (2002). Practice parameter for the use of stimulant medications in the treatment of children, adolescents, and adults. *Journal of the American Academy of Child and Adolescent Psychiatry, 41*(2, Suppl.), 26S–49S.

American Psychiatric Association. (2000). *Diagnostic and statistical manual of mental disorders* (4th ed., text rev.). Washington, DC: Author.

Eccles, R., & Wigfield, A. (1997); Young adolescent development. In J. L. Irvin (Ed.), *What current research says to the middle level practitioner* (pp. 15–29). Columbus, OH: National Middle School Association.

Fein, R. A., Vossekuil, B., Pollack, W. S., Borum, R., Modzeleski, W., & Reddy, M. (2002). *Threat assessment in schools: A guide to managing threatening situations and to creating safe school climates.* Washington, DC: U.S. Department of Education, Office of Elementary and Secondary Education, Safe and Drug-Free Schools Program/ U.S. Secret Service, National Threat Assessment Center.

National Middle School Association. (1995). *This we believe: Developmentally responsive middle schools.* Columbus, OH: Author.

Yalom, I. D. (1970). *The theory and practice of group psychotherapy.* New York: Basic Books.